B

W9-CCJ-230

DATE DUE

GAYLORD   PRINTED IN U.S.A.

ALSO BY MICHAEL ROSENTHAL

The Character Factory:
Baden-Powell's Boy Scouts and the Imperatives of Empire

Virginia Woolf

NICHOLAS
MIRACULOUS

NICHOLAS MIRACULOUS

The Amazing Career of the Redoubtable

Dr. Nicholas Murray Butler

MICHAEL ROSENTHAL

Farrar, Straus and Giroux

New York

Farrar, Straus and Giroux
19 Union Square West, New York 10003

Unless otherwise indicated, all illustrations were provided by University Archives and Columbiana Library, Columbia University in the City of New York.

Library of Congress Cataloging-in-Publication Data
Rosenthal, Michael, 1937–
    Nicholas Miraculous : the amazing career of the redoubtable Dr. Nicholas Murray
Butler / Michael Rosenthal.— 1st ed.
        p.   cm.
    Includes bibliographical references and index.
    ISBN-13: 978-0-374-29994-1 (hardcover : alk. paper)
    ISBN-10: 0-374-29994-3 (hardcover : alk. paper)
    1. Butler, Nicholas Murray, 1862–1947. 2. Columbia University—Presidents—
Biography. 3. College presidents—United States—Biography. I. Title.

LD1239.R67 2006
378'.0092—dc22

                                                                    2005014198

Designed by Jonathan D. Lippincott

www.fsgbooks.com

1   3   5   7   9   10   8   6   4   2

For Erik, Stephen, and Noah

I personally feel that Dr. Butler is the foremost American of his day.
— Bainbridge Colby, secretary of state in 1920–21, January 3, 1923

He is unique in so many ways that colleges might give a special course on his life up to now as an outline of academic, political and social history of the last half-century. — *Brooklyn Eagle*, April 4, 1937

He had come to seem . . . a public institution himself and independent of time, like the Constitution or the Republic of Plato.
— *Paterson News*, May 2, 1945

Contents

NICHOLAS
MIRACULOUS

The Sage

❧

There is a sage for Xmas turkey,
There is a sage to flavor cheese,
There is a sage to spice the lowly porker,
There is a sage that mother brewed in teas,
There is a sage that fills the prairies wide,
But the sage who makes our lunches delightful
Is the sage from OLD MORNINGSIDE.

Thus Number 25 in the 1939 songbook of the Occasional Thinkers Club, entitled simply "To the Sage." The book's inside cover exhibits the same kind of admiration but in a different rhyme scheme:

There is no man whose wit is subtler
Than our friend and sage, good Dr. Butler,
So let us drink to him this toast:
Some mean a lot, he means the most.
                    Chorus
Oh sage we feel this way for you
For all the things you say and do.

No mere purveyor of comic doggerel, the poet Robert Underwood Johnson evoked the greatness of his sage in a 1933 sonnet published in the *New York Herald-Tribune* after he had read several of Butler's addresses on the increasingly grim state of European politics:

To Nicholas Murray Butler

Let no man wait another hastening hour,
Nor unearned sleep enjoy, till he shall hear
These warning words that show thee sage and seer,
And breathe the secrets of the spirit's power.
Now, when the clouds of doubt more darkly lower
And Love and Hope contend with Hate and Fear
We listen for thy summoning trumpet, clear
And cogent, lest our very courage cower.

No time is this for the smooth prophecy,
For laggard rescue, rash experiment
As though no danger ever trod this path.
Nearest thou art unto a prophet sent
Bringing our needs—Lincoln's humanity,
Milton's full mind, Savonarola's wrath.

The things that Nicholas Murray Butler said and did as influential Republican, international statesman, and president of Columbia University from 1902 to 1945 made him a dominant American presence in his time, known, celebrated—and not infrequently vilified—throughout the world. The journalist Max Frankel, explaining why his parents chose to settle in New York after fleeing Germany in the 1930s, pointed out that the "three most famous symbols of America for every European—Franklin Roosevelt, Fiorello La Guardia and Columbia University—were New York institutions." Butler couldn't take credit for FDR and "the Little Flower," but he could for Columbia, which owed its status almost exclusively to his drive and flair. In building it into a world-renowned institution, Butler succeeded in turning himself into one as well.

The titles conferred upon him during his career by *The New York Times* suggest the magisterial sweep of his achievement: "the incarnation of the international mind" (1927), "Member of the Parliament of Man" (1931), "Prime Minister of the Republic of the Intellect" (1937). It is not likely that the author John O'Hara ever met him, and it is almost certain that Butler never read his novels, yet when O'Hara, in his 1934 bestselling *Appointment in Samarra*, has Caroline Walker document in a letter to Joe Montgomery the illustrious nature of the shipboard company on her first trip to Europe, her list begins with Nicholas Murray Butler (followed by the comedian Eddie Cantor, the actress Genevieve Tobin, J. P. Morgan's daughter Anne, and financier Joseph Widener). Whether Joe was impressed with all this talent, O'Hara does not say. But it is telling that he chose Butler as representative of the power and distinction he wished to claim for some of Caroline's shipmates. Bewildering as such a choice may seem today, when Butler appears to have vanished from human memory, his presence on board would have conjured for any middlebrow reader of the 1930s precisely the impression O'Hara intended.

Of course, no cultural seismographs are calibrated precisely enough to register the exact effect of an individual on any given era. For the opening decades of the twentieth century—once one is through with the Carnegies, Morgans, and Rockefellers, with Dempsey, Tilden, and Babe Ruth, with presidents and movie stars, inventors and war heroes—what method exists for determining the significance of a person's life?

In 1930 The New Yorker's Alva Johnston came up with a scientific breakthrough. A foolproof technique did in fact exist to calculate the magnitude of human achievement: merely count the lines in an individual's Who's Who entry, and the results will yield an indisputable rank order of importance. Applying this arithmetical model to the 1929 Who's Who, Johnston discovered the five greatest Americans to be Samuel Untermyer, Nicholas Murray Butler, the Reverend Dr. William Eleazar Barton, Nathan William MacChesney, and Bion Joseph Arnold.

Butler could not have been happy with his runner-up position (by only two lines) to lawyer Untermyer. And he would have been right. Johnston had overlooked a flaw in his objective approach: the discrepant nature of the information included in Who's Who. Whereas Butler's lines were limited to basic biographical facts and the array of positions he had held, honors earned, clubs joined, organizations headed, and books published, Untermyer's entry was primarily made up of lengthy descriptions of his legal victories. As a measurement of stature, Untermyer's padded ninety-nine lines cannot compare to Butler's lean, compelling ninety-seven. Had Johnston controlled for the verbose accounts of Untermyer's cases, his analysis of "The Fifteen Biggest Men in America" would have made clear that Nicholas Murray Butler was unquestionably the biggest.

Johnston's formula for determining cultural size is not the only method available. Beyond the prominence afforded by enormous wealth or political power or by the visibility given to entertainment and sports stars, America offers a host of other distinctions that help to define a person's status in the culture. Butler garnered a substantial collection of these: honorary degrees (thirty-eight); *Time* magazine covers (one); days in which his obituary appeared on the front page of *The New York Times* (two); memberships in foreign societies (thirteen); number of times a quotation from his writing provided the solution for the *Saturday Review*'s famous Double Crostic (one); occasions on which he received electoral votes as the Republican vice presidential nominee after the death of the actual candidate (one); public addresses delivered before various governmental bodies, such as the British House of Commons, the French Chamber of Deputies, the Italian Parliament, and the Hungarian Parliament (fourteen); issues of *The New Yorker* that included profiles of him (two); decorations from foreign countries (seventeen)—including Commander of the Red Eagle (with star) of Prussia, Grand Commander of the Royal Redeemer (First Class) from Greece, Serbia's Grand Cross of the Order of St. Sava (First Class), Grand Officer of the Order of Polonia Restituta (Second Class), Knight Commander of the Order of the Saints Mauritius and Lazarus from the Italian government, Grand Cross of the Order of the White Lion (First Class) from Czechoslovakia, and Grand White Cordon with Red Borders of the Order of Jade from China.

Inducted into the Bricklayers, Masons and Plasterers Union in 1923, Butler won the Nobel Peace Prize in 1931. He became president of the Carnegie Endowment for International Peace in 1925, president of the American Academy of Arts and Letters in 1928, and chairman of the Carnegie Corporation Board of Trustees in 1937. He was a candidate for the Republican nomination for president of the United States in 1920. His celebrity finally became commonplace: in 1928 the *Philadelphia Record* commented that Butler's receiving the Grand Cross of the Order of the Crown of Romania didn't cause much excitement

> for the reason that he already holds every nonstop, long-distance, endurance and weight-carrying record in this department of endeavor. His latest acquisition . . . is simply another scrap of adornment for the most lavishly decorated member of the human race. It may be, indeed, the last, for the supply must be about exhausted, and there

is only a remote possibility that new nations will be formed or new seats of learning founded for the purpose of adding illustrious initials to his name . . . Anyway, his possessions make him an influential factor in international affairs and the metal trades, although proposals that he incorporate himself as an individual League of Nations are not considered practicable.

Encrusted with honors, he was for H. G. Wells "the pearly king of academics."

Butler also collected—another sign of cultural influence—hordes of adoring friends and acerbic enemies. The friends included many of the world's most distinguished people, including the British statesmen Arthur Balfour, Lord Morley, Herbert Asquith, and Lloyd George; the foreign ministers Gustav Stresemann of Germany and Aristide Briand of France; the philosophers Henri Bergson and Benedetto Croce; Andrew Carnegie, who embraced him within the inner circle of his trusted "old shoes"; Theodore Roosevelt, whom he served as an adviser until a political dispute ended their relationship in 1908; New York governor and democratic presidential candidate Al Smith; secretary of state and first president of the Carnegie Endowment for International Peace, Elihu Root; the banker William Crocker; Presidents William Howard Taft and Warren Harding; and almost everyone else of note in America.

For those who admired him, there was hardly an American to compare. Superlatives competed to capture his immensity: "the greatest savant in America—if not in the whole world"; "no man in this country so necessary for the peace of the world and the guidance of humanity"; "of all the men in America . . . the best informed regarding the public life of Europe"; "nothing of human concern is foreign to his mind"; "one of the great intellectual leaders of today"; "one of the great shining lights in the world"; "the one outstanding supreme figure in our entire American university world"; "the master interpreter of nation to nation in our time"; "the nation's greatest unofficial statesman"; "the incarnate combination of the Greek and the Roman ways felicitously united"; "the most brilliant mind in the educational and political life of America."

William Nelson Cromwell, cofounder of the prestigious New York law firm of Sullivan and Cromwell, said it perhaps most fulsomely in birthday greetings to Butler in 1942:

The effulgence of your glorious career obliterates time which gave to the world the miracle of your existence. If my heart had voice, it would become speechless in the endeavor to convey to you my devotion, admiration and gratitude for the marvel of such a unique unparalleled life as you have exemplified to all mankind. Such work, such influence and such benefaction as your existence has manifested will never die. They possess the sublime gift of perpetuity. A revolving world is the type and you, Dr. Butler, are its most distinguished exemplar.

Honoring Butler on his eightieth birthday, his good friend Charles D. Hilles remarked, "It is indispensable that a man, to become great or famous, shall represent in a well-defined way the general aspirations of his times." Hilles was certainly right. Coming to power at the same time America was coming to power, Butler reflected the energy and optimism of a young country about to take on a position of world leadership, supremely confident in the rightness of its political and economic system. His values were unapologetically elitist, embodying the perspective of what he would call "the better classes," men entrenched in seats of influence and privilege, enjoying the benefits of good clubs, substantial incomes, and political clout. Butler flourished as the ultimate insider, really only comfortable with the well-to-do and the well-connected, with men who felt that the world would be better off leaving them alone to run it.

If his admirers came largely from the economic and cultural elite, his critics were a more diversified lot—writers, cranky professors, social activists. For them, "the Sage" represented an abhorrent strain of reactionary thought opposed to social or intellectual change. Catering to the rich, smugly confident in the rightness of his ideas, as tyrannical to those beneath him as he was obsequious to those above, their Butler was less exemplary icon than despicable caricature. The poet Ezra Pound, for example, considered him "one of the more loathsome figures of a time that has not been creditable even to humanity." No friend to university presidents, the economist Thorstein Veblen used Butler as a convenient model for his dissection of the species's most pernicious traits in his brilliantly dyspeptic *The Higher Learning in America*. The muckraking writer Upton Sinclair, who exposed the horrors of the meatpacking industry in his novel *The Jungle*, also sought to expose Butler as "the representative, champion, and creator of . . . false and cruel ideals . . . whose influence must be destroyed, if America is to live as anything worthwhile, kindly or beautiful." Charging Butler with serving as "the intellectual leader of the American plutocracy," he claimed that Butler was the most "complete Tory in our public life." For Butler, Sinclair argued, there were no people, only "the mob," and it was in opposition to the mob and in the interests of plutocracy's "instinctive greed" that he devoted his many talents. In the more direct words of the Communist *Daily Worker*, "Of Dr. Nicholas Murray Butler it may be said, paraphrasing Voltaire, that if he didn't exist, it would be necessary for the capitalist class to invent him."

The social critic (and Columbia College alumnus) Randolph Bourne mocked him as President Alexander Mackintosh Butcher of Pluribus University, a man who took pains every commencement day to warn "the five thousand graduates before him against everything new, everything untried, everything untested." Convinced of the absolute perfection of our Anglo-Saxon political system, Bourne's Dr. Butcher "never wearies of expressing his robust contempt for the unfit who encumber the earth." As America's outstanding "philosopher-politician," he is able to inject "into the petty issues of the political arena the immutable principles of truth."

Walter Lippmann shared Bourne's reservations about Butler's political acuity. He cited Butler as the extreme example of the man who wrote about politics without the slightest understanding of politicians, somone so committed to abstract principles at the expense of the nitty-gritty of reality that there was nothing left "but to gasp and wonder," Lippmann wrote, "whether the words of the intellect have anything to do with the facts of life?"

H. L. Mencken saw him as representing one of the two major strains of twentieth-century American thought:

> When the history of the late years in America is written, I suspect that their grandest, gaudiest gifts to *Kultur* will be found in the incomparable twins: the right-thinker and the forward-looker. No other nation can match them, at any weight. The right-thinker is privy to all God's wishes, and even whims . . . Butler is an absolute masterpiece of correct thought; in his whole life, so far as human records show, he has not cherished a single fancy that might not have been voiced by a Fifth Avenue rector or spread upon the editorial page of the New York *Times*. But he has no vision, alas, alas! All the

revolutionary inventions for lifting up humanity leave him cold. He is against them all, from the initiative and referendum to birth control, and from Fletcherism to osteopathy.

To which list Mencken might have added the income tax, woman suffrage, and the direct primary. At the same time, it must be noted that Mencken was mightily pleased when the right-thinker reviewed favorably (if briefly) his early book on Nietzsche. Right-thinking clearly has its moments.

Perhaps the most amusing instance of Butler's capacity to inspire antipathy occurred with the appearance of the "Draft Ode for a Phi Beta Kappa Occasion" in the June 1939 issue of *Poetry* magazine by the poet and classicist Rolfe Humphries. Richly veined in classical allusion and comically overwrought in style, the poem makes little sense until one reads vertically the first letter of each line, which clearly spells out its message: "Nicholas Murray Butler is a Horses Ass" (apostrophe assumed). Outraged at having been duped, *Poetry* castigated Humphries in the next issue for his "scurrilous phrase" and barred him from appearing in its pages again. (The prohibition was eventually rescinded, Humphries later admitted.)

Revered icon and reviled caricature, Butler was large enough to embrace both easily. Whatever else could be said about him, he was always noticed. During the first half of the twentieth century, few names possessed the potency of "Dr. Butler." Installing himself, in Supreme Court justice Benjamin Cardozo's words, "by sheer force of wisdom and learning and ability and character" as "one of the men that the world, the sick old world summons to its bedside when the fever pains and ague rack it too severely for endurance and it would learn the path to health," he ministered to it from on high, diagnosing its ills and prescribing his political, economic, and moral remedies. The press conspired with Butler in delivering his therapeutic counsel to a world in need. His addresses to Columbia and Barnard students, his welcoming speeches to summer school students, and even his annual reports to the Columbia trustees became instant news, reported by papers across the country and commented on by endless editorial writers. From 1923 on, his annual Christmas greetings to the world were published in *The New York Times*. When Dr. Butler spoke, everybody listened, hearing not a man so much as a venerable institution.

"The American Century," which Henry R. Luce proclaimed in 1941, was very much Butler's century, and he succeeded in imposing himself on it in a dizzying variety of ways. His ambitions were never parochially limited to Columbia, nor were they national or even international in scope. They were, finally, nothing less than intergalactic. The choice of "Cosmos" as the pen name under which he wrote a series of articles for *The New York Times* during 1916 on his program to end the war, tells us more about Butler than he understood, as does the quip that amused the British statesman Lord Halifax, to the effect that he had heard Butler had no intention of dying until a vacancy occurred in the Holy Trinity. Although it misses several dimensions of him, the best attempt to catch Butler's singularity in a few phrases was made by Alva Johnston, when he described him in the 1930 *New Yorker* profile as "the only member of his profession—that of consulting world adviser and liaison officer of the nations; the grandmaster of internationalists (non-Red) of all countries; the most comprehensively decorated private individual extant; the semi-official boss of American letters; the president of the most prodigious educational establishment on earth." Not bad for a boy from Paterson, New Jersey, whose father was a small-time manufacturer of floor coverings.

To understand the nature of Butler's ascent to cultural eminence, we must first appreciate the rather primitive state of higher learning in America in the late nineteenth century. At the end of the Civil War, the United States did not have a single institution committed in any significant way to original research. An 1869 report of the National Teachers' Association bluntly pronounced its absence to be a serious national liability: "We have, as yet, no near approach to a real university in America. No competent nation may stand acquitted before its own conscience and the enlightened judgment of the world until it can point to one such center of original investigation and educational power." It wasn't until the founding of The Johns Hopkins University in 1876 that the nation could legitimately claim to have an institution devoted to advanced instruction leading to a Ph.D. Hopkins changed the educational landscape as dramatically as the steel and oil and railroad monopolies were altering the economic one. It was, according to the sociologist Edward Shils, "perhaps the most decisive single event in the history of learning in the western hemisphere." Butler, slightly more moderate, pronounced it "the beginning of a new era in the history of higher education."

The rhetoric accompanying the arrival of the research university suggests the exalted aspirations attached to it. To use a term preferred by Butler, it was the "power house" that would drive the nation's progress. Daniel Coit Gilman, Hopkins's first president, did not intend hyperbole when he declared, "To be concerned in the establishment and development of a university is one of the noblest and most important tasks ever imposed on a community," any more than Stanford's David Starr Jordan did in asserting, "The foundation of a university . . . may be an event greater in the history of the world than the foundation of a state." Well beyond their practical value in supplying a rapidly growing industrialized nation with trained doctors, managers, professors, lawyers, and engineers, universities were hailed as agents of the country's material and even spiritual transformation. As opposed to the vitally important liberal arts college, with its avowed purpose of shaping moral character through the rigors of a prescribed curriculum, the university's sophisticated research methods and its gifted scientists and scholars promised to bring society closer to truth of all sorts, including the mysteries of nature itself.

The leaders of these institutions were invested with enormous cultural capital by an America eager to feel it could compete intellectually as well as industrially with the Old World. Unlike the relatively innocuous band of fund-raisers who head today's universities, the titans who roamed the campuses at the turn of the century—men like Jordan and Gilman, Eliot of Harvard, White of Cornell, Angell of Michigan, Harper of Chicago—were powerful figures of great influence. They ruled their academic empires in much the same way as Gould, Rockefeller, Carnegie, and Vanderbilt presided over theirs. Veblen, understanding how universities, with their complicated managerial and organizational challenges and their need for endless resources, resembled competitive business enterprises, contemptuously (if perceptively) labeled university presidents "captains of erudition."

In his carefully groomed annual *Who's Who* listing, Butler always identified himself first as a publicist, in the sense of being actively involved in and commenting on public affairs, and only second as a university president. This ordering neatly defined his own priorities, although it was only as a "captain of erudition" that the rest of his career was possible. Columbia's presidency supplied Butler with the platform he required in his implacable commitment to the Butlerization of America. He derived much of his initial authority from his university affiliation, and he understood brilliantly how to enhance it.

To begin with, Butler realized that if Columbia, and its president, were to be important, his institution had to be big—bigger, if possible, than its peers. To this end, he instituted an ambitious, one might almost say frenetic, building plan from the moment he took office. In the first ten years of his tenure he presided over the construction of eleven buildings. As the buildings went up, so did the enrollment figures. Increased numbers of students meant increased tuition dollars that Columbia badly needed to meet its operational expenses and help defray the costs of expansion. But apart from the financial necessity, Butler appreciated that higher enrollments signified an institution's health and prestige. Enrollment figures became the university's bottom line, as it were, the not-for-profit's equivalent of a business corporation's net income figure. Including all manner of enrollments — summer school registrations, home-study students, and the like — in his official total, Butler made sure the numbers ticked ever higher with each passing year. He proudly trumpeted the increasing size of the university, always careful to emphasize the connection between quantitative growth and qualitative excellence. Expansion was rapid and impressive. By the early 1920s, when "Dr. Butler spoke," it was as the president not just of a university but of one generally acknowledged to be the world's largest. Weighty as his words were in themselves, the public accorded them even more weight because of Columbia's size.

Columbia's transformation into a globally recognized university did not occur simply as a result of Butler's administrative skills, considerable as they might have been, or of the flourishing of the city around it, dramatic as that was. It was driven by Butler's view that Columbia had a sacred mission: to generate a civilizing force and intellectual power that would shape the modern world. Skeptics such as Abraham Flexner mocked his aspirations, deriding Butler's comparison of "the slight elevation called Morningside Heights on which Columbia University is situated" to the four most sacred and inspiring spots in the world — the Acropolis, the Mount of Olives, the Capitoline Hill, and Sainte-Geneviève in Paris. For Flexner, "Such language lapped up by the uncritical millions is a serious obstacle in the way of real progress."

Flexner's resistance to Butler's excessive claims was understandable, but it missed the extent to which such convictions can animate an institution's life and contribute to its success. Butler cannot seriously be accused of deluding the public or standing in the way of its realistic understanding of the nature of universities. He was simply articulating an ideal — unrealizable, as all ideals are — that defined his own vision of Columbia. In wanting Columbia to be much more than it could possibly be — a force affecting the spiritual and material nature of civilization—he made it into what it became, a great center of research and learning. John Sexton, the current president of New York University, is right to recognize the obligation of university presidents to create the institutional mythology that their schools require in order to know what they are about and where they are heading. "The greatest power of a university president is to be the Homer of the community," he argues, and in the history of American higher education no president has ever been more brilliantly Homeric in this sense than Nicholas Murray Butler. Flexner might have found the claim absurd, but Columbia could never have managed what it did without Butler's uncompromising belief in its greatness. Butler's declaration of faith at a trustee celebration of his seventy-fifth birthday helps us to understand why Max Frankel's family saw in Columbia one of the distinctive symbols of America:

> What was in my mind, and is in my mind still, is that Morningside Heights shall become the greatest capital of the mind that the world has ever seen—either ancient or modern—and that from it there shall go out to every part of this land and to every foreign land a steady and heartening stream of influence and inspiration in every field of thought and endeavor.

Butler's success in selling both his institution and himself to the world required capacities of a different sort from visionary ones, and he possessed them in abundance. Foremost was his intuitive sense of the need to keep the two products he was marketing—Dr. Butler and Columbia—constantly before the public. Like Andrew Carnegie, Butler had a genius for self-promotion. He grasped early on the insight, attributed to Carnegie by his biographer, "that a man and his business could be so identified in the public mind that whatever the man did became an advertisement for his product." Butler labored unceasingly on behalf of his image. Before the age of television, that meant using the press, whose resources he exploited with virtuoso skill. As the novelist Henry Morton Robinson commented while still a Columbia student in 1932, Butler was

> the originator of the idea that Higher Education must be sold Right, Constantly and in a Large Way . . . All this educational crusading is accompanied by the fanfare of Publicity's bold brass horn. Butler,

like every great modernist, thoroughly believes in the Front Page . . . Butler cannot munch a cruller or buy a Pullman ticket without "the papers" knowing all about it.

Or, put more sonorously by a hostile editorial writer in Indiana some years later, Butler was a man "who can merely gasp, wheeze or gargle and find himself quoted in headlines."

Not surprisingly, Butler numbered among his friends the editors and publishers of newspapers throughout the country—Maurice Sherman of the *Hartford Courant*, William Allen White of *The Emporia* (Kansas) *Gazette*, Alfred Holman of the *San Francisco Argonaut*. And most important of all, the young publisher of *The New York Times*, Adolph Ochs. Superficially, Ochs and Butler were quite different: Ochs, an uneducated Jewish outsider, and Butler, the WASP insider bedecked with academic titles and honorary degrees. But coming to power in New York at roughly the same time (Ochs bought the *Times* in 1896) and sharing a socially conservative view of the world—Ochs was said to "worship the God of things as they are"—each came quickly to cultivate the other. For Butler, it was a calculated matter of self-interest: the *Times* served as his own personal press agency. For Ochs, it was a question of unabashed hero worship. He revered Butler's culture and learning, finding in his intellectual achievements the embodiment of everything the untutored Ochs felt he himself lacked. According to Elmer Davis, who wrote a profile of Ochs for *The New Yorker*, Ochs put Butler on his very short list—along with Woodrow Wilson, Calvin Coolidge, and theatrical producer Morris Gest—of "radiant beings from a celestial world." A series of important *Times* editors and managers—Carr Van Anda, John Finley, Louis Wiley, Karl Miller—understood the paper's commitment to Butler and made sure that he received the attention that their publisher found appropriate for a figure of such distinction. The *Times* supported Butler's political positions, devoted countless editorials to celebrating his achievements, covered his speeches, addresses, and reports, praised his stewardship at Columbia, published the Christmas greetings Butler issued to the world each December, and permitted him space for sixteen pseudonymous articles in 1916 presenting his ideas for terminating the war. The paper even felt it newsworthy to announce when the Butlers were leaving for their European travels in the summer and when they were expected back in the fall. Butler never uttered a statement or made a decision the *Times* didn't like. It was no wonder that President James Angell of Yale, at a dinner honoring Butler's thirty years as Columbia's head, commented admiringly, "The metropolitan press has become little more than a diary of your daily doings."

Butler's ability to command press attention did not depend simply on the personal affection of editors and publishers, which, after all, would not explain the presence of his gargles and wheezes in small-town papers in Tennessee, Louisiana, North Dakota, and Montana. Butler's most casual utterance found its way into the national news because of the care he took to ensure that every paper in the country received an account of what he said or did. Butler was a master of the art of dissemination and saturation. Every speech he gave, whether to Columbia freshmen or Barnard alumnae, was grist for his advertising mill. He even sent the guest list for his parties at the presidential mansion to the press. Although he employed two press agents, Butler functioned effectively as his own public relations firm, committed to the notion that no day was satisfactory unless his name appeared in the newspaper. In pursuit of this goal, he proved to be an inexhaustible supplier of material to be publicized, producing at least one hundred articles, addresses, welcoming remarks, reviews, introductions, public letters, reports, and the like every year. The most substantial of these were regularly collected into books. Beginning with his undergraduate prize essay on the *Effect of the War of 1812 upon the Consolidation of the Union*, published in 1887, Butler went on to complete twenty volumes during his lifetime. He was successful enough in making himself into a recognized brand name that the *American Educational Review* assumed it would be understood when it characterized observations he made in 1924 as "truly Butleriolic."

Butler was particularly concerned that his work reach the world's political and intellectual elite. What newspaper coverage could obviously not guarantee, direct mailing would—helped along by the funds to which he had access through the Carnegie Endowment for International Peace. An exchange in 1933 with Henry Haskell, his assistant at the Endowment, reveals Butler's thoroughness: announcing in July that the subject of a September address would be "The Ship of State," an examination of some features of American government, he urged Haskell to prepare the appropriate mailing lists and make sure that enough copies were available for immediate distribution. Columbia would be responsible for his university, editorial, personal, and political lists, and Butler expected the Endowment to take care of the rest. Haskell checked back on August 2 to make sure he had understood what Butler wanted. Beyond the four groups handled by Columbia, the Carnegie mailing would go to:

Trustees of Carnegie Endowment
                      Foundation
                      Corporation
Justices of U.S. Supreme Court
Judges of U.S. Circuit Courts of Appeal
Judges of New York Court of Appeals
Judges of the New Jersey Court of Errors and Appeals
President of the United States, Vice-President, Members of
    Cabinet and Chief Assistant Secretaries
United States Senate—home addresses
House of Representatives—home addresses
Governors of all the States
Foreign Ambassadors & Ministers at Washington
Counsellors or chief secretaries of each Embassy or Legation at
    Washington
U.S. Ambassadors, Ministers, Consuls-General in Foreign Service
Carnegie Endowment foreign list
Bishops of the Roman Catholic Church
            Protestant Episcopal Church
            Methodist Episcopal Church
World Almanac: Presidents of all colleges
            Officers of Educational, Religious organizations
Old and New Correspondents
Comité d'Administration
Foreign Newspapers

A total, Haskell calculated, of nine thousand copies.

Although Butler always directed himself to a highbrow audience, he became a figure esteemed by lesser brows as well. Middle-class America adopted him as its best-beloved upper-class pundit. Butler had no problem with this role, happy to dispense his influence and sell his image wherever he could. At the beginning of 1945, for example, *Pageant* magazine asked various "prominent people" to share their New Year's resolutions with the world (or at least that portion of it that read *Pageant*). Butler, America's "Public Sage no. 1," according to the *Muscatine* (Iowa) *Journal*, was apparently not disturbed to appear next to the young Frank Sinatra, "America's number one crooner." And certainly his resolution was socially more significant than Sinatra's. While Sinatra was content to encourage people "to nourish a feeling of confidence in your own abilities. To acquire poise and charm, to develop your own individual personality is to learn to live," Butler offered a grand ambition appropriate to a serious international statesman: "Let us resolve to take leadership in the effort to unite the independent nations of the world in a movement to co-operate in the establishment of peace, prosperity and sound public morals, and to protect these by an international police force composed of the combined navies of the world."

Butler understood both the quantitative features of marketing as well the need to attract consumer interest in his intellectual goods. He instinctively appreciated from the start of his university presidency the opportunity every Columbia address gave him to reach a larger public. He used his annual reports to the university trustees, ostensibly in-house documents dealing with conditions at the university, as occasions for musing on the state of education generally, on manners, morals, ethics, history, economics, and the American way of life. The incremental attention earned by the regularly scheduled ceremonial address or report was also not lost on Butler. If a single speech was good, a speech given under similar auspices the next year was even better, and by the third year an eagerly anticipated event with a built-in audience had been created. Such was the case with Butler's Parrish Art Museum lectures in Southampton, the site of his summer home on Long Island. Having agreed to give a political talk there in 1926, Butler turned it into an annual address, usually in September, whose major significance was always noted by the press. The Oracle of Southampton, as he eventually became known, continued these lectures until 1944, when his physical infirmities required that he stop.

Butler's potent blend of the practical and the visionary is perhaps best analyzed not in a handbook of qualifications for university presidents, but in an article written in 2000 by Michael Maccoby for the *Harvard Business Review* on what makes successful CEOs of major corporations. Maccoby's description of what he calls "productive narcissists" is an extraordinarily accurate assessment of Butler's strengths. It demonstrates that Butler was intuitively functioning as a modern CEO long before the term was ever thought of. Maccoby argues that today's CEOs "hire their own publicists, write books, grant spontaneous interviews, and actively promote their personal philosophies. Their faces adorn the covers of magazines like *Business Week, Time* and *The Economist* . . . They shape public and personal agendas." At best, Maccoby's narcissists are gifted and creative strategists who seize opportunities and tend to see the big picture before others do. Critical to their success is their ability to attract followers through the power of their rhetoric. They are skillful orators who "believe that words can move mountains and that inspiring speeches can change people."

Butler's career testifies to the power of Maccoby's insight into the importance of language to an effective leader's self-creation. From his earliest years, Butler was effortlessly at home with words, reveling in his ability to dazzle listeners with his precocious verbal talents. At thirteen he gave the commencement day oration for his high school class, and at twenty, the class day address at Columbia.

"'Talking with Dr. Butler,' as one enthusiastic friend confided to another, 'is like listening to a symphony orchestra.'" Professor and inventor Michael Pupin referred to the "magic of Butler's winged words." Although he distrusted Butler's verbal facility, Roger Howson, a Columbia librarian and university historian, accurately diagnosed his president's ability to build a career out of language:

> For him words were things out of which one made sentences, out of sentences one made speeches and out of one's speeches one compiled a career and a life. Speeches made at the right place, at the right time and to the right people formed a balloon barrage to keep intruders and inquirers at a safe distance. There was always an adequate supply of such speeches and enough in each speech to assure approval and agreement. If one agrees to 97% of the statements in a speech the 3% that is questionable seldom gets questioned. And if the subject of the speech is sufficiently general one forgets what in particular is omitted.

His seductive skills from the lecture podium were legendary. Dean James Russell of Teachers College remembered a twenty-minute introduction Butler delivered without any notes: "There was a perfectly beautiful flow of language. He was an artist at this. He had the amazing ability of putting one word next to another and making it sound beautiful. He went on and on." Afterward, when a reporter who came late asked Russell what had been said, "I suddenly realized that I couldn't remember a thing that he had said. It just sounded so wonderful."

Butler was very much a man of words, but not everyone admired them. Skeptics like Walter Lippmann dismissed Butler's resonant language as essentially vacuous. Humorist Finley Peter Dunne claimed that the quality of Butler's oratory in his annual Southampton Labor Day talks was so rich that "it was possible to waltz to it"; the journalist Dorothy Dunbar Bromley thought his addresses "interminable miasmas of guff"; Robert Shafer, a critic, noted that "wherever windbags are in demand President Butler is still asked to speak"; for McAlister Coleman, Butler crafted his arguments "in phrases that glow with empty grace." The feisty *New Yorker* writer Joseph Mitchell declared that "even the semi-colons are pompous" in Butler's prose, noting that any list of occupational hazards faced by reporters would have to include "indigestion, alcoholism, cynicism and Nicholas Murray Butler."

Harvard professor Harold J. Laski, whose radical social views clashed dramatically with Butler's conservative ones, mocked what he considered his predictable conventionality. Laski headed a review of Butler's *A World in Ferment*, published five months after America had entered World War I, "Nicholas Murray Tupper," referring to Martin Tupper, the nineteenth-century British author of *Proverbial Philosophy*, whose name had become a synonym for the contemptible commonplace. College presidents, Laski concluded,

> must perforce burnish platitude to the semblance of thought. That is, perhaps, in ordinary times. But as President Butler himself will not deny, these are not ordinary times. May not the young men who crave some stimulation, some intellectual clarity, some insight into the justice of their sacrifice, legitimately be resentful? May they not rightfully ask more than that they shall be gathered together and told—"You are about to die, and two and two make four"?

Whether one was moved or appalled by Butler's words, they were indisputably the major source of the recognition he earned for himself. Their sheer profusion carved out a space in the American consciousness where the less loquacious feared to tread. When speaking, Butler also took care to pronounce them in a way that drew attention to their gravity. He employed what Jacques Barzun called the "Dutch Patroon Accent," in which words like "circle," "curve," and "first" were pronounced "coicle," "coive," and "foist." Easily mistaken for Brooklynese, this distinctive accent contributed to his aura of being a long-term, inbred member of Knickerbocker society—socially prominent descendants of New York's original Dutch settlers—instead of the parvenu from Paterson that he actually was. A brief exchange with Clark University president G. Stanley Hall in 1923 testified to the success of Butler's image making. Butler, in praising Hall's autobiography, had remarked on the similarities between Hall's rural childhood educational experiences and his own early schooling in northern New Jersey. Hall expressed surprise: "I did not know your boyhood was rural, but had an impression that you grew up in something like Fifth Avenue surroundings."

Appropriately enough for a man who never seriously entertained the possibility that he might be wrong about anything, Butler's autocratic bearing, like his words and his face, radiated self-assurance. "It has sometimes been remarked," the *Herald Tribune* said in acknowledging his thirty years as Columbia's president, "that Dr. Butler should have lived in an age of dictators." His enthusiasm for democracy stopped short of sharing with others any portion of his own authority. The reason why St. Paul's Chapel on the campus had not been consecrated, Butler explained to Columbia's long-term Catholic chaplain George Ford, was because the act of consecration would have invested the Episcopalian bishop of New York with authority over it—an intolerable situation: "'I,' said Butler, 'am the Bishop of Columbia. And I'll be Bishop of Columbia while I live.'"

He didn't merely hold opinions and issue judgments; he embodied them in an elegantly pugnacious physical self. Stocky and of medium height, Butler had as his defining feature a massive head, sitting, as one magazine described it, "like a dome on the shoulders of Atlas." A formidable forehead, wide-set gray eyes with heavy folds beneath them, a broad nose, and a full, drooping mustache that he liked to stroke while speaking, led the *Glasgow Bulletin* to describe him as "burly of figure and striking in headpiece." The *Times* of London observed that "energy exudes from his every pore. The robust, middle-sized frame seems to be always in motion, its movements are always alert; he couldn't walk from one end of a room to the other without giving the idea of a hasting and unresisting spirit within him . . . One of those positive, downright, thoroughly high-minded controversialists with a tremendous power over the opinions of others." One might compare him to Francis Prescott, Louis Auchincloss's fictional Rector of Justin, whose critics claimed he "looks too much like a great man to be one."

The cumulative distinction Butler fashioned for himself out of language, appearance, manner, and position was nourished by his prescient understanding, to use the mantra of today's technology-driven commerce, of the synergies of cross-selling. The triumvirate of Butlers—the Sage, the president of the world's largest university, and the international statesman and president of the Carnegie Endowment for International Peace—reinforced one another at every turn. His summer trips through Europe under the auspices of the Endowment spread Columbia's reputation abroad, just as his presidency added academic prestige to the Endowment. Both contributed to his stature as Sage even as they derived luster from it. Altogether, a unique combination: "a high priest of things intellectual" who was at once "a human power plant, a political live wire and a tireless dynamo of industry."

Butler gloried in the notion of being recognized as much more than a mere academic. For Americans, whose country was beginning to demonstrate its economic power, the image of a university president as an experienced business executive presiding over a large corporation was reassuring. The praise Butler frequently received for running Columbia like a railroad was serious indeed at a time when the organization of railroads gave America a perfect metaphor for its growing efficiency and industrial might. Even before he tried, during his quest for the Republican presidential nomination in 1920, to resist being classified as another college professor running for the presidency, like Woodrow Wilson, he preferred to be seen not as an academic, but as a manager with cutting-edge administrative skills. Years before Calvin Coolidge's famous declaration that the business of America was business, Butler had intuited what the country was about: BUTLER MEANS BUSINESS, his campaign pin announced.

"Polymath and politician," in Justice Cardozo's words, no university president achieved the worldwide celebrity Butler managed for himself, and no public or political figure acquired the intellectual distinction attributed to him. When the International Mark Twain Society (whose honorary president, surrealistically enough, was Benito Mussolini) awarded him its medal in 1937 for service to education, it was inscribed "To the American Plato." Lists of the great, the profound, the articulate, and the accomplished invariably contained the name of Dr. Butler at the very top: one of "the three greatest thinkers" in America, behind William James and George Santayana; "among the five leading figures of the country"; among "the best thinkers of our time," along with French writer André Maurois and Franklin Delano Roosevelt; among our "five greatest contemporaries" (ahead of Edison but behind Einstein and Mussolini, who were tied for first, followed by Gandhi and FDR); one of only "four good after-dinner speakers in New York"; one of "the two greatest living educators" (Vanderbilt's James Hampton Kirkland being the other); one of the fifty Americans "whom all high school students should know"; tied with several others in fifth place behind FDR, Sinclair Lewis, the Mayo brothers, and Will Rogers for title of "greatest living American." The newspaperman and press agent Edward Marshall explained to Butler in 1928 that he had been fortunate to have associated with many prominent people, among whom three stood out: Teddy Roosevelt, Thomas Edison, and Butler. Although the achievements of all three had already permanently influenced civilization,

> You and Edison are both light-makers, and therefore, probably of greater import than Roosevelt, who to me seems to have been a sort of public conscience. You two are constructive; he was corrective . . . The world, because of Edison, is living every year millions of months longer than it was able to before his creation of a competent illuminant . . . You have done more than anyone of whom I have knowledge to teach humanity how best to use the hours that Edison has given. I always think of you and Edison as unconscious perpetrators of the greatest piece of teamwork in the modern world.

The scope and richness of his career, as much as any individual achievement in it, constituted Butler's greatest triumph. As the *Brooklyn Eagle* commented in 1937,

> He is unique in so many ways that colleges might give a special course on his life up to now as an outline of academic, political and social history of the last half-century. During this period Dr. Butler

has been in the news more than any other American, and has made news more continuously than anyone else. He has been an initiator as well as a commentator, a participant as well as a spectator, a fighter as well as an instigator.

Although he was on occasion likened to Gilbert Murray, the Oxford classicist who actively involved himself, during the early decades of the twentieth century, in the search for world peace, the comparison is not finally useful. Murray was a far more subdued personality, lacking the manic energy that drove Butler. Perhaps the closest American parallel was a man whose background, flamboyant lifestyle, personal wealth, and political commitments were completely different from those of the Sage, namely "the Chief": William Randolph Hearst. They were opposed on almost all the issues— Hearst, the man of the people, a radical, pro-union Democrat, a fierce critic of class privilege, an unwavering isolationist who was against the League of Nations; and Butler, the conservative Republican internationalist, hostile to unions in his defense of corporations and entrenched moneyed interests, and an advocate of the League. What they shared, however, was arguably more important: an all-consuming narcissism, a love of power, a brilliant understanding of the art of self-promotion, and an abiding passion to influence the American political agenda. Both wanted to be president of the United States, and when they were stymied in this aspiration, they spent the rest of their lives using the institutions they commanded to try to shape public opinion. It was a measure of Butler's accomplishment that lacking the ready access to the nation that Hearst's newspaper empire afforded the chief, he still succeeded, as H. G. Wells said, in making himself into a figure who "speaks with the voice of America."

According to Garry Wills, the archetypal American myth celebrates the outsider, the anti-institutional figure who achieves his independence by cutting himself free from restraints and escaping to his freedom in the open spaces. Butler represented an American strain of quite another sort. A prophet of urban power and urban institutions, he earned his cultural centrality not by ambling out into the sunset, but by immersing himself ever more deeply in his metropolitan identity, by accepting yet more honors, affiliations, obligations. His career demonstrates the power of sociologist Georg Simmel's insight that "it is the decisive nature of the metropolis that its inner life overflows by waves into a far-flung national or international area." If John Wayne is Wills's American Adam—"untrammeled, un-spoiled, free to roam, breathing a larger air than the cramped men behind desks"—Butler can properly be seen as the institutional hero, a figure com-mitted to all those values of intellect and culture, of corporate power and in-fluence and social connection that the Wayne symbol equates with sterility and death. A less-resonant image perhaps than that of the unencumbered outsider, it nevertheless is also part of the mythic American experience.

Time has not been kind to Butler. Great and famous as he was ac-knowledged to be during his lifetime, caricature seems now to have effaced icon, and with it all traces of the man whom many of his contemporaries thought was guaranteed a distinguished and lasting place in the country's memory. Even current Columbia students, though they generally realize that their renowned Butler Library was named after somebody, are hard-pressed to identify the person. No one would have been more surprised than Butler at his total disappearance today. His view of his importance is perhaps best caught in a small typewritten chart located in a file of his pa-pers labeled PERSONAL ODDS AND ENDS. Most likely the product of a self-indulgent reverie that he had worked out in an idle moment sometime in 1940, it had no doubt been typed into its current neat form by a dutiful sec-retary:

	Mussolini	Stalin	Hitler	Roosevelt	NMB
Born	1883	1879	1889	1882	1862
Come to Power	1922	1924	1933	1933	1902
Years in Power	18	16	7	7	38
Age	57	61	51	58	78
Total	3880	3880	3880	3880	3880
Divided by 2	1940	1940	1940	1940	1940

Astonishing as this numerical confluence is, it is no less astonishing than the demands of an imperial ego obsessed with making a claim for its own significance. Suggesting rather more recognition than history has granted him, the chart nevertheless must have assured Butler—who was fasci-nated by numbers—that he really did matter as much as he thought he did.

If a man is known not only by his achievements but also by the company he keeps and the company he thinks appropriate for himself, Butler is a compelling American cultural figure of his era. His contemporary obscurity is as unmerited as his numerical fantasy of world leadership was implausible. Somewhere in between, majestic and imperfect, stands the Sage. It is time to rediscover "the foremost American of his day" and the roles he played in the drama of the age that nourished him.

CHAPTER ONE

Flying the Union Jack

✤

A lifelong Anglophile, Butler reveled in his purebred British ancestry. "Speaking some years ago in England," he wrote in *Across the Busy Years*, "I said jokingly that if any one was entitled to fly the Union Jack, I should be at liberty to do so, since there was in my inheritance a strain of Scottish, a strain of English, a strain of Welsh and a strain of Irish." Never mind that as a discarded draft of *Across the Busy Years* indicates, the comment was actually made *to* him in the summer of 1884 by his father's cousin, Lord Chief Justice Coleridge, who laughingly told him when they met in England, "I was the only person known to him who should have the right to fly the Union Jack." A good quip is a good quip, no matter who said it.

Attribution aside, Butler's prized British credentials were in fact impeccable. The English strain first arrived on American shores in the person of Benjamin Loxley from Yorkshire, who settled in Pennsylvania in 1730 and subsequently left his position as keeper of the king's stores in Philadelphia to help in the Revolution. A reward on his head from the British and a commission as captain in the First Artillery Company of Philadelphia followed. Promoted to major, he fought at Germantown and Valley Forge. In addition to his military contributions to the fledgling country, he helped produce twelve children, the youngest of whom married Morgan John Rhys, Butler's Welsh connection.

Rhys was admired by his biographer as "the Welsh Baptist hero of civil and religious liberty" in the eighteenth century. His liberal political and social views—he was sympathetic to the impulses behind the French Revolution, whose early stages he had witnessed in Paris—had not endeared him to Welsh authorities. After returning from Paris, he set about to enhance opportunities for children's religious instruction through developing the Sunday school system. When he learned that the government was not altogether relaxed about what he was doing, he thought it prudent to leave the country. He sailed from Liverpool on August 1, 1794, arriving at the port of New York on October 12. He was thirty-four at the time. He later made his way to Pennsylvania, where he distinguished himself as a community leader, judge, and inspired pastor and preacher. At his early death, in 1804, a monument was established in his memory at the First Presbyterian Church of Philadelphia.

The Welsh and Irish in Butler's background merged when Morgan's daughter, Eliza Rhees (Rhys changed the spelling of his name after arriving here), married Nicholas Murray of Ballynaskea, County Westmeath, in 1830. Nicholas, Butler's maternal grandfather, had traveled across the ocean from Dublin when he was sixteen, landing in New York in 1818. After attending Williams College, he eventually entered the Church, becoming nationally recognized as the pastor of the First Presbyterian Church at Elizabeth. The distinction he achieved during his thirty-seven-year service there was such that he was often referred to good-humoredly as the Presbyterian Pope. Eliza and the Reverend Doctor had ten children, of whom only one—Mary, Butler's mother—ever married. Nicholas died in 1861, a year before his grandson was born.

The next two arrivals were Butler's paternal grandparents, who came already married, and with two-year-old Henry, Butler's father, on February 13, 1835. Although John Thomas Butler-Buchanan (he dropped the Buchanan before landing) was born in Surrey, his family was originally Scottish, having come down from the Highlands to Glasgow sometime in the latter half of the seventeenth century. His wife, Elizabeth Lower, was born in Dorset. The two began their New World existence in New York. Butler's occupation on the ship's manifest was listed as mariner, and it was as a ship's officer that he supported his family while living in New York. It was also as a ship's officer that he died in a fogbound collision somewhere off the coast of Nantucket in 1837. In 1840 Elizabeth Butler moved with seven-year-old Henry to Paterson, where she supported herself by taking in lodgers to her small house on Market Street.

Although not genetically relevant, Butler's Union Jack diversity was reinforced in 1849 when Elizabeth married John Balfour Meldrum of Fife, Scotland. Meldrum had begun manufacturing jute in Dundee, and when he met Elizabeth Butler in Paterson, he had been serving successfully as the general manager of the jute mills of the Dolphin Manufacturing Company. He built a house for them on Clark Street, where they remained for the next thirty years, until he moved to Brooklyn to accept a position as general manager of the Barbour Flax Spinning Company.

Henry Butler and Mary Murray married in 1860. The leader of the intellectual plutocracy, as Upton Sinclair branded him, Nicholas Murray Butler made his decidedly unplutocratic entry into this world in Elizabeth, New Jersey, on April 2, 1862, child of Henry and Mary Butler. Six siblings followed, of whom four survived to adulthood: Henry (1864), William (1866), Eliza (1872), and Mary (1878). As befits a godlike figure of the sort Butler aspired to be, his beginnings were not without their mythological dimension. According to family lore, at least as passed on by Butler himself, several days after the infant Murray was born in his grandparents' house, his aunt Rosa took him up to the cupola, along with an American flag, a Bible, and a ten-dollar gold piece. Although no information exists about what occurred, it is clear that the purpose of the exercise was to baptize the newest Butler into the values of patriotism, piety, and wealth. Whatever incantations were uttered, their efficacy cannot be doubted. Aunt Rosa must have died a happy death in 1913, comfortable in the knowledge of what she had accomplished fifty-one years earlier at the top of Grandmother Butler's house.

Despite William Carlos Williams's assertion in the fourth book of *Paterson* that Butler was born there, he didn't in fact move to Paterson with his parents until he was two years old. Writers using New Jersey as settings for their work seem eager to lay claim to him. If Williams has him being born in Paterson, Philip Roth's *American Pastoral* locates his growing up in Elizabeth.

Always reluctant to reveal anything that smacked of the messily personal, Butler made sure that the "Recollections and Reflections" section of *Across the Busy Years* contained very little material about his parents. "It is not easy for a son to record with any freedom memories of his mother and father," he states without explanation. Stripped of any affect, his portrait of Henry at least records some of the pertinent facts. Henry grew up on Clark

Street with his mother and stepfather, and he graduated at eighteen from Burlington College, a tiny, ephemeral institution founded by a Bishop Doane who was head of the diocese of New Jersey. In its laudatory obituary, the *Paterson Press* noted that Henry graduated high in his class, but since, as Butler recalled, there were only four students in the one class that graduated from the school, perhaps this did not constitute a significant achievement. Following his college work, Henry, at his mother's insistence, apprenticed as a machinist in a Paterson locomotive shop in order to master some useful skills. After several years he left to become a salesman in a linen importing house in New York, moving from there in six years or so to starting his own importing business in New York. At the close of the Civil War he joined his stepfather in the manufacturing of jute carpet. When the firm of Meldrum and Butler dissolved, in 1880, he rented a new mill and continued on his own until the rigors of foreign competition forced him to close the business in 1892. From 1888 to 1898 he also owned a silk-manufacturing plant.

Henry's modest professional success—on several occasions in the 1890s he had to accept Murray's offer of a loan to help him over some financially rough times—did not begin to exhaust his status in the Paterson community. He was actively involved in the city's political and educational circles, serving on the board of education and the board of prison inspectors and narrowly losing as the Republican candidate for mayor in 1879. His Hamilton Avenue home provided a center of intelligent talk about books, politics, and ideas for his array of friends. According to Gardiner Cove, a textile-manufacturing colleague, Henry was "the greatest and most interesting conversationalist" he had ever met, "well posted on general business and world and domestic politics." Butler remembered with fondness listening as a boy to the intense arguments that took place on the porch during summer evenings or in the library when it became too cold to sit outside. The discussions were never trivial or gossipy, according to Butler, and never sank to mercenary matters: "They were as unconcerned with money as if such a thing did not exist." Serious issues only were engaged, providing the schoolboy with an education not available in the classroom. Young Murray might not have participated, but he certainly absorbed.

His fascination with politics, apparent at a precociously early age, was symbolically encouraged by his parents from infancy. Just as Aunt Rosa had initiated him into patriotism, piety, and wealth, so Mary carried him in her arms down West Jersey Street in Elizabeth to see Abraham Lincoln as he passed through on the railroad in 1864. Several years later, when Andrew Johnson's train stopped in Elizabeth and he appeared on the rear platform, Henry lifted Murray up so that Johnson could shake his hand.

The indoctrination was potent. "You seem to take a great deal of interest in the election in Paterson," his uncle Chalmers wrote to his ten-year-old nephew in 1873, "and I regret it did not go your way, but you will, I trust, have better luck next time." A year later, Republican luck had not changed, and Chalmers again sympathized: "I was sorry for your sake that the Republicans were so routed in New Jersey this fall." In 1876, as his father's political hero, James G. Blaine, struggled against Rutherford B. Hayes for the Republican presidential nomination, Butler was arguably the only thirteen-year-old boy who bothered to memorize Robert Ingersoll's nominating speech for Blaine. Butler's willingness to be seduced by Ingersoll's shameless excesses—"This is a grand year . . . a year in which they call for the man who has torn from the throat of treason the tongue of slander; the man who has snatched the mask of Democracy from the hideous face of the rebellion; the man who, like the intellectual athlete, hath stood in the arena of debate challenging all comers, and who up to the present moment is a total stranger to defeat"—tells us much about the origins of his own rich political rhetoric. In every way, the intellectual stimulation he received at 175 Hamilton Avenue contributed to his passionate adult interest in public affairs.

Butler's sparse account of his father seems positively flamboyant when compared to what he is willing to reveal about his mother. "It is not possible to put on paper what I feel and could say concerning the personality of my mother and that of my grandmother Meldrum," Butler wrote, a reluctance made the more emphatic by the next paragraph's declaration that "my mother's memory is too sacred to be made the subject of record." A refusal to speak about his mother did not prevent him from remarking that she was as well educated as a woman of that era could hope to be, enjoyed literature and music, was interested in the lives of her five children, and presided over a household "of great beauty and charm, marked by simplicity and entirely normal relationships." Beyond this rather scanty summary of Mary's life, Butler was not prepared to go: "This much can perhaps be properly recorded but more may not be said."

The sacred silence Butler was comfortable maintaining about his mother was not shared by his step-grandfather, John B. Meldrum. Meldrum's correspondence with his sister-in-law and her daughters in Scotland supplies us with a few glimpses of Mary beyond the image of the perfect mother. Wracked with endless headaches and always complaining about her ill health and the extent to which her family exploited her, Mary appears a far more plausible human being than the saintly maternal presence Butler allows. She makes demands and is bored by Paterson, wishing instead "to live in New York City amongst her father's rich friends, and jaunt about in summer time to watering places."

She was also extremely obstinate, a trait that Meldrum argued had fatal consequences for two of her children, Jack and Rhees, who died of scarlet fever in 1872. When Henry, Butler's father, contracted the disease, Meldrum and his wife begged Mary to let the two boys live temporarily with them in Brooklyn until Henry recovered. She refused to consider it, convinced that "to have them removed was to distrust Providence." Meldrum's Providence, he later confided to his sister-in-law, tended "to help those who helped themselves." Henry apparently had no say in the mattter, which was not surprising. Although Henry might have been a revered public figure, fully engaged in Paterson's civic life, it was Mary who essentially ran things in the home, forged the personal bonds with the children, and provided the emotional nourishment necessary for their growth. However stimulating the conversation of Henry's friends, 175 Hamilton Avenue comprised Mary's turf.

Despite the insistence of some that Butler sprang fully formed into this world, formidably mustachioed, wearing a three-piece suit and spouting perfect paragraphs, compelling evidence exists that he did indeed experience a normal human childhood. "Henry's boys are getting the upperhand of everyone save their Pa," Grandpa Meldrum complained. "Mur and Har are the most rebellious and disobedient little varlets so far as their mother is concerned." His affection for them was marred by an appropriate grandfatherly impatience at their rambunctiousness: "I am always glad to see them come and equally pleased to have them go. Their shouting and screaming at dinner table and general lawless behavior would make your eyes open wide—the rude and sometimes profane language they pick up in the streets is at times distressing."

While Mary seemed exhausted by the behavior of "her young wolves," she suffered even more when their father disciplined them. "Her boys are more hopelessly disobedient and rude than anything that you can conceive of," Meldrum grumpily remarked when Murray was ten, "and when Henry punishes them, which he is by no means slow to do, she hugs and kisses them and undoes all the good that the punishment has been productive of."

Her maternal protectiveness did not entirely obscure her equally maternal ambitions to help Murray achieve perfection. On his first real absence from home, attending his uncle Chalmers's graduation from Williams College with his grandmother in the summer of 1869, she reminded him to be a good boy, rejoicing "that you are so well and happy, and I think you will be such a man after having been to College, that we shall have no more trouble with you." "Be a little more careful of your spelling," she cautioned eight-year-old Murray while he was on vacation with the Meldrums, including with this exhortation a list of his school's "distinguished and meritorious pupils" from which he was noticeably missing. "I am sorry not to see your name," she rebuked him, "but you see that your deportment has told against you very seriously."

His behavior perhaps kept him off the honor list, but his academic work never posed a problem. Butler always found school congenial and never encountered any difficulty with its demands. Years later he was fond of extolling the "good, old-fashioned education" he had received in the Paterson school system, first at age five and a half, at the small school run by Elizabeth Calkins, then in 1870 to 1872 at Public School #1, and finally as one of the two boys (out of thirteen students) graduating from the first class at Paterson High School in 1875.

Although from the perspective of twenty-first-century curricular reform one might question the goodness of his early training, its solid old-fashionedness was indisputable. Butler's high school entrance examination, which he took in December of 1872 (he would have taken it in September, but an attack of scarlet fever—the same that killed his two brothers—caused him to miss several months of school), came from the Paleolithic era of educational theory in which students were actually expected to know vast amounts of information. (In 1936 Butler came across his examination and sent copies of it, without his answers, to twenty-five school superintendents from Massachusetts to California, asking if they would submit them to students of the appropriate age. Their answers, according to Butler, were "too amusing to be printed anywhere except in a comic almanac.")

Defining the fundamental rules of arithmetic, listing the principal parts of a verb, naming the major rivers, lakes, and mountains of North America, parsing sentences—Butler drew upon an immense amount of rote learning simply unimaginable today. It is safe to say that few contemporary college students could begin to match the information asked of Butler in the geography section, where he had to name the boundaries of Europe and the major rivers, seas, gulfs, and mountains of Asia, Africa, and Europe.

> Europe is bounded on the north by the Arctic Ocean, North Sea, Bay of Biscay, Black Sea, on the east by the Atlantic Ocean, North Sea, Arctic Ocean, Meditterranean [sic] Sea, and a small part of Asia, on the south by the Meditterranean Sea, Black Sea, Caspian Sea, and part of Asia, on the west by Asia, Meditterranean Sea, Black Sea, Caspian, Arctic Ocean, Dover Straits, English Channel and the St. Georges Channel, & Irish Sea and North Sea. The principal rivers are, the Volga, Nile, Cambodia, Amoor, Obe, Niger, Rhine, Rhone, Vistula, Saoone, Seine, Tiber, Arno, Danube, Dniester, Dnieper, Don, Elbe, Weser, Main, Thames. The principal gulfs are the Gulf of Bothina, Gulf of Guinea, Gulf of Aden, Gulf of Aegina, Persian Gulf, Gulf of Siam. The principal seas are Meditterranean, North, Arabian, China, Java, Yellow, Black, Caspian, Kamschaka, White.
>
> The principal mountains are Alps, Appennines, Pyrenees, Ural, Scandinavian, Atlas, Kong, Himalaya, Stanovoy.

Hardly the kind of learning John Dewey most esteemed, but still not unimpressive for a ten-year-old trying to get into high school. Miss Gall, the "excellent and efficient" teacher who graded his examination, awarded Butler a nine (out of ten) for his geography answer, and a ninety-eight for his overall performance.

For the mature Butler, the examination was historically interesting in providing insight into an age that believed in the powers of mental discipline and in "instruction for the purpose of conveying facts which human experience had taught were of value." Butler's running argument with progressive education (or at least his version of it) held that it encouraged children to feel that they were discovering the world for the first time and that no previous human experience existed that could teach them anything. The learning, however disembodied and mechanical, that Butler poured out on his examination paper embodied an educational ideal he never relinquished.

Praising the strict academic education he received at Paterson High School in *Across the Busy Years*, Butler at the same time condemned the corporal punishment that accompanied it. The beatings, with a belt studded with copper rivets, administered by Principal McIntyre on the offending student's hand were painful and bloody, and Butler in 1939 had nothing good to say about such behavior. Whether Butler's 1939 criticism of this violence was influenced by the world situation at the time, it is difficult to know, but it was certainly the case that in earlier decades he spoke quite fondly of classroom punishment, endorsing it as part of the "old-fashioned" structure of values he found attractive.

Butler's academic prowess notwithstanding, he could only achieve the third rank in class, the first two going to Nancy Dillistin, daughter of a grocer, and Mary Graham, daughter of a contractor and builder. At the high school commencement exercises of June 28, 1875, in which most of the students performed, he was therefore relegated to delivering what the *Paterson Daily Press* somewhat portentously called an "oration," the salutatory and valedictory addresses being reserved for Graham and Dillistin.

By any standards, "The Age in Which We Live" must be considered an extraordinary instance of precocity and pomposity. A "resume of the triumphs of man," as the *Paterson Daily Guardian* commented, Butler's analysis bore little resemblance to the voice or vision of a conventional thirteen-year-old. Surveying all of modern science and the world's social and economic progress, the young orator proclaimed it a good time to be alive—and American. "This is indeed a wonderful age," Butler began. "Science and culture joined hand in hand, have changed the face of the world and revolutionized life and society."

Butler's survey found vast improvement in all areas of human endeavor. Science had unearthed the mysteries of nature, the slave trade had been stopped, cities had sprung up, the steam engine had transformed travel and commerce, the science of agriculture had increased the yield from the land, and refinements in the art of war had been more than matched by progress in the arts of peace. Books were available to all, and public school instruction, once so rare, was now available to everybody. The result of this latter development, in perhaps the speech's most compelling formulation, was that "ignorance is no longer looked upon as a misfortune, but regarded as a crime."

In its confident pronouncements, broad sweep, and healthy Americanism, Butler's oration was the exemplary miniature tune-up for the fully orchestrated rhetorical performances regularly delivered by the mature Butler. Whether it was the oration's tone or theme, even Butler admitted that it was "a never-ending subject of teasing on the part of my mother and father for many years."

Given the lack of correlation between college admissions requirements and high school curricula, graduation from high school in 1875 did not necessarily qualify a student for college. However much Butler admired his "good old-fashioned education," it was not so good as to have included Greek and Latin, without which he could not pass (or even take) the entrance examinations for the kinds of elite schools he would be interested in. So before the problem of college choice stood the need for college preparation.

Butler spent 1875–78 remedying his deficiencies. Studying Greek and Latin primarily at home, he also relied on the supervision provided by James D. Donnell, headmaster of a private school for boys in Paterson, and the Reverend J. C. Wyckoff, who ran a private school for girls. Butler spent an hour each day with Wyckoff, who corrected his daily recitations. His uncle Chalmers, who became the first professor of Semitic languages at Johns Hopkins, contributed much encouragement. During this three-year period Butler and his family also spent a great deal of time considering his college options. Despite Butler's lifelong identification with Columbia and his frequently repeated quip that if you cut him open he would bleed Columbia blue, Columbia was not his first choice. In fact, it wasn't even his second.

The Butler "family" college was Williams, attended both by Butler's grandfather, Nicholas Murray (class of 1826), and by his two uncles, Nicholas and Chalmers. It was always assumed that Butler would follow. As Chalmers wrote him from Göttingen, Germany, in 1873, while studying for his Ph.D., "I hope you have already commenced with Latin and I suppose by the time I get back to America you will be quite ready for college. When you do go to college you must go to Williams to keep up the succession of your grandfather and uncles and it would disappoint me greatly to have you go anywhere else."

As appealing as Williams was, the local merits of Princeton were also attractive. The Butlers were impressed with Princeton's academic seriousness and the quality of the students being drawn to it, many of whom came from families well known to them. A detailed comparison of the two was undertaken, with careful attention paid to their programs of study, costs, faculty, and the like. Before any conclusion could be reached, however, one of those unexpected events occurred that entirely changes the course of a person's career. Step-grandfather Meldrum's deteriorating health mandated his retirement from his post at the Barbour flax spinning plant, causing Butler's father in turn to reassess his own business plans and responsibilities. Suddenly a less-expensive Columbia seemed more inviting than either Williams or Princeton. A thorough examination of Columbia's curriculum and faculty seemed to argue that it offered good value, and the decision was made to forgo Williams and Princeton and send Murray to Columbia instead.

In order to do this, of course, he had to pass the college's entrance test in June. His three years of intensive language study prepared him well for his three days of examination on "four books of Caesar's *Commentaries*, on Sallust's *History*, on six orations of Cicero, on six books of Vergil, on three books of the *Iliad* and on Xenophon's *Anabasis*, together with Latin and Greek prose composition."

Columbia also required an examination in ancient history and geography lasting one hour. Dr. Schmidt, author of the standard book on ancient geography, asked Butler only one question: "to name, beginning at the Adriatic, the rivers of Europe going from east to west and around to the north, giving both their English and their Latin names. That meant that I was to be able to say without omitting any: 'Podanus, the Po; Tiberis, the Tiber; Rhodanus, the Rhone; Rhenus, the Rhine'; and so on." Failing to include a half dozen, Butler received a "condition" in the subject, though Schmidt assured him that as soon as he learned the names in correct order, it would be removed, as indeed it was. Entering Columbia with a "condition" was no disgrace, however, and in the fall of 1878 Butler began an affiliation with Columbia that would not end for another sixty-seven years.

The Columbia College that Butler found that fall bore little resemblance to the university he left behind him in 1945, physically, academically, or in any other way. Having moved north from Park Place in lower Manhattan in 1857, the School of Arts, as the liberal arts undergraduate division was then called, occupied the block between Forty-ninth and Fiftieth streets, stretching from Madison to Fourth avenues, on a site purchased from the Lexington Institution for the Deaf and Dumb. Initially conceived of as a temporary location, it remained Columbia's home for forty years. Its neo-Gothic campus, completed during Butler's four years there, included a library, a chapel, a house for the president, a building for the School of Mines, and one for the instruction of the School of Arts students. There were no dormitories and no playing fields. Although the surrounding environment had improved by the time Butler arrived, it was still not entirely salubrious. Before the bodies were removed during 1858, students coming across Lexington Avenue and Forty-ninth Street, one block to the east of the campus, could occasionally see the bones of the indigent sticking up out of Potter's Field. The Bull's Head Cattle Yards, several blocks south on Fifth Avenue, lent olfactory pungency to the academic enterprise when the climatic conditions were just right.

Butler was one of seventy-eight entering students in the class of 1882; four years later, forty-eight graduated. We have become so accustomed to thinking of elite colleges as intellectually rigorous places, admitting only a lucky few from the hordes who apply, that it is important to realize that in Butler's time — and for a number of decades thereafter — the problem facing colleges was not the contemporary challenge of deciding among qualified students, but rather the need to convince qualified, and even not so qualified, candidates to apply in the first place. Only a small number sought admission; of these, few were rejected. In Butler's freshman class, for example, one hundred initially applied, and seventy-five were accepted. Three additional students joined somewhat later. In the late nineteenth century most undergraduates attended schools within one hundred miles of their homes. The absence of dormitories guaranteed the parochial nature of Columbia's student body. Of Butler's original seventy-seven colleagues, only sixteen were not from Manhattan, coming instead from such exotic places as Brooklyn; Yonkers; New Jersey; Greenwich, Connecticut; and even Tarrytown, New York.

Butler's commuting experience divided itself between Brooklyn and New Jersey. During his first two years his travel from Step-grandfather Meldrum's house on Sackett Street involved his walking to the Brooklyn terminus of the Hamilton ferry, taking the ferry to the foot of Whitehall Street in Manhattan, and then boarding the Third Avenue El for a twenty-five-minute ride to Forty-seventh Street, two blocks from the campus. After two years of this, Butler decided to move back to Paterson, where a longer, more complicated journey awaited him: an eight-block walk from 175 Hamilton

Avenue to the Erie Railroad Station, a train trip to the Pavonia Street station in Jersey City, and a twenty-minute ferry ride across the Hudson to West Twenty-third Street, followed by a horsecar across town to Fourth Avenue and another one north to Columbia. In order to arrive in time for the morning chapel service, Butler had to be sure to catch the 7:25 train from Paterson to Jersey City.

Once admitted, and for an annual tuition fee of $100, Butler and his fellow students immersed themselves in a required curriculum (with the exception of some senior-year electives) taught by a faculty consisting of ten professors, two adjuncts (today's equivalent of assistant professors), and a half dozen or so assorted tutors and assistants. The precise syllabus for each year, semester by semester, was set out in the informational handbook. The freshman studies Butler encountered in the fall, for example, included the *Odyssey*, Greek prose composition, Greek scanning and prosody, Horace's *Odes* and *Epodes*, Latin prose composition, Latin syntax and prosody, Grecian history, Roman antiquities, geometry, and rhetoric, with German as an optional choice. The spring continued Greek and Latin prose composition, Grecian history, and rhetoric and Roman antiquities, but substituted Herodotus or Xenophon for Homer, algebra for geometry, and Cicero and Pliny for Horace.

If one actually had to know something to get into Columbia, little was expected after that. Classes ran for three hours a day only, from 10:00 a.m. to 1:00 p.m., following the mandatory chapel service that started at 9:40. Students sat in alphabetical order in the chapel, and class officers specially appointed by the president took daily attendance. The four officers of the roll were each provided with a seat permitting a full view of his particular class. Anyone absent from more than one fourth of the chapel exercises for a term was "debarred from being any longer a candidate for a degree." (Other infractions that could terminate enrollment included leaving the college premises before the end of the third hour and missing more than one quarter of the classes in any single department.)

The classes themselves were never intended to be intellectually challenging. They consisted almost entirely of students spewing back in recitation sections that they had previously memorized from the textbooks or the professor's lecture. Independent thinking was rarely a requirement, and academic standards were practically nonexistent. Whether standards should exist at all had in fact provided a legitimate issue of trustee inquiry some twenty years before Butler entered. In a report published in 1858, a committee of five trustees debated "whether public opinion would sanction a strict course, and whether, to avoid a large diminution of students, allowance ought not to be made for defect of intellectual capacity, imperfect elementary training and inattention or indifference of parents as to the studies of their sons."

Should standards be set too high, it was argued, "you might exclude students of dull or slow minds, who are yet faithful and diligent." Such an exclusion would clearly affect the tuition revenues on which the school depended. On the other hand, although enforcing standards could result in a loss of potential students, it might also prove beneficial by convincing skeptical families that Columbia was actually trying to train their sons to some purpose, thereby attracting students who might otherwise have been sent elsewhere. A similar argument presented itself concerning admissions: Should Columbia admit even the deficient, on the grounds that they might improve, or should applicants be held to a serious level of preparation and achievement? In both cases the claim for some form of standards triumphed, but that these issues should have been debated at all raises disturbing questions about what sort of institution Columbia was at the time.

A major part of Columbia's difficulties could be traced to the largely moribund body of trustees reluctant to make changes or exercise any kind of creative leadership. They were controlled by their treasurer, Gouverneur M. Ogden, who tended to think of Columbia more as a real estate holding whose funds had to be meticulously husbanded than as an academic institution that needed to grow if it was to stay alive. The diary of the splendidly acerbic New York lawyer George Templeton Strong best expressed the despair of the progressive trustees at the suffocating mediocrity around them. When Wolcott Gibbs, because of his Unitarianism, was denied a professorship of chemistry in 1854 in favor of a less-qualified man, Strong deplored the "Boeotian fogyism, the abyss of inert, stolid, obstructive, and obstinate, mulish, willful stupidity revealed in the talks and acts, the theories and policies of the five fossils."

His contempt for the shortsightedness of the board was profound: "I have come to the conclusion that the College is hopelessly given over to coma, stupefaction and probable poverty for the present generation." Strong's enthusiasm for the college and his sense of its possibilities kept him on the board despite his instincts to flee: "It is the Castle of Indolence, the College of Non-Feasance . . . It is a hopeless case of corporate paralysis and I wish I had never been honored with a seat on the Board." He was horrified at the proposal to consider moving the college to Westchester, away from the city's vital currents: "Imbecility, stagnation, lethargy and torpor, genteel non-feasance, dignified conservative urban paralysis for all good Works. These constitute the fundamental character, essence and idea of our corporate being. So much is clear, so it has been for thirty-five years at least."

However heroic their obtuseness, the hard core of reactionary fogies among the trustees—William Betts, Thomas Wells, Gerrit Van Wagenen, Gerard Morris, and Ogden—finally could not resist the impulses toward progress, and the 1857 move uptown from Park Place marked the first step of Columbia's uncertain stumbling toward the twentieth century. The next step was taken with the appointment of Frederick A. P. Barnard as president in 1864. The choice of Barnard proved to be one of those happy miscalculations of which even the worst-intentioned search committees are capable. The relatively elderly (he was fifty-five at the time), deaf onetime southern gentleman, a respectable scientist sporting a ponderous ear trumpet, hardly seemed the type to cause a largely fossilized board any trouble. And surely the board thought that as well. Appearances notwithstanding, however, Barnard turned out to be a dreamer, an academic visionary full of strange notions, such as teaching modern languages, offering education for women, enriching the curriculum with electives, and, most unsettling of all to trustee inertia, developing the sleepy, insular college into a genuine university. The combination of the radical president, endlessly coming up with subversive ideas, and the reactionary board, steadfastly resisting them, was not the best recipe for institutional success.

It must also be added that Barnard was politically inept and administratively erratic, so that his tenure was vexed from the beginning, a strain for his supporters as much as for his opponents. Articulating his conviction of the college's manifest destiny to be "one day the great university of the city—possibly of the continent," he had to struggle even to get French and German into the curriculum, over the trustees' objections that such an innovation would require classes to go past 1:00 p.m., a change they were reluctant to make. Trustee unwillingness to consider that there might be fruitful academic life after 1:00 p.m. was evident in a rather poignant note that trustee Bishop Horatio Potter wrote to Hamilton Fish regarding the quixotic effort of their colleague, Dr. Cornelius Agnew, to extend the hours:

> Dr. Agnew in his zeal has carried a resolution requiring the work at the college to go on not only to *one* but to 2 p.m. What good can it

do? It will only keep the young men longer from going home to resume their studies. There is no place at coll. in which to study & the
profs can do no more than they are now doing with their present
means and rooms.

Barnard's annual presidential reports, in which he defined his sense of the
college's mission and offered a number of specific recommendations concerning curriculum and administrative structure, soon became so troublesome to the trustees that they at first reduced the number published from
approximately a thousand to fifty, and then for several years refused to publish them at all.

Although the establishment of the faculty of political science in 1880
(see Chapter 3) represented the first stage in Barnard's plan to raise the college "from the level of an elementary school to that of a grand institution of
the highest learning," Columbia was still, during Butler's undergraduate
days, essentially "a school for small children." Without dormitories or even
offices for its ten professors, efficiency of operation with low cost was the
aim: chapel, three hours of classes, students out by 1:00, gates closed, and
college shut down until the next day. (It was thought imperative, for purposes of behavioral decorum, that the students always be occupied in
classes while they were on campus. If they were prohibited from leaving the
premises before one o'clock, the first of the college's general regulations
also declared it out of order for students "to linger about the grounds, the
passages or the vacant rooms" while classes were in session.) A library,
presided over by a librarian who resented anyone's using it, never remained
open for longer than an hour and a half each morning. Under such circumstances it is not surprising that the intellectual life available on Forty-
ninth Street was meager at best. According to Brander Matthews, who
graduated from Columbia in 1871 and went on to become a distinguished
professor of dramatic literature, "You can't imagine the Columbia of that
day. A modern high school probably gives a better all around training.
Though all our instructors were gentlemen, scholars and learned, there was
not a good teacher in the lot . . . All the men were popular, but they just did
not know how to teach."

Into what he later characterized as "a very simple and naive sort of
place," Butler brought a prodigious memory and ferocious desire to succeed. The latter was nourished by family expectations. After the sudden

death of his uncle Chalmers, the burdens of achieving Butler distinction passed to Murray. A letter from Uncle Chalmers's father during the spring of Murray's freshman year declared the responsibilities he was now expected to meet:

> I was very much pleased to learn from your mother's card this morning of your success during your first year at Columbia.
>
> I was very proud and happy to hear of the appreciation accorded to your faithful work and high aims.
>
> You are our rising star now.
>
> I hope and think that you have caught the inspiration which animated your dear uncle, and will do for the world and for those that love you, what he aimed to do.

Murray took seriously his obligation to excel, working hard to remain always at the top of his class, even if it meant putting his health at risk. "Murray we see only on Sundays," Step-grandfather Meldrum reported in 1881. "He is thin, and troubled a good deal from nose bleeding, but sticks to his work as determinatedly [sic] as ever." Butler's obsession with getting the highest grades—a trait that earned him, in the student jargon of the time, the title of "champion bun-yanker"—did not, however, preclude his participation in a variety of collegiate activities. Despite the lack of facilities, undergraduate existence, according to Butler's good friend Harry Thurston Peck, "was full of interest and color and animation," and Butler enthusiastically engaged as much of it as he could. As an editor of *Acta Columbiana*, the college newspaper, he praised the freedom Columbia men could enjoy without the constraints of dormitory living, and he criticized coeducation for turning out "brazen, mannish and unfeminine females." He served as sophomore class secretary; edited the *Columbiad*, the junior class yearbook; and created the fictitious S.P.Q.R., a nonexistent organization intended to draw attention away from the Gemot, a real club to which he had not been admitted. He was a member and officer of Peithologia, one of the two literary debating societies on campus. He drafted the 1882 class constitution and wrote a resolution passed unanimously by the senior class against admitting women to Columbia, which held that "it is the fixed opinion and firm conviction of the Senior Class of Columbia College that the coeducation of the sexes is undesirable from an educational as well as from a social and a moral standpoint, and that its introduction here would be a fatal blow to the future welfare and prosperity of the institution." He played cricket (badly), was rejected for football and crew because he did not weigh enough, and acted as secretary of the college meeting to form a football association. (His role in helping form the association is particularly interesting in light of his presidential decision, in 1905, to ban the game.)

Before he became appalled by its professionalism and violence, in fact, he seemed particularly to enjoy football. He wrote his mother with obvious relish in 1879 about a trip to Princeton to see Columbia play. As Princeton "'runs the racket' on football," little was expected of Columbia, and Butler delighted in his team's gritty effort: "Dave said he never saw such 'tackling' as Henry and DeForest could do; it was funny to see those comparatively little fellows catch Ballard & Pease round the neck & throw them 'heels over appetite.'" Columbia's inevitable loss didn't diminish the expedition's pleasure: "'We went, we saw, we (got) conquered,' but we got a good day's fun."

Perhaps the most lavish event involving Butler was the annual sophomore "Burial of the Ancient" ceremony, whose origins dated back to 1860, in which the textbook deemed most hateful to the sophomores was consigned to flames amid much elaborate ritual. For a number of years the book so honored had been Bojesen's *Grecian and Roman Antiquities*, but Butler's class chose instead March's *Anglo-Saxon Reader*. Butler was elected chairman of the burial committee in charge of the extensive preparations necessary for a successful burial. As the *Acta* cautioned in April—the event was scheduled for May—"The sophomores must take care to deck themselves out well at the burial. Every man should wear a high hat and a gown with emblematic figures attached. It gives more tone to the procession, and looks well to outsiders, besides the over-awing effect it has upon the freshmen. A burial is a grand thing when every minute detail even is carefully attended to, but if only the principal points are looked after, many things fail to harmonize, and the general effect is marred."

With Murray at his organizational best, everything proceeded flawlessly, particularly the two-hour march up Madison Avenue to the campus, including a platoon of police, a German brass band, a trumpeter, twelve mourners wearing academic gowns adorned with skulls and crossbones, four pallbearers chanting funeral songs and carrying in a small bier on their shoulders the loathed Anglo-Saxon reader to be consigned, and three hundred torchbearing students wearing their coats inside out. Accompanied by masses of spectators waving, singing, and cheering, the procession arrived on campus at midnight, where the Deadly Orator addressed the crowd, expressing his feelings about the soon to be cremated text. At the proper moment, the Gravedigger committed March's reader to the flames, after which the Poet, wiping his eyes with a huge black handkerchief, celebrated the many virtues of the recently departed. Following appropriate cheering and lamentation, people repaired to the Terrace Gardens, where the twenty previously purchased kegs of beer were consumed. "Thus," commented the June 1 *Acta*, "passed off the best and most successful Burial that Columbia has ever seen, and it will be a long time before it is surpassed."

The class of '82's distaste for its mandatory confrontation as sophomores with Anglo-Saxon and its instructor, Charles Scott, involved Butler in yet another way. As the unofficial class slogan chanted repeatedly throughout the burial— "Who was the great Scott? Last in peace, last in war, Last in the heart of the soph-o-more"—made clear, Mr. Scott did not have a large following among the students. (The sophomore animus against Scott was such that after the burial, *Acta* reported, "A few men returned to the college at three o'clock, burst in the door of Mr. Scott's room and removed his table and its contents to the campus where it was destroyed in the flames.") Had there been any doubts about Scott's reputation, the 1881 *Columbiad*, featuring a dramatic satire entitled "A Glimpse of Hell; or an Hour With the Anglo-Saxons," would have put them to rest. A thoroughly puerile spoof, it mocked Scott and his incapacities, ending with him being knocked senseless as the chorus sings, "Charles Scat's body lies a mould'ring in the grave." Scott was legitimately aggrieved over the drama's publication, and even though he wasn't especially popular, the faculty took up his cause. As chairman of the *Columbiad* and anonymous author of the piece, Butler was fully responsible, but in a way that pointed to some of the future personal skills he would display in easing his way past blame, he managed to stay above the controversy that ensued. Robert Arrowsmith, the business manager, was instead chastised by the faculty, which insisted that all copies of the issue be destroyed. Most were, but as Butler later admitted with a malicious twinkle, not quite all. Why Butler escaped censure, or, worse, why he permitted Arrowsmith to absorb all the criticism, remains unclear.

Andrew Carnegie, in some of the instructions for worldly success he endlessly dispensed to the young, advised that "the battle of life is already half won by the young man who is brought personally in contact with high officials; and the great aim of every boy should be to do something beyond the sphere of his duties—something which attracts the attention of those over him." Butler instinctively understood this; he possessed a sensitive tropism toward the powerful that was to serve him well throughout his life. It was not surprising, then, that the most significant relationship Butler formed in his college years was not with any of his classmates, but rather with President Barnard himself.

No record exists of how they first met. Certainly in a school of 250 or so boys it would not be unusual for the president to know a number of them, especially the outstanding ones. But it is also hard to believe that Butler would have been entirely passive in making this connection. Murray was not the kind to pass up opportunities, and Barnard, ear trumpet and all, was clearly an opportunity. Whatever the circumstances that brought them together, Barnard immediately took an interest in Butler. Having gotten to know him, Butler reported, Barnard "occasionally summoned me to his office during the afternoon to question me about various things or to offer me advice of one kind or another." *Across the Busy Years* describes the formative moment in Butler's life:

> This happened some time after the middle of junior year. Doctor Barnard sent for me one afternoon and, after a few preliminary words, asked me bluntly what I intended to do upon graduation . . . I answered rather conventionally that I expected to study law, to take an interest in politics and to do the usual things that went with those interests and occupations. Doctor Barnard, after hearing this statement, replied crisply and somewhat bluntly: "That would be a great mistake . . . Why not do something distinctive, something that is really worth while, something new and constructive?" He enlarged upon these questions of his by plunging into a really eloquent exposition of the subject of education and of the place which the study of education and its problems should and might occupy in the intellectual and political life of the American people . . . I listened with growing interest but without much understanding. Education I had always thought of as a mere process involving the teacher and the taught. To look upon it as a great social institution having a philosophical basis and a moral purpose and ideal was something that had never entered my mind.

Once entered, it stuck, and with the inducement of several volumes on education lent to him by Barnard, Butler "became an enthusiastic convert to President Barnard's ideas and hopes for me, and straightaway resolved to abandon all thought of the study of law and its accompaniments and to give my life to an academic career for the express purpose of understanding, promoting, developing and applying the subject of education, both as an intellectual discipline and as a human institution." In the process, though he certainly couldn't have fully appreciated this at the time, Butler latched onto what was to prove one of America's greatest growth industries in the twentieth century—the research university—giving him access to a career of unrivaled power and visibility. The rising star of the Butler family could not have chosen more wisely.

With his career goals firmly in place by the end of his junior year, Butler intensified his senior year efforts, as his step-grandfather Meldrum anxiously noted, to graduate at the top of his class:

> Murray now 20 is very near the end of the curriculum of 4 years at Columbia . . . His ambition to be the first of his year in all the classes is very great and the amount of hard study bestowed has been very great. We have been much alarmed that his physical health would break down under this excessive strain—indeed several times it looked as if this must happen. He is now within a few weeks of the termination and we are sanguine will come off well and triumphant.

Grandpa Meldrum's hopes were happily fulfilled. Butler's senior year performance earned him the distinction of being one of two men to achieve First Honor Class status. In addition he received the Chanler Historical Prize and, most important for his academic plans, the three-year Fellowship in Letters that would see him through to the Ph.D. at Columbia.

Butler was always proud of the fact that with the exception of his freshman tuition of $100, he financed his educational expenses totally by himself. Along with money earned as a campus correspondent for the *Tribune* and a part-time teacher of mathematics and classics at the Drisler School for Boys and of logic and ethics at Mrs. Sylvanus Reed's school for girls, the cash prizes he gathered in specific courses played a significant part in making this possible. Including his fellowship money, Butler accumulated $1,960 in academic awards (as well as seven honorable mentions) during his time in school. By comparison, Joseph Baker, his fellow First Honor classman, received $400 and five honorable mentions.

One prize that carried with it no stipend but nevertheless anticipated Butler's later successes was that designated by the Columbia College Talking Club, whose motto was "Too muchee damnee chin-chin." With a number of award categories available, including First Historical Parallelist, Unassisted Talker-to-Death, and Head Wild and Chivalrous Assertionist, Butler was granted Champion General Talker, a title for which, over the next sixty-five years, he had few rivals anywhere in the world. It was not a title that conflicted at all with Meldrum's insight into his eighteen-year-old grandson that "he is the most reticent person I ever knew—can hardly be got to speak of himself or plans in any degree, and does not like being questioned." A veritable talking machine in public, able to speak on any topic of any length under any circumstances, he was at the same time extremely reluctant ever to reveal personal feelings. In Butler, the Champion General Talker and the guarded, intensely private person existed in oxymoronic harmony. The Talking Club and Grandfather Meldrum were both right in their characterizations.

Appropriately enough, it was Butler's capacity for speech, not silence, that concluded his public career as a college student when he was chosen to give the class day oration on June 2, 1882. (When the faculty submitted to the class the names of twenty-two seniors as candidates for the valedictory address to be given on commencement, held on June 14, Butler was not selected for what was arguably a greater honor.) Its bittersweet tone of sadness and exhilaration was what one would expect from class day addresses by twenty-year-olds. Butler evoked the splendors of their past four years — "Our riotous rushes [cane rushes, competition between freshman and sophomore classes], those tempestuous times in Anglo-Saxon, the harrowing hours in mathematics, the boisterous burial, the canonical 'Columbiad' — all will form the topic of many an hour's pleasant reminiscence" — but then he acknowledged that it was time to look ahead. We seek to "pierce the future's veil," realizing that before "Old Sol rides high in Cancer we shall be scattered to the four winds of heaven." No longer pleasure-loving undergraduates, they were soon to be "plunged into the mad vortex of life." All this was standard stuff, although the rhetoric was perhaps somewhat more fulsome than most seniors would be capable of.

The tone might have been predictable, but the speech's concluding argument—an exhortation against overweening ambition, an insistence that we accept our limitations and refuse the temptation "to pass beyond the finite and attain the infinite"—was not. For a man whose own ambitions knew no bounds, it is fascinating to see him advocating the virtues of restraint. Correctly diagnosing part of the quintessential American aspiration, or even pathology, at the end of the century—"In these days and especially in this country we are far more likely to be led astray by that 'vaulting ambition which o'erleaps itself,' than by any baser motive"—Butler at the same time defined the very animating impulses of his own life. His urging that we "keep steadily before us the motto of the ancient sage . . . 'not too far'—and rest content with the satisfactory attainment of a reasonable ambition as our ideal of human happiness" seemed a message more designed to tamp down future competition than anything else. In the "fight first for existence and then for prominence" that he informed his classmates they were all engaged in now that school had ended, the gentle voice of moderation, whispering "not too far," was not one Butler much heeded.

CHAPTER TWO

"An Indubitable Genius"

❧

With his fellowship for graduate study at Columbia in hand, Butler still had to decide whether or not to obtain a Ph.D. locally. American scholars seeking advanced degrees in the 1880s ordinarily made their way to the prestigious universities of Germany and France to obtain them. After some deliberation, Butler chose to continue his philosophical work at Columbia instead of abroad, largely through the urgings of Archibald Alexander, Columbia's one-man Philosophy Department. Alexander convinced him that it would be prudent to get the degree first before going to Europe for further study. Butler cast the decision in intellectual terms—"the requirements for this degree in Germany were so very minute and so very technical that the time and effort necessary to comply with them would be largely wasted"— but the practical advantages of a domestic degree were certainly not lost on him. Since he would be working only with Alexander, the path to the degree would likely be less onerous than if he were to enter the German system. Butler's Ph.D. two years later, in 1884, confirmed the wisdom of this calculation.

An 1875 graduate from Princeton, Alexander had begun teaching at Columbia in 1877; in 1881 he was appointed professor of philosophy, ethics, and psychology. His main virtues, as far as Butler's development was concerned, were less his academic gifts than his physical frailty. A neurasthenic sort who was chronically ill, Alexander rarely got through an entire school year without frequent absences. Butler did not have much regard for him as a teacher, finding that his lectures on the history of philosophy "lacked form, consecutiveness and adequate interpretation." But he more than compensated for these flaws by his affection for Butler and his need to rely on him to cover his classes when he was too sick to meet them. Even as a college senior, Butler had taught the junior class in logic and psychology when Alexander was indisposed. In addition to giving Butler useful teaching experience, Alexander's inability to meet his classes encouraged the trustees to view Butler as a healthy, energetic alternative to Alexander, a perception with major consequences for Butler's career.

Alexander's 1884 annual report to President Barnard on the state of the Philosophy Department documented Butler's skill in making himself indispensable:

The study of logic to the elective class of Juniors has been unusually complete, owing to the assistance rendered by Mr. Nicholas Murray Butler, a Fellow of the College and candidate for the degree of Doctor of Philosophy . . . Mr. Butler's lectures treated on the origin of Logic, and its development from the period before the time of Aristotle to the present.

In addition to doing his own work and much of Alexander's as well, Butler spent a good deal of time organizing and directing the Columbia College Philosophical Society, whose avowed aim, as Butler's 1882 flyer announced, was "to add interest to the study of philosophy in the college." Beyond furthering interest in the subject, the society also enabled Butler to call attention to himself. Alexander mentioned the society as a significant event in his report to Barnard, noting, "At certain intervals cards have been printed and distributed by Mr. Butler among students in the department giving a list of articles on the subject of Philosophy which appeared from time to time in the periodicals of Europe and America."

The society helped Butler's "fight for prominence" in yet another way. One of the most influential figures in American philosophy and education at the time was William Torrey Harris, editor of the *Journal of Speculative Philosophy*, who would go on to become United States commissioner of education. On December 27, 1882, Butler, who had never met him, sent him a belated notice of the society's first meeting in a letter that began:

I enclose you a notice—which will explain itself—of a meeting recently held here. It was successful in every way. An attendance of about fifty—comprising members of our faculty, graduates, graduate students and undergraduates—was obtained. We propose to meet at the same place and hour on the last Saturday of each month from October to May. The next paper will be read on January 27th, 1883, by Francis Speir, Jr., A.B. Princeton, 1877, on the "Relations of Pascal to Modern Agnosticism."

The real point of telling Harris about a meeting that had already occurred and in which he could not possibly have much interest was to allow Butler to introduce himself to the most important man in his field. Explaining that he was pursuing a Ph.D. under the guidance of President Barnard and Professor Alexander, Butler asked Harris if he might "spare a few minutes of the time at your disposal . . . for any advice or assistance which you can give me as to my studies."

Harris agreed, and though no record exists of questions asked or advice dispensed, the point of the meeting was effectively accomplished: Harris was charmed by Butler, and the two went on to become fast friends, each outdoing the other in mutual admiration. By 1894, well before Butler had achieved his full glory, Harris was writing that "a bare outline of the history of this young man shows what ample material there is for a Plutarch who could make a biography that would inspire young men to a high career."

Butler made sure that the important business of meeting the right people did not interfere with his philosophical progress. He worked conscientiously under Alexander's direction, receiving his M.A. in 1883 and his Ph.D. in 1884. As interesting as it would be to read his master's essay, "The Permanent Influence of Immanuel Kant," or his doctoral dissertation, "An Outline of the History of Logical Doctrine," neither exists. Since Butler was scrupulous in saving all manner of trivial material relating to his career, it is odd that these important documents are no longer available. Butler himself commented on the absence of his dissertation in *Across the Busy Years*, noting that he recalled depositing a copy in the college library, as the rules required. "I assume that, perhaps with other unimportant material of like character, it was lost or destroyed when the university was moved from the Forty-ninth Street site up to Morningside Heights." Such an explanation is reasonable, but it still seems peculiar that Butler wouldn't have kept a copy of each. Another explanation, equally reasonable, is that Butler, who carefully monitored his past, decided in retrospect that the hurried nature of these productions made them best forgotten. In any case, their disappearance remains a mystery.

Butler's doctoral examinations were unique in that they took place at Alexander's home in Hoboken over three or four days: "We discussed and debated for two hours or more each morning, and then after luncheon he resumed the grilling, which ended only late in the afternoon." Butler was responsible for the general history of philosophy, emphasizing the philosophical literature since the seventeenth century, as well as "the whole theory and practice of logic from the time of Aristotle, and the literature of that subject, including the new theories just then being brought forward in England and France."

Butler completed his examinations, submitted his dissertation, and received the Ph.D.—the first ever awarded by Alexander—at commencement in the summer of 1884. He was now free to take advantage, as Alexander had counseled, of the intellectual richness of European universities without needing to worry about satisfying their time-consuming requirements. With savings he had accumulated and money from the third year of his Columbia fellowship, Butler embarked on June 19 on the S.S. *Servia* to Liverpool for what, quoting Hegel, he later called "A Voyage of Discovery."

Butler's European year began with two months of travel in England, Holland, Belgium, and Switzerland, followed by six months of study in Berlin and four in Paris. Butler's public reminiscence, recorded in *Across the Busy Years*, testified to the exhilaration he felt from the moment he landed in Liverpool until the day he departed from France. The intellectual high point was Berlin, in which "every hour of the day and evening was an educational influence." Berlin offered the stimulation of the Royal Opera House and the Royal Theater—both accessible at nominal prices with a student card—and above all, the glories of the lecture hall at the university. It was here that Butler encountered the second pair of great men (along with President Barnard and Professor John W. Burgess of Columbia) whom he later claimed helped to shape his life: professors Fredrich Paulsen and Eduard Zeller. From Zeller he learned his reverence for Greek thought, from Paulsen his understanding that "without a critical examination of the process of knowing it is quite useless to attempt to discuss knowledge." Paulsen in particular reinforced his conviction that education was too important a subject to be left simply to teachers. It was instead a study worthy of the strictest methods of scientific investigation.

Butler's published account of his year stressed the cultural enrichment, the intellectual growth, the personal encounters with the great that made his time in Europe so memorable. If we had only his official rendition of the trip narrated in the pages of *Across the Busy Years*, we would have no reason to think that Butler experienced anything other than what was described there. But in 1978, a Mrs. Alexander C. Bell donated to the Columbia University Library a set of letters preserved by her grandmother that told a more complicated story.

Butler's departure in June 1884 meant the temporary suspension of the relationship he had been developing with Susanna Edwards Schuyler of the Schuyler family of Bergen Point, New Jersey. Susanna's lineage was exemplary. Her father, J. Rutsen Schuyler, who married a descendant of Jonathan Edwards, had been born on the estate in New Jersey that had been owned by his family since 1700. His mother was a Van Rensselaer. He added to the considerable family fortune first by importing, later by manufacturing, fancy goods; when he retired, in 1876, he was the senior partner in the firm of Schuyler, Hartley and Graham. The Butlers of Paterson were certainly not the social equals of the Schuylers of Bergen Point, but they were well enough established to make appropriate the connection between Murray and Susanna. By all reports, Susanna, the second youngest of six Schuyler children, was gentle, quiet, and loving—a perfect complement to the supercharged young Butler. In addition to her personal charms, she clearly represented to Butler's mother—the unquestioned general manager of the Butler family franchise—the right kind of investment for her son. Marriage into the Schuyler family would enhance the Butler status.

Although no evidence exists of a formal engagement or even informal commitment, Butler left on his journey assuming that he would return and marry Susanna, an assumption shared by members of both families, notably his mother. Mary's letters to him during his year away included gentle maternal reminders of what she expected, referring to his brother Will's affection for his "sister-in-law" and to her own need to get a new dress "for your wedding, whenever that may be."

Mrs. Butler was not disappointed: in February 1887 the two married. As important as that day was for Butler, however, it could not obliterate the poignant memory of the moment—or place—in 1884 when he first met Miss Alice Haven of Chicago. "It is twelve months next Sunday," he wrote to her on October 21, 1885, "since I was introduced to you at the foot of the stairs in the American Chapel in Berlin. It seems a lifetime." Butler's correspondence with Alice permits an access to the private Butler that he normally took pains to obscure. His letters to her suggest a spontaneous, attractive, and vulnerable young Butler, rather different from the formidable presence of public record, and perhaps explains in part how the older Butler came to be.

When Alice met Butler in Berlin, she was traveling through Europe with her sister and several friends. Butler was taken with her, and a pleasant, bantering friendship quickly developed. "My dear Miss Alice," he wrote to her in December 1884, while both were in Germany,

> If you and your sister are not tired out, and if you are not mediating a descent upon some opera, ballet, theatre or concert, and if there is no danger of herr Otis dropping in upon you, would it not be well for us to hold a consultation over the illustrated edition of our great modern epic this morning?
>
> Provided that any one, or more, of the above "ifs" stands in the way, or if any other objection, overlooked by me, occurs to you, you have merely to mention the fact and our meeting will stand adjourned—postponed is doubtless a more accurate word.
>
> If you find that nothing will interfere, then do not trouble to send any answer, but we will act on the good old Latin policy of "Silence gives consent."

The initial letters, written first while Alice was in Berlin and then early in 1885 after she had moved to Paris but before Butler arrived there, were gossipy and innocuous, filled with the kinds of details of daily activities that friends exchange with each other: Butler going to parties; suffering from the "blues"; being embarrassed (and secretly pleased) that his revered Professor Zeller introduced him as "Professor" Butler; maintaining his social poise when a dish of ice cream was spilled on him; continuing the arduous process of trying to appreciate Wagner's operas: "I am constrained to believe that he and his followers claim too much for him. To me he seems to mistake the grotesque for the genial and the formless for the sublime; although I willingly admit that he has invested the grotesque with meaning and made the formless interesting." They also express a playful sensibility. He tells jokes; plays with language ("But you may be thankful that I had not already directed a missilve—that is a new word and is a cross between a missile and a missive—at your head"); and even displays, most unexpectedly, occasional flashes of self-deprecation. The playfulness extended to Butler's putting himself coyly in thrall to Alice's rules about his work schedule. Explaining that all he did was "sleep and eat and study and walk and study and eat and study," he wrote on February 2 to ask a favor: he wanted her

> to raise the quarantine that shuts down on my reading and writing at half after ten. Only once have I exceeded this limit and then I was reading Mark Twain, which I am sure you will not consider an over-extension of the intellect. Please change the time to eleven or abolish it altogether, for in my loneliness I enjoy sitting up late and sleeping late in return thereafter.

The gentle dominatrix refused to compromise on her concern for his health, however, and on March 6 Murray noted that since he "never received any notice that my ten-thirty law was raised, I of course stood by my promise and kept it until the end. Perhaps it was just as well after all . . ."

The letters stopped when Butler came to Paris the second week in March to see her. When they started again, in June, with Butler back in Paterson and Alice in Chicago, they are astonishingly different in tone and content. Reunited with his Susanna, he appeared to be thinking only of his departed Alice. The arrival of her photograph, he wrote on June 21, "is the last straw, and I can put off writing no longer." Calling her now "My Dear Sister" instead of the "Miss Alice" of the European letters—a change of salutation perhaps designed to insulate him from the intensity of his feelings—Butler revealed that though committed to Susanna, his heart was with Alice:

> Well you know, sister mine, how often and how fully I would write were the world suited to your peace and mine, and you can understand as no one else the restraint that is upon me. The photograph, while not you at your best or in the most familiar guise, is an inexpressible comfort and is framed and standing on my study table before me whence it can look at and influence all my thoughts and work.

His longing for her, he continued, had taken its toll:

> The lines on my face are more numerous and deeper and those on my heart, where no one can see them, are even more painful, but

only one person in the world, besides myself, knows or shall ever know the cause. My condition of mind and body is a constant topic of conversation here, but happily no one has the slightest inkling of the trouble and I have grown accustomed to having my looks ascribed to worry over my work. In time I shall grow better able to control my external appearance, but to my dying day my heart will be as sore and as vainly longing as it is today.

Subsequent letters elaborated the theme of mutual longing that he knew could not be satisfied. "But for you, my sister," he wrote on July 7, "my heart aches with an ache that is intensified by the thought that willing—oh! so willing—as I am to aid and comfort you in your loneliness, I cannot do it." But what he could have done—which he did not—was to save her letters:

Of your letters I have of course kept every line, and they are to be the beginning of an unbroken series that will be put beneath the earth with me when I am dead and gone. Oh! sister, there must be relief some day for these heart sorrows, and sometimes I feel as if I would be glad to die. Then I think how cowardly and selfish it is not to be willing to shoulder my load and bear it silently and without complaint . . . Not for all the world would I forget my sorrow; it is too sweet, too sad, ever to wish it to be forgotten. I only ask for strength to bear it bravely and silently, unknown to all the world but you.

In the midst of the sorrow and silent suffering, this July 7 letter revealed the cause of it all: Susanna Schuyler. His mention of her was in terms that spoke primarily to dutiful concern for her health. Her selfless regard for others, evident in the attention she devoted to her seriously ill father, had taken its toll: "Sue has altered so much under the anxieties and cares of this past year, that her photographs are no longer anything like her . . . She is a wonderful woman and it puzzles me why God thinks me worthy of her. But he must know best." But if God's wisdom decreed that Murray was deserving of Sue, Murray also understood, in a favorite bit of Heine that he translated for Alice, "It is determined in God's plan that man from that he holds dear must part; yes, part." Butler's God thus managed both to endorse his commitment to Sue and to acknowledge the depth of his feelings for Alice.

Butler's unwillingness even to consider leaving Sue did not make any easier the thought of Alice's leaving him. In August he was suddenly overcome by anxiety at that possibility, and he wondered to her whether his "divination is a right one, when I think that perhaps my sister has found the seeds of a life's love growing in her heart." If so, Butler exhorted her not to spare him, but also advised her to be certain that she was giving her heart to one who would cherish her. We have no evidence of Alice's immediate response, though the fact that she didn't announce her engagement to Charles Requa until 1888 suggests Butler's fears were premature. But she did interpret Butler's feelings in a fashion he may not have anticipated. Alice's letter to Murray of September 21 is the only one of hers we possess. Butler did not himself keep her letters, and she specifically asked him to destroy this one; we know about it only because she made a copy ("As far as I remember, this is an exact copy"), so she clearly wanted it preserved for the record.

After some gossip and desultory talk about books—Charlotte Yonge's *The Daisy Chain*, one of Butler's favorites, and several of George Eliot's— Alice moved to the point:

Now Murray, dear Murray, how can I write what I think I ought to say. If you think it wrong in me please forgive it for I have struggled hard and prayed to do right and if I fail it will not be from want of thought or tears. Situated as you are do you not think it wrong in me to receive letters in which love is breathed in every page? Having a responsive heart you know what it is I like but now I am trying to put it aside and let my conscience do its work. Just suppose that I were Miss Sue and that I should some day see a letter that you had written to some one else like those of mine, do you not think my heart would be utterly broken? I have a woman's heart and I can not help but feel for her. We can not always keep on writing the way we do and I am fearful lest some time there should come a crash that would leave us something to regret utterly all our lives . . . I think you understand me better than any one else so I have not the strength to ask you not to write me, nor do I see the necessity of doing it, but will you not promise to try and let Miss Sue read all your letters to me or else have them so that I could hand them to her without a blush and she could read them without a pang. Dearest brother, do you not think I am right in saying this.

She concluded by asking him either to destroy the letter or to send it back to her.

Alice's plea had an instant effect. Butler's September 24 response devoted two sentences to the issues she raised, and though their correspondence continued for several years, these were the last two sentences that it would be complicated for Sue to read: "If you think it better to burn all my previous letters, please do so and let me know it. Your letter has been destroyed as you desired, and the highest tribute I can pay to your letter is to act on its advice."

Until it was prematurely terminated by her death in 1903, Butler's marriage to Susanna was a happy one, graced by the birth of their beloved daughter, Sarah, in 1895. But at the same time it is impossible to read Murray's letters to Alice without a growing sense of sadness. His "year of discovery," intellectually an opening up, appeared like an emotional closing down. Sue was admirable and made him a good wife. And yet his heart was elsewhere, even if family expectations and his own sense of propriety left him no real choice.

It would be fruitless to speculate on how different Butler's life would have been had he married Alice. The importance of his relationship with her, as we deduce it from their correspondence, lies not simply in his lamenting the fate that kept them apart, but in the candor with which he actually spoke about his feelings. As we know from Step-grandfather Meldrum's diagnosis of Murray, he was never a person happy to reveal things about himself, and these letters are one of the few instances we have of Butler allowing his emotions full expression. Their poignancy is not simply the story of an unrealizable love, but of a young man who seemed to have decided early in life to eschew the vulnerabilities of the emotional life for more manageable professional and vocational spheres. Butler's obsessive work habits and concern for his career did not spring from the pain of his relationship with Alice. They were built in and operating long before he met her. But the way he dealt with his inability to continue with Alice suggests a certain hardening of the emotional arteries. The valued private self he displayed in the letters would henceforth be stowed safely away as Butler's rapidly accomplishing public self began to make its mark.

Butler's return to Paterson in June 1885 was emotionally complicated not simply because of the still unresolved nature of his relationship with Alice but also because of the unresolved shape of his career. It was not obvious what he was supposed to do now that he was back, though what he wanted to do was eminently clear—teach at Columbia. And of course both Barnard and Alexander were eager to have him. The problem was money, as it had been for so many of Barnard's projects, or more precisely the lack of it. The trustees, struggling with their immediate needs, had no budgetary surplus to invest in the teaching of philosophy at Columbia.

Fortunately for Butler, Barnard's long years of frustration at trying to get things accomplished had not sapped his taste for battle. Working in cahoots with Alexander, he had already begun joint efforts to find a way to bypass trustee resistance before Butler returned to the United States. "If all the gossip is true," Butler's mother wrote to him on April 28, "Prof. Alexander is rapidly clearing the way for you to help if not fill his place." Mary was right about Alexander's intentions, but prematurely optimistic about his capacity to realize them. At a meeting on June 1, Alexander put before the trustees the case for supplying additional support for the Philosophy Department. As always with Alexander, the issue was his health, and he requested that an adjunct be hired to share the burdens of undergraduate and graduate instruction in logic, ethics and psychology, and the history of philosophy. The trustees were not pleased by the physical liability Alexander had become, but they authorized $500 for a Fellow in Philosophy to begin July 1, 1886. For the intervening year, however, they declined to make any new provisions: Alexander would just have to manage on his own.

With his powerful lobbying group in place, Butler could more or less confidently rely on the projected position of fellow for 1886–87, but how would he get through the current academic year? Pressure had to be maintained in the hope that something could be arranged for the present. On June 23 Alexander called his young protégé to the attention of Morgan Dix, rector of Trinity Church and chairman of Columbia's board of trustees:

> My special reason for writing is to tell you about Mr. Nicholas Murray Butler . . . I have mentioned his name in case it should be thought advisable to extend the philosophical course in the Senior year or in the graduate department at the College . . . I think it would be a good thing if some kind of appointment could be given to him before the opening of the next academic year, as he is pretty sure to be wanted elsewhere and it seems a pity to let a good man be lost to Columbia, particularly when he is a graduate. If it would not

be asking too much, I should like to have Butler call on you so that having seen him you can judge to some extent what value his services might have in case the suggestions contained in my letter to the Board were followed out.

To support Alexander's claim about the instructional needs in philosophy, Barnard then wrote to Dix on July 11, arguing that Columbia was falling behind its competitors in maintaining adequate provision in logic, ethics, and the history of philosophy. The remedy, happily enough, was right at hand, for "we have . . . just now, a young man the most remarkably qualified for such a position of all I have ever known." He elaborated on Butler's talents and achievements, noting his success at organizing a philosophical society in the college, his important work as a teacher in helping Alexander with his courses, and his diligence while studying abroad. "In short," he concluded, "I consider him an indubitable genius, and it would be a great grief to me to see him drawn away from us as I fear he will be . . . We have had nothing like him since my connection with Columbia College began."

The campaign for Butler reached out also to the Reverend H. Y. Satterlee of the Calvary Church in New York, where Butler had been confirmed as an Episcopalian in 1883. Writing to his colleague Dix about Columbia's need to resist the materialistic thought of the day, Satterlee put in a word for "Nicholas Murray Butler who has just returned from Europe and whose name has, I believe, been presented to your committee" as someone well qualified to teach ethics and theism. His Butler, one of the "best read and one of the most thoughtful young men of his age I have ever met," was primarily "a devout Christian and churchman" who could lead a curricular battle against the dread materialism of the day.

But no amount of arguing about Butler's brilliance, moral fiber, and plain usefulness could squeeze money out of trustees slightly panicked over the state of the budget. On July 16 Barnard confessed to Butler that the short-term prospects of hiring him looked slim. Financial concerns and the absence from the city for the summer of some trustees made it doubtful that anything could happen in time for the fall semester. Barnard assured Butler that he had no intention of giving up, however: "I have urged Professor Alexander to keep up a similar fire on these gentlemen. I feel very confident that we shall be successful in the end, but I am not very confident of immediate success."

The solution, worked out between Alexander and Barnard, involved getting Butler into the classroom even without a salary. As long as they weren't paying him, the trustees had no objections, and thus Butler's illustrious teaching and administrative career began on the unlikely note of his working for free in the Philosophy Department. It was not a position that he relished. "Columbia and 'Prof.' Butler are not getting on well at all," he complained to Alice on October 18, "and for the present I am only a 'Prof.' on sufferance." However demeaning it was to work without a salary, the work itself was therapeutic for Butler: "But work, work, work is hanging over me, and from it there is no escape. Perhaps it is just as well, for I am never happy unless I am busy, and an idle life would soon grow tiresome." Fortunately, with two newly organized graduate classes, one on Kant and another on Berkeley, idleness was not a temptation: "As I can not bear not to give the men my best energies, I am slaving away and my time is well taken up. The work is a pleasure, though, for I find that teaching others teaches me a great deal." But as the October, November, and December trustee meetings came and went with no authorization for a salary, it had to become evident that if Butler was to receive any remuneration, it would have to come from a source other than the currently approved budget.

At some point in the late fall it must have occurred to Barnard that the answer lay in the ever-frail Alexander, invariably failing to meet his classes because of physical incapacity of one sort or another. Knowing that Alexander had been considering requesting a brief medical leave, Barnard asked him on December 20 to take instead a leave for the duration of the academic year. Under such conditions, he argued, the trustees would probably be inclined to offer Butler compensation as Alexander's replacement for the spring semester; and given what Butler had done thus far without any pay, this would be the only honorable step for Alexander to take. Alexander did not appreciate being transformed from an ally in the Butler campaign into the solution to its biggest problem. He wrote rather querulously to Butler, complaining that he was reluctant "to ask for a leave of absence longer than that advised by the physician" and emphasizing that Butler's difficulty in gaining a formal place in the college was not his fault but "the fault of the Trustees. The line of duty, so far as I am concerned is perfectly plain."

Alexander's resistance could not withstand the pressure exerted on him by Barnard, his colleague Professor Van Amringe, and others. The January trustee minutes announced that Alexander had been given "leave of absence during the remainder of the current Collegiate year"—with the added twist that the "President of the College" was charged to "provide a substitute or substitutes at the expense of the Professor." Butler was ecstatic at the prospect of being paid, even if his salary was coming out of Alexander's pocket. "I feel quite chipper," he wrote to Alice, despite the fact that his workload had now doubled, as he was absorbing all of Alexander's classes as well as continuing with his own. But the combination of writing, giving public talks around the city, and "lecturing on various philosophical subjects eighteen times a week" at Columbia did not seem to bother him. If it made "your poor little bit of a brother . . . about as busy as mortals are," it also made him happy. Besides, as he reminded Alice, he would have time to relax in Heaven, where he "can talk quietly for ages and not worry. I hope so at all counts, for not this side of eternity will I ever know what rest is."

Barnard now focused on obtaining Butler a more appropriate rank than fellow for his appointment the coming fall. Butler was too talented and accomplished to have to settle for such a rudimentary status. Barnard's 1886 presidential report, published in the spring, assessed the enormous contributions Butler had made to the department over the course of the year, single-handedly ensuring that Alexander's absence had "not operated prejudicially to the interests of the students." But the future of the department was not guaranteed, Barnard stressed. Its well-being still rested entirely in the hands of one single professor whose precarious health made certain that the curriculum would always be vulnerable. Alexander had never attempted to teach the subject of ethics, for example, because he claimed it would overtax him. "On this account," Barnard continued, turning his report into an explicit plea for Butler, "it is greatly to be desired that there should be appointed an assistant in this department . . . The gentleman who has been in charge of the department *ad interim* since December last has proved himself to be possessed in an eminent degree of the qualities necessary to fulfil the duties of such a position satisfactorily, and the undersigned most earnestly recommends that the appointment asked for be conferred upon him."

The issue of a different appointment for Butler went back to the trustees. On June 1, Morgan Dix, chairman of the trustee Committee on the Course and Statutes, wrote to Alexander regarding Barnard's suggestion that either Alexander's duties should be split between a new professor and himself or he should in fact teach all the subjects included in the title of his professorship (philosophy, ethics, and psychology), which he had never done. By this time Alexander was most unhappy about having been coerced into taking a longer leave than he wanted, and by having to turn over his salary to Butler. He spoke so strongly against any changes being necessary or desirable that Dix decided not to pursue the issue.

Distressed by Alexander's intransigence, Barnard then made a radical suggestion to Butler: he should refuse the fellowship, leaving Alexander alone "to shoulder his own log." When Alexander failed to perform, as he surely must, the trustees would finally take action. "But so long as you are there, he will always know that the classes will be looked after, and will go on, I suppose, as he has been accustomed to do heretofore." Barnard concluded by advising Butler temporarily to take a position elsewhere, "so as to be quite out of his reach."

Butler could not bring himself to leave, however, and urged Barnard instead to continue the pressure. Barnard agreed to do so, and in addition enlisted Henry Drisler, a crusty professor of classics with significant trustee connections, in his efforts. Finally, on October 4, the rather bizarre spectacle of the president conspiring with one faculty member against another to influence the trustees came to a happy conclusion. Whether through sheer exhaustion or because of a genuine appreciation of Butler's value, the trustees capitulated: Butler was named fellow and assistant in the Department of Philosophy, Ethics, and Psychology, an appointment launching him on a career of uninterrupted employment at Columbia lasting fifty-nine years.

As a teacher of philosophy, the young fellow and assistant whom Barnard and Co. had secured for the Columbia department was more organized and thorough than provocatively brilliant. Lectures began on time and ended on time, covering comprehensively each subject—whether ethics or Kant or the history of philosophy. Butler was in no way an original thinker. He filled the classroom hour by imparting clear information about philosophical schools and ideas rather than confronting students with perplexing issues. There were no jagged edges left unsmoothed or contradictions that lingered. Everything was put into place, all doubts resolved. And he kept his own views to himself: Columbia professor John Erskine, class of 1900, remarked that Butler lectured "on Plato and Aristotle, on Spinoza and Kant, with such precise impartiality that we did not know where he stood."

Such flawless presentations, while easily absorbed, had a serious downside: they could be soporific. Author of the "Lassie" dog stories Albert Payson Terhune, a Columbia student in the 1890s, described the risks. Falling asleep in one of Butler's classes after a hearty lunch with lots of wine, Terhune kept hearing Butler's voice droning through his dreams. "Still two-thirds asleep, and wholly forgetting I was in a lecture room, I roared peevishly, 'How am I going to get a decent sleep with your damn jabbering going on? Shut up, can't you?'" Awakened by his own roar and acutely aware that this outburst might well have ended his Columbia career, Terhune was profoundly grateful that Butler simply continued on with his lecture, seemingly oblivious to the interruption. He never forgot what he considered Butler's act of extraordinary grace.

Commuting back and forth each day from Paterson, teaching eighteen hours a week, and dealing with the anxieties over his career, Butler still found the time and the calm to begin his writing career. Between his return to the United States in June 1885 and December 1886 he published 105 separate pieces: unsigned brief notes, short book reviews, and proper articles. Many appeared in *Science*, a magazine on whose board Butler sat, but he also published in the *Herald Tribune*, the *Journal of Speculative Philosophy*, *Churchman*, *Christian Union*, *Popular Science Monthly*, and *History of Pedagogy and History of Education*, among other journals. Even if their length consigned most of these pieces to the category of ephemera, the diversity of subject is nevertheless startling for a twenty-four-year-old: convict labor problems, suicides in England and Wales, progress in New Zealand, education in Spain, the election of the Yale president, chapel services at Harvard, the annual report of the commissioner of pensions, the English and German novel, hereditary inebriety, psychical research, and the educational institutions of Prussia, to name some of them. Butler was precocious, but the range of these early pieces perhaps indicates his intrepidness more than his capacity. He didn't achieve his status as pundit by hesitating to offer his opinion on every conceivable topic, as these early efforts suggest.

But neither the writing, the extensive teaching obligations, nor the time-consuming commuting could exhaust Butler's immense energy. Having been attracted to the academic world in the first place by President Barnard's vision of the vast, unexplored territory of serious educational thought in the United States, Butler was eager to lay claim to some of it.

Direct appropriation seemed the best method, and in the spring of 1886 he offered, with Barnard's enthusiastic support, two lectures on the science of education for a program of free Saturday lectures that Columbia had established for the public. Because education was not generally deemed a subject worthy of study at the college level, neither the faculty nor the trustees were happy with the idea. Butler was told that he was wasting his time, that no one would come. We can taste the relish in Barnard's 1886 presidential report, observing that "the demand for tickets rose in a few days to the extraordinary number of two thousand. After the first of these lectures had been given, moreover, letters to the number of two hundred were received by the lecturer, asking information as to the bibliography of the subject and instructions for reading."

On the basis of this success and with Barnard's active connivance, Butler tried to get a course in pedagogics into the curriculum, but the trustees, always suspicious of Barnard and his projects, diagnosed trouble. The course was nominally intended for seniors, but part of the proposal suggested that it be open to anyone interested in the subject. The trustees correctly understood the inevitable consequences of such an option. Their minutes of May 2, 1887, exposed what Barnard was up to:

> Mr. Butler . . . admitted . . . that his chief object would be to bring to the College a large number of persons not connected to it, for whose benefit in fact the scheme had been devised. Your Committee are not prepared to give their assent to the proposition . . . The outsiders whom the establishment of such a course would immediately attract to the College would be according to Mr. Butler's estimate, as many as 150 to 200 in number, and of these, by the same estimate nine-tenths would be women, either already engaged in teaching or in training for that profession.

Not only was the subject matter questionable, but worse, the course was designed to subvert the trustee prohibition against introducing women into Columbia, long one of Barnard's goals. Though Butler later would refer to this incident as indicative of the trustees' inability to appreciate the need to study education in a scientific fashion, it had less to do with their obtuseness than with their battle with Barnard over coeducation.

The rejection of the course did not rule out other ways to proceed. A group of philanthropic-minded women, intent on teaching domestic skills to daughters of the poor, might seem an unpromising place to begin, but it was the existence of such a group that led to Butler's founding and becoming the first president of an institution devoted to the scientific study of pedagogy: Columbia's Teachers College.

For some time, the question of how to teach working-class girls the art of household management had perplexed Emily Huntington, a well-to-do woman interested in education. In the fall of 1876 she visited a kindergarten class in New York City, and seeing how the children of the wealthy were being introduced to various academic skills through the use of toys and blocks, she had her insight: Why couldn't the children of the poor, for whom academic training would be inappropriate, learn how to wash and clean and set tables through the use of toy brooms and dishes and tables? Presided over by kind and supportive teachers, the children would master these skills through play and song and would also find pleasure in such activities. As they matured, they would be able to take care of their own homes and, equally important, have productive careers taking care of other people's.

With the image of these "bright courageous young faces and voices cheering me to the end," Huntington developed her method of instruction, which she called her Kitchen-Garden system, in order that it could be taught to others. First practicing it herself at the Wilson Industrial School in St. Mark's Place, within a year she had thirty-five volunteers teaching nearly two hundred students weekly. As interest in the method spread, Huntington decided that she needed some formal organization to monitor its growth and train its teachers. Meeting for the first time in the Madison Avenue home of the socially prominent Grace H. Dodge on January 14, 1880, eleven young women established the Kitchen Garden Association to provide such a structure.

A system of education whose central mission was to inculcate a love of housework (along with the requisite skills for it) in the hearts of working-class girls could not fail to arouse middle- and upper-class interest. Under the association's leadership, the method had spread, by 1881, to a number of eastern cities and to places as removed from New York as St. Louis and Cincinnati. In New York and its vicinity alone, according to the 1881 report, 990 children received instruction in 29 different classes, covering "kindling fires, waiting on the door, bed-making, sweeping and dusting, completely arranging a room with the manipulations of broom, whisk-broom, feather duster, etc. Also, all laundry processes, from the preparation of the tubs to the delicacies of polishing and folding," among the useful tasks.

By 1884, with classes in most of the states and parts of the system—especially its toys and books—in France, Italy, India, China, and Japan, the association's leaders thought that both the name of the organization and its scope of interest needed to be changed. A growing recognition of the importance of advanced manual and industrial training for older boys showed that the focus on homemaking skills for very young girls was far too limited. The association had to be flexible enough to incorporate some of the innovative techniques and new methodologies into its own system if it wanted to be influential in a rapidly changing educational and social world. On March 21, 1884, the members voted to dissolve the Kitchen Garden Association and transform themselves, with a new constitution, into the Industrial Education Association (IEA).

The all-female membership and board of managers immediately changed its gender composition, as it seemed important now, in Grace Dodge's words, "to have the wise counsel of men." The young Teddy Roosevelt, along with a number of others, was named to the board's central association; Seth Low and President Barnard became honorary members. General Alexander Webb, president of the College of the City of New York, was elected president and Grace Dodge, vice president. The IEA's new set of aims embraced interests that the Kitchen Garden could not have addressed in its old form:

First—To obtain and disseminate information upon Industrial Education and to stimulate public opinion in its favor.

Second—To invite co-operation between existing organizations engaged in any form of industrial training.

Third—To train women and girls in domestic economy, and to promote the training of both sexes in such industries as shall enable those trained to become self-supporting.

Fourth—To study and devise methods and systems of industrial training, and secure their introduction into schools; also, when expedient, to form special classes and schools for such instruction.

Fifth—To provide instructors for schools and classes, and, if necessary, to train teachers for this work.

General Webb's role was largely honorific, and most of the work was done by Grace Dodge and the association's secretary, Jane Cattell. In an office at 21 University Place, the IEA spent most of its first year organizing and publicizing itself, fund-raising, and exploring the problems and potentialities of industrial training in the schools. Its concerns—like those of the Kitchen Garden—were primarily social and philanthropic rather than exclusively pedagogic, seeing in industrial training the opportunity to improve the plight of the poor by equipping them to look after themselves and to pursue useful if humble careers.

Within a few years the IEA's focus had begun to shift. By 1886 it was arguing that its methods were designed not simply to teach trades. Industrial education offered training "which is neither technical nor professional, which is calculated to make better men and better citizens of the pupils . . . which affects directly, and in a most salutary manner the mind and character of the pupil, and which will be of constant service to him through all his life, whether he be a wage-worker or trader, teacher or clergyman." That it was now talking about the importance of industrial education for men rather than the women for whom the training was originally designed suggests the IEA was cognizant of how it had to sell itself if it wanted to be taken seriously.

With this evolution from the mostly philanthropic to the primarily pedagogic came the need for "a trained and expert educator" to direct the association's future development. Since Webb was not that person, he resigned in the winter of 1887. Led by Dodge, the IEA commenced a search for somebody who combined administrative abilities and a commitment to the importance of industrial training in the schools. After consulting with the presidents of Johns Hopkins and MIT, among others, the committee decided that the twenty-five-year-old Nicholas Murray Butler was the best candidate.

According to Butler, it was his friend John B. Pine who first suggested his name to the IEA. This of course is possible, though it is hard to believe that Barnard, an honorary member of the association, didn't influence the search. But in any case the selection of Butler could scarcely be questioned. As chairman of the Committee on Education of the New Jersey Board of Education, he had already been recognized for his efforts to modernize the state's school system. Energetic, responsible, and known to be interested in the adoption of manual training methods, Butler had all the necessary qualifications.

The position afforded Butler a marvelous opportunity on several grounds. First, it was always better to be president than not, and leading the IEA would be a brightly colored feather in the Butler cap. Second, it gave Butler the chance to formulate the kind of serious instruction in pedagogy whose importance Barnard had insisted upon some six years before.

In announcing the choice of Butler, the IEA's 1887 report sought to defuse potential criticism that the system of industrial education was in any way limiting. An "Articles of Faith of the Association" emphasized that its educational aim was not so much to teach children rudimentary skills as to nourish all their faculties. The problem with current education was that it trained "the memory too largely, the reasoning powers less, the eye and hand too little." Its deficiencies would be remedied by industrial education, which was intended to develop students' characters as well as their intellectual capacities.

The Articles of Faith did not mention the training of teachers, but appended to the same report was the prospectus of a college to be established for just that purpose. It would be located in the association's new home at 9 University Place, and it planned to offer

> systematic instruction to persons desirous of entering on the profession of teaching. For the present at least, the instruction given will be almost wholly confined to those hitherto neglected factors in education which may be included under the name of Industrial Training. Both male and female students will be admitted to the college.

The impetus for the college itself, and its long-term aims, owed much to Butler. He was explicit from the start that he would accept the presidency only if "the work of the Association was fundamentally changed and so broadened as to make it really an effective representative of President Barnard's ideals. This meant the whole movement must be converted from a philanthropic enterprise into one for educational advancement and reform"—in short, the fifth of the association's original goals, more or less to the exclusion of the first four. Not everyone welcomed Butler's new emphasis—some IEA members were reluctant to renounce the last vestiges of their philanthropic origins, others their particular concern for industrial training—but Butler prevailed. Henceforth, the IEA would be in the business of educating teachers in all aspects of their discipline.

With his usual energy Butler set about turning the association, as he wrote in his first annual report, into "a great educational force." He continued its work of educating the public about the importance of industrial training in the schools, but his real commitment was to producing teachers. Given his failure to convince the Columbia trustees that even a single course in pedagogics was appropriate, it was easy to imagine the immense satisfaction he took in designing a two-year curriculum for prospective teachers. "The recognition of education as a science" to be taught professionally—it was the dream he and Barnard had shared.

Butler took pains to distinguish the college, with its aim of providing "broad-minded, cultured, professionally trained teachers," from "normal schools," which at that time were supplying teachers across the country: "It is not a normal school and is not intended to be such. The normal schools of the country . . . are academies or high schools with a slight infusion of pedagogic instruction. They certainly are not to the profession they represent what the law school, the medical school and the theological seminary are to their respective professions."

Butler's projected curriculum included courses in psychology, natural science, teaching methods, and the history, science, and philosophy of education, among other subjects. Manual training courses would also be offered, but within a large methodological and historical context. To train teachers in only a single branch of instruction, Butler argued, "was not to train teachers, but tradesmen; the graduates of such a college could be artisans, but not artists." And he continued to praise the efficacy of manual training in the classroom. "Opposition to it," he declared, "is now confined to the sluggish, the stupid and the educationally blind."

Candidates for the New York College for the Training of Teachers (the name was changed officially to Teachers College when it received its permanent charter from the University of the State of New York in 1892) had to be at least eighteen years old and graduates of an approved high school or academy. Applicants had to pass entrance examinations in a number of academic subjects, including arithmetic, geometry, history, and English. (Graduates of colleges or normal schools were admitted without examination.) By the end of the first year (1887–88), 104 students were enrolled, a number that grew by 1890–91, Butler's last year as president, to 182.

A critical part of the college's program was its affiliation with a children's school, which would give students both the opportunity to practice

what they learned and a laboratory for demonstrating how manual training methods could be successfully incorporated into the usual school
studies. It was initially called the Model School, based on an established
school in Trenton that Butler knew about through his reform work on the
New Jersey Board of Education. But skeptical observers objected to the
notion of conferring on an unknown and untested school the name
"Model," and Butler and his colleagues cast about for another possibility.
They decided on Horace Mann, an appropriate name for two reasons: he
was at once a distinguished educator, an early advocate of the public
school system in America, and also, as Butler said with a nice touch of
irony, "nobody knew who Horace Mann was." Opening its doors the same
time as the college did, the Horace Mann School attracted sixty-four
students the first year.

"The whole history of civilization," according to Butler, "can be written — and only written — in terms of ideas building themselves into institutions." Translating Barnard's vision of the need to treat education as a
science into Teachers College and the Horace Mann School was an exemplary instance of this process, for which Butler deserves the credit he has
been given. Presiding over the initial growth of both was a major administrative and intellectual achievement. But it was only part of Butler's ambitions for himself. As his larger Columbia University career unfolded, he
found he had less time for the details of running the college for teachers, a
reality not lost on Grace Dodge and others for whom the interests of the
school were paramount. Trustee minutes of April 18, 1891, documented
the inevitable consequences:

> It was moved by Miss Dodge that it is the sense of this Board that it
> is in the interest of this college that the President should devote all
> his time and attention to the duties of the position. In view of the fact
> that the President has been asked informally whether he could de-
> vote all his time to the duties of the Presidency and to the interest of
> the college and having expressed himself as unable to do so and has
> sent in his resignation, the Board accepts Dr. Butler's resignation, re-
> gretting his inability to retain the position.

The resignation effectively ended Butler's relationship with the college
while it was at University Place. Although he agreed to continue on the

board at the request of the trustees, there is no evidence that he ever actually attended a meeting prior to his finally leaving in 1894. When it moved to Morningside Heights and became part of Columbia University, Butler actively reentered its affairs, but in an altogether different fashion, as we will see.

CHAPTER THREE

A University Is Born

❧

Even as he worked in the late 1880s to shift the Industrial Education Association from a philanthropic to an educational institution, Butler was caught up in the details of a more complicated and consequential shift, that of Columbia from a college to a university. Columbia's transition from one to the other was not unique to a small school in New York City. It was part of a larger process transforming higher education in the United States following the Civil War. Although no one at the time seemed to know exactly what an American university might properly be, everyone agreed that whatever it was, the United States didn't have one.

For American advocates of educational reform, the defining characteristic of a genuine university was not its size, administrative structure, or affiliation with technical or professional schools, but the presence of distinguished faculties of philosophy, political science, and natural science that were committed to original research. The exemplary instance of this ideal could be found in Germany, where Butler and other young American scholars flocked to pursue their advanced studies in arts and sciences. The freedom of German professors to teach what they wanted and of mature students to study with them untrammeled by the bureaucratic restraints of a prescribed curriculum—the condition of *Lehrfreiheit* and *Lernfreiheit*, as Butler always celebrated them—constituted the peculiar glory of the German university system.

The vast differences in secondary schooling between Germany and the United States, however, meant that wholesale importing of the German model was impossible. The freedom of the German universities to advance knowledge through independent investigation carried out in laboratories and seminars depended on the rigorous training provided at the secondary school level, where the *Gymnasium* prepared students for specialized university work in a way American high schools most decidedly did not. German professors could function exclusively as scholars and researchers, not college drillmasters, because they did not have to bother themselves with remedying undergraduate deficiencies. It was generally accepted that American students needed two years of college instruction to bring them to the intellectual level that German students achieved in the *Gymnasium*.

Although these differences prevented the pure embodiment of the German research university from ever taking root in American soil, they did not rule out the development of a distinctively American version of that institution, the single educational entity combining both undergraduate and advanced training—the college and what came to be known as the graduate school. This form for centers of higher learning didn't begin to get established in the United States until the invention of The Johns Hopkins University in 1876. American Ph.D.s were not unheard of earlier—Yale awarded the first American doctorate in 1861—but extensive formal graduate instruction of the sort we are familiar with today did not exist. American higher education in the mid-1870s offered instead various options for students of disparate backgrounds and training: colleges, academies, technical institutes, medical schools, theological seminaries, manual labor schools, adult extension initiatives, and community libraries.

The college was the most important of these, of course, differing greatly in quality, resources, and size. Most of the three hundred or so colleges throughout the country were engaged in the common task of exposing undergraduates to the bracing rigors of the "mental discipline" thought to be the goal of higher education. The psychological theory behind mental discipline held that each person had separate faculties or powers—will, observation, memory, attention, and reasoning—that required intense, protracted training in order to develop properly. The mind had to be exercised to reach its fullest potential the same way the body needed a strict regimen of activity. Nothing less than a person's mental and moral health was at stake.

Few serious educational theorists during the nineteenth century would have disputed this idea, and the mind-body analogy became a commonplace way of understanding the mission of college instruction. In 1890, for example, Middlebury's president, C. B. Hulbert, spoke for the age in asserting the virtues of vigorous mental bodybuilding:

> If you wish to develop physical power, put your physical organs to drill; if you seek to bring your mental powers up to a high degree of efficiency, put them to work, and upon studies that will tax them to the uttermost. When one has been mastered, take a second and a third; and so go on conquering and to conquer, victory succeeding victory in your march to mental conquests and triumphs.

The agency of such training was the prescribed four-year college curriculum dominated by the study of Greek, Latin, and mathematics. Although other subjects were included in most programs of mandated study—moral and natural philosophy, rhetoric, physics, psychology, religion, and history, to name some of the major ones—mathematics and the classical languages comprised the intellectual bedrock on which the defenders of mental discipline took their stand. As Noah Porter maintained in 1870, the year before he became president of Yale, "The prominence given to the classics and mathematics should never be abandoned. These two studies, we believe, must, and ever will, be regarded as the great pillars on which any education which deserves to be called liberal must always rest."

After the Civil War, changing social and economic conditions began to undermine the authority of the mental discipline tradition. The ideal of a well-crafted mind making its way confidently through Greek and Latin syntax seemed less attractive in a country whose industrial and business growth demanded managers with serviceable skills and a body of useful information. Advocates of academic reform, eager to aerate the American college curriculum, charged the mental disciplinarians with being interested less in what undergraduates actually knew than in guaranteeing that their minds were properly conditioned for adult living. In focusing on the need to toughen students' mental faculties through strenuous exercise, critics argued, colleges were not paying enough attention to the acquisition of new knowledge. Or, in F.A.P. Barnard's unsparing assessment of the mental discipline system he came to loathe, "A well-stored mind is *per se* of little consequence; a well-developed mind is the main thing, though it be stored with rubbish." The intellectual life of the nineteenth-century college was not as uniformly sterile as Barnard and other of its ferocious opponents insisted, but nevertheless it was becoming evident that schools promulgating Barnard's "rubbish" were increasingly perceived as being unable to meet the challenge of a rapidly evolving urban industrial society.

In addition to wanting a more substantial, varied, and even practical curriculum for undergraduates, a maturing America began to resent having to send its sons abroad to receive advanced training. A country aspiring to world-class status had to reform its system of higher education, and two specific dates mark the progress of that reform. It would take a number of years before it could be pronounced officially dead, but mental discipline suffered a fatal wound with the election of Charles W. Eliot as president of Harvard in 1869. Believing in the liberating power of an elective—as opposed to compulsory—curriculum, Eliot argued strenuously to free Harvard from the fetters imposed by the advocates of disciplinary training. Students who could choose what they wanted to study, he maintained, would approach their studies with a passion and enthusiasm not found when they were forced to proceed in lockstep through a prescribed set of courses. Real intellectual growth would result from this kind of freedom. An elective system would simultaneously encourage the faculty to develop new courses that expressed their own interests, thereby escaping the drudgery of the endless drill and recitation required in the traditional classroom.

Eliot was not immediately successful—the faculty proponents of a tightly prescribed curriculum by no means retreated at the first assault—but once the battle started, the outcome was inevitable. And gradually, as a rich fare of options began to replace conventional requirements at Harvard, other schools followed. The defenders of "mental discipline" could not withstand both the cultural pressures of a dynamic young country and the leadership of its most prestigious institution.

Eliot's concern was with the quality of undergraduate education, but Daniel Coit Gilman had a substantially different purpose in mind when he opened The Johns Hopkins University on October 3, 1876. His inaugural address stated simply and clearly the radical new principle on which Hopkins was founded: "A university is a place for the advanced special education of youth who have been prepared for its freedom by the discipline of a lower school." Although the purity of its definition was compromised from the start—local Baltimore politics and enrollment concerns required the existence of an undergraduate student body—the discovery of new knowledge and the training of advanced students in techniques of independent investigation were the university's first priority. Only faculty capable of making original contributions to their fields would be hired, and only those successful at their work would continue through the ranks. Hopkins thus became the first academic institution in America to distinguish between the restricted method and scope of college teaching and the independent work toward a Ph.D. that graduate students would pursue under the direction of senior faculty researchers. In its "recognition of the university as an entity distinct from the college," Hopkins permanently altered the American educational system.

Soft-spoken and gentle, more eclectic than single-minded, Gilman was an unlikely radical, and there was little in his career to suggest that he would be an educational pioneer. Neither his credentials as a professor of physical and political geography nor his experience as president of the University of California from 1870 to 1875 suggested that he was anything other than a competent administrator—a safe choice, in short, for the twelve trustees charged in the will of the businessman Johns Hopkins to employ the income from his $3 million bequest for educational purposes. Gilman had been recommended to them by three prominent college presidents—White of Cornell, Eliot of Harvard, and Angell of Michigan—none of whom was eager to champion research or graduate instruction at the expense of the undergraduates. It is doubtful that when Gilman came to Baltimore to be interviewed in 1874, the trustees were committed to the kind of institution he had in mind for them, but by the end of their session together, a new kind of academic enterprise had been born, with Gilman as its president.

Having invented the American research university, Gilman next had to discover the distinguished faculty necessary to convince qualified American students that they need not sail away to Germany to obtain advanced training. After a year of extensive travel, investigation, and cajoling throughout England, Europe, and the United States, Gilman returned to Baltimore with six professors in the fields of Greek and Latin, chemistry, physics, zoology, and mathematics. The fifty-four students holding college degrees who appeared at Hopkins in the fall of 1876 to study with them testified to the success of Gilman's recruiting skills.

Hopkins not only established a long-term structural model for the American university system, but more immediately, it stimulated colleges to compete for the high-powered researchers it was attracting to its faculty. Although committed to undergraduate instruction, for example, Harvard took particular notice of the intellectual excitement generated by Hopkins. Its push in the 1880s and '90s to find world-class scientists and scholars who would strengthen its graduate offerings was motivated in part by the sight of large numbers of students moving to Baltimore to earn doctorates.

Happily going about its business of dispensing the standard disciplinary fare for three hours a day, Columbia—at least as presided over by its comatose board of trustees—had no problem maintaining its old curriculum. It was only President Barnard who objected. The majority of the trustees were content with a small school that adequately prepared its two hundred or so students for the moral challenges of adult life, but Barnard wanted an institution "in which provision should be made at once for giving instruction of the highest order in every department of human knowledge, and for encouraging and facilitating original investigation in every subject of interest to man." For Barnard, it was a mission "of such dignity and grandeur that beside it [Columbia's] original function, as a school for the training of boys, shrinks into comparative insignificance."

Unfortunately, Barnard's tact fell far short of the majesty of his vision. Flailing trustees for their obtuseness did not persuade them of the rightness of his views. The more he pushed for adventurous reform, the greater became their attachment to the status quo. Barnard needed a faculty ally who shared his vision but also had the capacity, which he seemed to lack, to avoid alienating the trustees. In 1876 such a figure materialized in the person of John W. Burgess, newly appointed professor of history, political science, and international law.

Burgess had been teaching at Amherst, from which he had graduated in 1867. A native Tennessean, he did not like cities and was not eager to come to New York. He did so, however, in the interests of trying to establish, for the first time in the United States, a program of advanced instruction in political science. It was a dream he had been harboring for some time, ever since a nightmarish experience during the Civil War in the swamps of western Tennessee. Despite living in a secessionist state, the Burgess family supported the Union. To avoid impending conscription into the Confederate army, Burgess and a friend had ridden eighteen hours one frantic day in June 1862 until they encountered Federal forces, with whom Burgess promptly enlisted. Sent into the swamps some six months later to rebuild railroad bridges destroyed by the Confederates, Burgess and his Missouri regiment endured a month of rain—wading in water and sleeping with snakes and scorpions crawling over and under them while night birds assaulted them with their beaks and wings. In the middle of a violent storm early in January 1863 they were ordered to withdraw, and they stumbled back to an old fort that was shortly thereafter attacked by the Confederates. The battle lasted most of the day; at night, with the Union forces finally triumphant, Burgess was assigned to stand guard on the battlefield. Alone and terrified, surrounded by the awful sounds of mangled and dying men and animals, he vowed that if he should emerge from this horror, he would spend his life teaching men "how to live by reason and compromise instead of by bloodshed and destruction."

After graduating from college, he became a lawyer, studied for two years in different German universities, and then returned to Amherst in 1873 to teach, determined to use the college as a base for developing a school of political thought. Introducing the German seminar format and modern research techniques, he rapidly gathered around him a cadre of devoted undergraduates. Their enthusiasm for Burgess's methods was such that seven members of the graduating class of 1874 petitioned to be permitted to remain at Amherst for an additional year in order to continue to study modern history under his direction. Their request was granted, and during the 1874–75 academic year, five of them stayed on to work with him. In the spring of 1875 Burgess recommended that they go to Germany the following year for further graduate study, which all of them did. These five thus constituted Amherst's first group of graduate students—and its last. Full of excitement about the possibility of expanding his new enterprise, Burgess was soon informed by President Stearns that Amherst was about undergraduate training and discipline, not advanced, specialized instruction. The experiment promptly ended, and with it Burgess's belief that Amherst might welcome graduate education. When Columbia offered him the opportunity to teach in the Law School and the School of Arts in 1876, he accepted, hopeful that he could achieve in an uncongenial urban New York what he couldn't in his comfortably rural Massachusetts.

From the time he arrived, Burgess worked to include advanced instruction in political science in the curricula of the Law School and the School of Arts. Faculty and trustee opposition was determined, however, and progress in convincing people to consider change was painfully slow. He had supporters, of course, notably Barnard and, more important, a trustee named Samuel B. Ruggles, who had been largely responsible for bringing him to Columbia. Ruggles, who was then past seventy-five—at a time of life when conservative torpor might be considered natural—radiated pleasure at fresh ideas and stood totally behind Burgess. But even with Ruggles's help Burgess gradually realized that his plan for incremental change— adding a third year to the Law School and additional courses to the program in the School of Arts—would never happen. Radical rather than incremental change would be necessary, nothing less than "a new faculty and a new school for the study, teaching, and development of the historical, political, economic, and social sciences."

The idea was so extreme that he hesitated for a long time before discussing it with anybody. But when he finally revealed his plan to Ruggles in April 1880, he was delighted at the trustee's enthusiastic endorsement of the notion of a School of Political Science distinct from both the Law School and the School of Arts. Ruggles wanted a plan for the school as soon as possible, and he urged Burgess to go to Paris to study similar developments at the École Libre. Burgess drew up a plan and departed for France early in May, leaving Ruggles with the task of convincing his fellow trustees to authorize it. At 5:00 a.m. on June 7 in Paris, Burgess was awakened by a loud knock on his hotel door and handed an American cablegram. It was from Ruggles: THANK GOD, THE UNIVERSITY IS BORN. GO AHEAD. Ruggles had won, and now Burgess was free to hire the two additional instructors he thought he would need if the new school (really a faculty) were to offer instruction in the coming October.

But if a university was on its way, it was not yet there—as Barnard certainly understood. Despite the presence of the newly formed School of Political Science, which matriculated eleven students in the fall of 1880, he continued to press the trustees to realize that the undergraduates in the School of Arts needed not just to have their minds formed on the disciplinary model but to be exposed as well to advanced thinking and research. He drew a distinction between the "inferior" undergraduate level of disciplinary instruction and the "superior," research-based university kind. Columbia could only fulfill its destiny of becoming America's leading educational institution by engaging "the superior class of students" in "the business of proper university instruction."

The issue of the appropriate level of instruction for Columbia to be offering came before the trustees in 1887 as a formal question regarding whether or not the School of Arts should continue to exist at all. Barnard did not want to address the issue as long as the trustees were discussing it, though he did observe in his 1888 (and last) presidential report that the faculty could occupy itself even if it was devoted exclusively to the teaching of graduate students: "It would not be therefore educationally a misfortune if Columbia College should cease to exist as a school for undergraduate students. The city would still be fully supplied with educational advantages, while there could be no doubt that this institution could be more profitably employed by confining itself to the field of superior education."

Before any determination was reached, Barnard's poor health caused him to resign in May 1888. Needing an acting president while a search for his successor was conducted, the trustees chose the college's senior professor in point of service—Henry Drisler—for the post. From the point of view of the pro-university forces, led by Burgess, there couldn't have been a worse appointment. Drisler embodied those traits of the small-town college teacher that Burgess believed Columbia had to repudiate. According to Burgess, Drisler had no serious intellectual interests, no thoughtful ideas about education, no curiosity about the function of colleges in America's rapidly changing culture. Moreover, he was thoroughly parochial, having spent all of his student and teaching life at Columbia. Burgess claimed that Drisler knew of nothing outside of New York, nor did he care.

In the spring of 1888, with Drisler seeking to repel the advances Burgess had managed with his trustee supporters, the board decided to solicit the opinion of the separate faculties (School of Arts, Law, Mines, and Political Science) regarding the kind of instruction Columbia ought to be giving and the importance of continuing the School of Arts. The four responses came in over the summer and in the following fall. Predictably, faculty members of the School of Arts who drafted the majority report wanted the school maintained and strengthened; for them, it was self-evidently the heart of the college, commanding alumni support, binding together the various departments of instruction, and furnishing a good source of students for the other schools. Instead of ending undergraduate instruction, they argued for an improved undergraduate curriculum that could be a solid base for more advanced work. The long-term desirability of making Columbia into a real university, which the faculty endorsed, was not to be accomplished by a violent rupture with the past, "but by a gradual growth out of the college itself, in response to the needs of the community in which the college works."

The minority report, written by Burgess, began by noting that Burgess and his five dissenting colleagues had been excluded from contributing to the majority report (a point suggesting that perhaps Drisler was not quite as ineffectual as Burgess had made him out to be). It then proceeded to reject every claim in the majority report as to the importance, centrality, and unifying purpose of the undergraduate enterprise. The School of Arts, it argued, had been a distraction: "We consider that the faculty of arts, in its present form, is the greatest existing hindrance to a sound university development. It is not a bond of union, but an organized conflict." It emphasized that what the country needed was not more or even better undergraduate education, but enhanced "higher or university instruction," which American students seeking postgraduate training should not have to go abroad to get. Americans could now study political science in their own country, but those interested in philosophy, literature, or philology generally still had to approach them through the medium of a foreign language and foreign point of view.

The solution was not to eliminate the School of Arts—with its potential supply of students seeking advanced instruction—but to insist on a clean distinction between collegiate and university instruction. The report called for the creation of a new faculty of philosophy, on the model of the faculty of political science, to be responsible for all advanced instruction in literature, philosophy, and philology. Such a faculty would then be part of a different institutional model: one with four university faculties—law, natural sciences (mines), political science, and philosophy; and one undergraduate collegiate faculty, arts. Members of the university faculties would not be expected to supervise the mundane drilling and recitation chores in the School of Arts.

Rather than expanding the influence of the School of Arts, Burgess and his allies recommended its contraction. Disciplinary work should occupy the first three years of an undergraduate's career, preparing him to go on to serious intellectual work in the university faculties. In the fourth or senior year he would then undertake the specialized studies taught by members of those faculties, after which the bachelor of arts degree would be awarded. In place of the "illusory bond of union afforded by the existing faculty of arts," the minority report suggested that a university senate, with representation from each of the four graduate faculties, should determine all matters of university interest, including the first three years of the undergraduate curriculum.

Since Burgess was an influential member of the political science and law faculties, their reports made exactly the same points in exactly the same language. The political science report closed with the suggestion that the term "college" be restricted to the disciplinary department supervising the undergraduates in their first three years, and that the entire institution, hitherto called Columbia College, be known instead as Columbia University. The School of Mines, the one faculty whose membership did not include John Burgess, supported the majority position of the School of Arts, agreeing that while university instruction should be developed, it should grow out of the School of Arts rather than at its expense. The mines faculty did not see any necessary opposition between the two.

The ideological battle lines were thus clearly drawn between Burgess's university forces and the Drisler-led School of Arts loyalists. As Butler did not yet hold a professorial rank (during the 1887–88 academic year he was a tutor), he was forbidden by statute to sign a report. This temporary lack of status turned out to have had unexpectedly positive consequences for his career. Appointed an adjunct (in current terms, an assistant) professor the next year, he was now officially qualified to offer an opinion. Charles Da Costa, secretary of the trustees and a pro-university stalwart, knew that Butler could be counted on to make a strong case for the university, and since he hadn't had a chance previously to express his views, Da Costa invited him on March 18, 1889, to answer for himself the issues that had been put before the faculties.

Instead of merely being an additional signature on a report signed by others, Butler now could address the trustees in his own voice, to argue not just for his ideas but for his importance in the whole process of decision making. It was the kind of opportunity he relished. On April 5 he submitted a plan for reorganizing Columbia College into a university, together with a diagram illustrating how the different university faculties would relate to each other and the School of Arts. In *Across the Busy Years* and elsewhere, Butler took full credit for shaping Columbia into a modern research university, emphasizing that his views in the April letter "were, with a few modifications, accepted by the trustees and became the basis of the plan adopted shortly thereafter for the organization of an institution which is the Columbia University of today." Or as he wrote to W. T. Harris in April of 1890, "You will be glad to know that after a long fight my ideas about the organization of a university at Columbia College have prevailed and the formal announcement will be made in a few weeks."

The claim was not unwarranted—if slightly exaggerated—with the essential qualification that Butler's letter largely restated Burgess's position as expressed in the reports of law and political science and in the minority submission of the arts faculty. Butler's scheme followed Burgess's plan in all of the basic structural suggestions. The rhetoric and the historical context in which Butler framed his arguments made the document legitimately his own, but its recommendations could hardly be thought original. He was clearly working with Burgess to bring about what they both desired. Not that there was anything odd in this: next to President Barnard, it was Burgess who exerted the greatest influence on Butler at Columbia. Burgess had discovered him as a student at the Forty-ninth Street campus in the fall of 1881 in his course for seniors in American constitutional history. He was struck by Butler's intellectual gifts and energy, just as he was similarly impressed with another eager student, who listened attentively to what Burgess said in his constitutional law course at the Law School on Great Jones Street. He thought that both young men probably had the power and intelligence to be great presidents of the United States, though he concluded that Butler had more executive potential than the alert man in the first row of his law lecture, Theodore Roosevelt.

Burgess found Butler in most respects the most brilliant student he had ever taught, someone who might one day become a distinguished professor of political science. When Butler returned to Columbia in 1885 after his European sojourn, the student-teacher relationship turned first into a close one between a senior and junior colleague and then gradually an even closer one between devoted friends. The young Butler shared Burgess's enthusiasm for developing Columbia into a university, becoming, in Burgess's words, "one of my most powerful and efficient allies in this great work."

In doing Burgess's (and the university's) work, Butler did not neglect to do his own. He always maintained that one of his most valuable possessions was a copy of his April 5 trustee letter that he sent to President Eliot of Harvard in December for his comments. Calling himself to Eliot's attention as a university planner revealed the same instinct for career advancement he had shown when, as an undergraduate, he made the acquaintance of President Barnard, or when, as a graduate student, he asked W. T. Harris for advice. Butler rarely let pass an opportunity to introduce himself to men of importance who could be of use to him. Having gone to the trouble of constructing a scheme of university organization, he might as well make sure that the president of Harvard saw it. Eliot returned the document at the end of February with penciled marginalia so that Butler could erase them if he wished. But to Butler they were precious, defining the points on which the president of Harvard had taken the trouble to disagree with a lowly adjunct professor of philosophy.

The two were committed to developing their colleges into universities, but they differed radically in their views of the primacy of the college. For Butler—and for Barnard, Burgess, and, later, Seth Low—the college existed primarily to supply students for the graduate faculties. To use Low's metaphor, it was merely the seed out of which the great tree of the university grew. (Butler's metaphoric version stressed "the splendid university that has sprung from the loins of Columbia College.") While disciplinary training of the undergraduates was important enough to continue, it could not be confused with the genuine intellectual activity occurring at the superior or university level. The only question for Butler in sorting out the proper relationship between the college and the university was where to draw the line between the two. He, like Burgess, drew it after the junior year.

Eliot rejected this division entirely. Eliot's college was not a seed out of which something more valuable emerged, but the foundation on which everything else rested. For him, the natural educational divisions were the prescribed, disciplinary curriculum of secondary school, the free elective courses of four years of college, and the specialized years of graduate study leading to the Ph.D. He wanted to expand, not restrict, the intellectual options for college students. One year of electives made no sense to him, as it eliminated the possibility of putting together a coherent set of courses to be taken consecutively. He wanted to see departments establish a curriculum that would run smoothly from the first year of college through to the Ph.D. Charging different faculties with different responsibilities—as in Butler's model—fragmented things unnecessarily. And he objected to the exclusion of the arts faculty from representation in Columbia's proposed senate: "Arts faculty degraded—Why?" he commented in the margin. "Historically most serviceable of all." As for Butler's rather baroque term for the newly organized institution he was advocating—University of Columbia College—Eliot substituted the simpler "Columbia University."

Butler treasured Eliot's criticisms, though he did not let them, after the fact, alter his proposal, which remained as he had submitted it. But before any resolution could be reached on the various reports and letters received by the trustees, a new president had to be elected to direct the process. The choice would presumably determine the outcome of all the organizational proposals that had been unleashed by the trustees' earlier solicitation of faculty opinion about Columbia's future.

The two final candidates who survived the preliminary winnowing represented sharply opposed positions, mirroring the conflict among the trustees: for the conservative, pro-college wing, acting president and professor of classics, Henry Drisler; for the radical, pro-university forces, the trustee Seth Low. Unlike Drisler, who had some legitimate (if not very impressive) academic credentials and little else to recommend him, the forty-year-old Low had no academic credentials to speak of but lots of everything else. The son of a wealthy businessman, he was well connected, and energetic, and had been actively involved in Columbia affairs since his election to the board in 1881. His administrative capacities were known not only from his successful business dealings but from the two terms he had served as mayor of Brooklyn in 1881 and 1883.

Given the relative merits of the two men, it should have been no contest at all. But entrenched undergraduate loyalties were not easily overcome, and it was not clear that Low would win. At its October 1889 meeting, with Low absent on vacation and one trustee abstaining, the board revealed its uncertainty about Columbia's proper direction by barely nudging Low into office with a vote of 7–6.

Once elected, Low moved expeditiously to try to resolve the different issues and organizational interests. Understanding the need to allow all factions to express their views, he went to the extraordinary lengths of holding three days of meetings on March 12–14, 1890, in which all thirty-four professors on the faculty were invited to participate—the first such event in the history of the school. Butler opened the discussion following the Columbia custom in which the most junior member of the faculty was asked to speak first. It was one of those magnificent occasions to display himself in all his intellectual and rhetorical plumage that Butler always successfully exploited. Essentially presenting the substance of his April 5 letter of the previous year, Butler swept all before him, making a formidable case not just for his university views but, equally important, for himself as a major figure in the university's future. "No one who was present will ever forget the masterful way in which he handled the subject," Burgess later commented.

No one in the opposition did or could answer his arguments. His convincing presentation of the subject gave the university party the greatest encouragement, and the thought that came into my mind at the moment was that here was the proper and, for the University, fortunate personality for the deanship of the Faculty of Philosophy, to which position he was, upon the creation of that faculty, immediately and unanimously chosen by his colleagues of the faculty, and continued therein by their choice until his accession to the presidency of the University.

Not all the Burgess-Butler proposals were accepted. Low and the trustees put into effect the basic recommendations that started Columbia along the path to becoming a coherently administered research university: a single matriculation fee was established; a faculty of philosophy joined those of law, mines, political science, and the School of Arts; a University Council (initially with only advisory powers, to which shortly were added legislative ones) was created to oversee the university's academic operation and degree programs. And, more prudent and political than Butler and Burgess, Low refused to humiliate the School of Arts faculty, whose members would be entitled to the same representation on the council as the other faculties.

The organization of the faculty of philosophy brought with it, as Burgess indicated, the simultaneous elevation to the deanship of the man who had so passionately desired its formation. There was never a possibility that its ten members would choose anybody other than Nicholas Murray Butler as their leader. Thus, in 1890, to the title of president of the New York College for the Training of Teachers, the twenty-eight-year-old Butler added the impressive credential of dean of the faculty of philosophy. By this time the presidency of Columbia itself must have been in his sights, though it would take another dozen years before he achieved this further ambition.

CHAPTER FOUR

Educator

✣

In 1885, as a young philosophy instructor with an interest in pedagogy, Butler had joined the National Education Association, the country's largest professional organization of teachers and school administrators. In 1891 he was elected to the association's sixty-person National Educational Council, becoming its president four years later. He ended his affiliation as chairman of the board from 1906 to 1911. Until the early 1890s, the NEA had proceeded in the respectable, inconsequential way of most professional associations, bringing together its members for annual conventions at which a great deal of talk, and not much else, occurred. But at a meeting of the National Council in 1891, James H. Baker, principal of the Denver High School, addressed an issue of enormous significance: the lack of correlation between the admissions requirements of colleges and the curricula of secondary schools. More and more schools were being established for America's growing school population, but no general guidelines existed for advising them on how to prepare their students for getting into college. Instead of some coherent system linking the hundreds of colleges and thousands of school districts throughout the country, there was only the chaos of idiosyncratic arrangements, with no consensus about what a high school academic program should include, what comprised a course, how it should be taught, how many periods a week it should meet, or what its requirements might be.

In early July 1892 the NEA met in Saratoga, New York, to consider the issues raised by Baker. On Butler's motion, it decided to form a national committee—the first time such a body had ever been convened to deal with school problems—to study the situation and make recommendations. Butler then offered a second motion, nominating the committee, and that, too, passed. He did not place himself on it, but in choosing the membership of what became known as the Committee of Ten, he exercised considerable influence over its deliberations, making him, in effect, its eleventh member.

The committee consisted of Harvard's Eliot as chairman and included Commissioner of Education William Harris along with four university presidents, one college professor, and three school principals. Its makeup guaranteed that the committee's perspective would essentially be from the top down—a university and college-centered view—rather than from the bottom of the school system up. Meeting in New York at an event hosted by Butler in November, it decided to set up conferences in nine subjects: Latin, Greek, English, modern languages, mathematics, physics (along with astronomy and chemistry), natural history, history (including civil government and political economy), and geography. Each conference would involve ten participants, drawn from schools and colleges from different regions, and each was charged with examining how long, when, and how the individual subjects should best be taught in the secondary schools. The separate recommendations would then be digested into the Committee of Ten's final report.

Having suggested the committee and chosen its membership, Butler then succeeded in getting it funded. As a member (along with his friends Baker and Harris) of the NEA's Committee on Expenditure of Money for Pedagogic Research, established a year earlier, Butler supported a request he had made to the National Council for underwriting the cost. The allocation of $2,500 (the eventual cost of the total project was approximately twice that) was the NEA's first effort in subsidizing educational research.

The nine different conferences met from December 8 through 11 at seven locations across the country, and the following October their reports were submitted to the Committee of Ten. In November, working at Columbia for three days, the committee produced a draft of its overview and recommendations. The different subject reports, together with their conclusions, captured the interest of America's educational community. It was, in the words of Commissioner Harris, "the most important educational document ever published in this country." For the historian of education Theodore Sizer, the report's success in helping to standardize the way sec-

ondary schools taught the major subjects made it "the first such effective
document in the history of American education."

Its findings were controversial from the beginning—and have remained
so to this day. Supporters applauded its emphasis on studying the major academic disciplines in a sustained fashion; on insisting on the same kind
of strict academic exposure for all students, regardless of their interests in
going to college; on asserting that the newer curricular subjects—history,
science, and the modern languages—were as valuable as the traditional
stalwarts of Greek, Latin, and mathematics.

Conservative critics attacked it for dethroning Latin and Greek from required to optional status and, even worse, for urging colleges to admit students who had not studied them. Advocates of progressive education
excoriated it as an elite, university-led putsch on the secondary school curriculum, seeking to impose a narrow academic uniformity on a diverse student population with diverse abilities and motivations. They noted the
absence of attention to any practical courses or to instruction in the arts.
What the committee saw as the energizing power of a liberal arts curriculum extended to every student, some of its opponents saw as a gross failure
to recognize the indisputable fact of unequal human endowment. For those
not intellectually gifted, or to use the stronger words of the psychologist
G. Stanley Hall, one of the committee's sternest foes, for the "great army
of incapables, shading down to those who should be in school for the
dullards," such a common academic curriculum was sheer waste and folly.
Students whose "probable destinies" would lead them to the factory
shouldn't be asked to wrestle with physics and modern languages.

Whether denounced or admired, the report was widely read and discussed, acting as a benchmark for debate of academic reform for a number
of years. In practical terms, it influenced the structuring of secondary
school curricula and standardizing of the way the major academic disciplines were taught. With the growth of the progressive education movement and its child-centered focus in the early decades of the twentieth
century, the committee's findings gradually came to be dismissed as reactionary and elitist, its values demeaned as an obstacle to the development of
the child. But Butler's words about it in 1894, self-interested though they
might have been, were not without their point:

It must stand as the most important single discussion of the aims,
methods, and content of secondary education that has ever been

made. It will be eagerly studied, as it ought to be, in every college and high school of the country. If its suggestions are generally acted upon, as there is good reason to hope that they will be, there will result a most healthy reform of our secondary instruction, and a long-wished-for improvement in the relations of the secondary schools to the colleges.

The report could not itself address the strains that the different admissions requirements of colleges imposed on secondary schools. At the end of the nineteenth century, students got into college in two ways. The first, more generally in the West and Midwest than in the East, and more generally in public rather than private institutions, was through the certification process. In this system, a college would examine the academic quality of the schools in its geographic area; all applicants to the college (from those schools certified as academically sound) with a diploma and the endorsement of the principal were then entitled to automatic admission. The second system, more common in the elite, private institutions of the East, required passing an entrance examination in subjects devised by the particular college. From the secondary schools' point of view, this option posed an almost insuperable problem: regardless of how thoughtful and coherent their curricula, it was unlikely they could ready students for the various and distinct examinations set by the different colleges.

A common examination for college entrance had been discussed for many years, but it wasn't until the Committee of Ten established the guidelines for a common secondary school curriculum that it became plausible. Once some uniformity in preparation existed, then surely some uniform way of evaluating that preparation could be devised to help bring order to college admissions. The problem was to overcome the anxiety of the individual colleges that they would be relinquishing authority over the selection of their student bodies. Butler welcomed the challenge. With his usual zeal, he lobbied vigorously on behalf of this radically new idea of a single coordinated exam. Entrenched procedures were slow to give way, however. When he introduced a motion before the Columbia faculty in 1893, charging the president to enter into discussions with presidents of other eastern colleges to discuss formation of a college admissions examination board, the motion was tabled. But the Butler-led drive for change could not be diverted. In 1896 he submitted the resolution again, and this time it passed unanimously. Later that year, preliminary talks with Harvard, Princeton,

Yale, Cornell, and Pennsylvania were held at Columbia about the possibility of such an exam.

By 1899 Butler decided that the academic world—or at least the twelve
colleges and universities making up the Association of the Colleges and
Preparatory Schools in the Middle States and Maryland—was ready to
move on the proposal. On December 2, at the association's annual meeting
in Trenton, Secretary Butler (he had already served a term as the president
in 1895) presented a motion calling for the establishment of an examination board. Anticipating a contentious debate, Butler had asked Harvard's
Eliot—unquestionably higher education's most prestigious figure—to come
to Trenton to lend his support, even though Harvard was not a member of
the association. Eliot believed personally in the importance of Butler's proposal despite the fact that the Harvard faculty had voted against it, and he
took the trouble to get there in time for the meeting. According to Butler,
he made a critical difference. President Ethelbert Warfield of Lafayette had
just criticized the idea, stressing that Lafayette would never permit an external body to tell it whom to admit, when Eliot rose to speak. After some preliminary remarks in favor of the resolution, he turned to Warfield, sitting
near him on the platform:

> The President of Lafayette College has misunderstood Mr. Butler's
> proposal. This College Entrance Examination Board, if constituted,
> is not to admit students to any college but so to define the subjects of
> admission that they will be uniform, to conduct examinations in
> these subjects at uniform times throughout the world, and to issue
> to those who take the examinations, certificates of performance—
> good, bad, or indifferent. And, President Warfield, it will be perfectly
> practicable, under this plan, for Lafayette College to say, if it so
> chooses, that it will only admit such students as cannot pass these ex-
> aminations. No one proposes to deprive Lafayette College of that
> privilege.

Following an outburst of laughter, the several hundred members of the association voted unanimously to create the College Entrance Examination
Board. "This might never have happened," Butler noted, "if President Eliot
had not come down from Cambridge to support the proposal and make that
kind of a speech."

Within a year, under Butler's leadership, the organizational plan of the board had been completed. On November 17, 1900, it was formally approved by the association's twelve members: Barnard, Bryn Mawr, Columbia, Cornell, Johns Hopkins, NYU, Rutgers, Swarthmore, Union, Pennsylvania, Vassar, and the Woman's College of Baltimore (Goucher). Critical details remained to be resolved: the subjects for examination, the kinds of questions to be asked, the examiners entrusted with formulating the questions, the readers to evaluate the answers. But by early summer of 1901 everything was in place. During the week of June 17, in sixty-seven different locations in the United States and two in Europe, 973 applicants took the first College Entrance Board examinations. The 7,889 examination papers were promptly sent to Columbia, where 39 men and women seated around tables in Low Library read them. The modern era of college admissions had begun—in a limited way. Of the participating schools, only a few agreed to drop their own examinations entirely in favor of the board's (most permitted the students the option of taking either), and a number of influential colleges, like Harvard, Yale, and Princeton, chose to remain outside the association. Eliot's enthusiasm for the idea notwithstanding, Harvard didn't join until 1904. Still, although it took some years before the new system reshaped admissions procedures nationally, the organizational revolution had been successfully launched. For this considerable achievement, no one was more responsible than Butler, as the Examination Board itself stated:

> To him is due the conception of the Board. His eloquent advocacy of his plan before educational bodies prepared the way for its organization. His steady guidance, clearness of statement, resolution in holding to the original design, his maintenance of the importance of a dignified and solid basis of membership, and his wisely progressive conservatism in so enlarging the scope of the Board's work as to make it responsive to the needs of the schools and colleges, have laid broad and deep the foundations of success already achieved.

His national leadership efforts in coordinating college admissions examinations did not prevent Butler from also becoming the leading figure in the pressing local issues of New York public school reform. Dissatisfaction with public school education in cities has existed as long as public school education has existed, and certainly New York in the late nineteenth century proved no exception. Since the early 1870s, New York's schools had been functioning under a complex arrangement of overlapping and elusive centers of responsibility. The mayor appointed twenty-one commissioners of common schools who together made up the New York City Board of Education. They were expected to make general academic policy and exercise overall administrative supervision of the system. The board in turn appointed a superintendent of schools who acted as a general inspector and also prepared a list of those qualified to teach at individual schools.

The real power, however, lay not with the board, but with the five trustees it appointed to each of the city's twenty-four wards. Unlike the board members, who generally came from New York's social elite, the trustees were middle-class laymen who lived in the wards where they were appointed. They essentially controlled the schools in their wards: hiring teachers from the superintendent's list of those eligible, determining promotions and teaching assignments, and advising their school principals—whom they helped to choose—on matters of academic policy. Equally important, they were in charge of site selection for new schools, and managed the contracts for supplies, repairs, and construction. Both in personnel and budgetary issues, their influence was immense, terminally complicating anyone's capacity to discern a clear line of authority for rational decision making. The system's murky administrative structure was not its only problem. Insufficient funds, overcrowded classes, underqualified teachers, and the burdens imposed on schools by having to accommodate increasing numbers of immigrant children created desperately urgent difficulties.

As a president, a dean, and arguably America's most voluble advocate for the science of pedagogy, Butler had the perfect credentials to direct the forces pushing for change. He rapidly became, for historian of education Diane Ravitch, the "Field Marshal" of the battle for school reform. He had fired his first official salvo in 1889 while still living in New Jersey and serving on the New Jersey State Board of Education. In February of that year, as a member of the Public Education Society of New York, he helped draft a memo to the city's board of education that pointed out the defects in the current public school system, including the ineffectiveness of the ward trustees, and called for the state legislature to establish a special commission to investigate the schools' operations. Nothing came of this effort, but Butler and his colleagues were hardly discouraged. The board's indifference to the memo only emphasized to Butler the need to gather additional support among appropriate city organizations.

Before he could reorganize his campaign, however, his health required him to take a brief time-out. Even his prodigious capacity for work had its limits, and the burdens of simultaneously serving on the New Jersey State Board of Education as chairman of the Education Committee and on the Paterson School Board as its president; teaching at Columbia; publishing and lecturing; editing the *Educational Review*, a monthly journal he founded in 1891 devoted "solely to the scientific study of education"; acting as dean of Columbia's philosophy faculty; and engaging in his New York reform efforts, among his myriad other activities, managed to test them. Exhausted, he requested a sabbatical leave from Columbia in the fall of 1892 for the following spring. When Seth Low and the trustees granted it, he resigned from the Paterson School Board and set about planning a recuperative six-month trip with Susanna through the Middle East, Italy, France, and England.

In late January 1893, shortly before leaving, he wrote to his parents, asking them if they would permit their "ewe-lamb," Elizabeth (also known as Eliza and Betty), his twenty-year-old sister, to accompany them on the journey. Butler argued that it would be a wonderful opportunity for her, supplying her with enough experiences "to keep fire in her intellectual boilers for a long time to come." If wanting to include one's younger sister on a trip with one's wife might seem odd, Susanna clarified the reason in a postscript to Butler's January request. Given her own general frailty and desire not to do much of "anything except rest," Sue herself realized that she would not be much of a traveler. Eliza, on the other hand, full of enthusiasm and curiosity, would make the perfect partner. Butler wanted her along less out of concern to fuel her intellectual boilers than to equip himself with an energetic companion who could keep up with him. The benefits for Eliza were real, but less significant than what her presence would do for Butler. Henry and Mary, not surprisingly, were thrilled that Murray wanted to take his sister with them. Early in February the three left on their journey.

Butler's letters home revealed an exuberant American traveler, eager to see and experience everything. Unlike the solemn, slightly orotund prose he developed for his professional addresses, his reports to his parents were light, spontaneous, and even unself-consciously touristy as he tried to capture his impressions for them. With few exceptions, he found enchantment and beauty everywhere: "Cairo interests me immensely, as a city of contrasts" (March 11); "The Pyramids themselves and the Sphinx are not to be described. They far surpass one's expectations and nothing that has been written about them does them full justice" (March 13); Damascus is "the most interesting and enchanting place yet . . . The view of Damascus from the hills to the west of it . . . has been called the most beautiful in the world, and after drinking it in I am ready to agree" (April 13); "The view from the Acropolis, taking in as it does all the plains of Attica . . . & the sites made famous by Aeschylus, Sophocles, Euripides & Demosthenes, Pericles, Socrates, Plato & Aristotle, simply reduces one to silence" (May 7); Rome was "a most enchanting place" (May 21); Bologna, "far more interesting than the guide books had indicated" (June 11); in Venice, "evidence of present beauty and past greatness" was everywhere (June 18).

He even met, on the ship from Alexandria to Jaffa, the man who was to become one of his closest friends. In the midst of a debilitating seasickness, James B. Scott could only remember with envy the "tall, slender and youthful-looking person" who seemed utterly impervious to the demons assaulting Scott's innards. When they disembarked in Jaffa, Scott recalled stumbling "into the arms of this tall and slender gentleman wearing a felt hat, and his word of greeting made me his friend for life: 'I am sorry you had such a bad time of it.'"

Unhappiness was reserved for Constantinople, "the land of the passport-demanding, baggage-inspecting, bribe-taking Turk" who remained, in spite of the beauty of the land he possessed, "incommensurable, as the mathematicians say, with our point of view" (May 7). Betty proved the indefatigable adventurer Murray had anticipated, and he flourished in the company of both his women. Sue noted immediately how much better he became as soon as they had begun their trip. In early March, shortly after setting out, she wrote Mary that he was "quite like himself again, and as jolly and bright as possible" (March 5). At the end of March she conveyed the good news that not only was Butler eating and sleeping well, but she thought he was also "really learning to loaf" (March 30). And with four months still to go, Butler declared himself "quite rested out" and even admitted that he was beginning "to resent being away from college during term time" (March 31).

His recuperation from exhaustion was complete and more or less instantaneous, but he was plagued throughout his trip by the oppressive buildup of earwax that interfered with his hearing. He sought relief in Constantinople from an Armenian physician who diagnosed catarrh of the middle ear resulting from chronic catarrh of the upper nasal passages. He recommended a physician in New York for Butler to see when he returned and in the meantime prescribed a spray for his nose and a wash for his ears. Butler was delighted with the diagnosis, having always suspected that "catarrh was at the bottom of the trouble" (May 7). After one week's use of spray and wash, he was already feeling better. Spray and wash had their therapeutic limits, however, and by the time Butler reached Paris in mid-July, he was once again afflicted. Instead of waiting to return to New York before being treated, he decided to have the condition attended to while he could devote his time to getting better. The French specialist he consulted confirmed the earlier diagnosis and determined that before he would operate "to remove the seat of the disorder," the symptoms had to be addressed. This involved "a strong gargle for the throat, an equally fine sting-wash for the worse ear, a paint pot of iodine for the back of the ears to reduce the inflammation inside, & a mixture of phenol & vaseline to be shoved up the nose and drawn back into the throat." Somehow Butler survived this treatment, as well as the operation that followed, consisting of "cutting out of the rear nasal passages, through the mouth, the diseased portion which secreted the mucous & communicated the inflammation to the ears" (July 18). He took it all stoically, happy to endure the unpleasantness in the service of a permanent cure.

Rested, happy, and wax free, Butler, along with Sue and Eliza, returned home at the end of August. Within no time he reentered the maelstrom of reform activities. The lapse of six months had not dulled his love of political battle: the ward trustees still had to go. Working closely with the Wall Street lawyer Stephen H. Olin, Butler soon enlisted settlement houses and various churches in his campaign, along with the Association for Improving the Condition of the Poor (AICP), Good Government Club E, and the City Vigilance League. To focus on the school issue, Good Government Club E organized a women's committee (mainly composed of the members' wives), which by 1895 had transformed itself into an independent Public Education Association. Although the membership of the PEA was entirely female, they largely took their directions from a male advisory board chaired by Butler. As Mariana Griswold Van Rensselaer, the PEA's first president, commented, "A meeting of the Association without Dr. Butler was like the play 'Hamlet' with Hamlet left out."

Despite their organizational accomplishments, Butler and Olin still lacked the political clout to translate their reform agenda into law. In late 1894 they sought to bolster their support by involving in their cause the Committee of Seventy—an influential coalition of anti-Tammany Democrats, prominent business and professional leaders, and Republicans who had recently succeeded in getting a reform candidate, William L. Strong, elected mayor. The committee welcomed their interest and immediately appointed a small subcommittee, with Olin as chairman and Butler as a member, to explore ways of establishing meaningful school reform.

The first result of their collaboration was a bill, drafted by the subcommittee and endorsed by the Committee of Seventy as a whole, that was sent to the state legislature in Albany in the spring of 1895. Known alternatively as the Committee of Seventy Bill or the Pavey Bill (after state senator Frank Pavey, who submitted it), it recommended a range of administrative changes: the creation of a board of superintendents, trained experts who would be responsible for the educational administration of the schools; the nomination of principals and teachers by the board of superintendents; the complete separation of business affairs from educational administration; and the removal from the ward trustees of most of their powers, assigning to them only the responsibilities of visitation and inspection. Of these, the last was of course the most controversial. It became the contested battlefield of what Butler himself called the "School War," pitting the Butler-led forces for centralizing against the defenders of ward trustee status quo.

The actual merits of centralized authority as opposed to local or neighborhood control of schools were as difficult to resolve in 1895 as they are now. While there is always an argument to be made for efficient, direct lines of reporting and management by so-called experts, the decentralizers also have their persuasive claims. Centralized control is not always the most effective management model. It can degenerate into an unwieldy bureaucracy that rapidly grows out of touch with the living reality of what it is ostensibly supervising. Community involvement, whether through local school boards or ward trustees, can be more sensitive in detecting problems as they occur, and more capable of devising flexible solutions. The ward trustee idea was not devoid of substance.

The managerial pros and cons of the two systems, still being debated today, could not obscure the social, political, and religious dimensions of the conflict between Butler and his opponents. Whatever its objective administrative virtues, the movement to centralize represented an effort by the city's intellectual and economic upper crust to wrest control of the schools from what they considered to be socially inferior ward trustees. Butler and his troops were wealthier, educated more prestigiously (private as opposed to public colleges), better credentialed professionally, and far better connected than the largely middle-class trustees, many of whom had Irish or German roots. No degree of competence or conscientiousness (and there was plenty of both among the trustees) could make up for their obvious difference from Butler's patrician colleagues. School reform was thus as much a class issue as anything else.

It was also—given the inescapable connection of the two—a political issue. Part of Butler's campaign against the trustees rested on what he considered the need "to take the schools out of politics." In the artful language of a crusading politician, he extolled the nonpolitical interests of his reformers and condemned the intrigue and corrupt system of Tammany patronage that he attributed to the trustees. Cries of being above politics, of course, have always been an effective strategy for those outside of power trying to gain access to it. Butler's Republican centralizers were every bit as political as the basically Democratic Tammany ward supporters. "Taking the schools out of politics" really meant substituting Republican for Democratic control of the system. It meant, as well, liberating the schools from what was perceived as the Irish Catholic grip of Tammany Hall. Butler's reformers were overwhelmingly Protestant and included prominent leaders of the city's Protestant charities. Anti-Catholic bias, fed by the ever-increasing flow of new Catholic immigrants into New York City, made it seem all the more important to ensure that the schools were centralized so as to obviate the threat of subversive Catholic influences posed by the ward trustees.

Buoyed by their own reformist zeal and the enthusiasm of what Butler could permit himself to refer to as the city's "best men" (and women), neither Olin nor Butler adequately gauged the intensity of the resistance to change. Their contempt for the trustees, in the language of the Pavey Bill, as mere "dispensers of patronage" and "relics of a system long since outgrown" blinded them to their genuine popular support—for better or worse—from many quarters: school principals; a majority of the board of education; most of the city's four thousand teachers who, in spite of the Pavey Bill's insistence that they would relish their freedom "from the harassing control of local trustees," were quite comfortable in their relationship with the people who hired them; immigrant leaders who enjoyed influence in their individual wards; Catholic and Jewish religious spokesmen suspicious of Protestant encroachment; Tammany Democrats; and even the supporters of New York State Republican boss Thomas Platt, who shared Platt's anxiety about the intellectually elitist and socially well-connected people intent on curtailing his power.

Butler's initial efforts were not enough. In April 1895 the Pavey Bill died in the state assembly, defeated by the active lobbying of the opposition. Butler was determined to make sure that this setback was "only the Bull Run that points the way to an Appomattox." Ultimate victory would require a refining of strategy, designed to capture the public opinion that he always understood to be the key to political struggle. To begin with, the by now slightly stale Committee of Seventy, with its broad reform agenda, had to be replaced by a fresher, more formidable group, with school centralization as its single priority. This calculation resulted in the formation of the Committee of One Hundred for Public School Reform, whose membership, according to the historian David Hammack, "was a virtuoso exercise in list-making." It included prominent lawyers, physicians, businessmen, charity leaders, and educators associated with the development of the research university. The presence of investment bankers and directors of national corporations attested to their conviction that centralized administration was the approved, modern form of organization. Butler explained to Seth Low that he had left him off the committee to avoid the impression that "the reformers were college men and aristocrats," but it hardly comprised a cross section of the city's population. Of its membership of 104 (no one made a fuss about its erroneous title), 92 were listed in the 1896 *Social Register*. (The numbers would have been higher, but the committee's three Jews could obviously not be included.)

His support group in place, and having more or less co-opted the diverse interests of the city's reform movement on behalf of his centralization crusade, Butler then set his targets on influencing Republican legislators in Albany through press coverage of the issue. His success at this was perhaps the most spectacular feature of his campaign. Utilizing his impeccable credentials as an expert in educational matters, brilliant networking skills, and rhetorical powers as a supersalesman, he virtually controlled the way most of the city's major papers treated the story. In short order the *Evening Post*, the *Times*, the *World*, the *Sun*, the *Tribune*, the *Mail and Express*, and the

Commercial Advertiser slanted editorial and news coverage in his favor. When he couldn't himself make the necessary connections, he found someone who could. Mariana Van Rensselaer, for example, Butler's friend and president of the PEA, knew the newspaper publisher Joseph Pulitzer before Butler did. On December 4, 1895, she wrote to Butler, "Mr. Pulitzer has promised me that the *World* shall be run just as we want it to be in regard to the school question, and that he will publish any editorials, and as many of them as I choose to send in." To guarantee the correctness of what she would say, she asked Butler if he would spend some time going over them with her. Between December 8 and February 20, 1896, Pulitzer's *World* printed fourteen editorials advocating the abolition of the ward trustees, of which twelve were written by Van Rensselaer under Butler's close editorial supervision.

But only the *World* required such intervention. For the rest, Butler manipulated away, suggesting to the papers what and when to publish. To Palmer of the *Tribune*, thanking him for his editorial comment, he wrote, "May we not have the cooperation this year, as last, of the *Tribune* in this controversy? . . . If the *Tribune* will support the policy that it emphasized last winter I believe that we can win" (December 3). To Murlin of the *Tribune*: "I trust, therefore, that we may have your influence against the Strauss bill on this matter" (January 30, 1896). To Milholland of the *Tribune*, after he had located a temporarily misplaced earlier letter Butler had sent him: "I telegraphed you this afternoon to have it appear as a news article if possible. It will be far more effective that way than as a letter, because what I want to effect is public opinion at Albany and letters have no weight with them. Besides I should far rather have it appear without my name. It will do far more good" (February 4). To Bishop of the *Evening Post*: "Would you be willing to put a brief note in Thursday night's *Post* to the effect that the card calling the meeting of the Citizens Committee on Public School contained a misprint and confusion may result" (February 5). To Merrill of the *World*, encouraging it to continue to fight: "Our friends [in Albany] ask for further newspaper support during the next week or two and assure me that the *World* editorials have been more efficacious with members of the Legislature than those of any other newspaper" (March 4). To Milholland: "The school bill will reach the Mayor on Wednesday morning. Could you not have an editorial in the *Tribune* of that day or Thursday, strongly urging him to sign it promptly, and putting the responsibility for its success or failure on him" (April 6).

Butler also conducted an unyielding rhetorical assault on ward trustees in the pages of his own journal, the *Educational Review*. Understanding that in public relations warfare, moderation does not win the day, Butler never felt the need for restraint. Vilification was the sole note struck. The conflict between the reformers and the trustees represented a battle between "civilization and barbarism," between the pure motives of the centralizers and the self-interested "horde of bandits and barbarians" defending the current system. Trustees were "the forces of darkness," a mess of schemers, dishonest orators, the easygoing, the indifferent, and the narrow-minded. Their control of the school system "sheltered incapacity, favoritism, political chicanery and extravagance." In contrast to the "wire-pulling, jobbing lot of petty officials" capable only of "untruthfulness, blackguardism and demagoguery," the shining armies of reform embodied the nonpolitical virtues of "good citizenship and patriotism."

Ward trustee corruption and incompetence were never documented but merely asserted—and repeated over and over again until it was impossible to imagine any single justification for the trustees' existence. Altogether, a Butler blitzkrieg at its most irresistible. If the beleaguered forces of decentralization could be said to possess a commander, the job would have belonged to Henry S. Fuller, editor of *School*, a weekly newspaper intended primarily for the city's teachers. Fuller became the voice of the opposition, arguing for the importance of the trustees and criticizing Butler and his reformers for their arrogance and lack of comprehension about the actual workings of the school system. He saw their disagreement, correctly, as a form of class struggle, with Butler's economically privileged elite viewing with contempt the socially undistinguished trustees (and teachers) who toiled in the schools. Fuller rejected the notion that some kind of educational expertise was required of trustees. For him, the trustee was important in providing a form of "local home government in the school system." His task was

to look after the general condition of the school in the interest of the neighborhood of the school. He represents the constituency of parents whose children are pupils in the school, and if these pupils are largely of German, Jewish or Italian parentage, it is quite natural and right that they should prefer to be represented by a trustee in sympathy with them, and who understands them.

To be effective in this work, one needed not elaborate credentials but "intelligence, education and respectability"—qualities, according to Fuller, the trustees certainly possessed.

The issues of *School* in 1895 and 1896 teemed with denunciations of Butler as a high-handed "Continental expert" who was filled with theories but lacked any practical experience with public education. Fuller mocked his pretentiousness by referring to him as Nicholas Miraculous Butler, the first instance of the use of this name. So although Teddy Roosevelt popularized it as a means of celebrating him, Fuller gets credit for its invention. Fuller was capable of some rhetorical bite, but he couldn't hope to compete with Butler's academically sanctioned bluster. In the battle for the public opinion that mattered, Butler could scarcely lose. By the fall of 1895 the board of education also began to realize this. To try to deflect Butler, in January 1896 it proposed its own reform bill (the Strauss Bill) which included some of the provisions Butler had pushed for. It called for substantially modifying the powers of the trustees, but stopped well short of abolishing them. In fact, because the bill wanted to reconfigure and expand the individual districts served by the trustees, it actually recommended increasing their number from 120 to 225. Outraged by this notion of reform, Butler said he would settle for nothing less than total elimination of the trustees. When the board refused to consider that step, Butler and Olin decided to fashion a reform bill of their own with one major provision: to remove the ward trustees from the school system. Under the auspices of the City Club, Senator Pavey introduced it before the assembly once again; it bore the endorsements of the Good Government Clubs, the Committee of One Hundred, and the PEA.

With two competing bills now in Albany, Butler devoted his public relations talent to winning over the minds and hearts of the Republican legislators. Discrediting the Strauss Bill proved to be easy. Charles Strauss was a Tammany lawyer, and though only five of the fifteen members of the board who supported his bill were Democrats, Butler immediately began referring to it as "the Strauss or Tammany bill." Insisting on this connection in the Butler-influenced press and in the pages of the *Educational Review* welded the two together in the public's perception. Republicans in Albany who might have been inclined to see the virtues of local control thus found themselves in the impossible political position of seeming to support Tammany Hall.

Along with his active press campaign, Butler aggressively went after state senators, arguing his case for centralization with them by citing the enormous support he had been receiving from the popular press on the issue. He even sent the women of the PEA to testify before the legislature, causing trustee advocates to deride the Pavey Bill as "the Pink Tea Bill." Not only were the women effective in presenting their case, but they then paid a visit to Governor Levi Morton's wife, in short order capturing her for the movement as well.

Despite the fact that the opposition—including nearly all of New York's teachers and principals, American Federation of Labor president Samuel Gompers, and one hundred thousand parents—considerably outnumbered the forces of reform, the Butler-led juggernaut could not be stopped. On March 31, 1896, the state senate voted the Pavey Bill in and the trustees out by a vote of 31–13; on April 7, the assembly followed, 88–43. With the approval of Mayor Strong and Governor Morton, the bill became law on April 23. Nicholas Miraculous had triumphed; the ward trustees were no more.

One battle remained, however: to get the board of education to elect the right superintendent. In almost every essential, the incumbent, John Jasper, constituted the perfect anti-type of what Butler wanted. Undistinguished and poorly educated, he was himself a product of the decentralized school system that he strongly supported. Having worked his way up through the school ranks, he had already been chosen for sixteen consecutive terms. For Butler, Jasper would be an obstacle to, rather than an agent of, reform; the problem was to locate a compelling alternative whom the board would be obliged to consider. Unfortunately, Butler and his reformist colleagues could think of no serious candidate attractive enough to wrench support away from Jasper. Butler then had one of his tactically brilliant ideas. If no plausible challenger could be found, why not select someone entirely implausible whose excellence was such that he could not be dismissed? Arguably the most implausibly distinguished person Butler could conceive of for the position was Daniel Coit Gilman, an educational figure of international visibility who had once been the head of the New Haven school system and was for the past twenty years the president of Johns Hopkins. Butler's strategy did not require Gilman to accept the position, but merely to agree to run for it. Faced with a candidate of Gilman's distinction, Butler reasoned, the board could not possibly choose Jasper. A Gilman memo recounted Butler's approach on May 18:

Gradually, to my complete surprise, he led up to the remark that he came, in behalf of many influential New Yorkers, to say that they desired to have me accept the office of Superintendent. He unfolded the possibilities of the situation and said that whether I accepted finally or not, it would be a great boon to the public if I would allow my name to be presented and considered. I told him that I could not say "yes" and would not say "no" to any such overtures. He said that even if I declined, they could use my name in such a way as to make it easier to secure a suitable person.

Saying neither yes nor no, Gilman consented to Butler's plan. The results were precisely what Butler had hoped for. "New York has been swept off its feet," he wrote Gilman on May 20, "by the mere suggestion that we may have you to lead our great city's new civilization. Everywhere it is the topic of conversation among bankers, merchants, professional men; they are red-hot with enthusiasm." Having permitted himself to be used as a pawn in Butler's game, Gilman now found, notwithstanding Butler's assurances to the contrary, that he was expected to accept the position if it was offered. Seth Low was quite explicit: "What I want to lay before you now as earnestly as possible is this;—that, having consented to the use of your name, I do not think you are any longer free to decline an appointment, if tendered to you upon conditions that you are justified in accepting."

Guilt was heaped upon him from all directions. The Hopkins trustees criticized him for thinking of leaving the university he had started twenty years earlier. Supporters of New York's reform movement, like Commissioner of Education Harris, told him that his refusal to accept the position would undermine "at one blow" all the good work done on behalf of good government in New York and restore power to Tammany. Even Butler thought it appropriate to remind him, "To lose you now would mean Jasper for six more years." Gilman continued to maintain his essential innocence, stressing to Low that he had done all that was asked of him by agreeing to have his name presented. Disappointed, Low finally accepted the reality that Gilman would not abandon Hopkins. Low then wrote him on May 26 that since he had made up his mind, he should tell board of education member Peaslee the truth before Peaslee embarrassed himself by submitting Gilman's name as a candidate. Low's call for honesty confused Gilman somewhat, as he had received from Peaslee, also on the twenty-sixth, a letter urging him to say that he would seriously consider the position of city superintendent if it was offered him. Gilman, opting for principle over expedience, informed Peaslee that he was not interested in the job.

Having lured Gilman into this against his will, Butler avoided the temptation to be graceful when informing Gilman of the results of his defection. He wrote to Gilman that just as he had anticipated,

> The members of the Tammany Ring feared the effect of delay and they pushed through Mr. Jasper's election. It may interest you to know that had your name been before the Board, the vote would have been, in my judgment, seventeen for you and four for Mr. Jasper. However, we cannot undo what has happened, and I wish to thank you most sincerely for having aided us in our campaign to the extent that you did.

Butler's efforts at reform were not in the end undercut by Jasper's reelection. With the passing of the Greater New York Charter in 1897, bringing together the five boroughs, a new central board elected a new superintendent, the admirable William H. Maxwell, whose qualifications certainly included being a good friend of Butler's as well as an editor of the *Educational Review*. Maxwell's appointment in 1898 satisfied Butler that the proper administrative system now had the proper man to lead it. The battle "to redeem the schools of the metropolis from politics, sloth, and low ideals," had ended victoriously.

The purging of Tammany influence in the restructuring of the public schools did not mean that Butler could allow himself to become complacent about possible relapses in the future. His alertness to any flare-up of Tammany infection led to one of the odder episodes in his career. On February 11, 1896, the *Educational Review* published a strong editorial criticizing Commissioner Joseph J. Little of the New York Board of Education for his unwillingness to permit funds set aside by the board of estimate for primary education to be used to build new—and desperately needed—high schools. Butler thought Little's position was retrograde. The editorial, entitled "Tammany in the Saddle," argued that Little didn't really understand the city's current educational problems:

That fine old educational mastodon, Commissioner Little, is Tammany's President of Tammany's new school Board for the boroughs of Manhattan and the Bronx. He is supported by two other representative ante-diluvians, Commissioners Livingston and Moriarity; but some of the other men named by Mayor Van Wyck belonged to a better and higher order of citizenship. In consequence we predict an early rift in Tammany's pet lute, for Commissioners O'Brien, Van Hoesen, Kittel and Davis are not men who can be held to a reactionary policy indefinitely, and they are not so easily impressed as are some others by the "cohesive power of public plunder."

Little admitted later that he didn't know what "mastodon" and "antediluvian" meant. He was, however, deeply incensed by the accusation. "I do not propose," he was quoted by the *New York Tribune*, "that any man shall call me names I do not understand." With the aid of Tammany district attorney Asa Bird Gardiner, who was determined to teach Tammany Hall critics a lesson in civic propriety, Little appeared before a grand jury on March 28 to seek an indictment for criminal libel against the editor and publishers of the *Educational Review*. On March 29, Butler and Henry and Charles Holt, the *Review*'s publishers, were arraigned before Judge Blanchard in the court of general sessions and released on $500 bail.

The ludicrous nature of the case, especially when Little revealed his ignorance of the offending term's meaning, delighted the press. Cartoons of the commissioners' faces affixed to prehistoric tusked mammals and strange flying reptiles appeared, along with editorial comments lampooning "the absurd and monstrous indictment" that only provided "conclusive proof of the District Attorney's unfitness for his place." The *St. Paul* (Minnesota) *Pioneer Press* suggested that the entire spectacle was "one of those amazing things which occasionally cause us to wonder whether we humans are a race of intelligent beings or whether we are merely a part of an extensive Punch and Judy show."

But while the press hooted, Butler and the Holts had to fashion their defense. Butler's old friend John Pine represented him, and on March 30 Pine gave notice that he would make a motion to inspect the grand jury minutes to determine on what testimony the indictment was based. The motion was granted on April 7, and on April 18 he moved that the indictment should be dismissed for insufficient evidence as well as in the interests of justice. Meanwhile, public scorn continued to descend on District Attorney Gardiner. The *Milwaukee Sentinel* argued that the whole affair had to be an elaborate joke:

> It is becoming plainer and plainer every day that the New York papers have combined to hoax the country at large. They have conspired together and invented an utterly impossible person, whom they call Asa Bird Gardiner, and upon whom, in a spirit of playfulness, they have conferred the office of District Attorney.

Jacob Mack, former chairman of the board of education's finance committee, objected to Butler's characterization of Little: "President Little has been called a 'fine old educational mastodon,' when as a matter of fact, there is nothing fine about him. Nor is he old, nor is he educational. Therefore, gentlemen," he insisted at a meeting of the City Club, "the epithet 'dodo' is manifestly more fitting."

Although he had to go to the serious trouble of defending himself—engaging Pine and inserting an editorial in the April issue of the *Review* stating that the original comment was obviously jocular and that Little's probity had never been questioned—even Butler got into the absurd spirit. While the case was still pending in April, he couldn't resist producing a jolly doggerel version of the incident:

How Gardiner hurled a thunderbolt
That fell kerflop on me and Holt

———

I was sitting in my study
    Writing puffs of Harry Peck
Which would give him lots of pleasure
    And would yield me quite a check.

Then the bell went jingle-jangle,
    And the hired girl appeared,
With the word that I was wanted
    By a gent who dyed his beard.

While she spoke, a person entered
    Red of eye and thick of speech,

Saying are you Murray Butler,
　　Him who teaches how to teach?

In my taking way I nodded,
　　"I am he whom all should know."
"Ho!" said he, "You are my captive,
　　And to-night to gaol you go."

I was harrowed—yes, I shuddered,—
　　Yet I'm calm and could not whine;
So I asked him to be seated
　　Till I sent for J. B. Pine.

As the Cits were round the corner,
　　Drinking tea and making talk,
I was sure J.B. was near me—
　　Just within a minute's walk.

When John B. with six reporters,
　　Passed within my polished door,
Peace returned, and all grew quiet,
　　And I seemed myself once more.

Libel was what Little called it,
　　Just because I said my say
On cohesive power of plunder
　　In the mildest sort of way.

"Mastodon of Education"—
　　That was humor—durn their eyes!
Can't the fools admire good writing?—
　　In my prose there ain't no flies.

"Courage!" quoth my noble counsel,
　　"You will never land in gaol—
This is easy, they will grovel;
　　Now we only need some bail."

Thus the horrid Gardiner hurled a bolt
That fell kerflop on me and Holt.

After embarrassing Little and Gardiner more than anyone else, the bolt
fell harmlessly to earth. On April 28 Judge Cowling, who had no sympathy
for plaintiff or district attorney, dismissed the indictment on the grounds
that since no legal evidence was presented at the hearing that the alleged
crime was committed in the county of New York, the court had no jurisdiction over it. Gardiner protested that the case had been thrown out on a tech-
nicality and threatened to bring it up again. But given the figures of fun the
two had become, both were satisfied to allow Butler's libelous assault to remain unpunished.

Not all of Butler's later relations with the National Education Association
were as untroubled as when he was directing the forces of curricular and admissions reform in the 1890s. In July 1903 he ran afoul of the determined
Margaret Haley, a teacher from Chicago, at an NEA meeting in Boston.
Butler's centralizing impulses, often sound organizationally, were also
tainted with the conviction that democracy was fine so long as it didn't interfere with the freedom of a small cadre of the right people to run things.
And the right people in educational matters could not possibly include a
horde of undistinguished, poorly paid teachers, a majority of whom were
women. Acting on this principle, and wanting to preserve the historically
all-male control of the NEA, he proposed a resolution at the Boston meeting to remove the selection of the nominating committee for president from
the delegates and place it instead in the hands of the president himself.
    But Butler had not reckoned with Haley, who had won her battle stripes
two years earlier when she led a successful campaign to increase the salaries
of Chicago teachers. Haley immediately saw past the arguments offered by
Butler and NEA president Eliot that such a system would dignify the proceedings to the blatant class and sexual bias beneath. Grilling Eliot in front
of the delegates, she forced him to admit that the resolution, if passed,
would institute a process in which the president appointed a nominating
committee that would then appoint a president who would then appoint
a nominating committee. In which case, she concluded triumphantly, the
NEA would have produced an efficient self-perpetuating machine.

Haley's determination not to permit the university-educated men to exclude the (mostly women) teachers from the nominating process succeeded. Butler's resolution lost, 123–43, and the press took pleasure in the unlikely triumph of one woman over the formidable duo of Eliot and Butler. This defeat rankled, both because it was a defeat and because it was administered by one of Butler's untouchables—a woman teacher.

Butler's next skirmish with the NEA involved another indomitable Chicago schoolteacher, Ella Flagg Young, who had risen from the ranks to become the much-admired superintendent of the Chicago school system. Sharing with her friend Haley a profound unhappiness at the patriarchal control of the NEA, she resolved to challenge the old-boy network by becoming the association's first woman president. In an election muddied by allegations of voter fraud, she achieved her goal at the Boston meeting in July of 1910. The allegations were brought by the association's secretary, Irwin Shepard, Butler's closest ally at the NEA (though not himself a trustee, as Butler was), who shared Butler's anxiety about female control of the NEA. Shepard charged that the Chicago schools, in an effort to stock the meeting with voters sympathetic to Young, had illegitimately purchased association memberships for teachers not technically entitled to them. He pointed out that although Haley had not violated any rules in 1903 when she resisted the Butler-Eliot proposal, she had engaged in the same technique of bringing in voters at the last minute to guarantee a victory. The difference, for Shepard, was that Haley's actions, though tawdry, were legal, while Young's were not.

Shepard's arguments, though not without merit, did nothing to undermine Young's election. She remained very much the president. They did manage, however, to deepen her hostility to the association's male leaders, and particularly to Butler, who had been chairman of the board of trustees since 1906. She retaliated in several ways. Butler had gone abroad in the summer of 1910 uncertain whether he wanted to stay on as chairman, despite the desire of his fellow trustees that he remain. His European travels caused him to miss the July 8 annual trustees' meeting. At the board's membership committee meeting on July 7, Augustus Downing, one of Butler's friends, told the board that before Butler left, he had instructed Downing to report that if he was reelected, he would decline the nomination. Nevertheless, after extended discussion about Butler's importance to the association, the directors present voted to have him succeed himself for another four-year term.

At the annual trustees' meeting the next day, attended by Young in her ex officio capacity, she moved that in light of Butler's absence and uncertain availability, trustee Henry B. Brown, president of Valparaiso University, be elected the board's temporary chairman. No stenographer was present, but the secretary, J. M. Greenwood, a Butler supporter, later produced minutes indicating that Brown was "to serve during the absence of Chairman Butler." Young and her supporter, Milwaukee school superintendent Carroll G. Pearse, disputed this language, insisting that Brown had been elected instead to serve temporarily "till further action by the Board." The distinction was critical: if Brown was only serving while Butler was away, then Butler could, if he chose to, come back and immediately become chairman again; if Young and Pearse were right, then Brown remained acting chairman until the board officially moved to return the position to Butler. On the basis of these unresolved (or nonexistent) minutes, there ensued a somewhat farcical but also bitter controversy.

Responding to urgent requests from Shepard, Brown, and Greenwood not to let Young and Pearse gain control, Butler agreed to keep open the option of accepting his election and exercising his rights as chairman upon his return. Young, however, refused to acknowledge that he had any such rights, asserting that the board, without Butler, would have to meet to determine his claim to be chairman. Since Butler's absence meant that the five-member board would be split—Young and Pearse against Butler; Greenwood and Brown for him—it was unlikely that "further action by the Board" would restore Butler to his position. In the meantime, Brown would remain acting chairman, and Butler would not even have the authority to call a meeting. While Butler was still debating what to do, Young ratcheted her anger up a notch. On September 23 Chicago newspapers featured an interview with her in which she questioned whether the $170,000 of securities belonging to the NEA were intact in a Chicago savings bank. She claimed to have been misquoted, acknowledging only that she had told a reporter who asked her about the rumor concerning the possible misuse of the securities that she too had heard it. Whether misquoted or not, Young had managed to cast doubt on the integrity of the trustees, who were responsible for supervising the association's permanent fund. Such aspersions were particularly offensive to Butler, whose friend Newton C. Dougherty, a former NEA trustee (1900–1905), was currently serving a jail term for embezzlement of funds while superintendent of schools at Peoria. Butler was appalled at the reports of the interview sent him by Shepard:

I have read them through with mingled feelings of amusement and disgust. It is amusing to see a woman who has been elevated to high place by disreputable methods making such a fool of herself, and it is disgusting to think that her knavery is great enough to lead her to try to discredit the good name of the organization of which she is for the moment the head.

Young had no grounds to encourage the rumor, beyond the fact that it helped torment the male hierarchy that had done its best to keep women like Haley and Young out of it. One unintended consequence of her remarks, however, was to make Butler all the more determined to take over the chairmanship. "I am now much more inclined than I was to accept my re-election in order to oppose and denounce this woman officially," he assured Shepard. Returning from Europe at the end of October, he immediately informed Shepard of his binding decision to fulfill his obligations as chairman. Much as Butler would have preferred not to, the wickedness of an upstart woman and his commitment to the association compelled him to defend it against the unjust accusations: "Personally I cannot afford to be engaged in a public squabble with people of the type of Mrs. Young and Pearse," he complained to Brown. "I have nothing in common with them or they with me. I have consented to continue on the Trustees only with profound reluctance and in order to stand by Secretary Shepard, yourself and Mr. Greenwood."

Upholding the integrity of the association, in Butler's mind, required that he insist on his chairmanly prerogatives in the face of Young's insistence that he wasn't chairman. This standoff had serious consequences when Butler tried to pay some NEA bills, a process normally initiated by the trustees and endorsed by the president. Young refused to recognize the legitimacy of Butler's signature and returned bills to the trustees unsigned, preferring to let them go unpaid rather than acknowledge Butler's authority. When she called a meeting of the executive committee (on which the chairman of the trustees sat) in November, she invited Brown, not Butler, noting that Butler "has not been elected to the chairmanship of the board and consequently he is not a member of the executive committee. In July, our last meeting, there was no chairman elected." Equally intransigent, Butler refused to allow Brown to stand in for him.

The conflict between the implacable Young and the immovable Butler had to be resolved, but it was evident that neither compromise nor negotiation could manage it. Someone had to act decisively. As Young wouldn't retreat, Butler decided to attack. Avoiding the trap that he was not entitled, according to Young, to call a regular meeting, he arranged instead for a special meeting of the trustees in New York on January 23, 1911, authorized by secretary Greenwood, acting chairman Brown, and himself, to settle the chairmanship question. (In a calculated affront to Young, Brown's announcement of this meeting referred to Butler as *Chairman* Butler.) Young refused to attend, and she asked Pearse (who did) to read a letter of protest; it objected to the choice of the twenty-third, which Butler and Greenwood knew would be inconvenient for Young and Pearse. "I cannot understand," her letter to Brown concluded, "why two members of the Board should be consulted and their convenience taken into consideration, and two other members utterly ignored."

Pearse followed with his own protest that the meeting was irregular and illegal. Brown, Butler, and Greenwood listened calmly to his dissent, then proceeded to do exactly as they intended, either defeating or refusing to second all of Pearse's motions, and voting in all their own. A 3–1 majority restored Butler to the post he had always thought was his, but it didn't quite end the verbal sparring. "I came on expecting to be swallowed, and I was," Pearse commented to the press afterward. "Dr. Butler has been elected chairman, but he is no more chairman than he was before. He has usurped the place at an illegal meeting and it is only the beginning of the fight." Ella Young affected a more indifferent response: "I am too busy with the public school budget to talk about Dr. Butler and his trustees . . . Dr. Butler has run the NEA ever since it was started, so what can I, a mere woman, do to check him in his wild career, anyway?"

The press looked forward to more pyrotechnics at the annual meeting in San Francisco on July 9, where the fight would be resumed. The *Record-Herald* anticipated it would be "a case of the Young Amazons against the Nicholas Murray Butler mercenaries." But the leader of the mercenaries had had enough. Claiming that he needed to care for his ailing mother, Butler told Shepard that he could not attend the San Francisco meeting. The association rules, Butler noted, called for automatic forfeiture of trustee membership for those who missed two consecutive annual meetings. Since he had also missed the 1910 Boston meeting, he declared his own seat immediately vacant. (His insistence on this rule was pointed. Several years before, he had unsuccessfully argued that Pearse had disqualified himself from his position because of a similar violation.) In case the automatic forfeiture was not sufficient to deter his supporters, who might be tempted still to try to reelect him, he included a letter of resignation, which he asked Shepard to read to the board at the appropriate time.

The final year of Butler's NEA trusteeship had not been gratifying. In winning the battle to reclaim his title as chairman, Butler had expended too much energy and shed too much blood to take pleasure in the victory. "I am sorry, deeply sorry," he apologized to Shepard, "not to be able to work longer by your side for the association that we have served and loved for so long; but if the fate of that association is to become the football of political schemers and educational politicians and demagogues, then I have no regret at ceasing to be one of its officers."

At the San Francisco meeting, his sworn enemy, C. G. Pearse, succeeded Young as president.

CHAPTER FIVE

The Twelfth President

🙏

In 1889, as the youngest dean of the newest faculty in an institution transforming itself from an old-fashioned college into a modern university, Butler must have seen in Columbia's pinched, inadequate Forty-ninth Street campus a vast continent of personal and professional opportunity. Who better able to mine its potential riches than the energetic, visionary dean who had already claimed responsibility for having drawn up Columbia's blueprint for university expansion? The problem was that Seth Low, not Nicholas Murray Butler, ruled over its small campus and large future. As long as Low remained in place (and he was only twelve years older than Butler), all Butler could do was to work hard, make himself indispensable to Low, and wait.

Butler was not designed by nature for the loyal adjutant's role. The circumstances of his career were now very different from what they had been when he ranked as an assistant in the Philosophy Department, but a certain structural similarity remained: he was still professionally dependent on a mentoring older man whose position he actually sought. Low stood in the way of his presidential aspirations just as Archibald Alexander, some years before, had stood in the way of his professorial ones.

Not that, in either case, he was anything other than conscientious and dutiful. Toward Low, however, loyalty stopped short of affection—or even much respect. After Butler gained the presidency, he managed rather successfully to avoid saying anything complimentary about his predecessor. His enthusiasms were always saved for Barnard, to whom he assigned all credit for the vision of the modern university. For Low, who in fact provided the leadership cement and administrative steel that started a small college on its way to becoming a university, and who presided over the decision to leave the Forty-ninth Street campus for the grander space of Morningside Heights, there was only grudging acknowledgment that he too had occupied the office.

A number of factors account for this, the most important being that Butler felt himself in competition with Low, so that to praise him posed the risk of diminishing his own achievements. Barnard's tenure was sufficiently in the past, and he was sufficiently idiosyncratic and administratively erratic as not to constitute any threat. Low's achievements, however, required some calculating disregard. Butler also found it irksome that as a genuine patrician of enormous wealth and social status, Low possessed—by virtue of the unfairness of birth—all those qualities that Butler had struggled to acquire for himself through his own exertions. Coming from a family that manufactured jute carpets didn't quite measure up to one owning a fleet of clipper ships that plied the tea and silk trade with China, and Butler was not above resenting such disparities.

Low's lack of any proper credentials as an educator did not escape Butler. His 1898 piece in the *Educational Review* on the qualifications for a college presidency (written well before he decided to redefine himself as a businessman running a business), in addition to providing an idealized portrait of himself, delivered a none too subtle dig at Low:

> The supposition that the merely successful business man can develop into a satisfactory college president is nonsense. He never has and he never will. The illustrations usually relied on to prove the contrary are not to the point. The men referred to were much more than business men. They were men of cultivation, intellectual sympathy and educational ideals. Their business training has been the least useful part of their equipment. No university can be run on business principles, any more than a business can be run on university principles. A university must be run on university principles or not at all.

And it is true that during the ten years of Low's presidency Butler acquired a national reputation as an educator that far outstripped Low's. However explicitly Low acknowledged from the start that he came to Columbia not as a professor, but as an administrator, his honesty failed to diminish Butler's unhappiness at having to serve someone who lacked the appropriate academic qualifications.

Butler's harshest criticism of Low was his most unwarranted. Overlooking his own dreams for national office, he frequently distinguished his steadfast loyalty to Columbia from the cavalier attitude of Low, who twice ran for mayor of New York (1897 and 1901) while at Columbia. In answer to a question about Low put to him in 1940, Butler incorporated Low's alleged political aspirations into a consummately delivered bit of faint praise: "I think that Seth Low had very excellent tact in dealing with difficult matters and with conflicting opinions and arguments. His real limitation at Columbia was that his mind was fixed on public service in public office. He did a good job, nevertheless."

Butler knew better. Low had an acute sense of social responsibility, and he was willing rather than eager to stand for election if the community felt it needed him. Running for public office was an obligation he was prepared to honor, not an obsession he couldn't subdue. Indeed, if anyone was interested in a political career for Low, it was Butler, who was always looking for a chance to ease Low out to open the Columbia presidency for himself. Early in 1900 he wrote to his good friend Teddy Roosevelt, then McKinley's vice president but clearly on the way to the White House himself, extolling Low's merits as a future vice presidential possibility. "He would make a very strong candidate," Butler suggested, "and would, if elected, be an admirable incumbent of the office." Roosevelt was not interested in the suggestion, however, and in 1901 Butler turned to the more practicable, more immediate option of getting Low elected mayor of New York. He enthusiastically explained to lawyer Frederick W. Holls that Low was the only serious Republican candidate who commanded any significant popular support. As to whether or not Low would leave Columbia should he be nominated, Butler accurately diagnosed why he would: "While Mr. Low has not authorized me to speak for him in any way, yet I know that he will accept the nomination if it comes to him in the form of a duty to be performed."

Despite his appreciation at the time of Low's principled reasons for running, Butler never restrained his subsequent attacks on Low for harboring political ambitions and never overlooked an opportunity to diminish him. When the trustees sought, in 1917, to honor Low with a tablet in the chapel with the letters LL.D. on the inscription—referring to the honorary degree granted him by Columbia—Butler objected to the inclusion of the degree. The clerk of the trustees, John B. Pine, argued with Butler that "in view of Low's position as President and his personal peculiarities and the suscepti- bility of some of his family and friends, I think we should give him his title. Besides, the additional three letters will help fill up space where needed." In the face of such compelling logic, whether about the space or the sensi- bilities, Butler relented.

Butler's mean-spirited stake in posterity's negative view of Low expressed itself only after Butler became president. As dean, he worked compatibly with Low, their relationship remaining cordial if largely professional. What- ever competitive instincts secretly roiled him, Butler kept them firmly in control as he helped Low run the fledgling university. For his part, Low came to rely more and more on Butler's efficiency and energy, trusting him with increasing amounts of administrative responsibility. Minor skirmishes over the years revealed certain tensions between the two, but none that would be unexpected in the case of a talented, ambitious subordinate work- ing closely with his superior officer. Most suggest Butler's obsessive concern for his status and the frustration he must have felt at not being in charge. Writing to Low, for example, while on his recuperative trip through the Middle East in 1893, Butler noted that he was "surprised and not a little cha- grined" to find in a circular of new education courses "the horrid word 'Pedagogy' substituted for 'Education' in the caption." Objecting to the word as "evil-sounding" and inappropriate, Butler concluded that he couldn't "conceive how the change was made." The answer, needless to say, which Butler no doubt anticipated when he wrote the letter, was that the deci- sion had been made by Low himself. In a letter of May 22 Low apologized, explaining that the suggestion for the change had made sense to him because all the departments in the college could be thought of as departments of education, and this would clearly distinguish the courses in pedagogy from the rest. Low assured Butler, however, that "Alma Mater is entitled to all the privileges of her sex," and there was no reason why they couldn't change back the following year if it was thought desirable.

Low saw no reason to apologize when, the following fall, Butler com- plained about the order of deans appearing in the general catalog. Indicat- ing to Low that Section 3, Chapter I of the Statutes called for deans to be listed according to seniority, Butler noted that the current arrangement was "apparently a haphazard one," by which he meant that his own name should have appeared second instead of fourth. The order, Butler was informed, was not arbitrary but consciously determined by Low himself, who spelled out his reasons to Butler "so that you may know that the question raised by you has had consideration." The polite dismissal of his grievance could not have pleased Butler, but fourth in deanly order he was to remain regardless of the dates of appointment.

Perhaps the most serious and sustained disagreement between the two occurred during the summer of 1897, when Teachers College set about to find a new president to replace Walter Hervey, who had suddenly resigned. After leaving the Teachers College board in 1894, Butler no longer had any official connection to the school, but the school's founder and first president had no intention of leaving its future to a group of uninformed trustees. In Butler's mind, at least, there was no one better qualified in the country—even the world—to select the next president than himself, and he was determined to make sure his wisdom prevailed. Besides, as chairman of the Department of Philosophy and Education, it was his moral obligation to guarantee that Columbia's professional school of education develop along the proper lines.

The trustees, needless to say, did not share Butler's vision of his centrality to their process. They considered themselves perfectly capable of conducting an intelligent search and discovering a suitable candidate on their own. However much Butler's real agenda was his personal desire to control the board's deliberations, he did raise some legitimate administrative questions regarding the somewhat murky connection that had existed since 1893 between Columbia and Teachers College. Did the Teachers College trustees have the right to function independently, or were they obligated to see themselves as part of a larger university and evaluate all candidates in the light of this broader perspective? Was Teachers College a freestanding school, with the authority to chart its own destiny, or one of several professional divisions of a complex institution, its freedom constrained by the responsibilities of that relationship?

Recognizing both the force of Butler's organizational concerns and the fragility of the Teachers College affiliation, Low was eager to avoid any rift between the two schools. He understood that Butler's previous history with Teachers College made it hard for him to stay out of its affairs, and he cautioned Butler that restraint and patience were the appropriate responses. By proceeding with tact and due regard for the good sense of the trustees, Low remained confident that an agreement could be reached on a mutually acceptable candidate.

But while Low gently tried to placate and negotiate, Butler simply fumed. The two recommendations from the trustees struck him as ridiculous. One was "simply absurd . . . distinctly third-rate . . . a very inferior superintendent." He would "not do at all." Why he should even have been considered "is a mystery." Mere mention of his name in connection with Teachers College "would hurt the college with the best people in the country." Almost as bad as the first man was Butler's friend, Dean Andrew West of Princeton's graduate school, whose opposition to everything Teachers College was trying to do would make his selection "ludicrous" on July 3 and "preposterous" on July 5. Butler's "only consolation is that I cannot believe he would dream of accepting."

Early in the process Butler had decided that Charles DeGarmo, president of Swarthmore, represented the best choice, and he could not understand how there could be anything more to say on the subject. "It is a matter of curious interest," he complained to Low, "that had this situation arisen in almost any other college or normal school in the land, my judgment as to the men would have been asked and accepted without demur or discussion. Indeed, it happens so, many times each year."

No one at Teachers College did in fact listen, and finally Butler felt compelled to act. Alarmed at learning in early July that West was likely to be offered the job and to accept it, Butler dispensed with the tact enjoined on him by Low and entered the fray directly. On July 5 he wrote to West, explaining how supremely unqualified he was and how enormous a mistake it would be for him to take the position.

Both the trustees and Low were furious with Butler's blatant intrusion. Low's characteristically polite censure could not conceal his anger: "Your own letter to Prof. West was an interference at long range with a matter that you ought to have left entirely in my hands; and you have written, as it seems to me, too much as though we were in a position to demand concurrence in our wishes, without regard to the views of the Teachers College . . . Before anything further is done," he cautioned Butler, "I shall expect to have an opportunity to talk with you. Then we can go into all the questions involved much more fully than is possible by correspondence." He concluded by regretting that this situation should have occurred in the summer, when everybody was exhausted by the rigors of the school year, "and perhaps for that reason more than ordinarily likely to make mistakes."

Not even Low's polite way of forgiving (and thereby simultaneously declaring) Butler's guilt in the last sentence could get Butler to admit his fault: "I am not able to regard my personal and confidential letter to West as an interference in any sense," he quickly responded. He had done nothing more than send West the kind of frank letter Butler would have appreciated receiving himself in a similar situation. With an astonishing display of moral virtuosity, Butler suggested that if anyone was to blame for upsetting the Teachers College trustees it was West, not himself, for revealing the contents of a private letter: "Of course I wrote him frankly and fully because I wrote him confidentially. Should he see fit to make my letter known that would be an unfortunate event, for which the responsibility would not be mine."

West's refusal to honor the claim of confidentiality Butler tried to impose on him was not surprising. West was unhappy not only with the judgments themselves but with Butler's discourtesy in not discussing the issues with him before writing his July 5 letter. Under the circumstances, he told Butler, he could not "accede to your request that I shall treat the letter as confidential."

Butler immediately tried to correct West's notions both about his motives in writing and about the nature of his specific observations. West should appreciate that the frankness of his initial letter revealed the depth of his affection for him, Butler explained. He never would have troubled to write to a stranger in such a direct way: "Had the situation been reversed, I should have felt badly [sic] had you not written to me with as much candor as I have written to you." Butler had only wanted to convey to West his sense that the trustees were primarily interested in appointing a fund-raiser rather than a genuine intellectual leader. Such a desire was abhorrent to Butler, and he thought it important to warn West that the institution had its values badly skewed. Butler assured him that in casting doubt about the adequacy of West's training for the position at Teachers College, he was merely noting that the "proposition to call you from your work at Princeton to this place struck me very much as would a proposition to call me to the presidency of a medical college or a polytechnic institute." Simply a case of "putting a round peg into a square hole" and not to be taken as a reflection on West's ability. Indeed, Butler had long harbored the hope that one day West would himself be chosen president of Princeton, a position in which he could do more good for American education than at Columbia. West, in short, had no more reason to be angry with him about the contents of the letter than Low did at the fact that he had written it.

The incident once again displayed Butler's gift of avoiding the imputation of wrongdoing even when guilty. Butler's ability to believe in and even insist upon his own innocence was an extraordinary talent, serving him well repeatedly throughout his career. Whether a result of his "non-interference" or not, the outcome of the Teachers College conflict was agreeable to Butler: West declined the position, and an alliance with Teachers College was forged that brought it as a separate professional unit, like the Law School, under the administrative control of the university. The newly appointed head of the school, James Russell, bore the title of dean, not president.

Despite his anger at Butler's behavior during this time, Low never lost confidence in him and never ceased relying on him for administrative support. When Low had to go on a fund-raising trip for several weeks during early January 1901, he asked Butler to attend to his correspondence while he was away. (In typical Butlerian fashion of making the most out of every opportunity, Butler asked Low if he would like him to keep office hours as well for those who might need to speak to the president. Low assented, and Butler then had the chance not just to affix his signature to presidential letters but actually to practice for an hour on Mondays, Wednesdays, and Fridays, and for thirty minutes on Tuesdays and Thursdays, the role he longed to play on a full-time basis.)

Low's admiration for Butler couldn't change the reality that as long as Low remained at Columbia, he would necessarily frustrate Butler's all-consuming ambition to be its president. It was not as if Butler didn't have other presidential options. In *Across the Busy Years* he said that between 1886 and 1899 he had been approached to be the president of Stanford, in addition to the state universities of Ohio, Indiana, Illinois, Wisconsin, Iowa, Colorado, Washington, and California. Butler was not always the most accurate reporter of his own achievements, and it is unclear what to make of this claim. Written evidence seems to exist only of California's interest, which does not mean that these other institutions did not also consider him, as they might have done so informally, without leaving any kind of documentary trail. However accurate the number, it is the case that Butler's national prominence as an educator would have put him on the short list of many universities searching for a president. But nothing could tempt him to leave Columbia for another school.

Low was finally removed as an obstacle in Butler's path not by accident or disease, but by the corrupt hold on New York City politics of Tammany Hall. The opposition to Tammany was always searching for a mayoral candidate who could unite the disparate reform factions in the city. It settled on Low for the 1897 election, but the Tammany grip proved too tight, and Low lost to the Tammany-backed Democrat, Robert A. Van Wyck. (Despite his criticism of Low's political ambitions, Butler as early as the 1897 campaign was suggesting strategic moves for Low to follow, if "you believe it your duty to lead the forces of good citizenship this autumn." As George McAneny, who became Low's director of the Civil Service Commission, later commented, "Seth Low . . . hated to give up Columbia. Mr. Butler was always anxious to have him give up Columbia."

By the summer of 1901 Butler's eagerness to have Low anywhere but at Columbia, as well as his own analysis of the New York political situation, led him to conclude that Low was in fact the strongest anti-Tammany candidate available. Although in theory an independent Democrat would have been more attractive, there didn't appear to be one whose popular support would be as strong as Low's. Butler thought he would appeal not just to mainstream Republicans who would never vote for a Democrat but also to Bryan Democrats who would vote against Tammany as long as they didn't have to back anybody they thought had betrayed William Jennings Bryan in his campaigns for the U.S. presidency in 1896 and 1900.

To win, Low needed all the city's reform organizations behind him, though techinically he would be running as the formal nominee of the Republican Party and the Citizens Union. Herein lay Butler's strategic problem. While the Republican leaders unanimously favored Low, the Citizens Union, to which Butler belonged, did not. Or at least its leaders did not. The rank and file enthusiastically supported him, but the officers, put off by Low's defeat in 1897, preferred city comptroller Bird S. Coler as first choice and any appropriate independent Democrat as second. Butler's ability to pry Low out of Columbia would require galvanizing the entire Citizens Union in the effort. He devoted himself to this goal with a fierce intensity. Their final endorsement of Low testified not only to an accurate recognition of his admirable qualities but also to Butler's manipulative and persuasive powers. As an admiring reporter for the *Philadelphia Press* wrote, referring to Butler (though not mentioning his name):

> Now the leaders in the Citizens Union and many men of indepen-
> dent inclinations who are not active are saying to the quiet, unas-
> suming, really modest man, a man of profound scholarship and
> extraordinary achievements in other than practical fields, "You have
> carried your point, we take off our hats to you . . ."

Low understood that accepting the nomination would mean leaving Columbia. In 1897 the trustees had agreed to defer action on his resignation until the outcome of the election was known, but he realized they could not be expected to do this a second time. As his resignation letter of September 25, 1901, to the trustees stated, with typical humility, "Columbia University can-not teach men to be patriotic if it will make no sacrifice in the public inter-est; and not even Columbia's President can expect to be exempt from the obligation to illustrate good citizenship as well as to teach it." On October 7, his resignation accepted, Low officially said goodbye to students and faculty in a packed University Hall. Stressing his deep feeling for the university, Low explained the pull of duty that required him to "burn his bridges be-hind him" so that he could function in the coming political campaign with-out compromising the institution that was so firmly embedded in his heart. After his farewell, with a cry of "Six Columbias for 'Prexy Low,'" followed by "Low, Low, Low," Seth Low left University Hall, his twelve-year presidency over.

The choice of acting president was no more complicated than had been the choice of the man to sign Low's letters in his absence some ten months before. Trustee conversations in September, as they contemplated Low's impending resignation, had never seriously questioned that Butler was the obvious temporary replacement while a search was conducted for a perma-nent president. As chairman of the board William Schermerhorn wrote to John B. Pine, "Professor Butler is undoubtedly our best man, and indeed his qualifications for the higher office seem to be not a few."

Butler began his new job on October 8. Earlier in the week, Schermer-horn appointed a search committee consisting of himself, Morgan Dix as chairman, Edward Mitchell, George Rives, and Pine to bring before the entire board one or more names to fill the vacancy caused by Low's departure. All five were predisposed to Butler, but Pine, his college friend and clerk of the board, would have to be thought of as an active agent on his behalf. However judiciously Pine conducted himself with his colleagues, it was apparent from the beginning that he intended to guarantee that the search would end with the election of Nicholas Murray Butler as the next president. Even before the committee held its first meeting, Pine asked Low to help influence its deliberations in a way that almost bordered on the unethical:

> If I am correct in my impression that Dr. Butler is the successor you would wish to choose, I think that a line from you to that effect would serve a most useful purpose, if read at the first meeting of the committee. I fully believe that he is their inevitable choice and I hope that they may come to share my feeling of deep thankfulness that we have at hand a man so admirably qualified for the position . . .

Such support from Low at the start, Pine continued, would have the further benefit of enabling Pine "to be able to state when a conclusion is reached, that the Trustees have chosen the successor whom you yourself selected, not only as a mark of respect to you, but because such an announcement will be gratifying to the Trustees and to your successor."

On November 2 Low told Pine that he did not yet have the time to give his letter proper attention, but that his general principle was to refrain from becoming

> the advocate of any particular solution of the problem at the present time, for I think it is a question that all of us ought to address with an open mind . . . You know how highly I think of Prof. Butler; but it remains to be determined whether he can command the cordial and hearty support of the teaching force and of the governing and teaching bodies of Barnard College [the women's college of Columbia University, opened in 1889] and Teachers College.

Meanwhile, as Low skillfully avoided taking a position on Butler's candidacy, enthusiastic letters of praise reached Pine from Butler's friends around the country. And not just any friends, of course, but people like the freshly minted president of the United States, Theodore Roosevelt; commissioner of education William T. Harris; Presidents Harper of Chicago, Eliot of Harvard, and Draper of Illinois; Newton C. Dougherty, superintendent of schools in Peoria, Illinois; and Irwin Shepard, secretary of the National Education Association. It is difficult not to feel the encouraging presence of Pine (and, of course, Butler himself) behind these "unsolicited" recommendations. In addition to the president of the United States and the commissioner of education, they happened to represent all the different educational constituencies of the country in whose opinions the trustees might be interested: public universities (Draper); private universities (Eliot and Harper); and the thousands of public school teachers, administrators, and educators involved in the grassroots problems of secondary education (Dougherty and Shepard). Hardly a random group supporting Butler's candidacy.

Together, these letters helped assuage whatever doubts the trustees might have had. Befitting his position, Roosevelt's was the most sedate, merely acknowledging that it would be a good thing for the country as a whole if Butler was made president. The others endorsed Roosevelt's conclusion in rhetorically more compelling ways: "He has won the right to be regarded as the most versatile, resourceful and accomplished man of his age in the educational work of America" (Draper); "There is no man in our country whose leadership in educational matters is so universally recognized by the educational men of this state as that of Pres. Butler" (Dougherty); "To professional teachers in school, college or university, Professor Butler is the best known man connected with your university" (Eliot); "Dr. Butler in my mind is one of the providential leaders in education at this particular epoch . . . I think Dr. Butler is the man of all men to be selected for the President of Columbia University . . . He has come to be the defender and expounder of a spiritual interpretation of our civilization" (Harris).

The search committee had been charged to present to the trustees "one or more names," but no evidence exists that any candidate other than Butler was ever genuinely considered. Several possibilities were raised by the press. The *San Francisco Chronicle* suggested that the trustees were thinking about George Edgar Vincent, who taught sociology at the University of Chicago. Less plausibly, *The New York Sun* mentioned Pine himself as well as Columbia dean John Van Amringe. Least plausibly of all, the *New York Post* stated that Andrew Carnegie was reputed to be on the short list. Despite these reports, none of these names appeared to surface in the trustees' recorded deliberations. The issue from the start seemed only to be about the appropriateness of Butler.

By late December, Low finally wrote to Dix, as Pine had requested he do in October, urging that Butler be appointed as soon as possible:

> I have never had any doubt as to his fitness, except upon the question of his ability to command the co-operation of his colleagues. If the feeling of apprehension that greeted the announcement of his name as Acting President had grown stronger, week by week, that would have been good cause to look elsewhere; but so far as I can learn, precisely the reverse is the case, and, if so, the best way to dispose of the question, now, is to elect Prof. Butler at once.

To delay, Low worried, would make it harder to fill Butler's professorial place and would suggest that the trustees had entertained doubts about their decision. For Low, the sooner the better; he saw no reason why Butler couldn't be elected in January.

Low's letter was decisive. Pine got it from Dix on December 28 and distributed it to the rest of the nominating committee in time for its scheduled meeting on December 30. Rives could not attend, but he permitted his name to be added to those of the other four in unanimously agreeing that after "mature deliberation and a full discussion . . . they have concluded to nominate Dr. Nicholas Murray Butler to the office of President, and accordingly, they now present his name for the consideration of the Trustees." On January 3, 1902, Pine reported to Low the good news about the nominating committee, adding, "Your letter to Dr. Dix was undoubtedly influential in bringing about this happy result, and I have taken the liberty of sending copies of it to many of the Trustees as well as to members of the Committee."

Having heard that Low might not be free to attend the full trustee meeting on January 6, Pine expressed his hope that he would manage to stop by, if only during the early part, when the nominating report would be considered, "to help launch your successor." Whether because of strict compunction about his mayoral duties, or whether he had at the last instant a twinge of doubt about his successor—or at least the propriety of voting for him—Low declined to miss or cancel a board of estimates meeting that same afternoon. In an oddly reluctant way, he advised Pine to "make my excuses. You are at liberty to say, if the report of the comtee. comes to a vote, that if I were present I should vote for Dr. Butler for the presidency, with pleasure." Low's absence notwithstanding, his pleasure at Butler's election apparently was real. "The morning after Nick Butler was elected," George McAneny reported, "Low came in rubbing his hands and was greatly pleased. He said, 'It isn't given to every man, McAneny, to be able to choose his own successor so well and so happily.'" With Low's support, then, but without his actual vote or presence, Nicholas Murray Butler shed his "acting" title to become the twelfth president of Columbia on January 6, 1902.

Saturday, April 19, 1902, was crisp and sunny, the perfect day for a garden party—or the inauguration of a new university president. The trustee committee responsible for choosing Butler's installation date could not take credit for the lovely weather, but they did have a serious reason for selecting this particular Saturday. The decision, Pine laconically commented on February 3, "was influenced somewhat by the fact that the committee were able to obtain assurances of the presence of the President of the United States, the Governor of the State and the Mayor of the city at this time." Roosevelt's attendance, courtesy of his friendship with Butler, itself guaranteed the auspiciousness of the occasion. More than simply a personal tribute to Butler, Roosevelt's participation also spoke to the significance of Columbia. As one editorial writer noted, it was most unusual to have a mayor, governor, and president sitting on the same platform celebrating a university that all three had attended. (Low had graduated from the college; Governor Benjamin Odell had taken an engineering course in the School of Mines; Roosevelt had spent a year in the Law School.)

The formal ceremony was scheduled to begin at 2:30 p.m. in the University Hall gymnasium, but the day's festivities began when Roosevelt, sporting a brand-new top hat and yellow spring coat, arrived in New York by ferry from Jersey City at 6:30 in the morning and went immediately to his aunt's house on the East Side, where Butler joined him for breakfast. Shortly before noon, after Butler had left to deal with university business, Roosevelt, along with former mayor Abram Hewitt, entered a horse-drawn carriage to begin their procession up Fifth Avenue accompanied by four troops of Squadron A, a cavalry unit of New York's National Guard, in full-dress uniform. Brandishing swords held stiffly upright against their shoulders, swaddled in tightly fitted double-breasted tunics, festooned with quantities of braid, and wearing large black fezlike hats jauntily displaying a kind of feathered cockade sticking out of the top, they looked like nothing other than extras from a Franz Lehár operetta. They inadvertently added a touch of useful old-world pomp as they escorted the carriage to Morningside Heights.

Following three separate luncheons—one given by the trustees for Roosevelt and those speaking at the ceremony, one by the University Council for the participating college and university presidents and their representatives, and one for university marshals and the men of Squadron A—the members of the academic procession assembled in Low Library and shortly before 2:30 marched around the library to University Hall, located directly behind it.

The *Times* pointed out that New York had never seen an academic pageant quite like it. In addition to the president—the first time since the first year of George Washington's administration, it was noted, that a president of the United States had paid an official visit to Columbia—and the governor and mayor, distinguished marchers included Senator Chauncey Depew; the German ambassador; the British scientist Lord Kelvin; forty-eight college and university presidents; the U.S. commissioner of education; the postmaster general; William Howard Taft, then governor-general of the Philippines; and the librarian of Congress. Andrew Carnegie, not part of the procession, sat in the audience.

Altogether, close to three thousand people packed the beribboned and bedecked University Hall (whose preparation and dismantling cost $4,008) for the installation. They witnessed a dignified program, framed by opening and closing prayers and containing the presentation to Butler of the University Charter and Keys. Ten separate speeches were delivered (including Butler's inaugural address) as well as greetings from the presidents of Harvard, Yale, Princeton, and Chicago, and Butler's old friend William T. Harris. Throughout the proceedings Butler remained prominently seated, except when giving his address, in the "President's Chair," once the property of Benjamin Franklin. President Roosevelt did not speak but instead silently endured the two-and-a-half-hour ceremony, surely one of the few times that the president had been invited to attend a public event of this importance without being asked to say anything.

At 5:00, after the singing of "My Country 'Tis of Thee" and a closing benediction by Bishop Horatio Potter, five hundred selected guests left the proceedings for Sherry's restaurant and an elaborate banquet hosted by the alumni for Butler. Amid much blue and white bunting—Columbia's colors—and the flags of other American universities, more encomiums were lavished upon Butler. Songs were sung, oysters and filets of bass and boeuf were devoured, and of course more addresses—eight this time—offered. Here TR at last got his chance to orate, stressing his favorite theme of the importance of character over intellect. By the end of the evening, as the well-fed and well-talked-at alumni and guests dispersed, it would have been difficult for them not to have been caught up in a haze of warm feelings for Columbia and its new president.

The enthusiasm for Butler that united the lucky five hundred who dined at Sherry's was also shared by those who didn't make it to the restaurant. With one exception, Butler's election produced rhapsodic responses from newspapers around the country, whose editorial writers tended to settle upon the same basic set of superlatives—"foremost educator"; "distinguished record as an educator"; "one of the most widely known and competent of American educators"; "one of the ablest pedagogues in the United States"—to celebrate Columbia's choice. The exception, oddly enough, was Butler's hometown newspaper, the *Paterson News*. Angry over a spat some years earlier when Butler, as president of the New Jersey Board of Education, had refused to pay the paper what he considered an illegitimate bill, the *News* entered the sole editorial caveat after learning of his selection: "When Mr. Butler gets to be President of Columbia, he will either be a great success, which the *News* does not believe, or an ignominious failure, which the *News* thinks the most probable." This repeated a previous expression of skepticism over his choice as acting president: "Nicholas Murray Butler always did have a swelled head of huge proportions. If his appointment to the $15,000 job of President of Columbia College does not cause an explosion before long the *News* will confess that it has done the distinguished gentleman a great injustice."

The *News*'s demurral notwithstanding, the country, Columbia, and Butler all exulted in the outcome of the search. Butler had his dream job, Columbia had attracted the best of all possible men to develop it in the twentieth century, and the United States could look forward, under Butler's leadership, to a university of international distinction. In its lavishness and gravity, the inauguration became in effect a national occasion, not merely a parochial gesture of self-congratulation. It was less Columbia itself than the importance of the American university that was being acknowledged. The *School Journal* of April 26 understood that the day's real cultural meaning lay in demonstrating how "our great universities are established and believed in as essential institutions in our national life . . . The procession bore eloquent testimony to the high honor in which the worthy institutions for higher education are held in this country."

The presidents of these emerging research universities faced challenges different from those running a traditional liberal arts college. Universities were complex entities with large ambitions, requiring amounts of money unheard of in a small school—to support scientific research, to house burgeoning professional schools, to hire more faculty. However learned and accomplished they were as academics, presidents had to become shrewd and tireless fund-raisers. The spectacle of intellectual leaders conducting themselves as businessmen seeking money offended some, like Thorstein Veblen, who viewed it as degrading. H. L. Mencken was even less forgiving, characterizing the university president as a "perambulating sycophant and platitudinarian, a gaudy mendicant and bounder, engaged all his life, not in the battle of ideas, the pursuit and dissemination of knowledge, but in the courting of rich donkeys and the entertainment of mobs." But despite the criticism of academic purists like Veblen of the debased nature of presidential behavior, it was only through such behavior that their schools were able to survive. In the competition for prestige that rapidly developed among the proliferating institutions, any serious president had to be obsessed both with growth and with obtaining the money that made it possible.

Beyond their roles as competent administrators, efficient businessmen, and persuasive academics capable of earning the respect of their faculty colleagues so as to influence institutional priorities, presidents had to be skilled marketers of their educational product, able to explain to a variety of audiences the importance of the university's vision, its needs, its future. An unlimited appetite for talk thus became an essential ingredient for the heads of universities. Understanding this too, much as he lamented it, Veblen described the necessarily loquacious president as "an itinerant dispensary of salutary verbiage."

Butler came well equipped to join the ranks of these industrialists of the mind, especially in his capacity to dispense verbiage, salutary or otherwise.

The "Champion General Talker" of his undergraduate years, whom Joseph Mitchell would later classify as one of "the fanciest ear-benders . . . in the world" (along with George Bernard Shaw) who had ever tortured him, Butler was never happier than when he was glorifying the mission of the university. His inaugural address, ranging down centuries and across continents and rich with allusions to Charlemagne, Emerson, Aquinas, Socrates, and Marcus Aurelius, proclaimed its centrality to everything valuable that bears upon the human condition:

> Today, in the opening century, the university proudly asserts itself in every civilized land, not least in our own, as the bearer of a tradition and the servant of an ideal without which life would be barren . . . To destroy the university would be to turn back the hands upon the dial of history for centuries: to cripple it is to put shackles upon every forward movement that we prize—research, industry, commerce, the liberal and practical arts and sciences.

Lest pursuing knowledge for its own sake might seem too theoretical and otherworldly, Butler emphasized that the university's practical idealism can be found in its commitment to service: to students, community, country. Scholarship and service—the title of the address—thus became Butler's formula for selling the university to the public, one he used effectively for the next forty-four years.

Butler accepted his new responsibilities without any discernible doubts or anxiety. Nothing appeared alien to him, and there was nothing, Butler made it seem, he couldn't accomplish. Henry Fuller, Butler's uncompromising enemy during New York's public school wars of the 1890s, put it as well as anybody by suggesting that "if the Higher Powers would entrust him with the task of constructing a new universe, Professor Nicholas Miraculous Butler would enter upon that undertaking with equal confidence, unabashed and unaided." It cannot be known whether Butler, if given the necessary materials, could have created a new universe, since for some unaccountable reason the Higher Powers decided not to risk it. What is clear is that the Columbia trustees were more daring than the Higher Powers. Handing Butler the materials of a small school, they watched admiringly as he made for himself a powerful empire of education, not unlike "The Empire of Business" forged by his friend Andrew Carnegie. In turning Columbia into one of the largest and best-known universities in the world, he served the longest tenure of any university president. "The surest pledge of long remembrance among men," Harvard's president Eliot wrote, "is to build one's self into a university." Eliot was wrong about the perpetuity such a connection guaranteed, but it is the case that no one ever built himself more tightly into an institution than Butler did at Columbia. Once there, he had no intention of leaving. Had the trustees understood the tenacity of his attachment, it would have come as no surprise to them that more than four decades later, blind and deaf, Butler had virtually to be pried out of his position by the next generation of the board. Retirement from Columbia was never part of his plan. He would have much preferred to die in office.

CHAPTER SIX

"Great Personalities Make Great Universities"

❧

As Butler settled into the presidential office in Low Library that was now legitimately his, it would not have been lost on him that the rising star of the Butlers had fulfilled the family hopes thrust on him after the death of his uncle Chalmers. At forty, his long apprenticeship as professor, dean, and acting president was finally over: the university he loved, with all its problems and potential, now belonged to him. His $15,000 salary ($310,000 today) not only took care of his needs but indicated the confidence the trustees had in him that he was the man for the job. The task, however, was daunting. Although the 1897 move from the Forty-ninth Street campus to the four blocks between 116th and 120th streets bordered by Amsterdam Avenue and Broadway (the "Boulevard" at the time) opened up possibilities for Columbia's growth, it did not bring along the funds for achieving it. Instead, it burdened Columbia with a $3 million debt.

Columbia now occupied a lot roughly 960 feet long by 775 feet wide (approximately 16.8 acres), formerly the grounds of the Bloomingdale Asylum, which Columbia had purchased in 1892 from New York Hospital. It contained nine buildings, three of which—all quite small—had been retained from the asylum. The other six had been built between the time the trustees bought the site and the opening of classes in the fall of 1897. The most impressive of these was the magnificent domed Low Library, given as a gift by Seth Low (at a cost of more than $1 million) in memory of his father. Designed as a library, it also temporarily housed the Law School and the School of Political Science, as well as various administrative offices.

Four classroom, laboratory, and faculty office buildings—Havemeyer, Schermerhorn, Fayerweather, and Engineering—and the never-to-be-finished University Hall, meant to include a grand dining hall, auditorium, and gymnasium, completed Columbia's campus.

From the southern exposure of his office window in Low, Butler looked out across the beautiful open plaza of South Court to the broad commercial thoroughfare of 116th Street, bordered by a ragged two-block plot of land also owned by New York Hospital, known as South Field. Stretching beyond that lay some of the small farms and undeveloped land that characterized the northernmost development of the city. Seeing the physical limitations of what was there, he saw with equal clarity a vision of what was not there:

> What we do here, what we say here, is part and parcel of the Great Tradition which the Mount of Olives, the Acropolis, the Capitol and Mont Sainte Genevieve have made for all mankind. May it not be said, a thousand years from now, when even Macaulay's traveler from New Zealand will be in a distant past, that the human spirit had found a fifth capital hill, not unworthy of those that had gone before, to be remembered, like them, for what human endeavor and human insight had been able to do here in the spirit, the true spirit, of America?

Butler's capacity to invest himself emotionally and intellectually in the prospect of its future grandeur made Columbia a different institution than it would have been had Low remained as president. Although Low had put its administrative structure in place and had orchestrated the move to Morningside Heights, he lacked the insatiable need for power and recognition that drove Butler. Low had come to Columbia as a fully formed, widely accomplished businessman and politician. Not a calling nor an identity nor a base for personal ambition, the presidency was for him a job—albeit one that he loved and worked at devotedly, in the process never transgressing the boundaries between self and institution. It was otherwise for Butler, for whom Columbia was the visible sign of his distinction. Once he was president, he ingested the university, becoming, for all emotional purposes, the very thing he was running. His identification with it was total. The comment he was fond of making during the long course of his tenure—that if you cut him open you would find his blood to be Columbia blue—was truer than even he realized.

Butler's goal of establishing Columbia as a prestigious research institution known throughout the world, as opposed to one rooted in the culture of New York and primarily serving its needs, has not met with universal acclaim. Thomas Bender, in *New York Intellect*, criticizes Butler for turning his back on the city in his obsession with national and international recognition. Bender much prefers the civic responsibility of Low, the genuine patrician who was determined to have Columbia engage the city's social diversity in interesting ways—"seeking a multi-voiced conversation among the many elements of the United States' unique metropolis"—to the vast ambitions of the middle-class Butler, committed instead to asserting "the authority of university expertise in the city and the nation." Noting that Columbia's official corporate title declares that it is *in* the city of New York, Bender wonders to what extent Butler cared if it was *of* the city as well.

Before concluding what urban responsibilities properly devolve upon Columbia in making the claim to be "in the city," it might be well to consider the origins of the phrase. After all, Johns Hopkins doesn't officially declare itself to be in Baltimore, or Yale in New Haven, or Harvard in Cambridge. It goes back to the formulaic legalese of the original charter granted King's College in 1754, in which it was stated that "the Governors of the said College and their Successors forever shall be one body Corporate and politick in deed fact and name and shall be called named and distinguished by the name of the Governors of the College of the Province of New York in the City of New York in America." The charter of 1787 "fully and absolutely ratified and confirmed" the 1754 charter "in all respects, except that the college thereby established, shall henceforth be called Columbia college: That the stile of the said corporation shall be, The trustees of Columbia college, in the City of New York." The official corporate title of "Columbia College in the City of New York" was not very much thought about until roughly 1895, when Columbia began to take seriously the notion that it was no longer a simple undergraduate college. In November 1895, after substantial discussion among the faculty and at the University Council, Low proposed to the Trustee Education Committee that Columbia should change its official title from Columbia College to Columbia University. His argument was the self-evident one that Columbia's growth into a complex institution of different parts made it essential that it adopt a name that would encompass the entire organization rather than one that was associated with a single school. In addition, he pointed out that continuing to refer to the whole as Columbia College required calling the college proper "the School of Arts," a term unique in the country that no one really understood. Low stressed that the name Columbia College misrepresented the scale of the institution, leading people to question him why, if Columbia was as much a university as Harvard and Yale, it called itself a college.

At the Education Committee's meeting of November 18, 1895, five of the six trustees supported Low's proposal. The one dissenter, S. P. Nash, criticized the idea on various grounds. To begin with, he thought there was no need for a change; second, he worried that if the trustees wanted to change the statutes, they would then have to alter the corporation name as well, involving Columbia in the legally uncertain business of obtaining a new charter, a step he opposed; third, "There is now a Columbian University in the city of Washington," Nash argued, "and although we may have a legal right to adopt a similar name, it would be unfortunate to have a complaint made that our institution was infringing the 'trade-mark' of another."

The majority response to Nash's dissent stated that "college" simply failed to describe the current reality of Columbia and ought to be corrected. As for the "trade-mark" issue, they suggested that "possible complications growing out of the name 'Columbian University' adopted by the nascent institution at Washington, can easily be avoided by adding to 'Columbia University' the words 'in the city of New York.'" Thus the university's full title—less a proclamation of obligatory shared interests and concerns with the city than a geographical specification to avoid having it confused with Columbian University, and not one committing Columbia to any particular set of values or social attitudes.

Certainly Butler saw Columbia's role in the city quite differently from Low. In Bender's terms, instead of Low's "collaboration" and "democratic dialogue" with New York's problems and population, Butler offered the "authoritative, expert service" of an institution training a leadership elite. Butler distinguished between "service institutions," which lived on tuition income and extended basic instructional opportunities for a local population (like NYU), and "endowed institutions" (like Columbia), which needed vast financial support to achieve international renown in scholarship and research. It never occurred to Butler to confuse the two. "Every city," he said in his inaugural address, "which, because of its size or wealth or position, aims to be a center of enlightenment and a true world-capital must be the home of a great university." In return, Butler expected New York to help Columbia, materially as well as spiritually. For Butler, the exchange of expertise and distinction for financial and other kinds of support constituted the real working relationship between university and city.

Butler understood that to make Columbia into the civilizing force he intended would demand not just faculty excellence but even faculty celebrity. "Great personalities," as he declared in his first presidential report, "make great universities." It was for this reason that he welcomed John Dewey to the Philosophy Department in 1904, even though Butler had little interest in pragmatism and was firmly opposed to Dewey's ideas of progressive education; that he offered positions to Nobel Prize–winning physicist Ernest Rutherford in 1911 and to Albert Einstein in 1923 (neither of whom came); that, as he informed chairman of the board G. L. Rives in 1911, he wanted to hire Henry James as a lecturer in the English Department for several years to deliver some lectures on literary history and literary criticism. Such an opportunity, he argued, "would add to our own repute and give new distinction to New York as a center of literary thought and activity . . . For about $2,500 or $3,000 we could have a series of brilliant lectures from him during the height of the New York season, and kill several birds with a not very expensive stone." Butler was right, of course, but Rives was not up to it. The idea, Rives responded, "does not appeal to me. That sort of lecture seems to me a sort of intellectual dissipation . . . I question whether it will be worth what we should have to pay James."

As this exchange demonstrated, Butler's vision of Columbia would also require—in addition to the inspired leadership that he was supremely confident he could provide—lots of money, which he did not have. In his first annual report to the trustees Butler employed an image to which he would frequently return: Columbia was "a giant in bonds." Bursting with energy and admirable purpose, it was shackled in place by an absence of funds: "In plainest language, Columbia University in 1902 is without adequate grounds and buildings and without sufficient income to care properly for the work that has already been undertaken, even if not a single extension of the work now in progress be planned."

Butler's analysis of Columbia's plight was designed to encourage his trustees to help solve the problem through their own personal gifts, but it was not exaggerated: Columbia did have a plan for the coherent development of the campus, carefully prepared by the distinguished architectural firm of McKim, Mead and White, with a number of empty rectangles drawn on the blueprint waiting to receive their projected buildings. Instead of the resources to fill them, however, there stood roughly $3 million in debt caused by the move to Morningside Heights. In addition to eliminating the debt and accrued interest, Butler listed Columbia's immediate needs: a Law School building; the completion of University Hall; expanded facilities for the School of Political Science and for the Philosophy, Chemistry, and Engineering departments; and a building for the academic life of Columbia College. Even if money were somehow found for all of these, the university would still be without a chapel, dormitories, and an astronomical observatory, not to speak of the general-purpose endowment funds required for the health of any growing educational institution. Columbia required, in Butler's calculation, the riveting figure of $10 million.

Butler's first task, to obtain the necessary moneys, was the more difficult because fund-raising as such had never really occurred before at Columbia. Money coming to Columbia in earlier years came largely in the form of bequests rather than gifts from the living. Despite the graduates that Columbia had been producing since the mid-eighteenth century, there was no organized alumni association of the sort that is common today, nor any tradition of alumni support. Having existed essentially as a day school, lacking the dormitories and dining facilities that foster the warm memories of the "collegiate experience," Columbia had not earned the loyalty of its students as Harvard and Yale had.

Without a nostalgically committed alumni body to fall back on, Seth Low himself had chosen to become Columbia's largest benefactor, donating the money for the new library—an extraordinarily generous sum in its own right that was also tactically designed to stimulate the generosity of others. In this it succeeded. At the same meeting on May 6, 1895, in which Low announced his intention to build the library, William Schermerhorn, chairman of the trustees, followed Low with a declaration that he would contribute $300,000 for a new science building. But such splendid individual acts were not easily replicable and did not in any case constitute an organized system of fund-raising on which an institution could depend. Butler did not have Seth Low's personal wealth, nor the easy access to the city's affluent citizens permitted by that wealth. He had instead to create a constituency to whom he could appeal for help—along with an argument that would elicit its support. In addition to trustees and personal acquaintances, he determined his audience to be those prominent New Yorkers who would be sympathetic to his vision of bringing the city an elite institution that might cast glory on them all. Low had already started to make such a case—having convinced J. P. Morgan and Cornelius Vanderbilt to contribute $100,000 each toward the purchase of the Morningside Heights property—but it was not one that Low, the self-confessed businessman and administrator, lacking academic credentials, could have plausibly sustained. But when Dr. Butler, the country's prominent educator, spoke of intellectual ideals, of the cultural role a great university could play in the city, his words carried professional credibility. No one was better equipped to persuade the city's influential business community that it was not only in their interest, but was actually their obligation, to support his university.

Although his method of approaching them was slightly ham-handed, institutional fund-raising at the turn of the century was hardly the subtle art it has since become. There were no vice presidents for development directing well-staffed offices, skilled in the techniques of identifying prospects and setting up individualized appeals designed to cajole money from them. There was, in the case of Columbia, simply one hungry president rather bluntly asking people he barely knew or didn't know at all for help. Butler launched his campaign by sending a form letter, starting in early November and December of 1902, to various businessmen, lawyers, bankers, and newspaper editors—August Belmont, Meyer Guggenheim, Joseph Milbank, Henry Phipps, William Whitney, George Hearn, Henry Frick, Archer Huntington, and Adolph Lewisohn, among numerous others. It possessed the virtue, at least, of directness:

> You are in position to know and to appreciate how heavy is the task which has been imposed upon me as President of Columbia University. For its successful accomplishment there is no hope whatever unless I am able to secure the sympathy and generous support of those men and women who care for the highest things in our American life, and who intend to do all that in them lies to make secure, beyond peradventure, the position of higher education in this great metropolis.
>
> I am causing to be sent to you a copy of my Annual Report, which I trust you will find time at least to examine. After you have

done this, I beg that you will accord me the privilege of a half-hour of your time, in order that I may have the opportunity of discussing with you more fully than I can do by letter my hopes and plans for the immediate future.

His initial fund-raising burdens were made more onerous when Susanna became critically ill that same December. Following a bout of childhood rheumatic fever, she had struggled all her life with a case of chronic endocarditis, which accounted for her general frailty and frequent exhaustion. But when the chronic suddenly turned acute, her condition became desperate. Aware of the gravity of her illness, Butler nevertheless remained resolutely optimistic, reporting to his friends, particularly Teddy Roosevelt, on those moments in which she seemed to be improving. But his hopes for her recovery were vain. Two months short of her fortieth birthday, on the morning of January 10, 1903, Susanna died. Of the many condolence notes Butler received, President Roosevelt's was perhaps the most moving:

> Few things are as idle as the effort to express sympathy for even one's dearest friend in the name of bitter sorrow, yet I am not willing that you should doubt how both of us have thought of you and mourned with you in these your days of darkness. We have grown to love you dearly, and all that concerns you concerns us also.
>
> May the unseen and unknown powers be with you always.

Faced with the care of his eight-year-old daughter, Sarah, Butler could be excused if he temporarily lost his fund-raising focus. But he was not the sort to permit the death of a wife to interfere with the obligations of his job. His sisters Eliza and Mary took over the domestic duties at 119 East Thirtieth Street, where he had been living since his marriage to Susanna, and Butler continued his pursuit of potential donors. He appreciated from the start that some rich people were more equal than others, and he treated them accordingly. John D. Rockefeller, whose money had founded the University of Chicago in 1891, received his own special, more elaborate, version of the Butler form letter. On February 5 Butler wrote him concerning the range of problems confronting Columbia, emphasizing his basic theme that "great cities of the world are the natural homes of great universities." On February 25 he received a rather curt letter from John Junior, noting that most large universities have many needs and indicating little enthusiasm for the strategy of Butler's general appeal for support. Should Butler present a definite plan to meet specific needs, Rockefeller was sure it would at least receive his father's careful consideration. Somewhat chastened, Butler responded a month later with a request for a $3 million endowment for the medical school, a proposal in which John Senior was not interested.

Another unequal rich person worth a special approach was J. P. Morgan, whom Butler appealed to in March 1903, six months before making him a trustee. Three years later, Butler reminded him of his 1903 stated "intention and purpose" to give Columbia $1 million and suggested that now the time was right for a permanent endowment whose income could be used to satisfy pressing current needs. Morgan, unfortunately, did not recall making any such explicit promise. He responded that he feared Butler had "misunderstood" his intention and what he had said three years earlier, but he agreed to consider the matter when he returned from a trip he was about to take; he wanted it "distinctly understood," however, that he was "under no actual commitment, either written or implied." He had not changed his mind upon his return: the million was still not forthcoming.

Over the next several years Butler continued to remind Morgan of the various moments in which he had promised money—"on two occasions you have been kind enough . . ." (January 30, 1908); "You have more than once indicated your intention to do something . . ." (January 13, 1909)— moments that continued to elude Morgan. The clarity of Butler's memory failed to convince Morgan of his earlier pledge: he remained a dutiful trustee until his death, in 1913, never giving Columbia another penny beyond his $100,000 gift to Low in the 1890s and never attending a single trustee meeting.

Bungling and rejections notwithstanding, Butler's energy and persuasive powers did start to attract funds. Gift giving to all branches of the university increased dramatically in Butler's first year to more than $1 million, growing to more than $1.7 million in the next several years. Between 1890 and 1901, gifts to the university totaled $5.45 million; between 1901 and 1911, $16.55 million. With additional money (and the issuing of additional debt), Columbia began to break the shackles Butler had decried in his 1902 report. In the first ten years of his presidency, Columbia erected eleven new buildings: a chapel, three dormitories, a building for the School of Mines (funded by a gift from Adolph Lewisohn but not named after him, as he was a Jew), a building for Columbia College, a Law School building, the School of Journalism (donated by Joseph Pulitzer), a classroom and faculty office building (Philosophy Hall), Avery Library to house the art history collection, and an elegant house on Morningside Drive for the president himself.

Of all the buildings Butler planned for the campus, arguably the one that most fully embodied the grandeur of his aspirations for Columbia was a structure he failed to build. In 1906 the architectural firm of Palmer and Hornbostel, two Columbia graduates, came to Butler with the idea for an athletic stadium, recreational pier, and ceremonial "water gate" built on landfill in the Hudson River at the foot of 116th Street. Butler was delighted with the suggestion, enthusiastic about both the marvelous new space for student athletics and the notion that Columbia's facility would be New York's official welcoming site for distinguished visitors coming up the Hudson by boat. He praised the conception in his presidential reports, sought (and obtained) permission from the mayor and state legislature to fill in the Hudson for the project, and set about trying to raise funds for it. Unfortunately, Butler could not find benefactors who shared his vision, and the proposal eventually died for lack of support.

The building program Butler oversaw would not have been possible had Columbia not been willing to go further into debt by acquiring, in 1903, South Field. In 1901 the trustees, under Low's influence, had previously rejected an option to buy it. Low had been reluctant for several reasons: he thought the plot was too expensive, that it wouldn't appreciably enhance the university's development and status, and that in the long run Columbia's growth would inevitably require it to expand in other parts of the city anyway. He was also concerned that if the university were to use its credit to buy the land, it would create the impression that it was rich, thereby undermining his efforts to convince the city that it needed vast amounts of financial help to survive. Low's prudent and responsible position was worthy of a prudent and responsible businessman, and it was completely wrong. Had Low's conclusion, in May 1900, "that any other land in the city available for our uses is almost as valuable to the University as these blocks," been endorsed by his successor, Columbia would have seriously crippled itself. Fortunately, Butler shared neither Low's qualms nor his conviction that the land didn't really matter. In June 1902, when the Butler-led trustees were again invited to purchase South Field, they did so enthusiastically (the deal was completed in 1903) for $2,020,071.18.

Butler recognized that his ambitious building plans required equally ambitious plans to expand the student body—and only partly because tuition income was needed to defray the building costs. The public would use the size of Columbia's enrollment, Butler realized, as a means of assessing the university's health and influence. Insist as he did that the quality of Columbia's education was all that mattered, he was never for a moment indifferent to the impact of numbers.

Along with raising money, then, Butler also had to raise students. The question was: How? Butler's enduring commitment to the university as a research institution notwithstanding, he understood that the vital student expansion would have to come through the undergraduate college. For this to happen, undergraduate life needed to appear a higher priority for Butler than he actually believed it to be. "I find myself in hearty agreement with the recently expressed opinion of President Jordan of Stanford University," Butler wrote in his 1902 report, "that 'in the long run, the greatest university will be the one that devotes the most care to its undergraduates,' and for that reason I believe that too much care and attention cannot be given to the students in Columbia College." It was a prescient comment, but for Butler it was more strategic than real. It placated the college alumni, concerned that the trajectory of the university proper would efface the college, while at the same time declaring to the outside world that undergraduates mattered and would be well looked after at Columbia. What finally mattered to Butler, however, was less the thoughtful taking care of them—Columbia never really got around to doing that very successfully—than just getting them to Morningside.

Butler wanted more students not just to swell the size of the college but also to feed into Columbia's graduate and professional schools. At this point in his career he conceived of the college largely as a valuable source of university enrollment, though this view was to change substantially. His enthusiasm for funneling undergraduates into graduate and professional schools can be seen as early as 1897, when Columbia was considering an affiliation request from Hobart College, a small school in Geneva, New York, that was finding it difficult to survive financially. Low had asked Butler to prepare a memo dealing with the essential administrative understandings to be included in any such agreement. Butler's report stressed that the merging of small schools with large universities was an inevitable development of American higher education, one which he strongly supported; his concluding paragraph explained the payoff of such an arrangement for Columbia:

> It would tend to increase very largely the number of College students who would look naturally to Columbia as the university in which to carry on their post-graduate or professional studies. The value and importance of securing a number of sources of supply for university students cannot be overestimated. It should be a constant aim of university policy.

Butler began his presidential tenure with a radical proposal intended to make Columbia attractive to students who might be interested in pursuing advanced degrees, as well as to those who wanted an undergraduate degree in less than four years. Instead of a single four-year program leading to the B.A. degree, he proposed two different undergraduate paths: a two-year track leading to the B.A., and a four-year route to the M.A. A four-year bachelor's degree was appropriate in earlier eras, when America did not offer any opportunities for advanced study, Butler argued, but now that more and more students were seeking technical or professional training, it was too much time to devote to the first degree. Improvements in the secondary school system, he claimed, also rendered redundant some of the work currently undertaken in college.

Butler was not alone in wanting to truncate the college experience in order to expedite the obtaining of advanced degrees. Harvard had already established a plan to let students get their degrees in three years, and other colleges were considering similar arrangements. Such a compromise did not interest Butler. He objected that allowing students to complete four years' work in three only shortened the course of study without officially restructuring it. Furthermore, the popular option of substituting a year of professional work for the senior year of college, which Columbia had permitted since 1891, divided the students' interests in ways that were satisfactory neither to the college nor to graduate school faculties. Worse, it undermined efforts to establish a coherent program of purely liberal study.

Butler's suggestion for a two-year B.A. coexisting with a four-year M.A. avoided these shortcomings. Accommodating both the traditional student and the student eager to earn one or more degrees quickly, his plan, Butler stressed, "would certainly . . . increase the total number of students taking a college course of one length or another," not to speak of those who might be encouraged to move into some form of graduate training at Columbia. But despite Butler's arguments, the faculty remained unconvinced. No one was happy with the idea of awarding two different degrees, and though there was general agreement that too much time was spent in school getting both undergraduate and graduate degrees, few actually wanted to shorten the college experience. After protracted discussion, the faculty voted against altering the degree requirements. Columbia would continue to offer a four-year bachelor's degree, and students could continue to take professional school classes as seniors, thereby reducing the time spent earning an advanced degree. As it turned out, and even without Butler's streamlined track, the flow of students to Columbia (and elsewhere) steadily increased throughout the early decades of the twentieth century, a consequence of simple demographics as well as the perceived importance of a degree for social respectability and professional success. Whether they were, in Columbia's case, exactly the right *kind* of students was another story.

One of Butler's earliest administrative decisions, which he had no intention of submitting to a faculty vote, was to ensure that the system by which he had become dean of the faculty of philosophy be permanently eliminated. As the new CEO of an institution that he instinctively sought to organize along corporate lines, Butler the president was unhappy that Butler the dean had achieved his position through faculty election. The democratic tradition of faculties electing their own leaders had no place in the business model Butler felt comfortable implementing. For the university to mimic the efficient structure of the corporation, the managers of the separate divisions had to be answerable solely to the president—and be appointed directly by him. His 1902 presidential report approached this issue tactfully, with a declared concern that scholars and researchers not be unfairly burdened with extraneous obligations. Instead of asking active faculty to take on administrative work, Butler suggested that deans should be full-time administrators standing "in increasingly close relations to the policy and the votes of the Trustees." Whether creating a competent board of education to run a city's public school system or choosing United States senators, Butler always preferred the control of an appointment process to the uncertainties of an election. The trustees promptly endorsed his plan, and in 1905, when the terms of the sitting deans had expired, Butler gained the power to select those he wanted, men whose primary loyalty would be to him rather than to the constituencies they represented. The university was now located squarely where any ambitious, aggressive president wanted it—in his own hands.

As money came in, buildings and enrollment went up, and Butler began to fulfill the promise of dynamic leadership the trustees and Low saw in him. But Low had also detected an intransigent, arrogant side to Butler, unwilling to accept criticism or to question his own decisions, a side that had initially made him wary of Butler's capacity to work productively with his colleagues. Low's reservations were not unjustified. Butler's successes—administrative, intellectual, promotional—in guiding Columbia to its educational distinction were accompanied by some painful failures in his dealing with faculty, particularly early in his career, from whose taint his reputation has never entirely recovered.

When Butler became president, in 1902, he inherited a problem created by the hostility between two distinguished literature professors—George Edward Woodberry, a gentle, retiring, spiritual poet and literary critic, and Brander Matthews, a flamboyant playwright, man-about-town, and professor of dramatic literature. After Seth Low brought Woodberry to Columbia in 1891 and Matthews in 1892, the two had conceived a profound dislike for each other that deepened over time. Their personal antipathy began to erode the capacity of the Literature Department, in which both were housed, to function responsibly, eventually making it clear that one department could not contain these two personalities. To remedy this, Low in 1899 had split the Literature Department into two, assigning Matthews to a larger, better-funded English Department and Woodberry to a smaller Comparative Literature Department, hoping thereby to keep two valuable men at Columbia. It was a precarious solution, but it worked—at least as long as Low was available to guarantee its success.

Before resigning from Columbia, Low had made certain budgetary commitments to Woodberry, assuring him of enough money to hire two tutors for his department. On January 2, 1902, four days before Butler actually became president, Low (now Mayor Low) wrote to him that he had learned from Woodberry that the 1902–03 budget for Comparative Literature contained no provision for a second tutor. He rehearsed the history of his negotiation with the trustees, noting that he had himself furnished the salary for the current year on the explicit understanding that thereafter it would be assumed by the university. Had the trustees not agreed to this, he would not have provided the salary for 1901–02. He ended by urging Butler to recall this arrangement to the trustees.

Butler, however, a dear friend of Matthews's did nothing about it, and in March he told Woodberry that financial exigencies made it impossible to honor the level of funding for Comparative Literature that Low had promised. Unless Woodberry could raise the $1,000 salary himself, he would have to get along without a second departmental tutor. Woodberry objected strongly, but to no avail. When his plight became known to the alumni and students, who loved him, it incited them to action: letters and editorials were written, meetings held, outrage expressed. The issue was picked up by a number of papers, including *The New York Times* and *The Nation*. Students organized in support of him, signing a petition to Butler protesting the loss of courses. An April 25 editorial in the *Columbia Spectator*, emphasizing that Woodberry had been "a mighty factor in inculcating a hearty, manly, democratic tone in student character," pronounced the situation "nothing short of a calamity."

Butler responded briefly several days later in the *Spectator*. There was no reason why the Comparative Literature Department couldn't offer the same number of courses next year that it was currently offering, he claimed. Woodberry would simply have to raise the money himself for the second tutor. In the same issue of the *Spectator*, Woodberry described the agreement Low had worked out with the trustees and revealed that when he told Butler he couldn't raise the money himself, Butler had replied that Woodberry would have to make plans to get along without the second position. The explanations and accusations only increased the anger of the students and alumni. The *Spectator*, in an April 29 editorial, declared that it knew of no other department expected to raise its own money for faculty salaries. Alumni expressed their grief: in the words of a member of the class of 1899, "It is not too much to say that for many at this time Professor Woodberry and Columbia College are practically identical, so completely his teaching seems to sum up Columbia's highest spiritual and intellectual ideal."

Butler issued his official and final statement on the matter in the May 9 *Spectator*. It was no more than an elaboration of his earlier position, along with the charge that student indignation was based on a total misunderstanding of the situation. The administration had the highest regard for Woodberry and his contribution to the intellectual life of the college and had in fact authorized the second position—as long as Woodberry would raise the money for it. Since he refused to, it was Woodberry's decision to have only one tutor in the department.

Butler's declaration of support for Woodberry was rendered somewhat less credible when it was learned on May 6 that Butler had received a pledge of $3,600 from Harry Harkness Flagler, a former student of Woodberry's and scion of the Standard Oil fortune, to underwrite a tutor's salary for the next three years. Butler had thanked him for his generous letter but regretted that he could not accept its terms for two reasons: first, since Woodberry had initially refused to agree to the position being carried on gift money, Butler could hardly ask him to change his mind now; and second, since the Comparative Literature Department had already announced its program for 1902–03, it was not possible to make any changes. Flagler immediately suggested that perhaps if Woodberry understood the unsolicited nature of the gift, he might well give up his reluctance to funding the salary in such a fashion. In that case, would Butler accept the money? Butler remained adamant that the publication of the courses for next year prohibited any change. Flagler's $3,600 notwithstanding, there would be no second tutor.

The students were not satisfied with Butler's published explanations, seeing the administration's behavior as an effort to discourage Woodberry from remaining at Columbia, as indeed it was. After Woodberry disclosed in the May 13 *Spectator* that Butler had rejected Flagler's offer to pay for the tutor, the *Morningside*, another undergraduate paper, published an editorial on May 22 wondering why Columbia was trying "by slights and innuendoes before the public, and by other means elsewhere" to get Woodberry to resign. Butler, incensed at student temerity in challenging his rendition of the facts, summoned the editor, George Sutton, to his office four days later. A stenographic record documents Butler in his full autocratic splendor. There were three limits to permissible student criticism, he explained to Sutton:

> First, there must be absolute truthfulness; second, there must be freedom from malice; and third, there must be freedom from vulgarity. This editorial offends in the first two particulars. It is untruthful and it is malicious. It is untruthful in that it imputes motives to the administration of the University and states facts which are in direct contradiction to an official signed statement made by the Presi-

dent on behalf of the University; and it is malicious in intimating that there is an attitude on the part of the administration of the University toward a department, which attitude has been expressly disavowed in public by the University speaking through the President. Now, that being the case, that statement cannot be permitted to stand without action on my part. I can only offer you two alternatives,—first (and which I would prefer) a written retraction of the statements and of the implications and inferences contained in the editorial, and an apology for them; or, second, the severing of your connection with the University this afternoon.

In response to Sutton's question as to whether it made any difference that he hadn't written the article, Butler said it did not. As the editor, Sutton was responsible for what appeared in his paper. After he had seen Butler's "complete and final" account of the incident on May 9, Sutton should have appreciated that "neither the facts in the case nor the motives of the administration are open to question or challenge in the student papers." Butler told Sutton he was not interested in the identity of the author, for that was purely a matter between *Morningside* and the editor. Butler in fact did know that the offending editorial had been written by George Henry Darnton— whom he promptly expelled but then reinstated after he had apologized.

Faced with expulsion or offering an abject apology, Sutton chose the prudent course and then prudently inquired what form of apology Butler would like. Butler answered that a simple retraction would be fine, something that would "ask the pardon of the Trustees, the President, and the Faculty of Columbia College, for permitting to appear in the journal of which you are editor a series of statements as to the administration which are unfounded in fact and which are not becoming in a gentleman and a loyal student of Columbia; and I would like your expression of regret and apology, and that will end the matter as far as I am concerned." Sutton delivered it as ordered that afternoon.

But if the matter of the tutor was now definitively closed, the question of Woodberry's future at Columbia was still very much open. Would he be willing to remain in a place that had treated him so shabbily? A demeaning letter from Butler on May 13 made the answer unfortunately clear. Butler rebuked him for his uncooperative attitude toward the English Department, his alleged habit of criticizing his colleagues in the presence of students, his insistence that his own teaching program be supported by a core of junior subordinates, and his conviction that both faculty and trustees were conspiring against him. In addition, Butler warned him that he must absolutely desist from any effort, "active or passive, direct or indirect, now or hereafter," to involve the press in any of his concerns about the department or the university. Even a less-sensitive spirit than Woodberry would have found such criticisms and injunctions insulting. His dignity had been violated, but he nevertheless resolved to honor his commitment to Columbia for 1902–03 and then go on leave for the next academic year to consider his options. Although he told friends he would avoid any precipitous act, he had already made up his mind to resign. On January 14, 1904, while on leave, and for reasons, as he wrote to his Columbia colleague J. E. Spingarn, "that I think my position (as I have long done) impossible," he sent Butler a letter informing him of his decision.

Four days after Woodberry resigned, another Columbia professor, the distinguished American composer Edward MacDowell, also submitted his resignation. The issue in this case was not budgetary manipulation or departmental politics, but pedagogic frustration. MacDowell had come to Columbia in 1896 as the first chair of the Music Department, determined to integrate art and music into the university curriculum. Distressed at undergraduate boorishness, he entertained such radical ideas as trying to convince the Columbia administration not to admit students unless they could demonstrate some familiarity with the fine arts, or not to permit them to graduate without having taken some arts courses. He envisioned a faculty of fine arts, including music, painting, sculpture, and "Belles Lettres," granted parity with the other faculties to offer courses, make appointments, and grant degrees. Butler, however, viewed this as unworkable, and he vetoed the scheme. Instead, as MacDowell discovered when he returned to Columbia after a sabbatical leave in 1902–03, the Music Department had been confined, by Butlerian fiat, to a "Division" of fine arts, along with architecture, comparative literature, and work involving kindergarten studies, with the entire operation housed in Teachers College.

The move was not capricious. Butler had initiated discussions with the National Academy of Design about cooperation in a new School of Fine Arts, and he wanted to liberate music and architecture from their traditional faculties so they could participate in a new one. But he had not bothered to consult MacDowell, who resented the change. He disliked especially the connection with Teachers College, which he considered undignified, and he accused Butler of associating music with kindergarten activities. According to MacDowell, in this new arrangement music had acquired "somewhat the nature of a coeducational department store," tending "towards materialism rather than toward idealism." He feared that music had been prevented from becoming part of an influential faculty with the power to vote on its own future. After eight years of struggle to bring the fine arts into the university in a serious way, he concluded, "I was wasting my time," and decided to leave Columbia.

Butler spoke with MacDowell several times after receiving his resignation letter of January 18. MacDowell said he would not change his mind, but he promised to send Butler and the trustees a report he was preparing on the Music Department. On February 3, as rumors of his resignation began to seep out, three undergraduates visited MacDowell to ask him about what they were hearing. Insisting that the conversation was off-the-record, MacDowell foolishly confided in them—only to have the three go immediately to the *Evening Post* with their scoop. The next day, MacDowell was shocked to see the story prominently displayed in the paper. Embarrassed, he immediately apologized to Butler, explaining that he had not authorized the leak.

The loss of a man of MacDowell's stature was a blow to Columbia's image; the press speculated on whether Butler and his university were in fact hostile to the arts. The issue became uglier and more damaging when Butler, incensed that MacDowell's account had made its way into the news, whether inadvertently or not, wrote a letter to the *Times* on February 8, stating that MacDowell had decided to resign to devote more time to composing, and adding that the trustees had offered him a research professorship to induce him to stay. MacDowell, in turn, horrified at this version of his departure, retaliated with a letter on the tenth to the *Evening Post*, enclosing his report for the trustees. It was the futility of his efforts to change Columbia that motivated his return to full-time composing, he charged. The research professorship carried with it neither duties nor salary, and he immediately refused it, "as I was unwilling to associate my name with a policy I could not approve of."

The trustees were furious with MacDowell for permitting the story to appear at all and for releasing the private document he had written for them. They chastised him for his treachery in dealing with the newspapers, characterizing his act in making an official report public "as an offense against propriety, a discourtesy to the Board, and a breach of that confidence which the Board always seeks to repose in every officer of the University." Mac-Dowell retorted that when "a man's honour is at stake he does not stop to consider rules of etiquette." Butler's deliberately misleading letter about the reasons for MacDowell's resignation required him to defend his name. For MacDowell, Butler's dishonesty was "a far graver breach of . . . confidence than my using the only means in my power to correct his statement."

The Columbia administration was not fond of MacDowell when he left. Institutional irritation, however, rarely is permitted to stand in the way of institutional self-interest. On April 27, 1937, with MacDowell now fully recognized as an important American composer, Columbia put on an exhibition celebrating the life and work of the man it enthusiastically embraced as its own. It was jointly opened by Butler and MacDowell's widow.

CHAPTER SEVEN

An Old Shoe

❧

Andrew Carnegie didn't participate in Butler's installation on that lovely April day in 1902, but watching it from the audience was nevertheless pleasing to the eminent figure whose friendship helped extend Butler's influence beyond the academy and across the globe. It confirmed Carnegie's earlier judgment that Butler was destined to be the kind of successful, ambitious young man he wanted to know.

When, on December 14, 1910, Carnegie announced his commitment of $10 million to fund an Endowment for International Peace, with Butler as trustee and director of one of its three divisions, Butler's life began a new trajectory. Becoming president of the Carnegie Endowment in 1925 and chairman of the board of the Carnegie Corporation in 1937, he succeeded in folding his interest in peace into the power, prestige, and economic clout of Carnegie's vast resources, leveraging his connection with the Endowment into an international influence and visibility that would not have been possible simply as a university president. The fully formed, iconic "Dr. Butler" figure drew on both identities in its capacity to command the world's attention.

If character is fate, as Heracleitus declared several thousand years ago, it is fair to say that Butler and Carnegie were fated to meet each other. Although Carnegie's "simple and direct style," in the words of one writer, was vastly different from Butler's "baroque personality," the old steel magnate and the young professor were fundamentally very much alike. More important even than the passions they shared regarding peace, the sacredness of private property, the value of education, the pleasures of golf, the horrors of American football, the importance of the simplified spelling movement, and the splendors of Kaiser Wilhelm, to name a few, was their overriding desire to spend time in the company of people like themselves. For both men, the workings of Herbert Spencer's social Darwinism documented the moral excellence of the rich, successful, and powerful—those fittest who survived the competition—and justified the necessary inequalities in America's economic system. Carnegie's celebration of the glories of American free enterprise in his *Gospel of Wealth* might have been written by Butler:

We might as well urge the destruction of the highest existing type of man because he failed to reach our ideal as to favor the destruction of Individualism, Private Property, the Law of Accumulation of Wealth and the Law of Competition; for these are the highest result of human experience, the soil in which society, so far, has produced the best fruit. Unequally or unjustly, perhaps, as these laws sometimes operate, and imperfect as they appear to the Idealist, they are, nevertheless, like the highest type of man, the best and most valuable of all that humanity has yet accomplished.

Carnegie's admiration for these "highest types" led him to express his shock that at Butler's inauguration, President Eliot did not first bow to Theodore Roosevelt before speaking. "I cannot understand how a man can be in the presence of the President without being awed. I have known three presidents intimately before they were presidents, but when I entered their presence, after election, they were surrounded by a halo and I was somewhat of a worshipper." He then gently rebuked Butler for also failing to recognize the president before he began his own address. Butler, never one to accept a criticism lightly, promptly responded, "It rather pleases me to notice that you must have been sleeping when I arose to speak on Saturday, for I addressed the President by name first, before turning to the Trustees, the Faculty and the audience."

Their fated encounter occurred on December 17, 1891, as they traveled with other guests on J. P. Morgan's private railroad car to attend the opening of the Drexel Institute in Philadelphia. Understanding the opportunity Carnegie afforded him, Butler made sure to speak to him about educational issues of mutual interest. Several months later he followed up with a letter, reminding Carnegie of their conversation and asking if he might take a half hour of his time to discuss a pressing educational matter. Whatever the subject was, it was less important than the chance it gave him to speak to Carnegie again. Twice was all Butler needed. Carnegie was charmed by the young dean's energy, ambition, and intelligence, perceiving him to be someone worth cultivating. Their relationship deepened with Butler's own growing distinction, and by the time Carnegie donated his $10 million for peace, Butler had moved to the innermost circle of Carnegie's dozen closest friends, known as his "old shoes," along with two other Americans: the Cornell president and diplomat Andrew White and the journalist and editor Richard Gilder. British shoes included the distinguished statesmen Herbert Gladstone and John Morley, as well as Lord Armistead, Frederic Harrison, and Sir Henry Fowler. Besides the high regard of Carnegie, membership rights involved frequent invitations to stay at Skibo, Carnegie's castle in Scotland, which had its own golf course and an organ located at the foot of the castle's magnificent staircase. Feeling that every day should begin with music, Carnegie employed an organist to play for thirty minutes each morning, starting at 8:30. To guarantee that his guests be awake to hear the music, the Skibo day was officially announced by a kilted bagpiper piping his way around the castle at 7:45.

Butler's route to the Endowment for International Peace first passed through Carnegie's 1905 establishment of the Foundation for the Advancement of Teaching. With his interest in education and his pleasure in giving away his money in $10 million chunks (as with the Carnegie Institute of Pittsburgh in 1896 and the Carnegie Institute of Washington in 1902), Carnegie had for some time been thinking about what he might do to support higher education in general. Already maintaining a number of private pensions, he concluded that a retirement fund for college and university teachers would make the academic profession more attractive to talented people. He asked Henry S. Pritchett, president of MIT, and Frank Vanderlip, president of National City Bank, to estimate how much money was required to support a pension system for those private American colleges and universities that were free of denominational control. Their report, given to Carnegie in March 1905, indicated that there were about fifty such institutions and that the annual cost of a retirement fund for their faculty would be somewhere between $400,000 and $500,000.

Convinced by these figures that his idea was viable, Carnegie then set about enlisting a group of distinguished men to serve as trustees for the foundation he was now committed to establish. His admiration for American university (and college) presidents led him to appoint, on a twenty-five-member board, twenty-two presidents, including Eliot of Harvard, Jordan of Stanford, Hadley of Yale, Woodrow Wilson of Princeton, Harper of Chicago, and, of course, Butler of Columbia.

On April 16, 1905, Carnegie announced the transferral to the trustees of $10 million in 5 percent first mortgage bonds of the United States Steel Corporation, the revenue from which was "to provide retiring pensions for the teachers of Universities, Colleges and Technical Schools in our country, Canada and Newfoundland, under such conditions as you may adopt from time to time." The trustees met for the first time on November 15 in Carnegie's Fifth Avenue mansion, electing Pritchett as president and a seven-person executive committee that included Butler. Butler was thus closely involved in the gradual evolution of Carnegie's endowed pension plan into the contributory Teachers Insurance and Annuity Association (TIAA) system in effect today for colleges and universities throughout the United States. He was important in persuading Carnegie to bring tax-supported schools into the ranks of those receiving foundation pensions; and in spring 1908, when Carnegie decided to increase his endowment gift for this additional expense, Butler thanked him profusely for enabling the foundation "to take under its wing the whole field of American college and university work."

Football, Andrew Carnegie, and Nicholas Murray Butler might seem an odd trio, but their congruence produced an interesting episode in Butler's career. Although intercollegiate football in the early twentieth century was hardly the national obsession it is today, it was on its way: unhealthy alumni investment in winning, questionable admissions practices, and allegations of brutality were already beginning to taint this quintessential American collegiate sport. The center of football activity at this time was not the Big 10 or the PAC 8, but those small, elite eastern schools that turned into the academically prestigious "Ivy League" colleges—Harvard, Yale, Princeton, Penn, Columbia.

Concern for its violence actually led to a 1905 White House conference among representatives of Harvard, Yale, and Princeton to discuss football. President Roosevelt thought that if the "Big Three" could agree on a strategy of reform, the rest of the country would follow. The bland commitment the three finally settled on—essentially to uphold the rules of the game did little to change anything. According to the *Chicago Tribune*, the 1905 season saw 18 players killed and 159 seriously injured while playing.

Carnegie could never bring himself to understand how football had anything to do with higher education. His opposition to it was shared by a number of illustrious academic figures, including President Eliot of Harvard, who criticized its stress on "strength and prowess to the detriment of more intellectual interests" and objected to its savagery, trickery, and intentional harming of players. He stopped short of calling for its prohibition, however, feeling that its popularity was such that reform of its excesses was preferable to elimination.

Although he had been an avid fan of football (and the football club's secretary) while an undergraduate, Butler had also come to dislike it. It was not just the violence that made it reprehensible to him, but the distorted emphasis placed on winning, the increasing reliance of schools on football's gate receipts, and the extent to which the lust for the game "makes athletics impossible" by turning college students into passive spectators of "the gladiatorial struggle between two trained bodies of combatants." Instead of taking exercise themselves, students were happy to stand and watch their muscular colleagues bash each other. Butler charged football with "moral and educational evils of the first magnitude."

Unlike Eliot, Butler chose to act on his objections. On November 28, 1905, Columbia abolished football. The announcement came from the University Committee on Students' Organization, but the decision was Butler's, and not one that contributed to his popularity. Students and alumni protested vigorously, but the president refused to budge. Football, Butler insisted, was not an addition to the life of the school, but a distraction. Nothing would change his mind. It took a good deal of courage, Butler later declared, to stand on principle and deal with the howls of outrage unleashed by the elimination of football. As it was clearly the right thing to do, however, he never regretted it: "Columbia has gained for itself a proud preeminence by an act of conspicuous moral courage, good sense and high intelligence."

To resist cultural sanctities is never easy, and Columbia's pathbreaking decision to do so (a few, but not many schools followed) was admirable. But a letter of March 21, 1906, from Andrew Carnegie's secretary, James Bertram, to Butler raises the intriguing question of whether principle in this case had not been delicately flavored with a touch of calculation. Bertram told Butler that Carnegie was giving $100,000 (approximately $2 million today) to Columbia "on account of Columbia's noble stand against the present brutal and dishonest football."

Butler's view of the country's unhealthy football mania was no less accurate because it elicited Carnegie's financial support. Who can quarrel with those special moments when principle and expedience work happily together? Principle, in any case, was not forever. By 1915, alumni and student pressure caused Butler to announce that as the game had now been reformed (its moral and physical evils having apparently disappeared), Columbia in good conscience could return to intercollegiate football, which it did for the 1916 season. Once Columbia started competing, Butler liked to win as much as anyone. In 1925, for example, Columbia tried to lure Knute Rockne, the legendary Notre Dame coach, to bring his genius to Morningside, at the then unheard-of salary of $25,000 (plus an additional $7,500 for teaching chemistry). Rockne went so far as to sign an agreement to come, but then backed out.

It could not have been easy for Butler to be the close confidant of one of the world's richest men. Temptation to try cashing in on the relationship—for the greater good of the university he led—was always present, and Butler did not always manage to resist. One flagrant instance came early in January 1908, when Carnegie, eager as usual to find productive ways to dispense $5 million or $10 million, wrote to a number of his good friends, including Eliot and Butler, asking for their ideas. Eliot responded with a range of suggestions, recommending that Carnegie support constructive, stable institutions such as libraries, schools, and universities that "propagate good influences," and that he initiate promising experiments—like the Carnegie Foundation and Carnegie Institute—that might benefit society. While the description of the kind of long-established, efficiently run, and socially useful institution precisely defined the university of which he was president, Eliot nevertheless omitted the word "Harvard" from his two-page letter.

Butler, in sharp contrast, began his response with the statement that it would be "sheer hypocrisy" for him to claim that he could conceive of anything more urgent than endowing Columbia with such a sum: "I know of no other way in which more useful work could be done for the civilization of the United States and of the world than by making it possible for the one

great metropolitan University to do the work of leadership and enlightenment which lies ready at hand." Complete with four enclosures, notably a
five-page memo on how Columbia would employ the endowment, Butler's
letter was a passionate brief arguing for Columbia's importance to the
world. As one of the four great international universities connected with
great cities (along with Paris, London, and Berlin), Columbia could "be a
real lighthouse of humanity," to influence and illuminate the world. If
Butler had his way, not $10 million but "up to twenty millions" would be
devoted to Columbia.

But institutional self-interest worked no better than ostensible institutional selflessness in prying money out of Carnegie. His pleasure at hob-
nobbing with educational and intellectual elites did not mean that he was
interested in funding elite universities. He thought they had sufficient resources without him, and was happier supporting schools like Tuskegee
and Berea. Neither Eliot's genteel plea for efficiently managed, stable institutions nor Butler's aggressive case for Columbia appealed to him. What
he did find appealing was the idea of using his immense wealth to rid the
world of war. The problem was how to achieve this. In the memo Butler
had sent Carnegie, he had cagily suggested that Columbia was part of the
answer. With proper funding (say, $10 million or thereabouts), it could
help generate "a great body of international opinion which would not tolerate the brutalities and immoralities of war, with all that war means and
involves."

Carnegie rejected this particular solution, but the fact that it was Butler's
carried with it substantial weight, for by 1908 Butler had already made himself into a significant presence in the American peace movement. At the
turn of the century, peace, like education, was turning into a great growth
business. The emergence of the United States as an imperial power in
1898–99—achieved through the Spanish-American War and the conse-
quent annexation of Hawaii, the Philippines, Guam, and Puerto Rico—
infused the venerable peace movement, which had been trundling along
inauspiciously for decades, with a new urgency. Abstract principles about
the immorality of war—the goals of the American Peace Society, for example, the country's oldest peace organization, formed in 1828, were "to illustrate the inconsistency of war with Christianity, to show its baleful influence
on all the great interests of mankind, and to devise means for insuring universal and permanent peace"—gave way to practical concerns with arbi-

trating international disputes and projecting American national interests onto an international stage.

Of all the rapidly expanding peace organizations and conferences (one historian notes the formation of twenty-five new peace societies between 1904 and 1912), perhaps the most prestigious was the annual Lake Mohonk Conference on International Arbitration, held every May from 1895 until 1916 at Alfred Smiley's Victorian resort hotel in the Catskills, about a hundred miles from New York City. Smiley, a Quaker reformer who owned the hotel with his twin brother, Albert, had for a number of years hosted a summer conference for Friends of the Indians. In 1895 he concluded that the Indians had received sufficient attention, and decided to focus instead on issues of international arbitration. May of that year saw 35 people attend the first three-day conference, a number that steadily rose to 190 within a decade, the maximum number the hotel could accommodate. Explicitly not a pacifist himself, Smiley insisted that the conferences dwell solely on concrete questions dealing with processes and difficulties of arbitration, not on predictable denunciations of the horrors of war or celebrations of the glories of peace.

Smiley's emphasis on the practical gradually drew to Mohonk powerful, well-connected men in a position to shape national policy. In place of the clergymen who had dominated the earlier meetings, there began to appear lawyers such as Elihu Root and William Morrow; businessmen such as the publisher Edwin Ginn and the retailer Edward Filene; educators such as Charles W. Eliot, University of Michigan president James B. Angell, and Andrew White of Cornell; bankers such as George Perkins of J. P. Morgan and Frank Vanderlip; and all manner of politicians. They came not to debate the universal verities, but to discuss the complexities of foreign policy, trade agreements, international law.

Butler was by now thoroughly at home in this world. His Mohonk colleagues were the eminent, wealthy, influential men he always sought out, and the issues ones he had been engaged with for a long time. In *Across the Busy Years* he traced his internationalist impulses back to his 1884 "year of discovery," when he studied and traveled in Europe and when he began to appreciate how interconnected the world was culturally, economically, and politically, and to distrust the notion that any single nation could make its way in isolation from the rest.

The American peace movement in general, and Butler's aspirations for a system of international arbitration in particular, received unexpected and dramatic encouragement in August 1898 when Tsar Nicholas of Russia called for an international conference to discuss disarmament. Historians have since come to see the proposal as a rather self-serving effort to compensate for Russia's growing sense of its own military vulnerability, but it was welcomed by peace organizations as a historic breakthrough. Butler later called it "a magnificent appeal" that might open the door "to the building of a new federation of civilized nations which would make possible prosperity and peace for them each and all."

The First Hague Conference, held in 1899, hardly lived up to such expectations. It delivered to the world not disarmament or a workable international tribunal, but only a modest plan for choosing judges for the tribunal should several nations actually consent to go to arbitration. Failing to bring about any new judicial system, it did at least produce an important ally for Butler in his quest for a judicial basis for international order. In 1900 Butler's friend Frederick W. Holls, a lawyer who was secretary to the American delegation at the Hague Conference, introduced him to Baron d'Estournelles de Constant, a member of the French delegation (and later Nobel Peace Prize winner) who shared Butler's passion for international cooperation. The two became close friends. D'Estournelles along with several other French senators founded the Association de Conciliation Internationale in 1905, dedicated to promoting mutual understanding among the intellectual elite of different countries. Two years later, with funding from Carnegie, Butler set up an American branch, with himself as president. Under Butler's editorship, the association published a journal, *International Conciliation*, until 1924, when it was taken over by the Carnegie Endowment's Division of Intercourse and Education, whose director was, of course, Butler.

By 1908, then, as a (vastly superior) golfing partner of Carnegie's and esteemed old shoe, Butler was as well positioned as anyone to influence Carnegie's thinking about what important causes he might support, though his bald assertion in *Across the Busy Years* that he "had persuaded Andrew Carnegie to establish the Carnegie Endowment" is too facile. Butler was encouraged to focus specifically on peace by Hamilton Holt, a journalist and ardent world federalist who was managing editor of *The Independent* and a founder of the New York Peace Society, a leading peace organization. Working with Butler late in 1908 to arrange a Peace Society dinner in honor of Secretary of State Elihu Root, Holt suggested to Butler that perhaps Carnegie might, on the model of his institution in Washington and the institute in Pittsburgh, be willing to put one of his $10 million endowments to promoting peace. Butler responded enthusiastically and devised a strategy: Holt and another peace advocate, Edwin Mead, would draft a letter to Carnegie with the endorsement of a number of internationalists whom he admired, and then Butler would send it on to him. The letter was prepared. Holt rounded up the signatures of a number of Carnegie favorites—the old-shoe Andrew White, a member of the American delegation to the Hague Conference of 1899; Elihu Root and his predecessor as secretary of state, John W. Forster; Albert Smiley; Samuel Dutton; and several others. On January 8, 1909, Butler sent it to Carnegie with a covering note that acknowledged Carnegie's lack of enthusiasm for his previous proposal. He would not be bothering him again, he said, except that the suggestions in the enclosed document seemed so important that he deemed it his "duty" to submit them. As contained in a single sentence, these "admirable" ideas turned out to be a vague, rather insubstantial vision of how the new fund would help to rid the world of war:

> By persistent public demonstration, by the promotion of international visits and other courtesies, by the spread of literature, by the enlightenment of the people thru [sic] the press, the pulpit and the platform, and by the aiding of existing agencies, this fund could be made potent in developing a public opinion not only in America, but in Europe and Asia, that would in time reduce the martial and Jingo elements of the several populations to comparative impotence.

Carnegie was still not persuaded: "I feel that it is too much in the air," he responded to Butler three days later. "Much talk about bringing people together, and all this sort of thing, and nothing of a definite character." If Carnegie was going to spend his money, he wanted to know exactly how it would be used: "The avenues of expenditure should be distinctly stated," he insisted.

Butler and Holt went back to work, discussing more precisely what the purposes of such an organization would be and exactly how it would attempt to implement them. Butler drafted a new proposal, incorporating many of Holt's ideas. He submitted it to Carnegie on April 6, explaining that it attempted to meet his requirements that "the plan should be made more definite and the avenues of expenditure distinctly stated." The new document was far more elaborate than the previous one. Its eight numbered paragraphs spelled out in considerable detail how a "Carnegie International Institute" would be organized and administered, what its varied goals would be, and what specific steps it would take to achieve them. It represented an amalgam of Holt's desire to establish a world parliament and international police force and Butler's for a world court and an educational and research operation that would address itself to world public opinion. It concluded by asking not for a permanent endowment, but for operating expenses for five or ten years, or until Carnegie had had an opportunity to evaluate it.

Carnegie remained noncommittal. Whether he was skeptical that the plan's vast aspirations could be achieved, or reluctant to finance something that at this point appeared to be someone else's idea, is not clear. But the result was the same: no money.

Two rejections (or even three, counting the Columbia proposal with its peace argument) were not enough to discourage Butler. If written documents didn't work, there must be other ways. A month later, another way was found. Presided over by Butler, the 1909 Mohonk Conference expressed its dismay over the lack of coordination among peace societies and resolved that Butler should appoint a committee of ten, with himself as chair, to explore the possibilities of establishing a national council for peace and arbitration. There is no doubt that this resolution was crafted, at Butler's direction, to meet Carnegie's concerns about the problem of the disorganized peace movement; Carnegie had already complained that he was financing sixteen different peace societies. Its real agenda, however, was to interest him in funding what Elihu Root would later call a "peace trust." Carnegie, needless to say, was chosen by Butler to serve on the committee.

Butler had done what he could do, but Carnegie's 5 percent U.S. Steel bonds were still not forthcoming—until the confluence of two unexpected events. The first was the speech President William Howard Taft gave on March 22, 1910, at the Astor Hotel in New York City, to an audience consisting largely of fervent supporters of military preparedness. Taft assured them of his commitment to continue building battleships and of his conviction that armed strength was essential for the maintenance of peace. At the same time, he spoke of the virtues of arbitration, noting that while some people argued that there were certain questions of national honor that should never be brought to a court for judgment, he could find no grounds for any such exceptions: "But I do not see why questions of honor may not be submitted to a tribunal supposed to be composed of men of honor who understand questions of national honor, to abide by their decision, as well as any other question of difference arising between nations."

Taft's comments ignited Carnegie as all the complicated persuasion by Butler and his colleagues had not. He liked the notion of a practical man speaking practically. Carnegie's belief that a genuine system of international arbitration could be the key to perpetual peace now seemed not a dream, but an actual political possibility. He immediately wrote to Taft, praising him for his courageous statement: "No words from any Ruler of our time, or indeed of any of the past, so heavily laden with precious fruit, not for our nation only, but for mankind, as those you have just spoken in New York."

The second event, considerably less exalted than Taft's vision of a world adjudicating its disagreements, occurred in July 1910, when the millionaire book publisher Edwin Ginn founded what he called the International School of Peace with a $50,000 annual budget, promising a million-dollar endowment upon his death. Ginn and Carnegie were philanthropic rivals, each jealous of the other's eminence, and Carnegie had previously turned down a Ginn offer that the two together raise a $10 million endowment for a national peace organization. Predictably contemptuous of Ginn's meager funding and dismissive of his new organization as just another body dedicated to producing ineffective peace propaganda, Carnegie nevertheless felt threatened by its arrival on the scene, fearing it might obscure his own philanthropic status in the peace movement. The time had come to act.

Inspired by Taft and goaded by Ginn, Carnegie began to formulate plans of his own, clearly influenced by the earlier documents of Butler and Holt. Consulting with Butler, Root, and various others, Carnegie was able in early November to tell his British old-shoe John Morley that he had an important new idea, shortly to be announced, that had the backing of both Secretary Root and President Taft. The rest of November was spent polishing drafts and enlisting twenty-eight patrician lawyers, diplomats, educators, and businessmen, including Butler, to serve as trustees of a new organization that Carnegie could claim as his own. On December 14, with the board in place, Carnegie announced the creation of his Endowment for International Peace, with its declared aim to "hasten the abolition of international war, the foulest blot upon our civilization." Its means of achieving this would be through empirical investigation into the causes and conditions of war, as well as an examination of the best educational methods to influence public opinion to repudiate military solutions of international disputes.

In Butler's own words, the trustees

> believe that the time has come when the resources of modern scientific method and of modern scholarship should be brought to bear upon the problem of international relations. They believe that the leading jurists and economists of the world should be set at work in the service of humanity to ascertain just what have been and are the legal and economic incidents of war and just what are the legal and economic advantages to follow upon the organization of the world into a single group of friendly and co-operating nations bound together by the tie of a judicial system resting upon the moral consciousness of mankind, from whose findings there can be no successful appeal.

Research, in short, leading to practical action, not the uplifting exhortation that Carnegie felt had trivialized so many other peace societies.

The Carnegie Endowment's efforts would be focused on three areas: a Division of Intercourse and Education, a Division of International Law, and a Division of Economics and History, headed by Butler, James B. Scott, and the Columbia economist John Bates Clark, respectively. Together, Butler and Carnegie prevailed upon Root to become the Endowment's first president.

Carnegie's optimism that his money could bring about the end of war knew no limits. In his original deed of trust, he actually informed his trustees that after the possibility of war had been eliminated, they should determine "what is the next most degrading remaining evil or evils" threatening human happiness and turn the Endowment's attention toward abolishing them. But if two subsequent world wars demonstrated that even $10 million couldn't quite eradicate that "foulest blot upon our civilization," the Endowment's budget nevertheless effectively licensed Butler as an official international statesman charged with setting the world right.

Butler's ardent internationalism, like that of most of the eminent internationalists of his era— Elihu Root, Woodrow Wilson, A. Lawrence Lowell, Hamilton Holt, Joseph Choate, and Theodore Marburg, among others— grew out of an equally ardent nationalism. Whether because of Aunt Rosa's incantations with the flag at his birth or a mysterious imprinting of patriotism that occurred when, as an infant, he was taken to see Abraham Lincoln pass through New Jersey by train, Butler maintained an uncompromised belief in the virtues of this country and its political system. For Butler, America—its Constitution, its people, its values, its method of governance— represented as much an ideal to be emulated as an actual nation. In declaring at a 1920 Columbia Alumni Club meeting in Buffalo that "the enemies of America are the enemies of the human race," he was simply articulating a basic tenet of faith that he never questioned.

At the heart of America's greatness stood the Constitution, a document reflecting "the fundamental laws of human nature upon which all government and civilization and progress rest." In its guarantees of civil and political liberty; its careful allocation of power among the executive, legislative, and judicial branches; and its deliberate avoidance of statute making in focusing exclusively on the principles of representative government, the Constitution embodied for Butler the highest genius of what he called the Anglo-Saxon mind. If we had to build the country over again, "the result would be precisely the same. These principles can never grow old; they are everlastingly young and new and true."

From the perfection of the Constitution stemmed the perfection of American democracy, scrupulously distinguishing between legitimate governmental authority and personal liberty and extending the educational and economic opportunities of freedom to everybody. Not for Butler an America whose promise was in any way constrained by social or income inequalities. Butler reserved his greatest scorn for those who suggested that the country might be riven by class distinctions, that the system might in fact be skewed in favor of the rich. In Butler's classless America, the wage earner and the owner happily worked together in taking advantage of the mutual opportunities afforded them. Under such admirable conditions, any accusations against the American system must necessarily be both baseless and mad: "Who is it that has the temerity to wish to undermine the foundations of so noble and so inviting a political and social structure as this!"

The American fortunate enough to live in such a country was similarly idealized. In a series of lectures at the University of Copenhagen in 1908,

Butler portrayed "The American as He Is" for his Danish audience. Rugged, self-reliant, ambitious, and disciplined, Butler's American perfectly embodied the virtues of Butler's America. Astonishingly, he seems also to have studied with Professor Burgess, for he well understood the dangers of governmental incursion into the sphere of personal liberty. He would resist with all his might, for example, any effort "to regulate or curtail private business, to limit personal fortunes for purely punitive purposes." His insistence on making his own way without the paternalistic oversight of government—so common a feature of European society—meant that the ascent to distinction from humble origins was the characteristic trajectory of American life. Heads of universities, judges, leaders of railroads and industry—all began as struggling teachers, lawyers, employees of railway companies, and other businesses. Their careers demonstrated the fact that in America there were no "fixed and permanent social and economic classes." Although American hard work had produced substantial fortunes for its citizens, money as such was not a goal, even for those who had amassed it. "The American cares much less for money than the Frenchman, less even than the Englishman or the German." After taking care of their families, Americans were interested in using personal wealth for public good. Hence the strong tradition of private benefaction for schools, hospitals, libraries, and the like. Practical and efficient, the American was also highly emotional, open to the shaping powers of literature.

Above all, he was driven by an unassailable idealism, which perhaps accounted for the "scrupulous honesty" of his country's business leaders, particularly those who managed its large corporations. The occasional abuses of trust were rare, for overwhelmingly America's leading bankers and businessmen "hold fast with jealous care to the high traditions of honor and conservatism which have lasted for more than a century." Butler's American was intelligent, law-abiding, and incurably optimistic, and he never lost faith in his political institutions.

Embodying the purest strain of American exceptionalism, Butler never doubted for a moment that every country looked to America for moral and political leadership. Butler's interdependent world had no room in it for interests and needs other than those understood and promulgated by Americans. "As our brother's keeper, as the keeper of the conscience of democracy," Butler exhorted at a 1915 address in Philadelphia, America had obligations it could not fail to meet. If Butler had his way,

I would try and show Europe the fact that a national policy of hospitality and of equal opportunity solves problems.

I would make a world figure of Washington. I would make world figures of Hamilton and Jefferson, of Marshall and Webster. I would make a world figure of Abraham Lincoln. I would make their names, their faces, their public acts and the great tendencies and institutions that they organized and represented the property of the whole civilized world for the benefit of all mankind. For this or for any such policy of international influence this nation must prepare.

For mankind to understand its interdependence, which the projection of American values across the globe would achieve, it would be necessary to cultivate what Butler called "the international mind," a concept he defined in his opening address at Mohonk in May 1912. Critical to the peace and prosperity of the world, the international mind

> is nothing else than that habit of thinking of foreign relations and business, and that habit of dealing with them, which regard the several nations of the civilized world as friendly and co-operating equals in aiding the progress of civilization, in developing commerce and industry, and in spreading enlightenment and culture throughout the world.

Butler was extremely proud of this definition—a kind of Butlerian version of globalization—investing himself in it to such an extent that it seemed he had copyrighted it. He saturated the country's press with the formulation, had it translated into many of the world's languages, printed small cards with it that could be dropped off in offices or handed to individuals, and endlessly invoked it in his articles and addresses. The Carnegie Endowment gave the international mind access to a global audience. For the next four decades Butler's Division of Intercourse and Education functioned as a kind of advertising agency for selling it, bearing the distinctive label MADE IN AMERICA, throughout the world.

CHAPTER EIGHT

Teddy Roosevelt and a Horse Called Nicoletta

🌿

Another powerful figure who welcomed Butler's election as president of Columbia was the president of the United States, Theodore Roosevelt. "My close friend, my valued advisor," Roosevelt described him when addressing the Columbia inaugural dinner at Sherry's in 1902. Butler had in fact been in demand at the White House from the earliest days of Roosevelt's tenancy there. In a note to Butler in October 1901, a month after McKinley's assassination had put him in office, Roosevelt affectionately mocked Butler's own newfound importance: "I suppose the Acting President of Columbia can hardly come to see me. On the other hand, I am afraid of putting it off, lest a real President of Columbia might be still less able to come. Could you not some time soon slip down for a night at the White House and let me show you some parts of my message?" Butler was more than up to the good-natured ribbing, asking that Roosevelt instruct him on arrival protocol, "for I am not accustomed to visiting royalty. Do I have the impudence to go straight from the railroad station to the front door of the Executive Mansion, just as if it were Oyster Bay [TR's Long Island residence]; or do I go to a hotel and send over my card?"

They both had sparkled as students in the front rows of their respective classes with Professor Burgess in the fall of 1881, but Teddy the law student and Murray the college senior had not known each other then. They first met in early June 1884 at the Republican National Convention in Chicago.

Roosevelt, the vigorous, highly visible state assemblyman from New York's 21st District, scurried about as a delegate, futilely supporting the cause of Senator George F. Edmunds from Vermont. Butler, as he had in 1880, quietly observed the proceedings as a correspondent for the *New York Tribune* and the *Paterson Daily Press*. Their introduction to each other was no more than cursory, though Butler could not have failed to notice the excitement provoked by Roosevelt as he worked the crowds. He was clearly someone to watch.

And watch Butler did, as Roosevelt made his way up the local and national Republican ladder as U.S. Civil Service commissioner, New York City police commissioner, assistant secretary of the navy, and, finally, after his glorious interlude as "Colonel Roosevelt" of the Rough Riders in the Spanish-American War, New York's governor in 1899. It was then that the subdued acquaintance the two had maintained blossomed into a genuine friendship. Embroiled in all his educational reform efforts, Butler delighted in his new access to gubernatorial power, while Roosevelt drew upon Butler's familiarity with the minutiae of Republican politics as a source of reliable information and political guidance. More important was the confirmation of their own identities and values each found in the other. The two soon-to-be presidents were young (Roosevelt was four years older), already successful, energetic, in love with power, hugely ambitious, intensely idealistic. Although Roosevelt later derided Woodrow Wilson as a "logothete," a man of words who lived in a universe of language, it was hard to find two greater logothetes than TR and Butler, with their fine-tuned understanding of how language shaped reality and their ability to use it for their purposes. Above all, the two shared a robust Americanism, an unquestioned belief that America was on its way to becoming the world's dominant industrial, intellectual, and moral force, and the conviction that they were themselves uniquely qualified to lead the triumphal progress into the future.

Despite their occasional battles, the feisty governor and the learned dean enjoyed a harmonious relationship. On questions of national politics, the complexities of the new Charter Bill for New York, or the nature of his appointees, Roosevelt listened carefully to Butler's advice. Dispensing it freely in long letters and private conversations in Albany, Butler in turn relished his capacity to effect policy and his growing influence in Republican circles, as Roosevelt's inscription in a volume of his public papers that he gave to Butler demonstrated: "To Nicholas Murray Butler, who has watched these papers in advance on the installment plan, and has helped prepare not a few of them."

The first major crisis that precipitated disagreement between them had the unforeseen consequence of putting Roosevelt in the White House. Roosevelt loved being governor and judged himself, with characteristic humility, the best New York governor of his time, better than either Samuel Tilden (1874–76), the outstanding reformer whose successful tenure had led to his being chosen the Democratic presidential candidate in 1876, or Grover Cleveland (1882–84), who earned a national reputation by resisting the machine politics of Tammany Hall and was twice elected president of the United States. Not everybody shared this view, particularly Thomas Collier Platt, head of the New York State Republican Party. Platt, an old-style political boss (he was in fact known as "Boss" Platt), had ruled Republican state politics as his own personal fiefdom for a number of years. He had reluctantly backed Roosevelt when TR initially ran for governor, concerned that Roosevelt's quirky independence might threaten his own power. Platt's fears were justified. Roosevelt refused to defer to his elder's authority, clashing with him over policies and appointments. With Roosevelt's first term coming to an end, Platt was eager to ensure that he would not seek reelection, but he was trapped by Roosevelt's popularity. He could not be seen opposing the man the Republican Party enthusiastically supported. Then a perfect solution presented itself: as Roosevelt's gubernatorial term expired in 1900, when a national election was to be held, why not push him for the vice presidency on the William McKinley ticket?

There were two difficulties with this brilliant vision. The first was Ohio senator Mark Hanna, the Republican National Committee chairman; the second was Roosevelt himself. Hanna ran Republican national politics the way Platt did New York's, and he fiercely disliked Roosevelt for the same reason Platt did: the governor was uncontrollable. He didn't want Roosevelt in Washington any more than Platt wanted him in New York. As Platt tried to maneuver Roosevelt onto the national ticket, Hanna maneuvered to stop him. The spectacle of two political bosses, each trying to shuffle Roosevelt off on the other, was not without its comic dimension. "Some one said," Mark Sullivan noted, "that every time Platt and Hanna met and parted, Hanna used to search his pockets carefully to make sure Platt had not dropped Roosevelt into one of them."

Roosevelt had mixed feelings about the possibility. He resented the effort to dislodge him from the governor's office, but he couldn't deny the lure of Washington. With his eye set on the presidential nomination for 1904, the question was which job best led to that goal—as a popular two-term governor of the most important state, or a trusty but not very visible vice president with at least some proximity to the White House. Roosevelt struggled with the decision, but his uncertainty was not shared by Butler, who urged his friend to resist the unrewarding position of vice president. After a long discussion in early March 1900, Roosevelt dispatched Butler to go to Washington and tell both McKinley and Hanna that he would under no circumstances accept the nomination. Butler performed his duties, reporting back that McKinley received the news with some indifference and that Hanna roared that he never would permit Roosevelt to have the nomination in any case. Roosevelt was distressed to find that McKinley didn't seem to care and that Hanna was strongly against the idea.

Ostensibly not a candidate, Roosevelt couldn't entirely extinguish his interest in the vice presidency. His indecision was not made easier by the enthusiasm of the national press and numerous Republican leaders for his nomination. But if he equivocated, Butler did not. In May, a month before the Republican convention in Philadelphia, Butler pleaded with Roosevelt to reject any move to put him on the McKinley ticket, arguing that he would be in a better position to deliver New York's thirty-six electoral votes to the Republicans if he ran again as governor:

To put you on a ticket for the Vice-Presidency . . . means in my judgment to weaken the ticket by thousands of votes. Everyone will know that you do not care for the Vice-Presidency and that you have been forced into it, and they will resent the resultant failure to re-nominate you for Governor. I am as clear about this as I ever was about anything in politics. However let us keep up our coverage and fight to the end.

As the convention approached, Butler told TR that he and two other friends of Roosevelt's, the lawyer Frederick W. Holls and the editor Albert Shaw, were going to take an apartment in Philadelphia for a week, and that he should feel free to use it as a refuge. Roosevelt thanked him and asked that they stay close to him at the convention to explain to the delegates and press why he was unwilling to leave the governorship. Nothing the three said, however, could still the clamor for his candidacy. His national popularity was such that delegation after delegation implored Roosevelt to accept the nomination.

At lunch on Monday, June 17, with his wife, Butler, and several others, Roosevelt discussed the growing pressure. Butler tried to impress on him the need to make his refusal absolutely clear, adding that if he failed to be explicit with the press, who were due to arrive at four that afternoon, he would surely be nominated at the convention on Thursday. Anxious at the approaching deadline and feeling coerced by his wife and Butler, Roosevelt finally growled a request that Butler draft a statement for him. Butler shortly produced an unambiguous "am not a candidate and would not accept" declaration. Handing it to him, Butler said, "If you will sign that paper and give it out this afternoon you will not be nominated."

Roosevelt, frowning, affirmed its content but said he thought he could improve its phrasing. He then sat down and rewrote Butler's note, carefully purging it of all of Butler's finality. Its last sentence, expressing the earnest hope that "every friend of mine in this Convention respect my wish and judgment in this matter," was nothing less than a thinly veiled announcement that Roosevelt would accept the vice presidency if the convention desired it. Butler understood this immediately: "Theodore, if that is all you will say, you will certainly be nominated." A half hour's argument failed to change Roosevelt's mind, and Butler grasped for the first time that TR was in fact willing to renounce his governorship to join the Republican ticket.

Platt had won; Hanna had lost. New York would no longer have its governor, and the Republican convention would get the man it wanted. Hanna was appalled, but realized it would be politically inexpedient to try to resist the will of the convention. He prophetically warned his supporters, "The best we can do is pray fervently for the continued health of the President."

Hanna's prayers were efficacious for only six months from McKinley's inauguration for his second term, in March 1901. On September 6 Leon Czolgosz, a young anarchist, gave reality to Hanna's worst fears by firing two bullets into McKinley during a presidential appearance at Buffalo's Temple of Music. Butler immediately wired TR, who responded the next day, thanking him for his characteristic concern and offer of help, but saying that he had complete confidence that the president would recover. Six days later, while climbing with some companions in the Adirondacks, Roosevelt learned from a frantic ranger that McKinley was dead. The man Butler had urged to continue as governor of New York had suddenly, on September 14, 1901, become president of the United States.

As soon as he heard the news, Butler wasted no time in sending another telegram offering his services, followed by a longer comforting letter sent the same day:

> Words cannot express how fully and how anxiously you are in my mind and heart today. This fearful calamity, so much the more terrible because so surely escaped, puts upon your shoulders the greatest burdens known to civilized man — that of guiding the administration of the public affairs of a nation of nearly eighty millions of freemen, a power in the world's life and activities. How fully you will meet the tremendous crisis in the nation's life and yours, no one knows better than I . . . I am confident of the future.

Roosevelt replied, as he would innumerable times in the coming years, that he wanted Butler to come to the White House as soon as possible, as "I wish to talk over many things with you."

They met later in September at the Washington home of TR's sister, Mrs. W. S. Cowles, where the president was staying as the White House was being prepared for him. Roosevelt, arriving in the evening in a frock coat and silk hat, told Butler he needed to take a walk before dinner. They briskly set out along Sixteenth Street for nearly two miles, with Roosevelt talking volubly all the time. "Our intimacy was such that he could let himself go," Butler noted in *Across the Busy Years*, "and so relieve his pent-up feelings." According to Butler, Roosevelt expressed serious doubts about his capacity to do the job, and fears that his administration might fail. Butler finally interrupted his lamentations, declaring emphatically that he would be an enormously successful president: "Your youth, your vitality, your many-sided interests, will all captivate the American people, so soon as they come to know you better." Roosevelt's real problem, Butler cautioned, was his youth. At forty-three, and assuming a second term, would he be able to flourish as a contented sage at fifty?

Having assured Roosevelt that he was splendidly qualified, Butler attempted to assure the country of the same thing. In the October issue of the influential *Review of Reviews*, Butler contributed an unsigned piece on Roosevelt. Beneath the requisite fare of standard praise—"Theodore Roosevelt has never learned to tell or act a lie"; "Theodore Roosevelt is genuine"; "Theodore Roosevelt's tenderness and gentleness, his devotion to home and to family . . . make him preeminently lovable"—the article shrewdly addressed the two major concerns Butler believed the country had about TR: that he didn't deserve to be in the White House, because no one had voted for him to be president, and that he was an irresponsible, glory-hunting adventurer, in love with war.

Butler's skill in putting these reservations to rest demonstrated considerable intellectual adroitness. Roosevelt was not, he maintained, "a political accident." He had been chosen as vice president because the Republican Party and a majority of the people wanted him to be president. The party couldn't very well have unseated an incumbent president, but no one at the Republican convention would have denied that its commanding presence was TR, not McKinley. Roosevelt was the future: "He was not nominated to satisfy or to placate, but to succeed." Czolgosz had simply made the future arrive sooner than expected.

A political inevitability, Butler's Roosevelt also had to be separated from his rather flamboyant image as colonel of the Rough Riders in the Spanish-American War. The new president's famous advocacy of the "strenuous life," Butler suggested, had nothing to do with an enthusiasm for war or an impetuous love of adventure. Roosevelt detested war, and had volunteered himself, "against the urgent appeals of his family and of every intimate friend he had, not from love of fighting or of glory, and not from ambition, but from the sternest sense of duty." Moreover, TR's conception of the strenuous life ought not to be confused with hunting bears or swimming rapids; it had to do with disciplining oneself to produce work that in some way would benefit mankind. Admirably strenuous figures included those poets, artists, and thinkers whose writings helped to shape our understanding of human existence. The philosopher Kant, for example, who never left his native town and who doubtless never descended to arduous exercise, led as strenuous a life as Napoleon or Cromwell.

Butler's portrait of Roosevelt emphasized his thoughtful, scholarly nature, his integrity, his administrative efficiency. He was a leader of heroic stature prepared to rescue the country in its time of need. Butler concluded, "This strong, honest, experienced, lovable man has 'come to help' our great nation and his,—a nation confident in its truth and power, humble in its great grief for him who is gone. May God guide and guard." Roosevelt was properly grateful for this stellar effort to sell the novice president to a shocked and somewhat skeptical public: "I liked your *Review of Reviews* article," he wrote Butler on October 1, "better than anything that has ever been written of me. You said the very things, old man, that I would like to feel I deserve. I shall keep your article . . ."

With his friend in the White House, Butler plunged energetically into national politics, happily exercising his influence where he could. By late November he was busy persuading Roosevelt not to permit the establishment of a national university in Washington—an idea in which Andrew Carnegie had recently become interested—since he feared that its existence might threaten the stream of benefactions that private universities, Columbia among them, were becoming increasingly dependent on. Butler's vigorous lobbying efforts helped direct the $10 million Carnegie was prepared to give to such a project to go instead to endowing an institute in Washington for scientific research. Whether as reward or punishment, Butler had to write the draft of TR's brief message to Congress regarding the gift.

When the Columbia trustees removed the "acting" from his title in 1902, Butler made sure that his new university responsibilities did not interfere with his duties as presidential confidant. The calls to visit at the White House and Roosevelt's Oyster Bay home continued, and Butler continued to answer them. He even consented to confront Roosevelt on the tennis court—a precarious undertaking at best. For despite Butler's insistence on a spiritual and intellectual interpretation of TR's "strenuous life" ideal, it had a legitimately physical and sweaty side to it, which found full expression in the violent contortions, grimaces, and expostulations that Roosevelt brought to the game. Butler's willingness to endure them qualified him to join Gifford Pinchot, James Garfield, Robert Bacon, and several others in what came to be known, by those who couldn't gain entrance to it, as "Teddy's Tennis Cabinet." This appointment made Butler a member in good standing of all of the president's personal cabinets: "tennis," "kitchen" (along with Holls and Albert Shaw), and "literary kitchen" (writers and intellectuals Roosevelt admired, such as Booth Tarkington, William Allen White, Henry Cabot Lodge, and Holls).

Hardly a month went by without a Roosevelt request for a Butler visit. Roosevelt relied on Butler for general impressions and information about the national political scene—"I simply report rumors and statements that reach me from time to time, partly for your education and partly for your amusement," in Butler's words—as well as for specific counsel. The two men didn't necessarily agree about every problem, but Butler's input was always taken seriously. The political advice might have flowed exclusively from New York to Washington, but the currents of personal affection moved in both directions. In the spring of 1902 Butler received an invitation to deliver a lecture at the University of California the following year. Learning in April that a presidential train excursion to the West Coast was also being planned for that next summer, Butler asked George Cortelyou, Roosevelt's secretary, if the president would like Butler to accompany him. "I hope to heaven you can arrange to come," Roosevelt responded three days later. "I think it would be a particularly good thing for me to have you along—so you see I am selfish in begging you to come. It would also incidentally immensely add to my pleasure." Over the next several months Butler arranged and re-arranged his schedule, while Roosevelt kept up his gentle pressure: "I most earnestly hope you can accompany me, if only for a short part of the trip. I do want you to be identified as much as possible with my term as President."

Butler did not let Sue's death on January 10, 1903, shocking as it was, dis-suade him from the trip. He could not pass up an opportunity to travel with the president, and he finally decided that he would spend from April 29 to May 19 with him (TR would be away from April 1 to June 5), of which four days would be spent horseback riding in Yosemite National Park. Butler was excited about visiting Yosemite—"I should be willing to make any sacrifices to see it"—but this feature of the trip made it hard to plan his wardrobe: "In view of the fact that one sort of clothing will undoubtedly be needed in the Yosemite and elsewhere, and another sort for occasions of social character," he wrote Roosevelt's secretary (now William Loeb), "and since there will be no opportunity for laundry work, would it be too much if I took two steamer trunks in addition to my handbag?" Assured that any amount of luggage was fine, Butler left his daughter in the capable hands of his two sisters and set out for Kansas City to join the president's party. With Roosevelt giving nu-merous speeches to the public and Butler much advice to Roosevelt, they passed through Kansas, Colorado, New Mexico, and Arizona on their way to various stops in California. Riding and camping out in Yosemite from May 15 to May 18 concluded their California visit, after which Butler went to Reno, returning home in time for Columbia's commencement.

The three weeks he spent with the president had been both satisfying personally and important politically. They succeeded, as Roosevelt had intended, in declaring Butler a presidential intimate, a position that guaranteed him respect in Republican Party circles. The challenge now was to ensure that this status would extend through another presidential election. The summer of 1903 was none too soon to begin to attend to the business of getting TR nominated and elected in 1904, and it was to these efforts that Butler directed himself upon his return. Back in New York, he resumed his role as general political intelligencer, informing Roosevelt of all rumors and information that came his way. He carefully monitored the Republican scene, intent on neutralizing any pockets of resistance to Roosevelt's renomination. He praised Roosevelt for keeping Senator Hanna in line with a sharp rebuke, and he noted that in New York both Boss Platt and Governor Benjamin Odell seemed to be loyal, "provided appearances are not deceptive." Hearing of an attempt by Republican opponents "to create a prejudice against you among the Hebrews," Butler recommended that Roosevelt make himself available to give a public talk of some sort under the auspices of James Speyer, a Jewish banker. Roosevelt answered that he would be pleased to speak at "some typical Jewish gathering."

Butler remained especially anxious that Roosevelt himself do nothing to undermine his own cause, worried lest his anger at the moral abuses by the wealthy (or some of the wealthy) get the better of his political prudence and cast him as an unyielding foe of privilege. Seth Low's defeat in the 1903 mayoralty election at the hands of Tammany Hall elicited TR's predictable rage against the corruption of the rich: "The dog has returned to its vomit, as far as New York is concerned," he complained to Butler in November. "Wealthy capitalists who practice graft and who believe in graft alike in public and private life gave Tammany unlimited money just as they will give my opponent, whoever he may be next year, unlimited money." TR found it unsurprising that the rich should act that way, "for the criminal and violent poor and the criminal and corrupt rich are in essentials of character alike." Butler cautioned patience and discretion: "The danger, of course, is lest, smarting under the sense of wrong and injustice, you and all of us may be forced into sayings and actions defensible enough in themselves but, from a public point of view, unwise." He obliquely emphasized his concern by recounting to Roosevelt what he considered an "amusing incident" in which a *New York Post* reporter said he had learned from "Wall Street that

I was the emissary chosen by the financial magnates to go down on their behalf and make terms with you for the future." No such appointment had taken place, but the reporter's story had its point.

The start of 1904 found Butler still on the alert, warning Roosevelt about "the diabolical skill with which your opponents have set about undermining public confidence in you." Because of these fears, Butler remained ever vigilant to what might be "going on so adroitly beneath the surface." By early February, however, Butler announced the all clear: Republican opposition to TR's nomination had collapsed, and now it was time to start thinking about defeating the Democrats. Butler's first thoughts dealt with the need to moderate Roosevelt's image as a rash moral crusader indifferent to the country's business and banking interests. Roosevelt's intervention in the coal strike of 1902, when 150,000 anthracite miners walked out of the eastern Pennsylvania mines in May to protest low wages and the length of their working day, was one of the defining moments of his first term. He had begun with no intention of involving himself in the dispute, nor was there any precedent (or legal justification) for his doing so. But as the strike dragged on into the fall, Roosevelt foresaw the social and economic catastrophe awaiting the country when winter arrived and there would be insufficient coal to heat homes, sustain industry, or run the railroads. As politically risky as failure might be, he decided that he had to put his authority on the line and act. Summoning representatives of the miners and owners to a White House conference in early October, he persuaded them to accept the binding arbitration of a commission whose contentious membership he also got them to agree to. It was Roosevelt at his best: the miners won their shorter working day and their 10 percent wage increase, while the operators were given a 10 percent increase in the price of coal and were not required to recognize the United Mine Workers union. Both sides got something, but the real winner was Roosevelt, who had demonstrated his ability to use his presidential powers in the interests of the nation's welfare. Butler applauded TR's involvement—"Your relation to the matter has been really superb"— but at the same time worried that his participation in settling the strike would be seen as supporting organized labor, whom many regarded as disturbers of law and order, against the legitimate claims of mine operators and nonunion workers. To remedy this perception, false though it might be, Roosevelt had to make every effort to get through to the business community that he was on their side. Sound politics, instead of expressions of intemperate outrage, would be the key to his staying in the White House.

With Butler doing his best to restrain any untoward excesses, Roosevelt rolled on unimpeded toward the Republican convention in June. By May, when it was clear that Roosevelt would be nominated, Butler decided it was time to return to the pages of the *Review of Reviews* to sell him again to the public. Unlike his effort three years earlier, when he was pushing a largely untried product on a suspicious and traumatized nation, Butler was now dealing with a successful track record of a man whom the entire world knew. It was a much easier task, and as Roosevelt himself observed, there was no one better qualified to do it: "I am so pleased that you are to 'write me up' for the *Review of Reviews*; I would rather have you do it than any one else, of course."

For Butler, there were no political issues in 1904. The election was simply about Theodore Roosevelt, who had already demonstrated that he was "absolutely the best fitted to meet the problems and fulfill the duties of the Chief Executive . . . He has proved this abundantly, and the American people know it." If anyone doubted this, Butler rehearsed some of Roosevelt's political successes: the settling of the coal strike, the establishment of the reciprocal trade treaties with Cuba, the dissolving of the Northern Securities Company, in which the Sherman Antitrust Act was used to break up the railroad monopoly, which J. P. Morgan had illegally contrived with the help of E. H. Harriman of the Union Pacific and James J. Hill of the Great Northern. In all of these achievements Roosevelt had exhibited his keen moral vision, his wonderful capacity to act, his "intuitive insight into the mind of the plain people."

Butler praised Roosevelt's battle on behalf of decency and honesty against "every powerful selfish and exploiting interest in the country." Roosevelt was someone whom the plain people—and the plain voter—could trust. Beyond the record of legislative triumphs and effective leadership stood the irresistible energy and glory of the man himself, finally larger than any of the niggling criticisms that might be brought against him. Butler claimed that not since Lincoln had such a powerful personality entered the political scene. He welcomed the notion that the Democrats might attack him precisely on the issue of his personality, for to do so would only be to "emphasize its attractiveness." Roosevelt transcended conventional politics, Butler concluded, and had only to "leave his case with the American people" in order to win.

Butler was right, of course. No Democrat could measure up, certainly not the unexciting Alton Brooks Parker, chief justice of the New York Court of Appeals, who became the Democratic nominee in July. Just to be sure, however, Butler showed that he was not above the timely use of the political smear. In early August, Butler asked Roosevelt if they shouldn't try to pin the "'Standard Oil' tag on Parker early in the campaign and make him wear it . . . 'Rockefeller' and 'Standard Oil' are two of the most unpopular names in the country and deservedly so." Roosevelt was enthusiastic about the idea, saying he would ask George Cortelyou, formerly his secretary and now Republican National Committee chairman, if he could "get the Standard Oil tag put on as you suggest." He also wondered if Butler, with his New York press connections, could not help in the process.

One of the first postconvention issues Roosevelt had to deal with concerned the Republican choice of a candidate for New York's gubernatorial race. Because Parker was also from New York, it was important that Roosevelt have a strong man with whom he could work to help secure the state for the Republican ticket. He had lost confidence in the two-term incumbent, Benjamin Odell, who was competent but somewhat out of touch and whose waning popularity in the state made him more of a liability than an asset. The obvious choice was the smoothly efficient, impeccable lawyer Elihu Root. Unfortunately, having already served as secretary of war under McKinley and Roosevelt, Root had no desire to immerse himself in state politics. Even TR's attempt to persuade him by suggesting that the governorship would almost certainly lead to his being the Republican nominee for president in 1908 had no effect.

The Republicans had to turn elsewhere and, looking around, seemed to settle on Morningside Heights. On August 25 Butler received a brief note from Roosevelt stating that both Root and Cortelyou were "red hot" for him to run. Roosevelt claimed to know nothing about it, merely asking Butler not to reject the idea without careful thought. TR followed this on the twenty-seventh with a serious personal plea. He had just learned that Odell, who remained influential as the chairman of the state Republican Committee, had also decided on Butler, and he was now himself asking Butler to accept:

> If the Republican leaders do ask you to be the nominee for Governor, I most earnestly hope you will accept. The Governorship is a great and dignified office, and though it would at the moment interrupt your career as an educator, it would enable you at the close of

your term of service, if you so desired, to go back to that career with immensely added weight. I have always, as you know, felt that the part you had taken in politics—your being delegate to national conventions, etc.—had greatly strengthened your power for good in your educational work, and I think this would strengthen it still more. Moreover, if you are asked, it will be because there is a genuine need of you; and I hope you can make up your mind to fill this need. It is not often that we get such a conjunction as a man ideally fit for the office whom the powers in control desire to nominate for the office; and I hate to see a failure to take advantage of it.

Roosevelt ended on a note of strategic caution. Since it was important that he not be thought TR's special ally (Roosevelt originally wrote, then scratched out, "protege"), he warned Butler not even to come down to Washington to see him should he decide to run.

Although it was not without its narrowly political dimension (Odell, for example, supported him in part to oppose Boss Platt's candidate, former lieutenant governor Timothy Woodruff), Republican interest in Butler was completely understandable. He would be a candidate requiring no apologies and little introduction, having already managed to impress himself upon the public as a unique blend of erudition, managerial sophistication, and political acumen. By August the press had begun to mention him favorably. The *Times* on August 21 mentioned that Governor Odell viewed him as an attractive choice who would appeal both to the independent voters of the city and to upstate Republicans. The *New York Evening Journal* thought it a choice of such quality that it would force the Democrats to come up with a really distinguished person of their own and was thus valuable both for the Democratic Party and for the people as a whole. The *Philadelphia Press* was the most lavishly enthusiastic:

No one in the Republican Party who has watched the career of President Nicholas Murray Butler has doubted the calling of him some day to very high official place by the Republican Party. He is a masterly politician in the better meaning of that term . . . President McKinley once said that with one or two exceptions he regarded Dr. Butler as the ablest politician of a high order of whom he had any knowledge.

Butler expressed proper gratitude and amazement at Roosevelt's letter but insisted that he could not consider the position. Had he wanted a political career, he told his friend, he could have launched one twenty years earlier when Garret A. Hobart, a ranking New Jersey Republican who went on to become vice president, urged him to run for Congress from a safe Republican district in the state. Had he wanted the money and influence of Wall Street, he could have had that when he was offered the presidency of a trust company "at a salary nearly as large as yours." But what he really wanted was precisely the career he had established for himself as publicist and university president. Butler's explanation indicated that in his own mind he was choosing a life of more, not less power:

> A great University in a democracy is one of the most powerful engines of modern times. Most of them are administered by half-baked fellows who could not possibly get another job. My ambition is to make it a great University, to have it preserve and inculcate the highest ideals and also to keep it in touch with sound public opinion. That, if accomplished, is a public service that goes way ahead of being Governor of half a dozen states.

To which he might have added the appeal of lifetime tenure and a freedom to do his job without having to worry about making voters happy. Roosevelt regretted but understood his decision. Denied its first two choices, the party then turned to the drab lieutenant governor, Frank W. Higgins, who was carried into office in the wake of Roosevelt's easy reelection.

Butler exulted in Roosevelt's overwhelming victory, which he called "one of the most astounding triumphs in modern politics," attributing it to the president's "own personal character and achievements." He also praised him for asserting that he would not seek another term—words Roosevelt would later wish he hadn't uttered. Butler thought that his disavowal would eliminate any possibility of Roosevelt's being tempted to break with presidential custom, and that the moment to announce this decision was as the country enthusiastically embraced his election.

Butler was also aware of the implications of Roosevelt's declaration for his own career. There was no need for precipitous action, but he would certainly have to begin to think about his future in the party without Roosevelt. In the meantime, the personal friendship between the two endured, and Butler's role as active kitchen cabinet adviser continued as before. Still,

Roosevelt was not wrong to notice that on certain subjects, Butler had for the last year or so gradually been disengaging from parts of the president's political and social agenda.

The disengagement largely took the form of Butler's willingness to speak out against what he perceived to be Roosevelt's excessive sympathies for the labor movement. In a 1906 speech in Chicago, Butler attacked teachers unions, insisting that any teacher who joined one should immediately be removed from service. He criticized the strictness of the Sherman Antitrust laws, arguing that in ending certain abuses, they failed to take into account the public benefits of corporations, and threatened to "wreck the whole economic basis on which our prosperity and our happiness rest." Perhaps most pointedly, he organized the resistance to Roosevelt's attempt to get an anti-injunction plank included in the 1908 Republican platform. Roosevelt had become increasingly agitated by what he considered to be the complicity of the courts in cooperating with management to cripple legitimate labor protest. Issuing injunctions at the behest of management to forbid strikes had developed into a powerful means of denying labor its capacity to effect change. The issue roiled the country—and both political parties— expressing as it did the basic tension between labor and capital. Roosevelt, on the side of labor, sought to limit the power of the courts to use injunctions in this way; Butler, determined to protect the rights of capital, successfully undercut Roosevelt by maneuvering the argument into a discussion about the integrity and independence of the judiciary itself. The compromise plank that emerged from the Republican convention struggle—affirming the right of courts to issue injunctions without prior notice only when irreparable damage to property could be demonstrated—did not satisfy Butler, but at least it prevented TR from putting through a stronger measure.

The growing split between the two men turned into a terminal break early in 1908, when Butler found himself abruptly cast out of Roosevelt's affection. The president's rejection of his longtime intimate friend was swift and brutal. Writing to his son Archie in February, Roosevelt explained that Archie's mother had become so angry with Butler that she had named the new mare she was riding "Nicoletta."

Butler's transformation from trusted member of Roosevelt's kitchen cabinet to a horse galled by Mrs. Roosevelt's spurs began with his response to a special message Roosevelt delivered to both houses of Congress on January 31. With only one year left in office, Roosevelt was frustrated by his failure to achieve all his reformist goals, perhaps the most pressing of which was to ensure that the authority of the federal government (otherwise known as Roosevelt) to stem corrupt and illegal corporate practices not be interfered with by a timid Congress or a meddlesome judiciary. In the inevitable warfare "between the great corporations and the public," Roosevelt was always comfortable defining himself, rhetorically at least, as the champion of the public. Recent decisions of the Supreme Court invalidating an employer's liability law, together with the difficulties his administration was encountering in enforcing interstate commerce and antitrust regulations, had convinced Roosevelt of the need to ask Congress for stronger laws—in what he called his "campaign against privilege."

In his rambling ten-thousand-word congressional address the president railed against the abuses of the rich and powerful, calling on Congress to join him in preventing the liars and the stock manipulators, the sly corporate lawyers and the aggressive monopolists, from exploiting the honest wageworker. As was generally true with Roosevelt's assaults on the Establishment, the moral ferocity of the attack tended to go hand in hand with a rather more moderate set of political and legal prescriptions. After the initial impact of the subversive rhetoric, what he actually advocated was far more measured than his fulminations might have suggested. His thunder against the system led to curbing some of its excesses rather than an apocalyptic overthrow of the whole.

But thunder it was on January 31. We must silence "the apologists of successful dishonesty"; we must punish "those most dangerous members of the criminal class—the criminals of great wealth"; "our purpose is to secure national honesty in business and in politics"; "against the embittered opposition of wealthy owners of huge flocks of sheep, or of corporations desiring to rob people of coal and timber, we strive to put an end to the theft of public land." Roosevelt ended his diatribe with a reference to Abraham Lincoln's sacred sense of mission in the Civil War:

> In the work we of this generation are in, there is, thanks be to the Almighty, no danger of bloodshed and no use for the sword; but there is grave need of those stern qualities alike by the men of the North and the men of the South in the dark days when each valiantly battled for the light as it was given each to see the light. Their spirit should be our spirit, as we strive to bring nearer the day

when greed and trickery and cunning shall be trampled under feet
by those who fight for the righteousness that exalteth a nation.

Butler was quick to indicate his displeasure. On February 4, in a letter labeled "Strictly Confidential," he volunteered himself as the one friend
"fond enough of you to tell you what a painful impression has been made
on the public mind by your Special Message." The specific recommendations, he conceded, were generally reasonable, but the tone was not. Butler
upbraided Roosevelt for "descending into the arena of ordinary newspaper
and hustings debate" to attack his enemies, for haranguing Congress as if he
were a private citizen and not the president of the United States. Should he
read his statement over, Butler insisted, he would "see how lacking it is in
the dignity, in the restraint, and in the freedom from epithet which ought
to characterize so important a state paper." More self-control would have
made the substance of his message more palatable to Congress. The unhappy result of his speech, Butler concluded, was "to bring Mr. Bryan
[William Jennings Bryan, perennial Democratic presidential candidate running again in 1908] measurably nearer the White House than he ever has
been before."

Roosevelt's answer was unsparing. The rebuke did not surprise him, he
emphasized at the start, as he had understood for several years that Butler
had been "steadily growing out of sympathy with my purposes and policies."
Classifying Butler among those "lukewarm friends" who were upset by his
address, Roosevelt condemned him to the darkness of the morally obtuse,
from which there was no return. He found Butler's criticism "incompre-
hensible":

To me it seems that I have the right to the fullest and heartiest
support of every good man whose eyes are not blinded by unhappy
surroundings, and who has in him a single trace of the fervor for righteousness and decency without which goodness tends to be an
empty shame. If your soul does not rise up against corruption in politics and corruption in business, against the unspeakable degradation and baseness of a community which will accept Rockefeller and
Harriman, Foraker and Black and Chancellor Day, as its leaders in
the business world and in political thought, and which will tolerate
the vileness of the New York Sun and kindred newspapers in its fam-

ily—why, then naturally you are out of sympathy with me. If you felt, as I do, that the interests which these men and papers represent . . . if left unchecked and un-offset would work a ruin such as was worked in the last days of the Roman Republic by similar forces— why, then, you would naturally support my action.

Butler replied the next day that he was by no means out of sympathy with Roosevelt's purposes and policies; it was precisely because he still supported them that he had taken the trouble to write. His soul rose up as violently as did the president's against corruption in all its forms, he assured him, but it was only by assuming an "appropriate and dignified and effective attitude" that Roosevelt could hope to be successful. Butler's explanation of his motives, while continuing to deplore Roosevelt's "most serious blunder," was not the best means to asssuage the president's anger. This February 7 letter effectively marked the end of the relationship between the two men. Roosevelt never bothered to answer it, and though there was some desultory correspondence over the next decade, it had none of the intimacy or affection that had characterized the previous ten years of their friendship.

As Butler could not have intended his criticism to end his friendship with Roosevelt, it is worth speculating on why he wrote it. One would feel more comfortable with Butler's account that he acted only as a friend, if he hadn't sent blind copies of his explicitly labeled "Highly Confidential" letter to at least two (and perhaps more) powerful men, Andrew Carnegie and banker John S. Kennedy. Private rebukes to trusted friends inescapably become public statements of a sort when surreptitiously delivered to others. What message was Butler sending to the outside world through the agency of Kennedy, Carnegie, and possibly others?

To begin with, taking the step of distributing blind copies suggests not a mere unhappiness with tone, as Butler maintained, but a real desire to separate himself, in the eyes of his moneyed friends, from Roosevelt's attack on privilege. Roosevelt was certainly right in sensing that Butler was disaffected with his presidential agenda. Although Roosevelt's progressivism was more conservative than it appeared, his outrage at corrupt corporate practices was genuine. For Butler, on the other hand, the corporation represented all that was best in the American economic system. Problems were the fault not of the corporations, but of malign labor unions, endlessly fomenting class struggle and damaging the interests of the workers. Roosevelt's anger at the use of the injunction to interfere with labor's legitimate right to strike was matched only by Butler's unrelenting objection to strikes themselves, which he thought acts of economic warfare, aimed at destroying democracy. Butler's captains of industry, far from being symbols of the business community's "unspeakable degradation," embodied a glowing American ideal.

Butler was not prepared to confront the president publicly on these disagreements, but he was also not prepared to permit his banking and industrial friends to believe he approved of the president's allegations. The private objection, privately distributed to others, supplied Butler with a neat solution. It also suggested a larger calculation: an awareness that his Roosevelt connection was becoming less valuable for his own status in the Republican Party. Roosevelt was, in a sense, the past. The party's future, in which Butler fully intended to be engaged, lay not with Rooseveltian progressivism, but with Taft's mainstream Republicanism. Distancing himself from the lame-duck president was not the worst idea for a man with Butler's ambitions. The severance of the relationship was not what Butler expected, but the personal loss was at least compensated for by a significant political gain. Having become important in Republican circles in part because of his ties to Roosevelt, he would grow even more important without him.

With President Taft established in the White House after 1908, Butler no longer had to worry about Roosevelt as he began building his influence within the Republican Party. Roosevelt made it all the easier by leaving the country in March 1909 on a yearlong big-game-hunting journey through Africa. Despite his avowals in 1904 that he would never run again for president, Roosevelt's ego, energies, enormous popularity, and youth (he was only fifty-two) made it difficult for him to resist the lure of national politics when he came back in June 1910. The Taft-centered Republicans, pursuing their respectable and far from reactionary domestic agenda, suddenly found themselves threatened by the reemergence of a charismatic Roosevelt whose views had grown appreciably more extreme since he had left the White House. Unable to honor the vow he made to Taft that he would keep his "mouth shut" when he came back from Africa, Roosevelt set out in late summer on a speaking tour throughout the West and the South. He returned to some of the populist notes he had sounded during the last years of his presidency, especially his theme that the courts were being manipulated for class purposes against the interests of the workers. The rules were discriminating against equality of opportunity, Roosevelt maintained, so perhaps it would be necessary to change them. The "vulpine legal cunning" employed by "malefactors of great wealth" to avoid punishment had to be stopped.

The "New Nationalism" Roosevelt began selling called for a reexamination of the relations between property and human welfare. The radical notions he endorsed—voter initiative (the right of the public to cancel unpopular laws), recall of the judiciary, and review of judicial decisions—alarmed Butler. He thought Roosevelt's rhetoric smacked of the most abhorrent strains of socialism, putting into question the entire structure of representative democracy; in Butler's mind, the country had never been confronted by so severe an intellectual challenge. As Roosevelt moved closer to making a run for the Republican nomination throughout the fall of 1910 and 1911, Butler decided to take on the obligation of defending American political principles—as well as the aspirations of the incumbent Republican president for a second term—against his old friend's intemperate assaults.

He struck the first blow in New York on November 16, 1911, at the 143rd annual banquet of the Chamber of Commerce. Before an economically elite audience including Morgan, Carnegie, and Rockefeller, Butler rose to defend that institution which Roosevelt loved to hate: the corporation. Extolling its merits required superlatives:

> I weigh my words, when I say that in my judgment the limited liability corporation is the greatest single discovery of modern times, whether you judge it by its social, by its ethical, by its industrial or, in the long run,—after we understand it and know how to use it,—by its political effects. Even steam and electricity are far less important than the limited liability corporation, and they would be reduced to comparative impotence without it.

Butler launched a more sweeping attack thirteen days later at the Commercial Club in St. Louis in an address entitled "Why Should We Change Our Form of Government?" Without once mentioning his name, Butler managed a sustained, almost point-by-point rebuttal of all the major reforms Roosevelt advocated, reforms that, if implemented, would "change our representative republic into a socialistic democracy." The impulse to bypass the people's elected representatives and vest power in the people themselves was not a progressive but rather a thoroughly reactionary step, he claimed. Butler argued from the model of evolutionary biology that progress always developed from the simple to the complex. Movement from the lower to the higher organisms brought with it specialization of functions not found in the more primitive forms. The simple structure of the amoeba, for example, could hardly be thought to be an advance on the complicated organization of the mammal. As in biology, so in political systems: "The movement to substitute direct democracy for representative government is a movement back from the age of the mammal to the age of the amoeba. Such a movement may have merits of its own, but they cannot be the merits which we attach to genuine progress."

Having established the retrograde nature of all such efforts, Butler then examined the threat to representative institutions posed by the referendum and voter initiative proposals and, perhaps most dangerous of all, the use of judicial recall, which he termed "much more than a piece of stupid folly. It is an outrage of the first magnitude." None of these measures, for Butler, could be imagined as constructive: they effectively tore down the foundations of American liberty and its functioning democracy, which had been painstakingly built over more than a century. What social and political problems there were could be solved not through revolutionary change in the form of government (by implication, what Roosevelt was intending), but by trying to perfect what we already possessed. The proper direction, Butler suggested,

> leads, in my judgment, not to more frequent elections but to fewer elections; it leads not to more direct popular interference with representative institutions, but to less; it leads to a political practice in which a few important officers are chosen for relatively long terms of service . . . ; it leads not to more legislation, but to infinitely less; it leads to fixing public opinion on questions of vital principle, and not to dissipating it among a thousand matters of petty administrative detail; it leads to those acts and policies that will increase the desire and interest of public-spirited men to hold office, and not drive them away from it as with a scourge.

No amount of rhetorical lambasting in Commercial Clubs and chambers of commerce could dim Roosevelt's luster or deflect the grassroots enthusiasm for his candidacy building around the country. It might have helped had Taft been more aggressive, but he could not bring himself to attack his former friend and political mentor. Roosevelt remained tactically noncommittal on whether he would seek the Republican nomination, even as he helped create the pressure on him to challenge Taft. Finally, in early February 1912, he declared he could no longer resist the popular will, announcing in Ohio that his hat was indeed in the ring.

For Butler, the official declaration of his candidacy officially turned Roosevelt into an archenemy of the Republican Party and all it stood for. His insistence on running against Taft also guaranteed, as most political observers understood, that no matter who won the nomination, the hopelessly split Republican Party would be crushed in the election. Butler was enraged, and his fury erupted in an address he gave as presiding officer at the New York State Republican Convention held in Rochester on April 9. Later published separately as "The Supreme Issue of 1912," it was, once again without including his name, a withering, mocking, abusive attack on Roosevelt and his policies.

The "genuine" Roosevelt of Butler's 1901 *Review of Reviews* portrait— "natural not affected; frank, not deceptive; true, not false"—and the "honest, fearless, sympathetic and just" president of 1904 had now metamorphosed into "an itinerant political patent medicine man," a member of the "fussy and petulant minority," one of those "declaimers and sandlot orators and perpetual candidates for office" belonging to "that large group of socialists and semi-socialists who are waging relentless war on representative government." In listening to them, "one wonders whether he is really listening to the speech of sane men or to the incoherent ravings of Bedlam." Ignorant of the perfection of the American political tradition, with its constitutional principles rooted in human nature, they would rather "press upon us the odd and curious nostrums of their own making" that promised to cure all human ills and "to bring about that happy and blissful Utopia of which certain types of men with nothing to do habitually dream."

The national press recognized that Butler had declared war on Roosevelt. Responses to his speech predictably split along partisan lines. Taft supporters, representing the mainstream of Republican sentiment, praised his denunciation of Roosevelt, while TR's followers argued that Butler displayed a "refined and developed ignorance of political science and contemporaneous history in his unwillingness to allow any criticism of the American social and political system." New York State comptroller William A. Prendergast dismissed Butler's attack as "the most astounding exhibition of reckless judgment that I have ever listened to . . . Oblivious of the fact that the followers of Mr. Roosevelt and other progressive leaders number millions of American citizens, he proceeded to read them out of the Republican party."

With the battle lines drawn, Roosevelt prepared for the Republican convention in Chicago in June, initially announcing that he would "bow cheerfully" to the will of the convention should it reject him. Although he went to Chicago with greater popular support than Taft, the party leaders—and even the party rules—were against him. Elihu Root, who like Butler had been recently excluded from Roosevelt's friendship, was elected temporary chairman of the convention, and in the preconvention deliberations about delegates' credentials he helped to resolve most of the disputed cases in favor of seating Taft loyalists. By the time Roosevelt arrived for the start of the convention on June 18, his previously stated willingness to abide by its decision had given way to a deep resentment and a determination to leave the Republican Party and run on his own should he lose.

Butler did his best to make sure that no one would confuse Roosevelt with a Republican. As the most influential member of the platform committee, he drafted a version that included some explicitly anti-Roosevelt principles regarding the party's intention to "uphold at all times the authority and integrity of the Courts, both State and Federal," as well as the assertion that the recall of judges was both "unnecessary and unwise." And going well beyond the formal language of the platform, he continued his own personal assault. To charges that Roosevelt's policies were socialist, he added the somewhat peculiar accusation that Roosevelt was in fact intent on establishing a monarchy. "Roosevelt is no longer a Republican," he said in comments reported from Chicago on June 16.

> He is an imperialist democrat. The Colonel is the Louis Napoleon
> of 1912. But he is much more dangerous than Napoleon, because of
> his virility and aggressiveness in inflaming the passions of the near-
> politicians, down-and-outers and cranks, who have flocked to his
> standard . . . As did Louis Napoleon in 1849 in France, so Roosevelt
> in 1912 seeks by a third term crusade to upset the republic and estab
> lish either limited or absolute monarchy in America.

Butler lamented the distress Roosevelt's deterioration caused him: "I am much grieved that that Colonel, for many years my intimate friend, should have suddenly abandoned his belief in a Republican constitutional form of government, and as I suggested in my Rochester speech, begun to advocate a Cossack form."

Roosevelt didn't require Butler's rhetorical thumpings to help him lose. There was no possibility that the party's influential leaders would permit him to grab the nomination away from Taft. He went to the convention a Republican, albeit an idiosyncratic one, and left a Progressive, committed to his own third-party campaign. Butler was sophisticated enough to understand that Roosevelt's defeat in June still added up to a Republican disaster in the fall, but he nevertheless took satisfaction in what he considered to be the convention's successful response to "the greatest crisis which has confronted the American people since the Civil War":

> Had the forces of law and orderly progress been overthrown in that convention, we should have been well on the way toward establishing in the United States an imperialistic democracy. It is my own opinion, as it was that of many delegates, that no equally serious attack upon the Government has been made, save in the doctrines of Nullification and Secession.

But despite Butler's claims, the Republican establishment gained only the hollowest of victories. Incumbent though he was, the stolid, gentle Taft proved no match for the irrepressible TR. The party was split, with Roosevelt actually beating Taft by almost 650,000 votes, paving the way for Woodrow Wilson, whose total was less than that of his two opponents' combined. Four terms of consecutive Republican presidency came to an end in an Electoral College landslide of 435 for Wilson to 88 for TR. Although Butler had nothing to show for it other than in his opinion having saved the Republic, he had fought the good fight on behalf of his party and his president, and deserved some recognition. But there appeared to be nothing to give him—until on October 30, two weeks before the election, vice presidential candidate James Sherman suddenly died. The election went off without a running mate for Taft, but one was officially needed for whom the Republican electors, such as they were, could cast their votes on January 13. On January 5, *The New York Times* noted that a White House conference decided that Butler should have the honor of receiving the Republican electoral votes. It quoted Taft as arguing that Butler deserved it, "not only as a man worthy of the honor at the hands of the Republican party, but as a New Yorker who shared with the dead candidate the love and respect of the Republicans of the Empire State." The *Times* added that "Dr. Butler has long been regarded as a warm personal friend of the President, and is greatly admired by the latter, not only as a man of letters, but for his disinterested efforts for the advancement of the people of the United States." Butler refused to comment on the possibility, but Taft's support of him proved decisive. On January 13 the Republican electors of Utah and Vermont met in their separate states to cast their four ballots each for Taft and the man appointed to accept the vice presidential vote in 1912, Nicholas Murray Butler.

CHAPTER NINE

"Dear Tessie"

✣

Although Roosevelt's scheduled return to America in two weeks after his yearlong safari was about to complicate Republican politics, Butler was in fine fettle on the morning of June 2, 1910. Discussions with Andrew Carnegie that would eventually lead to the funding of his Endowment for International Peace had already started; the school year was safely behind him; and he was preparing to leave the following week on a five-month tour of Europe in which he would make important contacts and be feted by important people. Perhaps even more important, he was to play golf that very afternoon with his friend Henry Pritchett.

Butler had his good mood shattered while on the train to the golf course around noon, when a faculty colleague, Professor H. E. Crampton of the Zoology Department, handed him an early copy of the *Evening World*. Bold headlines—"Letters of Professor Peck Figure in $50,000 Suit His 'Dear Tessie' Brings"—announced a lurid tale of lust and dishonor scandalizing Columbia's name. Professor Harry Thurston Peck, one of Columbia's most illustrious faculty members and an old college friend of Butler's, was being sued by his former stenographer, Esther Quinn, for breach of promise. The article detailed the allegations that Peck had proposed marriage in September 1908, the very month in which he divorced his first wife. Esther's distress was considerable when she learned, according to the action she was currently bringing in New York's Supreme Court, that Peck had instead married someone else in August 1909.

Most of the *World's* coverage consisted of a selection of letters that

Quinn and her attorney claimed Peck had written her during their ten-year friendship. Hyped by the *World* as "filled with expressions of adoration, declarations of unswerving devotion and sobriquets of endearment," they hardly amounted to titillating reading. But with salutations like "Dear Tessie," "My Darling," and "Dearest Esther," and varieties of gooey thoughts regarding her heavenly qualities, her marvelous letters, and his objections to being thought a vampire by her, they certainly must have horrified Butler, even if it is worth noting that they spoke not a syllable of anything attesting to Peck's interest in marrying his Tessie.

There is no evidence of how Columbia's public disgrace affected Butler's golf game that afternoon, though he did discuss the gravity of the issue with Pritchett. Having read the sampling of the letters, Butler "was morally certain that Peck had written them," and that was sufficient, regardless of whether he was guilty of anything other than impropriety and smarmy prose. Upon his return from golf that evening, Butler called Edward R. Coe, a trustee, and set up a meeting of the Trustee Committee on Education for the next afternoon at 3:15. He then called Peck and asked him to come to his office at 11:00 a.m.

It could not have been easy for the Anthon Professor of Latin Language and Literature to be summoned before his friend to explain behavior that was at the very least embarrassing. Peck's relationship with Butler extended back to 1879, when the young Butler, an aspiring sophomore journalist on the college newspaper, looked to Peck, a sophisticated editor a year ahead of him, for advice and support. Peck was already an accomplished classicist and literary figure while still an undergraduate. He had built *Acta Columbiana* into a prominent college paper, affecting the noms de plume Smintheus and Spinx for his own contributions in poetry and prose. "Most Endeared Smintheus," Butler had begun one letter to him requesting editorial counsel.

With his learning and literary flair, Peck was perfectly equipped for an academic career, and by 1888 he had been appointed professor of Latin at Columbia. The Anthon Chair followed in 1904. He wrote effortlessly, churning out serious scholarly publications such as *Latin Pronunciation* (1889), *Roman Life in Latin Prose and Verse* (1895) and *A History of Classical Philology* (1911), as well as children's books, translations, travel books, and essays on every conceivable topic. Using his own name for his academic writing, he preferred pen names like Richard W. Kemp, Merton J.

Forrester, Lindon Orr, Walter Eaton, and Rafford Pike for much of his immense journalistic work.

Elegant and fastidious, he had manufactured for himself a prominent position in New York's cultural life. President of the Latin Club of America, founder (and editor) of *The Bookman*, trustee of Columbia University Press, member of the editorial board of *Munsey's Magazine*, and editor of *Harper's Dictionary of Classical Literature and Antiquities*, among other editorial positions, Peck basked in his reputation as one of Columbia's most brilliant literary men. In 1904 Columbia awarded him an honorary degree. In 1908, when the authorship of the popular American poem "Casey at the Bat" continued to be unresolved after twenty years of controversy, it was Peck who was asked by a magazine editor to investigate the issue and render his definitive judgment. (Ernest Lawrence Thayer, Peck concluded.)

So the man who came to Butler's office on the morning of June 3 was not simply a faculty colleague and longtime friend but an eminent man of letters, highly respected both inside and outside Columbia. What Butler saw, however, was only a person who had humiliated his university and in consequence had to be excised from it, irrespective of the niceties regarding due process or the presumption of innocence. Butler made clear, in a letter to another trustee several months after this meeting, that the Peck who appeared in the office embodied dissolute shame: "He moved slowly and heavily, his face was bloated, and his eyes were blood-shot and steadily turned away from me. I wondered whether perhaps he was not under the influence of liquor or of some drug."

Butler told Peck that at the trustee meeting scheduled for that afternoon he would be expected to discuss Peck's behavior. What could he say on his behalf? According to Butler, Peck sullenly replied that a man was innocent until proven guilty. Butler answered that such a formulation "would not quite do." Had he in fact written the letters published in the *World*? After an initial denial, claiming that they were all forgeries concocted by Quinn's lawyer, Peck grudgingly admitted that he had perhaps written ten or twelve of them. This was the issue, Butler said, that "seriously affects your usefulness here." Peck could only intone once again that a man had to be held innocent until proven otherwise.

Fueled by Butler's "moral certainty" that Peck wrote the letters, the Education Committee speedily concluded that Peck had to go. When Butler wrote to Peck on the committee's behalf, he did not discuss the justice of Quinn's accusations, but simply informed him, without giving any reasons, that he was being asked to submit his resignation as of June 30. Failure to do so would result in his being suspended until the trustees could meet to determine final action.

After summarily dispatching Peck from his Columbia existence—the only life he had known since his graduation from the college almost thirty years before—Butler boarded his ship six days later for the start of his European tour, confident that the ugly episode had been closed by his decisive action.

When he arrived in London, he seemed astonished to learn from cables, letters, and reporters that Peck had not accepted the termination of his Columbia career with gentlemanly grace. Not only had he refused to resign, but he was giving virulent interviews to newspapers, filled with accusations about Butler's moral and administrative failures. The papers delighted in the gobbets of malevolence he produced for them: "'You can say for me that Dr. Nicholas Murray Butler . . . is the greatest liar in the United States'"; "'There is a great fight on at Columbia . . . between the faculty on one side and the president on the other . . . His greed for power has got the better of him. In this fight I think the faculty are on my side'"; "'The trustees of the institution know nothing about the high-handed manner in which the affairs of the college are being managed. The finance committee is the only body that acts independently. Small matters like education are entirely overlooked'"; "'This idol with feet of clay and tongue of brass . . . is sure to be overthrown soon . . . I have been in this university for thirty years and I know as much about it as Mr. Butler, and I am going to use that knowledge to deprive him of the reputation of having power which he really has not'"; "'The trouble up here at Columbia is . . . that President Butler is the whole thing. He scares the kids in the faculty and lies in wait for the older men whom he does not like, and the trustees don't know that he is running the place to pieces.'" Peck claimed that Butler had already driven away from the university a number of professors who had challenged him, and he pointedly observed that the Latin address Butler was planning to give in Berlin was in fact written by Peck himself.

Butler appeared bewildered at Peck's behavior, apparently unable to fathom its cause. "The newspaper men here tell me that Peck is kicking up an awful fuss at home, and is now abusing me and the University generally. His troubles must have deranged his mind; I can think of no other explanation." Butler's sense of himself as the aggrieved party—"Knowledge of this fuss at home is spoiling my holiday"—was reinforced by letters from trustees and friends expressing similar dismay over "Peck's utter degeneracy" in turning so inexplicably on his good friend. Brander Matthews spoke for all of Butler's supporters when he sympathized with him for having his vacation "disturbed by the unspeakable conduct of Peck. I knew that he had a yellow streak, but I did not think that he was a treacherous cad. His conduct is worthy only of a . . . skunk."

Except for the shadow cast by Peck, Butler's London visit was totally gratifying. Distinguished British statesmen attended formal dinners in his honor, reporters asked his opinions about international issues, and he was invited to testify before a Royal Commission on the nature of American university administration. In the midst of all this nourishing activity, dealing with Peck from afar constituted an enormous distraction for Butler, and he urged the trustees to act expeditiously to conclude the matter: "You are cutting out a cancer and can not do it too soon."

Peck refused to go easily, however, vowing to fight his suspension in the courts, and Butler continued to be amazed at the personal hostility directed toward him. He focused exclusively on the wrongs done him by Peck's hysterical attacks, casting himself heroically as Peck's defender over the years in the face of much morally dubious (if unspecified) behavior on the part of the Anthon Professor. Little did Peck know what the president had done for him. Butler wrote to his friend J. B. Pine on July 13,

> I have in my possession a packet of letters from his first wife, written several years ago, and which I have not shown even to you because of my feeling that somehow or other he might be saved to the University and his undeniable talents put to good use . . . Perhaps I was wrong in not showing them to you and to the Committee on Education when they were first received, but I acted in what I thought was a generous and friendly way to a long-time colleague and a brilliant scholar.

Tactically, Peck's truculence only made things worse for him. Faculty in 1910 did serve at the pleasure of the trustees, who with or without due process had the power to terminate a professor's employment. His protests were futile, and the shriller his newspaper claims, the deeper the enmity he earned for himself. "Of course, he is now finished absolutely now and forever," Butler wrote Pine in regard to Peck's ongoing accusations, "not only at Columbia but elsewhere." Whatever he might have done to help Peck,

Butler somewhat disingenuously emphasized later, he no longer considered because of the outrageous interviews with the press: "They revealed to the Trustees, as they did to everybody, a state of mind and character which made his staying at Columbia an utter impossibility. Even had I been home, I could have done nothing to save him. He had been a traitor to the University in which he had spent his life, and the punishment had to be academic death."

It only remained for the trustees to determine how best to administer the sentence with the least amount of public repercussion. But before they could address that issue, some damage control was necessary regarding Peck's accurate statement that he had written the Latin address Butler was to deliver in Berlin. Despite the trustee insistence that he had "completely misled the press and led to much unpleasant comment," it was judged prudent to discard Peck's address and ask two other Columbia Latinists to prepare a new one. Both were competent and available, and as Pine noted, they had already found a number of errors in Peck's original document. The crisis of using the text of the disgraced and suspended Peck was thus avoided.

Butler continued his triumphant tour through Europe, and the trustees continued to ponder the strategy they should follow when they reassembled in the fall. Should Peck be offered an official hearing before them? Should his dismissal letter (regardless of a hearing, *that* conclusion was not in dispute) refer to the charges pending against him or not? What should be the exact wording of the resolution? From Butler's point of view, it was imperative to dispose of the matter definitively at the first scheduled trustee meeting in early October. Butler's argument that the "honor of the University" was at stake only thinly disguised his rather more self-serving desire to have everything over with by the time he came back in late October. In any case, there was no opposition to an early fall resolution except on the part of Seth Low, the only trustee who seemed the least bit concerned with Peck's rights.

In response to trustee chairman George Rives's suggestion in mid-September that Peck should be offered the option of resigning, Low pointed out that for him to accept that would be close to acknowledging the justness of the charges brought against him by Quinn. Chiding his fellow trustees for having obviously prejudged Peck, Low emphasized that a more appropriate procedure to have followed would have been to suspend him pending the outcome of an investigation. But having initially insisted upon his resignation and then suspending him when he refused, they could hardly expect him to resign now, thereby tacitly confessing his guilt. Sympathetic to the impulse to conclude the issue at the fall meeting, he nevertheless saw no compelling reason why Peck couldn't be given more time for a graceful departure.

Low's qualms about the haste and fairness of trustee behavior were dismissed, attributed to his usual muddleheadedness. Eager to return to a Columbia without Peck, Butler explained to Pine the need to act sooner rather than later: "Rives writes me that Low is disposed to 'compromise' & to postpone action. That would be quite fatal to the authority and prestige of the Trustees. It seems to me quite as vital to act at the first opportunity as to act at all."

One other Columbia figure attempted to intervene on Peck's behalf: Robert Arrowsmith, a good friend to both Butler and Peck, who wondered if there was not something to be done. Could Peck not be given a second chance, placed on some kind of probation so that he could demonstrate that he had been chastened by the experience? Having spent an evening talking with him, Arrowsmith was confident that Peck could once again become a trustworthy member of the Columbia community. "He is human like all the rest of us," Arrowsmith plaintively noted, "and I think he can be brought back to be of value."

Butler would have none of it, as Peck understood better than Arrowsmith. Referring to that peculiar episode in Arrowsmith's college career when Butler contrived to have him take the blame for the parody in the *Columbiad* that Butler himself had written, Peck reminded Arrowsmith that the man he was appealing to was "precisely the same Butler who got you into so much trouble in '81 over the *Columbiad*—the same liar, sneak and cur."

On October 3, when the trustees met, Peck was not permitted to be present, though a letter he had written to them (and simultaneously released to the newspapers) was read. It invoked his distinguished scholarship, teaching, and service to Columbia and claimed that he was innocent of all the charges Quinn brought against him, stating that they represented, as he had told Butler, "'Blackmail, backed up by perjury and forgery.'" The trustees listened dutifully and then unanimously passed their carefully worded resolution:

Whereas the Trustees are of the opinion that the best interests of the University require that his official connection shall cease:

> Resolved, That the appointment of Harry Thurston Peck as Anthon Professor of the Latin Language and Literature in this University be, and the same hereby is terminated on the adoption of this resolution, and it is the pleasure of the Trustees that the employment of the said Harry Thurston Peck as such Professor cease and determine forthwith; and the said professorship is hereby declared vacant.

An additional resolution, offered by Seth Low, authorized the payment of the salary that Peck would have drawn for the current academic year.

The next day, Butler received a cable in Berlin with pleasure, happy to learn "that the disagreeable business is over." Peck's career was indeed ruinously over, but the business was not quite. Instead of following Butler's advice that the "best thing for him now is to go to a foreign land and bury himself," Peck remained visible and voluble. In December he initiated action against Butler for $50,000 on grounds of slander in claiming not only that he was immoral but that his attacks on Columbia indicated that he must also be deranged. Butler was quoted in the *Times* as saying that he could find no letter in his files making such allegations, presumably being unable to locate those letters in July to Arrowsmith, various trustees, and others, in which he referred consistently to Peck's "mental trouble," "unsound mind," "disordered mind," and "gravely disordered mind," to name a few instances. The following June, Peck filed an amended complaint, specifically citing a letter Butler wrote to James Egbert of the Classics Department sometime in July that included the defamatory sentence, "I have been autocratic only in shielding Professor Peck's immoral acts from the knowledge of the trustees." Peck's anger here did lead him astray, as the actual sentence, which he had remembered imperfectly, read only, "From my personal standpoint it appeals to my sense of humor that he should pour out the vials of his wrath on me, since it is due almost wholly to what he is pleased to call my 'autocracy' that he was not requested to retire several years ago."

The case never came to trial, however, any more than Esther Quinn's did. The only suit that managed to reach a jury, in fact, was one for $100,000 that Peck brought against the *Boston Post* for libel in March 1911. Peck claimed that a defamatory article about him with an accompanying photograph, published on July 24, 1910, caused him to be ridiculed and that it resulted in a loss of income from magazines no longer willing to publish his work. A brief trial produced a $2,500 finding for Peck—a nugatory amount that was hardly cause for celebration.

The $2,500 settlement from the *Post* and the dismissal of Quinn's charges provided no sustaining vindication for Peck. The dashing man of letters and brilliant Columbia professor who had been a much sought after contributor to all kinds of journals and magazines now found himself a disgraced outcast shunned by editors who had previously welcomed him. Peck's friends and income gradually disappeared. Depressed and unable to work even if work were available, he filed for bankruptcy in January 1913. His list of assets, totaling $265, included fifteen copyrights worth $50; four suits of clothes and four suits of underwear, a stickpin, cuff links, and a nickel watch with a gold chain, valued at $105; four pictures at $10; and five hundred books worth $10. He testified that he had no cash, stocks, insurance, horses, cows, or sheep.

Without resources of any kind, he moved to Ithaca to stay with a family friend, Dr. C. H. Gallagher. In April he suffered a nervous collapse and was taken to the city hospital. As befitting the moral dissolute he was generally assumed to be, he was initially diagnosed as suffering from terminal syphilis. In the words of a friend, writing to Bob Arrowsmith, "Harry is a hopeless imbecile, in the last stage of paresis. Dr. Gallagher thinks he cannot possibly live a month . . . Nothing can save the man." Dr. Byron Caples, who had examined him in January, was somewhat less pessimistic, suggesting at the time that he was only suffering from "a probably beginning paresis." When Caples next saw him, in July, he noticed that Peck appeared to be in perfectly reasonable health, and as paresis only gets worse, not better, he had to conclude that his original diagnosis had been incorrect.

Credit for his recovery was claimed by Peck's loyal first wife, Cornelia Dawbarn Peck, who had learned of Peck's illness and the grim prognosis a week after he entered the hospital, and had decided to take over his care herself. A staunch Christian Scientist, she presented herself at the hospital, insisted that he be taken off the large doses of chloral he was receiving, and summoned the services of a Christian Scientist healer, whom she charged by telegraph to "Treat Professor Peck against death."

Whether it was the cessation of the chloral, the presence at his bedside of a human being who believed in him, or indeed the mysterious powers of J. H. Cooke, reader of the First Church of Christ, Scientist, who supplied absent treatment from Connecticut, Peck immediately began to improve.

He was shortly eating steak, taking exercise, and talking lucidly—behavior no one thought him capable of only a week before. After presiding over nineteen days of hospital rest and energetic absent healing from Cooke, Mrs. Peck bundled her former husband into her car and took him back to her home in Sound Beach, Connecticut, to continue monitoring his recovery. Because his physicians had not been inclined to release him, Peck later described himself as having been "benevolently kidnapped" from the hospital.

Peck remained noncommittal about the curative abilities of Christian Science. Meanwhile, the second and current wife, Elizabeth du Bois, whose marriage to Peck had precipitated the breach of promise suit in the first place, was nowhere to be seen. Her major effort on her husband's behalf was to send him a telegram of sympathy while he was in the hospital, regretting that she could not get to Ithaca herself. For her part, the first Mrs. Peck seemed content with nursing the patient back to a condition in which he would be strong enough to rejoin his wife. When asked by a reporter why she had gone to Ithaca to be with Peck, she replied simply that she conceived of it as her duty.

However peculiar the arrangement between Peck and his present and former wives, his recuperation proceeded steadily. By mid-May he felt strong enough physically—and in sufficient control emotionally—to initiate a correspondence with Butler, thanking him for the interest he took in his illness and evoking the warm memories of their shared past. A friendly exchange followed over the next several months in which each refused to allow one unfortunate episode to taint his regard for the other. Butler urged Peck to return to his literary work outside of the frenetic boundaries of the city. Peck apologized for his abusive behavior and informed Butler of the progress he was making. Peck's letters were upbeat and contrite, Butler's sympathetic.

By July, Peck had moved in with friends in Riverside, Connecticut. On the wall of the sleeping porch in his new lodgings he displayed the proofs of a magazine article that began, "Harry Thurston Peck, who died on May . . . ," taking pleasure in reading the positive things the premature obituary went on to say about him. The return of his strength and powers of concentration enabled Peck to find some occasional journalistic work to occupy himself with. One bizarre assignment he took on was to rewrite entirely the inadequate biographical entry in *The New International Encyclopaedia* on none other than Nicholas Murray Butler. Peck, aware of the ironies, wrote Butler that his editors had some trepidation lest he should approach it in a peculiar way. He assured Butler that he had no intention of doing that and would in any case send a draft for Butler's perusal.

One problem with encyclopedia articles, he noted, was their tendency to cover only the past and present, a treatment that would impoverish a piece on Butler because as much as he had accomplished in the past, it was just a "prooemium" of what was to come. Therefore, "I shall touch very lightly the sphere of prophecy. This is not because I want an easy consulate when you become President of the United States or possibly Secretary of State—as a purely personal and non-political appointment—but because I think this is the way in which your biography ought to be written at the present time." Butler approved the draft, only advising Peck, with his characteristic punctiliousness about his own achievements, that "it would be appropriate to add something about international interests, including the Directorship of the Division of Intercourse and Education of the Carnegie Endowment for International Peace, and the Presidency of the American Branch of the Association for International Conciliation."

Despite his cheery banter, Peck was a broken soul, and neither his renewed civilities with Butler nor his sporadic editorial assignments could put him back together again. Columbia had been everything to him; his expulsion from it, and accompanying disgrace, had inflicted a mortal wound. The man who had grown accustomed to the dignity of his position as Anthon Professor was bereft of status, of sustaining work, and even of the meagerest of resources. The optimistic outlook he exhibited in his letters to Butler proved illusory. By early 1914 he had sunk into a serious depression, exacerbated by what he considered to be the failure of his friends to help him find a teaching position or some other form of appropriate literary endeavor. In March, without real work or any hope of any, he moved out of a hotel he could no longer afford and into a four-dollar-a-week furnished room in Stamford, Connecticut. Taking his meals alone in a small Greek restaurant, he obsessed about his accomplished past and his grubby, indigent present. "I am at the end of my rope," he confided to Margaret MacDougall, a loyal stenographer whom he had recently let go because he had no work for her.

On the morning of March 23, MacDougall, who continued to care about Peck even though she was no longer employed by him, called his landlady to ask about him. She replied that he was still sleeping. Receiving the same answer after two or three more phone calls, MacDougall went to the boardinghouse at noon and entered his room. There she found him lying in bed, still clasping the revolver that approximately a half hour before (according to the coroner) had discharged a bullet through his brain. Peck had chosen to carry out himself the academic death penalty that Butler decreed for him in 1910. One wonders whether Butler, in the midst of the shock and grieving that followed, recalled the remark he had tossed off to Pine four years earlier, that he wouldn't "be surprised to read in to-morrow's paper that he [Peck] had taken his life."

If the distinguished Latinist's fall from grace into despair and suicide followed a classically tragic course, the interaction of the two Mrs. Pecks over the disposition of his body contributed a comic epilogue. To which Mrs. Peck did he properly belong: Mrs. Peck 1 (as the newspapers referred to her), who had rescued him from the hospital and healed him, but from whom he was divorced, or Mrs. Peck 2, who was legally his wife but didn't use his name? Speculation was rife about possible conflict. The *New York American* put it best:

> Mrs. Peck No. 2 departed immediately for Stamford. She made no statement before leaving, but she is known to have felt keenly the part that Mrs. Peck No. 1 has been playing to her own exclusion, and it is believed she will insist upon her rights. It is claimed in behalf of Mrs. Peck No. 2, a former school teacher, that she has been willing all along to care for her husband, but his preference has always been for his first wife.

In the end it was money, not adjudicated moral claims, that resolved the case. Mrs. Peck 1 agreed to pay all funeral costs; Mrs. Peck 2 consented. The service accordingly was held at Cornelia Dawbarn Peck's Sound Beach bungalow. Elizabeth du Bois Peck did not attend.

On December 9, 1910, soon after Peck's dismissal, and just before Andrew Carnegie announced the establishment of his Peace Endowment, the following one-sentence resolution was introduced at a Columbia University faculty meeting: "Resolved, That the Faculty of Philosophy place on record

its sense of the academic services of Harry Thurston Peck, who was connected with the University for twenty-two years, and was a member of this
Faculty from the date of its organization." Unexceptionable as it was in tone
and content, it was nevertheless tabled at the motion of Dean James Russell
of Teachers College, a member of the faculty. On January 16, 1911, the resolution's proposer, Joel Elias Spingarn, a young but internationally recognized professor of comparative literature, received a letter from Butler
informing him that because of budgetary difficulties, the Trustees' Education Committee had moved that his professorship be discontinued as of
June 30. On March 6 Spingarn learned that not only had the trustees accepted the recommendation to abolish his professorship, but in addition
had voted to end his connection to Columbia as of that date.

If there was one Columbia faculty member willing to confront authority over an issue of principled decency, it could only have been Spingarn.
He was in many ways an authoritarian president's nightmare. Brilliant,
handsome, personally compelling, and of sufficient independent means
not to be beholden to the university, Spingarn was deeply committed to
ideals of social justice. Following his expulsion from Columbia, he would
devote a large part of his energies to working for racial equality, becoming
by turns chairman of the directors, treasurer, and eventually president of the
NAACP; in 1914 he founded the Spingarn Medal, to be awarded annually
to an African American in recognition of outstanding achievement. Along
with a kind of spiritual purity and uncompromising idealism came a stub-
born personality prepared to resist any exercise of power he found illegitimate or constricting. W.E.B. Du Bois, who came to know him through the
NAACP, called Spingarn "a natural anarchist of the spirit."

Spingarn's anarchism had led him to run away, or more properly walk
away, from his New York family at the age of fifteen. He lived in Philadelphia for a time, until private detectives hired by his parents located him,
having traced him through a letter he had written to his parents requesting
additional clothing. After graduating from Columbia College in 1895 and
spending the next year studying comparative literature at Harvard, he returned to Columbia to work with George Edward Woodberry. Spingarn
became enthralled by Woodberry's moral power and deeply spiritual response to literature. His relationship with Woodberry rapidly changed from
that of simple student to adoring disciple, so profoundly influenced by the
older man's views that he was himself unsure at times where his own ideas

originated. In the Woodberry-Butler dispute of 1904 that led to Woodberry's resignation, Spingarn's strong support of his mentor and his concern for the future of comparative literature immediately marked him in Butler's eyes as someone to be monitored. Despite his best efforts to behave judiciously, his involvement in an issue that did not cast Butler in an attractive light led some at Columbia, including Butler, to question his loyalty. A memo written by Professor E. R. Seligman at the time of the Woodberry controversy, summarizing a conversation he had had with Butler about Spingarn's faculty appointment, revealed the degree to which Spingarn was viewed as a suspicious character:

> It appears that the only objection made by any of the trustees to Dr. Spingarn's appointment was the question whether he had not, at one time or another, been involved in certain newspaper correspondence which was generally considered derogatory to the University. I told the President that so far as I could see, Dr. Spingarn had, in a very delicate situation, conducted himself with fairness and dignity. The President was glad to hear that this was so, but advised that his attitude be carefully watched. If he showed any signs of acting in a particular fashion, contrary to the interests of the University, the President declared that he would be at once dropped.

From the beginning of his tenure at Columbia, then, Spingarn—without being aware of it—had been designated for special scrutiny. It probably didn't help that he was Jewish and a dashing enough figure to have been nominated by Republicans in 1908 to run for Congress from the 18th Congressional District. Spingarn realized that his chances of winning were slim, but he nonetheless had thought it appropriate to inform Butler of his candidacy. Butler praised him for the honor of the nomination and then made sure that Spingarn appreciated its absurdity, adding, "While I dare say your election is impossible," it might at least help the Taft vote in that district.

For the next several years Spingarn managed to avoid any administrative confrontations. He became one of the country's best-known comparativists, publishing widely on the history of literary criticism in the Renaissance, and editing, to great acclaim, an important three-volume collection of seventeenth-century critical essays. The English Department, however, had never been happy with the gerrymandered creation of the Comparative Literature Department, over which it had no control, and in 1910 it attempted to consolidate the two. This effort, motivated by politics rather than intellectual issues, was precisely the sort to provoke Spingarn's principled intransigence. Spingarn argued to Butler the need for a department of literary study that transcended national boundaries. He made a compelling case for strengthening comparative literature rather than permitting it to be absorbed by an English Department whose literary and scholarly interests were so different from its own. But Spingarn could not content himself merely with a reasoned argument. Anger at the injustice of the projected takeover contributed to this concluding unpleasantness in a 1910 letter to Butler:

> If the Trustees . . . carry into effect the recommendation of the English Department . . . it would be idle to deny that I shall feel aggrieved at what seems to me a kind of breach of faith and infidelity to its ideals on the part of the University. My own feelings are of no moment in a question that affects the general welfare; but I must frankly confess that my interest in my work would be seriously dissipated at finding it in a subordinate and no longer independent place; that I cannot promise any whole-hearted cooperation with my new colleagues, or take any interest whatever in any committees created by them.

Threats of noncooperation, particularly from someone whose institutional loyalty was considered shaky, were not the best way to appeal to Butler. In any case, the president and the trustees were not about to defer the amalgamation sought by the English Department because of one dissenting voice. In April 1910 the trustees officially created the Department of English and Comparative Literature. Spingarn remained opposed, and a November complaint from the new department to Butler described his inappropriate behavior, alleging that he refused to serve on departmental committees or in any way acknowledge the authority of the department. Rejecting his administrative responsibilities, the report went on, Spingarn was also effectively disregarding the needs of the students. The memorandum, written by Chairman Ashley Thorndike, concluded with an urgent request that the situation of one professor choosing to place himself outside the authority of his department be resolved sooner rather than later.

Butler asked Spingarn to respond to the department's account of the unsatisfactory relations existing between them. Characteristically, Spingarn took pains not to make things substantially better for himself. He reiterated his criticism of the merger, saying that he could see no reason to stop protesting until the arrangement was changed. But he claimed that he had at the same time remained faithful to his ideal of placing his intellectual gifts at the service of his colleagues and students—a slightly evasive answer to the charge that he wouldn't participate in departmental affairs. And he insisted that he could not permit administrative obligations to interfere with the time he had for productive scholarship.

It was in this climate of presidential suspicion, departmental indignation, and professorial intransigence that Spingarn decided to offer his resolution noting Peck's twenty-two years of service. However principled, politically naive, or spiritually pure Spingarn might have been, it is difficult to imagine that he didn't understand exactly what he was doing when he dropped his delicately worded motion before the faculty. He must have derived considerable pleasure anticipating the response its calculated innocuousness would inspire.

The fervent innocence Spingarn attributed to the motivation behind the resolution was matched by Butler's fervent denial that the resolution had anything to do with his dismissal. In an acerbic exchange of letters, Spingarn argued that it had to have been his resolution that was held against him, since he and Thorndike had met in January and resolved their differences. According to Spingarn, Thorndike had promised to tell Butler that the department no longer had problems with him. With that matter closed, Spingarn could only conclude that he was being punished for his desire to recognize, through what he called "a slight act of generous pity," Peck's twenty-two years of employment at Columbia. He reminded Butler that when the two spoke on January 6, Butler had told him, referring to the tabled resolution, "If you don't drop this matter, you will get into trouble." Rising to an exalted pitch of principled self-destruction, Spingarn apparently replied, "I am not in the habit of altering my conduct because of the prospect of trouble, Mr. President."

Butler did not take kindly to any of this. He replied testily, saying that when they had begun considering his case, neither he nor the trustees had any knowledge of Spingarn's motion, and at no point did it influence their deliberations. He also rejected Spingarn's version of the talk the two had in January concerning the resolution:

> I observe, for example, that you say that I told you that you would get into trouble if you did not drop the whole Peck matter. What I really told you was that you would get into trouble if you persisted in your intention to send to Professor Russell the letter of which you read me a draft, which I regarded as very impertinent.

Butler also pointed out that Thorndike told him that Spingarn's description of the conversation he and Thorndike had was entirely misleading.

Neither account is particularly credible. It is doubtful that Spingarn's attitude toward the department could have changed so thoroughly and so instantly that Thorndike would have assured him that it would drop its complaints against him. It is more likely that in their January discussion Thorndike listened politely to Spingarn's analysis of what he was and was not prepared to do and then told Butler that nothing much had changed. Spingarn's assessment, published later, that all of their "differences were amicably settled at a conference with the Chairman of the Department," must be regarded as a form of special pleading.

On the other hand, Butler's denial that the Peck resolution had anything to do with Spingarn's being fired in the middle of the term is impossible to accept. Certainly Butler and the trustees had started their deliberations about Spingarn *before* the December faculty meeting, but they had not yet concluded them when Spingarn offered his motion. For Butler, the resolution had to have been interpreted as a public flaunting of his authority, a flagrant display of insubordination. Butler's insistence that he was concerned not with the resolution itself, but only with Spingarn's intemperate letter to Russell, constitutes a bit of hairsplitting. As Spingarn commented, "A threat that I should drop this letter was therefore in any case a threat that I should drop the Peck resolution."

When the resolution was not dropped, Spingarn was. Like Peck, he chose not to go quietly. In newspaper interviews he stressed his serious commitment to his teaching duties and noted that his students, begging him to continue his classes outside Columbia, had just presented him with a testimonial inscribed on parchment expressing their gratitude. In a written statement to the press, he declared himself a victim of Butler's personal animus. And it was not just his own personal situation that was at issue but the health of the entire university:

> He has stifled all manly independence and individuality whenever it has exhibited itself at college. All noble idealism and all the graces of poetry and art have been shriveled by his brutal and triumphant power. He has made mechanical efficiency and administrative routine the goal of the university's endeavor. The nobler ends of academic life will never be served so long as this spokesman of materialism and plutocracy remains in power.

Likening him to a Tammany boss, Spingarn repeated his charge that by the time Butler fired him, he had already patched up his relations with his department, and that he had been removed solely because his resolution had threatened Butler's supreme authority. Butler, for his part, was content to insist, through an unsigned editorial in the *Alumni News* which he drafted, that

> A resolution introduced by Professor Spingarn at a meeting of the Faculty of Philosophy held on December 9 had nothing whatever to do with his separation from the University, and was at no time spoken of or discussed in connection therewith. The record shows that the fact that he had introduced such a resolution was not known either to the President or to any member of the Committee on Education until the consideration of the case was approaching a conclusion.

Incensed at what he considered Butler's blatant dishonesty, Spingarn claimed the last two public words. First, in October he published his Butler correspondence, accompanied by an acerbic introduction in which he attacked Columbia's dysfunctional organization, with an autocratic president presiding over a self-perpetuating board of trustee know-nothings who invariably took their instructions and sense of the university from him. Such a structure, Spingarn argued, guaranteed the sycophancy of those surrounding Butler, since "sycophancy is a condition of official favor; small wonder that intellectual freedom and personal courage dwindle, explaining, if not justifying, the jibe of European scholars that there are three sexes in America, men, women, and professors."

For the university to work properly, Spingarn insisted, the president had to represent its condition faithfully to the trustees who were responsible for it. Butler's failure to do so in this case was typical of his entire executive career. Spingarn regretted that he had to announce that

> the word or promise of President Butler is absolutely worthless unless it is recorded in writing, and that even a written document offers no certain safeguard against evasion or distortion. It is to this executive, with this code of honor, that Columbia entrusts all avenues of communication between the subservient Faculties and the governing Trustees.

"The spokesman of materialism" was not obliged to respond, and did not. Spingarn was gone, and Butler had no need to perpetuate the controversy.

Nor did Butler react to Spingarn's second and last public engagement with the issue, a 1914 poem published in *The International*, a journal edited by George Sylvester Viereck. "Harry Thurston Peck" proclaimed Peck's goodness at the expense of the president who had hounded him to his death and the seven hundred Columbia faculty members who stood idly by and said nothing. The thwarted resolution's "slight act of generous pity" had transformed itself in three years into three stanzas of rhymed rage. An excerpt gives the flavor:

This is the man they condemn, this is the man they defile,
But by all the gods of justice, not his the craft and guile!
For another poisoned his honor, and all the rest stood still;
Seven hundred rats obeyed the fox's will;
Another cast him out, another struck him dead,
But never a word of protest the seven hundred said.

Unlike Peck, Spingarn went on to a distinguished career after Columbia as a writer, critic, publisher (he joined Alfred Harcourt and Donald Brace in their new publishing venture as general editor of their European Library), and social activist. Also unlike Peck, he never effected any kind of reconciliation with Butler. There is no evidence, in fact, that he ever spoke to him again. Spingarn died in 1939, a few months before the start of the war. In 1953 a high school in Washington, D.C., was named after him in honor of his contributions to education and the cause of human equality. At the dedication ceremonies, the historian John Hope Franklin called him "one of the century's bitterest enemies of segregation."

CHAPTER TEN

"Mr. Butler's Asylum"

❧

Once Butler helped polish off Teddy Roosevelt's aspirations for the Republican nomination at the Chicago convention in June 1912, he was off to Europe in July to receive honors and preach the gospel of international understanding. In Paris in July to be named a Commander of the Legion of Honor, he talked about the new vision of international unity taking over the world. He announced that he could "confidently predict international peace. It will be accomplished through no panacea but through a higher, truer adherence to the common principles of morality." The high point of his trip was a lunch with Kaiser Wilhelm II in August. Butler had first met him in 1905, when he and his Columbia colleague, Professor John Burgess, had been invited to the castle in Wilhelmshohe, where Butler had been impressed by what he saw as the kaiser's charm and broad learning; his active engagement in political, literary, educational, and scientific issues; and his concern for his people. Butler had dismissed notions that the kaiser was in any way eccentric. On the contrary, he was "the most far-sighted and scholarly ruler in the world."

As purveyor of the international mind and minister without portfolio for world peace, courtesy of the Carnegie Endowment, Butler thought he had no greater ally than the kaiser, and he was not alone in this belief. In June 1913, the twenty-fifth anniversary of his taking the throne, *The New York Times Magazine* devoted a lengthy article to celebrating Kaiser Wilhelm's efforts on behalf of world harmony, featuring brief, laudatory testimony from such as Teddy Roosevelt, William H. Taft, and the Duke of Argyll, among others. Because of his friendship with the kaiser, Butler had been asked in January of that year by Adolph Ochs, publisher of the *Times*, to inform the emperor of what the *Times* was planning and to inquire what photograph or portrait of himself he would like to see reproduced. Butler was delighted to do so. Communicating via Chancellor Bethmann-Hollweg, he emphasized that although the *Times* article had no political significance, the admiration for the kaiser was strong throughout America, the whole country being enthusiastic about honoring his anniversary. Butler's own contribution to the issue outdid the other testimonials in both length and fervor. He praised him as a man of action and a student, judicious in temperament, guided by high ideals, and above all caring profoundly for the "welfare, the happiness, the comfort and the morality of his people." To have ruled over millions of people for twenty-five years, during a time of industrial unrest, territorial expansion, and commercial development, and to have done so without permitting armed conflict abroad or domestic turbulence at home, was an achievement "which rises almost to the heights of the miraculous." Butler concluded, "If the German Emperor had not been born to monarchy, he would have been chosen monarch—or Chief Executive—by popular vote of any modern people among whom his lot might have been cast."

Butler's marketing of the international mind, optimistic prognostications about world peace, and respect for the kaiser were rudely undercut by the outbreak of war on August 14, 1914. Appropriately enough for someone who didn't think a European war was a possibility, Butler found himself in Venice on August 1, the day Germany declared war on Russia. As soon as he realized how rapidly the political situation was deteriorating, he tried to get to Paris as the first step in returning home, only to discover that the French frontier was closed. Along with his wife and daughter, he instead made his way to Milan and then, on August 4, to Genoa, where he learned from the harried American consul that there was nothing the U.S. government was prepared to do to bring stranded travelers back. Butler and three others—Frederick Vanderbilt, the engineer Gano Dunn, and an American shipping official named R. A. Smith—decided to take things into their own hands. If the American government wouldn't help, they would simply obtain a ship themselves to make the voyage to New York. Butler and Smith met with the executives of the Lloyd Sabaudo shipping line, and after complicated negotiations, not in the least hurt by the presence of Vanderbilt in their group, succeeded in chartering the *Principe di Udine* for 500,000 lire (roughly $100,000), financed by credit and personal checks. Butler and his friends then chose which Americans (399 in all) could accompany them, fixing the rates at $250 for first class, $100 for second, and $50 for third, arranged to have two food services for lunch and dinner, and set sail on August 12.

They landed in New York on August 24, culminating what was for Butler a rather jolly adventure. He was proud of the fact that from the time he arrived in Genoa to his departure, he and his family (not counting the credit bestowed on him) had managed to subsist on the twenty-eight cents he had in his pocket. He indicated his delight in this economic feat in the interviews he gave upon his return. Years later, in *Across the Busy Years*, he continued to revel in the achievement, reducing his liquidity in this version to twenty-seven cents. President Butler, it was clear, could handle financial adversity as well as anyone.

Back home, Butler set out to find the silver lining to the "murky clouds of cruel, relentless war," which he evoked for Columbia students at his opening address in the fall, "lit by the lightning flash of great guns and made more terrible by the thunderous booming of cannon." He located that lining in several different places. First, Butler was convinced the war could not last long, as a shortage of food supply would make it impossible for nations to continue with it. Germany, in his view, would be the first to be ravaged by hunger, requiring it to sue for peace. Second, the horrors of war bolstered Butler's argument that strong armies and navies could not guarantee peace. As he had been insisting for years, the only civilized means of resolving international disputes was through judicial arbitration, not force of arms. Most encouraging of all, Butler detected in the terrible chaos of war the seeds of a new world order. The *Times* of October 18 published an interview with Butler accompanied by this unusual editorial note: "In view of the importance that will be attached to anything that Dr. Butler says in regard to the European crisis, the *Times* submitted this interesting interview to him for revision before publication to insure its accuracy." The interviewer, Butler's own personal press agent, Edward Marshall, also announced the significance of what was to follow: in Butler's thoughts "may be found the most important speculative utterance yet to appear in relation to the general European War."

The importance attested to by both the *Times* and Marshall concerned Butler's conviction that from the shambles of a divided Europe would eventually emerge a United States of Europe, modeled after the federal government of the United States. There was nothing radically original in this idea—from the mid-nineteenth century on, many Americans assumed that eventually Europe would see the light and follow the American path to unification—but Butler infused it with a new urgency to make it his own. A federated Europe would understand that one country could not afford to assault another, any more than New York could seek to resolve a dispute with Pennsylvania by invading it. The war thus represented the "birth-throe of a new European order of things." In place of a system based on nationalistic misunderstandings and racial antagonisms, Europe would rebuild itself into a harmony of federated states, with each state, in the interests of its own well-being, willing to give up some portion of its sovereignty in order to bask "in the sun of unity." A world, in short, organized according to the precepts of the "international mind."

Butler, viewing the future positively, carefully stayed away from any judgments about what was currently taking place. Concerned about the terrible destruction, he refused to assign blame, except to stress that the war was made by kings and cabinets, not by the people. He remained strictly neutral both because it was America's own stance and because in his Carnegie work he thought it essential that he not be seen to be favoring one side or another. He was interested only in supporting the rapid transition from the old order of parochial nationalisms to the new world of a flourishing internationalism. For this goal to be reached, the war somehow had to be stopped.

Starting on November 20, 1916, and running through to December 18, the *Times* published sixteen short pseudonymous articles examining how a lasting peace might best be achieved. Their author, a distinguished authority who "would be recognized in both hemispheres," wrote under the pen name "Cosmos." Three days before the appearance of the first article, Butler had told Ochs that he could not think of a suitable nom de plume for his contributions: Did Ochs have any suggestions? Butler understood that the simple attribution "by a special correspondent of the *Times*" could be used, although he realized it might tie the articles too closely to the paper. Whether it was Ochs or Butler or Ochs's editor, Karl Miller, who chose the splendidly resonant Cosmos is unclear, but rarely has a nom de plume more accurately caught the character of its author—his range, his aspiration, his narcissism.

The articles, all written from the perspective of an eventual Allied victory, proposed a formula for peace involving both specific commitments and a general reorientation in the way nations regarded the world order of which they were a part. The former belligerents would have to agree to two fundamental principles: the right of every nation, no matter how small, to its own unhindered development without threat of external interference; and the immunity of private property (not contraband) from seizure at sea, even in time of war. These guarantees, preserving the autonomy of small countries amd permitting all countries to trade without restriction, would establish the political and economic framework necessary for a satisfactory international understanding. The next step in Cosmos's plan required the return to France of Alsace-Lorraine, annexed by Germany in 1871. Germany's willingness to restore this territory to France would be dramatic proof of its intention to work toward an enduring peace. At the same time, Germany had to renounce the Prussian militarism that had for so long characterized its national state of mind in favor of a more liberal, democratic ethos. This was a job for the German people themselves, and though Butler was confident it could be achieved, he offered no practical suggestions as to how.

These steps introduced Cosmos's central prescription for peace: the organizing of the world into a new international order, served by an international court of justice to which all nations would submit their disputes. Once again Butler summoned the American juridical model to the rescue. The court would be invested with the power to issue binding decisions the same way the Supreme Court functioned in the United States. This new structure could only come about if the will of the people insisted on making it happen. "What the world is waiting for," Cosmos argued, "and what it must achieve before the foundations of a durable peace are securely laid is what Nicholas Murray Butler has called the international mind," whose definition Cosmos then proceeded to quote. "Then all dreams of world conquest will fade forever, as well as all schemes to extend Anglo-Saxon, or Latin, or Teutonic, or Slavonic culture over the whole world." Peace, American style, would descend upon all civilized nations. Cosmos called for a third Hague Conference to meet at the end of hostilities to work out the details of the court.

Cosmos was not alone, of course, in thinking about the possibilities of a new world order. Woodrow Wilson, for one, had already been talking about the need for an effective international organization to avoid plunging the world into future cataclysms, talk that culminated in his proposal for the League of Nations. For Americans, the sticking point in these discussions—which succeeded in keeping the United States out of the League—always revolved around the sanctions that might be brought against this country, or the military obligations it might face in enforcing sanctions against other nations. Cosmos understood this resistance and with deft equivocation eased his way around the problem. Although there was to be only one international law, he argued that for the sake of efficiency, the world should be divided up into separate "areas of jurisdiction for the enforcement of international law and for the administration of the international order." Europe was one such area; the Far East, with Japan granted chief responsibility for oversight, the second; and the United States, presiding over its sphere of influence, the third. Cosmos didn't dwell on what would certainly be the terminal political complexities of these arrangements. He was content to have found a model that both integrated America into a world organization and preserved for it the freedom from foreign intrusion it historically claimed for the Western Hemisphere through the Monroe Doctrine.

Cosmos absolved himself from having to address the questions of when and how much force was justified in implementing the judicial decisions of an international court by arguing that military sanctions were finally not the point. The solution could not be found in the employment of an international police force, but rather in educating public opinion: "As a matter of fact, the only practical sanction of international law is the public opinion of the civilized world."

The Cosmos articles revealed the two unquestioned (but highly questionable) assumptions on which Butler's system of international cooperation rested: the moral sagacity and power of the people, and the idea that countries functioned exactly as individuals did. In Butler's political universe, one could always rely on the wisdom of public opinion and on the reality that countries, like individuals, didn't want to be isolated or earn the rebuke of others. The ultimate constraint on the behavior of nations was not the threat of military intervention, but that of moral condemnation. Cosmos concluded his analysis on a hortatory note. A durable peace would finally depend not on political compromise and courts of law, but on

domestic policies of justice and helpfulness, and the curbing of arrogance, greed and privilege, so far as it is within the power of government to do so. It depends upon the exaltation of the idea of justice, not only as between men within a nation, but as between nations themselves; for durable peace is a by-product of justice. When these things are accomplished there will be every prospect of a durable peace because the essential prerequisite will have been provided—the Will to Peace.

The readers of the *Times* comprised an adequate first audience for this blueprint for peace, but now the rest of the world awaited it. Butler moved quickly to remedy the deficiency. J. B. Scott, the Carnegie Endowment's secretary, arranged to have Scribner's publish it as a separate volume, *The Basis of Durable Peace*, written by Cosmos. A month after the last article appeared, Butler was flogging his staff at the Endowment to get foreign translations started: "Perhaps it would be better to arrange without waiting to get the French, Spanish and German editions under way. With regard to the German translation perhaps Prof. Braun and Mrs. Haskell could suggest someone. We want it to be well done and smooth." Getting the book translated was one problem, but getting the translations across an ocean patrolled by German submarines was an even more serious one. Butler, however, was up to the challenge: "I think it is desirable to call up the post office and ask the foreign department about the mails. Perhaps it will be just as well to release the foreign Cosmos books. Distribute them over different ships. Keep a record of each batch that goes out to each ship, then if it goes down you can replace the books lost."

In short order, Butler succeeded in making his personal solution to the war emerge as the public agenda of the Endowment itself. The book's distribution costs were folded into its budget, and Carnegie personnel were put in charge of ordering and shipping. Above all, the Endowment had to maintain a steady flow of books. Extra copies should always be on hand, Butler cautioned. "It is very desirable to send to the leading French and English newspapers for review," he noted on February 21, 1917. Three days later he instructed that

Cosmos is to be distributed as widely as possible. We've got $15,000 additional. I want a sub-budget on Cosmos taking that $15,000 as a basis. We expect to spend more but we want to use up our balances before transferring anything to it. Begin by including everything we have spent already. Then the separate editions, French, English,

Spanish, German. I don't care anything about the postage. We know what it costs, how many distributed in each language. We want 3,000 French, 3,000 Spanish and 3,000 German . . . Put in an order for 10,000. Keep them going.

By the end of March he was considering the possibility of Russian and Japanese translations.

Before Butler's prescriptions could be tested, the United States chose to enter the war to help bring about the defeat of Prussian militarism. On April 6, 1917, the day America renounced its neutrality and joined the war, so did Butler, his previous objectivity instantly replaced by a militant patriotism that defended American participation in what had been solely a European conflict. Butler's eager embrace of the American war effort was simultaneously principled and practical. He did indeed think that German despotism had to be smashed before a new world could develop. At the same time, he knew that his well-known pro-German sympathies, notably his enthusiasm for the kaiser in his 1913 letter to the *Times*, did not enhance his public image. The more outspoken his patriotism, the less likely that people might hold him responsible for his earlier admiration. Purging himself of any imputation that he was reluctant to use force against old friends would also help placate Columbia's conservative trustees, for whom Butler's alleged "pacifism" was not an endearing trait. While silently enduring it, men like Marcellus Hartley Dodge, head of the Remington Arms Company, could not be expected to be happy over Butler's belief in the art of conciliation.

Committing Columbia to the war effort by establishing on campus the Student Army Training Corps (SATC), Butler also committed its faculty to support of the American military involvement. At the June 6 commencement luncheon, in an astonishing speech worked out in advance with the trustees, Butler announced the constraints on freedom of expression and behavior that Columbia now felt justified in imposing on the faculty. Henceforth, any professor (or student) who criticized America's engagement in the war would be found guilty of treason and promptly dismissed from the university. Trustees concerned about the views of some faculty dissidents would no longer have to worry:

What had been tolerated before became intolerable now. What had been wrongheadedness was now sedition. What had been folly was

now treason. In your presence, I speak for the whole University . . .
when I say . . . that there is and will be no place in Columbia University, either on the rolls of its faculties or on the rolls of its students,
for any person who opposes or who counsels opposition to the effective enforcement of the laws of the United States, or who acts, speaks
or writes treason. The separation of any such person from Columbia
University will be as speedy as the discovery of his offense.

The exercise of freedom of speech, in short, previously recognized as fundamental to the university, could now guarantee instant removal from it.
The high crime of treason, with its severe sanctions, would be determined
not through any judicial process, but by pronouncement of the president of
Columbia and its trustees. Anyone they deemed not "with whole heart and
mind and strength committed to fight with us to make the world safe for
democracy" might well be found guilty of it. This official threat would be
Columbia's "last and only word of warning" on the subject.

Butler's speech produced some volatile and unexpected consequences for
Columbia in its vexed relationship with one of its outstanding faculty
members. When H. T. Peck began giving his inflammatory interviews to
the press in the summer of 1910, Butler had said that he could reach only
one conclusion regarding this erratic behavior: Peck had to be acting under
the influence of Butler's inveterate faculty opponent, professor of psychology James McKeen Cattell. Despite statements from Arrowsmith and others that this was not the case, Butler could never be convinced. For him,
such severe assaults on his character and competence had to be coming
with Cattell's encouragement. Butler was wrong about Cattell's involvement—he did not support Peck's behavior—but in Butler's mind, when bad
things were being said about him, Cattell could not be far away.

Butler's suspicions were understandable. Formidably talented and formidably contentious, Cattell was an even more unsettling presidential nightmare than the obstinately principled Spingarn. The problem for Butler was
that Cattell was like him: gifted, firmly committed to the rightness of his
views, reluctant to acknowledge a fault or to renounce a position. If his ability as a research scientist revealed itself gradually over the course of a long,
productive career, his abrasiveness seemed fully developed from the start.

When as an aspiring graduate student he appeared on the verge of being re-fused a fellowship for the second time to the Johns Hopkins program, Cat-tell threatened to sue. He also felt comfortable, during this admissions dispute, informing President Gilman that he thought "a better president of the university could be found than you."

His prickliness, nourished by a not unjustified estimate of his own tal-ents, did not interfere with his professional distinction. Appointed professor of psychology at Columbia in 1891, having previously taught at the Univer-sity of Pennsylvania, he was generally regarded as one of the preeminent experimental psychologists of his day. His honors and accomplishments supported the claim, made by Teachers College professor Edward Thorndike, that he ranked as one of "the twenty leading scientific men in America"— the only psychologist at the time who was a member of the National Acad-emy of Sciences; founder and president of the American Psychological Association; former president of the American Society of Naturalists and the New York Academy of Sciences; editor of four significant professional jour-nals; teacher of a number of America's best younger psychologists; and the man most responsible for the national prestige of Columbia's department.

At the same time, as a self-proclaimed "radical democrat," he was an ar-ticulate, outspoken advocate of faculty control of universities—a position that made a clash with Butler inevitable. His 1913 book, *University Control*, decrying the power that trustees and presidents exercised in university man-agement, could almost be taken as a specific attack on Butler. Celebrating the fruitful anarchy of the medieval university, in which professors and stu-dents ran their institutions without administrative interference from above, Cattell objected to the hierarchical structure of American universities that invested all authority in the president and trustees. He believed passionately that power should legitimately rest with the faculty, to whom the president should be responsible. Degradation and demoralization occurred, accord-ing to Cattell, when the president (with faculty complicity) had been al-lowed to usurp faculty prerogatives. Instead of the ideal "democracy of scholars," running itself freely and openly, the university, for Cattell, had be-come an autocracy, presided over by an individual who answered not to the people over whom he ruled, but to the trustees who chose him. Cattell's suspicions about the men who assumed such power was boundless: "I once incited one of my children to call her doll Mr. President, on the esoteric ground that he would lie in any position in which he was placed."

Butler embodied all the despotic traits Cattell lamented in American university presidents. Two strong spirits vying over every inch of contested academic ground, their relationship could hardly have been congenial. Whether Butler's decisions concerned administrative procedures, professorial salaries, or the membership of the faculties, Cattell consistently took issue with them. The most flagrant instance of Butler's abuse of power, for Cattell, was his 1902 decision ending the separate faculties' practice of electing their own deans, so that he could appoint them himself, a change in the statutes that Cattell thought a gross violation of the principle of democratic governance. It guaranteed his unceasing opposition.

Hostile professors tend not to earn the admiration of trustees, and as Cattell continued to harass Butler over issues large and small, the Columbia board grew restive with their irritating psychologist. By 1911, J. B. Pine concluded, "So long as he remains in the University it is perfectly certain that he will be a source of disturbance." The problem, Pine went on, was that Cattell had so far given no grounds for discharging him. But perhaps, Pine speculated, thinking strategically (if somewhat fiendishly), there might be a way. Noting that Cattell had just submitted a confrontational resolution at a faculty meeting, Pine wondered whether, if the trustees summoned him for an explanation, he could be provoked into creating reasons for his dismissal: "He is at heart such an anarchist that he could hardly fail to betray himself."

Refusing to moderate his obstreperous ways, Cattell at the same time managed to avoid trustee retribution, until the publication of *University Control*. Its subversive nature must have struck the trustees as a public act of disloyalty, its criticism of general administrative practices a disguised attack on Columbia's circumstances and personnel. And it couldn't have helped that at about the same time the book was published, Cattell distributed a letter to all the members of the Century Association (whose membership included trustees, friends of trustees, and Butler himself), rebuking them for rejecting the candidacy of the distinguished scientist Jacques Loeb—the same Jacques Loeb to whom Butler refused to give an honorary degree in 1909, and for the same reason, that he was a Jew.

As the 1912–13 academic year was ending, the trustees determined to endure no more. On May 9 Butler was told to inform Cattell that at the June meeting a resolution would be moved retiring him from active service as of July 1. Cattell was not inclined to take such arbitrary dismissal lightly. He immediately wrote to George Rives, chairman of the trustees, asking that they rescind their projected motion. Butler's letter contained no reasons for retiring him, he said, and given his achievements and national distinction, they could not possibly be for any deficiencies as a teacher, researcher, or university citizen. The only possible grounds could be his opposition to some of Butler's policies, as well as his own recently published book. But surely, Cattell maintained, "the expression of my social and political views is as legitimate as are the political activities of the president."

Cattell listed fourteen points of disagreement with Butler—over professional salaries, the abolition of football, and the transformation of deans from elected representatives to appointed officials, among others—but insisted that he had always urged his own views in an appropriate manner. And if it was the book that had offended Butler and the trustees, "there could be no more coercive argument for its publication."

Cattell was not popular with his colleagues, but they could see that dismissing a professor for no compelling reason did not constitute a precedent in their own best interests. A number of them protested, including the influential dean of the graduate faculties, Frederick Woodbridge. Among the trustees, only Seth Low expressed dissatisfaction with what appeared to be an act of punitive censorship. The Cattell he remembered could indeed be difficult, he acknowledged, but in the long run, the university was threatened less by the difficulty of individual professors than by the public's perception that the faculty "are not free in what they teach, or to criticize the policy of the University." For this reason he urged the trustees not to retire Cattell.

Both the weak grounds and the bad politics led Butler to realize that it would be preferable to live with Cattell than to be implicated in an unpopular effort to get rid of him. Accordingly, he requested that the Education Committee not present its resolution regarding Cattell to the entire board for its action. On May 21 Rives informed Cattell that the trustees had decided not to move on the issue of his retirement. This, however, was not to be the end of the matter. Cattell might have had a genius for irritating the trustees, but their dyspepsia extended to anybody in the university perceived as a troublemaker or who espoused social or political views different from their own. With the outbreak of the Great War, and even before the American entry in 1917, they became especially sensitive to issues of patriotism among the faculty, intent on guaranteeing that the university remained immune from any "un-American" or radical teachings.

The publication of *An Economic Interpretation of the Constitution of the*

United States in 1913 had placed American historian Charles Beard in the forefront of those to be viewed with concern by the Columbia administration. Neither Butler nor the trustees could accept with equanimity the possibility that the Founding Fathers might have allowed their economic self-interest to influence the shaping of the Constitution. Despite his national status, Beard, like Cattell, was someone whose behavior would have to be carefully scrutinized. When it was reported in the newspapers in April 1916 that Beard had endorsed a speaker at a public school forum who allegedly said, "To hell with the flag," trustee alarm was triggered. Beard was immediately told to account for his actions before the Education Committee. (The explanation was simple. He had been speaking at the National Conference of Community Centers, in which he advocated using public schools as venues for discussing public issues. Several weeks before in such a forum, a speaker had apparently uttered the inflammatory words, and on that basis a number of people had urged the practice be stopped. In his address, Beard was simply arguing that the schools had to accommodate these events even if people could use them to express controversial sentiments.)

After satisfying the committee as to what he had said, Beard was about to leave the meeting when two trustees, F. S. Bangs and Frederick Coudert, suddenly initiated a spontaneous grilling of him regarding his political views and his conduct in class. Butler, who was present, did nothing to intervene. At the end of an unpleasant half hour in which Beard was forced to defend the substance of what he taught, he was advised to warn his colleagues of the dangers in promulgating any ideas "likely to inculcate disrespect for American institutions." The faculty was appalled by this inquisition, and treated with derision the warnings dutifully reported to them by Beard. Only the assurance of Dean Woodbridge that such trustee intrusion would never be repeated kept them from making a noisy scene. The trustees, for their part, aware of the brewing public relations disaster, backed down from their implied threat of investigating the faculty's political views and classroom conduct. But they remained on high alert for any new faculty provocation.

Cattell was happy to provide one. The issue seemed trivial enough at the start—Butler's notification to members of the Faculty Club in January 1917 that they would have to vacate their current premises and move to less-desirable ones. But no issue regarding faculty-presidential relations was so trivial that it could not arouse Cattell's principled wrath. He was furious at the cavalier way in which Butler had unilaterally dismissed the men from their club, seemingly indifferent to the club's importance in creating faculty loyalty to the university. For Cattell, it was just another instance of the presidential abuse of power he had criticized in *University Control*. It was not an abuse he could passively accept.

In a confidential memo to the club's resident members, he objected to Butler's actions and suggested, with varying degrees of seriousness and offensiveness, four ways an attractive new club building could be made available at no additional cost to the trustees. The second idea was the least serious and the most offensive: turn the president's house, recently built (in 1912) with general funds that might otherwise have gone to faculty salaries, into a faculty club that would at least return some value to the faculty. And while a $300,000 building was arguably too expensive for a faculty club, it was equally too expensive for a president's house. (Cattell exaggerated the number for dramatic purposes. The cost was closer to $165,000.)

The archness of the attack on trustee and presidential profligacy in spending so much money on the house was bad enough, but Cattell's final point went over the top: "If our many-talented and much-climbing president should be swept into the national vice-presidency by a reactionary wave," he wrote, "it is not likely that his successor will care to live in such a mausoleum. I certainly should not be a candidate for the job under such hard conditions."

Cattell's later characterization of his remark as merely "frivolous" seemed accurate, but the notion of a "much-climbing" president could not be taken as idle good humor by either Butler or his trustees. Still, Cattell might have escaped unscathed had not some member of the Faculty Club released the memo to the press on March 2. Public disclosure of the accusation required a public defense, and on March 3, at the instigation of the acting dean of the graduate faculties and highly respected economist, E. R. Seligman (and almost certainly with Butler's support), a letter signed by twenty-eight Columbia deans and professors objecting to Cattell's comments was sent simultaneously to Cattell and the New York press. Even as he organized the faculty rebuke of Cattell, Seligman urged Butler to take no administrative action against him, recognizing that the principle of academic freedom required that professors be able to express their views without fear of retribution.

But while Butler was considering this plea for moderation, the trustees had already decided to act: Cattell was ordered to appear before the formidable Education Committee on March 5 at 3:45 p.m. (It is difficult to believe that Butler, a member of the committee, knew nothing about this summons, but that always remained his position.) At 2:15 Cattell called Seligman to demand an explanation for what was happening. Seligman disapproved of what Cattell had done, but he was committed to protecting the faculty from summary judgments made without adequate procedural safeguards for their rights. He called Butler at a few minutes before 3:00, arguing that it would be harmful to the university if Cattell had to appear alone before the Education Committee, and reminded Butler of his pledge, made at the time of the Beard incident, that no professor would ever have to answer questions before the trustees without the presence of appropriate faculty representatives.

No answer was forthcoming from Butler, but at 4:45, after waiting outside the trustee meeting room for an hour, Cattell was told he could go home. In honoring the faculty desire to protect their own from star-chamber intimidation by not taking action against Cattell, the trustees instead announced they would conduct a full-scale investigation "into the state of teaching in the University." That afternoon they passed a resolution calling for the formation of a special committee to do just that.

Officially a trustee initiative, the special committee was in fact created at Butler's request; he was intent on enhancing trustee authority without being implicated in doing so. As he wrote several months later to Pine,

> I had a definite purpose in urging the appointment of a special committee of the Trustees last winter and in asking the Committee to hold its early meetings at a time when I was absent from the University. That purpose was to restore in the University the authority of the Trustees as a body which during the past five years had been attacked openly or covertly by many members of the University and which, when not openly attacked, was constantly sneered at . . . I think that for at least a decade to come there will be no more such sneers and sarcasm . . . as was quite too common not so long ago.

The trustees were not oblivious to the dangers of a besieged faculty organizing to defend itself, and they were shrewd enough to recognize that the political risks could be minimized by the tried-and-true method of co-opting the faculty in the review process. On March 15 the trustees told

Seligman that the University Council had been asked to set up a faculty committee to advise the trustees, and a week later the so-called Committee of Nine—five deans and four faculty members, with Seligman as chair—was created.

Seligman welcomed the establishment of the committee, seeing it as potentially useful in negotiating conflicts between faculty and trustees. A loyal Butler admirer—who viewed him, in Cattell's words, "as much beyond criticism and suspicion as Caesar's wife or the Constitution as interpreted by the cleptocratic classes"—Seligman believed it was only the trustees, and not the president, from whom the faculty needed to be protected, and he was pleased when the trustees, in their initial request to the committee, asked it to report on Cattell's behavior. Here indeed was the opportunity to have the faculty take on the disciplining of its own. He decided on a strategy of eliciting a straightforward apology from Cattell, which the trustees would have no choice but to accept, thus in one stroke both ending the issue and legitimizing the mediation powers of his committee. Cattell was reluctant to apologize, but he bowed to Seligman's pleadings and consented to sign a brief written apology (actually drafted by Seligman) to the Committee of Nine, with the strict understanding that the letter would be shown to no one but the trustees, and only then if it was believed that it would help the cause of faculty independence.

On May 14 Seligman sent the trustees a copy of the apology along with his committee's report, asking that no punitive measures be taken against Cattell. When the trustees accepted the recommendation in early June, the incident appeared happily over, with everybody satisfied. And so it would have been if Cattell hadn't then learned that Seligman, in direct contradiction of the terms on which Cattell had consented to sign the apology, had sent it to every member of the Faculty Club. Cattell was outraged at Seligman's perfidy in violating their agreement, turning a politically negotiated private apology into a public declaration of guilt. Seligman's defense that he was instructed to do so by the Committee of Nine did not help matters. It simply demonstrated to Cattell that the committee ostensibly formed to support the faculty was in fact doing the trustees' bidding by humiliating one of them. Cattell's only recourse, as he informed Seligman, was to make clear to the members of the Faculty Club the conditions surrounding his signing of the apology. For this purpose he would send to them several of the explanatory letters he had written to Seligman over the issue.

Now it was Seligman's turn to be angry at Cattell's breach of confidentiality. He didn't need much prodding to turn on him. The consummate university insider, he never liked the abrasive, radical Cattell; it was only in the larger cause of faculty freedom that he had become his advocate. With Cattell's challenge to his integrity, he no longer had to pretend. His transformation into an implacable foe was instantaneous. Cattell's conduct, Seligman wrote to him on June 18, demonstrated "the impossibility of any useful cooperation between you and your colleagues . . . The reason why one after another of your colleagues has fallen away from you is because you have shown that it is impossible for you to respect the ordinary decencies of intercourse among gentlemen." The letter concluded with the dread dismissal formula, "I regret to have to come to the conclusion which is shared by not a few of your colleagues that your usefulness in the University has come to an end." And just to make sure that the trustees understood that the Committee of Nine no longer viewed saving Cattell as a vital free-speech issue, Seligman got seven of the nine to repeat to the Education Committee the same language Seligman had used to Cattell: "It is impossible for Professor Cattell to respect the ordinary decencies of intercourse among gentlemen. We believe that his usefulness in the University is ended."

Nothing now stood in the way of Cattell's likely academic death except the fact that it was summer and no official administrative action could take place until the fall. But Cattell's vulnerability had never succeeded in the past in deterring him from his principled causes, nor did it now. Once Butler had delivered his threat on June 6 against any member of the Columbia faculty seen to be opposing the United States' war effort, it was only a matter of time until Cattell seized the moment to transgress. It took little more than two months; on August 23 he wrote the following letter, on Columbia University stationery, to several members of Congress:

> I trust that you will support a measure against sending conscripts to fight in Europe against their will. The intent of the Constitution and our consistent national policy should not be reversed without the consent of the people. The President and the present Congress were not elected to send conscripts to Europe.

In expressing his views to Congress on a matter pending before it, Cattell was merely exercising the normal rights of democratic citizenship, but the letter was taken to be the very embodiment of the disloyalty that was now prohibited. Representative Julius Kahn, one of its recipients, protested to Butler that the use of Columbia letterhead implicated the university in this scurrilous act: "I do not think that you will approve of the action of this man Cattell in sowing seeds of sedition and treason with the apparent sanction of the Institution of which you are the honored head."

Cattell's enemies—at this point, many of the faculty—rose to the occasion in calling for his ouster. Complaining about the disgrace he had brought to Columbia, various members of the Committee on Instruction of the Faculty of Applied Science implored Butler for immediate relief from Cattell's embarrassing presence, stressing how he had "lessened the power of our work and our influence in this national crisis." It was all welcome cacophony to Butler's ears. Having done nothing except announce Columbia's blameless criteria for treason, he was blessed to witness his arch-irritant engage in what was generally acknowledged as willful violation of them. Decisive action now was required, the quicker the better. "Words without deeds are futile," he wrote to trustee F. S. Bangs in September while still vacationing in Vermont, insisting that Cattell be preemptorily dismissed. "If this is not done, the whole world will laugh and laugh loudly at our pretence of patriotism. My patience is exhausted. I am not disposed to spend any more time in arguing about this matter with anybody, and feel sure that the Trustees will be substantially a unit in taking the same view." Indeed they were. As J. B. Pine crowed to Butler in plotting the trustee response, "We have got the rascal this time and must leave him no loophole."

The earliest the trustees could act would be at their first meeting, on October 1. On September 21 Pine prepared a preliminary report, calling for Cattell's dismissal, indicating that he would also consult with the Committee of Nine to elicit its views. Not surprisingly, the committee voted to notify the trustees that Cattell should be retired. And several days later Butler recommended to the Education Committee the immediate termination of Cattell on grounds of his blatant disregard of the public warning concerning seditious behavior. No mention was made of his other previous offenses. At the October meeting, without any opportunity for Cattell to testify in his own behalf, the trustees endorsed Butler's judgment that Cattell's presence in the university was prejudicial to its welfare. After twenty-six years of distinguished service and vexed interaction, Cattell was gone.

At the same meeting, the trustees also dismissed assistant professor of comparative literature Henry Wadsworth Longfellow Dana, grandson of the author of *Two Years Before the Mast*. Unlike Cattell, Dana carried with him no contested personal history. His transgression was singular and purely political: membership in the People's Council, a radical group that had for some time been questioning the appropriateness of America's involvement in the war. When Dana remained in the organization past Butler's announced June 6 deadline, he automatically triggered its treason sanction. Because he had not otherwise alienated anybody, Butler offered him the less-ignominious option of resigning. He refused, however, and therefore joined Cattell in the ranks of the disloyal, freshly terminated faculty.

As with Peck and Spingarn, little protest followed the firings. Professor of philosophy John Dewey had resigned in September from the Committee of Nine out of disgust for its weakness, but he made no fuss after the expulsion. Other faculty members were too cowed or too disaffected with Cattell to make a public display, and Dana, the young assistant professor, was perhaps too insignificant to merit concern. The one exception was Charles Beard. Although Beard was a strong supporter of the war against Germany, he also supported the right of professors to hold views without fear of administrative retribution. On October 8 he shocked the academic world by resigning his professorship at Columbia. He explained to Butler that he had come to believe that "the University is really under the control of a small and active group of trustees who have no standing in the world of education, who are reactionary and visionless in politics, narrow and medieval in religion." He expressed his astonishment that a small band of trustees could dominate and terrorize a university of Columbia's stature. "I am convinced," he wrote, "that while I remain in the pay of the Trustees of Columbia University I cannot do effectively my humble part in sustaining public opinion in support of the just war on the German Empire."

The consternation in the academic world over Beard's sudden departure from Columbia was not shared by Butler's friends at *The New York Times*. In an editorial that some suggested Butler had drafted, the *Times* exulted in the marvelous gift Beard had bestowed on Columbia by leaving it: "As every man of sound sense and unclouded vision knows . . . Columbia University is better for Professor Beard's resignation." It praised the university for its tolerance in enduring the irresponsibility of its faculty as long as it did. Fortunately, the *Times* concluded, the trustees know that they must ultimately answer to a sane public opinion that will not permit the universities to harbor those purveyors of false doctrines "sheltering themselves behind the shibboleth of academic freedom." It should perhaps be noted that "sane public opinion" had no problem with The New School for Social Research that Beard helped to found after leaving Columbia.

Butler was himself unwilling to acknowledge that Beard's departure spoke to any serious tensions at Columbia between faculty and trustees, nor that the sacred principle of academic freedom had been infringed. As he wrote to his friend Ben Lawrence, "If Columbia University has any fault in the matter of freedom it is that it gives too much freedom rather than too little. In my judgment it is safer to err in this way, if one must err at all, even at the cost of such an episode as has recently taken place."

Although Beard did not deign to respond to the *Times*'s editorial criticism, he felt he needed to clarify the reasons for his resignation. The December 29, 1917, issue of *The New Republic* published his analysis of the institutional conditions that had led to his decision. Unlike his polite resignation letter to Butler, in which he attributed his dissatisfaction at Columbia to the manipulations of the trustees, this account implicated Butler quite directly in what Beard found intolerable.

Beard accused him of sharing the trustees' suspicion of unsettling ideas and their penchant for summary judgments. Their contempt for the faculty, their commitment to driving out professors who were guilty of any semblance of liberal or unconventional thinking on political issues were at the very least unhindered, if not actually aided, by Butler. Despite Butler's insistence that nominations for appointments and promotions always stemmed from the faculty, Beard said that this admirable theory was modified in practice by information coming from the president's office regarding the trustees' views of potential candidates: "Mr. Butler cannot conceive of a scholar's entertaining progressive ideas. Once, in asking me to recommend an instructor to a neighboring college, he distinctly pointed out that a man of 'Bull Moose' proclivities would not be acceptable."

It was not a sense of personal injustice, but the orchestrated demeaning and demoralizing of the faculty that accounted for Beard's resignation. And it was not the trustees alone who were responsible, as Beard's concluding sentences made explicit: "These facts I submit to the candid and impartial reader. I believe that they constitute a full and unanswerable indictment of the prevailing method at Columbia University under the administration of Dr. Nicholas Murray Butler." Although many years later Beard would testify to the greatness of Columbia under Butler, at this time he expressed only pleasure at his escape. Two weeks after his resignation he wrote to Senator Albert Beveridge, "It is certainly a relief to be out of Mr. Butler's asylum."

The expulsions from the asylum of Cattell and Dana—and, in different ways, Peck and Spingarn—were not distinguished moments for academic freedom or for Columbia. And certainly not for Butler. Despite his insistence that harmony reigned, the friction between trustees and faculty at Columbia was real and debilitating. As Dean Woodbridge, a Butler supporter, wrote in the aftermath of the Cattell and Dana firings, "The source of our trouble is that the Trustees and the Faculties in their zeal for what they believe to be the good of the place are working at cross purposes and are failing to understand and sympathize with one another." True, Butler didn't create this antagonism, but he also didn't use his considerable influence to lessen it. In every case he sided with trustee authority against the expression of individual faculty opinion. His rhetoric honored the importance of freedom, but his actions opted for suppression and elimination of the troublesome.

And not only on the faculty. Several students were dismissed for various infractions in 1917 as well, most notably Morrie Ryskind, who would go on to write Animal Crackers and A Night at the Opera for the Marx Brothers, among his many screenplays, and who shared the 1932 Pulitzer Prize for drama with the Gershwin brothers for the musical Of Thee I Sing. A senior in the School of Journalism, Ryskind was the editor of The Jester, Columbia's humor magazine. After Columbia had refused one of Leo Tolstoy's sons permission to address a student group because of his supposed radical views, Ryskind published an editorial criticizing Butler for his willingness to make sure unpopular ideas were not presented on campus. He suggested the formation of a club of "The UnAmerican Members of the Columbia Faculty," among whom he listed as the first charter member "Czar Nicholas Murray Butler."

Butler was not amused, judging Ryskind to be guilty of "the conscious commission of a flagrant ungentlemanly or vulgar act" deemed worthy of dismissal from the university. Lest there be any doubt as to what Butler thought the sentence should be, he explained in a letter to Talcott Williams, director of the Journalism School,

The mode of dismissal, should dismissal be pointed to as a result of the inquiry, is by formal letter addressed to the offending student. A copy of such letter should be sent to his parent or guardian and one to the Registrar of the University, who will arrange for the refunding of such payments as the student may have made in advance on account of the work of the present Spring Session, or that portion of it which remains after his dismissal.

As only six weeks remained before Ryskind's graduation when Williams expelled him, the refund, if any, would have been quite small.

Expelling the unruly and the disrespectful, Butler himself was expelled from the discussions of 1917–18 that led to the building of the Columbia-Presbyterian Medical Center at Broadway and 168th Street. Since early in the century, Butler and his trustees had been attracted by the idea of a great medical center in New York, bringing together the clinical facilities of a hospital with the teaching and research capacities of a medical school. After negotiations with several other hospitals had failed, Columbia settled on an arrangement with Presbyterian Hospital in 1911 in which, among other kinds of cooperative endeavors, Columbia's medical school—the College of Physicians and Surgeons—would have access to the hospital's wards in order to train its medical students. As the specific details of the affiliation agreement were being worked out, both Columbia and Presbyterian informally agreed to the long-term goal of finding a site in which the two could form a single modern complex offering unrivaled resources for the care of patients, the training of doctors, and the support of medical research.

Among the interested parties involved in the talks, the single figure perhaps most eager to create the center was the man prepared to fund a substantial portion of it: the philanthropist Edward Harkness, who had joined the hospital's board precisely because of his commitment to establishing such a facility. Under his leadership, the decision was reached in the spring of 1915 to locate it in Washington Heights, on land formerly occupied by the New York Highlanders baseball team before they moved east to the Bronx and became the New York Yankees. The option on the property required that a down payment of $725,000 be made by September 16, a sum—as it was understood by Presbyterian officials—to be split between Presbyterian and Columbia. When Harkness informed Columbia on August 20 that Presbyterian had raised its half, Butler had bad news: Columbia didn't have its part. Harkness was irritated at Butler's failure, but he managed to extend the option until November 20. On November 18 Butler announced that he expected a large gift that very day, and hospital and university negotiators drew up concrete plans for allocating the land and apportioning costs. The next day, Butler revealed that he hadn't gotten the gift and that Columbia did not have the funds to continue the project or even to help with the cost of extending the option.

The failure to honor Columbia's financial commitment was shocking but can be explained in several ways. First, it was not easy to raise money, and Butler, despite his reputation, was not that good at it. Moreover, he was reluctant to put funds needed for current operating costs and priorities into a project that would require years to complete. But probably most important was Butler's strategic bet that if he delayed and admitted to problems in finding donors, Harkness, or the Carnegie Foundation, which was also interested in medical education, might just pick up Columbia's piece. Neither did, however, and the talks stalled.

Desultory conversations between Columbia and the hospital over the next year produced no new initiatives. In late January 1917 John D. Rockefeller, Jr., whose General Education Board was thinking about the educational possibilities of a large medical center, had suggested to Harkness that he engage Abraham Flexner to study the problem and recommend ways to enhance the training of physicians in New York. Author of an influential 1910 report on medical education in the United States and Canada, Flexner was the unquestioned world authority on the subject, a man whose acknowledged expertise invested his personal judgments with the weight of law. There was no one better qualified to examine the Columbia-Presbyterian relationship—or designed to enrage Butler more. For Flexner was every bit as formidable as Butler—aggressive, outspoken, unyielding, and confident he had all the answers. In 1908 he had written a scathing criticism of the American college, faulting it for its incoherent course of study, its lack of pedagogic seriousness and focus, its willingness to sacrifice all responsibility for liberal learning in the interests of furthering the narrow specialization of graduate instruction. It was not a book calculated to please university presidents like Butler, and the *Educational Review* dismissed it as naive and ignorant. The attack on Butler's educational turf was bad enough. Worse, however, this autodidact, who possessed only a B.A. degree, knew more about medical schools, their organization, curricula, and shortcomings than did Dr. Butler, who actually presided over one of them. And worse yet, the Flexner whose findings Butler would have to take seriously was a Jew.

Butler's dislike of Flexner was matched by Flexner's contempt for him. Flexner judged him to be "'a Tammany politician,' who lacked both ideas and common sense," as well as "the vainest human being in existence." Nevertheless, as Flexner worked throughout the summer and fall of 1917 on his report, Butler grudgingly supplied him with the information and data he needed. In November, Flexner finished his report, which recommended that the hospital and Columbia's medical school be rebuilt on a single site and that Presbyterian function as a university hospital. To achieve this smooth amalgamation, Flexner made specific recommendations, the most important of which were that the medical school be limited to four hundred students; that its faculty move onto full-time academic salaries, turning over all fees from private patients to the university; that the medical school sever its teaching relationships with other hospitals and focus exclusively on Presbyterian; and that the power of faculty appointments not be totally in the hands of the medical school.

The Presbyterian board of managers welcomed Flexner's report, and as Butler showed no dissatisfaction with its main points, discussions continued between the two sides. Then suddenly, in April 1918, Butler wrote to President John Sloane of Presbyterian objecting to the report and emphasizing that Columbia had not yet decided on an appropriate site and had no funds for the move. He suggested that Presbyterian make its own plans without counting on Columbia's participation. Sloane was astonished, for he had plausibly assumed, in the absence of any negative response, Columbia's endorsement of the Flexner memorandum. On May 2 Butler told Sloane that he could not accept the mandated enrollment limit of four hundred students, the forced resignation of the dean and all current members of the medical faculty, the required termination of teaching relationships with hospitals other than Presbyterian, and the demand that medical faculty relinquish to the university the private fees for their services. His conclusion left little hope that Columbia would ever consider a union with the hospital:

We deem all four of these proposals so reactionary and so antagonistic to the best interests of the public, of medical education, and of Columbia University, that they will not, under any circumstances, be approved by us. Were the Trustees to assent to the suggestion that, as a condition precedent to receiving a large sum of money they would invite or require the resignation of the entire medical faculty, they would thereby inflict a blow upon Columbia University from which it might not recover for a generation.

The absolutism in Butler's rejection of Flexner's suggestions, and even his distortions of them—Flexner had not, for example, ever hinted at the resignations of the medical dean and faculty—can only be seen as a product not of a deliberate negotiating strategy, but of an intensely emotional reaction to personal pique and frustration. Instead of viewing Flexner's positions as the starting points in a discussion, as they were intended to be, he treated them as fiats challenging his authority. Butler must have found it intolerable to be told by an outsider how to run his institution—the first time such a thing had happened. And not just any outsider, of course, but a contentious, irritating one whose experience with matters of medical education could trump Butler's own and whose connections with the Rockefeller and Carnegie foundations made it difficult to dismiss him. Butler realized that Flexner held all the cards—a situation that had to provoke him.

The Presbyterian response was swift, passing a resolution calling for the cancellation of the 1911 affiliation agreement. But Harkness and other hospital trustees were not prepared to give up their hopes for a modern medical center so easily. Instead, they demanded at a meeting with Columbia's representatives that Butler be replaced in the negotiations. Harkness then made the same point with Columbia's trustees: progress toward the medical center could not take place if Butler was involved in the ongoing talks. Committed more to the project than to the feelings of their aggrieved president, the trustees agreed to remove Butler from Columbia's three-person subcommittee, substituting instead trustee Frederick Coykendall.

With Butler gone, the talks immediately resumed in a constructive way; ten years later the Columbia-Presbyterian Medical Center opened. On October 12, 1928, Butler spoke at the center's formal dedication, which he characterized as "this most notable happening in the life of the University, the State, and the Nation." Awarding honorary degrees to the four men who contributed most to the building of the Medical Center, including Edward Harkness, Butler did not mention the significant contribution that his own absence from the deliberations made to its completion.

Meanwhile, Butler continued to pursue his personal war on Germany vigorously throughout 1917–18. At a Columbia summer school convocation on July 12, 1917, he defended American involvement in a "war against war; a war against the instruments of war; a war against the apparatus of war." It was not only, in President Wilson's words, a war to make the world safe for democracy, it was for President Butler "a war to make democracy safe for the world." Failure to persevere in this effort, he declared at the Commercial Club of San Francisco in August, would require this nation to "prepare to arm itself for 100 years, as upon arms alone will depend our very existence." He reserved some of his most inflammatory language for those—such as Wisconsin senator Robert LaFollette—who opposed America's joining the Allies. LaFollette's progressive views had always plagued Butler, particularly when he supported Roosevelt against Taft in 1912, but now they had become unendurable. In September, before three thousand New Jersey bankers, Butler called for LaFollette's expulsion from the Senate:

> What are they thinking about, those honorable, patriotic men, to sit there and be contaminated by having Robert M. LaFollette breathe the same air with them? Have we no courage? Are we so mealy-mouthed that we are afraid to make trouble with an object like that?
>
> Gentlemen, you might just as well put poison into the food of every boy that goes to his transport as to permit this man to make war upon the nation in the halls of Congress.

After enrolling Columbia in the Allies' cause, Butler next signed up the Carnegie Endowment. Its aims of international peace could only be achieved, he insisted, through the successful implementation of war. In November 1917 Butler got the Endowment to adopt unanimously the resolution that "the most effectual means of promoting durable international peace is to prosecute the war against the imperial German government to final victory for democracy." This was not the kind of resolution Butler had in mind when he first became the director of the Division of Intercourse and Education.

The end of the war in 1918 left Butler and his division in a peculiar position. Having taken on the job of educating people to rid the world of war, Butler had not only witnessed it breaking out but had finally found himself endorsing it as the means to peace. And now, before he could see his own elaborate program for peace acted upon, the fighting had stopped. He had failed both to prevent the war from starting and to help bring about its conclusion. Unlike the "scientific" work of the other two Carnegie divisions, whose research into the causes and consequences of the war and the issues connected to the development of international law was arguably more urgent than ever, it wasn't immediately evident how Butler should deploy the Carnegie resources at his disposal.

To maintain his division's educational mission, of course, was an obvious priority. The world was ostensibly at peace, but the best guarantee that it would stay that way was to continue to market the virtues of the international mind. Before the war, Butler had begun the process of trying to get people to think internationally by establishing International Relations Clubs in schools and universities across the United States and by creating "International Mind" alcoves in libraries everywhere. Stocked with books sent by the Carnegie Endowment dealing with international issues from different perspectives and in different languages, these alcoves permitted venturesome readers to trade in their national parochialisms for a wider worldview. Peace now made it possible for the Endowment to move ahead with a European expansion of these programs, and Butler enthusiastically reported on their growth.

But neither discussion groups nor library alcoves could be considered the kind of substantial undertaking that Carnegie had envisioned when he devoted $10 million to the Endowment. Something more visible, more dramatic was needed. After protracted discussion, Butler and the other Carnegie trustees decided to concentrate on raising money for reconstruction work, particularly in countries that had suffered most from the war. Determining what countries and which specific projects was left to Butler. He decided, after consulting with his friend Baron d'Estournelles de Constant, that Belgium, France, and Serbia should be the objects of the Endowment's efforts and that the focus should be on the restoration of two libraries badly damaged in the fighting—at the University of Louvain and the University of Belgrade—and on building a new municipal library in Rheims.

What was the connection between these activities and the Endowment's mission to rid the world of war? It is not clear that Butler understood, but he did see the opportunity to exhibit the kind of concerned internationalism he had advocated for so long. No vivid example of the international mind at work could be found than the willingness of the American people, in league with the Endowment, to respond to the suffering of their European neighbors. American fund-raising for European restoration demonstrated both the proper conception of how a country should act in an interdependent world and the moral authority Butler declared America had been prepared to assume in such a world. But equally important was the favorable publicity Butler could anticipate for the Endowment and for himself.

Of the three, Louvain was Butler's favorite—and for reasons that had little to do with the effects of a rebuilt library on Louvain or world peace. "It is a sentimental proposition," he stated at an Endowment meeting in October 1918, "to restore Louvain University which was the first institution to be ravaged by the Germans. It is an international affair started by the government of Belgium. It ought to make a good article." He exhorted his staff in November:

Get all the publicity you can. Take it to one of the syndicates, E.J. Edwards, or Marshall if he is home. You ought to get a very good syndicate article written for the Sunday papers, get it as a descriptive article with one or two pictures, Louvain as it was, Louvain destroyed, etc. Marshall would be a good man. Get it into all the papers some Sunday.

Butler also committed ten thousand pounds to aid in repairing London's Westminster Abbey, a building he esteemed as "the most notable structure associated with the history of the English speaking peoples." In addition, the Endowment asked the French government to identify a commune that needed rebuilding and whose population needed help. The commune of Fargniers was recommended, and the Endowment participated in providing it with funds to build schools, homes for those of modest means, and government buildings.

In *Across the Busy Years*, Butler wrote,

These interesting and highly important acts of reconstruction were hailed throughout Europe as an evidence of generous interest and sympathy of the American people with those of their fellows in other nations who might be suffering or in want. They led to a new and most affectionate attitude towards the United States, which has fortunately lasted until this day.

Whatever one makes of this claim, it is true that the Carnegie building agenda was a personal triumph for Butler, earning him the gratitude of foreign nations and burnishing his international status as an important cultural leader. In July 1921 he laid the cornerstone at Louvain in the company of the king, queen, and crown prince; the president of the French Republic; assorted cardinals and diplomats; and the French war heroes Marshals Joffre, Foch, and Petain. A mural depicting Butler and the others at this ceremony, later included in the grand hall of the new library, conferred permanent recognition upon his act of generosity.

CHAPTER ELEVEN

At Home—and Away

❦

When Butler left for Europe after the tumultuous Republican convention of June 1912, he was living in the comfortable three-bedroom house at 119 East 30th Street, which he had purchased in 1895. When he returned in the fall, he moved into a grand home that he had convinced the trustees he would require to lead Columbia on its world-civilizing mission. Built to Butler's specifications across the street from the campus on 116th Street, 60 Morningside Drive was a castle, of sorts: an elegant four-story brick and Indiana limestone building designed by McKim, Mead and White at a cost of $165,000 ($3.1 million in today's dollars). With its sweeping central staircase, high ceilings, oak wainscoting, luxurious formal rooms, leaded windows, personal elevator, and staff of nine, it served as a visible symbol of Butler's majestic aspirations for himself and Columbia, both a private home and a public space. A visiting professor from Europe commented that evenings there reminded him of "a formal reception at the court of some minor German royalty."

From the beginning, Butler actively involved himself in the plans for the house, commenting on decorative and architectural details and urging the trustees to keep pushing the builders forward so that it might be ready by the fall of 1912. He delighted in the prospect of how he would be able to treat his guests. The second-floor music room was, he told Pine, "exactly such a room as they have in the best English houses and in half a dozen of the best New York houses where entertaining is properly done." And he was pleased that McKim, Mead and White had modified the design to include "a dining-room that is big enough for a reasonable sized dinner, and a library that is not too petite." Butler's enthusiasm for its opulent possibilities caused Pine some concern. He cautioned Butler that if the house was in part meant to allow him to mingle informally with his faculty, its grandiosity might make a professor "who finds it difficult to pay for a $1500 flat" feel out of place. Pine was all for warmth and comfort but alarmed lest the craving for "impersonal magnificence" produce a setting that would alienate the struggling faculty from their august president:

> When you really think of it, and imagine how it will look, does it seem to you that marble corridors, and marble stairs and white and gold French salons afford an appropriate and congenial setting for the members of our Faculty, or of any Faculty? Cannot you recall rooms and halls at Oxford or Cambridge which were far more attractive and far more suitable, which helped to create the sort of social atmosphere which you desire?

Butler finally acknowledged this point, and if the finished building was not exactly the English "manor house" Pine would have preferred, at least it wasn't the "Italian Palazzo" he deplored.

Once the Butlers found their social rhythm, 60 Morningside became, in the words of Alva Johnston, Butler's *New Yorker* profilist, a "clearing house of celebrities." Butler teas, receptions, and dinner parties soon became the most sought after of high cultural invitations, proof that the privileged recipients had arrived in New York society. Well before New York's *Journal American* declared it so in 1942, it had been the case that the Butlers were recognized as

> New York City's official host and hostess to the foremost celebrities visiting Manhattan Isle. Truth to tell, matters have reached the point where if you're an overseas notable, are in New York and aren't entertained by the Butlers—you just don't rate. Only the creme-de-creme [sic] of the metropolitan social world ever find "bids" to Butler prandial events on their breakfast trays.

Butler himself once estimated that between 2,500 and 3,000 people came to the presidential house for receptions, lunches, and dinners every year.

Butler dinners were never casual events. Formal dress and strict rules prevailed. Young faculty, lucky or unlucky enough to be invited, found the evenings exhausting, their wives traumatized in worrying about the quality of their gowns and the appropriateness of wearing arm-length white gloves. Guests arrived promptly at 7:30 p.m. A seating chart was shown to them upon entering, so that when dinner was announced at 8:00 and it was time to form the line to move across the hall from the library to the dining room, each man knew which woman he was to escort and where they were to sit. People chatted in the library and drank sherry, never hard liquor, during the half hour before dinner. George Ford, the university's Catholic chaplain for many years, reported that Butler normally had a Scotch and soda at his place at the head of the table, and though wine was served to all the guests, no one was invited to have a highball. Smoking was prohibited during the meal.

Butler always led the way to the dining room. For dinners of thirty—the largest number that could comfortably be accommodated—the guests, once seated, were served by six butlers. Ellen McGrath, who came to work as Mrs. Butler's parlor maid in 1939, said that women were not permitted to work in the dining room until the early 1940s. The service was impeccable—"just about as perfect as any service could be," emphasized Ford—but the five-course dinners tended to proceed crisply. The historian Allan Nevins remembered that "plates were changed with such rapidity that slow eaters found their food snatched away," as Mrs. Butler was eager to finish by nine so the servants could be sent home. Butler, of course, dominated the dinner with his conversation and anecdotes, generally rising before its end to make a brief speech extolling the merits of the company. The dinner over, the women repaired upstairs to the drawing room for their coffee, the men to the library for cigars and brandy. Shortly before 10:00, Butler conducted the men upstairs to join the women—the signal that the evening was over. He said goodbye to everyone at the top of the stairs, never descending to the ground floor to see them out. Butler formality, it should be added, was not limited to the entertainment of others. On the occasions of the Butlers' eating alone, they dressed formally for dinner. And even at the very end of their lives, in 1947, when his wife was too sick to come downstairs and join him, Butler still ate his solitary dinner in his tuxedo, after which he took his coffee and brandy alone in the library.

Presiding with icy efficiency over the presidential dinner parties was

Kate La Montagne Butler, who set the rules (the prohibitions about smoking and liquor were hers) and attended to the details. Kate, whom Butler had married in 1907, was in many ways the anti-type of his first wife, Susanna, the warm, gentle, supportive woman whom everybody loved. Warmth could not be included among Kate's attributes. Born in 1865 on Staten Island, one of the six children of Annie Davis—whose father, Thomas E. Davis, was a prominent New York businessman—and Auguste La Montagne, a Frenchman involved in the liquor trade (a "champagne salesman," scoffed Mary Brown, Butler's niece), Kate had spent her early life in France, returning to New York after the death of her father, in 1894. Butler met her in the summer of 1906 while vacationing in Newport, Rhode Island. Kate was forty-one, a handsome, socially ambitious, no-nonsense woman whose fantasies, it is safe to say, did not include meeting a husband—no less one who was president of Columbia University—on a Rhode Island beach. Butler's arrival in her life must have come as something of a miracle. No one quite understood why Butler married her—Jacques Barzun called their relationship "utterly undetectable"—though she seemed to satisfy his need for a proper companion to grace his public life and a woman to give Sarah maternal care. Butler's letters to his friends and family announcing his engagement stressed this latter point.

The two were married on March 5, 1907, in the home of Kate's sister and brother-in-law, Mr. and Mrs. Francis Key Pendleton. Because Kate was Catholic, special dispensation had to be obtained to have the ceremony performed by a priest during Lent.

Butler's judgment of what Kate could bring to the marriage satisfied at least half of his expectations: she proved a flawless household organizer and professionally skilled party giver, discharging to perfection her responsibilities as presidential wife and official university hostess. Personally, however, she was abrasive, aloof, humorless, and controlling, disliked by most of Butler's friends and abhorred by his family. The family's view was understandable, since Kate from the start resented all Butlers, including her twelve-year-old stepdaughter, Sarah. She saw the Butlers, particularly her sisters-in-law Eliza and Mary, who had lived with Butler and taken care of Sarah after her mother's death in 1903, as threats to her relationship with Murray. "From the word go she made life with his family very, very difficult for Uncle Murray," Mary Brown commented. Dean Virginia Gildersleeve of Barnard, a great admirer of Butler's and a good friend of Eliza's, recalled the harrowing comment Kate made to her new husband at the start of their marriage: "'Before I can help you to be a really great man . . . I must amputate you from the Butlers.'" In practical terms, the amputation meant that once the president, Kate, and Sarah moved into 60 Morningside Drive, no other Butler family members were allowed to call or come to the house. Family appointments with him could be made only through Butler's Low Library office. Mary Butler objected to this appalling arrangement and challenged her brother about why he endured it. He begged her not to make life complicated for him, explaining that his wife "makes me very comfortable."

The comfort Kate apparently provided was more physical and social than psychological. The perfect, attractive companion in Butler's public life, she was privately, according to Gildersleeve, "a jealous, hysterical tyrant," endlessly haranguing him about the need to stay away from his family. When the Butlers weren't entertaining, the major right Kate granted her husband at home was the right to remain silent. Lindsay Rogers of the Political Science Department, a good friend of Butler's who once planned to write a biography of him, acknowledged that Butler "was a very henpecked man" who could never confront Kate on any issue, especially any issue related to his family. This was true even when it came to his own daughter, whom he adored. Once Sarah had married (in 1933) and was officially out of the house, she was no more free to enter 60 Morningside Drive than were her aunts. Rogers described an incident in which Sarah, knowing Kate was in church one Sunday, came to visit her father. Told by one of the staff that Sarah had arrived, Butler came downstairs, tears streaming from his eyes: "Sarah, you shouldn't have come here: Mama will find out about it and not like it." Rogers was struck by Kate's total intimidation of her husband and his inability even to lie to her:

> [She] determined the number of times that he would see the daughter, and where. He never had gumption enough to say to his wife, "Well, now, I'll be downtown all afternoon at some meeting," and have his daughter come to the Waldorf for tea with him. I don't think the daughter ever spent a night in 60 Morningside Drive after she was married.

Fortunately, Kate didn't have to worry too much about surreptitious visits, because in 1933 Sarah married an Englishman, Neville Lawrence, and until her early death, in 1947, lived in Woking, outside of London. But Kate's hostility never flagged, even though an ocean separated father and daughter. From the time Sarah moved to England, Butler wrote regularly to her—long, personal letters apparently quite different in content and tone from those in his immense correspondence with political and public figures, letters that might have given us the same sort of access to Butler's private self as those to Alice Haven did, written half a century earlier. But when Sarah died, the distraught Neville destroyed many of her possessions, including the letters from her father. And after Butler's death, Kate made sure no record existed of the correspondence by throwing away copies of the letters he had written to Sarah as well as those he had received from her.

It would have been nice to have Kate's view of things, but she made sure this was not available. A manila envelope in the Columbiana archives contains her diary—with all of its pages torn out. And Ellen McGrath recalls that after Kate's death, her lawyer, Tom Christie, asked Ellen to witness the burning of a packet of letters bound, according to her, with a pink ribbon— the love letters Kate and Butler had exchanged prior to their marriage. Christie explained that he was following Kate's instructions in destroying them.

Kate's austere presence turned Butler's castle into something of a prison, with Kate as stern warden and Butler as cowed inmate. Rogers thought the high-handed, autocratic manner of Butler's public persona was a refuge from the debilitating constraints Kate imposed on the private Butler at home: "He'd get away from 60 Morningside Drive, where he'd have to say, 'Yes, yes, Kate; I'll do that, Kate,' and he gets out into the university world, or the world downtown, and he just has to express himself." The theory seems a bit strained—Butler, after all, met Kate when he was forty-four, with his drive for recognition and power already in full throttle—but if she can't properly be held accountable for his behavior when he was away from her, it was certainly the case that she dominated him when they were together.

Whatever pain he felt at Kate's interfering with his family, Butler did not allow it to threaten the marriage. Sarah told Rogers's wife that she didn't think her father ever considered leaving Kate. In the long run, comfort and companionship won out over sensitivity to feelings. Cozy family gatherings were not to be, but even Rogers admitted that Kate "ran an excellent establishment, and she really worked to earn part of the salary that Columbia

University paid him." Much of the work was devoted to supervising the nine staff—cook, butler, kitchen man, waitress, parlor maid, lady's maid, chambermaid, laundress, and houseman—Columbia employed to help her run it properly. Her general managerial competence must have reminded Murray of the way another strong woman, his mother, had directed affairs on Hamilton Avenue in Paterson while he was growing up—perhaps another reason for his willingness to endure Kate's control with so little complaint.

Despite his protestations to the trustees that 60 Morningside was necessary for his work, Butler required its grandeur to satisfy his own needs. Few people loved the trappings of power more. In the conviction, for example, that people who lived in castles shouldn't be expected to enter them unattended, he insisted that household staff be available to open the door for him whenever he returned home: it was a matter of aristocratic principle not to be required to use his key.

Butler might have been pathetically beholden to Kate for her capacities to look after him, but he was himself a master at it. He even managed to find medical sanction for taking care of himself as carefully—and lavishly—as he did. In the fall of 1903, when Sarah was suffering from some minor childhood illness, Dr. Nathan Oppenheim was called to treat her. After examining Sarah, he turned his attention to Butler, concerned that he looked somewhat fatigued. He asked Butler what time he arose in the morning, when he got to work, how many days of the week he went to the office. Alarmed at the answers he received, he suggested that Butler was working much too hard, and he laid down a strict regimen of self-cosseting that Butler was to follow all the rest of his life. He instructed him not to get up before 8:30 in the morning, and then to proceed very gradually through a leisurely breakfast, reading the newspaper and perhaps taking a brief walk, being sure not to get to the office earlier than 10:15 or 10:30. Butler could then work as hard as he wanted, with or without lunch, as long as he stopped at 5:00, went home, undressed, and went to bed for an hour. Such a system, Oppenheim explained, meant "going up to your work by an inclined plane and coming down from it by an inclined plane, instead of getting up and hitting it in the face, or jumping from work to dinner."

Even more important than the moderated daily routine was the need to take time away from the office. Administrators should understand, Oppenheim cautioned, that since they can do twelve months' work in less time, they should never devote all twelve to it. He insisted that Butler take two days off each week (besides Sunday), recommending that on Wednesdays and Saturdays he play golf or "otherwise divert your mind and nervous system, and get the advantage which that rest will bring." At least two months' summer vacation and two or three weeks' holiday in midwinter completed the Oppenheim prescription for healthy living.

Except for the afternoon nap, which his schedule couldn't always include, Butler tried to adhere scrupulously to Oppenheim's advice, modifying it only by adding a third (and occasionally a fourth) month to the summer and a fourth week to the winter break. He spent his summers traveling through Europe with Kate (and often with Sarah) on Carnegie Endowment business and then retreating to their cottage in Southampton, Long Island. Carnegie business was underwritten by a Carnegie expense account, a resource Butler felt comfortable using to the fullest. The Butlers stayed only in suites at the best hotels—for twenty-five years the Berkeley in London, for example, until the noise drove them to Claridge's. And always, when booking his "usual" suites in these hotels, Butler requested a "convenient room for Mrs. Butler's maid," a requirement that also had to be filled on the Cunard ships taking them across the ocean. Butler was not about to ask Kate to dress herself without help when she was abroad.

When Butler wasn't on holiday, he worked with prodigious efficiency in attending to the interests of the three major institutions he ran: Columbia University, the Carnegie Endowment's Division of Intercourse and Education (and later the Endowment itself), and Dr. Butler. He organized his day to manage all three. After slowly ascending the inclined plane to activity in 60 Morningside through bath, breakfast, and newspaper reading, he would go downstairs for his personal and political dictation to three or four waiting stenographers. He next went around the corner to the Endowment's 117th Street office, where he spent an hour or so handling his international business with a different batch of harried stenographers. He generally arrived at Low Library by 11:00 a.m., reaching his office in a private wood-paneled elevator. Nothing was scheduled for him until 12:00, so he could devote the first hour to answering his Columbia mail. From noon on, Butler toiled in his office, went to meetings, kept appointments, pondered Columbia's problems, and unleashed a new torrent of words to yet more stenographers as he produced the stupefying number of speeches he delivered every year before every kind of commercial, political, and academic audience. If Butler had done nothing else than write, the twenty volumes of addresses (in addition to the many hundreds not republished in book form) would have earned him a lasting place in the pantheon of this country's most prolific authors.

Good or bad, whether "miasmas of guff" or the best American prose since Benjamin Franklin, Butler's addresses were always his own. He wrote them without benefit of speechwriter or public relations office or helpful professor (except for those in Latin). The method was dictation, delivered while Butler paced about his office, hands clasped behind him, speaking in well-constructed paragraphs. Sometimes he spoke without benefit of text— but never without preparation. If there was no written copy, Butler would insist on being left alone for a half hour before his appearance so he could think through what he wanted to say, and the talks he produced under these circumstances tended to be as smoothly put together as those he read. On such occasions, when no text was available beforehand, his staff would hire the Master Reporting Company to send a stenotype operator to take down the talk as he gave it and then present it to Butler for his editing. It normally needed only minor changes before Butler made it available for public distribution.

Butler also did his own research. He liked to boast that he used the library more than any other professor, and he may have been right. When preparing an address, he would send for books—according to his secretary Frank Fackenthal, sometimes by the hundreds—to browse through for relevant material. Marking the passages he wanted, he would gather his ideas—the process might take a week or a month—until they achieved a satisfactory coherence. Then the stenographer was summoned to receive, in one sitting—or walking—the completed text. The books were promptly returned to the library and a new batch ordered for the next address. Without an official research assistant, he did have access to two extraordinarily competent university librarians who were devoted to him. Isadore Mudge worked as a Columbia reference librarian from 1911 until 1942. When she retired, Constance Winchell, who had come to Columbia as a reference assistant in 1925, replaced her as the head of the reference division. Butler depended on them to supply bibliographical data, check dates and spellings, and track down elusive facts.

The immense range of the subjects Butler wrote about required an endless supply of information that he did not have time to get for himself—

hence the inexhaustible requests for help flowing from Low Library over the years to the unflappable Mudge and Winchell. "Could Miss Winchell possibly find for the President the full text of a clever bit of verse written for the purpose of making it easy to learn the names of the English sovereigns in their historical order?" "Can Miss Winchell tell the President how the phrase 'perfidious Albion' originated?" "For Miss Mudge: The President wants very much to have the name of the river in Syria which flows into the Mediterranean at its northeast corner at the town of Alexandria." "Why is the Archbishop of York the Primate of England and the Archbishop of Canterbury the Primate of *all* England?" "Description of the streets and buildings of Nineveh and Babylon (in comparison with the Empire State Building)." "How old was the Princess Victoria, daughter of the Kaiser, in 1905?" "Can you give me the reference to Abraham Lincoln's criticism of the Mexican War, which he made either in debate or otherwise while a member of the House of Representatives when that war broke out?" "Was Mr. Buckle's first name George?" However obscure the query, Mudge and Winchell would find the answer, and Butler was quick to admit that his work would not have been possible without them.

Like many men of his generation, Butler found welcome relief from the rigors of his domestic life in the comfort of private clubs. Butler flourished in a variety of educational, political, and cultural settings, but he was never happier than when enjoying the selected male companionship of his clubs. They offered far more than simple escape from Kate. As Max Weber and others noted about American society in the first half of the twentieth century, membership in the right clubs indicated one's standing in the best upper-class circles. Like battle ribbons for military officers, club affiliations defined a man's theater of social operations. Prestige was afforded by quantity as well as quality. One good club was fine, but a half dozen were even better.

Butler's list of memberships in officially sanctioned clubs, compiled for his 1947 *Who's Who* entry, made clear his status in the eastern social establishment: the Union Club, the Century Association, the Metropolitan, the University, and the Lotos, of which he was president from 1923 to 1934, all in New York City; the National Golf Club, the Links Golf Club, the Garden City and Englewood golf clubs, the Bohemian Club of San Francisco, the University Club of Washington, D.C., the Atheneum and Reform clubs of London, and the American Club of Paris. With the exception perhaps of the Knickerbocker and the Brook in New York, a pretty complete coverage of what sociologist E. Digby Baltzell called the "strongholds of our traditional and Anglo-Saxon metropolitan upper class."

Luxuriating in their leather-chaired elegance, Butler found in these exclusive clubs the pleasures that well-to-do men have always enjoyed in them: the support of affluent male company; the reassurance that they matter; a shared sense of power conferred by the distinction of individual members; the illusion of a social coherence immune from the unsettling forces of change occurring outside club walls. But in addition to these generic comforts, the club ethos encouraged Butler to reveal features of himself otherwise obscured by the demands of the austere, even pompous self he cultivated for public display. The clubby Butler was more relaxed than he would ever permit himself to be when on display as university president or Carnegie Endowment head. Just as the banker Winthrop Aldrich commented that in order to preserve his forbidding image, he never smiled south of Canal Street, so Butler might have safely said that he never smiled north of Fifty-seventh Street, home of the Lotos. But his humor, irreverence, and sense of the absurd were readily apparent to his companions in the sacred precincts of the club. The comment of Frank Fackenthal, who worked closely with him as university secretary and provost for more than thirty years, that Butler "didn't have a well-developed sense of humor," demonstrated his success in maintaining strict barriers between public and private selves.

Butler's commitment to club life embraced two different kinds of affiliation: the official "old-money" New York establishments housed in their impressive buildings and cited in his *Who's Who* entry; and special groups, created by Butler and his friends without benefit of clubhouses, dues, or written constitutions, that met at regularly scheduled times throughout the year. And while membership in the former was obviously critical to Butler's sense of his own cultural standing, it was really the latter (with one major exception) that he cherished. The Gin Mill Club, the Occasional Thinkers Club, the Round Table, the Little Mothers, the Conversation Club, and the Philosophers supplied Butler with structured opportunities to practice what he did best and most enjoyed: talk. The Saturday before Christmas was reserved for the annual Gin Mill luncheon; the first Friday of each month between November and May witnessed the Round Table dinner; and the Occasional Thinkers met every Saturday for lunch (except, of course, the Saturday before Christmas) from November to May, when golf was not in season. Thomas Bender's comment—that conversation as the traditional medium of intellectual life has now been almost entirely displaced in the modern world by the reliance on the printed word—suggests a way of understanding Butler's uniqueness. However sophisticated a business executive he claimed to be, using his up-to-date management skills to run a large corporation, he was temperamentally at home in a context that esteemed the old-fashioned glories of good conversation.

Suspending the Occasional Thinkers Saturday lunches during the golfing season was no sacrifice for Butler; far from a trivial entertainment, golf was a passion for him, "not a game," as he said, "but a career." Playing for the first time in 1900 on a primitive course in Rye, New Hampshire, he had rapidly become addicted to the sport, religiously going at it twice a week (Wednesday afternoons and all day Saturday), weather permitting, during the school year, and every day except Sunday while vacationing in Southampton. Striding around a golf course with his pals was for Butler the outdoor, perambulating version of the satisfactions available within his clubs: good friends, good conversation, and a physical space offering at least a temporary escape from the turmoil of the outer world. His enthusiasm for the game was of the sort he normally reserved for the American corporation or Columbia University: "Golf has changed the psychology of the American man of affairs more profoundly than anything else in the last fifty years . . . It is the best exercise ever invented for middle age."

In 1998 Graef Crystal, an executive compensation expert, compared the published golf handicaps of CEOs of leading corporations with his own data on the performance of their companies. He found a direct correlation between company success and low handicaps; the best-performing companies, in other words, were led by the best golfers. Crystal didn't attempt any glib explanations but merely documented a correlation that he argued could not be due to chance. Whatever the reason—perhaps the capacity to concentrate in an intense way—it is interesting in light of Butler and Columbia. Where Butler's handicap of twenty-two would place him vis-à-vis his presidential peers is unknown, but it is safe to say that it would probably be low enough, in Crystal's theory, to make sense of Columbia's success. Certainly it would be hard to imagine him losing at his favorite game of three-ball match with Eliot of Harvard or Harper of Chicago.

In addition to his twice-weekly games while Columbia was in session,

Butler went every March (when he wasn't on a cruise) to the Hotel Bon Air in Augusta, Georgia, for a month of golfing and conversation among the regulars—men, he notes in *Across the Busy Years*, who were frequently "of exceptional importance in Washington." Here the metaphoric connection between golf life and club life occurred in the creation of "the Little Mothers," an assemblage of the important golfers such as Warren Harding, Senators Eugene Hale of Maine, Gilbert Hitchcock of Nebraska, Frank Brandegee of Connecticut, and assorted governors who met every night at 10:00 in one of the hotel's lower rooms to discuss the critical issues of the day. The Little Mothers earned their name from a woman who joked that when the group came together, it was with the intention of rocking the cradle of the universe. After fifteen years of happy rocking, they met an unwanted end when Prohibition eliminated the liquid refreshment that had always been deemed essential to the evening's success. But the group shortly resurfaced, with a somewhat different set of Bon Air golfers, as the Conversation Club, which avoided the constraints of Prohibition by meeting in the morning, after breakfast but before golf. This, too, lasted some fifteen years.

The smallest and arguably most precious to Butler of his personal clubs was the Gin Mill Club, established on May 24, 1878. On that day— according to the chronicle of the club composed in Biblicalese by Butler's good friend and club member Bob Annin—two Columbia law students, Billy Forbes and Moses Pyne, went off to lunch and "both went together into a cave which is in the street of the Beaver, wherein were many steins and kegs, and when the spigot was turned there came forth beer . . . And they called that place 'Dirty Dutch' for the sake of him who kept it, and because it was so." Forbes and Pyne soon became friendly with two other law students, Francis Speir, Jr., and J. B. Pine:

Full oft they met,—in Dirty Dutch at first
To lunch together, and to slake their thirst:
Not common food their want, so much as beer
And that good company which makes good cheer.

Dirty Dutch in time was succeeded by the Silver Grill, and when that was destroyed by fire, they finally "came unto Beilby's, which is in Stone Street near the Lane to the Mill, and there they gathered together in a corner; and there they tarried many days. Wherefore, they are called the Gin Mill Club."

It is not known when Butler became a Gin Miller, nor precisely when the Saturday before Christmas lunch became the club's defining ritual celebration. The first mention of Butler is at the 1892 lunch, but given his Columbia friendship with Pine, it is likely that he joined in the mid-1880s, after he had returned from Europe and begun teaching. The group remained small, rarely including at any one event more than twelve or thirteen celebrants. In addition to the four founding fathers, the regular membership, such as it was, comprised Butler; the Annin brothers from Princeton; Andrew F. West, who had a distinguished career as dean of Princeton's graduate school; the zoologist Henry Fairfield Osborn; a Columbia professor of classics, Edward Delavan Perry; the historian William M. Sloane; the writer Rollin Lynde; and businessman William T. Innes.

Over the forty-nine years of the club's existence, the locations changed— the Downtown Association, the Century, and finally the Lotos—but the strict observance of the Saturday Christmas ritual did not. The group sang, joked, told stories, read poems, performed skits, ate, drank, and engaged in all the pleasures of high-spirited fellowship. Records were kept of every lunch, detailing all the witticisms and irreverence. They would have been a useful trove of material for any biographer if they hadn't been deliberately destroyed at the insistence of Andrew West.

The story of their destruction reveals Butler in a surprising light. By 1925, with the original four members dead and various other regulars too frail to be counted on, Butler and Bob Annin began to question how long the tradition could be continued. Realizing in early December as they approached the 1925 lunch that they had only six of the old crowd coming, Annin suggested someone he might invite and urged Butler to think of others worthy of inclusion: "If you have anyone in mind that would fit in as an eighth man, I am frank to say I would be greatly pleased. I am not one of those who would let this meeting dwindle year by year until only two should meet. That would be too dismal. I think eight is better than six." Butler and Annin managed to find two more to attend, but it was evident that time was running out for the Gin Millers. By November 1926, as the two began to consider the possibilities of another lunch, Butler could no longer maintain the fiction that the Saturday Christmas lunch was still a viable enterprise. Reluctantly, a month later, he asked Annin to draft the letter announcing the club's demise.

Given his usual instinct to suppress the purely personal, it is curious that on the very day he determined it was useless to go on, he began lobbying Annin to produce a record of the past: "It seems to me," he told Annin, "that the G.M.C. is of sufficient social and general interest to warrant a little sketch by way of a small review of its composition and happy days." Annin did not respond, but several years later Butler returned to the theme, wondering "what had become of all the records and papers . . . Surely they ought to be brought together and deposited somewhere with an introduction and explanation written by you, in order that those who come after us may get some little notion of what the G.M.C. was all about." Annin's argument against preserving them tantalizingly points to the kind of material they contained. They should be destroyed, Annin maintained, because of their personal nature:

> More of it would be quite unintelligible except to the G.M.C. members; and those parts which might have a pseudo-historical significance are too intimate to be opened to the outside world . . . I hate to think of destroying it but there can be no bad mistake made in *not* preserving it . . . The most interesting stuff to outsiders would be the ragging of N.M.B. when he came into his Kingdom of Columbia and the stuff about the West-Wilson fight; which are at least undignified in spots, and which no one could appreciate who was not of the crowd. Bill Forbes [*sic*] passion for laxatives and Mo's crack at sundry Princeton Trustees, were and are good for the crowd but for no one else . . .

Butler took his battle directly to West, urging him to recognize the papers' unique value: "Think what we would give to have something of that kind out of the life of ancient Greece or Rome, or even out of eighteenth century England. To destroy such a record is like the capital punishment of a man whose guilt is in doubt. Once done, it can never be undone."

Butler's insistence as to the historical significance of the records was unavailing. West, like Annin, was resolute. The papers had to be destroyed for three reasons: "The contributions to the G.M.C. were intimate confidences among close friends. They were not meant for publication—at least not without the members' consent. Moreover, many of them are satirical comments of persons, most of whom are now dead and gone." His sentence: death by burning.

The Round Table Dining Club, which occupied Butler's first Friday evenings of the months from November to May (except for the March interlude in Augusta), had an even more ancient lineage than the Gin Mill Club. It was established in the winter of 1867–68 by seven friends whose leader was the crusading liberal editor of *The Nation*, E. L. Godkin. All were committed free traders, a cause for which, as one member later quipped, many people were ready to dine. Unlike Gin Mill Club, it had one fixed home—the Knickerbocker Club—and a rather more solemn goal of serious conversation, as opposed to the the Gin Millers' varied jocularities. Brander Matthews, whom Butler persuaded to write a privately printed brief history of the club, described it as "an amorphous entity, a freak of nature, since its structure is apparently no more organic than that of a jellyfish. It has no constitution and no by-laws. It has no elected officers. It has no waiting list and no limit to its membership. It demands no initiation fee. It issues no year book and it owns no club-house."

Elected in 1902, Butler delighted in the companionship and conversation of its "oddly distinguished membership" for more than forty years. According to Matthews, by 1926 that membership had included

> 2 Presidents of the United States, 2 Secretaries of State, 1/2 dozen Assistant Secretaries of State, 2 Attorneys General, 1 Secretary of War and 1 Secretary of the Navy, 5 American envoys to foreign nations, 2 Senators, 2 members of the peace commission in 1918, 2 Bishops, Directors of the New York Public Library, Metropolitan Museum of Art, American Academy of Rome and the Smithsonian Institute, 1 admiral, 4 generals.

Always assiduous when it came to documenting his personal associations, Butler updated Matthews's list in a piece he wrote for *Scribner's Magazine* in 1935 to mention one ambassador from a foreign nation; eight, not five, American envoys; one member of the Permanent Court of International Justice; one justice of the Supreme Court; one judge of the Second Circuit Court of Appeals; three presidents of Princeton and one of Yale (Butler modestly omitting one from Columbia); three editors; three astronomers; two geologists; half a dozen bankers; and many executives of great corporations. Twenty Round Table members, Butler also pointed out, had been chosen for the American Academy of Arts and Letters, and five were elected to the National Academy of Science.

Members, generally no more than two dozen, were permitted to bring a guest with them, on the assumption that he—and of course there were only he's—would be interesting enough to merit the honor of attending, with the single stipulation that guest and host were not to sit together. The presence of outside celebrities added luster to the dinners, and Butler noted in 1935 that some of the famous guests included President Masaryk of Czechoslovakia, H. G. Wells, and the British novelist John Buchan, then governor-general of Canada.

The combination of prominent members attracting yet more prominent guests to dinner made the evenings extravagantly appealing to Butler: "Perhaps the nearest approach to the Round Table is the sort of conversations which Greville describes as having taken place at Holland House when that was the social center of Whig Society in England, and when Sidney Smith and Macaulay were frequent visitors." All the more gratifying, it seemed that regardless of the eminence in attendance at any single dinner, the one irreplaceable presence was his own. Henry S. Pritchett, president of the Carnegie Foundation for the Advancement of Teaching at the time, spoke for the group when he explained to him in 1933 about a dinner Butler had to miss: "The Round Table—ten present—had its regular session tonight, and I was officially designated to inform you that under no circumstances will the Round Table consent to your absence again any time in the next ten years. The Round Table, sans Butler, is not itself. You are requested to take notice. Tom Lamont brought Lord Lothian and he and Norman Thomas did their best and mighty interesting they were, but no excuse for your absence will be accepted in the future."

The Round Table's admiration for Butler was as nothing compared with the reverence in which he was held by the Occasional Thinkers. Honored, as we have seen, in verse and song, the Sage of Morningside, or more informally just "The Sage," as he was generally known, basked in the permanent affection shown him by his Occasional Thinker friends. "Leader of Educators and Educator of Leaders, and our Sage and Beloved Friend" reads the invitation from the Thinkers for a lunch honoring his eightieth birthday:

Caesar had his Brutus
Charles the First his Cromwell
The Occasional Thinkers
The SAGE.

The origins of the Occasional Thinkers went back to the moment Butler first met, in 1900 or 1901, the charming, energetic California banker William H. Crocker. The young banker and the young soon to be university president immediately took to each other, launching an affectionate relationship that would end only with Crocker's death, in 1937. A group of friends gradually developed around the two and by 1910 or so had formed themselves into the "William H. Crocker Amusement and Exploration Co., Ltd." whose announced purpose, according to Butler, "was to induce Mr. Crocker, whose home was in California, to come to New York as often as possible, to see to it that he was entertained at luncheon, at dinner and at golf with practically uninterrupted continuity, and to plan excursions of one kind or another to different parts of the United States." The core group consisted of the same Henry Pritchett of the Round Table, Jerome Landfield and Joseph Redding of San Francisco, and Butler's old friend Carl "Ole Olson" Ahlstrom of New York. Butler termed Alanson Weeks of San Francisco their "medical and spiritual advisor." Meeting as often as they could for lunch, they also began, over time, to expand the company's membership to include Boris Bakhmeteff, the Russian ambassador to the United States from Kerensky's provisional government, who stayed on in the United States and became a professor at Columbia; editor and correspondent George B. Baker; Newcomb Carlton, president of Western Union; Charles D. Hilles, chairman of the Republican National Committee; the lawyer and diplomat James R. Sheffield; Martin Egan, an international journalist and financier; and New York governor Alfred E. Smith.

Eventually the lunches became a regular feature of Saturdays in New York—except, of course, when golf was in season. Sometime in the early 1920s the Amusement and Exploration Company transformed itself into the Occasional Thinkers Club. No documentary evidence exists as to the origins of the new name, though we do have one—possibly apocryphal—explanation. Discussing the length of the original title, the six charter members agreed that they should look for something shorter and more apt, since amusing Crocker had ceased to be their mission. Butler felt it should be grandly pretentious, and he made some appropriately elaborate suggestions. Redding favored something facetious and offered several examples. Crocker said nothing, and when asked what he thought, "replied that he didn't want to think unless he had to," adding, "'Most of us don't think much, anyway. Most of the time we just *think* we think.'" This was all Butler needed. He quickly popped up with the "Occasional Thinkers Club," which the group applauded and affirmed.

True or not, the story points up the significant differences between the Occasional Thinkers' slightly rowdy and exuberant proceedings and the more responsible, sober dinners of the Round Table. Butler was completely at home in both. Each offered, from his perspective, a version of "the best traditions of conversation in our American social life." Butler admired the "perpetually juvenile spirit and temper" of the Occasional Thinkers as much as he praised the seriousness of the Round Table. If Macaulay might have had problems with a club whose motto was "Thank God, we never lived to grow up!" and whose Hymn to Action, sung at the start of every lunch, was "Don't let the old jokes die," Butler had none. Under the proper conditions, he could allow his residual juvenile instincts to work their way to the surface through the stuffy maturity he normally displayed to the outside world.

For someone who took his elitism as seriously as Butler did, election to the American Academy of Arts and Letters was an absolute necessity. By no means a social club, the academy made up the most prestigious core (50 members) of the larger (250 members) National Institute of Arts and Letters, whose self-appointed mission was to advance the country's art, music, and literature. The Institute was created in 1898 out of the American Social Science Association. Its original members, anointed by a committee of the Social Science Association as America's finest artists, composers, and writers, included Henry Adams, William and Henry James, William Dean Howells, Augustus Saint-Gaudens, Edward MacDowell, and Mark Twain. In 1904 it was decided that for fund-raising purposes, as well as to supply additional recognition for which the already accomplished Institute members might strive, a subset of the *most* accomplished members should be culled, hence the American Academy. In 1909 Butler was elected to the Institute under the category of writer. He ascended to the elite fifty of the Academy in 1911, becoming its president in 1928.

Butler had little in common with the artists he met through the Institute and Academy. Although making Butler president revealed the Academy's desire to achieve the kind of cultural centrality its previous president, Professor William Milligan Sloane could not manage, it was a little like appointing a blind man head judge in a beauty contest. Painting and music played no part in Butler's life; his taste in fiction ran to the sentimental effusions of Charlotte Yonge, and the poem he most esteemed was John

Greenleaf Whittier's maudlin "In School-Days." Establishing as goals of the Academy the need "to set standards, to defend ideals," the ideals and standards Butler defended were largely those espoused by the poet Robert Underwood Johnson, the highly reactionary man of letters and former ambassador to Italy who served for thirty-two years as the Academy's influential permanent secretary. (Johnson's literary rigidities matched perfectly his behavioral peculiarities. When he was elected secretary of the Academy in 1905, he informed himself by letter of the honor, to which he dutifully replied in writing, accepting with pleasure his appointment.)

Inspired by Johnson's distrust of the modern, Butler joined him in a kind of geriatric rearguard battle (Johnson was nine years older than Butler) against permitting new trends in art, literature, and music to infect the Institute. After one Institute meeting, the writer Stephen Vincent Benét noted in his diary, "Stuffed imbecile R.U. Johnson & other incompetent old men try as usual to elect mediocrities and suppress ability." It was a struggle they were destined to lose, but they resisted gallantly. Johnson warned the conductor Walter Damrosch in 1934 of the "impending degradation of the Institute," lamenting the quality of the members newly admitted and currently being considered. In addition to the recent nomination of the Nobel Prize–winning novelist Sinclair Lewis, whom Johnson detested most of all, he complained that "[Carl] Sandburg, a wretched poet, and [Archibald] MacLeish a flash poet are already members and the Committee now proposes [Theodore] Dreiser, who avows there is nothing in life but sex . . . [H. L.] Mencken the mocking and flippant poseur, [Ernest] Hemingway, lacking in taste and distinction . . . Truly we are headed for Gertrude Stein, thought worthy of consideration by the Yale Review."

Butler was distressed when he and Johnson failed to keep Sinclair Lewis out of the Academy (he was elected in 1935), but at least he could take some satisfaction in having overturned the unanimous decision by the Pulitzer Prize jury to award its 1921 prize for fiction to Lewis's *Main Street*. Butler found Lewis's scathing depiction of American life deeply offensive, and he led the Pulitzer Advisory Council, of which he was chairman, to reject the jury's selection in favor of Edith Wharton's *Age of Innocence*. He couldn't do it twice, however, and when the 1925 jury chose *Arrowsmith* for its prize that year, the Advisory Council said nothing, though this time Lewis said something by refusing the award. Butler intervened again on behalf of American values in 1934, when he led the council to nullify the jury's selection of Maxwell Anderson's *Mary of Scotland* as the prizewinning drama, preferring instead Sidney Kingsley's *Men in White*. The issue, according to Walter Winchell, had nothing to do with the quality of the two works—Anderson's was clearly the superior—but with the council's insistence that an American subject matter be honored.

Out of his intellectual depth in rendering aesthetic and critical judgments, Butler felt very much at home as head of an institution with a nationally important cultural agenda, understanding how adding the arts to his portfolio of education, American politics, and international peace contributed to his luster. Until the loss of a silly argument forced him to resign, in 1941, he enjoyed his tenure—however inappropriate in some ways it was—at the Academy's stately building on Broadway and 155th Street.

But nothing could compare with the joy of participating in what Herbert Hoover called "the Greatest Men's Party on Earth": the two-week summer encampment run every year in a northern California redwood grove by the Bohemian Club of San Francisco. Begun in 1872 as a club for journalists, artists, writers, and actors—those for whom the term "bohemian" was a fitting label—it soon had to admit decidedly non-bohemian businessmen with the resources to pay the bills. Gradually it developed into what is arguably the most powerful private association of men in America. Most of its members were—and are—ordinary (but generally wealthy, always highly successful, and mostly conservative and Republican) businessmen, professors, scientists, and authors, but over the years the club has been defined by such high-profile celebrities as Teddy Roosevelt, Hoover, Eisenhower, Nixon, Ford, Reagan, George Herbert Bush, Walter Cronkite, William Randolph Hearst, Laurence and David Rockefeller, Tom Watson, Bob Hope, Joseph Coors, Henry Ford II, Henry Kissinger, Bill Buckley, and George Schultz, to name a few of the illustrious, if not altogether bohemian Bohemians.

It is not the club itself so much as the extraordinary summer camping experience that has been irresistible to the American political, financial, and industrial Establishment. Like its original membership, the club's camping origins were inauspicious, beginning with a simple picnic in Marin County for a departing member. But the idea of a summer outing took instant root, and a year later food and other supplies were carted sixty-five miles north of San Francisco to a redwood grove on the south side of the Russian River for the Grove's first camping event. By 1925, when the last of the 2,800 acres of lush redwood forest had been purchased, the Bohemian Grove had been catering to the physical needs and male-bonding fantasies of its upper-crust members for more than forty years.

Early in its history the encampment was invested with rituals that persist to this day. The most important of these is the Cremation of Care ceremony, first performed in 1880. Originally enacted on the camp's last weekend, the logic of its message decreed that it be moved back to the camp's opening night. For if dull care is to be cremated to allow the members the fullest happiness in one another's company, it makes sense that it be cremated at the start of the experience and not at the end, when everybody is about to reenter the workaday world. The ritual remains today essentially as it was in 1880. As the members sit about in the open-air dining hall after dinner, a funeral procession comes into view, led by men wearing robes and pointed red hoods. They are carrying an open coffin containing the body of Care, a wooden skeleton wrapped in black muslin. The diners, some presumably still carrying cigars and brandy snifters, fall into the procession and march together with the pallbearers and hooded priests to the side of a small lake, where priests and Care move off to the right, the followers to the left, around the lake, to a good vantage point from which to view the ceremony.

After welcoming the audience and urging them to "shake off your sorrows with the city's dust and scatter to the winds the cares of life," along with other exhortations concerning the healing powers of nature, the head priest makes ready to set Care alight. It is then borne aloft and brought to a funeral pyre in front of the Owl Shrine, symbol of the camp. Just as Care is on the verge of being destroyed, a floodlight suddenly illuminates a dead tree, and the hideous voice of Care shrieks out:

> Fools! Fools! Fools! When will ye learn that me ye cannot slay? Year after year ye burn me in this Grove, lifting your puny shouts of triumph to the stars. But when again ye turn your feet toward the marketplace, am I not waiting for you as of old? Fools! Fools! To dream ye conquer Care!

The priest retaliates that he will indeed burn it, but before he can act, Care, shouting that he will spit upon the fire, extinguishes the flames held by the eighteen torchbearers. It looks bad now for the priest and for all the campers, but there still remains the power of the Owl, repository of wisdom and the Grove's presiding spirit. The priest, accordingly, falls to his knees and beseeches the Owl for its guidance. The Owl points out that Care cannot be defeated with fire from the outside world, but only with the flame from the Lamp of Fellowship—which fortunately is at hand on the Altar of Bohemia. Understanding now what he must do, the priest takes an extinguished torch from one of the torchbearers and lights it from the Lamp of Fellowship. He then ignites the funeral pyre. As the flames roar upward and the music from the band grows louder, the chorus rejoices in their victory: "Hail, Fellowship. Begone Dull Care! Midsummer sets us free!" With that, fireworks light up the sky, and the band strikes up, "There'll Be a Hot Time in the Old Town Tonight." Liberated by the will of the priest and the wisdom of the Owl from the burdens of Care, the men celebrate their freedom by singing, hugging, and dancing.

The incineration ceremony dramatically enacts the meaning of the club's motto, taken from A *Midsummer Night's Dream*, "Weaving spiders, Come Not Here"—a warning that the anxieties of work are not welcome in the Grove. The shedding of adult responsibility to recover the boy lurking within the bosom of even the most haggard businessman is what the Grove is about. A 1922 Grove announcement put it clearly:

> We are grown men now, but to most of us it seems as if we have done little more than progress from one schoolroom to another. And we have found to our dismay that the big school of life isn't very different from the little grammar school we knew when we were eight. But each year, in the hard procession of our days, there comes, thank God, to us Bohemians, a recess time—it is upon us. Come out Bohemians. Come out and play.

Answering this call, the Bohemians come forth for two weeks in late July to enjoy the emancipating pleasures of outdoor living. Musical performances and various formal and informal addresses by guests and members occur during the retreat. Good humor and high spirits are the only behavioral restraints imposed upon those present, with one minor exception. As might be expected in an all-male gathering in the woods, where men are encouraged to be boys, phallic activity of various kinds becomes a source of conversation and humor, with much attention paid to the activity of urinating in the redwoods. As Hampton Sides has noted, "Tacked to a redwood tree near the dining area is an admonition to campers: GENTLEMEN! PLEASE NO PEEPEE HERE." Sides suggests that perhaps the fullest expression of Bohemia's fascination with the phallic is a version of William Blake's "The Tyger," written by a member whose prostate condition kept him from the Grove in the summer of 1982:

Prostate, Prostate, burning bright
Up there where the plumbing's tight
What in hell persuaded thee
To plug the pipe through which I pee?
In what ocean, on what land
Grew the tissues of this gland?
What dread ailment fed increase
That caused my fluid flows to cease?

The Grove consists of individual campsites ranging from cabins with attractive furnishings and amenities to primitive structures that presume no elegance. When Joe Redding told Butler in 1918 that the tents where they had previously stayed had been improved with hot water, Butler confessed, "It disturbs me somewhat, as it will probably not cause Will Crocker to emit the same kind of morning noise which the cold water shower always induces." The different camps, generally housing between ten and thirty men, bear names like Woof, Shoestring, Toyland, Silverado Squatters, Rattler's Camp, Cave Man, and Monkey Block Camp and are known for particular artistic, musical, or gastronomic talents. The Jungle Camp specializes in mint juleps. Owl's Nest, where Ronald Reagan was a member, offers a gin fizz breakfast. Perhaps the most famous culinary speciality is the Bulls' Balls Lunch at Poison Oak, with freshly castrated testicles supplied each summer by a California cattle rancher.

Butler's camp was the Land of Happiness, founded sometime around 1904–05 by Joseph Redding, a successful lawyer who was also an accomplished piano player, composer, and librettist. Every year the Grove presents, for one night only, an original musical play written and performed by Grove members. The Land of Happiness took its name from the title of the 1917 play—*Fay Yen Fa or the Land of Happiness*—for which Redding wrote the music.

Brought to the camp as one of Crocker's guests, Butler loved everything about the Bohemian Grove—its good-natured juvenility expressing itself within a context of tradition and ritual, the male bonding with men of the right sort, the natural beauty of the redwoods. For him, the Cremation of

Care was "one of the most solemn and inspiring ceremonies of which I know"; and the Grove play (or High Jinks) on the last weekend "invariably a stirring and inspiring performance." Altogether, he thought it no exaggeration "to say that not since Ancient Greece has there ever been such whole-souled and truly human devotion, on the part of a large group drawn from every walk in life, to all that is best in that life, including human relationships, letters and the fine arts, as is to be found each midsummer at the Bohemian Grove." Put more succinctly in a 1941 letter to Jerome Landfield, thanking him for a copy of the previous year's Grove play, Butler wrote, "Bohemia means everything to me."

The affection was mutual. The general rule that in any association of equally prominent men to which he belonged, Butler was considered more equal than the others applied at the Bohemian Grove as it did elsewhere. That status was confirmed in 1918, when the Grove's directors elected him an "honorary member," the highest category of membership reserved for only ten or so "renowned and world distinguished" men, such as the composer Pietro Mascagni, Luther Burbank, Teddy Roosevelt, and W. H. Taft.

The close friends at the Land of Happiness camp—Butler, Ahlstrom, Landfield, Pritchett, and Redding—gradually blended into the founding directors of the William H. Crocker Amusement and Exploration Co., Ltd., which in turn, as we have seen, evolved into the Occasional Thinkers Club. The group also managed an additional allotropic transformation into what the stationery of the Amusement and Exploration Co. listed as its eastern branch—the Lotos Club in New York.

First occupying an elegant building on West Fifty-seventh Street, later on East Sixty-sixth Street, the Lotos Club was established in 1870. Like Butler's other official clubs, it attracted an appropriately elite membership who enjoyed one another in predictably comfortable sitting rooms and over dependably good dinners. In this the Lotos was no different from Butler's other club affiliations. What distinguished it from the Union or the Century was not only its practice of giving dinners for celebrity guests, people such as Mayor Jimmy Walker, British prime minister Lloyd George, General Pershing, and songwriter George M. Cohan, for example, but the identification Butler forged between it and the Bohemian Grove. At a dinner held in his honor when he was elected president in 1923 (he had originally joined the Lotos in 1915), Butler elaborated on the powerful meanings he found in the metaphor of Bohemia. After explaining that Abraham Lincoln achieved his immortality by embracing the true spirit of Bohemia, he continued:

[It] is the place for a wise man to pitch his tent. Not in the market place, not in the theatre, not in the forum but here in Bohemia under the Lotos where it is always afternoon, and where there is time to loaf and invite the soul, where there is opportunity for man to meet man in spirit and in truth, for the affections to express themselves, for sentiment to come forth from its hiding places and for letters, music and the arts, the drama, and that greatest of all fine arts, conversation, to flourish among intelligent and right-minded men. That, my friends, would be my definition of Bohemia.

Butler's belief in the human and artistic values Bohemia came to embody for him actually led him to write the verses for a song, fittingly enough entitled "Lotos Land," which was faithfully sung by Lotos members before every dinner:

O, Come with me to Lotos-land,
Where care takes wings
And Fancy brings
Her treasures rich and rare
Of art and song and story—
O, Come with me to Lotos-land!

O, Come with me to Lotos-land,
Where fellowship
And friendly grip
Give cheer to brighten life
And banish dismal strife—
O, Come with me to Lotos-land!

O, Come with me to Lotos-land,
Our hearts all greatly grieve
When spiders come to weave.
Bohemia's call
Unites us all.
O, Come with me to Lotos-land!

Butler's enthusiasm for the Bohemian ideal of friendship and the rich inner life, unsullied by the base concerns of everyday living, could lead him to some absurd rhetorical excesses. At the 1923 dinner for former British prime minister Lloyd George, surrounded by the club's socially exclusive membership, Butler invoked the humble ideal of Bohemia, open to all on the basis of inherent merit alone. Butler's failure to sense the incompatibility between his classless ideal and the audience to whom he was professing it produced an unintentionally humorous moment. Having just explained how rank and station meant nothing in Bohemia, he ingeniously contrived to emphasize both as he welcomed Lloyd George "not as a former President of the Board of Trade and a cabinet minister . . . not as a Chancellor of the Exchequer . . . or as Prime Minister of England—one of the greatest titles ever known to history . . . but we welcome to Bohemia and to the Lotos David Lloyd George, human being."

Once he encountered Bohemia, Butler brandished it as a kind of metaphoric antidote to the struggle and aspiration, power and politics that characterized his professional existence. The experience of friendship that Butler found in Bohemia's happy grove was real, and he valued its emotional sustenance. But he seemed oblivious to the truth that the lush shade was available only to those privileged few who, like him, lived their lives in the scorching sun of ambition.

CHAPTER TWELVE

"Pick Nick for a Picnic in November"

❦

Polite applause greeted New York delegate Ogden Mills as he made his way to the podium through the red and green feathers released several hours earlier by General Leonard Wood's supporters. Given his mission and the temperature, not much more enthusiasm could be expected.

June 11, 1920, in Chicago was hot to begin with—90 degrees when the Republican National Convention at Convention Hall opened for political business at 9:30 a.m.—and by 2:50 in the afternoon the thermometer was approaching 100. The normal excitement of presidential conventions was heightened by the near certainty that whoever the Republicans nominated would win the election. After eight years of Woodrow Wilson, it was taken for granted that the country wanted the Democrats out of the White House. Anxieties about socialist agitation, labor unrest, unemployment, the high cost of living, and the perception that Wilson had been trying to drag the country into the League of Nations against its will made an easy target for the Republicans. As Butler later said, "a wooden man would have been elected President this year on the Republican ticket." With no obvious favorite, the field was crowded with aspirants: eleven in all, including Calvin Coolidge, Herbert Hoover, Governor William C. Sproul of Pennsylvania, and a relatively unaccomplished senator from Ohio, Warren Harding. On the basis of the primaries, there were three front-runners at the convention's start: General Leonard Wood, a dashing army officer who had helped organize and fought with Teddy Roosevelt's Rough Riders in the Spanish-American War and then served as military governor of Cuba, going on to earn a reputation as a ruthless military commander in the Philippines; Illinois governor Frank Lowden, a former member of the House of Representatives who had gained national visibility by successfully reorganizing the state's cumbersome bureaucracy; and California senator Hiram Johnson, a founder of the Progressive Party and TR's vice presidential candidate on the Bull Moose ticket in 1912.

Sweaty and somewhat disheveled, the 984 Republican delegates had already managed to perform with the calculated lack of decorum expected at a political convention. They had roared and stamped for forty-two minutes following Kansas governor Henry J. Allen's nomination of Wood. Governor Lowden's backers delivered forty-six minutes of cheering for their man after Congressman William A. Rodenburgh of Illinois had made clear why Lowden should be the next president of the United States. Hiram Johnson's people could only come up with a paltry twenty-seven minutes of raucous interruption for the California senator, but he was too radical for most mainstream Republicans anyway, even if he had emerged from the primaries trailing Wood by a scant twelve delegates.

The assemblage was visibly wilted when Mills began. They were gathered there, he assured them, not simply to nominate a candidate but to select the next president, who would face the enormous tasks of rebuilding the world following the destruction of the war. What sorts of qualifications must such a man possess? He must be "an American to the bone," thoroughly "imbued with the underlying moral and political principles upon which America rests." Although courageous critics will always be important, Mills stressed, the country now needed "a builder, not a destroyer," with a well-trained, disciplined mind, able to deal with complicated industrial and agricultural problems and problems of foreign commerce. More than an experienced executive, he must have a feel for the people, a capacity to understand their fears and aspirations, and the administrative skill to promote their welfare. He must appreciate the degree to which the United States is inextricably involved in world politics, with a "clean-cut conception of our international relations and of our traditional foreign policy." Finally, the Republican Party's choice could not be parochial: "He can not belong to any one part of the country, but must know and be known to all." Of the men vying for the nomination, only one "satisfactorily meets all these tests": Nicholas Murray Butler.

There was nothing Butler wanted more than to be president of the

United States. But his own party was not about to honor his campaign's exhortation to "Pick Nick for a Picnic in November." One disliked university president in the White House was enough. The public's disaffection with Woodrow Wilson guaranteed that Columbia would not follow Princeton to Washington.

The intensity of Butler's desire for the presidency was matched only by the intensity of his subsequent disavowals of any interest in it. Butler hated to lose — it is worth pointing out parenthetically that he almost never did — and he began several days after the convention to make clear that he never wanted the nomination in the first place. He admitted only to awkwardness in failing to suppress the outside enthusiasm for his candidacy until it was too late: "What I should have done was to put a stop to the matter at once, but not having done this then I did not see just how to do it later on." But it was less personal embarrassment than careful planning, driven by powerful ambition, that led to Ogden Mills's nominating speech.

It is impossible to locate the specific moment when Butler first began to think about the possibility that he might someday be the Republican presidential candidate, but the 1912 election could only have stimulated whatever dormant presidential impulses were already twitching within him. Butler's place on the ticket to receive the Republican electoral votes for vice president after the death of candidate Sherman (and after the election was decided), although purely ceremonial, surely had an impact. It meant, after all, that in some technical sense he had in fact been the vice presidential candidate. (Henceforth, all his *Who's Who* entries included the notation that he "received Rep. electoral vote for vice pres. of U.S., 1913.") The election of Woodrow Wilson was even more important: Butler had profound contempt for Wilson, seeing him as his intellectual and administrative inferior in every way. His judgment that Wilson boded ill for the country must have suggested to him what a man of real distinction could achieve in the White House. It is hard to imagine that these normal promptings of a competitive ego, fostered by the reverential circle of admirers who were always paying homage to "The Sage," didn't affect his musings on his political future.

Butler himself revealed that thoughts of national leadership were not unknown to him long before the 1920 election. As early as 1913 his name be-

Grandmother Murray's house at 156 West Jersey Street in Elizabeth, New Jersey, Butler's birthplace. Notice the cupola, where Aunt Rosa took the infant Murray several days after he was born to indoctrinate him into wealth, patriotism, and piety.

Henry, Mary, and two-year-old Nicholas Murray Butler

The earliest instance of Butler's presidential ambitions? The thirteen-year-old Murray dressed as George Washington for a family party

The Columbia College campus at Madison Avenue and Fiftieth Street in 1874, four years before Butler arrived as a student. The large building in the center was known as "Maison de Punk" in tribute to its ugliness.

Sketch of Columbia in 1891. St. Patrick's Cathedral is in the background at the left.

Butler as a college senior, 1882

The Reading Room of the Columbia College Library on the Forty-ninth Street campus, ca. 1887

On his "year of discovery" in Europe, Butler is at far right, next to Alice Haven, Berlin, 1884.

On a trip to Alaska in 1887, Susanna Schuyler Butler is seated at far left, with her husband standing to her left.

(ABOVE) Squadron A accompanies President Theodore Roosevelt and former mayor of New York Abram S. Hewitt up Fifth Avenue to attend Butler's installation as Columbia's president, April 19, 1902.

Their arrival at Low Library

Columbia's twelfth president, 1902

(BELOW) Farmland that Butler was soon to turn into the South Field of the new Columbia campus after becoming president

Artist's rendition of the athletic stadium and ceremonial water gate that Butler proposed building on the Hudson River between 112th and 120th streets

Kate La Montague (right) with her friend Countess Ernestine Ludolf in 1905, two years before she married Butler

Butler looking formidably presidential in his Low Library office in 1904, standing behind the Archbishop of Canterbury, Randall Thomas Davidson

Three who left Mr. Butler's asylum: the spiritual George Edward Woodberry, the fastidious Harry Thurston Peck, and the sophisticated J. E. Spingarn

The presidential mansion the trustees built for Butler in 1912 on Morningside Drive and 116th Street

Butler (at left) and fellow Bohemians leaving the Land of Happiness camp at the Bohemian Grove in the summer of 1916

Butler and Désiré-Joseph Cardinal Mercier at the laying of the cornerstone for the library that Butler and the Carnegie Endowment helped restore in Louvain, 1921

Four golfing friends at Augusta National in 1923: (from left) Edward B. McLean, Butler, President Warren Harding, and George P. James

Butler shaking hands with the legendary golfing champion Bobby Jones, Augusta, 1927

The form wasn't much, but the results were surprisingly effective. Butler at his favorite game, Augusta, 1928.

Opening of the Casa Italiana, 1927

The Nobel Prize winner, 1931

Three friends striding along confidently in Chicago, June 1932: Butler, William Crocker, and Carl F. Ahlstrom

Butler and his daughter, Sarah, plotting strategy before the Republican National Convention in Chicago, 1932

(BELOW) Butler speaking out against Prohibition at the 1932 Republican National Convention

Butler as Horace at the
Century Association's Twelfth
Night Revels in January 1933

Butler, son-in-law Neville Lawrence,
daughter Sarah, and grandson Murray,
Southampton, summer 1935

Butler receiving the Grand Cross of the Legion of Honor from Jules Henry, the French minister and chargé d'affaires in Washington, 1937

The berobed Butler pointing out the inscription on Low Library to King George VI and Queen Elizabeth on their visit to Columbia in 1939

When Butler's chauffeur wasn't driving the presidential car in the city, he was pedaling the presidential pedicycle in Southampton during the summer.

The dapper Butler with his "wet" friend Al Smith, former New York governor, at the Southampton Beach Club, 1940

Mr. and Mrs. Butler in Southampton, 1943

Butler at his last commencement, sitting in front of the statue of Alma Mater, June 6, 1945

The chairman of the board of trustees, Frederick Coykendall, escorting the president from the campus after the commencement

With Kate recuperating from surgery in 1946, Butler, blind and alone, listens to the radio in the library of 60 Morningside Drive.

General Dwight D. Eisenhower, Columbia's president-elect, arrives for Butler's funeral on December 9, 1947, accompanied by Frederick Coykendall.

St. Paul's Chapel,
December 9, 1947

(BELOW) Butler's casket is
carried down the steps of
Low Library to the waiting
hearse.

gan to appear in the newspapers as a possible candidate in 1916. When his press agent friend Edward Marshall wrote him in 1915 about the enthusiasm he had encountered for him across the country, Butler, in his usual guarded way, allowed that he was not surprised: "Accept my thanks for your very interesting personal note," he replied. "Some time when we have nothing more important to do, I will give you a little inside and confidential information regarding some interesting points in the political history of the last ten or fifteen years, bearing upon the matter you mention." That such talk was more than private whisperings is confirmed by a letter Butler received from his old philosophy teacher Archibald Alexander in the spring of 1915. Writing from Geneva, where he had settled after leaving Columbia, Alexander gently tweaked him about having learned that "it is on the cards to transfer you from Morningside to the White House." Alexander added that love of Columbia and respect for Butler would lead him to oppose such a step. Butler assured Alexander that someone "has been retailing some gossip that seems to me pretty baseless, at all events I hope so. My personal preferences and wishes are those which you so kindly and generously intimate to be your own, although for more modest reasons than those which you are good enough to describe."

But 1916, with the Democrats in solid control of the government and the Republicans in more or less complete disarray, was not the time to be other than flattered and elusive. By 1920, however, the political landscape was entirely changed. If Butler was ever going to give it a try, the time had come. On September 4, 1918, Henry Pritchett wrote from California to tell Butler how positively his August address on "The War and After the War" had been greeted by the Commercial Club of San Francisco: "You have made in your visit here a very marked impression on the more thoughtful and able men of this coast. A great number of them would like to do something to bring forward your name for the Presidency." Pritchett appreciated Butler's professed reluctance to seek such a position, but insisted that there was "no man in the country so well prepared as you, both as an executive and by reason of your background of knowledge of the fundamentals of politics and government, to take the Presidency." And he warned that "a year hence" Butler might have to permit "some of your wiser political friends to take some steps in the matter."

Butler responded that it was difficult to resist the support for his candidacy coming from all parts of the country:

My long time aloofness in reference to the matter of which you write, or anything leading to it, has been considerably weakened during the past few months by earnest and vigorous approaches that have been made to me from States as widely separated as Connecticut, New Jersey, Pennsylvania, Ohio, Indiana, Illinois, Minnesota, Kansas, Colorado, Utah, Washington, California and Oklahoma. As a practical politician of some thirty years' experience, I can see a good many conditions which are perhaps not so clearly visible to others.

Butler again showed his receptivity to the changed conditions several months later in correspondence with former Minnesota senator Edward E. Smith. Smith had praised him for his "clear vision of the real questions that will be discussed and rightly decided . . . in the campaign of 1920." The Republicans had to stop stumbling about, apologizing for their past, and organize themselves instead in a forthright, coherent fashion. What they need, Smith said, "is a well considered program, a candidate of presidential *size* and an intelligent, co-ordinated campaign. If we can have you as our candidate, with your equipment and power to express the real purpose of the party, I will have no doubt of success in 1920."

Butler answered that he was honored "by the suggestions," which he characteristically avoided specifying, adding that "whatever the future may have in store for any individual" was unimportant. What mattered—and here Butler set forth the campaign issue he would pursue for the next two years—was saving America from the dangers that beset it, fighting for the "preservation of the American form of Government, and against all forms of socialism, bolshevism and anarchism which threaten within and without."

As Butler, doughty defender of the American way of life, became the campaign figure who, he hoped, would reach the White House, Butler the university president remained the inescapable identity that ensured he wouldn't get there. Try as he might, he could never shed the label of "college professor," a definition that spelled political doom in a country that was eager to get rid of Professor Woodrow Wilson. The notion of being "merely" an academic was galling. When Franklin Murphy, former governor of New Jersey and a strong admirer, told Butler in 1918 that he hoped he would be the Republican candidate, he made the mistake of acknowledging that Butler labored "under the handicap of being a school master and, of course, every one cannot know you as your own friends do and so understand that there are school masters and school masters." The category of "schoolmaster" was even more demeaning, and Butler was more than irritated:

> Quite apart from anything political, it always amuses me to be taken by the public for a schoolmaster, since the duties of the post which I have held for nearly twenty years are about as far from those of a schoolmaster as it is possible to conceive. My duties as President of a corporation which owns and controls nearly $70,000,000 worth of property, has to do with about 25,000 human beings a year, and expends about $4,500,000 annually on maintenance and operation are about as remote from those of a schoolmaster as could possibly be imagined. It is curious how long it is taking the public to realise that the administration and business training gained in the office of President of a great University is quite unique in our modern life.

The irony of Butler, the visible academic administrator, busily expunging all traces of the academic was lost on him. But he was correct in understanding the political liability conferred by his university affiliation. "BUTLER MEANS BUSINESS," his campaign pin announced, speaking both to his seriousness and his preferred self-definition. Drafts of letters that he wrote himself for distribution under other people's signatures endlessly presented him as an accomplished business executive, not someone frittering his time away on the narrowly academic. Butler's efforts to transform himself into an executive free from the taint of the academic were not without their painful humor. Edward Marshall was particularly aggressive in seeking to refashion the Butler image. The letters he wrote to important people across the country on Butler's behalf—and with Butler's approval—emphasized that neither Butler nor his institution should be associated with anything so irrelevant as scholarship:

> If there is any general impression that Mr. Butler is an impractical scholar rather than a real, live man, it is, of course, as you and I know, inaccurate, for Columbia University which, under his guidance of ztrictly [sic] practical business method and appreciation of the public needs rather than of scholarship, has grown to be one of the world's great institutions of learning, is a quantity-production

democracy-factory rather than a retail output knowledge-of-dead-languages concern. Thanks to him it is a citizen factory rather than a scholar-factory.

The argument that "the nation has had enough of educators" didn't bother Marshall, because Butler was involved in running a school that cared for something more important than academic education—"It is a Ford-scale citizen builder." And he proposed other initiatives to enhance Butler's popularity: a photograph of him laughing, to offset the image of his severity, as part of a series called "Laugh and the World Laughs with You" that would include the deceased Teddy Roosevelt and others like Edison, Queen Mary, Ford, and the Prince of Wales; a film focusing on his campaign against Bolshevism, touched with just "the suggestion of romance necessary to catch the low-brows"; and a milk distribution scheme in Butler's neighborhood—understood as embracing "some tenement section"—designed to show how the elimination of waste and middleman profits could at once benefit the farmer while providing the best product at lowest cost to the consumer. Marshall thought this last idea might have a genuine national impact. Butler disagreed. He acted on none of them.

By the time Butler officially announced his candidacy, in late December 1919, he had effectively been running a campaign for more than a year. Its low visibility expressed both deliberate political strategy and stylistic preference. The strategy was to avoid getting caught in the vicious exchanges that were bound to ensue among the camps of Wood, Lowden, Johnson, Harding, and, even for a time, World War I hero General Pershing. Standing aloof from all that was vulgarly "political," Butler would instead focus on the issues, through the articles and addresses he was in any case producing in his work at Columbia. Then, with all the front-runners crippled by their mutual battering, he would walk into the convention as the proven business executive of impeccable integrity, known throughout America for his grasp of national and international problems, and come away with the nomination, leading the Republicans to a smashing victory in the fall. It could indeed be a picnic for Nick. Such were the tactical considerations that led Butler to run as what one observer called a "semi-dark horse"—visible enough to catch people's interest, but not enough to merit their criticism.

The personal impulses behind Butler's rather guarded entry into the campaign spoke to his grand sense of self. Making a public display of actively competing for the nomination would compromise his dignity. Butler wanted it—desperately—but he wanted it awarded on the grounds of inherent merit. To have to sell the mass of people on his desirability was beneath him. Men of Butler's standing did not conduct themselves in such a fashion. In addition, of course, a full-scale, hard-fought struggle might end in defeat—an intolerable notion.

So from the beginning it had to be a stealth campaign. He would run while doing his best to disguise that fact for as long as possible. Butler realized that if such a campaign was to produce the nomination for him, it would require delegates able to resist the blandishments of the other candidates and remain uncommitted until the convention—delegates, furthermore, who would respond to Butler's skill in articulating the issues and not be swayed by crude sloganeering and self-advertising. The importance of this "right sort of delegate" was from the start a central theme in his political calculating. A letter to Edward Smith early in 1919 sounded the concern: we must, he wrote, "select as delegates to the next convention our strongest and most independent men, leaving them free without definite instructions, in order that they may study the situation and, in conference with their fellows from different parts of the country, select a candidate competent to represent and force the dominant issue. In that case, I believe our success will be absolutely certain."

What Butler hoped for was a Republican convention resembling a large-scale, popular version of an evening at the Knickerbocker or Lotos Club, where his educated, prosperous, prominent friends would meet for stimulating political conversation. A group of the best men, in short, of the sort Butler felt most comfortable with, free from any parochial interest and eager to take the right position on every subject. If there were enough of these, Butler reasoned, he would be a shoo-in. At one point he thought that as many as 800 (of the 934) delegates might arrive uncommitted and uninstructed. In actuality, the number was considerably less. And as Butler was painfully to learn on that humid June day in Chicago, very few of those were the kind who would have necessarily enjoyed sitting around with Butler and his friends discussing the issues.

In his naïveté, imagining an idealized community of judicious delegates who would rush to support him, Butler was entirely serious about the nomination. Even if he was going to run while pretending not to, he understood that he needed an organization behind him. It could not be professionally staffed or well funded, for then it would call attention to what Butler was up to, but fortunately there were Butler loyalists available who enthusiastically formed themselves into a low-key, appropriately amateur committee to deal with publicity, lobbying, mailings, and the like. These included Edward Marshall; the Wall Street lawyer James Sheffield; Joseph Harriman, a banker against whom Butler subsequently brought suit to get back securities that he had improperly used as collateral for personal loans; and a young Columbia alumnus named Howard Osterhout, working in Albany as secretary to New York's secretary of state. The committee chairman was municipal court judge John R. Davies, one of Butler's old club and golfing buddies. All were emotionally committed to what Marshall would later call "the holy effort" to nominate Butler. As Osterhout's moving declaration put it,

> you are the only logical, and the best man the United States can take for its President in 1920. I believe this so keenly, Dr. Butler, that I cannot state it without a real feeling or sentiment accompanying the expression of the thought . . . I know no cause in which I would do more willing work, or in which I would more zealously and willingly enlist than one to help further your candidacy for President. This willingness and desire to work for you is entirely spontaneous, and is prompted by a sincere and patriotic desire to help our country choose the right man for President at a time, above all others, when we, as a country, cannot afford to make a mistake in the choice of our next Chief Executive.

During the spring and summer of 1919 Butler's inconspicuous quest for the presidency was limping along as he intended. Managing successfully to stay out of the primary fray, he tried in talks given across the country to define central issues, to garner backing from western Republicans (to avoid the stigma of appearing a parochial eastern establishment candidate), and above all to distance himself from the liability of being perceived as an academic. On May 22 he sent Marshall a list of sixty influential men from twenty-three states to get a "confidential" letter written by Marshall (and approved by Sheffield), inquiring as to how they thought the Republican Party in their state might regard Butler's candidacy. Presenting himself as the director of a newspaper service supplying European publications with news about American affairs, Marshall claimed that his interest "is principally journalistic," though he admitted that Butler did seem to him the best-qualified man, who would in all likelihood receive the nomination. "Of course my newspaper organization in its American expressions is strictly non-partisan and must remain so," he concluded.

The twenty or so responses Marshall's letter elicited from different regions of the country defined the difficulties Butler's campaign faced. While all spoke of the high personal regard their writers had for Butler (no surprise, as many of them were personal acquaintances), most noted that he was not well known in their states, and to the extent that he was known, it was as a college president. One respondent, North Dakota's attorney general, asked whether Butler might be seen to share the same failings of Charles Evans Hughes, the defeated Republican candidate of 1916, of not understanding "the common man and his problems."

Butler's peculiar campaign was ill equipped to address any of these issues. His decision not to enter the primaries and to keep the lowest possible profile meant that he lacked almost entirely the capacity to make himself known around the country. Explaining in his publicity that he was not a dry-as-dust academic, but a "real" man, even—that best of all things—a businessman, would not do the trick if he did not go out and confront the people. Nor would talks at selected Commercial Clubs and chambers of commerce convince the skeptical public that he represented their interests.

But Butler, like all great artists and politicians, possessed the facility of believing that reality actually conformed to the shapes he chose to impose upon it. His interpretation of national trends testified in his own mind to the shrewdness of his tactics. "You will be interested to know what the talk is about candidates for 1920," he wrote to Osterhout in the summer of 1919:

> The general feeling is that the man to be nominated has not yet been much discussed in public, and that he will be a man who can represent the real issue of 1920, viz., the preservation of our American form of government against ultra-radical and socialistic attacks, and who can present this issue clearly and persuasively to the people. Opinion is general that to bring forward the name of such a man now would lead all the favorite sons to unite to attack him and to render his nomination inadvisable.

The little-discussed man around whom Butler felt the party would eventually unite bore a suspicious resemblance to the president of Columbia, particularly in his diagnosis of the culture's need for an inoculation of healthy Americanism to combat the contagion of Bolshevist-socialist unrest. In all its manifestations, "Americanism" became the central theme of Butler's major addresses during most of 1919—the focus of his campaign. "Is America Worth Saving?" delivered before the Cincinnati Commercial Club on April 19 and later included as the title essay of a volume of his speeches published in 1920, may be taken as his initial campaign address. "What I would like to do," he wrote to a friend on March 31, "is to arouse the attention of the country, and particularly Republicans, to the fact that the campaign of 1920 must be fought on the issue of the preservation of the American principles of government which are being undermined and attacked on every side by vigorous and energetic people who do not believe in them." Given his insistence that his support originated in the Midwest, Cincinnati as site of the address was hardly accidental. *The New York Sun* commented the next day that the speech comprised "the strongest indictment against socialism that has ever been heard in the Middle West."

Butler did not mince words. American traditions and way of life were facing the greatest challenge they had ever known. Acknowledging that not every social and economic problem had been solved by the American system, he claimed that the socialist alternative was undermining the precious civil liberty of the individual, which American government protected. Socialism was perverse insofar as it curtailed the energies of the ambitious in the interests of the mediocre and inferior. Individual opportunity necessarily brought with it inequality, but "the one fact never to be forgotten is that pulling some men down raises no man up."

In the face of those carping naysayers who argued that in America the gap between the rich and the poor was growing ever wider, Butler unleashed an array of statistics to indicate it couldn't be true: 18 million dwellings in America housed 21 million families; 6 million families owned their houses without mortgages (3 million with them); 12 million people had accounts in mutual, stock, or postal savings accounts totaling more than $6.5 billion; 266,000 miles of railway tracks were traveled by more than 1 billion passengers. Socialists failed to appreciate that in the United States there were no permanent or inveterate conflicts between economic classes, because "the wage earner of today is the employer of tomorrow."

Excoriating the Democrats for their waste and extravagance in "The High Cost of Living," an address given in August at the Commercial Club of San Francisco, he located the remedy in an evocation of a kind of mythic American sensibility that could look reality squarely in the eye and make hard decisions. No namby-pamby, Woodrow Wilsonish equivocation, in short, but tough action by tough men: "Our task, as intelligent, self-respecting, patriotic Americans, is to ask for facts . . . This is no time for bravado; this is no time for cynicism; this is no time for violence or revolution. This is a time for clear, sane, courageous thinking on the facts of business, industrial, and political life."

Butler saved his most explicitly political address for a speech in November at the Union League of Philadelphia. "The Republican Party—Its Present Duty and Opportunity" restated the large, central themes of his campaign—the destructive nature of two terms of Democratic leadership, the need to resist the subversive nature of socialist propaganda, the urgency of bringing down the high cost of living, the threat to American democracy posed by strikes, and the misleading claim that the United States was torn by permanent, nonnegotiable class divisions. To these platform items he added some of the more specific issues that belonged to an election-year arsenal of concerns: the importance of establishing an international tribunal of justice and an industrial relations committee to settle internal industrial disputes; the incoherence of current foreign policy; the need to keep the government out of owning and running the railroads.

But by the end of the speech, the issues gave way to a deluge of good old-fashioned political rabble-rousing. Butler conjured up the glories of Republican days past to stimulate proper enthusiasm for the challenges ahead, reading American history through the lens of Republican achievements:

Take away Washington and your whole fabric falls. Take away Hamilton and your whole philosophy of government disappears. Take away Jefferson and the foundations of your foreign policy are swept away. Take away Marshall and the epoch-making judicial interpretation of the Constitution has gone.

The drumroll went on through Webster, Clay, Lincoln, and, most potent of all, his onetime patron, Teddy Roosevelt: "Oh, my friends, you cannot take out of the story of America these names . . . All that we can do is . . . to strive to be worthy of their example, of their counsel, and of our opportunity." One would have to be relatively tone-deaf not to feel that Butler had firmly in mind the next name to be added to this roster of illustrious Republicans.

As he continued to talk throughout the summer and fall, his campaign headquarters continued to pretend he wasn't actively campaigning. In August, John Davies assured him, "our candidate is in the position of a classy racehorse that by breeding and training and *private* timing, some insiders know to be the hardiest, but that is yet to get into the race." Once Butler started to show his stuff, Davies was confident that knowledgeable touts would welcome his entry. (Silence from the Butler stables notwithstanding, the press routinely commented during this period on Butler's interest in the nomination.)

Maintaining the posture of not running did not interfere with Butler's careful monitoring of his rivals' strengths. Letters from Butler to his supporters at headquarters and elsewhere throughout 1919 confirmed the declining popularity of the other candidates: General Wood had no chance, because the country wouldn't elect a military man; Lowden was a fine person but lacked national stature; Hiram Johnson's strict isolationism had cost him dearly. Meanwhile, Butler reported, enthusiasm for him was growing every day, notably in the vital West. Overflow crowds of "thoroughly representative, vigorous-minded Americans" embraced his views. An auditorium holding 4,500 people in Minneapolis, for example, "was packed to suffocation"; 3,500 additional people were turned away.

As the end of the year approached, Butler and his team decided it was time for the privately trained thoroughbred, with his racing colors displayed, to march onto the track and into the glare of official public scrutiny. The announcement was scheduled for the evening of December 23. Right up to the actual moment of the declaration, Butler remained coyly insistent that he didn't know what was going on. In an article published that day, *The New York Times* reported that "some of his friends were engaged in a movement to crystallize sentiment for him." But when asked about this, "Dr. Butler said last night that while he appreciated the kind interest behind the effort, he personally had done nothing to inspire it, nor was he familiar with what was being done." And the *Herald Tribune* of the same date quoted him as maintaining, "I don't know anything about Judge Davies starting a boom for me for President."

That evening, however, through a prepared statement that Davies issued at the Commodore Hotel in New York, Butler learned that he was after all a candidate for the Republican nomination. What the Republican Party needed, Davies proclaimed—aligning Butler with the man he had previously repudiated—was a worthy successor to Teddy Roosevelt who could lead the fight "to rehabilitate the United States, rescuing it from that chaos into which almost every department and activity of the national Government has been allowed to slump during the present Democratic administration." Nicholas Murray Butler was the man best qualified to do that, a "big, healthy, red blooded citizen—a positive American" who was a successful businessman, a brilliant speaker, an expert on the budget, a man of enormous international influence, someone who knew and was admired by the entire country. The strength of the Butler movement, Davies asserted, was "its spontaneous and national character. It has not been worked up or heavily or at all financed, and it is not merely local in its origin. It is warmly supported by Republicans of all types and factions, particularly by young men and soldiers in all parts of the nation."

With the significant exception that he could now no longer deny that he was seeking the nomination, candidate Butler conducted himself and his campaign precisely as noncandidate Butler had. He spoke on the issues, though the deluge of invitations required that he turn many down ("I am refusing them by the dozens every day," he wrote Marshall on January 2); he tried to whittle away at the university president bugaboo by endlessly referring to his business achievements; and he continued to convince himself and others that his rivals were self-destructing as he grew stronger.

While all his advisers seemed to share some portion of Butler's unflagging optimism, young Osterhout alone remained intent on pushing Butler toward a more professionally organized and financed campaign. In early January he insisted that Butler needed to make three appointments: a visible national campaign chairman; an experienced publicity man, to work full-time to convince people that Butler was not a muddled visionary of the Wilson type, but a "sane, practical, reasonably-progressive, positive, businesslike executive, with a mind unsurpassed by any living American"; and a national treasurer with a million-dollar budget.

Osterhout was right on all three counts, but Butler rejected them all, and bothered to respond only to the last: "I really do not believe that any considerable amount of money ought to be necessary for the purposes you mention, and my experience would lead me to feel that most of such expenditures is really wasted." To act like the other candidates was an option Butler never seriously considered. There was something demeaning about the process, to which he would not stoop. And the fringe benefits of not stooping were that if he didn't win, he would have less explaining to do—to himself and others.

Still, Butler remained attentive to unfolding political developments.

Lengthy analytic letters to such friends as Edward Smith, University of Washington president Henry Suzzallo, Henry Pritchett, Marshall, and others assessed his chances, which, according to him, were never less than very promising. On January 13, 1920, for example, he saw the critical moment coming on "the third ballot, and possibly on the second. If California, followed by Washington, should, on the second ballot, swing any considerable number of votes to us it would probably be decisive." Matters were moving smoothly in Connecticut, New Jersey, and Pennsylvania; New York seemed certain to act as a unit for him; offers of support were coming from Utah, Texas, and North Carolina. He even rejoiced at the huge amount of money that General Wood was rumored to have raised (more than $500,000), certain that when the public learned of this, it would turn against Wood for trying to buy the nomination.

Butler moved into 1920 feeling that everything was proceeding smoothly. Press coverage of his numerous addresses was providing him with the kind of national visibility he felt most comfortable with, one that cost nothing and was entirely devoted to issues. Suzzallo, in fact, was so pleased with the publicity that he recommended that Butler disregard the college president issue. Butler welcomed this advice, eager to believe that the problem had been solved. He reported back to Suzzallo that Marshall also agreed that the matter "has practically disappeared of its own weight and foolishness," and henceforth it would not be mentioned. It was a vain hope; he could never disentangle himself from his crippling academic image. The public continued to see him, he later wrote to a friend, as "suffering from an occupational disease."

Meanwhile, he took comfort from his bleak assessment of the campaign of General Wood, the candidate he most feared, keeping up a running commentary regarding what he took to be Wood's deteriorating position: "The Wood movement seems to us here to be going on the rocks in various directions and from various causes," he informed Smith on February 2. On March 1 he observed that "the Wood movement . . . is beginning to thin out as it has really not very much political substance behind it." And on April 30 he finally proclaimed its demise to his Tacoma newspaper friend John Rea: "The Wood movement is as dead as Julius Caesar. There never was much life in it, save what a lavish expenditure of money was able to accomplish."

Simultaneously, for his own peace of political mind, he performed a similar dismissive procedure on Governor Lowden, whom he actually liked. He was appropriately less virulent about Lowden's possibilities, merely predicting that a temporary wave of enthusiasm for him would disappear after a month or two, to be followed by a brief Harding surge that would last up to the convention. He never thought that the Lowden campaign had enough strength to survive. Nor did he spend much time burying Hiram Johnson, whom he always considered too eccentrically progressive to be a genuine source of worry.

At the end of April he exuberantly informed Suzzallo that "the situation from our point of view could hardly be better." Johnson had helped to destroy Wood, and the path to an open convention had now been cleared. Butler's confidence that such a convention would inevitably turn to him as the candidate led him to tell Smith in early May that "the dance goes merrily on and our friends are wearing a broad smile of satisfaction which grows broader as each day passes." In mid-May, Judge Davies's smile enabled him to declare that Butler's campaign had achieved all of its goals: it had never wavered in its dignity, had not alienated the public through raising and spending large sums of money, had not antagonized the other candidates, and had brought Butler's qualifications before the nation. It was generally agreed that the nominee would have to be "an Eastern man who has a western following, a wide western acquaintance and western influence," he said, and only Nicholas Murray Butler satisfied those criteria. He predicted strong support—though not on the first ballot—from Rhode Island, Connecticut, Vermont, New Jersey, Pennsylvania, Wisconsin, Minnesota, Iowa, Mississippi, Oregon, Texas, Georgia, North Carolina, and New York. Butler, he thought, would be nominated on the fourth or fifth ballot.

Butler was no less positive. "If I were at liberty to write you in detail," he informed Thomas Procter, "I think you would be immensely interested in the evidence which accumulates upon me every day that the State of New York can have the Republican nomination if it wishes it simply by closing its hand upon the support that will be offered it from the west after the first few ballots."

Neither Butler's nor Davies's optimism was shared by the press. Most newspapers considered Butler a distinct long shot, with very little popular support. The *New York Tribune* reported the consensus view of the state's political leaders that while he would receive 75 (of the 88) votes on the first ballot, that number would drop to 60 on the second and by the third would have disappeared entirely, with almost all of them going to Wood. Butler enthusiasts refused to be shaken, however widely felt the public skepticism. John Rea shared the news with him that the Wall Street odds against him were 20–1. He assured Butler he was prepared to take them.

When Butler arrived in Chicago on June 5, accompanied by Kate and Sarah, he did not find the 800 unpledged delegates he had hoped for; there were instead approximately 500 to whom he would have to appeal. The first step was to convince them that he was a serious candidate, not a favorite son looking for complimentary votes. He and Davies went to work immediately, declaring that they were not interested in New York delegates voting for him on the first ballot and then shifting: if they weren't prepared to stick with him for at least three or four ballots, Butler didn't want their support at all.

Despite the fact that he remained fully invested in his own chances, the convention's interest centered on Wood and Lowden, relegating Butler to the periphery of speculation. And yet as astute a political reporter as Mark Sullivan noted that the line between Butler the entirely dismissible and Butler the extremely plausible was quite thin: "One strong man, believing in Butler and making a speech that reflected his faith, might very readily transform the convention from one which regards Butler as an accepted impossibility to one that would regard him as an ideal candidate under present conditions."

That speech was not forthcoming, but on June 6 the New York State Republican train was arriving in Chicago with ample supplies of Butler banners, placards, buttons, badges, and laudatory editorials. The hoopla couldn't conceal the unresolved nature of the delegates' commitment to Butler. Would they support him past the first ballot, or would they merely stockpile their votes under his name and then see how things developed? Butler deeply resented the notion that he had come this far only to be satisfied with some perfunctory votes as a favorite son. "This is no time to be paying compliments," he said. "[I] want only the votes of those who have faith in my candidacy and who sincerely wish to support me. I am not willing to be made a pawn in any campaign for the nomination for the governor, or any other local political issue."

The open convention that Butler sought had in fact come about, and the uncertainty of the New York delegation mirrored the uncertainty of the convention as a whole. Rather than one obvious winner, there seemed to be an array of obvious losers. A consensus prediction of first-ballot results in the *Cleveland Press* the day before the convention opened had Wood leading with 253, followed by Lowden with 215, Johnson with 175, Butler with 107, Governor Sproul of Pennsylvania with 76, and Warren Harding with 57. (*The New York Times* of June 9 had much the same figures, but with 112 for Johnson and 88 for Butler). Closed-door deliberations began that would eventually invest Ohio's Republican boss and kingmaker, Harry Daugherty, with the legendary political insight to have commented in February that his candidate, Warren Harding, would be nominated "about eleven minutes after two, Friday morning of the convention, when fifteen or twenty men are sitting around a table."

Butler struggled from the start with a recalcitrant New York delegation. Despite his confident claim that he would receive almost all of New York's eighty-eight votes, the Wood, Lowden, and Johnson supporters among the delegates were reluctant to give their votes to Butler, out of fear of hurting their candidates' chances. After a meeting of the state delegation on the evening of June 7 in Lowden headquarters, Butler said he was grateful that no decision had been reached, thinking that this perhaps gave him time to demonstrate that he had substantial strength outside New York. Without bothering to be unduly specific, he insisted that "constant assurances of support were being received from every quarter."

But by the next day, James Wadsworth, the New York delegation's chairman, and Charles Hilles, Republican National Committeeman, heard Butler's request that the state's position be clarified. Would New York be unified behind him or not? The decision, he argued, was not simply personal. A delegation at odds with itself would lose the chance to affect the nominating process: only a unified front could give New York a decisive voice in what was to happen. Wadsworth, Hilles, and other state Republican leaders agreed that the muddle of dissension ought to be ended. Accordingly, Wadsworth announced that evening that he had "ordered" delegates to vote for Butler.

This order pleased Butler but few of the delegates. It also lacked statutory authority, so that no one was bound by it. When the delegates recovered from the shock of being told what to do, they reasserted their rights to be as leaderless and disunified as they had been upon their arrival in Chicago. The only concession that most seemed prepared to make was to agree to back Butler for the first ballot. Butler accepted this commitment, though it came precariously close to that complimentary vote he had always said he would reject. But finally, more support was better than less, and he continued to hope that to the New York total would be added those numerous but always elusive votes he had been promising would come from all over the country.

The enthusiasm with which Butler's managers greeted the delegation's position did not convince many others that Butler's chances had appreciably improved. According to *The New York Times* of June 11, "So far as it is possible to ascertain, the one thing that stands out with a degree of certainty in this otherwise complicated and uncertain situation is that Dr. Butler will be quickly eliminated from consideration." The paper's normal loyalty to Butler bowed before the priority for responsible political analysis:

> Little genuine sentiment for him exists among the New York dele-
> gates. His name is seldom mentioned among them as a candidate to
> be seriously voted for. After the first few ballots the delegates will
> desert him. However, Dr. Butler himself talks as if he takes an alto-
> gether different view of the situation and is convinced that he has a
> good shot for the nomination.

On Friday, June 11, General Leonard Wood was the first nominee, followed by Lowden, Johnson, Calvin Coolidge, Judge Jeter Pritchard of North Carolina, Butler, Herbert Hoover, Harding, Sproul, Senator Miles Poindexter of Washington, and, eleventh and last, Senator Howard Sutherland of West Virginia. When the actual balloting began, the 75 or 80 New York first-ballot delegates that Butler had counted on turned into only 68, and the vast support from the South and Midwest into one vote from Kentucky and one half vote from Texas. Three more ballots would follow, but he was effectively finished as quickly as the *Times* had anticipated. First-ballot results had Wood leading with 287½, trailed by Lowden with 211½ and Johnson with 133½. (It might have come as some satisfaction to Butler that his paltry 69½ was nevertheless four votes more than Harding managed on the first ballot.) The almost total absence of support from the rest of the country confirmed the already skeptical New York delegates in their conviction that Butler had no chance, and they quickly deserted to the camps either of those they really wanted or those they thought would win. On the remaining three ballots held that evening before adjournment, Butler's New York numbers steadily fell from 41 to 25 to 20.

When the convention closed for the evening at 7:00 on Friday, no one was close to the required 493 votes: Wood had 314½, Lowden 289, Johnson 140½. Some of Butler's friends wanted him to withdraw officially to avoid embarrassment, but he refused. The fantasy of his victory on an early ballot had been shattered, but his strategic sense that the convention was deadlocked told him to stay in the running. If no one else emerged, might not the wheel of fortune turn to the trusty Republican wheelhorse, still available to be discovered?

The discussions that ensued that night and early into the morning in a thirteenth-floor suite of the Blackstone Hotel had nothing to do with Butler. Amid much cigar smoke and the substantial consumption of Scotch, influential Republican senators, assorted party hacks, and campaign managers drifted in and out of Suite 404 trying to decide on a workable scenario for the next day. Compromises were explored—would Johnson agree to run as a vice presidential candidate?—and all manner of dark and darker horses considered: the seventy-year-old Senator Henry Cabot Lodge, chairman of the convention; Will Hays, chairman of the Republican National Committee; Charles Evans Hughes, who had not really figured in the convention thus far; and Pennsylvania senator Philander Knox, among others. The talk was scattered, sporadic, depressed. As James Wadsworth commented some years later, "It was . . . a sort of continuous performance. I was in and out of that room several times that night. They were like a lot of chickens with their heads cut off. They had no program and no definite affirmative decision was reached."

As the evening wore on, one name—that of Warren G. Harding—seemed to stay afloat as the others sank under a burden of negatives. It was not a name that inspired enthusiasm, but at least it seemed minimally plausible. Shortly after 1:00 a.m. the hard core of senators remaining in the room, including Lodge, McCormick, Calder, Curtis, Smoot, and Brandegee concluded that Harding should be nominated the next day. In response to a question from a reporter regarding Harding's qualifications, Connecticut senator Brandegee testily responded, in language that would have appalled Butler, "There ain't any first-raters this year. This ain't 1880 or any 1904; we haven't got John Shermans or Theodore Roosevelts; we got a lot of second-raters and Warren Harding is the best of the second-raters."

Neither a participant at the discussions nor a subject of them, Butler certainly learned what had transpired by the next day. When the opening four ballots on Saturday confirmed that neither Wood nor Lowden could go much beyond 300 votes, the transfer of support to Harding was about to go into effect. The eighth-ballot results of 307 for Lowden, 299 for Wood, and 133½ for Harding shifted on the ninth to 374½ for Harding, 249 for Wood, and 121½ for Lowden. The tenth ballot would be decisive, and given Butler's genius for knowing whom to be close to, it was no surprise that as the states began their calculated vault onto the Harding bandwagon, Butler was found in a small room in back of the platform of Convention Hall, sitting with Warren Harding and Frank Lowden. "We three were alone," Butler wrote in *Across the Busy Years*. "Suddenly, there was a tremendous roar . . . In an instant, the door of the room in which we three were sitting burst open and Charles B. Warren of Michigan leapt into the room, shouting, 'Pennsylvania has voted for you, Harding, and you are nominated!' Harding rose, and with one hand in Lowden's and one in mine, he said with choking voice: 'If the great honor of the Presidency is to come to me, I shall need all the help that you two friends can give me.'"

Harding's nomination drew appropriate good-soldierly support from Butler, though he had no illusions about Harding's abilities. But party loyalty (as well as self-interest) mandated delight at the convention's wise choice: "It is a keen pleasure," he wrote to Harding on June 14, "once more to report my personal pride and satisfaction in your nomination, and to assure you with the utmost heartiness that during the campaign no effort of mine shall be spared to bring about your election, and once elected, to uphold your administration of the government." He publicly applauded Harding as a practical, solid nominee who would get the job done. Privately, his thoughts took another direction, as he indicated to Stephen Olin:

> The New York Times thinks we would have to go back to Franklin Pierce to find so small a man intellectually as Harding in our list of presidents. I have a different notion. Harding is not a great man and knows it, but he has those extraordinary qualities of practical commonsense, patriotism and capacity to confer which mark so many of our public men of the type who are excellent without being geniuses . . . There will, perhaps, be no great enthusiasm for him, since he is not of the type that invokes enthusiasm, but, on the other hand, he imparts confidence, and I believe that confidence is, in the long run, a better political asset than enthusiasm.

Despite his brave facade, Butler found it hard to absorb the convention's cursory dismissal of him. His private pain produced a stunningly inappropriate—and uncharacteristic—outburst of public anger in an interview with the press on June 14. Without provocation, he assailed what he claimed was Leonard Wood's attempt to buy the election. Butler cast himself as the heroic defender of the Republican Party's integrity: "The chief task of the convention was to prevent the sale of the Presidential nomination at auction to the highest bidder," he stormed, and the "sixty-eight New York delegates who voted for me on the first ballot were the chief factor in stopping the Hindenburg drive to overwhelm the convention by the power of unlimited money and by strong-arm methods in preference primaries." Conveniently forgetting that he chose, for various reasons, not to raise money himself, he vilified Wood's supporters as "a motley group of stock gamblers, oil and mining promoters, munition makers and other like persons" who "seized upon so good a man as General Wood and with reckless audacity started out to buy for him the Presidential nomination." In Butler's account, only New York stood between Wood and the nomination. Realizing the danger, he "sent word to the New York delegation by James R. Sheffield that with me party success and party honor came first, and that no personal interest of mine should be considered until party success and party honor had been protected . . ." The defection of his delegates to Lowden after the first ballot had nothing to do with any perception that Butler couldn't win, but was rather his donation to the anti-Wood cause.

Wood's response was immediate and direct:

> The statement is a vicious and malicious falsehood. I would ignore it if it were directed at me alone, but I cannot remain silent when my loyal friends and supporters are vilified . . . The attack upon them is infamous.
>
> This action of Nicholas Murray Butler is an attempt to ingratiate himself with certain elements which exercised a determining influence at the convention and possibly to explain his own political weakness. It is a self-seeking, cowardly attack made under the cloak of an alleged public service which was never intended or rendered.

Colonel William C. Proctor, Wood's campaign manager, sent a stern telegram to Butler: "Statement in the morning papers credited to you, relative to General Wood's support, wholly false and made with the malicious disregard for the truth." The *Tribune* followed with an editorial rebuke, which concluded by raising the question of whether Butler was fit to lead a great university.

Things had clearly gotten out of control, and Butler, reluctant as always to take a step back, at first tried to roll over the mounting criticism. "I am sorry that General Wood lost his temper," he responded provocatively in the press, "it does not sound well." But the facts of the fund-raising, Butler went on to say (as if they were the issue), were well known, and all he had done was to point to what was already part of the public record. Butler's intransigence did not still the controversy, however, and Republican leaders became alarmed at the gratuitous rift his unnecessary comment had created within the party ranks. Bowing to growing pressure from his friends and other influential Republicans to end the issue, Butler, on June 22, did the unthinkable: he apologized publicly. "Answering your telegram of June 15," he cabled to Proctor, "I am convinced that my word, spoken under the strain, turmoil and fatigue of the Chicago convention, and in sharp revolt against the power of money in politics, was both unbecoming and unwarranted, and that I should, and do, apologize to each and every one who felt hurt by what I did."

But Butler was not the sort to offer a public acknowledgment of intemperate behavior without a simultaneous private disavowal of real culpability. The fault, he explained in a letter to William Crocker, lay with the New York delegates, who had been disturbed by the postconvention rumor that they had withdrawn their support from the popular Wood because of the influence of the Republican Old Guard; they wanted it known that they left Wood because they thought his fund-raising tactics would have made it impossible for him to be elected. "Against my better judgment" they had prevailed on Butler to make his charge. As soon as he had done so, he recognized that its language was "very unwisely chosen." And while he believed the accusation was justified, "I am convinced . . . it was not a statement that I, as one who had been voted for at the Convention, should have made, and that some of its language was based upon the hearsay of the Convention and not upon personal knowledge."

With his apology rendered and appropriate friends thanked for "skillful and untiring labors on my behalf at Chicago," there remained only the need to deny that he had ever been interested in the presidency in the first place. And that fiction he would spend the rest of his life maintaining.

CHAPTER THIRTEEN

"Kid" Butler, the Columbia Catamount, vs. "Wild Bill" Borah, the Boise Bearcat

❦

Putting aside his disappointment, Butler returned from Chicago determined to establish a close relationship with Harding. He immediately placed himself at the candidate's disposal, assuring him that "my time and strength are at your service throughout the campaign," even suggesting that Harding stay at 60 Morningside Drive should he ever feel the need "to eat and sleep away from the madding crowd." Harding was grateful for the offers of assistance, sufficiently aware of his own limitations to be pleased to have access to Butler's political wisdom. And certainly there were plenty of limitations to be aware of. Handsome, genial, and decent, the Ohio senator possessed few other qualifications to be president of the United States. No one knew this better than Butler, except perhaps Harding himself. As Butler admitted years later, Harding was "good-natured, lazy and weak," without any serious grasp of "public questions or of the foundations in history, economics and public law on which these questions rest." His inadequacy hardly mattered, however, as the country wanted the Democrats gone. Just how badly was indicated by Harding's annihilation of Democratic candidate James Cox, winning thirty-seven states by the largest electoral margin since James Monroe's victory of 1817.

In November the president-elect told Butler he would like to discuss the "foreign situation" with him, and asked him to choose a convenient date in mid-December for their conversation. Butler was delighted at the prospect of influencing Harding on questions of foreign policy; accompanied by Judge Davies, Butler arrived by train at Marion, Ohio, at 7:30 a.m. on

December 18. While Davies was shuffled off to a hotel for meetings, Butler was driven to Harding's home for breakfast. Afterward the two men moved to an adjoining house to begin their private conversation. With time out for a family lunch and some archival filming of the event, they spent seven hours alone together. Not since the heady days of his friendship with Teddy Roosevelt had Butler enjoyed such protracted personal time with a president.

A confidential memo published in *Across the Busy Years* described the range of topics they covered: cabinet appointments; tariffs; the future of the League of Nations; the interdependence of economic and political issues, nationally as well as internationally; the problems of the Versailles Treaty. Although he didn't necessarily take Butler's advice, Harding fully appreciated his passion both for understanding foreign affairs and for meddling in them. After Butler retired, in 1945, gossip columnist Walter Winchell revealed that when Harding was once asked about American foreign policy, "he said that foreign countries were frequently confused by the fact that the United States had two foreign policies . . . 'What are they?' he was asked. 'The Secretary of State's,' he said, 'and Nicholas Murray Butler's.'"

At one point in the morning, according to Butler, Harding turned to him and "looking at him straight in the face, said, 'Now, Murray Butler, look me straight in the eye and tell me what you would like in my Administration.'" Butler replied, "looking Senator Harding straight in the eye," that he wanted no appointment, his objective being "always and everywhere public opinion and not public office." He insisted that he would prefer to have the confidence of the administration rather than occupy a position in it. Harding was sorry, suggesting that if he wanted to be secretary of state, the office was his; if he did not want it, perhaps he would consider being ambassador to England. A curious ambivalence then creeps into Butler's account. Given the financial burdens of such a job, Butler said, his academic salary would not permit him to accept the ambassadorship "even for two or three years." But then he added that he would find "a reasonable term of office" very agreeable, that his wife would be an enormous asset to the embassy, and that he was sure he could obtain leave from Columbia to hold the post for a short time. Having just denied his interest in any appointed position, he seemed in the next breath to be hoping for the ambassadorship, although on his own terms. Perhaps the terms were too strict, or perhaps Harding determined later that Butler would not be right for England. Whatever the reason, nothing more was said about the possibility of Butler serving at the Court of St. James's. On June 7, 1921, Harding offered to nominate him as ambassador to Japan; Butler found the idea "out of the question."

At the same time that he rejected this last proposal, he was preparing for his annual three-month visit to Europe. The three Butlers—Kate, Sarah, and Murray—were to leave June 14 on the *Aquitania*. On June 6 and 7 the story broke across the country that Butler had been asked to address the premiers of the British dominions on the evening of June 22 at an Imperial Conference to be held in London during that time. Although the details of the speech were obscure, Butler let it be known that he would deal with the general topic of the relation of the dominions and colonies to the British Empire and, specifically, with the advantages and disadvantages of consolidated as opposed to federated governments. The press hailed the invitation as a tribute not just to Butler but to America. That Great Britain would want the opinion of a private American citizen on how to organize the British Empire revealed how much the Old World respected the New.

By June 8, however, editorial skepticism began circulating about the nature of the invitation and the body that had issued it. On June 9 *The New York Sun*, which had enthusiastically celebrated the event only days before, declared it all a misunderstanding: no invitation of any sort had come from the British government, and Butler would not participate in any of the conference's official proceedings. Butler, it turned out, along with a number of other men, had been invited to address a society organized for the betterment of relations among the Allied nations that had participated in the war. It was hoped that perhaps Lloyd George and some of the dominion premiers might attend.

Butler had been the initial source of the misleading information, and now he felt obliged to correct the false impression. On June 10 he issued a splendidly fudgy explanation, saying he had received an invitation (he doesn't say from whom) that had been understood (he doesn't say by whom) "to be part of the programme for the entertainment of the distinguished visitors from the colonies, and as such to have the full knowledge and approval of the Government." With this understanding, Butler had accepted. Shortly afterward, "inquiry was made"(he doesn't say by whom) "as to the precise character of the meeting" he was to address. "Until information on these points could be had it was impossible to make any definite statement in response to the inquiries that were received." Butler concluded superbly: "In any event, I feel sure that the public importance of the invitation has been exaggerated."

But the exaggerated importance of the invitation at the start of the trip couldn't compare with the exaggerated importance Butler claimed for the trip itself. Describing it in *Across the Busy Years*, Butler professed embarrassment at the glowing headlines his visit elicited in the European press, some both annoying and startling:

> Was Nicholas Murray Butler President Harding's Representative In Recent Tour? Unprecedented Official Reception; More Distinctions Than Were Given Either To Theodore Roosevelt Or To Wilson; Appeared Before House Of Commons For Hours In Extraordinary Session—Utterly Unprecedented; Weekend With King Of Belgium; American Traveller Who Was Given A Unique Luncheon By The Benchers Of Gray's Inn; Received Unheard Of Honors From The Academie Française And The Sorbonne In Paris; Weekend Guest Of The Prime Minister Of England.

Butler claimed to have been especially disturbed by "these very superlative comments" because many of the "conferences and visits to which they alluded were kept quite confidential." Yet all the headlines came from a memo he had written himself and given to Edward Marshall on September 26, five days after his return, wanting Marshall to distribute it across the United States through his news service: "The enclosed is a bare statement of facts such as you desire, and you will have to decide what to put in and what to leave out, and what mode of treatment to adopt." Written in the third person and headed "America's Unofficial Ambassador," a title Butler conferred upon himself, it revealed the source of the material Butler found so embarrassing:

> The above is the phrase used by the European press and frequently by European statesmen to describe N.M.B. during his 1921 visit to Europe, which has just ended. During these three months he has . . . enjoyed a series of experiences and exercised an influence on international relations that are said in Europe to be quite without a parallel . . . More distinguished honors were reserved for him than

were given either Theodore Roosevelt or Woodrow Wilson, despite the fact that one was and the other had been the head of his state. In Great Britain, in France and in Belgium, the three countries included in the visit, the story was the same . . . He had long and intimate discussions with the chief officials of the British and French Foreign Offices . . . and he met in the most intimate personal relationship every important political personality in Western Europe.

Butler detailed the honors reaped in each country he visited: the special luncheon given him by the Benchers of Gray's Inn in London, at which the lord chancellor "spoke in most flattering terms of his influence upon the public policies and international relations of civilized nations"; the "overwhelming" reception he received in France, "both in the character and the variety of the honors conferred," including a "personal reception by the Académie Française, an honor given for the first time in its more than 300 years of history"; the full discussions, at a private meeting with the king and queen of Belgium, "of the problems, economic, financial and political, that are confronting Europe and the world."

With barely enough space to cover the major episodes of distinction, the memo explained, those of lesser note had to be passed over, "although under ordinary circumstances any one of these might well have stood out as in itself remarkable." Butler included, at the end of the account, an updated list of his honorary degrees, orders, and decorations to document a French newspaper's contention "that N.M.B. had received a larger and more distinguished recognition by Universities and Governments than any other person in modern life." Transforming this memo into a proper press release, with all the headlines featured on its first page, Marshall sent it out in early October so that all of America could share in Butler's triumph.

Of the trip's many alleged significant events, none was more important to Butler than his July 9 weekend at Chequers, the British prime minister's country home. He had been invited by Lloyd George to spend time with the dominion premiers—the same group of men he had unquestionably *not* been asked to address earlier. According to Butler, the meeting was called because New Zealand, Australia, and Canada, dissatisfied with their position in the British Empire, were threatening to secede unless they were granted independence from the authority of the British Parliament; Lloyd George had asked Butler, as an expert in federated systems of government, to speak about the advantages of the commonwealth structure. After several hours of intense discussion, Butler succeeded in convincing the premiers to accept the British Commonwealth of Nations as a substitute for the empire. Lloyd George imposed a pledge of secrecy upon everybody until the complicated political arrangements could be worked out, accounting for the fact that the press didn't talk about it. The Statute of Westminster, formally recognizing the commonwealth, was passed ten years later.

Or so Butler would have it. But not everybody agreed with Butler's version of his timely intervention on behalf of the commonwealth. In 1947, when Butler revealed in a luncheon address what had happened twenty-six years earlier, two of the actual participants claimed that he had fabricated the entire story. Arthur Meighan, prime minister of Canada at the time, dismissed Butler's narrative as a "pipe dream"; and William Hughes, the Australian leader in 1921, said, "There is not a word of truth in it." When reached for comment, Butler simply said that Lloyd George had told him that the three countries were planning to withdraw.

The summer and fall of 1921 were intoxicating times for Butler. The triumph—both real and self-proclaimed—of his European trip was reinforced by Harding's obvious interest in listening to him. Butler's visits to the White House encouraged him to think he could obtain presidential backing for his most urgent international priority: getting the United States to renounce its opposition to the League of Nations. In a less partisan political world, Butler would have been strongly supportive of Wilson and his League idea from the very beginning, for their internationalist visions had much in common. Both men were convinced of the need for a new kind of global order—one based ultimately on principles of American liberal democracy—to ensure that international law be respected, international obligations honored, and the rights of all nations to peaceful self-determination accepted. Both argued for the reduction of armaments, freedom of the seas, and the removal of tariff barriers that impeded international trade. Both wanted to find ways to prevent international disagreements from developing into full-scale wars. And both were guilty of the kind of moral idealism—or political naïveté—that would later be derided by such hard-nosed political realists as George Kennan and Walter Lippmann.

But no number of common goals or intellectual affinities could compensate for the fact that Wilson was a Democrat; and from the moment Wilson submitted the Covenant of the League to the third plenary session of the Versailles Peace Conference on February 14, 1919, Butler mocked its sloppiness and imprecision, calling it one of the worst-drafted documents he had ever seen. At the same time that he objected to its obscurity, and to the potential threat to American sovereignty posed by some of its stipulations, Butler recognized the genuine hope such a society of nations offered the world. While party loyalty required him to find manifold fault with the president's formulation, his own philosophical convictions drove him to "endeavor to show how it may be transformed into a wiser and better plan."

The debate over American participation in the League of Nations raged for more than a year, until on March 19, 1920, the Senate refused by the necessary two-thirds majority to ratify the Treaty of Versailles, of which the Covenant was an essential part. During this time, a group of pro-League Republican senators known as the Mild Reservationists sought Butler's advice. In contrast to the Irreconcilables or Battalion of Death—a set of their Republican colleagues firmly opposed to treaty and Covenant—these Mild Reservationists, who included Porter McCumber of North Dakota, Albert Cummins of Iowa, Selden Spenser of Missouri, Frederick Hale of Maine, Knute Nelson and Frank Kellogg of Minnesota, Charles McNary of Oregon, and LeBaron Colt of Rhode Island, were inclined to support the League as long as the Covenant could be adjusted to protect American interests.

In May 1919 Hale asked Butler if he could come to Washington to discuss ways to make the League palatable to some skeptical senators. Butler responded the same day that he was too busy, but he agreed with Hale that the Republicans could not afford to break with what he called the party's "splendid tradition" of constructive involvement in international affairs. American participation in the life of the world must continue, even if "President Wilson has muddled the international situation in almost every imaginable way." He claimed that Wilson was "likely to be considered by history as the greatest marplot of modern times" for combining the Treaty of Versailles with the Covenant, but he argued that the Senate had to move beyond Wilson's incompetence to find a way to endorse the League idea. He concluded by suggesting some ways in which that might be done.

Hale showed Butler's letter to Frank Kellogg, and on May 31 Kellogg wrote to Butler that he, too, wanted to discuss the League with him. Invitations from two senators were hard to resist, and on the afternoon of June 11 Butler arrived at Hale's Washington house where a number of senators were gathered. The talk immediately focused on Butler's ideas of what modifications could be attached to the Covenant that might get it passed in the Senate. A long, intense evening followed, with Butler sketching out his proposed reservations in rough form, incorporating in them some of the suggestions offered by the senators. The next day he sent to Hale a more polished version of what he thought the group had agreed upon — essentially the recommendations he had made to Hale in his May 19 letter: that the Covenant not be construed to interfere with American control of its own domestic policies; that League membership would in no way affect America's "traditional attitude toward purely American questions" (i.e., the Monroe Doctrine); that the obligations imposed by Article X, requiring the use of force to guarantee the territorial integrity and independence of all members, would not supersede Congress's constitutional power to declare war. Included was a plea for the establishment of a Permanent Court of International Justice.

Although not every senator who met with Butler agreed with all his proposals, his formulation did help organize the Mild Reservationists' agenda. As Butler reminded Kellogg some six years later, "Do not forget that that was the beginning of the whole discussion. Until you and Hale assembled that group, nothing at all substantial had been done in reference to the reception of the Treaty when it returned." Despite Butler's attempt to make the Covenant acceptable, the opposition of the Irreconcilables, led by Henry Cabot Lodge, to any infringement of American sovereignty, along with Wilson's intransigence about compromise, made the Senate's rejection of the League inevitable.

But with the arrival of Harding and the Republicans in Washington, Butler became hopeful that perhaps the country could be made to understand the virtues of the League of Nations. Harding, after all, had maintained during his campaign that he favored joining, and Butler, with thirty other prominent pro-League Republicans, had signed a letter saying that a vote for Harding was the only way to guarantee America's entry into the League. Soon, however, Butler understood that the diffident Harding had no intention of taking on the League antagonists in his own party. Campaign rhetoric was one thing, political exertion quite another. Butler's assurances to the public notwithstanding, Harding exhibited no interest in the issue.

The realization that he could not shape the new administration's agenda was a painful shock to Butler. His hope that the United States would recognize the world's political and economic unity by participating in an organization intended to help solve its problems was not to be. Nor would the punitive German war debt be reconsidered or protective tariff rates lowered. The "international mind," in short, which Butler had patented in 1912 as the only viable way of dealing with a complicated world, was not in evidence in his own Republican Party.

Harding's sudden death, in August 1923, did little, in Butler's mind, to improve the quality of the presidency. His prompt telegram to Vice President Coolidge on learning about Harding—"In their great sorrow your countrymen turn to you for your leadership at this critical time in the world's history"—represented a pious hope that Butler knew Coolidge could not realize. As little faith as he came to have in Harding, he had even less in Coolidge or Hoover. Butler thought the progression from Harding to Coolidge to Hoover described an appalling downward spiral of competence and vision. All three failed to understand the need for international cooperation; none was willing to take a strong position against the national absurdity of Prohibition. Even before the crash of 1929 sent the country and the world reeling into depression, Butler was inveighing against the bankruptcy of the Republican Party. "The general feeling is that the Republicans will lose control of the Senate after the elections of 1926," he wrote Professor John Dyneley Prince in February of that year. "They certainly ought to, for they have shown themselves incompetent to act when they nominally had control. They are a poor lot and not more than six or eight of them are fit to be in the Senate at all." Butler's despair intensified as time went on. "During the past eight years," he complained to Henry Pritchett in 1928, "the government at Washington has reached the lowest intellectual and moral level recorded in our history." Everywhere he looked, he found mediocrity, cowardice, and hypocrisy. "The political situation grows gloomier and gloomier," he lamented to his brother William in 1932, "as each outgiving from Washington, whether executive or legislative, surpasses its predecessor in stupidity and incompetence."

Butler's condemnation of Republican failure was undoubtedly affected in part by his lingering frustration at not having been chosen to lead the party—and therefore the country. But his diagnosis went deeper than the simple inadequacy of the three Republican presidents. Butler saw party rot taking hold with the establishment of the direct primary and the direct election of senators in 1913: "The plain fact is that the developments of the past ten years, including the direct primary system, have blown the parties to pieces." This judgment might seem peculiar for a person as strongly committed to the democratic process as Butler, but his admiration for representative democracy as the ideal form of government was always at war with his desire for control. In Butler's view, the democratic system functioned most effectively when an informed elite were left free to manage things. Nominees for important public office should be chosen not through a public referendum, but by a small group of responsible, serious people: party leaders, whose concerns were congruent with those of the country, as opposed to the workings of the direct primary, which were vulnerable to the distortions of voter self-interest, the corrupting powers of money, the perversions of campaign advertising. (Why the caucuses of the sober and the thoughtful should remain exempt from these influences he did not say.) From Butler's perspective, the results were a country led by blundering executives, inept congressmen, and a party system that could no longer be counted upon to produce qualified talent.

From the time Butler first came to political consciousness, his loyal Republicanism had never been in doubt. Identification with a single party had always been for him an essential ingredient of the healthy political life. But now the steadfast Republican "wheelhorse" began to find himself at odds with his party's leadership and values. Flailing away at Republican policies, he turned himself into a kind of moral and political maverick. The columnist Haywood Hale Broun, a longtime Butler skeptic, joined *The Nation* and others in celebrating Butler's transformation. "One of the most amazing of modern miracles," Broun wrote, "is the second blooming of Nicholas Murray Butler." Recalling the platitudes Butler had spewed at him during his high school commencement in 1906 — "He was for everything powerful and smug and entrenched" — Broun marveled at his development into an indomitable truth teller, prepared to take on his own party in the interests of principle.

Not everybody approved. As Butler's dissatisfaction grew more vocal, he was chided for his lack of loyalty. How could he attack the party that had done so much for him, that had put him on the ticket in 1912 to collect the vice presidential votes after James Sherman died? The criticism was understandable, if misplaced. Butler's loyalties were not capricious, but they were finally inseparable from the needs of his powerful narcissism. He functioned as a dedicated team player as long as he could feel that he was the team. In Butler's mind, at least, Columbia and Butler were inseparable. "Columbia, *c'est moi*" was the only way he ever conceived of his institution.

Butler brought the same attitude to his connection to the Republican Party. His commitment was unquestioned as long as he could nourish the fantasy that he and his party were one. The 1920 nominating convention demonstrated that things were not quite so cozy, but he still hoped that through his relationship with Harding, he could bring the Republicans to do his bidding anyway. When that too began to prove illusory, Butler could find few compelling reasons to continue to play the party loyalist. Instead of achieving satisfaction by working to shape party policies from within its inner circles, he would take his positions directly to the public and bludgeon from the outside.

His outspokenness led one newspaper editor to pose a question many must have been thinking: "At the risk of being impudent and because you present an enigma to me," Rollin Kirby of the *New York World-Telegram* wrote Butler in 1932,

> I am curious to know why you stay within the Republican party. Your splendidly liberal ideas seem to clash at every point with those of your party . . . I daresay it is none of anyone's business except your own, but you, together with Newton Baker, Walter Lippmann and Al Smith (with reservations) seem to me to be about the only voices we have that are worth listening to and if we are to extricate ourselves from the mess in which we now stew and fret it must be with the help of such ideas as you four propound.

Butler was pleased that Kirby recognized the extent to which his "liberal ideas" differed sharply from those proclaimed by Republican Party leaders and officeholders:

> I have been trying for many years to turn the Republican Party into a truly liberal and progressive political organization, and every once in a while have seemed to be on the point of getting some success. Since 1919, however, the progress has been steadily backwards and the intellectual and moral bankruptcy of the Party organization is now substantially complete.

However unsatisfactory the Republicans, Butler pointed out, the inescapable reality of American political life permitted no significant role for third parties; the only way to achieve influence was to retain formal contact with the party of one's original choice. To leave was to renounce any possibility of redeeming it. Butler hoped that what he expected to be the Republican debacle in the forthcoming election in November would provide a catalyst for change.

Kirby was delighted with the forthrightness of the response and asked Butler if he could publish it. Butler refused permission, emphasizing its strictly confidential nature and claiming that all his delicate efforts to reform the party would collapse if it were made public. Kirby honored Butler's request to keep the letter private.

Butler would not desert the Republicans, but he was not averse to shaking up American political apathy. In a speech before the National Industrial Conference Board at the Waldorf-Astoria on the evening of May 19, 1932, he caught the attention of the country—and the front page of *The New York Times* (which published the entire text the next day)—by calling for new party configurations. Instead of the fraudulent and artificial distinctions that no longer separated Republican from Democrat, Butler proposed giving voters a real choice: a Constitutional Liberal Party, appealing to "the most intelligent men and women throughout this land who now call themselves either Democrats or Republicans without being in the least able to tell what those words mean"; and a (nameless) opposition party, which would attract "all those who prefer compulsion in any of its forms to the historic principles of civil, economic and political liberty," who prefer "persecution to tolerance, prohibition to temperance, and control or compulsion of individual thought . . . to liberty," among other questionable preferences. It would offer a haven "to the Ku, Klux, Klan, to the prohibitionists, to the doctrinaire Socialists and to the Communists," as he put it later.

Butler's speech, a dramatic way of publicizing his own urgent agenda to reinvigorate the country, drew on an idea that he had been playing with for years. He had first lamented the flaccid, indistinguishable nature of the political parties in an address to the Columbia Institute of Arts and Sciences in 1922, suggesting that the country would be better served if the meaningless distinction between Democrats and Republicans gave way to two new parties: a "Democratic-Republican" Party, embodying what he called the "predominant liberalism" of the American people, and a "distinctly radical party," strictly opposed to the Democratic-Republicans' policies. The country would then have a real choice—in Butler's rather heavily freighted rhetoric—between "constructive liberals" and "destructive radicals."

Ten years of frustration with the incompetent Republican leadership led Butler to supply the Waldorf-Astoria address with the crucial ingredient that had been missing from the 1922 version: "a definite, a constructive and a rational program" on which the new party could take its stand. Butler's platform, deliberately echoing Woodrow Wilson's outline for peace presented to Congress in 1918, consisted of fourteen points. They came ready made for his Constitutional Liberal Party from a speech he had given at the National Republican Club on November 17, 1931, entitled "What Should Be the Republican Program in 1932?" The fourteen points embraced all of Butler's major political concerns, including the need for the repeal of Prohibition; a balanced national budget; tariff reform; cooperation with the League of Nations; adherence to the Court of International Justice; reorganization of the federal government; reconsideration of war debt; genuine disarmament; examination of the world's monetary system; unemployment insurance; and farm relief.

With his fourteen-point program to move America forward in place, Butler concluded with a description of the human qualities necessary to implement it, qualities Butler was himself prepared to offer the country: "clear thinking, administrative capacity and outspoken moral courage." In his call for a new party, Butler's address in fact announced what various perceptive observers had already noticed: the emergence of the aspiring mainstream politico as fearless critic of American domestic and international abuses. Among the domestic issues, Prohibition had long been his primary obsession.

On December 5, 1933, at 5:32 p.m. eastern standard time, Utah delegate S. R. Thurman cast the ballot that brought to the necessary three quarters the number of states ratifying the Twenty-first Amendment to the Constitution. (Utah could have ratified as early as November, but it had delayed, intent on claiming for itself the honor of putting an end to Prohibition. Assured that Pennsylvania had already become the thirty-fifth state to endorse repeal, Thurman went ahead to invest Utah with its permanent place in American history.) Shortly thereafter, at 7:00, President Franklin Delano Roosevelt affixed his signature to the amendment. Thirteen years, ten months, and eighteen days after it began, Prohibition was no more.

Intended to save Americans from their basest instincts, Prohibition succeeded primarily in encouraging new ways to express them. At 12:01 a.m. on
January 17, 1920, when it became illegal to buy or sell alcoholic beverages,
the country plunged into a morass of hypocrisy and criminal activity that its
temperance advocates could scarcely have imagined. Drinking was not seriously affected, but only the country's moral fiber. H. L. Mencken's estimate, though exaggerated, catches the spirit of the social disaster wreaked
by the Eighteenth Amendment: "It seemed almost a geologic epoch while
it was going on, and the human suffering that it entailed must have been a
fair match for that of the Black Death or the Thirty Years War."

The prominent heroes of the wets in the struggle for repeal were numerous, including Governor Al Smith of New York, Pierre du Pont, the
banker Charles Sabin, the philanthropist Edward S. Harkness, Democratic
National Committee chairman John Raskob, and, late in the day (but not
insignificantly), John D. Rockefeller, Jr. Among the less distinguished—as
Alva Johnston wryly pointed out in a 1933 New Yorker article—were the en-
trepreneurs who demonstrated that Prohibition generated vast amounts of
crime while simultaneously depriving the government of much needed tax
revenues, men like Dutch Schultz, Waxy Gordon, Legs Diamond, and
Frankie Yale.

Of all of these players, legitimate and illegitimate alike, no one was so
insistent and articulate a foe of the Eighteenth Amendment as Butler. Arguing vociferously from every conceivable pulpit, Butler turned his hatred
of Prohibition—"I regard prohibition as a form of mental disease . . . I feel
about it as my father and grandfather felt about slavery"—into an urgent
personal crusade. "So wet he wears a bathing suit when he walks down Fifth
Avenue" and "wetter than the high seas," as several hostile editorial writers
wrote, Butler deserved as much credit as anybody for bringing the case for
repeal before the nation. The acknowledgment he received at a dinner in
1933 from the Association of Foreign Correspondents, as the one man "most
responsible for repeal," was a defensible assessment.

He did not begin actively battling until 1924, a fact he later attributed to
his desire to see whether or not Prohibition would actually work. The explanation is only partly convincing. He was not about to address the politically vexed issue while seeking the Republican nomination in 1920, nor did
he want to put at risk his close relationship with Harding for some time after that. But by 1924 he was resigned to the failure of his own presidential

ambitions (with Coolidge in the White House) and disgusted enough with the ditherings of the Republican Party to be willing, in his own words, "to take the risk of being unpopular for the sake of being right." He launched his first full-scale assault on April 29 at a dinner of the Missouri Society in New York's Plaza Hotel. In a passionate address entitled "Prohibition Is Now a Moral Issue," he denounced the Eighteenth Amendment (and its enabling legislation, the Volstead Act) as responsible for the "shocking and immoral" conditions currently ravaging the country. Instead of curing the liquor problem, Prohibition had encouraged "a nation-wide traffic in intoxicating liquors which is unlicensed, illicit, illegal, and untaxed . . . We have invited and induced a spirit and a habit of lawlessness which are quite without precedent and which reach from the highest ranks in the nation's life to the lowest and most humble."

For Butler, ratification of the Eighteenth Amendment guaranteed the disaster that followed: it "is the corner-stone of the whole vast immoral, degrading and law-breaking system that has been built upon it." Beneath the rhetorical excess to which he was prone—"Such is the pass of hypocrisy, of double-dealing, of cowardice, and of public and private immorality to which we have been reduced by the policy of prohibition"—Butler's argument was straightforward: the Constitution was intended to establish a form of government, not to enumerate regulations structuring people's lives. Attempting to dictate what people eat or drink was blatantly unconstitutional, "a form of oppression to which a free people will never submit in silence." The issue, he wrote to Pierre du Pont, was not alcohol so much as governmental principle. "I should be just as much opposed to it [the Eighteenth Amendment] if it dealt with spinach, or turnips, or beef." While combating the evils of the saloon had become a public necessity—and Butler was more or less obliged to sign on to this claim—it could be accomplished only through individual state regulations, not by amending the Constitution of the United States. Federal Prohibition laws allowed the sphere of government to invade the sphere of liberty—a moral violation of the highest sort and a threat to the very foundations of America's political and social order. Butler likened his mission to that of Abraham Lincoln reacting to the Fugitive Slave Law: "Like Abraham Lincoln, I shall obey these laws so long as they remain upon the statute book; but, like Abraham Lincoln, I shall not rest until they are repealed."

The speech pushed Butler to the forefront of the repeal movement.

Butler's leadership in the fight against prohibition was recognized in 1929 in cartoons from New York, Dallas, St. Louis, and Springfield newspapers.

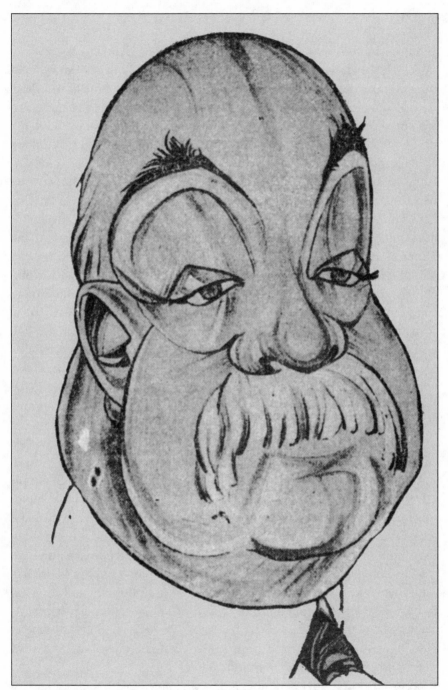

Gonzalez of the *Brooklyn Eagle* claimed that Butler's head reminded him of a ripe pear, August 1924.

Lionized by the wets, he was vilified by the drys. Georgia congressman W. D. Upshaw, a leading proponent of Prohibition, thought Butler should be sent on the next boat to Europe (with no particular destination), where he would feel at home with "more than half the women in the cafes smoking and drinking with the men and where whole nations had been sodden drunk for centuries." Wayne Wheeler, chief spokesman for the Anti-Saloon League of America, suggested that Butler was at one "with the boot-leggers, rum-runners, owners of speak-easy property, wet newspapers, underworld denizens, alcoholic slaves and personal liberty fanatics in his fight to bring back booze." (To which Butler managed the splendidly laconic, "It sounds as if something had happened to trouble him.") Less overwrought but rather more harrowing was Dr. Harvey Wiley's recommendation that Butler "should be tried as Socrates was for corrupting the youth of the nation." Butler relished the press attention his anti-Prohibition comments earned him, but at the same time his goal remained decidedly practical: to galvanize the country into demanding repeal. Educating public opinion through a steady stream of Dr. Butlerisms would be the way to influence party platforms and candidates' views. However heated his own rhetoric, he always kept one eye coolly fixed on the polling booth, knowing that was where the remedy lay. He began declaring as early as 1926 that Prohibition would be *the* issue in the 1928 election, thereby desperately hoping to make it so.

His outspokenness made it inevitable that he would again surface as a political candidate, this time for the New York gubernatorial race in 1928, but he declared, as he always did, that he was not interested. Unlike his alleged indifference to the 1920 presidential nomination, this disclaimer was legitimate, though the reasons were more complicated than those he gave—his usual insistence that he couldn't bring himself to leave Columbia before his work was done. First, it would have been demeaning for a man who sought the presidency to be seen aspiring for a lesser position; second, there was no way in which Nicholas Murray Butler was ever going to beat the four-time (and current) governor, the enormously popular Al Smith, one of the country's most charismatic politicians, should Smith decide to pursue a fifth term. Even if Butler wanted the position, he would never allow himself to risk the humiliation of losing.

Refusing to consider opposing Smith (who opted to run for president instead), Butler understood that he could use him to further his wet agenda, which Smith shared. At Columbia's 1926 commencement in June, Butler the staunch Republican conferred an honorary degree upon the Democrat Smith. Enraged New York State Republicans, appalled by such treason, stormed that Butler would now never receive the Republican nomination, missing the point that Butler, not interested in it, was implicitly endorsing Smith's repeal position by honoring him. When it came to the evils of Prohibition, Butler was only too happy to declare himself oblivious to partisan politics.

Soon Butler's harangues made him the object of official Republican hostility. Idaho senator William Borah, Butler's rhetorical equal and perhaps the most prominent spokesman for the drys, demonized him as more dangerous than the "ragged, unshaven bolshevist." Upstate New York Republicans accused Butler and former senator James Wadsworth of trying to impose their wet wills on a party that favored Prohibition. They were right, of course. Butler was explicitly committed to shifting the Republican position despite the opposition of its leaders, including, in 1927, President Calvin Coolidge. And as he was enjoying his notoriety as national moral therapist, his party's hostility could hardly deter him.

Coolidge's unwillingness to take a strong position on the question, out of fear of driving a wedge in the Republicans between wets and drys, moved him squarely into Butler's crosshairs. The president was now an obstacle to be overcome rather than the party leader to be supported. In an inauspicious setting—the Riverside Republican Club in New York on the evening of February 7, 1927—Butler burned many of his remaining Republican bridges before a small and unsuspecting audience. Conflating two separate issues—that of a possible third term for Coolidge and his refusal to take a decisive stand on Prohibition—Butler preempted Coolidge by announcing that the president had too much common sense to seek reelection. As if that weren't sufficiently presumptuous, he went on:

In 1928 no candidate for President can escape making known with definiteness and decision his attitude towards prohibition . . . If he endeavors to avoid committing himself, to pussyfoot and to please all elements, he will be even worse beaten than if, like a brave man, he comes out for what I believe to be the wrong and immoral policy.

Butler's comments provoked the country. Republicans were incensed at Butler's effrontery in injecting Prohibition into the forthcoming campaign

"An Embarrassing Moment. Butler: 'Your Hat and Coat Sir?'"

"Noisy, But Not Disturbing"

"The New Spokesman"

(ABOVE AND OPPOSITE) Responses to Butler's announcement in 1927 that Calvin Coolidge would not run for another term

Butler identifies himself with Patrick Henry in criticizing the policies of presidential candidate Herbert Hoover, 1928.

and in effectively making the sitting president of his own party a lame duck before Coolidge could speak for himself. Editorial writers across the nation examined the question of whether or not Coolidge had technically served two previous terms (since he had merely completed Harding's after his death in 1923) and if, in any case, he should be encouraged to seek another. Butler's argument that Coolidge would be violating the precedent against running for a third term if he sought reelection was clever, if not altogether compelling. He insisted that a term should be defined by the taking of the oath of office. No matter that Coolidge's first oath resulted from the death of Harding. Two oaths equal two terms, and in the American political tradition no one ran for a third.

It was a vintage Butler performance: sucking the air out of other political issues, putting himself on the editorial pages of every newspaper, inserting his personal agenda into the national discourse. The attention he earned was such that the *Times* of March 2 wondered:

> Is Dr. Nicholas Murray Butler, president of Columbia University, arriving at the conclusion that he is about to hear the call to sacrifice on the political altar? Is he at the crossroads that must lead to a decision in which the presidency is the goal? If not, he is uncommonly interested as a mere bystander. A few weeks ago he suddenly became his own spokesman on several matters that may have a bearing on the 1928 nomination in the Republican national convention.

The furor Butler had aroused did not lead to a call to the presidency, but it did produce, a week later, a call of quite a different sort. It came from Robert Washburn, president of the Roosevelt Club, a slightly moribund Republican club in Boston. Picking up on the challenge to debate that Borah had thrown down following Butler's February 7 talk, Washburn offered the auspices of the Roosevelt Club to bring together the two prominent Republicans with their diametrically opposed views. Butler, who had previously refused to speak at a meeting sponsored by the Massachusetts branch of the highly partisan Anti-Saloon League, welcomed the chance to debate Borah on neutral ground. The resolution over which the two would argue was uncomplicated: "Shall the Republican national platform of 1928 advocate the repeal of the eighteenth amendment?" The date was set for April 8.

Republican leaders were not happy at the prospect of the debate, because it drew attention to an issue they intended to obscure. Frank W. Stearns, a Coolidge confidant, resigned his membership in the Roosevelt Club to protest the importance being given to the question. But while Coolidge and Republican officialdom cringed and frowned, the public greeted the prospect of the Butler-Borah confrontation with enormous enthusiasm. The anticipated showdown between the two Republican heavyweights naturally gave rise to boxing metaphors. The *Newark News* hailed it as a bout between "Battling Borah and N.M. (Cyclone) Butler," listing Borah as 5'7⅞" and 182 pounds, and Butler as 5'6⅞" and 185. The *Seattle Post Intelligencer* preferred "'Kid' Butler, the Columbia Catamount vs. 'Wild Bill' Borah, the Boise Bearcat." The *Hartford Courant* saw it as a fight between "'Tousled-headed' Borah, the Nemesis of Nullificationists and 'Talkative Nick' Butler, the Protector of Personal Privilege." Others less pugilistically inclined placed it in the tradition of America's great debates, like those between Lincoln and Douglas, Webster and Hayne.

Washburn had obtained Boston's Symphony Hall as the venue and had arranged for radio coverage. (His motivation in staging this event was not simply public-spirited. It also thrust him into the national spotlight. Various editorial writers described him as the Tex Ricard—the legendary boxing promoter—of political debate. More practically, once it became known that all registered members of the Roosevelt Club would be assured of tickets, enrollment immediately soared to its full quota of 1,000. The previous summer it had languished at 375.)

Excitement over the Butler-Borah debate grew as April 8 approached. (With his punctilious attention to narcissistic detail, Butler had insisted that Washburn bill it as "Butler-Borah," despite the alphabetical primacy of Borah's name.) Whatever the metaphor or context, it was awaited as an event of national significance.

Every seat in Symphony Hall was filled on the evening of April 8. Three hundred additional people sat on the stage. Scalpers flourished, selling last-minute tickets at the exorbitant price of $20.00. Arrangements for nationwide radio coverage had not worked out, and the event was broadcast only in the local Boston area. Sharing the front of the stage with the combatants were Washburn and former senator William M. Butler (no relation) of Massachusetts, chairman of the Republican National Convention. Butler was dressed in formal dinner clothes; Borah, as befitted a rugged westerner, wore an ordinary business suit and sported a shaggy, round haircut known as a "badger." Newspapermen sat at the foot of the stage, ready to give their copy to messenger boys who were primed to scramble through the audience to deliver it to the telegraph operators waiting in rooms outside the auditorium.

In form, it was no more a debate than are the quadrennial American presidential debates. Butler spoke first, his affirmative argument restating the basic claim he had been making all along: the issue of Prohibition was only incidentally about liquor. "It is primarily and chiefly a question of government." Not only did the Eighteenth Amendment not belong in the Constitution, but it didn't work, representing "the worst possible way of dealing with the evils of the liquor traffic and the saloon." Lest anybody should have failed to notice, Butler referred to the prosperous bootleggers and the "murders, the entrapments, the solicitations to crimes" that had resulted from Prohibition.

The only effective cure was to place the responsibility for the control of liquor in the hands of the individual states, which could then pursue the sort of system he stressed had been successful in Quebec and Scandinavia, based on abolishing the saloon and private liquor traffic and putting the sale of liquor under government ("state") supervision. Should these measures be adopted, Butler argued, the country would be back on the way to "that progress in temperance" it was following before the "debacle" of Prohibition occurred.

Butler concluded by wrapping himself in the mantle of American political heroes, thereby enrolling them in his anti-Prohibition forces:

> For myself I claim the privilege and assert the duty to preserve and to uphold the great American tradition, and to follow after in the footsteps of Washington and Adams, of Hamilton and Jefferson, of Madison and Marshall, of Webster and Lincoln.
> "My country 'tis of thee,
> Of thee I sing."

Borah appealed to the sacredness of the Constitution and the duty of all to obey it. When the Supreme Court endorsed the constitutionality of the amendment, Borah insisted, the issue was resolved. It was not a question of whether it belonged or not; it was simply there. Retreating from upholding it was only to contribute to the lawlessness that his esteemed opponent had lamented.

Borah maintained that critics of Prohibition had to propose a sensible alternative if they were to be taken seriously. The problem with Butler's state control of liquor was that the dry states would be vulnerable to commercial invasion from the wets. In one of his better lines, which induced cheers, laughter, and applause, Borah noted that "the wet states can ship wet into the dry states, but the dry states can not ship dry into the wet states." He would have been happy supporting a better solution than the Eighteenth Amendment, Borah said, if one had existed. But as there clearly was none, national Prohibition remained the only answer. As to Butler's charge that it had failed, Borah retorted that not enough time had passed to make that determination. If after a quarter of a century no progress was made, then it might be time "to talk about a repeal of the Eighteenth Amendment and going back to the saloon."

Rhetorical pyrotechnics aside, the meeting on the same platform "of two of the most brilliant minds of the country" had no discernible effect on the public's understanding of the issue. Despite the boxing metaphors leading up to the debate, no real infighting occurred and no serious blows were struck. Butler's terse analysis of his differences with Borah is perhaps the best summary of the debate: "He believes the Eighteenth Amendment to be as germane to the Constitution . . . as those that have preceded it. I believe that it contradicts them all." Instead of slugging it out head-to-head, it was rather as if the two opponents were content to stand with their backs to each other, displaying their polished, carefully rehearsed combinations of lefts and rights to the spectators.

But as it was technically a debate, the *Boston Herald* had assigned nine ringside judges to score it. A smattering of lawyers and civic leaders, four were ostensibly wet, four dry, and one neutral. All were Republicans. The verdict? A 6–3 decision for Borah, a judgment that seemed to accord with the majority of the audience, at least as indicated by their applause at the announcement. Since Borah's central argument essentially held that the country had no reasonable alternative other than supporting Prohibition for at least twenty-five years, one wonders how damp the wet judges were, or how they responded to "Dr. Butler's" persona. Even as cynical and hard-nosed a type as Damon Runyon, however, who presumably had little affection for Prohibition, endorsed the decision. "I suppose a draw would be the safe decision, but being a bold man I must say I thought Senator Borah had a slight shade on points. He was not lingually as fast and graceful and shifty as Prexy Butler, from the big college on Morningside Heights, but he had the heavier punch."

Irrespective of who walked off with the prize, both Butler and Borah, with the connivance of Washburn, were pleased that they had embarrassed the Republican leadership, which had wanted to keep the subject quiet. Butler's disagreement with Borah (as well as personal dislike of him) did not prevent him from praising the senator for his willingness to debate publicly. In his mission to smoke out candidates' views on the question that dared not be mentioned, Butler acknowledged Borah as an ally. As much as he distrusted constitutional amendments, Butler was prepared to offer one more in the interests of honesty: "Resolved, all pussy-footers must wear rubber boots."

Butler never took kindly to losing, though, and he could not resist, nine years later, from throwing one last roundhouse right at his erstwhile foe. In 1936, while candidates for the Republican presidential nomination were jockeying for position, Butler knocked Borah clear out of the ring with a letter to a fellow Republican that found its way into the *Times*. Remarking that "of all those who have more or less coyly proposed their own names for the nomination," Borah was much the ablest, Butler added that unfortunately he was

a hopeless reactionary. He opposes, no doubt conscientiously, almost every progressive policy, national and international, upon which depend the future prosperity, satisfaction and peace of the American people. Moreover, he was the outstanding defender of the Eighteenth Amendment, the most anti-constitutional and demoralizing enactment ever written into the statutes of our nation.

This attack on Borah's plausibility as a candidate brought with it some unhappy consequences. Borah supporters resented the notion that their man was a "hopeless reactionary," arguing that he had voted for many important New Deal policies during the previous four years. The *Dayton News* commented that if Borah was a reactionary, "then it is certainly a case of the pot calling the kettle black." Republican backlash resulted in Butler's not being elected as a delegate from New York's 19th Congressional District; and in June 1936, for the first time in thirty-two years, he did not attend the national convention. (Butler contrived to put his best face on when the convention opened in Cleveland, saying only that "for reasons entirely satisfactory to myself . . . I shall not be a delegate.")

But in 1928 Butler continued to lecture the country—and the Republican Party—about the need to recognize the importance of the Prohibition question in the forthcoming election. If the Republicans didn't choose a candidate firmly opposed to the Eighteenth Amendment, Butler repeatedly warned, they would lose heavily. Such remarks were pointedly aimed at the evasive Herbert Hoover. Arriving in Kansas City early in June for the 1928 Republican convention, Butler announced that he wanted the party to "nominate a man with G-U-T-S." When asked if this included Hoover, Butler deftly sidestepped, saying that as a loyal organization man, he wouldn't discuss details or personalities. But he promised to do whatever was necessary to draft a wet plank for the platform.

The opposition, once again, was the indomitable Borah, equally determined to ensure a dry plank. Borah triumphed easily in the deliberations of the resolutions committee, but Butler vowed to continue the fight on the floor of the convention. The prospect of Butler's eloquence creating a rift did not please the party bigwigs, and plans were laid to keep it from happening. On the morning of June 14 Butler was entitled to speak for five minutes on behalf of his plank, but before he could, the convention chairman George Moses submitted the platform as a whole (instead of the separate planks) to be voted on, and the delegates promptly approved it. Moses then recognized Butler for his five minutes. At this point considerable noise and confusion broke out in the hall, as no one was sure what was happening. Moses made no effort to contain the disturbance, making it essentially impossible to hear what Butler was saying, though he did manage to propose at the end of his few minutes that his wet plank be substituted for the dry one.

Congressman Fiorello La Guardia, another wet delegate from New York, was scheduled to follow Butler, but Moses instead recognized Fred Dow, a dry Maine delegate, who moved that Butler's plank be tabled. Moses immediately called for a voice vote and declared, though not everybody in the hall agreed, that the "ayes" had it. Butler had lost again, outmaneuvered by the canny opposition. The young Arthur Krock, who went on to become a distinguished correspondent for *The New York Times*, was appalled at the dishonesty of the convention's manipulators:

The consideration of politics decided things for them. They do not agree with Dr. Butler that it is "safe to abandon cowardice and hypocrisy" on this issue. They believe it would have split their party and defeated their nominees if they had officially admitted the truth

that is clear to them, or proposed either amelioration or extension of
the enforcement provisions. So they stood by the same old formula,
chanted the same old words, dodged the same old obstacles. Then
many of them went back to their hotels . . . and had some drinks.

Hoover emerged from the convention with his dry plank and nomination in place, but Butler earned plaudits for his honesty and willingness to
take on the party establishment. H. L. Mencken, no great friend of Butler's,
exempted him from "the clown show" of hypocrisy and lying put on by the
Republicans, with its "unmitigated bilge, discharged in roaring streams
from red, raw necks" and its "old boozers moaning and slobbering for prohibition." In the midst of this "small-time vaudeville," Mencken found two
exceptions: "Dr. Nicholas Murray Butler, who made a cogent and dignified
appeal for honest dealing with the prohibition issue . . . and Bob La Fol-
lette."

Two months after the convention, Butler decided to give up even the
pretense of being a loyal organization man. In a blistering letter to the *Times*
of August 20, featured on the front page, he denounced Hoover's position
on the need for a strong navy, which Butler thought undermined the possibility of world peace, and on his refusal to consider repeal of the Eighteenth
Amendment. Hoover had "no conception of the real problem by which the
country is faced." To be against repeal was necessarily to be in favor of its
only alternative, "which is the continuance of the present reign of lawlessness, debauchery and Government-made crime"—a position endorsed by
every bootlegger in the country. Deriding Hoover for his absurdly inadequate views, Butler succeeded in making it "entirely plain . . . that no candidate of my party for the Presidency can commit me or countless others
like me to any such doctrines or to any such policies." Lest anyone should
fail to appreciate the momentous nature of this break with his party, Butler
concluded by associating himself with the famous words Patrick Henry had
uttered some 160 years earlier: " 'If that be treason, make the most of it.' "

The *Times*, always Butler's best advocate, applauded his courage, calling his letter the most "sensational" document of the campaign so far. His
comments, according to the paper, would at the very least make a powerful
impression on the voters of both parties and might indeed have a significant
effect on the outcome of the election. But beyond whatever practical consequences would follow, the fact that Butler was prepared to sacrifice his

lifelong Republican affiliation in the interests of principle served as a moral lesson to the nation: "Dr. Butler's statement of his unalterable beliefs which lead him away from his own party will go resounding through the country. It will be more than a sensation. It will be a great means of education in political morality."

Not everybody welcomed his forthrightness. Neither President Coolidge nor candidate Hoover deigned to respond, and various Republican leaders, such as Senator Arthur Capper of Kansas, emphasized that Butler did not speak for the Republican Party. The West, Capper insisted, stood solidly behind Hoover's Prohibition views. Press coverage was immense and predictably uneven. New York's *Herald Tribune* looked skeptically both at Butler and at the *Times*'s adulation of him: "The New York *Times* rhapsodizes over Dr. Butler as the Martin Luther of his age. Dr. Butler concedes his resemblance to Patrick Henry. To outsiders without specific gifts of insight he will appear even more like Dr. Butler being once more himself." The *Telegram*, however, remarked as "the most extraordinary development in American life" Butler's growth from conventional "good boy" to fearless, independent thinker:

> In a slightly earlier era the president was known to the student body as Ridiculous Hurry Nutler. To undergraduate eyes he was an old fluff who had a knack of raising endowments. Then things began to happen. Butler was almost the only man in his party who dared to tell the truth about prohibition. Nor did he state his case just once. He kept on telling painful truths when the demand for conformity was greatest.

Despite the fuss it created, Butler's criticism of Hoover didn't have the electoral impact the *Times* had predicted. Even without Butler's support, the dry Hoover went on to defeat the wet Smith handily, and Butler remained, at least nominally, a member of the Republican Party. Whether he actually voted for Hoover, whom he disliked, or crossed party lines for his Democratic friend and anti-Prohibition ally Smith, nobody knows. Butler never let on, but odds are that he permitted emotions to trump party loyalty and for the first time in his life voted for a Democrat.

His inability to convince the nation of Prohibition's complete failure distressed him considerably, but only strengthened his resolve to persevere.

In the interests of getting his message across, he even suggested in November to his wealthy wet colleague Pierre du Pont that it might be useful to "acquire a great organ of public opinion, preferably in Washington," for the cause. Butler informed du Pont that *The Washington Post* could be available at a "not unreasonable price" and that he could discreetly inquire about the possibility of a sale. Either the price was too high or du Pont simply wasn't interested, but in any case the *Post* did not fall into the hands of the repeal forces. The opportunities of the 1928 election had come and gone, but there was always 1932 to anticipate. While pussyfooting Republican politicians were his major targets, Butler flayed anybody who dared to support Prohibition. When Henry Ford, a devoted dry, maintained that he would cease making cars if booze returned, Butler accused him of appearing "to live in a land of dreams and to be wholly oblivious to the realities which surround us."

Though Butler always said he felt obliged to uphold the Eighteenth Amendment as long as it was the law, his hatred of it led him to flirt intellectually with the notion that perhaps not all laws had to be obeyed. In his 1929 annual presidential report to the Columbia trustees, he argued that law was only one form of social control. There were two superior modes: "The first is the conduct and manners of a gentleman, and this includes the second, which is conduct according to the highest standard of morals."

Obviously aiming at the pathology of Prohibition (although he never mentioned the word), Butler wrote that there were far too many laws for society's own good. Not only was it impossible to observe them all, but given their frequently contradictory nature, the social order would collapse into paralysis if one tried. It was therefore absurd to posit that all laws be respected. Contempt for one law in no way indicated contempt for the structure of law itself. In a key phrase, picked up by newspapers across the country, Butler distinguished between a "higher lawlessness and a lower lawlessness." The former was essentially the behavior practiced by the intellectual, moral, and economic elite—those upper-crust, private-club members for whom Butler was their sage—in choosing to disregard trivial, oppressive laws that served no good purpose. For Butler, such lawlessness was "law-abiding, and the law by which it abides is far higher as well as far more fundamental than any casual or temporary statute can possibly be. Much of this higher and deeper law finds its basis in morals, and much of it is firmly embedded—or was until recently firmly embedded—in the Constitution of the United States."

Opposed to this higher lawlessness Butler admired—the lawlessness, for example, of Antigone, whom Butler surely had in mind when developing this theory—was the reprehensible, criminal activity of the lower lawless, who broke rules purely for their own selfish advantage. Social progress could occur, for Butler, only when society distinguished between the two kinds of conduct. Altogether, a precarious argument to make, and one that reflected the urgency of Butler's desire to chip away at the edifice of Prohibition. Its class bias and complicated social applicability made the argument far from compelling. Butler must have realized this, for although he frequently recycled old ideas for use in new contexts, this was not one to which he ever returned.

Butler's new status as the renegade Republican, lambasting party stalwarts over their reactionary stands, earned him many kudos. It wasn't all kudos, of course. There was also much debris thrown at Butler for his position. Brickbats at him included the charge that he had formulated his anti-Prohibition stance because his wife's family was connected to the bootleg liquor business. Both Butler and Kate responded indignantly to the accusation, denying it any credibility whatever. Perhaps their rejection of any family tie had to do with a conviction that cousins really weren't family, for Kate numbered among her first cousins the four dashing La Montagne brothers—Montaigu, Rene, Morgan, and William—later described as "the only bootleggers of impeccable social status in the annals of prohibition." Polo players, inscribed in the *Social Register* and members of the best clubs, they had inherited an international liquor company from their father, Rene senior. When Prohibition came, they exercised their rights to pursue Butler's "higher lawlessness," supplying New York's best hotels and private clubs with premium liquors. A 1922 bachelor party at the elegant Racquet and Tennis Club, for which they provided the champagne, was their downfall, as one of their own disgruntled employees reported them to an assistant U.S. attorney. They were subsequently indicted, tried, and found guilty. Their socialite friends were appalled, not at the brothers' guilt, but at the prospect of a loss of a good booze supply. Pleas for gentle handing of their case came from every quarter. In the end, $2,000 fines and brief jail sentences were levied. As the brothers entered the Essex County jail to begin their terms, the warden observed, "We haven't had such a group of good fellows here for a long time." After they came out, President Coolidge himself restored the citizenship rights they had lost as convicts. But he clearly could do nothing about Kate's refusal to acknowledge them as family. Nor about the fact that soon after, they disappeared from the pages of the *Social Register*.

From the moment Butler began his active campaigning in 1924, he confidently announced from time to time that Prohibition could not possibly last more than four or five years. He continued to maintain this, even as the country continued to resist his arguments for repeal. At some point he clearly was going to be proved right, and by 1932, through the efforts of various repeal organizations, determined propagandists like Butler, and the absurdity of the Eighteenth Amendment itself, that time was approaching. In June of that year, as Butler was readying himself for the Republican convention in Chicago and another attempt to insert a repeal resolution in the platform, dramatic support arrived from an entirely unexpected source. On June 6, in an open letter to Butler published in *The New York Times*, John D. Rockefeller, Jr., a teetotaler and longtime advocate of the Anti-Saloon League, announced a complete change in his position. Having observed that the effort to keep alcohol from people not only did not solve the liquor problem but rather seemed to contribute to the increase of drinking and crime nationally, Rockefeller had finally concluded that Prohibition had to go. To this end, he strongly endorsed Butler's resolution to ask Congress to "submit a proposal to repeal the Eighteenth Amendment." For the man whose family had over the years donated $350,000 to the Anti-Saloon League to be now publicly criticizing it caused general jubilation among the wets: "Wet leaders from every walk of life, men and women representing business, labor, finance, society, the professions, the schools and the churches, expressed satisfaction that such a notable recruit as Mr. Rockefeller had joined the wet ranks."

Rockefeller had been reconsidering his support of Prohibition since April, with Butler acting as one of the major influences on his thinking. On June 3 Butler had attended a meeting in Rockefeller's office, along with Nelson, John D. III, the Rockefeller family lawyer Thomas Debevoise, and several others, in which he eloquently presented the case for repeal. Butler left the office feeling encouraged about Rockefeller's response but with no sense of what precisely Rockefeller was planning to do. When asked what he thought about the letter on the morning of June 7, the day it appeared, Butler said he hadn't yet read it, though he was thrilled to learn of its contents. His claim of ignorance was technically correct and only mildly disingenuous. The day before, having discovered that Butler's phone in Southampton didn't work, Debevoise had telegraphed him that "our friend" had sent a letter to the *Times* regarding Prohibition, to be published the next day, whose contents would please him. Butler wired back that he was looking forward to reading it. So it wasn't exactly a surprise for Butler to find that wets had landed their biggest catch since the start of Prohibition.

The timing of Rockefeller's letter—a week before the Republican convention—was designed to give Butler maximum leverage in his assault on the Republican platform. With Rockefeller's backing, Butler entered the platform fray in Chicago with his usual enthusiasm, determined to make the party take a stand. "The bell has rung for the pussy-footer and the trimmer," he solemnly intoned. "There is something more important than party harmony and that is party honesty." Butler soon discovered that pussyfooting could at least be intransigent in its own interests. Anxious not to divide the party or embarrass Hoover, party strategists were intent on making sure that honesty did not interfere with party harmony. In place of Butler's proposed plank demanding unconditional repeal, they preferred the evasion of a "resubmission" plank, suggesting the issue be taken up again by state conventions. The word "repeal" would not be mentioned. This had the virtue of presumably satisfying the wets without threatening the drys—the perfect trimmer's resolution.

Butler fumed, maintaining that he had 640 delegates (out of 1,156) prepared to endorse an honest call for repeal. "Resubmission means nothing," he raged. "It is a fake word and everyone who mouths it knows it is a fake word. Senator Borah himself says it is hypocritical, and that is one proposition upon which he and I are in complete agreement." Despite his threat that if the Republicans failed to push for repeal and the Democrats did, "the Presidential nomination will not be worth the paper it is written on," the Republican pussyfooters were not intimidated. They insisted that as opposed to Butler's figure of 640 delegates seeking a repeal plank, 90 percent of the delegates were in fact delighted with the temporizing tactic. In the end, Butler could not prevail against party timidity and the active politicking of what Mencken termed "Lord Hoover's agents." The moderate plank— "sired by Muddlehead out of Cowardice," Butler later called it—went through. Standpattism had won the day, producing what Butler said was the "worst plan he had heard of yet advocated by any responsible source."

Butler's postconvention attack on the Republican leadership rivaled in intemperateness his excoriation of Leonard Wood's backers following the 1920 convention. He laid the blame for this "political blunder of the first magnitude" squarely on Hoover, charging that every word of the Prohibition plank "was passed upon by the President." Hoover manipulated the delegates, according to Butler, by the "most shocking exhibition of patronage control of a convention since 1872, when Ulysses S. Grant won his second nomination . . . In effect they said, 'We expect to be in power, dispensing patronage for another four years. What jobs can these repeal fellows hand you?' It worked."

In the months following, Butler kept up a steady stream of criticism at Hoover and Republican cravenness. He dismissed the notion that repeal should not be addressed as a partisan issue because it was divisive, pointing out that slavery, woman suffrage, the tariff, and the gold standard were also controversial issues that the party had fought over. In October he savaged Republican hypocrisy at a Detroit meeting sponsored by the Women's Organization for National Prohibition Repeal, calling the party's platform "a declaration for obscurantism." Instead of disappearing, as the prohibitionists had promised, "all the saloon has done," he mocked, "is to marry the speakeasy and take its wife's name."

He diagnosed the country in general and the Republicans in particular as suffering from "an infectious disease which may best be described as candidatitis. It attacks both the seat of intelligence and the seat of courage. It thrives upon platitudes, the more sonorous the better, and upon rhetorical expression of truths so old and so universal that one must wonder why they are repeated." The remedy was straightforward: "when the sufferer from it is sternly rebuked by an aroused public opinion." Lest the message be missed, as he left for his annual summer voyage to Europe, he pronounced that the Republican failure to endorse a repeal plank would make it impossible for Hoover to win in the fall.

Public opinion spoke clearly in the 1932 election. Roosevelt's trouncing of Hoover constituted a kind of personal triumph for Butler. From "unrepentant old guardsman" of twenty years earlier, he had turned himself, in large part through his anti-Prohibition campaign, into "as sane and effectual a progressive spirit as may be found in the Republican party or in any party for the matter of that."

If Prohibition still lingered on, its death rattle could clearly be heard in

Roosevelt's election. The driving issue behind his victory had been the Depression, not the saloon, but everybody knew that FDR had no particular sympathy for the Eighteenth Amendment. The path to swift repeal lay open. One of Roosevelt's first decisions as president was to legalize the sale of 3.2 percent beer. Real beer followed shortly, and in early December 1933 delegate Thurman did the rest. Almost six and a half years after he first stepped into the ring against the Boise Bearcat, the irrevocable decision was rendered: Kid Butler had finally won.

CHAPTER FOURTEEN

"Jastrow Is, I'm Sorry to Say, a Hebrew"

In addition to a powerhouse, Butler liked to think of the university as civilization's skirmishing line, fighting the forces of ignorance and complacency while pushing courageously into the future. But at the same time as he led his faculty armies in their metaphysical battle against the powers of darkness, he found himself embroiled in a rather less-exalted struggle within the confines of New York City against a raggle-taggle foe largely unaware that it was actually involved in combat: aspiring eastern European immigrants, predominantly Jewish, whose sons sought admission to Columbia College.

Butler's anti-Semitic credentials, as commander in chief in this effort, were not the virulent sort displayed by such people as Henry Ford, who, along with his Model T, mass-produced hatred against the Jews through his weekly newspaper, *The Dearborn Independent*, which promulgated his rabid views about them in ninety-one consecutive issues published in 1920 and 1921; or Father Charles Coughlin, the Roman Catholic priest who argued for the existence of a Jewish world conspiracy and attacked the malefic influence of Jewish bankers in radio broadcasts from Detroit during the 1930s and in his magazine *Social Justice*, which ran from 1936 to 1942; or even M. Carey Thomas, president of Bryn Mawr from 1894 to 1922, whose antipathy toward Jews—"a most terrible set of people to my thinking"—led to her excluding them from the college's faculty. They were more discreet, the kind found in the proper drawing rooms and the poshest clubs, where men of refinement thought the insistent, unscrupulous behavior of the Jews sadly offensive and who took pains to avoid encountering them socially. The frown of disapproval, in short, rather than the overheated rhetoric of uncontrolled denunciation.

Butler's frown—and the polite but firm judgments accompanying it—was essentially consistent throughout his career. It was there when he regretted that he must inform Low in 1897 that Joseph Jastrow, a distinguished psychologist being considered for an appointment to Teachers College, "is, I'm sorry to say, a Hebrew." It was there in 1909 when he responded, "Do you not think we ought to pass over the California Professor in view of his race and of the fact that he has been getting a lot of degrees lately," to J. B. Pine's suggestion that Jacques Loeb, a Stanford scientist and Nobel Prize candidate, be given an honorary degree. It was there when he resisted (until he could resist no more) the advent of a Jewish trustee on the Columbia board, complaining to Pine in 1913 that Adolf Lewisohn, who gave substantial money to Columbia, would have been a fine trustee "if he had been born a Methodist"; or when he assured trustee William Barclay Parsons that his analysis of Jews—as being distressingly persistent, seeking special privileges by law, and supplying "leaders for anarchistic, socialistic and other movements of unrest"—was as "true as gospel." It was still there twenty years later when he suggested that Columbia invite a German-Jewish scholar named Arnold Brecht, living in New York, to give a lecture, assuring Dean Howard McBain, "Personally, he is most agreeable and not, so far as I can see, a Jew or Jewish in any way." (McBain, in fact, shared Butler's enthusiasm for Brecht, agreeing that he "could discover nothing of the Jew about him.")

These attitudes in no way distinguished Butler from the class of people with whom he associated. On the contrary, Butler's views expressed values shared by many of them—many, but not all: Seth Low, for example, was one striking exception. Anti-Semitism flourished unapologetically in New York during the early decades of the twentieth century, and it is not surprising that Butler believed what he did. Even before the "Jewish problem" actually existed at Columbia, there seemed to be one. Or at least fears that there might be. As early as 1902 Pine wrote to Butler "in regard to what threatens to become one of our most dangerous problems, viz: the Hebrew question." Lamenting the disappearance of instruction in Christianity and the mandatory chapel, Pine was worried lest Columbia might in the future cease to be a Christian university (as it was intended to be) and devolve willy-nilly into a "Hebrew Institution." The trustees were responsible, in

Pine's view, for not having taken an explicit stand reaffirming the school's Episcopalian origins.

More alert than others at the university, Pine clearly saw the demographic handwriting on the wall. "You know as well as I," he cautioned, "that we are in danger of being overwhelmed by the number of Jewish students who are coming to us, and who are certain to increase in number." As in his mind there was no moral or legal way to restrict Jewish enrollment, the solution was to reassert the university's traditional Christian values by vitalizing the chapel experience and reintroducing the study of Christianity into the curriculum. Although "we cannot keep the Jews out . . . we can bring Christianity in." By so doing, Pine concluded, "we can also, I believe, interpose the most effective check to increasing Hebrew influence, and to the often repeated assertion that Columbia is a 'Jew college.'"

Butler thanked Pine, stating that he was in full sympathy with his analysis and hoped to find ways of putting his ideas into effect. And we can surely hear at least an echo of Pine's suggestions in Butler's assertion, in his 1906 annual report, that "Columbia University is a Christian institution and by its charter and traditions its Christianity is truly catholic." Nothing, however, was done about the chapel or the curriculum.

But if Pine's diagnosis was correct (though premature), his remedy was futile. No preemptive rhetorical strike in favor of Christianity could stem the flow of qualified Jewish students seeking to attend Columbia. Indeed, nothing could, of Jews or any other group, because no mechanism existed to determine either the number or types of students who could enroll. At the turn of the century, Columbia admissions was a relatively straightforward procedure, only requiring the passing of one of three tests: Columbia's own admissions examination, that of the New York State Board of Regents, or that of the College Entrance Examination Board. No other criteria were involved.

Like other burgeoning schools of the time, Columbia had no interest in limiting its enrollment. The admissions process was not designed to distinguish among academically qualified applicants, but simply to admit, on the basis of objective performance, those deemed capable of doing Columbia work. The more boys passing the tests, the happier (and larger) the school would be. It was this totally unregulated system, based simply on one specific measure of achievement, that led to the crisis: too many socially undesirable Jews seemed to be passing the tests. Concern about Jewish enrollment, of course, was not limited to Columbia. By the early 1920s a number of elite eastern private institutions—MIT, Harvard, Yale, and Princeton, for example—felt threatened by the specter of hordes of anemic, socially awkward, and ferociously competitive Jewish immigrants swamping the congenial, well-proportioned men of solid American stock who traditionally composed their undergraduate student bodies. All these schools shared the same anxiety, but Columbia's was the more urgent because of its location in New York, the veritable home of the Jewish immigrant. Butler's conception of Columbia as a prestigious national school training America's elite leadership did not entertain the possibility that ambitious, bright immigrant children would seek to better themselves through access to that prestige. The Free University of New York (City College) and New York University were sufficient, in Butler's mind at least, for such aspirations, and he saw no reason for Columbia also to have to admit them. In the absence of any preexisting guidelines, it would have to invent its own strategies as it went along to dissuade too many Jews from applying.

Butler's first step in his campaign was to centralize the admissions process, which he managed in the spring of 1909, when he created a single Committee on Undergraduate Admissions. Responsible for the acceptance and rejection of all candidates to Columbia College, Barnard College, and the School of Mines, Engineering, and Chemistry, it was chaired by a member of the Philosophy Department, Adam Leroy Jones. Butler wasted no time in supplying the committee with his suggestions. In April, a month after it was formed, he recommended that candidates' suitability be determined not just on the basis of exam results but also on an evaluation of high school records as well as interviews. These additional sources of information might help Columbia "escape . . . from the difficulties and perplexities of the existing system," Butler told Jones.

The more flexible method, with its new discretionary power, could not by itself be expected to work miracles. Frederick P. Keppel, dean of the college from 1910 to 1917 and one of Butler's chief advisers on the enrollment issue, argued in a fall 1910 letter that strong administrative will would have to be exercised. He repeated to Butler the caution he had communicated to Jones when learning that the incoming class would be slightly larger than the previous year's:

I told him that personally I was not greatly interested in the matter of numbers and that where an undesirable citizen could, with justice, be left outside the walls, I was sure that in the long run his room would be more advantageous than his company. The particular trouble at this time is that a number of ill-prepared and uncultured Jews are trying to obtain a cheap College degree by transferring, usually in February, from the City College, which they entered after only a three year High School Course.

In the midst of these admissions concerns, another Jewish issue arose that caused Butler some distress. At a trustee meeting in December 1910, Butler proposed a resolution offering Columbia's Earl Hall and St. Paul's Chapel as sites for the fall meeting of the Episcopal Church's General Convention. Seth Low was the only trustee to oppose the resolution, worried that it suggested (as Butler perhaps meant it to) the essential Episcopal nature of the university; unless the invitation to use Columbia's facilities was extended to members of all religious faiths (which Low knew would not happen), it should be extended to none. The glory of the university, Low asserted, was precisely that it "makes no discrimination against the Jews, either in its faculty or its student body." Jews contributed to the economic vitality of the city as much as any other group, thereby indirectly benefiting Columbia. In addition, Low pointed out, the university had received important gifts from them. If Columbia would not extend the same hospitality to them as to the Episcopal Church, it should also refuse their money. Unhappy with having to disagree with the action of the current president, the former president thought it appropriate that he retire from the board of trustees.

For Butler and G. L. Rives, chairman of the trustees, nothing would have given them greater pleasure than to be rid of the troublesome Low. But they both knew that if he left now, people might ask embarrassing questions. Rives suggested that a better solution would be to have Low remain a member but relieve him of any obligation to attend future meetings. Eager not to harm the university he loved, Low agreed. He stayed on the board until he could retire inauspiciously in 1914, but he never appeared at another meeting.

Despite the efforts of Jones and his committee, the perception of Columbia as a Jewish college persisted. Both Butler and Keppel were alert to all possibilities of discouraging Jewish enrollment without courting the public relations disaster of engaging in blatant discrimination or use of a quota system. In 1912, for example, thinking about how Columbia might implement a scholarship fund provided in the will of the newspaper owner Joseph Pulitzer, Keppel wondered if preference could be given to boys who came to the college with the express purpose of continuing to the Journalism School. It might please the Pulitzer family, Keppel argued, "and it might also give us a larger proportion of Gentiles among the scholars; for Journalism is not sufficiently lucrative a profession to be particularly attractive to the Jew."

Nothing came of this suggestion, and Butler followed up with one of his own in 1913, proposing that the college consider imposing a residential requirement on all its matriculated freshmen. Dean Keppel rejected the idea as not feasible. If the point of the plan, Keppel argued, was to make the school more attractive to the "right" kind of New York parents, it couldn't possibly work. The tendency for New York society families to send their sons to the best schools far away from the temptations of the city would not be affected by the residential requirement. "To put it frankly, I do not think such a plan, or any other, would bring to us the sons of men like Mr. Rives, Mr. Cutting and Mr. Parsons." And if it wouldn't attract the desirable students, it also wouldn't dissuade the undesirable ones. Already, according to Keppel, of the students in the dormitories, "a fair proportion are Jews." If the plan were put into effect, the rich Jews would simply take rooms but continue to spend most of their time away from the campus with their families. And the poor Jews, even less desirable, would still somehow manage to attend.

Another suggestion, also from Butler, was to subject all candidates to a physical examination, so that Columbia would not be tempted "to spend our narrow income" upon those who were physically unsound—hardly a measure he would have thought necessary had the applicant body been free of boys whose parents had only recently arrived on American shores from Eastern Europe. The motive was to find grounds to eliminate socially unappealing Jews smart enough to have passed the entrance examination. Jones objected to wholesale testing, wondering if perhaps it could be insisted upon only in doubtful cases. Butler consented, adding that it was "particularly desirable to determine and to exclude cases of tuberculosis, hereditary syphilis and marked part or other functional weakness"—conditions attributed to the immigrants crowding New York's Lower East Side. The system was never put into place, however, even for the "doubtful" cases.

By 1914, college administrators thought it imperative to assure the respectable gentile families of New York that Columbia's Jewish character had been exaggerated and that their sons would still feel comfortable with their fellow students. Keppel thought it best to take the question on directly. His *Columbia*, published in 1914, defined the situation without embellishment:

> One of the commonest references that one hears with regard to Columbia is that its position at the gateway of European immigration makes it socially uninviting to students who come from homes of refinement. The form which the inquiry takes in these days of slowly-dying race prejudice is, "Isn't Columbia overrun with European Jews who are most unpleasant persons socially?"

Keppel's answers were designed to soothe gentile anxieties. First, the "proportion of Jewish students is decreasing rather than increasing." (How he arrived at this comforting conclusion he does not say. Presumably, names and noses provided clues.) This putative decline was a healthy development for the college and for the Jews themselves, showing that Jewish parents were beginning to understand the virtues of sending their boys away from home, thereby minimizing the dangers of social inbreeding that existed in their intense family life.

Second, the Jews who did come to Columbia tended to be "desirable students in every way," "entirely satisfactory companions." Unfortunately, "there are Jewish students of another type who have not had the social advantages of their more fortunate fellows." These did not make "pleasant companions," but their numbers were small, and in any case, every reputable institution was obliged to accommodate some of these who were making such sacrifices to improve themselves. Having initially said that there was no problem, Keppel warned that the problem would not go away. Improved economic conditions for Jews throughout the country meant that every first-rank college—and they will accept nothing less—would have to confront the issue of how to assimilate Jewish students. Keppel expressed optimism that the nation would somehow meet the challenge.

Keppel's reassurances to the public notwithstanding, Butler's anxiety— that Columbia was viewed as the "Jew college," which Pine had feared some years before—remained undiminished. (Accurate data on the exact numbers are impossible to gather, but it is not likely that Jewish undergraduate enrollment from 1912 to 1918 ever exceeded 25 percent. The issue, however, was always more perceptual than statistical.) Columbia would need more imaginative solutions to alter its image. In his 1917 presidential report Butler proposed an idea that he and Jones had been thinking about for some time: dividing the college into two separate schools to meet the different needs of what he argued were two entirely different kinds of student. For the traditional variety, who wanted to devote three or four years "in pursuit of those liberal and elegant studies which have long since established their primacy as instruments for the education of a scholar and a gentleman," Columbia would provide a residential college experience leading to the bachelor of arts degree. For those students, "rapidly increasing in number," whose sole purpose was to prepare "themselves as speedily as possible to meet the requirements for admission" to professional schools, Columbia would establish a two-year nonresidential junior college offering the degree of bachelor of science.

The distinction between the scholars and gentlemen on the one hand and the anxious professional aspirants on the other equipped Butler with both a polite code to speak about the Jewish problem and a polite way to solve it. If the narrowly focused, unpleasantly career-minded Jews couldn't be prevented from applying, they at least could be relegated to their own institution. Creating a full residential college, abetted by scholarships designed to attract to Columbia "the best type of American student from all parts of the land" (as opposed to the immigrant-infested New York), would return the school to the Protestant idyll of its earlier incarnation:

> Such a prospect must make strong appeal to the imagination of those who, looking back upon the old College of thirty or forty years ago, wish the Columbia College of the future to represent everything that was good in the college life and work of the last generation and to add thereto everything that is helpful and uplifting in the life of the present.

With the junior college in place to address previously unanticipated needs, the real Columbia College would then be "free to resume without farther [*sic*] interruption or hindrance the natural lines of its own collegiate development."

Butler then left it to Herbert Hawkes—the mathematics professor who replaced Keppel as dean after he left for Washington to become an assistant secretary of war—and director of admissions Jones to refine the proposal as to administrative procedures, admissions criteria, and the like. Jones addressed the qualifications for the residential college. Intellectual ability, of course, was paramount. But in the list of essential "qualities of character and capacity for leadership" that followed, Jones carefully put together the opposite of all the defamatory stereotypes attributed to Jewish behavior. They included native strength and uprightness, independence, initiative, capacity for cooperation, balance and sanity, public spirit, and the ability to enlist others in work for the general good. As anti-Semitic thinking has always accused Jews of being shifty, dishonest, weak, unwilling to cooperate, unbalanced in their priorities, involved in their own affairs at the expense of the public good, and unwilling and unable to work with others, we can see the exclusionary agenda behind these criteria. They added up to a NO JEWS NEED APPLY sign. (Or at least so few as not to constitute a threat to the character of the college.)

"You are on the right track beyond question," Butler responded enthusiastically to Jones, asking him to make his report even more detailed. Despite the promise it held for solving the vexed question, however, the idea came to nothing. Two institutions, separate and very much unequal, together on the same campus must have seemed too administratively bizarre—and perhaps even too blatant—to try to implement.

America's 1917 entry into World War I significantly influenced Butler's thinking about his admissions battle. The start of the 1917 fall semester saw him criticizing the quality of the incoming class as "depressing in the extreme," which he attributed to the fact that the desirable "boys of old American stock" had either enlisted in the army or volunteered for public service, leaving behind a college-bound cohort "largely made up of foreign born and children of those but recently arrived in this country." Immigrant refuse, in short, in place of upstanding native youth. This perceived deterioration of the applicant pool led him to reconsider a suggestion Keppel had made several years earlier, that the college should limit the size of the entering class. In place of a negative admissions policy seeking only to exclude the unfit, then, an affirmative procedure to select only the best among a larger group of academically qualified applicants.

To achieve this, Columbia would have to be willing to forgo increased income each year from an ever-expanding student population—no trivial matter, since every tuition dollar counted—and, even more important, devise some sensitive mechanism lending objective authority to those subjective assessments that would have to be made about the desirable candidates. If the former could be accomplished by simple administrative fiat, the judgment issue was more complicated. Columbia could not afford to be accused of distinguishing among capable students on the basis of elusive, highly suspect social criteria.

Butler's 1917 presidential report demonstrated the necessary administrative will. It was time, he argued, for the university to become selective as to the students on whom it would expend its limited fiscal and intellectual resources. Sufficient other options in the country meant that Columbia's stricter admissions policies would not deprive anybody of the chance for a higher education. He indicated that Columbia would both limit the number of students in each class and work toward developing a new admissions process that would take into consideration students' academic potential, personality, and school achievements.

As Columbia began to formulate a new set of nonquantifiable criteria, the War Department contributed to Columbia the gift of training potential army officers through the Student Army Training Corps (SATC). The more than 150 schools involved in the program were permitted to select their students from the applicants who met the minimum requirements—evidence of graduation from high school—established by the War Department. Jones found many of the Columbia candidates to be a sorry lot, deficient in personality and character. Because their academic preparation could not be tested by Columbia's traditional entrance examinations, the decision was made to require them to take the Thorndike Tests for Mental Alertness, devised at Teachers College by E. L. Thorndike. Purporting to measure innate capacity to learn rather than any acquired skills or knowledge, the tests offered themselves as accurate prognosticators of future academic success. Columbia had been skeptical about their reliability and had previously rejected their use as a means of assessing the strength of applicants. But the first SATC class, entering in the fall of 1918, now offered the perfect opportunity to examine the tests' predictive powers. The results were startling: of the fifty SATC students who were asked to withdraw by the end of the year, only three had earned a Thorndike score as high as a B. In other words, there seemed to be a high correlation between performance on the Thorndike and performance in the college: a mediocre score on the former led in almost all cases to an unsatisfactory record in the latter. Columbia apparently had discovered the instrument it sought to evaluate the "real" intelligence of its applicants. With the Thorndike now able to supplement the three different admissions examinations Columbia used—all of which merely determined students' knowledge about particular subjects—college authorities would presumably no longer be fooled by the exemplary results of dedication and hard work. Grubby immigrant overachievers, of the sort Columbia wished to find grounds to reject, would now be found out. Natural talent, rather than external achievements earned by obsessive drive, would henceforth be the hallmark of the Columbia student.

While Butler and his colleagues stressed the diagnostic power of the mental test in determining a boy's fitness for college work, at the same time they charged the Admissions Committee to request a broad range of non-quantifiable material from candidates to enable the college to obtain the class it wanted. In addition to submitting school records and character recommendations, an applicant now had to supply information as to his father's place of birth and occupation, his own religious affiliation, his school activities (athletics, publications, musical organizations), and his "patriotic activities, both inside and outside of school." In short, the modern process of selective college admissions was created. Henceforth, with an enrollment limit now imposed, the Admissions Committee had the capacity to choose, from the pool of qualified students, those they judged most desirable.

In the summer of 1922, when Harvard's President A. Lawrence Lowell had precipitated a national furor through the mistake—which Columbia had carefully avoided—of trying to implement an explicit Jewish quota at Harvard, Hawkes received a letter from Professor Edwin B. Wilson of MIT (not to be confused with Columbia biologist Edmund B. Wilson), inquiring about Columbia's experience with its intelligence test. Wilson had heard that the test discriminated against the "grind" type of student in favor of the naturally bright one. And since so many of the grinds, according to Wilson, were Jews, he concluded that the test perhaps "actually and entirely appropriately" discriminated against them, even if it hadn't been intended for that purpose. However, Wilson went on, he had been told that the tests did so not because Jews had done less well on them than gentiles, but rather because the results were kept secret, so that the "officers of Columbia could thereby discriminate at their own sweet will against the Jew." Wilson asked Hawkes for any statement about the issue that he might feel comfortable making, assuring him that its confidentiality would be protected; he suggested that Hawkes could answer on blank paper without a signature, so that nobody could identify him.

Hawkes responded that Columbia had nothing to hide. The facts were simple. The admissions office had no intention of trying "to eliminate the Jew from Columbia College." Given its New York location, Columbia should in fact "furnish the very best education we can to a good many of them . . . I believe that we ought to carry at least 15% of Jews and I do not think that 20% is excessive for Columbia College." It was true that since the Thorndike test was incorporated into the admissions process, the percentage of Jews had been reduced. This was not part of a scheme to get at the Jews, Hawkes said, but rather a direct consequence of Columbia's effort "to eliminate the low grade boy":

> We had 1200 applications for admission last fall and could accommodate only 550. This meant that somebody had to lose out. We have not eliminated boys because they were Jews and do not propose to do so. We have honestly attempted to eliminate the lowest grade of applicant and it turns out that a good many of the low grade men are New York City Jews. It is a fact that boys of foreign parentage who have no background in many cases attempt to educate themselves beyond their intelligence. Their accomplishment is well over 100% of their ability on account of their tremendous energy and ambition. I do not believe that a College would do well to admit too many men of low mentality who have ambition but not brains. At any rate this is the principle on which we are going.

Neither the Thorndike nor the more inclusive admissions process solved the problem: Columbia still couldn't change its reputation as primarily a city—as opposed to a national—school. More Jews might be rejected than before, but more Jews continued to apply, and the academically qualified, desirable boy from the rest of the country did not show up in sufficient numbers to reshape the school's image. Lurking beneath its praiseworthy arguments in favor of diversity, Columbia's real goal of gentile homogeneity continued to elude it.

The luxury of no longer having to admit the academically plausible but socially unfit also came at a cost: tuition dollars. The loss in incremental revenue for every student now turned away who might once have been added to the student body could easily be calculated. With Columbia endlessly struggling to find the resources to meet its expenses, it was not a calculation designed to please Butler's heart, nor the even flintier hearts of his trustees. Butler was not one to give up easily, however, and in 1927 he returned to his earlier idea of creating some form of parallel but separate college whose nonelite student body might leave Columbia College free to cultivate a more exclusive one, uncontaminated by the other.

Two circumstances, one general and one local, presented Butler with the ingredients of his solution: the popular junior college movement, which had been expanding throughout the United States since the beginning of the century, and the premedical and prelaw instruction Columbia had been offering in Brooklyn for some time. In 1915 Columbia had responded to a request from the Long Island Medical School for help in setting up a course of premedical study to qualify students for admission to the school. Columbia was pleased to establish a small educational beachhead in Brooklyn, and it quickly put together first a one-year and then, by 1918, a two-year program of liberal arts study, housed at the medical school but under the administrative control of Columbia's Extension Teaching division. (A college degree was not at this time a requirement for entry to medical school.) In 1925 the dean of Brooklyn Law School, knowing of Columbia's involvement with the medical college, approached Columbia to set up an appropriate program of preparatory liberal arts courses for students interested in attending the law school. A one-year program, housed in the Brooklyn Law School's building, was immediately begun. When the New York Court of Appeals ruled in the summer of 1927 that two years of college study would be compulsory for law school by the fall of 1929, Columbia expanded its initial offering into a two-year curriculum.

Thus, by the summer of 1927 Columbia was running two separate academic enterprises in Brooklyn. The obvious conceptual leap between offering two distinct programs for students not one's own and bringing the two together into a single coherent institution with a structured two-year curriculum, designed for tuition-paying Columbia students with preprofessional aspirations, was not difficult to make. Models for such an institution were readily available in the variety of junior colleges that were springing up across the country. Junior colleges today bear the stigma of often being perceived as intellectually suspect places, giving either a terminal, not very challenging collegiate exposure for those who want to go no further or some basic remediation for those who aspire to a four-year college but lack the credentials. Such, however, was not the vision behind their creation. They developed not as the low-end academic option they seem to be now, but as part of the growth of the decidedly upscale research university system. The "father" of the junior college movement was the University of Chicago's altogether serious president, William Rainey Harper, who, like other university (not college) presidents, including Butler, saw undergraduate education falling into two distinct parts: a general liberal arts training in the first two years, and more specialized studies during the last two. His initial description of the two were "Academic College" for the lower years and "University College" for the upper. These terms were not entirely satisfactory (suggesting that the more-advanced work of the upper years was somehow not academic, for example), and never received popular acceptance. In 1896 he proposed the simpler contrast of "junior college" and "senior college" as a way of distinguishing the two different educational priorities within the four years of undergraduate instruction. Soon the term "junior college" spread to any freestanding institution that offered some form of preparatory work, eventually becoming the designation of two-year schools of all kinds that were not entitled to award the bachelor's degrees. Harper thought that they could help relieve traditional liberal arts colleges of the burdens of introductory instruction. The more junior colleges of academic merit there were, the less universities would have to worry about, or put teaching resources into, freshman and sophomore programs. Harper's enthusiasm for what he called these "shock absorbers" between high schools and universities encouraged their development throughout the country.

With Butler's two preprofessional programs working smoothly in Brooklyn, it didn't take him long to think about the plausibility of blending them into Columbia's own institution. In November of 1927 he asked Dean Hawkes to put before the Committee on University Undergraduates, which he chaired, the question of the usefulness of developing a number of junior colleges under Columbia's auspices. To guarantee that it reached the right conclusions, Butler wrote to Hawkes two weeks later requesting that the committee defer submitting its study until it read his discussion on junior colleges in the 1927 presidential report he was currently preparing, which argued for the merits of establishing them "at certain of the larger centers of population which University Extension serves."

Not surprisingly, on January 25, 1928, Hawkes's committee produced a document unanimously calling for the organization of a junior college in Brooklyn. But unlike the grand claims for social utility found in Butler's report, the Hawkes memorandum rather more specifically addressed the pressing local issue simmering beneath Butler's rhetoric: the Hebrew problem. "The student body that such a college would be likely to attract for the present would undoubtedly be of foreign parentage," its opening paragraph declared. "Many of these boys ought not to take a full college course and most of them will probably find their way into law and medicine." Ambitious boys, in short, whom Butler, Keppel, and Hawkes were eager to keep away from Columbia's ideal student body of leisured gentlemen, but whose capacity to pay tuition had not lost its appeal. Now they would have a school of their own, miles away from Butler's Acropolis. Columbia congratulated itself for taking on a critical national responsibility in helping such boys gain "a more intimate insight into our social and economic life"; and the committee recommended that the university proceed expeditiously to implement plans for opening the school.

On March 5, 1928, the trustees endorsed its establishment. Columbia's movement into Brooklyn coincided with an educational incursion northward, up the Hudson River, to Annandale, New York. In July, Butler announced that Columbia was affiliating itself with St. Stephens College, a liberal arts Episcopalian school of 125 men, on the same terms that applied to Barnard College—as a freestanding undergraduate college with its own faculty, curriculum, and trustees. Incorporating small colleges into large research universities represented, for Butler, the inevitable development of American higher education. As long as there was no drain on fiscal resources, he conceived of a time in which first-rank urban universities might be surrounded by a variety of these colleges, catering to separate needs and populations, whose teaching staffs, values, and administrative oversight would be provided by the home university. A future, in short, organized around the Harvards, Yales, Chicagos, and Columbias presiding over a series of satellite schools whose academic status would in a sense be certified by their university affiliation. In their different ways, both Columbia's venture into Brooklyn and its inclusion of St. Stephens fitted into this vision of what was to come. Butler was wrong about the trend, but St. Stephens remained a part of the Columbia system for sixteen years, shedding its Episcopalian identity and name in 1934 for the secular Bard College, honoring

St. Stephens's founder, John Bard. In 1944 the insistence of Bard's trustees on admitting women came up against Columbia's ban on undergraduate coeducation, and the relationship between the two institutions was severed.

In September 1928 Seth Low Junior College—inevitably named after the former mayor of Brooklyn—opened for business on the fifth and sixth floors of Brooklyn Law School's new building on Pearl Street, still relegated by Butler's insistence to a branch of the Extension Teaching division rather than being permitted any independent status within the university's organizational structure. Boys who completed the two-year curriculum would receive a certificate testifying to their achievement; those who wanted an actual college degree, and whose records qualified them for further study, could finish two additional years of evening courses at Morningside Heights in order to earn a B.S. These students were known as "university undergraduates" to ensure that the vital distinction between them and the "real" college students was maintained. (Initially, few students were attracted by this possibility, although the numbers increased over time. Of the 308 boys admitted in the first semester, for example, only 13 indicated an interest in the degree.)

In addition to a curriculum taught largely by junior faculty members from Morningside Heights, what the students found on the two floors of the Pearl Street building was a small library; psychology and zoology laboratories; a large lecture room and eleven smaller classrooms; a faculty room; space for a student newspaper; small accommodations for faculty advisers to meet with students; and a student recreation room. As there was not adequate space for physics and chemistry laboratories, arrangements were made for the premedical students to take these necessary courses in the evening at the Columbia campus. There were no physical education activities at first, but shortly thereafter Seth Low was able to use the facilities of the nearby Plymouth Institute, and by the school's second year a modest intercollegiate athletic program was established. A smattering of clubs and activities for the nonathletic also evolved, including *The Scop*, the weekly newspaper; premedical and prelaw societies; debate, foreign language, and glee clubs; and even college dances and a college boat ride.

What the students most certainly did not find was anything approximating an institution with a clear, independent identity. Despite the urgings of its first director, James Egbert, that it be granted administrative equality with other Columbia divisions, Butler steadfastly refused. Nor would he drop the

"Junior" from the name, which many of its students wanted. He was determined that the marginality of Seth Low not be compromised lest it begin to obscure the distinction between the quality of the enterprises on Morningside Heights and Pearl Street.

The result was that even the students at Seth Low remained uncertain as to what kind of school they were attending. On the one hand, it bore an obvious connection to the prestigious Columbia University. On the other, the nature of that relationship remained shrouded in ambiguity. Was it a separate college or not? *The Scop* asked on February 17, 1930. Administrators avoided any straightforward answer, murkily asserting only that the school was "independent of, and yet closely articulated with the other parts of the University."

This unwillingness to clarify Seth Low's status grated on students, accounting in large part for the massive dropout rate. About half of them left when they became aware of their second-class or even third-class status within the university. They were offended, for example, when they realized that if they wanted to spend the two additional years to earn the B.S. degree, they had to be approved by the University Council, an obstacle not put in the way of Columbia College sophomores on the way to their B.A.s. When asked about their experiences at Seth Low, many alumni said they would never have enrolled had they known what exactly it was—or, perhaps better, wasn't. They believed that Columbia had deliberately deceived them about the institution's character.

The students, of course, were right. The trappings of college life, such as they were, that grew up around Seth Low could not disguise the fact that it never was intended as a real college. It was painful to believe that a university of Columbia's prestige would mislead students the way it did, and not all Seth Low students could bring themselves to recognize the truth. One who did, however, was Will Katz, who left after a year for Ohio State, which he felt would improve his chances of getting into medical school. Responding to an alumni survey in 1932, Katz explained why:

As far as educational facilities go, I believe that Seth Low is by far the superior of Ohio State. But is that fact generally recognized? Not as long as Seth Low is generally laughed at as being the sewers of Columbia University by prominent men I have spoken to about it.

Also, I was constantly irked while at Seth Low because I was not attending Columbia College. With an 87% Regents average and a score of major extra-curricular activities to my credit I believe myself to be fully qualified for entrance into Columbia College. I know a number of gentile students of lesser ability than myself, with lower averages and with fewer activities who were admitted to Columbia. Why wasn't I? It is true that I did not apply to Columbia originally (I was a February graduate from High School and therefore couldn't apply for admittance the same year), but when I did apply later I was rejected because I was already attending Seth Low. I can see only one reason for this action of the entrance board of Columbia College in rejecting me—even after I offered to throw away my Seth Low credits and enter as a freshman again . . . My pride was hurt at the insult that Seth Low throws to the Jewish race.

Another student who eventually came to understand Seth Low's real function was arguably its most prominent alumnus, the science-fiction writer Isaac Asimov. His Russian immigrant father wanted him to be a doctor but needed him to go to school in New York so that he could help in the family candy store. Although he was admitted to tuition-free City College, he really wanted Columbia, "the most prestigious college in New York City." In the spring of 1935 he was granted a Columbia interview. Fifteen years old, riddled with adolescent acne, and without the least shred of self-possession, Asimov knew from the outset he never had a chance. If the prime purpose of the interview, as he later reflected, "was to see if I were too Jewish to give at least the appearance of a gentleman," his interviewer had only to look at his skin to reject him.

The interviewer told him that Columbia had a minimum age requirement of sixteen and recommended Seth Low instead. Eager to ally himself with the university's power in medical school placement, Asimov, despite his disappointment, consented to have his application shifted. (Once there, he found that Seth Low had the same minimum age stipulation as Columbia.) He also found that of the many virtues of Seth Low the interviewer had enumerated, one point that had somehow not been mentioned "was that the Seth Low student body was heavily Jewish, with a strong Italian minority." It gradually became clear "that the purpose of the school was to give bright youngsters of unacceptable social characteristics a Columbia education without too badly contaminating the elite young men of the College itself by their formal presence."

All his life Asimov resented having been duped, having been made to accept, as part of the "Seth Low rabble" earning a four-year degree, the inferior B.S. as opposed to the B.A. awarded to the real Columbia College students. He admitted that when asked where he went to college, he would always answer "Columbia"—not Columbia College, which would have been a lie, but simply "Columbia," which, while not precisely the truth, at least avoided the embarrassment of trying to explain the nature of Seth Low. And given his sense that it was the condition of his skin that had immediately pronounced him unfit for Columbia College, he undoubtedly would have taken some ironic satisfaction to learn that it remained an issue for the Seth Low authorities. Evaluating the credentials of the premedical candidates in the spring of 1938, a confidential memo noted about Asimov: "Very high Thorndike. Not too good on appearance due to bad complexion which may clear. A+ scholarship."

Disgruntled though many were with their obscure status and lack of serious collegiate facilities, the students—mostly Jewish and mostly premed, like Asimov—endured the indignities of Seth Low for the sake of professional school placement. Of course, placement at good medical schools was not guaranteed, and the Seth Low advisers were sometimes less than helpful in promoting the careers of their charges. A 1934 letter from M. M. Chappell of the Department of Psychology to the University of Chicago Medical School testified to how some faculty at least regarded the peculiarly homogeneous student body. Explaining that several of the Seth Low boys had asked for his endorsement, Chappell proceeded to rate them in descending order. Starting with Kraftman and Mariaskin—"the best type of men"—and moving through Wollman, Dibbs, Workman, and Zehner, "who in my opinion rank only a little below these two," Chappell ranked them candidly in relation to each other. The following group of four were "good" men, if not quite up to the standard of the first. The next to last man had compiled a mediocre record but probably had the ability to be a competent physician. Then the single-sentence judgment of the letter's penultimate paragraph: "The last man, Louis Ryterband, is a supercilious kike." (Such a terse assessment of Ryterband's qualities perhaps casts some doubt on the claims made by director Edward Allen, who had succeeded Egbert, that at Seth Low, recommendations for professional schools are "written on the basis of the most careful analyses of the candidates and judicious consideration of the merits of each man.")

Seth Low continued to channel intellectually competent but socially undesirable students away from Columbia College until 1936. A clear trend in declining enrollments—from the more than 400 during Seth Low's first year, 1928–29, to 304 in 1933–34, to 206 in 1935–36—meant that the school was losing its viability as a revenue-generating institution, and in March 1936 the trustees voted to stop admitting any new students to Seth Low. Those already in the school were permitted to finish their work at Columbia (in the afternoons and evenings), and Seth Low officially went out of existence on June 30, 1938.

The reasons for its demise were various. Word of mouth of disaffected students, accompanied by the substantial dropout rate, played a major part, as did the perception that the best professional schools viewed the Seth Low applicants with some skepticism. Like Will Katz, students came to understand that their chances for admission were better if they attended an established college rather than the murky, anomalous place on Pearl Street. As the professional schools continued to upgrade their own standards of admission, the Seth Low two-year certificate or even the four-year B.S. exhibited diminished potency when compared with the traditional B.A. offered by a four-year college. In the end, the school could no longer successfully argue the case for the benefits it could confer on the professionally ambitious student. And with the failure of Butler's hope that the community would generate financial support to nourish Columbia's presence in Brooklyn, he had no choice but to recommend its closing.

The disappearance of Seth Low marked the end of any serious attempt by Butler to manipulate Columbia's Jewish enrollment through structural or administrative innovation. The two floors on Pearl Street might have temporarily lessened some of the admissions pressures on the college without costing it any potential income, but it didn't finally solve the Hebrew problem, any more than the imposition of the Thorndike test did. Although the popular fraternity drinking song of the 1920s couldn't have been more wrong about who controlled Columbia,

Oh, Harvard's run by millionaires,
And Yale is run by booze,
Cornell is run by farmers' sons
Columbia's run by Jews—

it accurately embodied a generally held notion about Columbia College that Butler could never entirely dislodge.

It is part of his peculiar genius for self-promotion that, having spent so much of his time devising ways to keep Jews out of Columbia, perhaps the best-known incident regarding Butler and the Jews was his success in keeping one in the university: the young instructor of English, Lionel Trilling, who would become one of the country's most esteemed literary critics. Trilling was not popular in the department. In 1936, as he worked on his dissertation, he was told by his chairman that as "a Freudian, a Marxist, and a Jew," he would probably be happier elsewhere. Although Trilling managed to resist the invitation to leave, his future at Columbia was precarious. In the spring of 1939 Butler invited the Trillings to a formal dinner at the presidential house. Lionel had just published his dissertation, an intellectual biography of Matthew Arnold, and Diana Trilling related how, after they were let in by the footman and announced by the butler, the president congratulated him on the excellent English reviews of the book. Following dinner, while the women repaired to the upstairs sitting room, the men gathered in the library, where the president engaged in his usual monologue. Speaking of Columbia's faculty exchange program early in the century with the University of Berlin, Butler remarked how the German university's chancellor had protested when he learned that Columbia intended to send Felix Adler, a Jew. Fixing his eyes, according to Diana's account (who obviously got it from Lionel, as she was upstairs), on Ernest Hunter Wright, head of the English Department, Butler intoned dramatically, "'And I, gentlemen, I wrote back: At Columbia, sir, we recognize merit, not race.' Silence. The party rose to join the ladies and move on to the Faculty Club reception. In the summer, 'under his summer powers,' President Butler appointed Lionel an Assistant Professor of English, the first Jew of that department to become a member of the faculty."

Mrs. Trilling's admiration for Butler's securing her husband for Columbia is deserved, but it hardly modifies, as she suggested, "the image of Butler that has come down to us." It was rather another instance of Butler's unerring capacity to seize the moral high ground when it served his purposes. The glowing reviews of the Arnold book had alerted Butler to the prize he had in Trilling, and he was always eager to ally himself with distinction. Moreover, Trilling was an elegant and graceful man, not one of those Jews whose actions could embarrass. The opportunity to honor principle while enhancing the quality of his faculty was not one Butler would ever pass up. The Trilling appointment does not alter our view of him or his anti-Semitism; it simply shows him at the top of his game, making himself look good as he got what he wanted.

CHAPTER FIFTEEN

The Path to Peace

In 1925 Elihu Root, arguably the man most responsible for getting Andrew Carnegie to establish his Endowment for International Peace, decided to give up the Endowment's presidency. At eighty, having led the organization since its inception in 1910, Root thought it time to step aside for youth. There was no serious question as to Root's successor. The trustees immediately chose the youthful, sixty-five-year-old Butler, the person who played the second most important role in encouraging Carnegie to invest $10 million toward peace. Moving to the presidency, Butler did not relinquish his directorship of the Division of Intercourse and Education. Instead, he would function simultaneously as director and president.

Butler delighted in his promotion. Taking over the Endowment helped assuage the old pain of having lost the White House to the mediocre Harding, and the fresher pain of seeing the equally mediocre Calvin Coolidge in control of the Republican Party and the country. If the grubby realities of national politics had forced Butler to scale back his aspirations for a significant voice in the highest Republican circles, the prominence of his Endowment position freed him from the need to harbor such ambitions. His new international prestige and power gave him less cause to worry about his status within the party. He could criticize Republican values and direction with the impunity conferred by a vast pulpit, a worldwide audience, and access to the income produced by $10 million.

Butler the Endowment president continued the efforts of Butler the director to proselytize for the importance of the international mind and the peaceful settlement of international disputes. Toward these goals he directed every conceivable kind of educational activity: lectures, seminars, conferences, book and magazine publication, exchange visits between journalists and professors of different countries, and the proliferation of International Mind alcoves in libraries and International Relations Clubs in colleges and universities. But from the moment he replaced Root, Butler also waged an educational campaign of a different sort, an effort to convince the trustees of the Carnegie Corporation that the Endowment needed more money to enable it to rid the world of war. At issue was not simply the Endowment's budget, but the relationship between the Corporation and the different trusts Carnegie had also created, including the Foundation for the Advancement of Teaching, the Carnegie Institution for Science in Washington, and the Carnegie Institute at Pittsburgh.

Butler's view was simple: the Endowment, representing Carnegie's fondest dream for the world, stood far above the rest in importance; as the moneyed parent, the Corporation had been explicitly intended by Carnegie to address all of the financial needs of its favorite child. If the cost of the Endowment's activities exceeded the $500,000 income produced by its $10 million principal, the difference should be made up by the Corporation. But the Corporation's trustees did not share this understanding of Carnegie's vision. They found no evidence that Carnegie preferred the Endowment to his other trusts or that the Corporation had been designed to support any of them. With its own charter and its own mission—essentially "to promote the advancement and diffusion of knowledge among the people of the United States"—it had always been willing to consider financial appeals from the other Carnegie enterprises, but it was not obliged to do so.

Butler did not begin the dispute. In 1916 the Corporation had asked the four organizations to assess their future plans and budgetary needs. Root responded for the Endowment that it was impossible to speak in specific terms about programs and projected costs while the war was still going on, but he felt confident that after the war was over, substantial amounts of money would be necessary to reform international relations in constructive directions. He therefore refrained from making any concrete proposals for the present, but suggested instead that "not less than $5,000,000" of Corporation funds be set aside for Endowment use at the close of war. The need for such an enormous sum spoke to the structural problem with the Endowment's budget. By 1916 the fixed administrative and programmatic costs of running its three divisions amounted to $300,000, leaving only $200,000 for all other initiatives. Given the work to be done after the war, such a sum would certainly be inadequate, and Root wanted to ensure that the Endowment had the resources to pursue whatever new opportunities it thought productive. The Corporation declined his request, though it responded to particular appeals: between 1911 and 1925 it granted $1,050,500 to the Endowment.

But no amount of money was enough for Butler, who justified his insatiable demands by appealing to what he claimed had been one of Carnegie's favorite exhortations: "Don't save; spend, and ask me for more." That was the reason, Butler maintained, that Carnegie had established the Corporation: "In order that where he had underestimated . . . the necessities, this great trust would be at hand to take care of it." When Butler became, after Root's death in 1937, the sole survivor of the original group of Endowment trustees, it was impossible to refute his insistence that he knew from firsthand conversation precisely how Carnegie had envisioned the Corporation's purpose. In his hagglings, Butler always played this card of personal knowledge: whatever the arguments adduced by Corporation trustees, he would counter them by asserting that he alone had been privy to Carnegie's deepest wishes.

Complaining about inadequate budgets, whether at Columbia or the Endowment, became a central activity for Butler in the late 1920s. Unlike at Columbia, however, where no ready solution was available, Butler saw the Corporation as the easy answer to the Endowment's needs. Early in 1927 the Endowment asked for $425,000 (later increased to $580,000) for a variety of projects—including five new Carnegie professorships in addition to those already in Paris and Berlin; an American system of cataloging for the Vatican Library; sending thirty editorial writers to study the Permanent Court of International Justice and to visit Berlin and Prague during the summer—among a number of other specified items. The additional $155,000 was to be used to develop productive relations between the people of the United States and the Latin American countries, in response to a request from Secretary of State Frank Kellogg. Several months later the Corporation approved a grant of only $150,000, having found much of what Butler proposed unconvincing.

Disappointed, Butler nevertheless continued to push for sizable grants for his European programs. In 1928, Corporation lawyers ruled that as its charter directed it to serve the people of the United States, it was not legally entitled to fund activities abroad. At the same time, the trustees, understanding the extent to which the Endowment was already heavily invested in European enterprises, were reluctant to undermine it. They sought a way around their own strictures, finally deciding to support the Endowment's domestic ventures, fully aware that the money was being used to release income for work elsewhere. Corporation grants to the Endowment were all worded so as to apply to the United States, despite their explicit international destination. Between 1927 and 1931 the Corporation gave $525,000 to the Endowment.

But even this did not satisfy Butler. In 1930 the Endowment argued that it needed the assured income from an additional $5 million in order to fulfill its responsibilities to the world. In 1932 it doubled that estimate to $10 million. The Corporation continued to deny any such massive infusion of funds—implying that part of the Endowment's fiscal difficulties stemmed from its own failure to restrict the growth of fixed expenditures—but it also continued to entertain (and fund) annual specific proposals, labeled domestic but in essence foreign, of not more than $100,000.

The tension between the endlessly needy Endowment and the skeptical Corporation was exacerbated by the complicated relationship between Butler and Frederick P. Keppel, who became president of the Carnegie Corporation in 1922. Keppel had worked under Butler at Columbia after graduating from the college in 1898, first as assistant secretary of the university (1900–1902), then as secretary (1902–10), and finally as dean of the college (1910–17). When Secretary of War Newton Baker asked him to come to Washington as his assistant in 1918, Keppel felt he must go, expecting to resume his Columbia position once his "national service" had ended. Returning to New York after the war to discuss his university future with Butler, he was devastated to discover he had none. "Butler looked him in the eye and said, 'Fred, there's no place now for you at Columbia,'" reported Robert Lester, Keppel's assistant at the Carnegie Corporation. Keppel later told Lester of "his great surprise and shock at Butler having taken that attitude towards him."

It's hard to know what lay behind this treatment of Keppel, for there had been no previous indication that Butler harbored doubts about Keppel's character or competence. An unassuming man who came from a well-to-do family—his father was a successful art dealer—he had married a niece of J. P. Morgan's and lived on a large estate in Montrose, New York. His popularity among students, faculty, and alumni gave him every reason to assume he was destined for a long-term university career. There seem to be only two possible explanations for Butler's behavior. The first is that Butler, angry at Keppel's departure, resolved to teach him a lesson about the consequences of disloyalty by not permitting him back. The second, more likely, is that Butler saw Keppel's administrative talents, popularity, and success (he rose quickly in Washington to the newly created post of third assistant secretary of war) as a threat to his own control at Columbia. Lester suggested that the idea that Keppel was secretly nurturing ambitions for the Columbia presidency might well have troubled Butler. If so, it is interesting that as trustee of the Carnegie Corporation, Butler did not oppose Keppel's election as president in 1922, almost as if he was pleased to have him safely lodged there rather than humming about the Columbia hive as a ready alternative to Butler. It must also have been the case that Butler would have anticipated little difficulty handling his former subordinate.

Once Butler became president of the Endowment, however, he found it offensive to deal as an equal with someone he once regarded, in Lester's words, as a "glorified office boy." Being forced to request funds from the man he previously ordered about could not have been easy for Butler, and no doubt contributed to the low-grade hostility that he directed at Keppel, treating him, according to the Corporation's John Russell, "as if he didn't amount to anything." Keppel, naturally enough, found Butler's dismissive attitude painful. But it was hard for him to overcome the vulnerability caused by seventeen years of seeking his formidable boss's approval, and even though he was now in a position to endorse (or deny) Butler's budgetary requests, he never stopped wanting to earn Butler's respect.

It was a vain hope, the more so because Keppel refused to appreciate that Butler alone understood the true nature of Carnegie's wishes for the Endowment and Corporation. "Butler just changes not only his own mind, but he changes his memory about things," he commented. Keppel nevertheless showed both patience and tact in keeping annual grants of $100,000 or so going to the Endowment. He simply had too much regard for Butler—in spite of the disdain Butler exhibited toward him—to cut the Endowment off entirely. And he stayed consistently loyal to Butler, reluctant to hear any criticism of him: "If anybody made a snide remark about Mr. Butler in front of Keppel, he'd get cut down. He would just not have any," one junior Corporation officer said.

The disagreements between Butler and the Corporation could not be resolved. "Of all the trusts, large or small, with which I have ever been associated," Butler complained to Henry Pritchett, "the Carnegie Corporation is far and away the most incompetently managed . . . The Corporation is pouring Mr. Carnegie's money down a hundred different ratholes." By which he meant simply that Keppel and the other trustees were not honoring what he knew to be Carnegie's priorities. "Everything they proposed and had been recently doing," he wrote Pritchett a month later, "was in flat contradiction of Mr. Carnegie's hopes, plans and ideals. I suggested that the name of the Corporation be changed to the 'Anti-Carnegie Corporation.'" Butler's unhappiness with the Corporation was such that he confided to Pritchett that he would himself have resigned from the board except for the commitment he felt to honor Carnegie's memory and ideals. The Corporation never acceded to Butler's argument about its obligations, and Butler never ceased making the case. It remained a standoff to the end of Butler's regime, in 1945, when he retired from both Endowment and Corporation.

As opposed to the controversy that marked the relations between the Endowment and the Corporation, Butler presided with very little turmoil over the workings of the Endowment itself. Much like the frictionless way he managed the Columbia board, cajoling, coercing, and even just issuing pronouncements to get his way, so the Endowment's trustees tended obediently to conform to Butler's will. Given Butler's preference for unhindered authority, it is not surprising that his favorite biblical passage was Psalm 19. Exalting divine authority and grandeur, verses 7 through 9 define the ideal way a strong CEO would like to be understood by his board:

The law of the Lord is perfect,
converting the soul;
The testimony of the Lord is sure
making wise the simple.
The statutes of the Lord are right,
rejoicing the heart:
the commandment of the Lord is pure,
enlightening the eyes.
The fear of the Lord is clean,
enduring for ever:
the judgments of the Lord are true
and righteous altogether.

More articulate, more distinguished, and more confident than almost anybody else, Butler was difficult to withstand. In his own mind he became the Carnegie Endowment, just as he had become Columbia. According to one Endowment trustee, "he ran it almost untrammeled in the most extraordinary manner." He was not inclined to spend much time debating priorities and strategies. For E. Berthol Sayre, Butler's secretary at the Endowment for twenty years, "His method was direction from above . . . Under Dr. Butler's administration, so far as I know, there was very little consultation of staff even among the Trustees." The self-doubt that occasionally assailed lesser souls did not trouble Butler: "He was *absolutely* definite about what he wanted—there was never any indecision, never any playing with ideas." And certainly never any anxieties about the conduct of the Endowment. Butler remained an unabashed booster both of the importance of its mission to educate public opinion and of its wholehearted success. He was quick to assure his trustees at their biannual meetings that they were doing invaluable work in ridding the world of the possibility of future wars. In answer to the question, "Do we matter?" Butler replied resoundingly,

We have mattered enormously . . . There is no other agency for peace in this world which is fit to be mentioned in the same decade as the Endowment, from the standpoint of recorded accomplishment, of public confidence, of reliance, and that statement I am prepared to back at any time and buttress it by the most complete evidence.

Butler's testimony aside, did the Carnegie Endowment matter? According to his successor as president of the Endowment, not much. Alger Hiss—whose career at the Endowment was abruptly ended by Whittaker Chambers's accusations that he was a Soviet spy—dismissed Butler's direction with a curt, "He didn't do a damn thing. Ran it as his own show for his own purposes," but this judgment was certainly colored by the restrained Hiss's dislike of Butler's egotism. When Hiss took over, in 1945, the establishment of the United Nations provided him with a concrete opportunity—not available to Butler—to help bring about a new era of world order, and Hiss channeled all the Endowment's energy and resources into supporting the fledgling institution. But the aims of the UN as set forth in its charter—to maintain international peace and security, to cultivate friendly relations between states, and to work cooperatively to solve social, economic, and humanitarian problems—were essentially those that Butler had been pursuing for twenty years. And though Butler's hopes were doomed by the context of the times—an unstable Europe and an ineffectual League of Nations (made even more ineffectual by the unwillingness of the United States to join it), he nevertheless persisted in trying to educate people to understand the necessity of forging a viable political community out of the world's separate states. Protesting against narrow economic nationalism (but perhaps failing to recognize its appeal), stressing the need to think internationally and recognize the interdependence of all countries, and trying to find a mechanism to resolve disputes peacefully, Butler articulated admirable— if perhaps naively optimistic—goals. The cataclysm of World War II can hardly be attributed to the Endowment's failure to propagandize forcefully enough for peace and international cooperation.

It can be argued, however, that the presumption that educated public opinion will shape actual political agendas is an expensive exercise in futility. What matters are not innumerable conferences, International Relations Clubs, and inspiring rhetoric, but hard-nosed political lobbying and the implementation of specific, concrete proposals designed to make governments act in responsible ways—practical intervention, in short, not ongoing discussions about the ideal. Such at least were the views of some Endowment critics, who objected to the vast amounts of money being spent on very little return, and on the high-handed way Butler determined priorities. Foremost among these was Ramsay MacDonald, British Labour M.P. and prime minister in 1924 and again in 1929–35, who became a member of the Endowment's European Advisory Council in 1913. In May of 1925, Butler, on behalf of the trustees, solicited some two hundred statesmen around the world for their confidential assessments of the Endowment's policies and administration. The responses tended to be benignly supportive with one pungent exception: MacDonald replied that a letter could not begin to do justice to his views:

> I have been so amazed at the way the Fund has been administered
> that I have often considered it my duty to ask that my name should
> be removed from the lists of people who are supposed to have some
> responsibility. I doubt if I have been consulted in any way for ten or

twelve years, although being a member of the European Advisory Council assumes that I know something regarding it . . . I doubt if the Fund has really done a particle of good in the promotion of peace. It would probably have been difficult enough at best but your failure has been pre-eminently conspicuous . . . My dear old Friend Carnegie, should he still be watching the ways of men, must be painfully aware of how easy it is to waste money . . .

If I am to remain in even a nominal connection with the Fund, its European organisation will have to be reconstructed so that my name is not given in support of an expenditure of money in ways of which I know nothing more than any man in the street of whom you would ask information by accident.

Butler immediately wrote back, thanking him for his frank views and explaining that he was eager to talk to him to involve him more actively in the affairs of the Endowment. Attempts to meet in London failed, however, and with it any possibility that Butler might have been able to convince MacDonald to stay on the Advisory Council. On November 6 MacDonald told Sir Donald MacAlister, at the University of Glasgow, that he had finally made up his mind to resign:

> In the whole course of my experience I have never known anything so bad as the Administration of this Fund. One or two people seem to settle the whole distribution of the money and how it goes, except in salaries, nobody seems to know. If poor Carnegie knew he would turn in his grave. That Nicholas Murray Butler has been made Director was a calamity.

That same day, he notified Butler he was leaving the Advisory Council. He complained that the money had been used foolishly, that there had been no serious consultation, that the Endowment had contributed nothing to the continental peace movement. "In a sentence," he concluded unsparingly, "I think the administration has been perfectly scandalous, and is a warning to everybody who wishes to leave money for a good purpose to take precautions not to allow it to fall from one pair of dead hands into twenty others." Four years later, describing to the Endowment trustees the nearly unanimous approval of their policies found in the 1925 survey, Butler explained away MacDonald's dissatisfaction by claiming "he thought we had made occasional statements that were antagonistic to the doctrine of socialism."

Butler might have misrepresented MacDonald's criticism, but he genuinely believed in the Endowment's accomplishments. Responding in 1929 to the unhappiness of one of its trustees, Frederic Delano, Butler confessed that

> it staggers me to have you write that you are disappointed at the way things have been going. So far as I know, the substantially universal opinion of the world accords with my own in believing that never in history have things gone so well as they have during the past few years . . . The Carnegie Endowment has established itself in practically every land as a major influence in the enlightenment and instruction of public opinion in all that relates to war and peace.

Butler's enthusiasm was less self-deluded than born of his profound need to think that informed public opinion would lead to sensible governmental policy. Saturating the public with the arguments for peaceful arbitration and disarmament, Butler could properly take satisfaction in the sheer number of educational programs the Endowment was running, but at the same time he remained unwilling to confront the reality that they didn't, in fact, make a difference. The case was brutally put in a 1938 letter by Butler's friend Lord Davies, an active supporter of the League of Nations who, in November of that year, gave as a gift to the Welsh people the Temple of Peace, dedicated to the memory of those who lost their lives in World War I: "From the purely academic standpoint no doubt it may be argued that the money has been spent on projects connected with peace. But when our civilization goes up in smoke, people may ask themselves whether, after all, it has been spent to the best advantage." His survey of the grim condition of the world in that very grim year left him with nothing to celebrate in the Endowment's accomplishments: "What of all the peace movements; what have they done; are they worth a rap? I wonder. What practical results can they show for all the speeches, literature and money expended in the cause? Very little, I fear."

It would not be reasonable to blame the failures of a private philanthropic organization for the outbreak of war at the end of the 1930s. But it was also true that by limiting itself solely to the instruction of public opinion and staying free of any political involvement, the Endowment vitiated some of the moral clout it might otherwise have exercised. Its official reluctance to condemn German anti-Semitism was an example of the bind in which the policy of impartiality had placed it.

In May 1933, two months after Hitler took power, Butler brought to the Endowment's trustees the concern of three "very important Jews"—Herbert Lehman, then a judge on the New York State Court of Appeals; Joseph Proskauer, a prominent lawyer and former judge of the state supreme court; and one Mr. Strupp, head of the Hebrew Charities—over the persecution of the Jews in Germany. Distressed by the news they were receiving about conditions there, and with the world seemingly indifferent, they at the same time were worried by the emotional response that outspoken leaders like Rabbi Stephen Wise were encouraging in their followers. With a kind of pathetic desperation, they had come to Butler in the hope that perhaps there was something—a "policy, statement or action"—the Endowment might undertake on behalf of Germany's Jews. Butler didn't think there was anything the Endowment could do that might not make matters worse, but he said he would raise the issue with his trustees. Not surprisingly, they were reluctant to say anything that would be seen as censuring the German government, a step that might endanger their own capacity to work effectively with it. Eager not to take any action, Butler was nevertheless looking for a way to make "some kindly reply to these three distinguished Hebrews." James Sheffield replied that it would be undesirable for the board to go on record. John W. Davis thought that Butler could say that the board "has heard their communication with the utmost sympathy" and would, if they saw an opportunity, be glad to do something, though at this moment they didn't see that they had any options. Henry S. Pritchett suggested that it "might be well to be careful about the sympathy," and Davis added that perhaps it would be best if Butler communicated with them orally. David Barrows noted that since the oppression of the Jews was technically a "domestic and interior" affair, the Endowment was not entitled to intervene in any case. Finally, it was agreed that the appropriate response was for Butler to offer "an assurance of the proper amount of sympathy without any commitment of policy." Attempting to organize public opinion without taking positions offensive to foreign governments was the delicate line Butler kept the Endowment treading. Large moral and economic principles could be espoused as long as unpleasant political issues were politely avoided. If such a tactic could not necessarily justify the importance Butler claimed for the Endowment, he did manage to direct public opinion, with the aid of the Endowment, toward one personally significant achievement.

On April 6, 1927, the tenth anniversary of the entry of the United States into the Great War, French foreign minister Aristide Briand delivered a message to the American public through the Associated Press. It appeared without fanfare in the middle pages of many American newspapers, though its contents perhaps deserved more prominence than the editors allowed. For in it Briand proposed that the United States and France provide a "solemn example" to the world by resolving never to resort to war as a means of settling international disputes between them. To this end,

> France would be willing to enter into an agreement with America mutually outlawing war, to use your way of expressing it. The renunciation of war as an instrument of national policy is a conception already familiar to the signatories of the Locarno Treaties [a series of treaties signed in 1925 between six European nations and Great Britain endorsing national boundaries and the commitment to arbitration]. Any engagement subscribed to in the same spirit by the United States toward another nation, such as France, should greatly contribute in the eyes of the world to enlarge and fortify the foundation on which the international policy of peace is being erected.

The proposal caused no stir until April 25, when *The New York Times* published a long letter from Butler, accompanied by a supportive editorial, wondering why the American people had "failed to hear the extraordinarily important message addressed to them," an offer made not through the normal diplomatic channels but directly to the people. Understanding the American hesitancy to get involved in European entanglements, Butler cagily distinguished the Briand proposal from other controversial alliances and institutions. It did not require, for example, accepting the Covenant of the League of Nations, with its obligations to use force, if necessary, to protect the territorial integrity of the member nations. All it called for was the assent of the American government that "in no case will they employ war to enforce their policies with reference to France." And what more fitting moment for the United States to agree to this than during the tenth anniversary of America's sacrifice in the First World War? The letter ended on a rhetorical note practically demanding some kind of American response: "M. Briand, speaking the voice and expressing the soul of France, has called out to us across the ocean. What answer is he to hear? What evidence is he to have that these noble words have been heard and understood?"

In the light of all that was written about the origins of Briand's offer and the complex negotiations that followed, Butler sought, in *Across the Busy Years*, "to set down in the simplest possible form the actual history of this epoch-marking public document." His "simplest possible form" located himself squarely behind the inception of Briand's idea, tracing its origins to a conversation the two men had in 1926. According to Butler, they were discussing the progress toward peace that the world seemed to be making, and Briand queried Butler as to what should be done next. Butler replied that he was just reading Carl von Clausewitz's famous book on war, with its extraordinary chapter entitled "War as an Instrument of National Policy." "Has not the time come," Butler suggested, "for the civilized governments of the world formally to renounce war as an instrument of policy?" Briand expressed interest in learning about Clausewitz's argument, and it was on this basis that Butler concluded that it had been "the reading of von Clausewitz's book by Briand which led to the celebrated statement made on April 6th."

Butler attributed the nineteen-day lapse of time between Briand's letter and his own to his being caught up in the preparation for and the aftermath of his April 8 Prohibition debate with Borah. It was only after he was able to settle down and consider other events that the astonishing reality of American indifference occurred to him, moving him to act. Even allowing for its necessary brevity, Butler's narration is a bit too simple. His conversation with Briand took place in a context in which arguments for outlawing or renouncing war were already well recognized in Europe, in substantial part owing to the strenuous propagandizing of the burly Chicago lawyer S. O. Levinson, who had been campaigning for the outlawry of war over a number of years. It is hardly credible that a casual remark about Clausewitz would have suddenly stimulated Briand into making his proposal. More important, there is documentary evidence that it was not Butler at all who was responsible for influencing Briand, but James Shotwell, Butler's colleague at the Endowment, and that it was Shotwell, not Butler, who recognized the need for an American response and drafted the April 25 letter. In a memo filed in *The New York Times* archives, Adolph Ochs described what happened:

> On April 20, 1927, Professor J.T. Shotwell lunched at the Times. He told us of his disappointment at the manner in which a speech of M. Briand's, made on April 6th, had been received.
>
> Dr. Shotwell said that he had suggested that Briand make this public statement, but that unfortunately neither the news agencies nor the correspondents of the Times had paid any heed to it.
>
> The importance of the statement was of course appreciated and ways and means were discussed at the luncheon table for bringing the matter to life again. It was finally suggested that Dr. Nicholas Murray Butler, as head of the Carnegie Peace Foundation, be requested to write a letter to the Times in which he would call attention to the oversight of Briand's proposal, and on April 25, 1927, his letter was published as attached.
>
> In the meantime, we arranged to secure comment on the letter from the various interested capitols and in this manner the proposal which subsequently developed into the Kellogg Treaty for the outlawry of war was started on its path.

If Shotwell, not Butler, deserved credit for wanting to mobilize the American public behind Briand's peace initiative, he deserved even more credit for knowing that the way to accomplish this required Butler's leadership, not his own. Sharing a commitment to world peace and the League of Nations, as well as to Columbia (where Shotwell taught) and the Endowment, they were nonetheless not friends. In many ways, they could have not been more different. Unassuming where Butler was imperious, dowdy where Butler was elegant, Shotwell was stylistically a kind of Butler anti-type. Although he admired Butler's conviction and courage, he found him at the same time condescending, aloof, self-involved. A man very much without pretensions of his own, Shotwell was put off by Butler's intellectual and social snobberies. Butler's grand manner led Shotwell to refer to him as the "Shah of Persia." But it was precisely these qualities, Shotwell also knew, that made him such a powerful presence in the peace movement. If the country was to be exhorted to clamor for acceptance of Briand's pact, "Dr. Butler" would have to lead the charge. Butler's letter (it seems easier to call it this) had precisely the effect Shotwell intended: Briand's disregarded offer suddenly became a prominent national agenda item, commented on by the press, celebrated by peace groups, strongly supported by public opinion. The Butler mystique guaranteed that Briand's "noble words" would be both heard and clearly understood.

One small and influential group of Americans, however, was decidedly not pleased with either the words or the favorable public response they elicited: the State Department, and most especially Secretary of State Frank B. Kellogg, who chafed at the prospect of governmental policy being conducted openly in newspapers and shaped by the uninformed passions of the people. No fan of bilateral treaties in general, he was angry at having his policy-making prerogatives eroded by an outpouring of public sentiment. Additionally, he thought the whole business of countries signing oaths against war was ridiculous.

Kellogg's skepticism was not entirely misplaced. Beneath Briand's elevated rhetoric about renouncing war, one could discern a sliver of parochial French self-interest: to ensure that if France was involved in a European conflict, the United States would not give aid to its enemies. The likelihood of France and the United States ever going to war with each other was infinitesimal at best, so there was hardly any point in signing a treaty to that effect. But as a strategy to keep the United States from supporting any opposing side should France get embroiled in a military struggle, it made eminent sense, part of the security policy France had been pursuing throughout the 1920s, forging agreements with Belgium (1920), Poland (1921), Czechoslovakia (1924), Romania (1926), and Yugoslavia (1926). For the wily Briand, adding the United States to the list of "friendly" countries could only be a boon.

While America applauded, Kellogg fulminated and fiddled. When Butler realized in early May that Kellogg was intending to do nothing about Briand's offer, hoping to stall until the enthusiasm died down, he undertook his own program to keep public opinion aroused. At the American Club in Paris on June 16 he suggested that the pact between France and the United States need only include three simple articles, "each of which can be learned by children in school": that war as an instrument of national policy be renounced, that both countries accept the definition of an aggressor country as stipulated by the Locarno Treaties, and that they agree not to aid an aggressor in case of war.

Actually, Butler's three paragraphs, which themselves represented a vast scaling down of an earlier draft treaty he had commissioned from Shotwell, were still one paragraph and many complications too long for the French foreign minister. Briand was convinced that the shorter and simpler the wording, the more likely to avoid the senatorial doubts that finally sank the League of Nations in the United States. Briand's attitude toward Butler's early role was caught by Harrison Brown, one of S. O. Levinson's peace colleagues, summarizing a conversation he had with Briand's confidential secretary, Alexis Leger:

> I mentioned Butler and Leger said that Briand had not intended to see him but that he (Leger) had insisted. Butler was talking a lot of bunk about his mile long effusion. Briand had him up and changed his whole tone so that after the interview Butler was stressing the need for simplicity, and saying that only two articles were necessary! Briand seems to have said roughly [sic] "No doubt you mean well but you keep saying that I want this and that and the other but you have not seized the idea that I want the simplest thing possible which will outlaw war between us."

With his slimmed down (if still bulky) scheme, Butler, during the next ten months, gave by his own accounting fourteen major addresses and many minor ones in "twenty-two states, reaching tens of thousands of persons directly, and hundreds of thousands, perhaps millions, over the radio."

He considered "The Path to Peace," his annual Parrish Art Museum speech in Southampton on September 4, his "first step in the campaign." It contained most of the basic arguments and analysis that he repeated in subsequent talks. Beginning with an apocalyptic and prescient view of what the next war would bring—"huge bombs dropped from the air to wipe out in an hour the industry and achievement of generations. In such a war there would be no non-combatants. Every man, woman and child would be in instant danger"—Butler then examined what he took to be the three major causes of war: a nation's need to achieve a substantial ethnic unity, to occupy a geographic unity, and to gain economic independence. These three natural impulses must be moderated and negotiated if war was to be avoided. How could this be done?

Not, Butler emphasized, by trying to outlaw war. Although outlawing war and renouncing its use might seem to the casual observer to come to much the same thing, the distinction was critically fought over by the various factions of the American peace movement during the 1920s. S. O. Levinson and Butler's Prohibition foe Senator Borah were fervent outlawrists, Butler and Shotwell determined renunciationists. Butler opposed attempting to outlaw war on two grounds. First, he saw it as completely useless: "We might as well pass a resolution to outlaw hypocrisy." Second, even if war could be outlawed, it raised the question of punishing the transgressors. Butler rejected the concept of outlawry because he felt it was necessarily tied to the notion of enforcement. The better path was renunciation, which, like temperance, was a voluntary act with "large moral consequences and effectiveness." The outlawing of war, by contrast, was like Prohibition, "vain and futile . . . resting not on morals but on brute force." (The outlawrists were not delighted by this comparison. Levinson suggested that Butler's fanaticism on the subject had rendered him unable to think straight. Anybody finding a similarity beween Prohibition and outlawing war was clearly in trouble.)

As Butler continued to whip up public support for his position throughout the fall and winter of 1927, Kellogg waited for it to die down. But with both peace camps—the outlawrists and the renunciationists—coming together in support of Briand, and with Butler's determined advocacy, popular feeling for a positive American response to Briand only grew. (The peace movement's practically unanimous enthusiasm for a Franco-American treaty did not entirely still the hostility between its two major factions. When outlawrist philosopher John Dewey of Columbia heard that Butler had given a talk in London in which he referred to "those admirable and amiable persons who would outlaw war—admirable and amiable but quite hopeless," he wrote to Levinson that Butler's remarks were not surprising, as he "had been born with a reserved seat on the band wagon.")

The contentious, temperamental Kellogg found himself in a quandary. His opposition to the bilateral agreement with France had seemingly placed him in opposition to the will of the American people on an issue as unexceptionable and wholesome as peace. Not a good position for a man who did not like losing—and who had done little of it during his career. Kellogg's was almost a clichéd American success story, as he had risen by sheer drive and native ability, without benefit of any but the sketchiest education in rural Minnesota, to become president of the American Bar Association, a senator, ambassador to the Court of St. James's, and then secretary of state. Needless to say, he and Butler did not like each other. He resented Butler's high-handed meddling; Butler scorned him as uneducated.

Despite the increasing pressure for an official answer to Briand, Kellogg and President Coolidge steadfastly refused to commit themselves. Finally, on December 28, Kellogg issued the government's response. In a consummate stroke of diplomatic ingenuity, he avoided what he considered the bilateral trap of the initial proposal by countering with a multilateral suggestion. Instead of limiting the renunciation of war to an agreement between two countries, would it not be a more significant achievement to extend the commitment to all the major powers?

At a stroke, Kellogg transformed himself from a crabbed critic of moral progress into a visionary architect of world peace. He had suddenly become the leader of public opinion rather than the object of its censure. In calling for all countries to renounce war, Kellogg had also effectively outmaneuvered Briand. Instead of the defensive alliance with the United States he had really wanted, Briand was trapped into a more inclusive treaty embracing all the major nations of the world. As Assistant Secretary of State William Castle noted in his diary on February 28, 1928, "We have Monsieur Briand out on a limb . . . I do not think the French will agree [to the multilateral proposal], but I think they will have an awful time not to agree."

After three months of diplomatic sparring, Briand finally consented to the larger framework. Several months later, the treaty that Briand never really wanted and Kellogg initially dismissed as some sort of pacifist nonsense was ready for signing. On August 27, 1928, at the Quai d'Orsay palace in Paris, representatives of fifteen nations assembled to affix their signatures—with a difficult to handle foot-long gold pen given to Kellogg by the grateful citizens of Le Havre—to the two simple substantive articles:

(1) The High Contracting Parties solemnly declare in the names of their respective peoples that they condemn recourse to war for the solution of international controversies, and renounce it as an instrument of national policy in their relations with one another.

(2) The High Contracting Parties agree that the settlement or solution of all disputes or conflicts of whatever nature or of whatever origin they may be, which may arise among them, shall never be sought except by pacific means.

The signing of the Pact of Paris by fifteen nations (with thirty-one adherents added later) unleashed a torrent of energy in the United States for prompt ratification. However ideologically opposed to one another the outlawrists and renunciationists still remained, all—the Levinsons and the Borahs, the Shotwells and the Butlers—joined together in calling for Senate endorsement. Every variety of peace organization, from Butler's Carnegie Endowment to the American Committee for the Outlawry of War to Carrie Chapman Catt's Committee on the Cause and Cure of War began actively lobbying for swift action. On January 15, 1929, Senator Borah moved the vote, and by 85–1 (Blaine of Wisconsin being the sole nay) the Senate ratified the treaty. Robert Underwood Johnson's "miracle," celebrated at the time of the Quai d'Orsay signing, was now an officially documented world fact:

Lift up your heads, ye peoples,
The miracle has come,
No longer are ye helpless,
No longer are ye dumb.

Not altogether improperly, Butler took the passage of the treaty as a personal victory. And he viewed the miracle of the world's ostensible renunciation of war without any of the cynicism that marked others' commitment to it. Even as they voted in the affirmative, a number of senators did so not because they believed it might accomplish anything, but because it smacked of apple pie (who, after all, could be against peace?) and seemed harmless enough. If it had little to do with establishing permanent peace, at least it did not constrain America's freedom to act in it own interests or entangle the country in any of the complications of the World Court, for example, or the League of Nations.

Butler nevertheless did not regard it in this way. Shotwell always maintained that Butler's investment in the peace movement was more "in the moralistic side of things than in the detail of political and structural thought," and in this sense the pact, with its vision of an international community voluntarily subjecting itself to the processes of peaceful negotiation to solve problems, embodied the goal for which Butler had been working all his life. Whatever its effectiveness (or ineffectiveness), its very existence signaled for Butler an extraordinary development in human civilization. He was perfectly serious when he spoke of it as "the most stupendous and most revolutionary change that has ever taken place at any time in the history of the world."

However much Butler applauded it as a symbol of mankind's spiritual progress, he also seemed prepared to take literally the fact that war was no longer a serious possibility. The treaty became in a sense the centerpiece of Butler's political thinking in the late 1920s and '30s, the intellectual foundation for a number of concrete proposals he advocated during this time. His call for the abolition of compulsory military service and the reduction of existing armies to small police forces; his suggestion that now that war had become an anachronism, the United States should replace its Departments of War, Navy, and Aviation with a single Department of National Defense; his lobbying to replace the war-making capacities of the world's large navies with small navies for peacekeeping; his urging that the authority of the Permanent Court of International Justice and the Permanent Court of Arbitration at The Hague be strengthened and that the prestige of the League of Nations be enhanced—"All this the Pact of Paris suggests and makes possible. It is a Program of Peace for the constructive statesmanship of today and tomorrow."

Even the discussion of key issues not directly connected to it, such as the need to renegotiate the German war debt of World War I and to reduce the high level of American protective tariffs, were invigorated, Butler thought, by the fresh possibilities of international cooperation implied by the treaty. Its passage became the opportunity for Butler to attack, in a phrase the press loved, the plague of "pharisaical nationalism" that prevented countries from understanding their proper relation to one another in an increasingly inter-dependent world. The new political realities required new kinds of national policies. In an interview in the Sunday *Times*, Butler declared that the Pact of Paris "is of so stupendous importance that it is even now most imperfectly understood." For Butler, people were slow to recognize that everything was changed:

Gone is the fear of national security; gone is the argument for compulsory military service and huge standing armies; gone is the plea for the protection of sea-borne commerce and a navy as powerful as any in the world; gone is the haste to build bombing planes and to store up vast supplies of poison gas; gone is the whole gospel of preparedness for a war which is promised never to be fought—gone are all these unless all men and all governments are liars.

Not everybody shared Butler's optimism. More skeptical souls pointed to the spate of interpretative reservations that many nations had tied to their pact endorsements, explicitly reserving for themselves the right to wage defensive war. Great Britain, for example, insisted on a kind of "British Monroe Doctrine," which declared that its right to defend itself included any attack on any of its far-flung dominions. Political columnist Harry Elmer Barnes wondered that since wars of self-defense, wars in defense of special interests, such as the Suez Canal, and wars in fulfillment of previous treaty obligations all seemed to be exempt in various degrees from the strict renunciation program, what other professed reasons existed for going to war? Concluding that "no war ever likely to arise in practice is really 'renounced' by the Kellogg pact," he dismissed it as "a hollow sham and an especially glaring bit of international hypocrisy."

But critics—and even awkward events, such as the Japanese invasion of Manchuria in 1932—aside, Butler continued to laud the Pact of Paris as a watershed in human history, and he never forsook his belief in it's importance. It spoke to an impossible moral ideal—people and governments, after all, do lie—but still it managed, in the face of countless obstacles, to turn the ideal into a concrete diplomatic reality that engaged global assent. That it existed at all was a significant accomplishment. It is easy to say, of course, that Butler should not have been surprised, as he noted in *Across the Busy Years*, by the fact that as soon as governments ratified the pact, then "at least half of them began arming for war, under the pretence of arming for defense." But if he was credulous, at least it was in the pursuit of a vision for which he need not apologize, a vision of a world at peace shared by many in the aftermath of the slaughter of the First World War.

Before the path to peace ultimately proved illusory, it contributed some enduring rewards to architect Kellogg and chief advocate Butler. Honors were immediately showered upon Kellogg. Having never himself attended college, he particularly cherished the degrees he received from Harvard, Oxford, Brown, Princeton, and several other universities; in 1929 France conferred on him its highest honor, the Grand Cross of the Legion of Honor; and in 1930 he was elected to replace Charles Evans Hughes as a judge on the Permanent Court of International Justice. Butler, who already

possessed most of the medals and honorary degrees available, simply became even more internationally acclaimed. In the spring of 1930 he was
invited to speak in the German Reichstag—which he said was "quite unprecedented in their parliamentary history"—as one of three representatives of a foreign power (Viscount Cecil of England and Briand were the
other two) during a formal session. Butler stressed the uniqueness of this
event in interviews and press releases, but the invitation was not quite what
he made it out to be. Although he did speak in the Reichstag chamber, he
was not addressing the sitting members of the Reichstag, but instead an
audience attending a special evening lecture under the auspices of the
German Committee for International Conciliation. An honor, to be sure,
though not the "extraordinary step" Butler proudly claimed.

Medals, lectures, and degrees, however, were one thing, the Nobel
Peace Prize quite another. For ridding the world of war, the Nobel Prize was
the least a person deserved, but the question was, which person? The secretary of state who negotiated and signed the treaty and whose name was associated with it, or the unofficial spokesman who had raised the nation's
consciousness about its importance? Butler, who never forgave Kellogg for
what he called his violent opposition to the treaty when it was originally proposed, was contemptuous of his qualifications for the prize. Early in January
1930 Representative Andrew Montague of Virginia wrote to Butler about being approached by some of Kellogg's friends who wanted to enlist his support
to secure the Nobel for Kellogg. Montague told Butler he had refused because he thought Butler deserved it, adding that he would be happy to associate himself "with any of your friends to this end." Butler answered:

> As you well know, it never occurs to me to take much interest in who
> gets credit for any public act or undertaking provided we can get it
> done. I feel just that way about the important matter which you so
> kindly and so generously mention. One smiles at times at the mis-
> takes which the public makes in its rewards and recognitions, but is
> it not better to suffer these mistakes rather than to leave the things
> undone?

These genteel protestations of indifference were as serious as his claims not
to be interested in becoming the president of the United States. He wanted
it as much as he wanted anything, particularly since he felt his com-

petitor was undeserving. His campaign manager in the quest was his old friend James B. Scott, whose own peace credentials were well established: president of the American Society of International Law, president of the American Institute of International Law, and secretary of the Carnegie Endowment for International Peace.

Even as Butler was explaining to Montague his lack of interest in who gets credit for good deeds, Scott was putting together his seventeen-page letter of nomination for Butler and organizing his list of seconders and supporters. On January 17 Scott cabled the Nobel Prize Committee in Oslo that he was formally nominating Butler and that the supporting document would be delivered before February. The nomination was accompanied by seconds from Elihu Root, a Nobel Peace laureate himself in 1912, and Montague. On the same day, Scott sent cables to Lord Balfour, Viscount Grey, and Austen Chamberlain in England, as well as statesmen in France (including Briand) and Germany, asking them to send letters to Oslo on Butler's behalf. On the eighteenth, Scott informed Butler that all the material had gone out, and he expressed the hope "that the Lord will soften the hearts of the Pharaohs of the Peace Committee and turn their eyes westward to Columbia."

Butler thanked Scott for his loyal friendship and "splendidly phrased and energetic proposal." He was right to be pleased with Scott's nominating letter. In a lucid and thorough way, it summarized Butler's immense range of activities, affiliations, and publications dealing with issues of peace and international arbitration, and took especial pains to ensure that the history of the Pact of Paris was properly understood:

> Without intending to detract in the slightest degree from the undying credit of the responsible statesmen who negotiated and signed the Pact of Paris renouncing war as an instrument of national policy, this section of the memorial in behalf of Dr. Butler's nomination for the Nobel Peace Prize sets forth facts showing his interest and familiarity with the subject antedating the public discussion of it, some of them known only to his intimate friends and associates, and his services in furthering the project to the point of official consummation.

The name of Frank B. Kellogg did not figure in this analysis.

The Pharaohs did indeed look westward. The Peace Prize had not been awarded since 1927, and in 1930 the Nobel Committee announced two awards: for 1930, it went to Nathan Söderblom, archbishop of Uppsala and primate of Sweden; and for his efforts in convincing the world to renounce war, the 1929 award went to Frank B. Kellogg (the fifth American, after Theodore Roosevelt, Elihu Root, Woodrow Wilson, and General Charles Dawes to receive it).

Unhappy at "losing" to Kellogg, Scott and Butler were not about to give up. A new year represented a new opportunity, and in late January 1931 Scott sent off another letter, whose draft Butler had approved, to the Nobel Committee. Butler's materials were still on file from the previous year, so Scott did not feel he had to reargue the case for Butler's merits. Instead, he emphasized what he felt had been the reason for the committee's passing over Butler in favor of Kellogg: its preference for people holding official government posts. Of the five American Nobel laureates, as he wrote to Butler, there was not a single case of a winner who hadn't held public office. Scott built his letter around this fact: "To such an extent is this so, that it occurs to me that the political element, as the more evident, may have overshadowed the less noticeable but none the less permanent services of the advocates and promoters of international peace, to international opinion and international conduct, who have not had the good fortune to occupy such exalted political posts." Lest the committee failed to comprehend how exclusionary this practice had been, Scott identified one "non-political advocate of peace in the United States" who never got the award but whom most would have considered deserving: Andrew Carnegie.

Whether it was the force of Scott's argument or the simple understanding that Butler's lifelong commitment to international arbitration and conciliation was indeed worthy of recognition, the Pharaohs again turned westward for the 1931 prize, this time splitting it between two nongovernmental figures: Butler, and Jane Addams, former president of the Women's International League for Peace and Freedom and founder of Hull House, the settlement house in Chicago. The announcement on December 10 pleased Butler enormously. "Prussia once had a Great Elector," he telegraphed Scott as soon as he heard. "America now has a Great Nominator. Accept my grateful congratulations upon the success of his enterprise."

Congratulations came from all over the world. From Aristide Briand to Adolph Ochs, from the Vatican Library to General Pershing, ambassadors, presidents, writers, and foreign ministers hailed Butler. Of all the letters and telegrams praising Butler's deserved honor, one particularly stood out. On December 11 Henry Wadsworth Longfellow Dana, the young assistant professor Butler had dismissed from Columbia for his radical peace organizing in 1917, produced one sublimely cutting sentence: "Let me be the first to congratulate you on receiving the Nobel Peace Prize." Missing or deliberately overlooking its irony, Butler responded with his standard formula: "Accept this expression of my grateful appreciation for your generous and kindly message on the occasion of the Nobel Peace Prize. I appreciate it to the full."

CHAPTER SIXTEEN

Perils of Bolshevism, Promises of Fascism

The Nobel Peace Prize winner was as staunch a foe of Communism as could be found in the first half of the twentieth century. In Butler's view, any political system that sought to raise some people up by pulling others down, that asserted an inevitable conflict between labor and capital, and that denied the sacredness of private property had to be resisted. His antipathy did not prevent him from initially endorsing the Russian Revolution as a vital expression of liberty on the part of a vast people who had been living for centuries under the yoke of the tsar's autocracy. Butler welcomed the Kerensky government and what he called the birth of "a new political era," in which the Russians had chosen to throw in their lot with the West's "idea of human liberty." If it could hold fast to its new trajectory, Butler saw Russia "speeding toward the high places that are in the possession of those human spirits who love liberty, who love justice, who preach righteousness, and who, with all their faults and stumblings and imperfections, will labor for the coming of that happy day when this earth shall be a better place to live in because men are all free and just together."

But when Lenin ended that utopian dream, Butler immediately turned on Bolshevism as the single greatest threat to the American republic. Its victory in Russia marked for Butler the starting point for the projected conquest of France, Great Britain, and the United States. The economic and social disruption following the end of World War I in the United States — high cost of living, labor unrest, strikes — exacerbated fears generally that conditions were ripe for a Bolshevik onslaught. The Palmer raids on New

Year's Day 1920, which Attorney General A. Mitchell Palmer ordered on suspected radical centers throughout the country—the police detaining six thousand people while discovering three revolvers—spoke to the anxieties of the period. "Public order," Butler declared, could "not be secure until civil and political liberty are finally and definitely protected against the assaults of Bolshevism." Butler feared that part of socialism's insidious appeal grew from people's inability to distinguish between it and social reform. Writing to banker James Sheffield in 1918, Butler emphasized that one of their most important tasks, as defenders of democracy, was to help the public understand that the two had nothing to do with each other. Socialism was a systematic philosophy of history and life based on two lies: that history teaches us that economic gain is the sole motive for human behavior; and that modern society is divided into two permanent economic classes, sharing no common goals or values.

As we have seen, Butler's warnings in 1919–20 about the perils of socialism became part of his campaign message as he pursued the Republican nomination. While he failed to convince his party that he was the candidate for them, he certainly succeeded in dramatizing the danger of the Bolshevik challenge to American democracy. He continued to preach vigilance and the excellence of the American capitalist system, and by the mid-1920s he had eagerly embraced a new ally in the struggle against Bolshevism: Benito Mussolini. The popular image of the later Mussolini as a posturing, strutting cartoon-character dictator has tended to obscure the genuine international stature he achieved as a politician who had rescued Italy from impending dissolution when he took over as premier in 1922. Despite his extreme right-wing views and the armed violence of the Fascist movement he had founded in 1919, he was hailed as the savior who had beaten back the threat of Communist revolution with an infusion of the "old-fashioned" virtues of moral rigor, willpower, and discipline. A man of intellect who was at the same time a pragmatic exponent of action, someone rooted in Italy's traditional values but also capable of administrative efficiencies and innovation, a tough guy with an affection for children and animals—Mussolini marketed a self that effortlessly resolved opposites.

He had his skeptics from the start, but Mussolini was rapidly invested with a heroic status in the United States. Once he had become premier, American reporters and intellectuals, publishers and professors—Ida Tarbell, Lincoln Steffens, Charles Beard, Anne O'Hare McCormick, Herbert

Croly, William Randolph Hearst, to name some—all fell under his sway, admiring his decisiveness, intelligence, and personal magnetism. In an age in which the absence of individuals of vision and power was often noted— by Butler, among others—Mussolini seemed an impressive exception. In 1927 *The Literary Digest* conducted a survey among newspapers to determine their views as to whether great men continued to exist in the dilapidated modern world. The results indicated that such men were still to be found, and the name most frequently mentioned was Mussolini's, followed by Lenin, Edison, Marconi, and Orville Wright, in that order.

Butler's enthusiasm began early, not long after the Blackshirt march on Rome in the spring of 1922 that caused King Vittorio Emanuele III to offer Mussolini the position of prime minister. Surrounded by what he saw as stasis and incompetence in his own country, Butler found in Italy the stirring example of a strong leader prepared to make things happen in the interests of the people. In 1923 the *Chicago Daily News* reported that Butler had become popular among Fascists for his recent statement that "the greatest lesson of the twentieth century comes from Italy, which has shown that there are forms of law which lead to illegal acts and a form of illegality which leads to law." As one inept Republican administration gave way to another, Butler continued to exult in Mussolini's energy. Speaking before the British Empire Chamber of Commerce in 1925, Butler claimed that "we have seen Italy on the verge of destruction and saved apparently by an Oliver Cromwell . . . A great personal force, violative of constitutional procedure and rising above those laws that are only imperfect laws, is working to save the nation in spite of itself."

Butler's excitement about the Fascist political, cultural, and economic transformation of Italy grew in direct proportion to his disgust at what he considered the abysmal failure of Republican policies. In a speech at the University of Virginia delivered on April 13, 1927, the 184th birthday of Thomas Jefferson, he asked Americans to meet the challenge other political systems posed by reaffirming their commitment to the Jeffersonian principles of civil and political liberty, local self-government, and popular responsibility at the heart of American democracy. Butler saw this as a sufficiently important address to merit tipping off Adolph Ochs at the *Times* that, as he was talking without notes, if it was "thought worthy of recording and reproducing it will be necessary for our newspaper friends to arrange to take it as spoken." Ochs, always ready to oblige, assured Butler that he would have a reporter in Charlottesville so that the *Times* could carry "a full and accurate report of your remarks."

"New Critics of Democracy" examined the plausibility of the American form of government in the light of the alternatives offered by Communism and Fascism. The radical experiment of Communism was in the process of falling apart, Butler said, and he predicted its imminent collapse. Fascism, however—"the amazing movement which under the leadership of Premier Mussolini has brought new life and vigor and power and ambition to the great people of the Italian peninsula"—was another story. Fascism, for Butler, consisted of three elements: sentiment, action, and theory. He had no quarrel with the first two. Fascism's insistence that every individual should seek his highest fulfillment "in the service of the state and of his fellows—not in selfishness but in service"—was an essential part of democratic rhetoric. And who could take issue with the dramatic change in Italy's physical infrastructure and spiritual and moral condition? Butler pointed to the extraordinary improvement in the health, safety, order, comfort, education, and satisfaction of the Italian people wrought by Mussolini's government in the short space of five years, concluding that it would be hard not to recognize its achievement. From a strictly pragmatic point of view, "there is no question but that we must accept the demonstration that Fascism is a form of government of the very first order of excellence."

It was only the theory that made it unacceptable. The efficiencies of the absolute state were real, but Fascism's capacity for short-term positive change could never justify its long-term suppression of human freedom and legitimate political process. For Butler, the question facing American democracy was whether it could be revitalized without permitting the loss of those indispensable political liberties as had occurred in Italy.

Despite his explicit and powerful reservations about the theory of Fascism, Butler's praise of Mussolini's leadership in restoring Italy to greatness could hardly fail to bring joy to the heart of a Fascist sympathizer. To have the president of Columbia University and the Carnegie Endowment for International Peace laud Fascism as "a form of government of the very first order of excellence" supplied the movement with an extraordinary propaganda gift. In a 1933 article in *Il Popolo d'Italia*, a Fascist magazine founded by Mussolini, Battista Pelligrini analyzed the criticism that Butler had levied against the desperate failures of American politics in the 1920s to show that he had grown from a stodgy believer in an outmoded form of representative government to a new-age, forward-looking Fascist.

No one was happier with Butler's pronouncements about the virtues of Fascism than Mussolini himself. Understanding the importance of cultivating pro-Fascist sentiment in the United States, Mussolini carefully monitored and massaged the American press coverage of his regime. He was always generous with his time in granting interviews to U.S. journalists, and had his embassy in Washington employ a "clipping bureau" to gather all the items written about Italy. In 1927 the Italian government established its own press service in the United States to counter criticism of Fascism by disseminating materials favorable to the movement throughout the country. As a former journalist, Mussolini even tried, with the help of a Hollywood publicity man, to get himself admitted to the National Press Club in Washington. The determined opposition of a few passionate anti-Fascists, the columnist Drew Pearson among them, assured that this wouldn't happen.

Mussolini was thus not about to lose the opportunity to establish a relationship with an influential American who had the good sense to appreciate some of Fascism's strengths. Not long after his University of Virginia speech, Butler was visited by the Italian ambassador, who said in the course of a casual conversation that Mussolini was upset by his criticisms of Fascism and wanted to discuss them in person. Would Butler be prepared to go to Rome for that purpose? Butler, needless to say, was thrilled at the prospect of meeting the newly emergent star of European politics, and immediately made plans to do so.

On June 18 Butler left Paris with Kate and Sarah, arriving in Rome the following evening. Much to his surprise—one wonders what he was thinking—he was met at the train station by a representative of the foreign office, along with several civil and military aides, who told him that he was a guest of the government. The three visitors were escorted to a lovely apartment at the Excelsior, Rome's finest hotel. Two days later Butler had his first audience with Mussolini. He recounted that after an initial exchange of niceties, Mussolini, glaring severely, challenged him (in French) as to what he meant by Fascism's inadequacies, banging hard on the table with his right hand for emphasis. Butler responded with his own emphasis, and the two went at it vigorously for the next hour. This summary of what occurred, in *Across the Busy Years*, is not entirely credible. It is hard to believe that Mussolini would have installed Butler in the Excelsior at the government's expense in order to bully him into repudiating his reservations about Fascism. The point, surely, was seduction, not conversion. Mussolini wanted a friend in the American Establishment, someone to be exploited, not argued with. It is more likely that instead of the strict polemical confrontation described by Butler, there was much congenial conversation about Italy in general and the Casa Italiana—Columbia University's Italian cultural center, which Butler would dedicate in the fall and which Mussolini had helped furnish—in particular. Irrespective of what actually took place, the cordial handshake at the end of the meeting signified that Mussolini's charm and intelligence had secured for Il Duce a valuable admirer. Butler might still have his doubts about Fascism, but not about its founder. "I must say of Mussolini," Butler said approvingly after their hour's talk, "that he is the only outstanding political leader or dictator whom I have ever met who would permit free and open debate with him on his doctrines and principles and yet keep up friendly relations. Both on this occasion and many times thereafter Mussolini has treated me with the greatest kindness and consideration, although he knows perfectly well what I feel and think about the Fascist philosophy." An honorary degree bestowed on Butler by the University of Rome shortly after their discussion contributed to his warm impression of the Italian leader.

In March 1930 Butler returned to Italy for another visit. From Mussolini's point of view, at least, their friendship paid precisely the kind of dividend he clearly had hoped it would. Butler had earlier appointed to the European branch of the Carnegie Endowment Count Carlo Sforza, a well-known anti-Fascist and distinguished former Italian diplomat and statesman who had been foreign minister and ambassador to France. Mussolini was unhappy that the Endowment's sole Italian representative should be opposed to Fascism, and he complained to Butler that Sforza should be balanced by someone sympathetic to the regime. Butler agreed, and at a meeting of the Endowment's European Center in Paris on May 30, he put before the group the idea of appointing a second Italian trustee, one agreeable to Mussolini. The British political journalist and Endowment member J. A. Spender objected that if a second Italian member was to be chosen, it should be someone Sforza would find acceptable; to appoint a Fascist as such would be detrimental to the work of the Endowment, particularly because "there could scarcely be less of 'the international spirit' than in the present manifestations of Mussolini and his regime." Spender even questioned whether there was any point in undertaking work in Italy, given the fact that "all expressions of opinion in lectures or publications are under censorship." And if the Endowment could not operate freely in Italy, what was the point of adding to the Italian representation?

Butler replied that for the Endowment to strengthen its hold on Italian public opinion, it had to appoint someone not explicitly anti-Fascist who was in touch with current Italian thought. Because Sforza was living outside of Italy, his reports were not dependable. Butler recommended Piero Misciatelli, "a distinguished man of letters . . . of the highest class," who, though perhaps not a card-carrying Fascist, shared Mussolini's vision of Italy. Butler's will to believe in Mussolini enabled him to insist to Spender that government censorship there "is about to be weakened and perhaps withdrawn . . . From what I was told, I am looking for an announcement almost any day." Spender remained (presciently) skeptical, but he accepted Butler's argument about the need for another Italian trustee. On December 8 Misciatelli was voted to membership of the Comité du Centre Europeen; two days later the Italian ambassador in Washington wrote Butler how pleased he was by the appointment, adding, "I have no doubt that his election will gratify Signor Mussolini."

On his March visit, in addition to talking with Mussolini, Butler had been introduced to the elegant, charming, rapaciously ambitious Margherita Sarfatti—political journalist, art critic, Fascist propagandist, biographer of Mussolini, and, by no means the least of her achievements, longtime mistress of Il Duce. Daughter of a prominent Jewish family, Sarfatti had moved with Mussolini from an early, shared commitment to socialism through the trauma of the war to the shaping of the nationalistic ideals that spawned Italian Fascism. Supporting Mussolini with her wealth and sophistication (he had neither), she contributed significantly to his political success and had assumed power with him. When Butler met her, she was unquestionably the most influential woman in Italy, equally involved in the realms of politics and culture. (She was also prudent enough, or so she thought at the time, to have converted to Catholicism in 1928.) Sarfatti and Butler each instantly saw the opportunity offered by the other: Butler, for access to Mussolini and the inner circles of Fascist thinking; Sarfatti, for a connection to the American cultural elite and perhaps even an escape route to the New World should things fall apart in the old. Together the two entered into a friendship that lasted until Butler's death.

Butler's admiration for Mussolini's Italy was only whetted by seeing him in March. Interviewed by *The New York Times* upon his return in May, Butler commented that "Mussolini has endowed Italy with a new sense of youth. They are young in spirit, young in feeling, young in ambition and young in enthusiasm. They wish to sit again in the seats of the mighty and to be hailed and looked upon as one of the great intellectual and political forces of the modern world." During the time that Mussolini gradually developed into the repressive political leader Butler ought to have despised, he continued to have faith in him, in part because he saw him as the only European statesman capable of handling Germany. By the early 1930s Butler thought that among the first-rate powers there were only two that had outstanding leadership: Italy and the United States. Franklin Delano Roosevelt and Mussolini constituted the twin hopes of a world in need, but since America was constrained from participating in European affairs, it was Mussolini who was "left alone as the one person on whose shoulders the burden of responsibility must rest."

Praising Mussolini to Sarfatti became a means of praising him directly, as Sarfatti read Butler's letters to Il Duce. "He thanks you very much," Sarfatti wrote to Butler in November, referring to the glowing estimate of Mussolini's achievements Butler had conveyed to Sarfatti in a previous letter. She shared Butler's reverence for Il Duce. "I think you are quite right," she assured Butler about his assessment of Mussolini's importance:

> What the world needs is power, responsible power, I mean, in someone who is able & willing to have, [*sic*] both a purpose & the will to put it into action. What strikes me as most wonderful in him, is that he seems to grow daily with the ever-increasing greatness of his task, not merely as a national affair, but as a world-business, such as you have so keenly described it now.

Nothing Mussolini did in the way of enhancing his dictatorial powers and infringing personal liberties seemed able to weaken Butler's belief in him as Europe's savior. Early in January 1934, after Hitler had ominously withdrawn Germany from a European Disarmament Conference and given notice that he intended to withdraw it also from the League of Nations, Butler learned through Sarfatti that Mussolini would be happy to talk to him again about the world situation. Making preparations for another

March trip, Butler appeared peculiarly anxious about how to act in Mussolini's presence, almost as if he had come to be awed by his own assessment of Mussolini's greatness. He consulted with Professor Dino Bigongiari in Columbia's Italian Department about issues of protocol:

> Should I, on the morning of that day [March 12th], go to the Foreign Office and leave a card . . . and ask at what hour the Premier wishes me to return in the afternoon? Of course, there will be no one accompanying me, so I am on my own resources and must be sure not to fail to do the correct thing in carrying out the Premier's wishes.

During the nine days Butler spent in Rome, he saw Mussolini three times. Returning on March 28, he confidentially proclaimed that there would be no war, because Mussolini "understands perfectly that another war would mean the destruction of our civilization."

Butler's public endorsement of Mussolini contributed to an unpleasant controversy at Columbia that erupted later in the year. On November 7 an exposé on "Fascism at Columbia" appeared in *The Nation*. It described Columbia's Casa Italiana as the Fascist propaganda center in the United States. Written by an anonymous "special investigator," it claimed that the Casa systematically excluded anti-Fascists from participating in the running of the Casa and its programs, suppressed free discussions in the interests of a partisan agenda, and in the guise of a social and cultural center was in fact functioning as an explicitly political institution committed to furthering Fascist goals. The article called upon Butler to investigate and act on these accusations. In a long letter to *The Nation* published a week later, Butler dismissed the charges with disdain. Basing his answer on a lengthy memo written by the director of the Casa, Giuseppe Prezzolini, Butler characterized the article as "a curious hodge-podge of falsehood, misrepresentation and half-truth, with the result that it ends in utter nonsense." He stressed that the Casa Italiana devoted itself solely to enhancing interest in Italian literature, culture, and civilization, and denied that it had any political purpose or significance whatever. Butler concluded his defense of the Casa in grand style by referring to himself in the third person: "My answer to your question is that Dr. Butler will not act for the convincing reason that there is nothing to act upon."

The Nation's charges that the Casa was in effect a subversive political institution, dedicated to sponsoring the cause of Fascism in the United States, were finally absurd, but so was Butler's defense that the Casa's mission of encouraging an appreciation of Italian culture was entirely free of any political implications. It is fair to say that the initial impulse behind the Casa Italiana had indeed been apolitical: several Italian undergraduates at Columbia had written a public letter early in April 1920 about their desire to raise funds for books on Italian literature and thought. Sensing development possibilities in the idea, Butler immediately asked whether the students might be interested in putting their energies into a more ambitious project: starting a campaign for an Italian house that could be a center for Italian studies, much as the Maison Française was doing for French. They agreed, and Butler shortly had gathered a group of Italian-American businessmen prepared to fund a building if Columbia provided the land. By 1925 enough money had been raised for the trustees to approve the plan and designate a site on Amsterdam Avenue and 117th Street, directly across from the main campus.

Mussolini was delighted at the prospect of a great university like Columbia establishing a center focused on the study of Italian culture. In January 1926, with the official dedication of the building projected—appropriately enough—for Columbus Day 1927, Butler told Mussolini that Columbia intended to acknowledge the occasion by honoring Saint Francis of Assisi, "whose high spiritual glory is today justly associated with the national ideal of the Italian people—of the Italian nation." Before they went ahead with specific steps, however, Butler wanted to "consult Your Excellency in order to learn whether I might, in general, count upon the support and approval of your government for this plan to inaugurate the house of Italian culture solemnly and officially with a notable celebration of the Italian genius." Mussolini expressed satisfaction at the depth of Butler's admiration for Italian culture, pleased that the opening would commemorate Saint Francis. He assured Butler he would be with him in spirit and would do whatever he could to make the occasion a success.

In addition to his spiritual participation, Mussolini's efforts included sending a substantial amount of furniture as well as modest amounts of money. The Casa even received a portrait of him, a gift not from Mussolini himself, but from L. Reni-Mel, president of the Center for French Art in Paris. (Butler already cherished an autographed photograph of Mussolini he had received in 1924 with a note thanking him for promoting friendship between Italy and America. Il Duce "has one of the most striking faces of modern times," he later commented to Mrs. F. S. Bangs, the wife of the trustee.) At the actual ceremony—in which the physicist and inventor Guglielmo Marconi represented the Italian government—Mussolini delivered a message to Butler expressing his hope that the Casa Italiana would initiate a new bond of sympathetic understanding between the American and Italian people.

There was nothing sinister in any of this. Mussolini was the legitimate head of the legitimate Italian government, and one could hardly quarrel with the goals of the Casa as Butler defined them: "As I have said on so many occasions, we have great need here in America of more of the Latin temperament, the Latin point of view, and the Latin love of beauty, whether in nature or in art. The Casa Italiana . . . can accomplish wonders in advancing all of these purposes." Prominent Americans who had been happy to be named to an honorary committee for Casa fund-raising included Governor Alfred E. Smith, Mayor Jimmy Walker, William Randolph Hearst, New York congressmen Sol Bloom and Hamilton Fish, Jr., eleven senators, and assorted editors, bankers, lawyers, and educators.

On the other hand, although Butler was not running a secret Fascist propaganda service, the neat distinction he insisted upon between culture and politics was hardly convincing. An institution devoted to "the study and teaching of all that relates to Italy and its civilization" could not help but be implicated, one way or another, in its politics. Butler was also not about to offend the strongly pro-Fascist Italian-American business community— whom he was continually badgering to help the Casa's finances—by permitting it to appear to be endorsing activities or programs critical of the regime. Despite the official position that Columbia was nonpolitical and nonpartisan—"We are a University in which free and fair discussion of all subjects that come within the proper range of our intellectual interest and activity is encouraged and promoted in the hope that thereby the cause of truth will be advanced and the highest public interests served"—Butler knew that when it came to the Casa Italiana, free and fair discussion was not always appropriate. Fascist sensibilities were more important than others and had to be treated with more care. A memo from Frank Fackenthal to Butler on March 24, 1928, demonstrates this concern. Butler had just appointed an administrative board, responsible for the supervision of the Casa, and proposed a larger advisory board, essentially to help with fund-raising.

Having informed Consul General Emmanuel Grazzi of what he was doing, Butler heard from Grazzi that he was pleased at the arrangement but wanted to meet with Butler to discuss it. Fackenthal's memo explained to Butler just how pleased Grazzi was:

> What the Consul General wants to see you about is, I think, to give polite expression to his disappointment that he was not consulted about the membership of the Administrative Board of the Casa Italiana. He objects to some of the members because they are not Fascists. This kind of question is coming up continually and is going to be a difficult one for us. The Italians in this country, even those who are American citizens, are taking their orders from Rome. We can hardly take orders from Rome, but at the same time the Consul and the Americans can block our efforts to raise money for the Casa if they become unsympathetic with our management of the House. When he comes the Consul General may talk about the weather, but the foregoing is really what is in his mind.

Invoking the purity of the Casa's cultural mission remained the explanation of choice in countering accusations of Fascist taint, as Fackenthal recommended to Butler in 1932 when a Fascist group in New York had offered Giuseppe Prezzolini, the director of the Casa, a bust of Mussolini:

> We run the risk of a row either way. Prezzolini's suggestion is that we accept the bust and that he, in a carefully prepared acceptance, express our appreciation of the gift and turn the matter away from a political question to a cultural one, redescribing the whole activity of the Casa as cultural. Mussolini is, of course, head of the State and we did accept his gift of furniture for the House. Do you see any difficulty with Prezzolini's proposal?

Butler finally decided it was wiser not to accept the gift, but he was obviously familiar, even before *The Nation*'s attack, with the usefulness of taking refuge from political storms in the safe harbor of the Casa's cultural ideals.

The Nation's allegations that non-Fascists were not welcome at the Casa prompted Butler to try to ensure that some did speak there. Count Sforza was a logical choice—as long as he did not say anything offensive. Butler cautioned him about the need for the university to avoid criticizing the regime, instructing Sforza that his "non-political" address, scheduled in the fall of 1935, should enable Columbia to greet him at the Casa "quite as warmly as though you were a member of, or representative of, the present Italian government." Only in this way could Columbia exhibit that kind of "balance which must be preserved in justice to the University's reputation and influence." The topic Sforza chose for his lecture—"The Italian Soul: Legends and Realities"—met the requirements. It would examine the psychology of the Italian people through its classics. It would raise, Sforza assured Butler, "no political questions."

The properly balanced view was not easy to maintain when Mussolini's armies invaded Ethiopia on October 3. Butler was deeply upset, not on behalf of Ethiopia—"I took no interest whatever in the Abyssinians," as he later told Sarfatti—but because his investment in Mussolini as a man of peace should have proved so misplaced. Butler had no difficulty with the notion of Italy's requiring additional land for demographic and economic reasons. Issuing a statement to *The New York Times* upon his return from his summer travel in July, Butler had declared his sympathy with the position that Italy, like Germany and Japan, was as entitled to an overseas empire as were France, England, the United States, and Russia. He was firm that these three new powers should have the same opportunity as the older four to acquire sufficient space for their growing populations, as well as access to critical natural resources and commercial ports. The pressing question the world faced, according to Butler, was how to find "a peaceful way to permit a rapidly growing nation which has inadequate territory to get what it needs by peaceful and orderly means and common consent."

In a letter to him of August 16 that Butler later claimed was written with Mussolini's knowledge and possibly even at his suggestion, Piero Misciatelli praised his analysis of Italy's defensible aspirations for colonial expansion. But observing that Butler had grouped Italy with Germany and Japan, Misciatelli felt obliged to say that unlike Italy, Germany had substantial resources of iron and coal, and that Japan had already begun to solve its problems through movement into China and Manchuria. Italy thus was uniquely disadvantaged in its efforts to assure "its own sacred right to live." Mussolini had done everything possible to come to a peaceful understanding with the emperor of Ethiopia about how Italy might "develop and civilize that rich country," but the emperor had not been forthcoming. Misciatelli argued that the situation was now grave because all of Italy had rallied around Il Duce, "determined to do anything to defend its honor and that of the white race against the negroes." Mussolini was motivated not by "imperialistic vanity," but by the "compelling need of solving the problem of vital expansion for his industrious and healthy people." Misciatelli ended by imploring Butler to use his influence as a prestigious political commentator to convince Americans as to the legitimacy of Italy's claim on Ethiopia.

A month before the actual invasion, Butler responded that he did not object to the perceived necessity of territorial expansion but only to the military means with which Italy seemed about to pursue its goal. He reminded Misciatelli that nearly ten years earlier, in conversation with Mussolini on the same issue, Butler had tried to interest him in solving his land problems by purchasing from Portugal—"a small and almost insignificant nation"— title to some of its vast holdings in West Africa. Although he had heard nothing more about that idea, Butler felt that peaceful options of that sort were still available. He assured Misciatelli that the world was entirely sympathetic to Italy's plight, filled with people who "regard Italy with something approaching reverence" because of its extraordinary contributions to civilization. But Italy must not violate that trust by throwing aside the arbitration treaty it signed with Ethiopia in 1928 or its solemn pledge in the Pact of Paris to renounce war.

Despite Butler's appeal for restraint, Il Duce launched his troops into Ethiopia shortly thereafter. Seven months later, on May 9, 1936, he proclaimed the establishment of his East African empire. Mussolini's failure to serve as the apostle of peace was a severe blow to Butler. Sforza was right all along and Misciatelli wrong: Mussolini was a violent, dishonest, self-serving dictator, bearing little resemblance to the administrative genius with the capacity to bring order to Europe whom Butler had supported. The conquest of Ethiopia was a criminal act—not, as Misciatelli stated, "a victory for civilization in the Black continent, full of fruitful promise for the Ethiopian population subjected for centuries to a feudal and slave-dealing regime." As president of the Carnegie Endowment, Butler believed he could not permit himself the luxury of issuing political judgments, but the conquest of Ethiopia definitively ended any illusions he harbored about Mussolini. Henceforth, he regarded the Italian dictator as part of the world's problems rather than as a potential solution.

Adolf Hitler, on the other hand, posed no such dilemma for Butler, though it was hard for him to reconcile his esteem for German culture of the past with his recognition of the degeneracy of contemporary Nazi policies. He was shocked that the country from whose philosophers he had learned so much and which had nourished him during his formative "year of discovery" as a young man should have fallen into barbarism under Hitler's leadership. Feeling constrained in his public role as international statesman not to sever his connections to Germany, however, he also was reluctant privately to reject the nation whose spiritual and intellectual ideals he once passionately admired. The tension between his commitment to the German past and the dreadful reality of the Nazi present produced an ugly scene at Columbia in the spring of 1936. While Butler was in Europe during February, Columbia, along with other universities throughout the world, received an invitation from the University of Heidelberg to send a representative to participate in festivities for its 550th anniversary in late June. In Butler's absence, the assistant secretary of the university, Philip Hayden, announced Columbia's acceptance. Students were instantly outraged at what they correctly understood would be a bogus propaganda occasion devoted to honoring the Third Reich. The campus immediately became alive with protest meetings. A petition containing more than a thousand names—including such distinguished faculty members as Franz Boas, the Nobel Prize winner Harold Urey, and the educational theorist George Counts—was presented to Butler upon his return at the end of March, asking him to rescind the Columbia acceptance.

Butler, for whom it was a temperamental impossibility to capitulate to student protests, agreed to look into the issue to see if the celebration possessed any political significance whatever. If he concluded that it did, he would cancel Columbia's participation. Predictably, as he was not about to give in to students, he determined that this artfully contrived event at which propaganda minister Goebbels, among other Nazi officials, would speak, was safely nonpolitical. Columbia, in short, would attend (along with, it must be added, Cornell, Yale, Harvard, Johns Hopkins, Stanford, Pennsylvania, Michigan, and Vassar). Oxford and Cambridge, either more skeptical or closer to the action, declined to send any representatives.

The university's position, announced on May 11, ignited more student anger. Columbia's chapter of the American Student Union voted the next day to demonstrate against the ruling that evening. After witnessing a mock "book-burning" ceremony to criticize Columbia's acceptance, three hundred or more students decided to continue the protest in front of Butler's house on Morningside Drive. One was Robert Burke '38, junior class president, amateur boxing champion, and a prominent figure in the American Student Union. The students marched to 60 Morningside, where, by all accounts, a relatively decorous protest featured several speeches (one by Burke) and appropriate amounts of denunciations of the president, including cries of "Castigate Butler." After about a half hour of this, the crowd dispersed.

Nine days later Burke was summoned to Dean Hawkes's office. Hawkes accused him of having led a rowdy demonstration that had violated the sanctity of Butler's home. Burke was also guilty, according to Hawkes, of insulting Butler, particularly of crying, "Castrate Butler." Burke denied using profanity himself and apologized if anyone else had, but he refused to apologize for the demonstration itself, asserting that the students had been responsibly exercising their political rights. But Butler and Hawkes were having none of it: on June 16 Burke received his letter of dismissal from Columbia. No amount of pleading on the part of Burke or Burke's father could get Columbia to change its mind. Hawkes charged that Burke had refused to apologize and that his behavior was so disgraceful as to merit no reconsideration. Burke insisted that he was singled out for punishment because he insisted on the right of the students to express their views through legitimate demonstrations. For him, it was a principled question of academic freedom. The *New York Journal* of June 29 drew the ironic moral by commenting that in expelling Burke, Columbia was "borrowing in advance some of the more efficient techniques of Nazi higher education. It shatters forever the pretense of Nicholas Murray Butler's liberalism. The University is rapidly becoming co-ordinated in the best Fascist pattern." Burke's case was taken up by Arthur Garfield Hays, prominent attorney for the American Civil Liberties Union, who brought suit before the New York State Supreme Court to get Burke readmitted. He failed, and Burke never finished college, becoming a labor organizer instead.

Butler's refusal to cancel Columbia's participation in the Heidelberg ceremonies represented a kind of last-ditch effort to believe that the rich contributions of German culture could overcome the horrors of Nazi politics. One year later, in May 1937, Columbia was again invited to honor the founding of another German university, this time at Göttingen. Butler knew enough to avoid attending, couching his apologies in a Latin letter of greeting to the university that emphasized Göttingen's contributions to the freedom of thought and absence of racial or religious persecution characteristic of old Germany. "May that which we now celebrate and salute quickly return to help steady this rocking world," he concluded.

It was not a hope that Butler himself took seriously. Having given up on Mussolini because of his Ethiopian conquest, and having decided that Hitler was not a temporary aberration who would shortly disappear, Butler had resolved by 1937 that Nazi Fascism, not Communism, was the leading menace of the times. In a welcoming address to the freshman class that fall, he argued that Communism, failing even in the Soviet Union, was so futile a system that "no matter how enthusiastically it can be preached and taught, it can never get very far." Fascism, on the other hand, which possessed a "seductive power that Communism lacked," posed the chief threat to democratic institutions. Absolving Communism of its aspirations for world domination in favor of Fascism clearly did not sit well with Butler, however, and by 1941 he had returned to his original position that Communism was the "philosophy of compulsion" most to be feared. The German invasion of the Soviet Union on June 22, 1941, gave Butler a chance to compare their respective evils and offer a pox on each. Five days after the start of Operation Barbarossa, Butler wrote to the *Herald Tribune* declaring Communism to be the great enemy "of everything in which our people have believed and of every principle on which our public institutions are built." While Nazism was surely destined to perish, Communism had agents everywhere and must be actively resisted. (Butler would no doubt have taken great satisfaction in learning that Alger Hiss, who replaced him at the Carnegie Endowment and with whom he never got along, was allegedly one of them.) Seeing in the unprovoked assault on the Soviet Union a wonderful opportunity to dispatch two abhorrent despotisms in a single stroke, Butler expressed his earnest hope "that this latest military contest between the world's two leading groups of barbarians will end in the destruction of them both." Henceforth, Butler would not feel it necessary to distinguish between their dangers.

CHAPTER SEVENTEEN

The Fund-raiser

All university presidents are by definition effective fund-raisers—or so university press releases would have it. Fiscal health, it seems, is the one certain gift outgoing presidents confer upon their institutions: rare is the presidential resignation not accompanied by an announcement of the vast growth in endowment and annual giving achieved during the incumbent's tenure. Decades ago, Butler and Columbia were no exception to this rule. When Butler stepped down from his post, in 1945, the university trumpeted the extraordinary numbers he amassed during his forty-four years: $120 million raised; an operating budget that had grown from $1 million in 1902 to $11,250,000; a tuition-paying student body that had gone from 4,400 to a peak, before World War II, of 31,400.

Impressive figures indeed, produced in the service of Butler's quest to make Columbia "the intellectual center of this country and of the modern world." Compelling as the gross numbers are, they don't tell the complete story. They don't reveal anything about what might have been or shouldn't have been, about lost opportunities or unexpected benefactions, about what administrative structures were or were not put into place to ensure long-term fiscal viability. The sum of $120 million does not in itself make the case for Butler's success in getting Columbia the funds it needed.

Myths about Butler's money-raising genius abound, abetted, needless to say, by his own refusal ever to quash rumors of his power over the rich. Most have to do with his calling up and ordering some stupendous amount of money from a Wall Street acquaintance as casually as one would phone in an order to a take-out restaurant. Professor Carlton Hayes's account of how, in 1923, Butler bought Columbia its football stadium on 218th Street is one such instance of his alleged capacity to summon money effortlessly over the phone. According to Hayes, Butler explained:

> He did it for the college . . . There was an opportunity to purchase this tract of land up at the northern end of Manhattan, and he called his friend George Baker on the telephone. "Baker," he said, "I want you to put down"—I forget the price—several millions of dollars—"I want you to do that to buy Baker Field for the College." And Baker said, "Mr. President, I will do it."

The truth of the Baker Field acquisition was decidedly less spontaneous. Columbia had taken an option on the land and had been looking to find a way to finance it before the option expired. A. Barton Hepburn, a Columbia trustee, had been talking to Baker for months about his possible interest in the project. Several days before the deadline, when he had completed his discussions with Baker, Hepburn sent Butler down to Baker's office to close the deal. Baker was friendly but noncommittal, suggesting that he would let him know his decision by letter. Returning to Low Library, Butler found the letter from Baker guaranteeing the $650,000 purchase price.

Sometimes, in the Butler mythology, a simple meal would suffice to pry vast sums from donors. Trustee Frederic Coudert, disregarding ten years of complicated and frustrating negotiations among Columbia, Presbyterian Hospital, and Edward S. Harkness that had become so bitter that Butler was finally asked to withdraw from them, concluded that he "had this marvelous way of raising money. If he wanted five million dollars for the medical school, he'd invite Mr. Harkness to lunch or dinner, and Mr. Harkness would give him five million dollars for the medical school."

Or, according to Butler's own testimony, $4 million for a library after he had briefly mentioned to Harkness the need for one. Fourteen months of detailed discussions concerning the importance of a new library were transformed, in Butler's account in the 1946 *Alumni News*, into a casual chat. The two were talking in Butler's office. "Mr. Harkness said, 'What is it that you need next year?' I replied, 'A university library' . . . 'Find out the cost and let me know,' said Mr. Harkness.'" Determining that it would cost not less than $3.5 million, Butler sent Harkness a letter containing the estimate.

"Two days later I received a personal telephone call from him in which he said, 'I have your letter. Go ahead.'" It is not to impugn Harkness's generosity to point out that when he agreed to fund the library in May 1931, he reached his decision after lengthy conversations that had begun in March 1930, during which Butler convinced both Harkness and his lawyer, Malcolm Aldrich, to support the project.

The perception that for Butler money was but a phone call or dinner invitation or informal talk away pleased him, as he actually found the business of fund-raising personally distasteful. For someone who saw himself as a member of the social elite, it was demeaning to have to forage among them for gifts, and he did his best to avoid the impression of doing so. He preferred, as he told the trustees at his last meeting as president, a more indirect method: "My plan has always been to come to know people personally and not ask directly for money, to have them come to know Trustees and leading members of our Faculties, have them at the President's House, and then before one knows it they begin to ask questions about our needs and it is possible for me to tell them what we plan to do." Cultivating the cultivated, in short, rather than pursuing a large-scale, organized campaign. Such an approach, was, in any case, in keeping with Butler's conviction from the beginning of his presidency that Columbia was a precious asset to the city that New Yorkers should be eager to support. Viewed this way, no argument about Columbia's needs should ever have to be made. Every resident of the city, understanding its importance and benefiting from its presence, would recognize the high priority of giving generously to it. Butler's suggestion, made on several occasions, that all New Yorkers should honor Columbia's contribution to their lives in the city by including it in their wills, was a serious recommendation, not a joke.

At the same time, Butler was reluctant to let anyone else in on the power and control that come with raising money. Butler might not have liked doing it, but he was not about to let anyone else do it. Effectively, this meant excluding the constituency that was presumably the most committed to Columbia's well-being: the alumni. Not until 1920 could Butler be persuaded to encourage the formation of an annual fund for alumni giving (Yale had started one in 1890, Dartmouth in 1907). Harvard had earlier developed its own structure, working with the twenty-fifth-anniversary reunion classes to secure a significant gift. In 1905 its class of 1880 donated $100,000 toward unrestricted endowment; these reunion gifts eventually matched in size the contributions of Yale's annual fund. Whatever the method, both Harvard and Yale understood the fund-raising potential of the alumni long before Columbia devoted any serious attention to it. Columbia paid a price for coming late to the game. By 1920, Yale graduates were contributing more than $100,000 a year to the annual fund, and the endowment fund they also established had grown to more than $1 million. On June 30, 1921, the accounting for the first year of Columbia's alumni fund showed a net balance of $24,856 (which included a gift of $12,000 from the class of 1896 and a special gift of $2,000 from the fortieth reunion class "for the maintenance of its historical flagpole").

Butler's eloquence did succeed in getting affluent New Yorkers to give money to Columbia, but it was never enough and it was never for precisely the right purposes. Even in the best of circumstances, there is an invariable tension between donor interests and university priorities. Donors like naming opportunities and visible evidence of their generosity, while universities require, above all, unrestricted funds to defray operating costs, pay down debt service, discharge loans, and address a host of other vital but unexciting needs to which no donor's name can be affixed. The necessity for unrestricted gifts was particularly acute at the start of Butler's tenure. With the purchase of its initial Morningside Heights location, followed in 1903 by South Field, Columbia entered the twentieth century with a debt of nearly $3 million. Paying off interest and principal while simultaneously developing the new campus imposed enormous financial strains that Butler struggled to meet. Beginning with his 1902 image of Columbia as a "giant in bonds," his annual presidential reports constituted a litany of concern about Columbia's severe undercapitalization. In 1902 he announced the minimal assessment of Columbia's immediate needs as $10 million, although he admitted that another $5 million could also easily be put to critical use. The number gradually grew to $30 million in 1916; $39,500,000 in 1929; and $50 million by 1943.

Beyond launching the alumni fund, Butler's response to the ever-increasing figure was to despair about the limited resources and to re-emphasize his desperate plea that the citizens of New York must take up their responsibilities. As he put it in his 1926 report,

No one who cares for the primacy of the city of New York, or who stands in close relation to its commercial and financial activities, can

consciously desire to remain aloof from generous and effective participation in strengthening the University's hands . . . It is now necessary to appeal in the most direct and emphatic terms to every man
and woman who cares for the higher life of New York and of the nation, to come quickly to the aid of this historic institution whose roots
are so deep down in the nation's life, and give it the strength which
the work of the years just ahead insistently requires of it.

But neither urgent appeals nor anguished laments made any significant difference in the level of giving. The people of New York, humble and privileged alike, did not seem inclined to come to Columbia's aid in quite the
way Butler hoped, and by the mid-1920s he began to feel a certain amount
of trustee pressure to do something more. At one of its regularly scheduled
meetings in early May 1926, Butler appointed a commission to study the
problem and recommend a plan "for the increase of [Columbia's] capital
resources which would provide an annual income sufficient to meet not
only its present needs but new demands and new conditions as they might
arise." At the same time, noting that at the upcoming October meeting he
would have served almost exactly twenty-five years as president, he issued a
confidential report on the strengths and weaknesses of the university. The
former heavily outweighed the latter, though he acknowledged that some
departments—Anthropology, Chemistry, Mathematics, Physics, and several others—lacked the highest intellectual eminence. Each, however, was
only one major appointment short of achieving national distinction. In assessing Columbia's current health and future prospects, he cited a $30 mil-
lion endowment increase as the goal to be reached for the university to
continue to flourish. Butler understood it was not an accomplishment that
could be managed by the president alone: "We must put on our thinking
caps," he argued, clearly referring to the commission he had just established, "and exert ourselves . . . to devise some careful, systematic plan to
bring to the attention of those who have money to give or to leave, the fact
that this University, despite all its prosperity, is faced with demands which it
can only meet, and meet in the fullest public interest, if these large addi-
tions be made to its productive capital funds."
    Despite wearing their caps for six months, the commission (which in-
cluded Butler) came up with no compelling ideas, and they rejected the
use of any "professionally organized movement" to get the $30 million.

Their failure to discover possible new approaches to solving Columbia's fiscal problems must have finally convinced the trustees that they could benefit from a fresh perspective. Early in January 1927 Butler got in touch with the John Price Jones Corporation of New York, professional fund-raisers, to discuss a plan of action. The Jones Corporation was uniquely well qualified to help Columbia. In 1919–20 it had organized a drive for Harvard that contained all the features of efficient, modern university fund-raising campaigns: thousands of volunteers working in different geographic areas; an appeal to all alumni, affluent and otherwise; income-based guidelines for giving and special treatment for rating the wealthier prospects; the solicitation of large "leadership" gifts to dramatize the importance of the enterprise. The results were staggering: more than 23,000 contributors (94 percent of them alumni) producing nearly $14 million.

For a president and a board of trustees not temperamentally disposed to share fund-raising with outside agencies, employing the Jones Corporation was a daring step to consider. At the end of January, Jones offered to prepare a report that would study what Columbia had done in the past and establish a strategy for the future, including the nature of the appeal to be made, the publicity to support it, the essential steps of the actual fund-raising process, a budget, and general recommendations. Jones said it would take six to eight weeks to compile and would cost $800 a week. On February 3 Butler assented to the terms and authorized Jones to proceed.

Jones submitted the report on April 14, having given Butler and the trustees plenty of time to become nervous about replacing Columbia's cozy, homegrown system—essentially Butler trying to seduce New York's rich into caring about Columbia—with a sophisticated, volunteer-driven organization devised by fund-raising professionals. Even before he had read the report, one trustee, Stephen Williams, told Butler he had reservations about the Jones target of raising $2 million from the alumni. Williams feared that a centrally directed effort to raise money might damage the currently functioning alumni fund, which had been showing modest but steady growth since its inception. (The last fund had provided nearly $71,000.) And furthermore, although a wealthy donor might be persuaded to give $100,000 now, he might use that gift as a reason to "cut out of his will a legacy to the University of say half a million dollars." Several other trustees, he assured Butler, shared his anxieties. Butler didn't need to be assured, as he had his own concerns about relinquishing control and tarnishing Columbia's dignity through a slick campaign. By May 2, when they met to discuss the report, most of the trustees (including Butler) seemed frightened at what they had contemplated doing. Willingness to consider new methods gave way to a reflexive embracing of the old. With all the trustees no doubt breathing a corporate sigh of relief at having managed to avoid any threatening incursion of the modern, Butler delivered the news to Jones the next day that after careful consideration of the report, the trustees thought it "preferable to continue the general policies in this respect which Columbia University has followed for some forty years past." Astounded at the rejection, Jones wondered, "in the light of many campaigns handled by us," if there perhaps had been some misunderstandings that further discussions might clarify. Butler, however, declared the matter closed.

Other options had to be explored. In addition to the obvious push for a larger university enrollment and the not-so-obvious step of creating Seth Low Junior College in Brooklyn, the trustees turned to their real estate holdings to see if more rental income could be obtained from them. A plot of land given to Columbia in 1814 by the New York State Legislature seemed particularly auspicious. In 1801 David Hosack had purchased twenty acres from the city of New York for $4,807.36 and an annual rent of sixteen good bushels of wheat or its equivalent in gold or silver. Hosack, a physician who had graduated from Princeton (although he originally entered Columbia in 1786), sought to develop the site, several miles to the north of the commercial and residential center of the city, into a vast botanical garden so that he could study the medicinal properties of the plants he grew. He named it the Elgin Botanical Garden after the Scottish birthplace of his father. By 1810, having poured $100,000 into this scheme, Hosack found he could no longer afford it. He put it up for sale, and various medical societies, interested in preserving the garden as an educational resource, persuaded the state to pay $74,000 to buy it from Hosack "for the benefit of the medical schools of New York." The cost of maintaining it, however, proved excessive. In 1814 the legislature held a lottery to support the different colleges in the state, and convinced Columbia, in lieu of the cash that went to the other schools, to take title to the property. (A specific constraint in the 1814 act requiring that Columbia move there within twelve years was nullified in 1819.)

The trustees were not thrilled with their acquisition. Although the state appraised it at $80,000, it had so deteriorated that most prudent observers thought its actual value closer to $6,000. Columbia's president, the Reverend John M. Mason, was publicly criticized for accepting an essentially worthless piece of land. Stuck with something they didn't really want, the trustees nevertheless set about to develop its commercial possibilities. In 1823 they rented it to a tenant for $125 a year and taxes; three years later they struck an even better deal—$500 a year plus taxes—although this new tenant in fact never paid any rent at all and the college was only able to recover $118 from the sale of his goods.

As Manhattan began its inexorable progress northward, the twenty acres that had been foisted on Columbia turned out to lie directly in the path of a major part of New York's development: the four blocks from Forty-seventh to Fifty-first streets between Fifth and Sixth avenues, known then as "the Upper Estate"—to distinguish it from Columbia's downtown holdings—and today as Rockefeller Center. The city's growth gradually transformed the unwanted property into the university's most precious asset. Its steady increase in value constantly tempted the trustees to sell off portions to meet operating expenses, but they succumbed only twice: in 1857, when they sold sixteen lots between Forty-eighth and Forty-ninth streets off Fifth Avenue to the Dutch Reformed Church; and in 1904, when they got rid of the entire block between Forty-seventh and Forty-eighth streets to defray the cost involved in moving to and developing Morningside Heights. Butler later condemned both decisions as grievous business errors.

Despite this insistence, had Butler gotten his way, Columbia would have dispensed with the whole property. In February 1908 F. S. Bangs became so discouraged by Columbia's mounting deficits and its seeming inability to manage them that he offered to resign as a trustee. He complained to Butler that the university's unwillingness to match its expenses to its resources meant that its recurring deficits would never be eliminated. Things were not as bad as Bangs made out, Butler said, but if there was an obstacle to Columbia's financial progress, it was the Upper Estate. The exaggerated worth attributed to it by New York's wealthy citizens made them think it superfluous to provide additional support: "We should be far more likely to get new aid if the Upper Estate were sold and the proceeds invested, first in bond and mortgage upon the same property, and second, in New York City or other bonds." The Upper Estate, for Butler, was simply "a constant source of irritation between us and the community. Every one of the scores of leases, whether the tenant agrees to the rent or not, is just like a little collection of pus in the human system." Fortunately, Butler's sense of the Upper Estate as obstacle and irritant was not shared by the other trustees.

By 1926 these eleven acres consisted of 202 residential and commercial lots, each with its separate lease drawn up by Columbia's treasurer, Frederick Goetze. Goetze was a tough-minded, irascible, remarkably competent man who had left Columbia School of Mines to work for the university in 1895. Beginning as an assistant superintendent of buildings and grounds, he became dean (of Mines, Engineering, and Chemistry), comptroller, and finally, in 1916, treasurer of the university, a position he kept for the next thirty-two years. Goetze liked to run things his own way. The technical fact that he reported to the president did not incline him to any kind of false subservience. Early in May 1926, as Columbia began thinking seriously about its income problem, Butler told Goetze he wanted to permit the city to put a street, running north-south through the Upper Estate property, from Forty-eighth to Fifty-first streets. Such a plan would create twelve new shopping corners, providing what Butler called "a literally stupendous addition to our productive capital." A week later Goetze replied that he was delighted by Butler's enthusiasm for the plan "which I submitted to the Finance Committee some eight years ago." Butler might have been the president, but Goetze the treasurer was not about to allow anyone to pilfer his initiatives. Nothing came, in any case, of the suggestion.

On January 22, 1929, Butler handed to a *New York Times* reporter a statement announcing what was "doubtless the most important happening from the viewpoint of both the city and the university that has taken place in a generation, perhaps in a century": Columbia was going to lease the entire Upper Estate for eighty-seven years to the Metropolitan Square Corporation, owned by John D. Rockefeller, Jr., at a rental of $3.3 million a year. Butler basked in the glory of the transaction, but it was Goetze who had handled all the complicated negotiations. (In honor of which, the trustees voted him a bonus of $25,000.) Neither man, however, could take credit for conceiving this extraordinary plan. Instead, it was a matter of Columbia's serendipitously finding itself, in 1927, at the juncture of high cultural aspirations and low real estate values. The depressed values embraced the three blocks of the Upper Estate holdings. In 1904, in an effort to increase rental income, Columbia had eliminated its earlier prohibitions against apartment houses (as opposed to single-residence homes) and buildings for commercial and industrial use. Ironically—but perhaps predictably—the result had been a rapid deterioration of the property into cheap rooming houses, speakeasies, repair shops, and other decidedly low-end businesses. By late 1927, with income down, seediness up, and a number of leases expiring, Goetze had been thinking about what to do with the site. He asked Harry Hall, president of William A. White and Sons, a prestigious real estate firm, to study the conditions of the Upper Estate and make recommendations.

The high cultural factor in Columbia's good fortune was the Metropolitan Opera, whose stockholders were looking for a new location for it. When he learned that the opera wanted to move, John Tonnele—an innocuous real estate broker working under Hall at White and Sons and assigned to the Columbia project—had the most striking idea of his career. Tonnele immediately saw the perfect fit between the stockholders' desires and Columbia's need for additional rental income from the Upper Estate. He proposed to R. Fulton Cutting, president of the Metropolitan Opera and Real Estate Company, that he consider building the new house on the northern end of the block between Forty-eighth and Forty-ninth streets, backing on Sixth Avenue. Cutting enthusiastically agreed. Goetze initially balked, however, worried that the building of a new opera house would further depress property value, as he claimed the old opera did at its adjacent site on Thirty-ninth Street and Broadway. Intense discussions with Tonnele and Benjamin Morris, the architect hired by the opera to help plan its future, finally persuaded Goetze. But his consent didn't come cheap: Goetze demanded $5 million plus income from parking fees and leases from the surrounding property. Morris quickly realized that a new opera house standing by itself in a decaying neighborhood could never be self-supporting; to flourish, it would require the redevelopment of the whole area. Morris allowed his architectural vision free play, and shortly had transformed all eleven acres of Columbia's land into a sleek, soaring, modern enclave, complete with an ornamental park, underground parking facilities, a double-decker system of elegant shops made possible by a huge mezzanine or balcony running along the front of buildings on Forty-ninth and Fiftieth streets as well as those on Fifth Avenue, and viaducts connecting the mezzanines, among other innovative design features. As Dan Okrent wrote in his absorbing history of the project, everything was now in place for Rockefeller Center: "It was missing only one thing: a Rockefeller."

That missing piece was soon provided by various people close to Rockefeller who were committed to the scheme, such as the legendary publicist and press agent Ivy Lee, and Charles Heydt, who had worked his way up from clerk to running the Rockefeller real estate operation. Rockefeller was seen to be the best person to make the whole thing happen, both because he could afford it and because of his own self-interest: living on West Fifty-fourth Street, he was clearly concerned about the quality of the area. It didn't take long to convince him, and in mid-June, Rockefeller gave Heydt permission to begin discussions with Columbia about taking over all the leases of the Upper Estate.

By late September 1928, with some details still to be worked out, the basic issues had been resolved: Columbia would lease its 202 lots to the Metropolitan Square Corporation for its development of the property, including, presumably, a new opera house. The initial lease was for twenty-four years, with three twenty-one-year extensions. The beginning annual rent was to be $3.3 million, rising to a maximum of $3.8 million. As leaks began to appear in the papers regarding the vast amount of money Columbia was about to make (no formal announcement by the Rockefellers or Columbia was permitted until the deal was completed), Butler became increasingly agitated over his inability to discuss the transaction. He feared that the reports of Columbia's impending windfall would convince prospective donors that their money was no longer necessary, and he was eager to explain both the realities of the lease and the fact that the additional income was already accounted for in Columbia's next budget. He pushed Goetze to bring matters to a quick conclusion, warning him on December 20,

> [The] damage being done to the University's interests . . . by reason of the exaggerated and preposterous stories that are current throughout the city is very great and steadily increasing. I must put a stop to it . . . Our new "hundreds of millions" are getting on my nerves.

Finally, on the morning of January 22, 1929, in Goetze's office on William Street in lower Manhattan, representatives from both sides gathered around the conference table at 11:00 a.m. to affix their signatures to the 110-paragraph agreement. Two men conspicuous by their absence were John D. Rockefeller, Jr., who had left the country the day before, and Nicholas Murray Butler, who had other things to do. According to Harrison S. Dimmitt, a Rockefeller lawyer who took notes on the occasion, the signing was interrupted by the discovery that someone had forgotten to bring the Metropolitan Square Corporation seal. Winthrop Aldrich, Rockefeller's lead lawyer, asked his secretary, Mr. Wilmot, for the seal; Wilmot tensed and asked his clerk. The clerk, startled, asked the younger clerk next to him; he, perplexed, asked Miss Primley the stenographer. She had no idea, but surely she could not be held responsible. The seal was nowhere to be found. A call was promptly made to the office to fetch it. As everybody waited for its arrival, suddenly a jolt of energy went through those assembled. In Dimmitt's words,

> And there in the doorway, as all eyes turned, stood Dr. Nicholas Murray Butler himself. Tall he was, smiling blandly. He looked into the conference-room with an expression quizzical, inquiring, and at the same time tolerant.
>
> The Treasurer of Columbia University was on his feet instantly, instinctively. "We fully understand, Dr. Butler," he said placatingly, evidently in reply to some unspoken message that he had received in some unheard-of-manner. "We understand, yes sir, and we will be out of here by noon. I am aware that you have called a conference here at noon."

Eventually the seal arrived, the document was signed, and Columbia's decaying Upper Estate began its metamorphosis into Rockefeller Center.

With newspaper headlines the next day blaring that Columbia had just closed a deal for $261 million ($3 million a year for 87 years), Butler conducted an aggressive press campaign to assure the affluent that it still required their support. "Our needs multiply as our means increase," he explained to the world through the *Times*. Improving academic salaries, building the new medical center, handling the debt produced in the construction of the new chemistry and physics laboratories, and meeting a host of other critical priorities had already accounted for the additional income, Butler stressed. Rich though the university might now seem, in short, it still needed money. At the same time that he was trying strategically to minimize the impact of the new rent, he was glorying in its achievement. "Perhaps no single act in the corporate history of Columbia," he wrote in his 1929 presidential report, "exceeds in importance the settlement of the leaseholds of the property included in the Upper Estate." Certainly the immediate infusion of several million incremental dollars into the Columbia budget was an enormous boon for which Butler could (and did) properly congratulate himself. The brilliance of having secured the constant flow of higher income from Rockefeller just before the Great Crash and the onset of the Depression must have been especially gratifying.

But if the self-satisfaction at having addressed some current fiscal problems was justified, the lease's long-term provisions raise disturbing questions as to whether it should be thought of as a triumph for Columbia or just another "grievous mistake of business judgment." However desperate the financial need, to sign an agreement leasing eleven acres in the middle of New York with a maximum rent increase of approximately $500,000 over the course of eighty-seven years seems to elevate myopia into a principle of cosmic blindness. Although inflation had been kept in relative check during the late 1920s, Columbia's neglecting to account in any significant way for its future ravages must be seen as a profound failure. When President William J. McGill, in 1973, insisted that the lease be renegotiated, Columbia was receiving $3.8 million a year, forty-four years after the initial rent of $3.3 had been determined. (To put this figure into its context, the maximum rent of $3.8 million that Goetze had negotiated in 1929 was yielding approximately $1.5 million of income in 1973 dollars; by 1985, when President Michael I. Sovern presided over the sale of the property to the Rockefeller group for $411 million, Columbia was receiving an annual rent of $11.1 million, or a 2.8 percent return on the estimated value of the land. Dan Okrent calculated that—on the basis of the original rental figure and taking no account of any increase in the land's inherent value—appropriate adjustments for inflation alone should have produced rental income of approximately $25 million by 1984.) It is impossible, of course, to speculate how the Upper Estate might have been developed had Rockefeller not acquired the lease in 1929, or what kind of income Columbia might otherwise have earned from it. But it is hard to resist the judgment that the Rockefeller team outsmarted Goetze, Butler, and the Columbia trustees.

With the new lease signed, Butler returned to the problem of insufficient annual giving. Choosing to continue to raise money the way Columbia had been doing since 1887—as he told the John Price Jones Corporation they preferred to do—did not guarantee that more of it would come in. As its 175th anniversary approached, in 1929, Columbia was still struggling with an accrued debt of more than $6 million. Instead of a professionally directed fund drive aimed at Columbia alumni, Butler and his trustees now settled on exactly the opposite: one endorsed by people who lacked any institutional identification, directed at those without any Columbia affiliation. The purported virtues of this plan were that it avoided harassing alumni with additional requests for benefactions and removed any possible taint of institutional self-interest from the appeal. In place of the usual strategy of a university presenting its own case, independent citizens now would make it objectively. Absence of connection would only attest to the credibility of testimony. The six distinguished men Butler enlisted in this task, whose names "will at once be recognized as those of highest authority and as representing practically every aspect of the social and business life of New York," included the financier Bernard Baruch; Walter S. Gifford, president of AT&T; Philip Gossler, president of Columbia Gas and Electric; Darwin Kingsley, president of New York Life Insurance; Morgan O'Brien, Butler's golfing partner and former justice of the New York Supreme Court; and Henry S. Pritchett, president of the Carnegie Foundation for the Advancement of Teaching.

On February 16, three weeks after the Rockefeller lease was signed, Butler wrote his charge letter to the six, asking them to conduct a "dispassionate and objective" study of the university and prepare a report "which would go far toward impressing the imperative needs of Columbia University upon the mind of the citizens of New York." On December 3, 1930, the committee submitted to Butler what he immediately called a report of the "highest importance and value and which will always be so regarded in the history of Columbia." There is no evidence that Butler actually wrote the text, but he almost certainly did: it was his usual pitch to the public, this time bearing six different signatures. It covered all the basic Butlerian themes: Columbia's status as a great urban university; its role in the city; its national and international importance; its prudent fiscal management. It summarized present resources, income, and expenditures, and—most critically—examined future needs. Looking ten years ahead at the cost of keeping Columbia the preeminent university in the world, the report determined that it would require $39.5 million—$9.5 for essential new buildings and a $30 million increase in the endowment. When Butler quoted the report's concluding paragraph in his own presidential report, one has the distinct impression that he was quoting himself:

> The fortunes that accumulate in the hands of our citizens come into existence by reason of New York itself, which gathers in extraordinary degree the forces—financial, economic, intellectual, and artistic—of a great new continent. Whoever has shared in the prosperity

of New York's marvelous development should consider it a privilege to aid by gift in his or her lifetime, or by bequest, the great agency of the intellectual life represented by Columbia University. Such remembrance, arising unasked from the idealism of its people, will be the finest fruitage of citizenship.

It is not easy to understand, beyond the fact that it would have provided a wonderfully simple answer to the problem, why Butler and the trustees thought that delivering the Butler message to the public through the agency of six non-Columbia people would produce a vast increase in giving. In fact—and not surprisingly—the document made no appreciable difference. Gifts and bequests continued, of course, but not at the enhanced rate Butler had hoped for. The Depression certainly dampened the philanthropic impulse, but it was also evident that the testimony of distinguished citizens regarding the greatness of Columbia was no more efficacious than his own in stimulating people's civic responsibilities.

The trustees had no difficulty overlooking the document's failure to produce substantial new levels of support, given the increased rental fees from Rockefeller Center. Delivering some $3 million of unrestricted funds annually into Columbia's coffers—once all the existing leases were settled, which took some time—was the equivalent of having added more than $70 million to the endowment (calculated on a 4 percent spending rule for the endowment's principal). But the Rockefeller lease also encouraged a certain complacency about the long term. It was as if, despite how loudly Butler proclaimed need, he secretly felt confident that Rockefeller had secured Columbia's fiscal well-being. With the new cash assuaging some of the old urgency, Butler felt no particular reason to change his comfortably indirect method of attracting money to Columbia. Ineffective though it was, the report of the six at the same time marked Butler's last innovative effort (if we can call it that) to bolster fund-raising. Thereafter he remained content to discuss the merits of Columbia at his dinners, stress the obligations all informed citizens ought to feel to support it, and wait for something to happen. Convincing himself there was little point in doing more, he declared in 1933 that the era of large gift giving had come to an end. Instead of the generous benefactions of the past, Columbia would have to "depend for its prosperous continuance upon thousands and tens of thousands of relatively small gifts."

In fact, it was not the day of the large gift that was over, but the capacity of a single person, essentially unaided, to meet the endless financial needs of a large university. Butler refused to acknowledge—and the trustees refused to insist—that he couldn't do it alone. "We had a psychology on the campus that we didn't have to raise money," observed provost Frank Fackenthal, who worked closely with Butler for more than thirty years. "All we had to do is ask the President. If he gets it, we get it, and if he doesn't, we go without." As development offices and paid professional staffs began to build endowments and run capital campaigns for colleges and universities across the country, Columbia soldiered on without such help, led by its solitary, gallant commander, unwilling to enter the modern era of fund-raising. "He didn't really like anyone to raise money for the University excepting himself. For decades, he did it extraordinarily well," Fackenthal commented, but after

> he had worked out his friends on the two avenues here in town, he was lost. He had not insinuated himself into the newer activities where the money was. The old family fortunes he knew, but he didn't know the pictures and foods and chemicals, etc. He thought when he had gotten what he could from the older family fortunes that there was no more money to be had in large amounts.

Despite having proclaimed that the era of large giving had ended, Butler entertained the fantasy, in 1942, that one enormous gift was headed his way. In a "very confidential" memo of August 24, Butler informed the trustees that the lawyer William Nelson Cromwell, who was eighty-eight at the time, had led him to believe in various private conversations that Columbia could expect to receive either the entirety or a substantial part of his estate, valued, according to Butler, at $50 million to $60 million. Cromwell had hardly been a Butler favorite, as he was the irascible figure who for years had obstructed the rental of the Upper Estate to the Rockefeller interests by refusing to sell the rights to the two properties he owned on the site. He eventually did, but not before costing Columbia a good deal of money in lost rent. Columbia had been reluctant to try to force him out, precisely because it didn't want to jeopardize the prospects of the will that Cromwell was shrewd enough to dangle before Butler whenever pressure began to be applied.

With Cromwell having already passed beyond all reasonable actuarial projections, Butler decided to entice the trustees with his grand plans for the use he would make of Cromwell's promised bequest: pay off the corporate debt; establish a $10 million endowment for general purposes; raise faculty salaries by 25 percent; complete University Hall; construct an engineering research building; purchase all the land and buildings between Morningside Drive and Amsterdam Avenue from 115th to 122nd streets; buy all the buildings on Claremont Avenue and Riverside Drive between 116th and 119th streets not yet owned by the university; acquire all the land and buildings between 112th and 114th streets between Amsterdam and Broadway, closing the property to traffic and creating out of it athletic fields for the use of the students. A magnificent architectural and financial vision, in short, which Columbia would realize because of Cromwell's admiration for the university and its president: "If the amount of his possible benefaction which Mr. Cromwell has suggested in his conversations with me, were as great as he indicated, then all these things could be readily done without much loss of time."

Unfortunately, this effortless solution to Columbia's fiscally assured future that Butler imagined for the trustees—his final gift to them—was not to be. When Cromwell died in 1948, his estate was valued at $17 million, not $60 million, and the amount of the bequest—given entirely to the Law School—was $600,000, almost the exact figure that Goetze had earlier calculated the university had lost because of Cromwell's intransigence regarding his Upper Estate properties. Instead of a windfall, Columbia had merely come out even.

The consequences of Butler's fund-raising failures were demonstrable. Although the numbers are not exact, as the actual value of university endowments is notoriously hard to calculate, figures from the American Council of Education show that between 1929 and 1939 Columbia's endowment decreased by $3 million, while Harvard and Yale increased theirs by $27 million and $18 million, respectively. Indeed, of the sixteen state and private universities covered in the 1940 study, Columbia was the only institution whose endowment declined during this period. When Butler stepped down in 1945, he left Columbia without any fund-raising structure in place, claiming for himself the sole prerogative of producing the moneys it required. Once he was named acting president following Butler's retirement, Fackenthal immediately tried to persuade the trustees of the importance of establishing a development office. Butler, still a trustee, fiercely opposed the idea. "'This is my responsibility, even though I've retired—this is my responsibility,'" Fackenthal recalled Butler saying to him. But Fackenthal persisted, finally convincing the trustees that such an office might be useful: "Harvard was getting seven and eight and ten million dollars a year, I thought. If Harvard can do it, why can't we get at least something? But Dr. Butler never seemed to have that point of view."

CHAPTER EIGHTEEN

"Morningside's Miracle"

❧

Whatever its disturbing long-term implications for the university's finances, the signing of the Rockefeller lease in 1929 marked a personal triumph for Butler in his leadership of Columbia, arguably the most important single event, as he suggested, in the institution's history. It capped a decade of dizzying growth in which he oversaw the transformation of the small school he had inherited into the preeminent research university he had always intended to deliver to Morningside Heights. With the end of the strikes and labor disputes that followed the war, as prosperity returned to the country and Columbia's real estate income, tuition income, and gift giving increased, Butler returned to building. The Faculty Club (1923), the Business School (1924), Johnson Hall (1925), John Jay Hall (1927), Pupin Hall (1927), Casa Italiana (1927), Chandler Hall (1928), and Schermerhorn Extension (1929) were all completed on the campus; and in 1925, five miles north on the Harlem River, Baker Field gave football its permanent home away from South Field. Perhaps most important, the opening of the Columbia-Presbyterian Medical Center in 1928 quickly took Columbia to the forefront of medical training and research in the United States. Although, as we have seen, Butler's unhappiness with the negotiations about the new complex finally resulted in his being excluded from them, his insistence that a first-rate medical school must be allied to a teaching hospital was the catalyst that led to the merger.

When the giddy days of the 1920s came to their catastrophic halt with the stock market crash of October 1929 and the ensuing Depression, Butler could at least take satisfaction in seeing that all his predictions about Hoover's incompetence had come true. "The collapse at Washington is so pitiful as to be tragic," he wrote to Henry Pritchett in 1930. "Hoover has managed in eleven short months to elevate James Buchanan to the rank of a statesman. Since I am one of those who expected nothing, but rather less than nothing, I am in no wise disappointed, but it is none the less shocking." Beyond the comfort of being right, there was little Butler could do about the consequences of the Depression for Columbia. The income that helped drive the expansion of the 1920s declined precipitously: Butler estimated in 1933 that the loss of student tuition alone since 1931 was close to $2 million, or roughly the interest from a $50 million endowment. And this sum didn't include the reduction in gifts and the decreased return from real estate investments. The Rockefeller Center money, initially thought of as an opportunity for Columbia's expansion, was now only compensating for losses. In the face of fiscal disaster and without a fund-raising infrastructure to help discover new sources of giving, Butler the builder had to become Butler the budget cutter. Austerity was not Butler's most congenial mode, but under duress he had no choice other than to embrace it. Working with Fackenthal and the deans, he slashed both fat and in some cases living tissue out of the budget: capital projects were stopped (with the exception of South Hall, a new library, which was funded entirely by Edward S. Harkness); maintenance deferred; salaries frozen; support services cut; open professorial lines left unfilled; funds for research and library acquisition reduced. What he refused to do on principle was to cut salaries or fire people. Savings were substantial but never enough, and mounting deficits were paid for in part out of shrinking endowments. Over the course of the 1930s, the university's operating budget declined by $3 million. It was a strategy for survival, not success, but it was necessary.

Fortunately, the one part of the university least affected by the Depression was the quality of the faculty. As jobs were scarce and competitive offers rare, the faculty excellence that Butler had helped stock during the previous two decades tended not to migrate elsewhere. In addition, Columbia retained some of its brilliant graduate students who blossomed into distinction in the 1930s, such men as the literary critic Lionel Trilling, the cultural historian Jacques Barzun, the art critic Meyer Schapiro. There were departures, of course, and the policy of not filling vacant lines meant that the faculty as a whole was substantially smaller by the end of the 1930s

than it had been at the beginning, but students coming to Morningside during this time continued to be taught by extraordinary people.

Early in 1932, as Butler was confronting his budgetary problems, Columbia decided to suspend its austerity regimen long enough to honor its
Nobel Prize–winning president on the occasion of his seventieth birthday,
the fiftieth anniversary of his graduation from college, and the thirtieth anniversary of his presidency. The worldwide celebration of Butler Day was
held on February 11 in New York's Waldorf-Astoria. More than fifteen hundred guests—Columbia's largest dinner ever—crowded into the grand ballroom with its two-tiered dais to pay tribute. Simultaneously, dinners and
meetings were held in Atlanta, Philadelphia, Boston, St. Louis, Los Ange-
les, Denver, Dallas, Cleveland, Detroit, Seattle, Memphis, and Little Rock,
to name but a dozen of the thirty-two cities in which Columbians gathered
for the occasion. The Waldorf speeches were broadcast to eighty-one American radio stations and to the rest of the world over two shortwave stations.
Alumni saluted him on the high seas, aboard the S.S. *Resolute* off Bombay
and the S.S. *Reliance* in the West Indies. Columbia engineers in Moscow
braved the Russian winter to come together to raise their vodka glasses to
Butler, and meetings were held in Sydney, Bombay, Paris, Geneva, London, Toronto, Havana, Montreal, Manila, Buenos Aires, and Mexico City.
Of all the international events honoring Butler, the small group meeting in
Shanghai as the Japanese were attacking the city was perhaps the most
poignant. The group's willingness to pay respects to the president, even as
the Japanese indicated the worthlessness of the Pact of Paris in which he
had invested such hope, must have made a complicated birthday message
for Butler. War had not been abolished, after all, as he had thought.

For those at the Waldorf, including Al Smith, General Electric's Owen
Young, Connecticut governor Wilbur Cross, Yale president James Angell,
and Chief Justice Benjamin Cardozo of the New York Court of Appeals
(who would be appointed to the Supreme Court in four days), the evening
began in the Astor Salon and Jade Room, where the famous Waldorf organ
and a three-piece band clad in Colonial garb entertained the guests. Once
in the ballroom, they encountered seven of the ten extant oil paintings of
Butler displayed on the walls, several of them depicting him in the honorary
scarlet doctoral robes of Oxford and Cambridge he liked to wear on formal
occasions. After all were seated, Butler's 1882 classmates led the dais procession to their places, accompanied by the tootings and thumpings of a fife

and drum corps. The lights were dimmed, and suddenly a spotlight illuminated, in a box looking out on the ballroom, the figure of Howard Osterhout, Butler's loyal volunteer during his 1920 run for the Republican presidential nomination, who led the crowd in a "spell it out" cheer for him.

As the diners turned to their délices of sole and breasts of milk-fed chicken, the orgy of celebration began. The cable and telegraph stations installed in the hotel by Western Union received messages of congratulations pouring in from European and American admirers, which were then flashed to those in the ballroom by three large Trans-Lux machines on the balcony. They came from more than three thousand dignitaries and statesmen, academics and politicians—from Chancellor Brüning and former foreign minister Curtius of Germany; from the Prince of Wales, the Archbishop of Canterbury, Lloyd George, and the Duchess of Atholl; from the chancellor of Austria, the president of Czechoslovakia, the prime minister of Greece; from the philosophers Henri Bergson and Benedetto Croce; from the ambassadors of France, Italy, Poland, Britain, Hungary, and Germany; from Rudyard Kipling, Marconi, Paderewski, and General Jan Smuts; from Governor Franklin Delano Roosevelt, Chief Justice of the Supreme Court Charles Evans Hughes, Adolph Ochs, the newly appointed ambassador to Britain (and former secretary of the Treasury) Andrew Mellon—and practically everyone else of distinction who happened not to be in New York that evening.

The toastmaster and former Columbia trustee William Fellowes Morgan reminded people of how far Butler had come since the days of *Acta Columbiana*'s class prophecy in June 1882: "It is positively announced that Butler . . . will talk less, and then when that difficult feat is performed, enter the Yale Theological Seminary with a view to going to Central America on a missionary racket." Yale's Angell praised Butler's "spacious intelligence," John Erskine his Emersonian understanding of the need for the true scholar to subject his knowledge to the test of everyday living. Columbia professor Dixon Ryan Fox, who prepared a short biography for the dinner program, extolled Butler as "perhaps the most eminent private citizen in the country." Columbia's official adoration of its president provided Fox with his concluding sentence: "We hail him now as he has long been hailed, as 'Nicholas Miraculous,'—and more miraculous each year." Along with the bracing infusion of sentiment, guests left the Waldorf with a party favor of a commemorative Wedgewood plate, recently shipped over from Liverpool, showing Low Library. Four days later Butler appeared on the cover of *Time* with an accompanying article entitled "Morningside's Miracle."

February 11 might have been declared worldwide Butler Day, but the pleasures he derived from November 8, 1932—the day the people of the United States voted his detested Hoover out of office—certainly exceeded those from his Columbia celebration. Franklin Roosevelt's 472–57 majority in the Electoral College and his seven million popular vote advantage gave Butler a treasured gift: the confirmation of his political acuity in warning Republican pundits of the disaster awaiting them at the polls unless they changed their policies. The specific issue he had brought to the 1932 nominating convention was the Republican failure to take a strong stand against Prohibition, but that was just part of a larger diagnosis that the party was losing touch with the American people, unable to offer the strong leadership the country needed. His pessimism about Republican chances turned out to have been premature in 1928, but henceforth it would be hard to argue with him about the party's health. As with the Hoover-Smith election four years earlier, no one knows for whom Butler voted. But it is likely that he made his own small contribution to the landslide by pulling the lever, for the second time in his life, in the Democratic column.

His initial view of Roosevelt as a presidential possibility was hedged with much faint praise (though not as much as he lavished on Calvin Coolidge when he died in January 1933, calling him "an exceptionally representative interpreter of the thought and feeling of him whom we call the average man"). Roosevelt "is in no sense a great man," he wrote a month before the election, "but he is an honest man and a gentleman and has the benefit of admirable advisors who genuinely understand the present world-wide situation." Faint praise developed into real admiration, however, when he found that Roosevelt shared many of his own foreign policy positions. He was especially happy with the appeal Roosevelt issued on May 16, 1933, to the nations participating in the Geneva Disarmament and London Economic conferences, urging the elimination of weapons of offensive war and the commitment to a pact of nonaggression. Butler characterized it as "epoch-making," both for its substance—"The wholly groundless notion that the United States is, or ever has been, isolated from the rest of the world is now laid at rest for ever"—and for Roosevelt's having addressed it, through the heads of government, to the peoples of the world. Butler thought reaching out to plain citizens instead of just their leaders, whether kings, presidents, or premiers, represented an astonishing precedent, showing FDR's "genius for democratic leadership."

The extravagance of Butler's response to Roosevelt's proposal—"one of the greatest and most influential state papers in the history of our government," as he wrote in the *Times* on May 20—strains credulity. Arguing that his message should be "included in that distinguished list with Washington's Farewell Address, with Hamilton's papers in the Federalist, with Jefferson's second inaugural, with Monroe's message of December 2, 1823, with Webster's reply to Hayne, and with Lincoln's Gettysburg speech and his second inaugural address," this extraordinary appraisal can perhaps best be understood as a kind of public love letter to the president of the United States proclaiming Butler's ardent support for him.

Butler's enthusiasm for Roosevelt's international commitments notwithstanding, both the Geneva and London conferences ended in failure. Mutual suspicion between the French and Germans resulted in paralysis, and the Geneva disarmament talks were adjourned from June to October. By the time they began again, Hitler had come to power, and Germany officially withdrew from them shortly after they reopened. Butler hoped that the London Economic Conference might help stabilize the international monetary system: "'It has got to succeed,' he said, 'or the world goes over the dam.'" But it too came to nothing, largely because Roosevelt refused to go along with the accommodations reached by his representative, Cordell Hull, and the French and British regarding measures to limit the fluctuations in the value of currencies. He thought the arrangements were putting American economic recovery at risk, and he instructed Hull—a man whose ardent internationalism Butler admired—to retract his consent. Ironically, in placing America's self-interest before the world's, Roosevelt was later criticized for the kind of economic nationalism that Butler himself always attacked.

Butler welcomed not just what he perceived to be the new spirit of internationalism that Roosevelt had brought to Washington, but also his economic and social programs, and he was delighted with Roosevelt's turning to universities to find his close advisers. It certified Butler's claim that the university was not a refuge from real life. Nor did it hurt Butler's reputation or Columbia's when Roosevelt plucked three professors from Morningside Heights—the political scientist Raymond Moley, the economist Rexford

Tugwell, and the lawyer A. A. Berle, Jr.—to form the core of his "brain trust." Butler had nothing but praise for Roosevelt's reliance on the expertise of the academy, noting that in earlier times Washington had "become so accustomed to the 'blockhead trust' that it sneers at the true scholar, the most practical person in the world."

Although Butler derided Hoover for his inability to deal effectively with the Depression, the two actually shared convictions quite opposed to Roosevelt's about why it happened and what could be done about it. Both felt that the Depression's causes were international rather than domestic and that they could be remedied only by adhering strictly to the therapy of a balanced budget. Indeed, it was this latter belief that led Hoover to scratch the expensive public works component of his first anti-Depression initiative. Butler, who had been extolling the virtues of balanced budgets, both state and federal, since the 1920s, seemed oblivious to the fact that what made sense during prosperity was perhaps not a solution during a time of crisis. In any case, it didn't seem to bother him that the frugality Roosevelt had preached when he was running for president was dispensed with once he was elected: between 1933 and 1936 governmental expenditures increased by more than 83 percent; during the same period, the federal debt ballooned from $19.5 billion to $33.8 billion. Butler valued Roosevelt's willingness to move aggressively to find solutions, viewing FDR's National Recovery Administration (NRA)—established to draft codes of fair wage and employment practices for industry—as "a magnificent and enthusiastic effort for economic recovery." He challenged critics "who carp at NRA stipulations" to consider the alternatives. Either Americans worked together to solve the nation's problems under the guidance and with the cooperation of the administration, Butler argued, or they ran the risk of losing their freedoms. At this point Butler still admired Mussolini's skill in using strong measures to save Italy from dissolution, and in his backing of Roosevelt we can feel that same enthusiasm for the political leader who can act decisively. The Supreme Court's decision in 1935 that the NRA was unconstitutional didn't alter Butler's judgment of its importance.

He remained a political supporter of Roosevelt's throughout FDR's presidency, in part because he felt that with the exception of his lack of interest in renegotiating the German war debt, the president had come to adopt Butler's fourteen points into his own priorities. Roosevelt, in turn, was grateful for Butler's endorsement but refused to let it develop into the kind of friendship Butler undoubtedly hoped it would. Butler never again had the access to the White House that had been made available to him during the tenure of Teddy Roosevelt and Warren Harding, and during Coolidge's early days.

Ranked ninth in a 1932 *World-Telegram* survey of ten people whose achievements suggested they would be leaders in the coming year— "Nothing in the world can prevent President Butler (of Columbia University) from being an outstanding figure until death. He certainly won't let us down in 1933"—Butler in fact began the new year in an unusual way. On the night of January 6, the Century Association revived a tradition that had lain dormant for sixteen years: the celebration of the Twelfth Night Revels, otherwise known as a Roman party of the time of the Caesars. Four hundred and seventy-seven Centurions arrived at their Forty-third Street building to be turned into ersatz Romans under the skilled ministrations of six professional costumers and makeup men. But since the Roman Empire extended over the entire world, as the instructions for the evening suggested, adventurous members also had the option of appearing in Persian, Arabic, Greek, Byzantine, Gallic, or Egyptian garb. Most opted for the complete Roman outfit, including toga, wreath, and sandals, supplied free of charge by the Century. (Those concerned about the expense to the club in providing the costumes could reimburse it $5.) At 9:30 p.m., dressed in a light green tunic with a forest green toga, green sandals, and a golden oak-leaf wreath around his imposing forehead, Butler, as the Latin poet Horace, led a procession of his Roman compatriots down the sweeping staircase to the art gallery, transformed into an open-air throne room of the Roman Senate. Behind Caesar's black marble throne, located in the center of the room on a raised platform covered by a zebra skin, sat twelve senators on twelve white "marble" seats. After saluting the Senate and the emperor, Butler occupied the throne to the right of Caesar. Following the reading of an ode to Caesar by Virgil, the entertainment began, featuring a Roman juggler, a Georgian sword dancer, the famous exotic modern dancer Ruth St. Denis and ten of her company, eight acrobats, and two comedians dressed as lovebirds and playing a comedy in bird language. The formal program ended with Horace delivering an oration to Bacchus and to the spirit of the Century. In his own notes for the performance, director and playwright Austin

Strong described Butler's concluding role in language that he would not have appreciated: "Nicholas, King of the Hebrews, pretending for once he was Horace, Mounted [sic] the rostrum and preached a sermon to end the depression." Informing the assembled Romans that he was there not to bury Twelfth Night but to praise it, Butler urged them to dispense with nagging worry and confidently embrace the future:

> Let care take wings and fly away. Let hope and courage, faith and constancy, control, direct, inspire us. Let faith drive out despair and confidence compel resolves of daring that will carry us to heights of understanding and of competence unmeasured yet by men. The world is ours to measure and to conquer. We shall not be defeated by its mounting difficulties. Excellence in thought, in words, in art, in act calls us forward, onward and upward. I sing it so:
> Oh, come with me to the Happy Isles
> In the golden haze off yonder,
> Where the song of the sun-kissed breeze beguiles
> And the ocean loves to wander.

While we can only wonder what Horace would have made of Butler's lyric gift, his indomitable spirit surely appealed to the elegant gathering. Butler's exhortation confirmed the wisdom of the revered Centurion, eighty-eight-year-old Elihu Root, who put the case for the Century's immunity from care two days before the Revels: "The spirit of the Century Club cannot be affected whether the country is on or off the gold Standard."

Optimism was in scant supply during the bleak early years of the Depression, and the country stood ready to embrace anyone who could give it hope. In 1932 one such figure suddenly appeared, spouting a gospel of salvation called Technocracy. Howard Scott was a purported engineer who had for many years been thinking about the organization of industrial society, particularly the problems of overproduction caused by increases in technological efficiency. The inability of consumption to keep pace with production inevitably meant, in Scott's analysis, ever-growing unemployment and huge debt, leading finally to the destruction of capitalism itself. The solution lay in balancing mass purchasing with mass production, a process that required eliminating the conventional pricing system and substituting instead a system based on the energy needed to produce goods.

Pricing them according to the kilowatt-hours needed for their manufacture would then permit the match of consumption to production, thereby doing away with the disjunction responsible for the Depression. Energy units, that is—ergs and joules—instead of dollars. Or so the argument went, in murky profundity, larded with obscurely resonant concepts such as "energy transgression," "decision arrivation," and "thermodynamically balanced load." Science, in short, in the person of Howard Scott, come to save the world.

Enthralled by Scott's messianic fervor, Butler invited him in 1932 to come to Columbia, working in the Department of Industrial Engineering, to conduct research into the history of American industrial development as seen through a complex series of energy measurements. When it became known in August that Scott and his fellow technocrats were established at Columbia, interest in Technocracy exploded. A dance was named after it, Scott became a sought-after speaker, and *The Nation* proclaimed his theories revolutionary. Butler tried to dampen expectations about its potential to solve serious problems by claiming that Technocracy was at this time "nothing more than a systematic and careful endeavor to assemble facts . . . as to how far machine production has displaced and is displacing man power, with a view to asking the question, what do we propose to do about it," but it was clear that he was excited to have captured it for Columbia.

Soon, however, as its methodology began to be questioned, and its findings—that with proper use of energy resources, for example, a worker would only need 660 hours of work a year to increase his current income—dismissed as absurd, Scott himself came under scrutiny. In place of a mysterious past replete with numerous foreign degrees and a vast family fortune, reporters found a Greenwich Village character who loved to discuss his ideas about social change in local coffee shops and had for a time been a partner in a New Jersey floor wax manufacturing company. Embarrassed by these revelations, Butler struggled to dissociate himself from the movement without having to acknowledge that he had himself been taken in by its quackery. "Columbia University has no more to do with Technocracy than it has with the fourth dimension," he explained. "As part of unemployment relief it gave working space to a group of engineers and architects who had nowhere else to go. Some of these men have been carrying on most interesting inquiries into the facts of technological development."

The spectacle of Butler's disavowing responsibility for Scott's project amused *The New York Sun*, which could not resist this parody:

I

Of these Technocrats I'm guiltless,
   I dislike this great furore:
All I know is that one morning
   They were left outside my door.
I retired late one evening
   Free from trouble and from care,
To discover in the morning
   That the Technocrats were there.

II

They were homeless, they were hungry
   In this big and cruel burg,
So I gave them food and lodging—
   And they went and laid an "erg"!
Of their plans to save the nation
   My endorsement I withhold;
Where would Butler get new buildings
   If they gave me "joules" for gold?

III

Life is full of great surprises,
   Sudden shocks and things like that,
But the doings of these lodgers
   Knocked your Uncle Nickie flat;
Never more will I be tender
   When strange roomers come to me;
What does kindness ever get you?—
   "Ergs" and "joules" and "energy"!

At the end of January 1933 Butler abruptly severed Columbia's connection with Scott and his researchers. "To use technical language," as the *London Daily Herald* wryly put it, Scott "has lost his 'energy certificates.'"

Three months later, at an event that gave Butler considerable pleasure but also significant pain, he saw his thirty-eight-year-old daughter, Sarah, marry British banker Neville Lawrence before an overflowing crowd at Columbia's St. Paul's Chapel. The legendary headmaster of the Groton School, Endicott Peabody, who had performed similar rites for Franklin and Eleanor Roosevelt thirty years earlier, conducted the ceremony, while Sarah exhibited a non-Butlerian piety by carrying a white satin prayer book throughout the service. Butler liked Neville, and his happiness at having Sarah married was real, but his paternal joy was tempered by despair that she would be moving to England, where Neville's banking career required them to live. Sarah was the person Butler loved most in the world, and her loss was irreparable. She was an affectionate daughter, a delightful traveling companion, an engaged Republican whose interest in politics was as passionate as her father's—at the time of her marriage she had risen within the party to vice-chairman of the New York State Republican Committee. As he wrote to a friend several months before the marriage, "It goes without saying that her leaving the household of which she has been an integral part so long and where she has been a dependence of a most exceptional kind, as well as a counsellor and helpmate, will be a terrible blow." She gave him the warmth and emotional nourishment that Butler could not find in the efficient Kate. According to Dean Virginia Gildersleeve of Barnard, a long-time friend of Butler's, Sarah's absence left a void in his life that led him to turn for solace not to Kate but to Columbia, helping to explain his reluctance to leave the presidency.

The betrayal of friends is perhaps not as distressing as losing contact with a beloved child, but it still hurts, and six months later Butler had to deal with this as well. In October he brought a suit against the Harriman National Bank, whose former president, Joseph Harriman, had been his friend and backer when he ran for the Republican nomination in 1920. The issue revolved around the status of personal securities—both stocks and bonds—that Butler had deposited in the bank in 1931 at Harriman's request. Butler charged that the bank refused to return the securities to him. The bank claimed that when Butler deposited them, he did so explicitly understanding that Harriman planned to borrow them to serve as collateral for two loans totaling $275,000 that he had taken out for his wife, Augusta. When Augusta defaulted on both, the bank argued that it had the right to cover its losses with Butler's securities. The question, then, was whether Butler realized the use Harriman planned to make of the securities when he put them in the bank. The bank asserted that Butler did and that he had been happy to transfer authority over them to his old friend without asking questions or imposing restrictions. Butler countered that he had never intended to have them used as collateral for someone else's loan and that Harriman had improperly taken them without his permission. Harriman himself, who had been removed from the bank presidency and was in the throes of what used to be called a nervous breakdown, was in no condition to clarify matters and did not testify.

When the trial began before Judge Grover Moscowitz, the defense tried to show that Butler, trusting Harriman to act responsibly, had ceded power to him to use the securities as he saw fit. Butler, who alternately napped and read the paper during the proceedings, simply denied having ever done so. Without compelling evidence either way, it was up to the bank to convince the judge that Butler would plausibly have allowed Harriman control over the securities. At one point, to suggest that Butler might have been beholden to Harriman for his financial support during the 1920 campaign, the defense attorney asked if he was aware of the extent of Harriman's backing. Butler replied that he had heard about it indirectly, but he never knew how much Harriman had contributed, and that Harriman had never spoken about it to him. The bank's lawyer seemed incredulous that Butler would not know, but failed to undermine his insistence that he was ignorant of the amount. Nor could he rattle him in commenting that Butler seemed preternaturally calm when he learned from the bank on August 11, 1932, about the disposition of his securities; his letter of response the next day contained not a word of protest. Had Butler truly not known about Harriman's use of the securities, would he not have been more upset? This line of questioning created a sublime opportunity for Butler: "One of the embarrassments of being a gentleman," Butler replied in accounting for his equanimity, "is that perhaps you are not violent when perhaps you should be." Butler's gentlemanly denials won the day; Judge Moscowitz ruled that Butler's securities had to be returned to him.

Personal issues, in any case, could never distract Butler from political ones, and just as he was about to win his battle against Prohibition, 1933 swept him up in another campaign to save America from itself: the need to resist the movement for a constitutional amendment granting Congress the right to regulate child labor. If Butler's protracted struggle for Prohibition repeal earned him the admiration of liberals and progressives, his equally determined efforts against the passage of the so-called Child Labor Amendment drew their ire. Celebrated for the one, he was generally reviled for the other, though both followed from his coherent view of the proper limits of constitutional authority. For Butler, just as the Eighteenth Amendment represented an illegitimate incursion into the private rights of individuals, so the notion that the Constitution should invest Congress with the power to regulate children's labor extended "the Federal police power to the invasion and destruction of the historic rights of our states and local governments as well as those of the family." Butler the esteemed social progressive and Butler the abhorred social reactionary argued from the same set of principles.

The country's interest in a constitutional amendment regulating child labor grew out of frustration at the inability to sustain federal legislation on the subject. The laws Congress had enacted in 1916 and 1922 to protect children from being exploited were declared unconstitutional by the Supreme Court, in 1918 and 1922, after which those committed to reform turned their attention instead to the possibilities of building protection for children into the Constitution itself. Thanks to the lobbying efforts of the National Council on Child Labor, Congress passed an amendment in 1924 that gave it the power to limit, regulate, and prohibit the labor of those under eighteen; and it stipulated that state laws dealing with the issue were superseded by the amendment.

Strongly supported in both House (297–69) and Senate (61–23), the Twentieth Amendment needed the ratification of thirty-six states, a process that would take place within state legislatures and conventions and on which Congress placed no time limit. Backers of the amendment anticipated little difficulty, as national polls indicated substantial approval of the measure, but within a year the proposal was effectively dead, with only three states moving to ratify. The opposition consisted of various groups, foremost among them the National Association of Manufacturers. Led by general counsel James Emery, they formed a National Committee for Rejection of the Twentieth Amendment and worked assiduously to convince state legislators of the harm to the economy that would result if the amendment passed. They were joined by farm organizations, which painted scenarios in which federal control would prevent farmers' children from milking cows or doing chores; by the Roman Catholic Church, which claimed the amendment was a means by which the federal government would undermine its authority in matters relating to the conduct of families; by much of the national press, concerned about the loss of a ready supply of newsboys; and by suspicious clusters of patriotic citizens who were convinced that the amendment was un-American, the first stage of a Communist plot to cede control of children to the state.

Although Butler's primary objection was what might be called more formal than substantive—holding that the Constitution was properly about governmental principles rather than specific rules and regulations—his involvement took on the coloration of his avowedly conservative anti-amendment colleagues. He joined, for example, the Sentinels of the Republic, an organization whose purposes included preventing the growth of socialism, opposing federal encroachment upon states' rights, and stopping the concentration of power in Washington. Founded in 1922 by Louis Coolidge, a Boston businessman, it devoted its energies from 1924 on to resisting the amendment, which Coolidge thought "the keystone of the Red program . . . It bears a hideous birth-mark—the spirit of the Soviet." Butler worked with him to educate the public to its dangers, as well as with Sterling Edmunds, director of the National Committee for the Protection of Child, Family, School and Church. He also shared Coolidge's rhetoric of paranoia, warning that if the amendment passed, it would bring about "a more far-reaching series of changes in our family, social, economic and political life than have heretofore been dreamed of by the most ardent revolutionaries." Ten years later Butler put it even more graphically:

> The Amendment in question would, once again, multiply the police powers of the Federal Government and bring the possibility of our finding in every home, every family, every school and every church a snooping agent from Washington, looking about to see what children were doing . . . It would, once again, undermine the foundations of our government.

Like every other clear-thinking American, Butler argued, he was firmly opposed to the exploitation of children in the labor market, but he insisted that the supervision of individual states had already dealt with it effectively. The amendment was therefore both insidious and superfluous.

It refused to go away, however. Congress had not put any deadline on the ratification process, nor did it stipulate that states could not change their minds. By the early 1930s, interest grew again in protecting children from exploitation while simultaneously keeping them out of the workplace so as not to take jobs away from adults. Between 1924 and 1932 only six states had ratified the amendment, but in 1933 fourteen more did, including eleven that had previously said no. Only sixteen more were needed for passage. With President Roosevelt enthusiastically supporting the amendment, Butler and the anti-amendment forces had to go back to work. On December 28, 1933, Butler published in *The New York Times* a long, two-column letter, really an essay, aimed at arousing the American public for the amendment's defeat. Butler's denunciation bordered on the hysterical: proponents of the amendment "had definitely in mind a Federal control of the population under 18 years of age quite equal to anything which has been brought about in Communist Russia"; "Nothing more indefensible or inexcusable than this amendment has been brought forward at any time in our nation's history." He concluded by calling upon his trusty Sentinels of the Republic and all other crusaders who labored to defeat Prohibition to rise to this new challenge.

Butler was delighted with the response, telling Louis Wiley of the *Times* several weeks later that the volume of letters and telegrams he received had convinced him that he had started a nationwide movement against ratification. But from different quarters it also earned him the charge that he had made himself "into a mouthpiece for the archconservatives." The *Columbia Spectator*, carefully calculating its words, wrote, "Dr. Butler's letter reveals himself to be the true nineteenth-century laissez-faire liberal. The tide thankfully runs against him today." Al Smith, on the other hand, who had shifted from being a defender to a critic of the amendment, praised Butler for his stand, noting that he had generally proven right in "attacking popular causes or defending unpopular ones."

In April 1934, with a number of other prominent New Yorkers, Butler helped to organize the New York State Committee Opposing Ratification of the Child Labor Amendment and became its executive chairman. The amendment was supported by both President Roosevelt and Governor Herbert Lehman; nevertheless, Butler persuaded the Judiciary Committee of the New York State Assembly to refuse to ratify it. His victory brought with it further condemnation: John Dewey characterized Butler's position as "sincere, honest, straightforward and completely wrong."

It was easy, of course—and totally unfair—to assume that Butler's opposition meant that he was indifferent to the abuse of children in the labor market. No group was more inclined to do so than Columbia's radical students, for whom Butler was deeply unappealing: a distant, punitive, reactionary figure. In May 1934 Ad Reinhardt, soon to be known to the world as a brilliant formalist painter and scathing political cartoonist, then a junior at Columbia, submitted an extraordinary watercolor for the commencement issue of *Jester*, the campus humor magazine. A consummate work of ridicule, it showed Butler brandishing a club at cherubic bare-bottomed infants crawling around him. Herman Wouk, the outgoing editor of *The Jester*, was horrified when he saw the proof of the cartoon, and he immediately summoned the *Jester* board into executive session. They soon released a statement that they would not publish a work in such bad taste. (The "taste" explanation was undoubtedly less important than the impulse for self-preservation. Two years earlier, Butler had expelled *Spectator* editor Reed Harris—a longtime irritant, for accusations he made in the paper about Columbia's dining services—only two months before he was due to graduate.)

Although disappointed, Reinhardt, who was also *The Jester's* incoming editor, defended the right of the old managing board to decide what to publish, as they were in charge until the end of the academic year. Wouk, when reached for comment, replied, "I can't be reached for comment." This brouhaha provided *Spectator* editor James Wechsler with a wonderful gift. Wechsler, a tough bulldog of a student who went on to become a formidably straight-talking journalist, disliked the Columbia administration even more than the unfortunate Harris had. He was especially unforgiving about Butler, charging in a book published shortly after he graduated, "There is no more loyal, devout and useful servant of vested wealth than Columbia's president. He has bitterly opposed the Child Labor Amendment, invoking the bogey of 'states' rights' to justify the exploitation of children." *The Jester's* decision not to include the cartoon made a fine front-page news story for Wechsler, and he took great pleasure in featuring it—along with Reinhardt's painting—in the May 17 issue.

Butler was undeterred. Having managed to take care of his own state, he continued to work nationally to guarantee that the sixteen additional ratifications would not be forthcoming. He was pleased with his triumph in getting the decidedly more pejorative "youth control" to be used, in place of "child labor," when talking about the amendment. As he wrote in 1937 to his friend Maurice Sherman, editor of the *Hartford Courant*, "I really think I did a good job when I invented the phrase, Youth Control, two years ago as descriptive of this so-called Child Labor Amendment. That phrase has caught the public and has the great value of being a really accurate description of the pending proposal."

In January 1937, several weeks after Roosevelt had written to the governors of nineteen states asking them for help in passing the amendment, Butler made public a letter he had written to the same nineteen, asking them to stand firm against the proposal's malign intentions. If it was passed, Butler cautioned, "the home, the school and the church would lose the protection which tradition and our fundamental principles have given them and would find themselves at the mercy of the Congress." States adopting some form of corrective legislation would be infinitely preferable to ratifying an amendment which "might, and almost certainly would, be used as an entering wedge for the development among us of policies which are characteristic of the reactionary and cruel totalitarian state."

Butler needn't have bothered. By 1937 the momentum behind the amendment had dissipated, and though four more states eventually opted for ratification, there it ended, twelve states short. With the passage of the Fair Labor Standards Act of 1938, however, an important piece of legislation that the Supreme Court this time permitted to stand, the National Child Labor Committee could claim their victory. But Butler could claim his, too, despite the hostility from his liberal critics that his rhetoric, tactics, and associates earned for him.

The energy Butler started devoting in 1933 to subduing the national specter of the Child Labor Amendment did not cause him to be indifferent to the growing problems of the world economy. The failure of the London Economic Conference of June 1933 encouraged him to organize his own meeting. In keeping with his principle that the Depression was an international phenomenon that could be solved only by international means, Butler decided in February 1935, under the auspices of the Carnegie Endowment, to host a conference in London at Chatham House during the beginning of March. The choice of London, to which Butler sailed on February 8, ostensibly to plan the meeting, was no doubt influenced by the fact that on that day Sarah gave birth to Butler's first and only grandchild, Walter Murray Butler Lawrence. Butler delighted in the event, reporting it to all his friends with the happy formula, "The doctors and the nurses pronounce him sound in wind and limb but are not prepared to make any statement as to his intellectual performance later in life."

Butler emphasized that this conference, unlike others, would not have airy, theoretical discussions, but instead would produce specific solutions that could then be openly considered by the public. A program of action, in short, not rhetoric, formulated by men entirely outside government— unofficial experts not subservient to any administration's point of view. Bringing influential scholars and practical men together to look at the issues without any distorting political baggage represented, for Butler, the best attempt "to see whether we can get rid of the hopeless outlook existing in the world today." Butler was pleased that sixty-two men from ten countries had responded to his invitation, glossing over the fact that thirty-two were English and eight Americans, the others coming from Italy, Belgium, Holland, Norway, Sweden, Canada, Germany, and France. The rest of the world remained unrepresented.

The Butler-made agenda dwelled on his three major concerns: the need to remove trade barriers, stabilize national monetary systems, and enhance international cooperation. The Marquess of Crewe chaired the daylong session on tariffs and trade, J. A. Spender ran the second day's treatment of the monetary system, and Sir Austen Chamberlain led the discussion about the best means of organizing nations to achieve the goal of international peace. At the end of the three days the conference issued unanimous recommendations that not surprisingly resembled what Dr. Butler had been prescribing for some time: the United States and Great Britain, the world's leading creditor nations, should work out measures to help the debtor nations meet their obligations through goods and services and the reduction of tariffs; led by France, Great Britain, and the United States, governments should establish a stable gold standard for all currencies; the League of Nations should be strengthened; judicial settlement of international disputes by use of the Permanent Court of International Justice and the Permanent Court of Arbitration should be encouraged; the growth of armaments should be checked; and the obligations of all those signatories of the Pact of Paris should be reaffirmed.

Long on vision, they were notably short on the specifics of implementation—no more practical, finally, than any other set of admirable ideas about how the world could and should be a better place. And none of their suggestions had the least effect on a belligerent Germany, Italy, or Japan, or on the unwillingness of any nation, including the United States, to take steps to lower trade barriers. Splendid as the words were, that is all they were. Of course, Butler did not see the meeting that way. For him, it was "the most important since the world war, since it was the first time a conference has not broken down." At a meeting of the Carnegie Endowment's board of trustees in 1939, he invoked "the applause which the Chatham House Conference has received everywhere, the reasonableness and practical character of its recommendations," the extent to which people have come to "picture the world as the Chatham House Conference outlined it and, as we have pretty well, I think rather unanimously among ourselves, agreed is a wise course to pursue."

If Butler's panacea of a revitalized internationalism seemed inconsequential to many—"the repetition of old exhortations," according to the *World-Telegram*—it nevertheless had the power to infuriate Butler's archisolationist foe, William Randolph Hearst. Following the publication of the conference's recommendations, Hearst included in his chain of papers on March 12 a blistering attack on Butler and the Carnegie Endowment. Entitled "Doctor Butler's Poison Mill," Hearst accused Butler of wanting to abolish the United States in the service of catering to European interests. For Hearst, Butler's enthusiasm for international cooperation would result in America's giving up its democratic institutions and liberties and submitting instead to the despotism of Europe. The Carnegie Endowment had been "founded by a sentimental Scotch crackpot, whose only use for America was what he could get out of it," and in Butler's hands it had simply become an instrument "for turning America back into a plundered colony of Europe." The only way to deal with such a subversive organization was for "the United States government to suppress it and sequester the fund for loyal purposes."

That the strongest response to the Chatham House proposals came from the man who most detested them suggests how inured America had become to Butler's moral hectoring. The problem was less that Butler was wrong about how the serious use of an international court of justice or an effective League of Nations might have addressed international tensions than that he had been harping on the same themes for fifteen years without recognizing that people no longer cared. As Europe began to find comfort in strong nationalist feelings and America to take refuge in the attractions of isolationism, Butler's message, devoid of a viable political agenda to help enact it, didn't seem to matter. Incapable of changing it, he was also incapable of understanding the passions of Columbia students who disagreed with him. In early April, following his return from London, Butler confronted the radical undergraduates who were pushing for an antiwar strike at Columbia. Butler warned them not to, and he adapted his usual antistrike position to this instance by claiming that student strikes against the war were simply forms of war in themselves. Butler told them instead to engage in the more appropriate (and Butler-certified) actions of supporting the Permanent Court of International Justice and making sure they voted for candidates for public office who did, too. The *Spectator*'s editorial response, dismissing the appeals to the Hague Court and the need to observe the Pact of Paris as "ancient shibboleths," pointed up the facts that Butler failed to grasp: "Is Dr. Butler unaware that his own faculty long ago laid bare the illusions that pacts, courts, and international conferences stopped the surge toward war?"

The answer was yes, Butler remained unaware. In the face of the world's deepening political and economic crises, he looked heroically backward, urging people, in a 1936 article, to return to the Republican national platform of 1920 and Harding's speech on August 28 of that year, affirming the need to strengthen international institutions supporting peace. He deplored the present-day moral deterioration, the absence of great leaders, the decline of governmental integrity, the loss of cultural idealism. If he can't be blamed for not having solutions, his repeated declaration that the Pact of Paris would have been the answer if only governments had honored it properly made him appear painfully out of touch with political reality.

Butler's internationalist rhetoric was perhaps becoming tired, but he wanted to make sure no one would think that he was as well, or that the time had come for the indomitable but no longer young president of Columbia University, the Carnegie Endowment, and the American Academy of Arts and Letters to consider retirement. In a virtuoso display of self-affirmation, he devoted his 1937 commencement address at Columbia to demonstrating that the age of a man's mind cannot be measured by years. Some men are stultified before they reach thirty, he remarked, yet creative, intellectual, and political contributions were made by those who might be old chronologically but whose minds remained everlastingly young: Pope Leo XIII, Gladstone, Bismarck, Cardinal Newman, Disraeli, John Marshall, Elihu Root, F.A.P. Barnard, General Smuts, Pope Pius XI. What comfort or illumination the twenty-one-year-old members of the class of 1937 derived from this was not clear, other than to realize that their seventy-five-year-old president still saw himself as fit and productive as ever. "May you stay always on the Morningside of life," he concluded, suggesting where he, at least, planned to spend the rest of his days.

CHAPTER NINETEEN

Resignation, Retirements, and Death

❧

Protest as he might, Butler was in fact growing older, and if his spirit burned as bright as ever, it could not prevent the inevitable physical decay of aging. By the late 1930s, Butler's vision (a 1925 operation for glaucoma had only temporarily restrained the disease) and hearing were deteriorating badly, making it harder for him to deal with all the details involved in administering his various empires. Not that he cut back on his responsibilities; he just paid less attention to them. But he continued to minister to the world's needs, and the world continued to revere him. German president von Hindenburg awarded him the Goethe Medal for his contributions to German culture, and Mussolini, as honorary president of the International Mark Twain Society, gave him theirs for "service in education," among other distinctions he earned.

And for a man who remained a passionate Anglophile all his life, the visit to Columbia in June 1939 of King George VI and Queen Elizabeth, although perhaps not technically a distinction, was at the very least a glorious episode, made all the more glorious because it was a gift unexpectedly bestowed. It began with a phone call from President Roosevelt in March, notifying Butler that their majesties had decided they would like to see Columbia when they came down from Canada on their forthcoming trip to the United States. Extensive preparations ensued, and the press was not told until several weeks before their arrival. At 5:00 on the afternoon of June 10, himself majestically attired in his soft cap and scarlet doctor of laws robe from Cambridge (he claimed he wore it because George had briefly attended Cambridge), Butler greeted them at the entrance to the campus on Broadway and 116th Street. Together they walked along the 103 yards of dyed red burlap the university had purchased for the occasion (at a cost of $65), across College Walk and up the stairs to Low Library. In the library's elegant rotunda, on a small stage erected for the event, an easel displayed the royal charter that King George II had issued to "King's College" in 1754. Six blue-brocaded French chairs from 60 Morningside awaited the king and queen, the Butlers, and the chairman of the trustees and his wife, but in the awkwardness of the moment, nobody bothered to sit. As Kate looked on rather sourly, Butler offered his official greetings, George admired the charter, and then the royal couple, with separate pens (never used before and never to be used again) that Kate had bought from a Fifth Avenue jeweler, signed the university guest book. Within a half hour they were off by car to Hyde Park to spend time with President Roosevelt.

Despite the honors lavished upon him for his sagacity, Butler seemed slow to recognize the impending European catastrophe. He failed to see the extent to which German and Italian support of Franco made the Spanish Civil War a kind of prelude to the larger conflict ahead. Concluding that there were no democratic issues involved—the Spanish Republic being too far to the left for Butler's liking—he dismissed it as a "typical contest between two reactionary forms of government—communism and fascism." Without taking sides, he simply issued an appeal through the Carnegie Endowment to the people of all nations, asking them to urge their governments to cease the bombing of civilians. Back in from his summer trip in Europe in July 1938, he told reporters that he didn't think war was imminent. He remained convinced that the Germans would rise up against Hitler to reassert traditional German spiritual and moral values and that Mussolini would make Hitler understand the virtues of peace. When neither of these happened, he took comfort, like many others, in the Munich Pact of September 1938, according to which Britain, France, and Italy permitted Germany to occupy Czechoslovakia's Sudetenland; he shared British prime minister Chamberlain's view that it had secured "peace in our time" and insisted that it did not spell "the abandonment of democratic ideals and principles." As chairman of the American Committee for Relief in Czechoslovakia, he was pleased to receive reports in November that the Czechoslovaks did not appear dispirited by having had a portion of their country signed away.

With the German invasion of Poland in September 1939, Butler had to renounce all of his hopes that public opinion or strong leaders could prevent the outbreak of war. Now that Fascism had launched itself on a path of conquest, there was no use talking about the obligations of the Pact of Paris or the efficacy of international tribunals. Before the world could be set right, Fascism had to be eliminated, and Butler believed that could only happen through a concerted use of force. He had no trouble understanding, before the rest of the country agreed, that the United States had to join Great Britain and France in the war. Putting aside his passion for arbitration, he minced no words about the need to fight.

On the afternoon of October 3, 1940, for the first time in Columbia's history, Butler summoned every member of the university faculties—eight hundred in all—to a special meeting in McMillin Academic Theater to hear a presidential address. On October 4 Senator Bennett C. Clark of Missouri interrupted the Senate's consideration of a pending sugar bill to discuss Butler's talk, a subject of such importance, Clark stressed, "that I do not think a day should be allowed to pass without its being called to the attention of the Senate and of the whole country." Clark requested that an article in the *New York Herald-Tribune* be included in the *Congressional Record*. It began:

> Dr. Nicholas Murray Butler, president of Columbia University, speaking yesterday before an unprecedented general assembly of the university faculties said that there could be no doubt where the university stood in "the war between beasts and human beings," and warned that those whose convictions were in open conflict with the university's doctrines should, "in ordinary self-respect," resign their faculty positions.

An ardent isolationist, doing his best to keep the United States out of the European conflict, Clark was incensed by Butler's pronouncement, charging that "never before in the long history of the struggle in the United States for academic freedom has so blatant, so outrageous, so arrogant a proposition ever been put to the faculty of any American college or university." Calling him the "old, senile, reactionary president of Columbia University, who for many years disgraced that institution by mixing up the activities of the president of a great institution with the activities of a pot-house Republican politician," Clark accused him of being a British propagandist, trying to coerce this country into going to war. For Clark, and for Senator Rush D. Holt of West Virginia, who joined in the denunciation, Butler was guilty of a capital offense: "When university professors, university instructors, no matter what they may believe, are required to teach their students that we are already in a war, and that we should get further in, that means that the American Nation is being polluted at its very source. I say better men than Dr. Butler have been tried for treason and hung for treason."

Rhetoric and rage aside, Butler's speech, "The True Function of a University in This World Crisis," was extraordinary even for Butler. Its ostensible purpose was perfectly appropriate: to explain to the faculty in what way Columbia would cooperate with the government in strengthening the nation's defense; the university could not affect military preparedness, but it could (and should) contribute to helping the public understand the political, economic, and social problems involved in the European war. Butler, however, had something more in mind beyond the university's traditional mission of education. Any faculty member who did not share his view that there was but one acceptable position in the war "between beasts and human beings, between brutal force and kindly helpfulness, between the spirit of gain at any cost and the spirit of service built upon common sense and moral principle," should voluntarily leave the university.

In delivering this astonishing message, Butler distinguished between academic freedom—the right of professors to engage in their scholarship and scientific research without religious or political constraints—and a freedom that for Butler took precedence: university freedom.

> Before and above academic freedom of any kind or sort comes this university freedom which is the right and obligation of the university itself to pursue its high ideals unhampered and unembarrassed by conduct on the part of any of its members which tends to damage its reputation, to lessen its influence or to lower its authority as a center of sound learning and of moral teaching. Those whose convictions are of such a character as to bring their conduct in open conflict with the university's freedom to go its way toward its lofty aim should, in ordinary decency and self-respect, withdraw of their own accord from university membership in order that their conduct may be freed from the limitations which university membership naturally

and necessarily puts upon it. No reasonable person would insist upon remaining a member of a church, for instance, who spent his time publicly denying its principles and doctrines.

Clark should not have been surprised at Butler's remarks. For the old recycler was playing a variation on a theme he introduced to the Columbia faculty in the summer of 1917, after the United States had entered World War I, to the effect that any professor who publicly opposed American participation in it would be guilty of treason. The two situations were of course not the same. In 1917 the country had just been committed by Congress to fight in the European conflict, while in 1940 much of the country wished to remain neutral. But both gave Butler an opportunity to display a bellicose patriotism rather different from the insistence on the need for judicious international consultation he normally preached. With his belief in the possibilities of a peaceful Europe shattered, Butler now entered the fray with the vengeance of the sorely disappointed. Even if the country had not yet declared war, he had.

Like most of the rhetorical bombs Butler loved to drop, this one caused a vast national—and international—explosion. Edward R. Murrow, broadcasting from London where real bombs were dropping, expressed his amazement that Butler would demand that his faculty support a university position, noting, "That will make strange reading to British scholars. No university head in this country has made such a pronouncement." Murrow added, "Even in wartime it's not customary for scholars to demand that their colleagues share their political or international views. It's still possible for British professors to pursue their search for truth without dictation."

Although Butler's speech elicited some editorial support across the country, praising him for his hard-hitting willingness to tell it like it is, most of those who commented were horrified by the ease with which he seemed prepared to deny people their civil liberties. Colonel Robert McCormick's *Chicago Tribune* titled its editorial "Hail Columbia's Fuehrer," suggesting that Butler had paid for his innumerable foreign distinctions "by delivering his university as its fuehrer. To him, at least, it means something that Columbia came into existence as King's College. Colonial days are here again." The columnist Max Lerner, in *The Boston Globe*, saw a comparison between the German despotism Butler was condemning and his own behavior in suppressing "the right of independent thinking." Should the

United States follow Butler's path, "there would be little improvement over Hitlerism." Bertrand Russell rejected Butler's argument as preposterous: "I cannot understand the logic of his reasoning in attempting to deny a man the expression of his opinion." John Dewey was similarly perplexed: "I do not know what a university is apart from students and its teaching staff. Placing the university in a realm so lofty that it is above faculty and students and can control their beliefs seems totalitarian." The Harvard scholar F. O. Matthiessen characterized Butler's words as "a complete denial of academic freedom, a black betrayal of the responsibility of an educator." Charles Beard, who had just returned to Columbia after twenty-three years for a one-year visiting professorship, refused to respond, declaring that the statement he issued in 1917 applied to the present situation, too.

The issue of academic freedom had long been a vexed one for Butler. Staunchly defending it in theory, as any self-respecting academic had to, he was never happy to accord it absolute authority. The abstract notion of academic freedom was fine as long as it was tethered to values Butler approved of. He seemed oblivious to the fact that the more constraints one puts upon freedom, the less meaning it has as a principle of any significance. Butler first enumerated these constraints in a 1910 letter to Edward Coe, a trustee, in a formulation that later found its way into his 1910 presidential report: "I hold that the four limitations upon academic freedom are those imposed by common morality, common sense, common loyalty, and a decent respect for the opinions of mankind." He made no attempt to explicate the standards against which the violations might be measured. It was enough to assert that anyone who "offends against common morality" or "against the plain dictates of common sense" is "in my judgment unfitted to be maintained by our University as a teacher or investigator." Similarly, a faculty member who could not share the university's stated ideals had no right to be associated with it. And the last stipulation, to honor the opinions of mankind, required that no professor hold "individual or extravagant views . . . in the face of the opinion of the civilized world, particularly as regards questions of religious belief, moral conduct, and the organization of society." Butler allowed people to articulate such aberrant views if they wished to do so as private citizens, "but without the added influence and prestige of a university name."

Butler admitted to Coe that the practical task of applying these principles in a specific university situation could be "one of surpassing difficulty and doubt." However difficult, in every case the judge of possible transgression would be Butler, both interpreter of the standards—of common morality, common sense, and common opinion—and the arbiter of the violations. In short, the academic freedom Butler endorsed was subordinated to his own values and priorities. He could invoke it when it suited his purposes, and he could show how it didn't apply when it conflicted with them. In the cases of professors like Peck or Spingarn or Cattell or Dana, he found it easy to prove that common morality or common loyalty was being traduced and that their behavior put the university's reputation at risk. Inflammatory speakers from the left, such as Count Ilya Tolstoy in 1917 or Robert Burke in 1937 (after he had been expelled), were not invited to campus, because Butler had already found them guilty of rejecting "civilized opinion" regarding social organization, but speakers from the right came under academic freedom's protective mantle.

Butler repeated in various of his presidential reports that academic freedom was alive and flourishing in the United States, and as long as faculty members expressed their opinions with "discretion, moderation, good taste and good sense," they were free to hold whatever opinions they wanted. He insisted that universities had an obligation to protect responsible professors from unjust criticism, and in this task they had largely succeeded: "Genuine cases of the invasion of academic freedom are so rare as to be almost non-existent." The Columbia turmoil of 1917 had required Butler to reassure people about the health of academic freedom. It was not in the slightest danger in the United States, he maintained: "Evidence to the contrary is quite too manifold and too abundant." But academic *obligation* was being eroded, the sense of loyalty to the institution, its traditions and purposes, which the faculty member ought to feel upon joining the university community. Butler worried over the decline of such commitments, disturbed that they were being disregarded in the service of showing "devotion to something that [is conceived] to be higher and of greater value."

In his 1917 report, the object of devotion that had upset Butler was the siren song of Communism. Its appeal had captured the minds of many "who, for lack of a more accurate term, call themselves intellectuals," and it must be resisted: "The time has not yet come . . . when rational persons can contemplate with satisfaction the rule of the literary and academic Bolsheviki or permit them to seize responsibility for the intellectual life of the nation." As Butler framed the issue, it was not a curtailment of academic freedom, but a failure of honoring academic obligation. Fortunately, the number of those guilty of subversive opinion and behavior were "negligible in number when compared with the vast body of loyal, devoted and scholarly American Academic teachers." A year later, reflecting on the dismissal of Cattell and Dana, he said that the action taken against them had solely to do with their public conduct as it affected the reputation of the University. He cited a special report prepared by the trustees in February 1918 indicating the "fealty" every new faculty appointment was expected to show Columbia, even if it was not an explicit contractual stipulation. Failure to live up to this "implied pledge" would destroy the essential mutual confidence between professor and trustees, making the termination of employment, voluntary or otherwise, the only appropriate response.

No one seemed to notice it at the time, but the formulation that Clark and others found so scandalous in 1940 originally appeared, practically word for word, in Butler's 1935 presidential report. In turning it from a declaration of principle into a kind of personal warning to the entire faculty about the single issue of the European war, Butler modified the text only slightly for emphasis and delivery. He also added the unfortunate sentence that compared university employment to church membership. The notion that university faculty were like voluntary chuch members who, if dissatisfied with the doctrines they are asked to observe, can blithely change their affiliations, was not one of Butler's compelling arguments.

His preference for "university freedom" over academic freedom had its Columbia adherents—though not surprisingly, most were deans. Dean Gildersleeve of Barnard found his remarks "safe, sound, true and interesting"; Dean Herbert Hawkes of the college thought his talk "was very appropriate"; Dean George Pegram of the graduate faculties claimed he had "no misgivings" about it. But professors and students were less kindly disposed. The students were angered by the president's assertion that academic freedom had nothing whatever to do with them, but only "the freedom of thought and inquiry . . . on the part of accomplished scholars"; and the faculty resented the modifier "accomplished," wondering why all of them couldn't share in its benefits. Students criticized the statement through the *Spectator*, while faculty expressed their opposition through letters, both individual and joint. Of these, the most influential was an open letter issued by the American Committee for Democracy and International Freedom, published in the *Times*. Its eight signatories were all Columbia faculty: Nobel

Prize winner Harold Urey, who was then chairman of Chemistry; Leslie Dunn, chairman of Zoology; Walter Rautenstrauch, chairman of Industrial Engineering; the distinguished anthropologists Franz Boas and Ruth Benedict; Wesley Mitchell of Economics; Robert Lynd of Sociology; and Clyde Miller, associate professor of Education. Their letter asked for clarification of the distinction between the two competing freedoms and also wondered why the university, if it was all about the extension of knowledge, should not consider all possibilities and protect minority points of view. And if the university was indeed a company of scholars and students, shouldn't the policies that governed them be formulated with their full cooperation?

The committee hoped that Butler would make a public reply. Provost Fackenthal responded that Butler was thinking about it. Meanwhile, *The New York Times*, as always a trusty friend, gently mentioned that Butler's address left many questions unanswered. But until such time as Butler could respond, it would be "a bit hasty to conclude that something in the nature of a gag rule is to be established on Morningside Heights." The paper looked forward to Butler's removing "what appears to be a rather extensive anxiety" that "conclusions reached on the basis of legitimate research" might be imposed or repressed.

On October 10, 1940, Butler sent a letter by messenger individually to the eight and simultaneously released it to the *Times*. Neither retracting, modifying, or clarifying anything, it was a masterpiece of Butler finesse:

> Are not the answers to the questions which you put quite obvious in any institution where academic freedom prevails? Our faculty members are certainly at full liberty to think and to talk as they please upon any subject which interests them, whether it be popular or unpopular. Moreover, it is clearly our duty to protect the opinions and judgments of minorities. Majorities can usually take care of themselves.
>
> We and our associates constitute the Columbia University of our day and generation. We make policies and we control them. Therefore, the University is not a foreign and remote thing; it consists of ourselves. This is why we ask for university freedom as a group as well as for academic freedom as individuals.

And as for the students' concern that they were somehow being denied their rights, given that academic freedom couldn't apply to them because it had historically covered only the work of scholars, Butler insisted they would always enjoy what he called "student freedom," which he made no effort to define.

Butler's comforting evasions succeeded in calming everybody. The eight Columbia faculty were relieved. Urey sent a personal note thanking Butler, saying that "your few sentences leave nothing to be added." The *Times* applauded:

> President Nicholas Murray Butler of Columbia University has cleared up handsomely the doubts surrounding his recent address on "academic freedom" and "university freedom." There is no point debating whether his original words were ambiguous. What matters is the message he intended to convey . . . He speaks out plainly for the right of faculty members to "think and to talk" as they please upon any subject which interests them.

As upset as the trustees must have been at the publicity, they loyally stood by their president, and at their regularly scheduled October meeting, several of them proposed a resolution approving the address. Although Butler would later maintain, in a letter to the *Columbia Review* in December, "that of all the addresses which I have made at Columbia during the past fifty-five years, none has received such unanimous approval and applause" as this one, he also knew it was not an issue he should push. Before an official vote could be taken, the trustee minutes record, "President Butler thought it better, in view of the misunderstandings and misinterpretations in the press, to let the matter drop." He was right, and he never again tried to assert the convoluted ways in which academic freedom might be constrained by the university's larger mission.

Of Butler's three major institutional presidencies, the first he relinquished — at the beginning of 1941 — was the American Academy of Arts and Letters, and he did so because of a dispute, not physical infirmity. As several of the participants observed, it was a veritable Platonic form of a tempest in a teacup. It developed out of the structural relationship between the National Institute of Arts and Letters, and the Academy, its elite "inner body." The Academy's bylaws stipulated that its august fifty members could be drawn only from the Institute. From time to time in the early 1930s Butler and the

Academy's high-culture and culturally conservative secretary, Robert Underwood Johnson, had grumbled about the pedestrian quality of some of those elected to the Institute. Deeply offended by all traces of modern slovenliness, Johnson feared for the decline of gentility in art, manners, and life. Together the two men worried, in Butler's words, that the highest artistic standards were being compromised by the admission of mere popularizers who "are quite below the plane of excellence upon which both Institute and Academy ought to move." Johnson had objected strongly, for example, to the election in 1933 of Carl Sandburg, whom he referred to as "Sandborg." Some day, Butler suggested, perhaps the Academy would have to break with the Institute and admit people from outside it.

Nothing came of this notion until suddenly, at a director's meeting of the Academy on October 13, 1939, a resolution was introduced and discussed (to be voted on at a later time) to eliminate from the Academy's constitution the sentence "Only members of the National Institute of Arts and Letters shall be eligible for election to the Academy." The resolution's proposer was Archer Huntington, inheritor of one branch of the Huntington railroad fortune, whose presence on the board was less a result of his writings on Spain than of the more than $3 million he had contributed to the Academy over twenty years. He had financed both the construction of the building on 155th Street and Broadway and the budget for maintaining it. But it was not at all clear that the new idea originated with the Academy's financial angel. He suggested it was Butler's; Butler insisted it was Huntington's. Given Butler's concern that his elite academy was in danger of becoming insufficiently elite, it is impossible to imagine that the two hadn't cooked it up together. Tactically, of course, it was a shrewd move to have Huntington offer it, as no one wanted to offend the man with the money. Butler warned repeatedly during the controversy that to reject the amendment would be to risk alienating the Academy's main financial supporter.

Perhaps because he thought that Huntington's name was sufficient to win the Academy's support, perhaps because he thought the change was too insignificant to matter, Butler had badly misread the politics of the situation. He failed to anticipate that the Institute would find the proposal demeaning and that the Academy would be distressed by the threat to the harmonious relationship between the two bodies. And he especially failed to reckon with the anger of the Institute's president (and Academy member), the conductor, composer, and radio celebrity Walter Damrosch, who resolved to resist what he conceived of as a gross insult to the Institute's members. Damrosch was aided in his efforts by eighty-seven-year-old Judge Robert Grant, the sole dissenter to the proposed amendment at the October meeting. Author of numerous unread books and Harvard's first Ph.D. in English, Grant was best known as the judge who upheld the execution of Sacco and Vanzetti as a member of Massachussetts governor Alvan T. Fuller's advisory board. He had written to the Academy members, informing them of what had transpired and urging them, if they opposed the new rules, to let their views be known. In short order, he elicited twenty-nine letters arguing against the change, including those from Stephen Vincent Benét, Walter Lippmann, and Ellen Glasgow. Later Hamlin Garland, Eugene O'Neill, and Ezra Pound added their protests. Not surprisingly, Pound, who hated Butler for his leadership of the Carnegie Endowment, produced the most memorable response:

> Whereas Nicholas Murray Butler belongs to a group of men unfit to live, and whereas under his presidency The Carnegie Peace Foundation has used its funds NOT to promote the cause of peace but to HINDER and neglect the valid investigation into the causes of war, I am against any action legal or illegal that cd/ place any further power to do evil in his hands or in the hands of any man or group of individuals of whatever sex who have not investigated Butler to the utmost in all his acts and relations.
>
> I trust that someday the legal forces of the country will find means of dealing with him, if he don't die first [added by hand: "& the sooner the better."] It took 'em some time to nab Capone. That the Academy as now constituted is a disgrace to the Institute might well be sustained, but that these fossilized old jossers shd/ be given any more power is against all decency.

As Institute and Academy opposition organized itself, Butler agreed to meet in late November with Damrosch; Arthur Train, the Institute's treasurer and an old friend of Huntington's; and Pulitzer Prize–winning American historian James Truslow Adams. Butler played the Huntington card forcefully, claiming that Huntington was prepared to cease all further contributions to the Academy and cut it out of his will if the resolution was not endorsed. The specter of a Huntingtonless Academy and Institute could not be lightly dismissed, so Damrosch, overcoming his anger, wondered how Butler would react to the compromise position that the Academy might be permitted to elect one member every two years from the outside. Eager to escape from his intransigence without damaging his credibility, Butler thought he could get Huntington to accept this splendid idea, and Damrosch promised to bring it to the Institute's executive council for its consideration.

But the council, still smarting and convinced that Butler had no legal basis for recommending any change, refused to allow their membership to vote on it. Butler continued to maintain that not only was it legal, but that the intended separation of the Academy from the Institute had been a matter of public record from the time of the Academy's incorporation in 1916. Henry Seidel Canby, the Institute's secretary, inquired where these discussions could be found. "I have no recollection as to just what form of record or public announcement, if any, may have been made by Mr. Robert Underwood Johnson in the matter to which you refer," Butler replied. "It was, however, a topic of frequent and sometimes violent discussion on his part."

Further attempts at negotiation and other forms of compromise possibilities failed, and Butler announced that the Academy's board would meet on April 12, 1940, to act on Huntington's proposed amendment to the bylaws. According to Judge Grant, who was still opposed, the choice of that date "was a clear case of rigging an election," as Butler knew that neither Grant, the literary critic William Lyon Phelps, nor Adams—three certain negative votes—could attend. Actually their absence made no difference, because Butler had the five votes necessary to carry the motion. In the end, the creator of the "Gibson Girls," the illustrator Charles Dana Gibson, cast the sole negative vote.

The minutes of the meeting, issued by Butler, contained the disingenuous statement that no protests had been received by the Academy between the time the proposal was made (February 7) and announced to the entire membership (February 23). The lawyer and historian Charles Warren, whose drafting of the espionage act of 1917 helped imprison radicals, was irate at what he called the "subterfuge" of this claim, noting that "practically a majority" of the Academy had opposed the action when it had initially been discussed. "Members of the Academy had a right to assume . . . that the earlier protests would be considered by the Board as applicable to the February 7th proposal." In Butler's struggle to keep the modern and the radical out of the academy, it is fascinating to see some of his resistance coming from figures as deeply conservative as Grant and Warren.

Butler's victory did nothing to calm the turmoil. Huntington tried to be conciliatory by having the board pass a motion that the "Directors, acting for the Academy, for the time being, waive the right to elect members outside of the Institute," but that only served to exacerbate the Institute's anger, as it was that very "right" that was being challenged. Butler's strategy at damage control expressed his characteristic puzzlement that people were so exercised. After all, he pointed out, Academy members could always vote down nominees from the outside. This did no more to assuage the unhappiness with him than did Huntington's conciliatory waiver.

Damrosch finally understood that the only remedy lay in bringing in a fresh slate of directors who would rescind the amendment. He, Train, and others worked over the summer and fall to guarantee that members sympathetic to their position would attend the annual meeting to elect the new board. On November 14 the Damrosch-led forces showed up in sufficient number to elect five new directors committed to returning the Academy to its old bylaws. With a majority on the board now assured, the insurgents sought to effect a reconciliation of their own by reelecting the three previous directors most responsible for the amendment: Huntington, Butler, and former Connecticut governor Wilbur Cross—an effort intended to keep Huntington's financial support. But it failed. When the new board met and voted 5–3 to rescind, all three men resigned, and Huntington vowed never to enter the Academy building again. Butler made his resignation effective as of January 14, 1941, when the board would choose a new president. Presiding over his last meeting (he did not go on January 14 to see Damrosch elected), he managed to end his tenure on a note of grudging respect from the man would would shortly succeed him. While "Cross and Huntington lost their tempers badly," Damrosch reported to Charles Dana Gibson, "Butler throughout acted with great fairness and courtesy."

His decorous behavior did not render him oblivious to the opportunity a Huntington disaffected with the Academy represented for Columbia. Less than two months later Butler asked him whether, since the Academy had demonstrated its lack of appreciation for his spendid generosity, he might not want to help Columbia meet its goal of adding $50 million to its endowment. Huntington politely declined, suggesting that he might be able to do something in his will. Butler thanked him for this "magnificent" pos sibility, hoped it would not become effective for a very long time, and rue-fully observed that he would simply have to "reconcile myself to living un-der the grave limitations which present circumstances have brought about."

No dispute could ever have persuaded Butler to step down from his presi-dency at Columbia. In fact, nothing could. And that was the problem. But-ler had for so long identified himself with the institution he ran that it was literally inconceivable for him to imagine life without Columbia. His jocu-lar comments to the press regarding his age, their jocularity notwithstand-ing, suggested the real anxiety he felt about not being permitted his final ambition of dying in office. He had no plans to retire, he stressed in 1941 on his seventy-ninth birthday, as there were still too many things left to do for Columbia: "They'll have to give me fifty million dollars before I'll talk re-tirement. That would solve our problem for the next half-generation." As he approached his eightieth, he reiterated that he was still not thinking of leav-ing: "Not until I die—the reason being, that if I did resign I would die right off." Until the mythical $50 million was forthcoming, Butler would stay right where he was—in his Low Library office. If they wanted to get rid of him, "they'll have to get a communist to shoot me." "What's the use of re-tiring?" he queried rhetorically on his eighty-first birthday. "I'd die if I had to retire, unless my physical or mental health gave out."

But if Butler was not contemplating his retirement, the Columbia trustees surely were. It could not have gladdened their hearts to hear the president of their university reviled on the floor of the Senate as old, senile, and reactionary. Although as a group they tended to be remarkably pas-sive—even obtuse—about their responsibilities for Columbia's well-being, even they had begun to notice that, like their president, Columbia was be-coming progressively infirm. The symptoms were evident: the value of the endowment, courtesy of the Depression, had declined since 1930; there had been no serious fund-raising for more than a decade, and no administrative structure had been developed to compensate for Butler's lack of interest in doing it; Columbia had stopped growing (its last project on the Morning-side campus was the 1934 completion of South Hall, renamed Butler Li-brary in 1946); deferred maintenance on both the medical school and Morningside Heights buildings had led to serious problems; enrollments were down; and the faculty was not being renewed at a healthy rate nor ad-equately protected from raids by other, more rapacious universities. Above all, no one was thinking about what sort of university Columbia ought to be; about how it should be funded; about the vexed but vital relationship between its research functions and its attention to undergraduate, graduate, and professional school instruction. The federated model of university organization that Butler preferred, with strong individual professional schools pursuing their separate courses, had essentially left Columbia a university without a center, a problem that no one was addressing.

Into the vacuum of presidential leadership, the trustees, in 1937, had inserted as provost Frank Fackenthal, the university's secretary since 1910, to help Butler with his administrative duties. Conscientious and competent but entirely bland, Fackenthal, who had in fact been running things for a long time from his less-elevated position, was hardly a substitute for a strong president. He could handle the university's day-to-day business, but he was not qualified to shape policy or provide direction. For that, there was only the progressively enfeebled Butler, ever less inclined to bother.

In a curious way, nothing quite became Butler like his heroic refusal to give in to his incapacities and acknowledge that he could no longer do the job. While his weaknesses produced their obvious embarrassing moments—the physicist I. I. Rabi tartly recalled that when Butler presented him with his Nobel Prize in Physics in 1944, he called him "Fermi"—they also somehow humanized the man who had spent so much of his life being always correct and perfectly in control. The spectacle of the imperious president being led to and from his office in Low Library by an attendant softened the hearts of many of his detractors, even if it didn't do anything for Columbia's management. And faculty and students alike testified to Butler's extraordinary ability to deliver flawless public addresses even when he could no longer follow a prepared text. Albert Jacobs, a law professor, recalled Butler's 1942 commencement address, when a windy day caused Butler to confuse the pages of his speech. Because of Butler's fragility, Frederick Coykendall, chairman of the trustees, had asked Jacobs several days before to be prepared to take over the ceremonies and deliver Butler's address should he falter. As Jacobs was deciding whether to move to the microphone and guide Butler to his chair, Butler "completely abandoned his notes and in an amazing fashion launched forth on an entirely different subject, delivering a brilliant address."

But Butler's remarkable rhetorical powers were not sufficient reason to maintain him as president of a university that needed an infusion of energy. The reluctance of the trustees to act had less to do with their failure to perceive the need to replace him than with their inability to oust the man who had put them on the board in the first place. Beholden to Butler for their socially prestigious appointments and awed by his status as Nobel Prize winner and America's wisest man, they had over the years essentially ceded all authority to him. Instead of the oversight they were supposed to exercise, they endlessly deferred to his judgment, making the board, in the words of the lawyer Frederic Coudert, a "non-debating Board." It did what Butler wanted. It did so, Coudert emphasized, not out of apathy or laziness, but because it had concluded that it simply could not improve upon Butler's understanding of an issue. Coudert explained the process. When a question was raised at a trustee meeting,

> Dr. Butler would get up, and in perfectly lucid and clear language, he would explain the proposition so clearly and so absolutely that nobody else had anything to say, because we'd only be wasting time.
>
> In that sense, and in that sense only . . . he knew so much more about Columbia and everything that's connected to Columbia, and the organization of Columbia, and he loved it so devotedly, and had done so much to create it, that after the older men—his own contemporaries—had disappeared, there really wasn't anyone who could intelligently debate with him. Things went very well that way for many years.

And when they stopped going that way, the trustees lacked both the heart and the courage to tell Butler it was time to resign. In the early 1940s, in an effort to get him to leave without actually confronting him, they enlisted the help of Virginia Gildersleeve, Barnard's dean and a confidante of Butler's. Her informal efforts to cajole him into retirement failed, however; he complained about the misery of his homelife and repeated to her his conviction that he would die without the position.

By the spring of 1945 it was clear that the decision could no longer be left to Butler: the trustees had to act. Finding people to tell Butler he was to retire must have been a little like asking for volunteers to go over the top during the vicious trench warfare of World War I. Two men finally agreed: IBM's Thomas Watson and Marcellus ("Marcy") Dodge. It must have been especially painful for Dodge, who had gone to Columbia College and been appointed a trustee by Butler only four years after graduating. Having inherited the Remington Arms Company from his grandfather and gone on to marry Geraldine Rockefeller, a niece of John D.'s, Dodge was one of the wealthiest men in the country from early in the twentieth century. An active supporter of the university, he also became a close friend and adviser of Butler's, who would frequently visit him at his remarkably unassuming estate in Morristown, New Jersey. Together with Watson, Dodge went to 60 Morningside to convey the unpleasant news. No record exists of Butler's reaction, but he had no choice. At a special meeting of the trustees on April 17, Butler's letter of resignation was accepted, to become effective on October 1.

The resignation of the man whom *Life* magazine called "the most famous figure in United States education" made the front pages of newspapers everywhere. Editorial writers extolled "the Butler era" at Columbia, noting the university's enormous growth in enrollment, endowment, budget, and physical plant. Dr. Butler, they agreed, had embodied the best America had to offer, at once a visionary educator and a fully engaged citizen whose passionate idealism had been devoted to trying to solve the world's most critical problems. Butler's hometown *Paterson News* commented, "He had come to seem . . . a public institution himself and independent of time, like the Constitution or the Republic of Plato."

Butler was concerned that the trustees not be tempted to overlook the worldwide significance of their newly installed president emeritus. Of the hundreds of laudatory letters he received on his retirement, he instructed Philip Hayden, the university secretary, to send to the trustees "copies of four which have been written by persons of high public importance who have no relation whatever to the work of Columbia University." The four were Secretary of Labor Frances Perkins; Assistant Secretary of State Nelson Rockefeller; the American diplomat Sumner Welles; and the former Archbishop of Canterbury, Lord Lang of Lambeth. Like the six wise men whom Butler enlisted to raise money for Columbia in 1929, their credibility could not be questioned, because they had no involvement with the university. In the midst of the adulation, of course, there were necessarily some dissenting voices, though none more majestically off target than that of actress Tallulah Bankhead—"the divine Tallulah"—who rejoiced, "At last they got the last Red out of Columbia."

Getting the last red out of the presidency did not mean actually losing him from the institution. Butler had no intention of giving up his influence. He made all of this explicit at the trustees' meeting of October 1, the last one at which he spoke as president. Reminding the trustees of his conception of Columbia "as the intellectual center of this country and of the modern world," he instructed them what needed to be done to keep it that way. He returned to some of the plans he had revealed three years earlier about how he would use the Cromwell money: buy up all of Morningside Heights to withstand "the invasion which has been threatened by Harlem on the east and north"; purchase the blocks between 112th and 114th streets, Broadway to Amsterdam, thereby protecting against invasion from the south, and turn them into modern athletic fields, complete with a gymnasium on the northeast (a transaction that would require the city to close off these blocks to the public); acquire the remaining buildings currently not owned by Columbia on Claremont Avenue and Riverside Drive between 116th and 119th streets for faculty housing. The obligation for funding these (as well as all other) priorities, Butler grandly announced, would be his and his alone. Laying claim as a blind president emeritus to a vital responsibility he had neglected as a healthy president represented a brilliant preemptive strike to remain important in university affairs. No one seemed to care that it was destined to fail. If Butler wanted to pretend to raise money, that was all right with the trustees. Besides, he did add that he "should be only too delighted to have suggestions from others."

Replacing a legendary presence like Butler after forty-four years would be difficult in the best of circumstances, but for a board of trustees that had become used to being supine, it was almost impossible. They began plausibly enough: in May of 1945 a subcommittee chaired by Thomas Parkinson, the head of the Equitable Life Assurance Society, was formed to present a slate of names to the full board. In turn, a committee of seventeen administrators and professors, under the direction of Dean George Peagram, was created to recommend people to the Parkinson Committee. Within three months Peagram and his colleagues had put together a list of eight candidates—four from within Columbia. The Parkinson Committee, unimpressed with all of them except perhaps the recently elected senator from Arkansas, J. William Fulbright, dithered among themselves before finally asking Peagram to submit additional names.

Trustee indecision was not helped by Butler's insistence that he be involved in the selection. He was anxious above all that the long-suffering, loyal, hardworking but undistingiushed Provost Fackenthal might be picked. Butler urged them not to permit his "clerk" (pronounced "clark" in the British manner) to have the job. Butler needn't have worried, as the trustees, beyond appointing him Acting President after Butler's resignation, had no interest in Fackenthal for the permanent job.

They also had no interest in Butler's candidate, Dean Willard Rappleye of Columbia's College of Physicians and Surgeons, an ambitious, capable man who had served Butler's own ambitions well by giving him a distinguished medical school during the fourteen years of his deanship. Rappleye had alienated many during his hard-driving tenure, including faculty at the medical school itself, and the trustees wanted nothing to do with him. But he was the dean who had, in a sense, done the most for Butler, and Butler would have been personally comfortable with his appointment. The inappropriateness of his lobbying for his successor did not seem to occur to him. In the face of the search committee's opposition to Rappleye, Butler argued to Coykendall in January 1946 that he was "the only one who ought to be considered," adding that the university "is being very much criticized for its apparent lack of capacity to deal promptly with this vital question."

Butler was correct that the trustees' inability to decide was embarrassing Columbia. In May of 1946, a year after the search had begun, the Parkinson Committee rejected the second slate of names provided by Peagram. In December 1946 one candidate, Robert G. Sproul, president of the University of California at Berkeley, seemed to have emerged, but he added to the growing sense of Columbia's incompetence by announcing in a speech, once his name had publicly surfaced, that he would not leave Berkeley.

By May 1947, the Peagram Committee still had nothing to show for two years' efforts. Meanwhile, though his name had not been included in either of the two Peagram lists, General Dwight ("Ike") Eisenhower, chief of staff of the United States Army and leader of the Allied forces that had defeated the Germans, had been privately approached by Tom Watson, who was not a member of the Parkinson Committee. Watson was eager to capture Eisenhower's celebrity for Columbia, even if Ike had few qualifications for the position. Watson's enthusiasm for Eisenhower soon persuaded Parkinson that he was the only choice, and together they set about to convince Eisenhower—the trustees, looking more foolish with each passing day, didn't need much convincing—that Morningside Heights was the place for him. To interest Eisenhower, who was considering a variety of other positions, including the presidency of the Boy Scouts, and who had no desire to live in a city or immerse himself in complicated administrative details, they had to assure him that the job would make no demands: he would not have to bother with curriculum, faculty, or academic matters (these would be dealt with by the provost), involve himself in extensive social obligations, or be concerned with fund-raising. In short, if he would just agree to be Columbia's president he would not be expected to take on any of the responsibilities of a university president. Absolving Eisenhower of fund-raising activities was perhaps the oddest exemption granted him, particularly given Columbia's deteriorating fiscal condition, but Watson doubtlessly thought Eisenhower's name alone would be sufficient to attract money to Columbia. Despite his reservations, Eisenhower could not bring himself to turn down Watson's misleading vision of what the job entailed, and at a trustee meeting on June 24, 1947, Eisenhower was elected Columbia's thirteenth president. Although Butler had been insistent that the next president had to possess academic credentials and be familiar with the achievements of the university over the last fifty years, Eisenhower's national and international status compensated for the glaring absence of both these criteria, and he accepted Eisenhower's election without complaint.

The announcement of Butler's retirement from Columbia came as good news to the trustees of the Carnegie Endowment, who had been hoping for a number of years that Butler would relinquish their presidency. By the beginning of the 1940s his blindness and deafness had rendered him a total liability at their meetings. The agenda had to be read to him; he could not recognize people to speak, and when they did, their comments had to be summarized in a loud voice by the Endowment's secretary, Robert Lester, who sat by his side. But no degree of debilitation could cause him to resign, and the Endowment's trustees—not unlike Columbia's—couldn't bring themselves to inform him that he had to. They tried—thinking that the lawyer and politician "Wild Bill" Donovan, a wounded war hero and Congressional Medal of Honor winner in World War I and organizer in World War II of the Office of Strategic Services (OSS), might be tough and formidable enough for the job. Lester described the results of this effort:

> Wild Bill Donovan . . . was a man of considerable courage and standing in the world. He was chairman of the committee to go up and see Butler, and he did. He came back and reported to the committee of the Endowment, "Well, I've been faced with a good many difficult situations. I've done many unusual things. I've taken a great

many chances. But I find I am just not man enough to sit across a table from Nicholas Murray Butler and tell him that we want him to get out. So I didn't mention it to him." And Butler stayed on and on and on.

According to James Shotwell, it was Thomas Watson who summoned up his courage (for the second time) to do what Donovan couldn't accomplish. Working, in Shotwell's words, "with extreme delicacy through Mrs. Butler," he persuaded Butler to give up the presidency. At a regularly scheduled meeting of the Endowment on December 10, 1945, Butler announced his retirement, as both Endowment president and director of the Division of Intercourse and Education, explaining that his blindness had made it impossible for him to discharge his duties. As with his Columbia retirement, he made clear that he was not about to sever his connection with the Endowment. Thanking his colleagues for their confidence in selecting him as president for "twenty-two years, I think, to be exact" (he was off by two years), he pledged to remain active on the board for as long as he lived. This commitment did not please the trustees of either the Endowment or the Carnegie Corporation, who "devoutly wished," in Lester's words, that he would leave, but they responded graciously, and Tom Watson's motion that he be named "President Emeritus" was unanimously affirmed.

As president emeritus, he continued to insist that he alone knew what Carnegie wanted. At a trustee meeting in December 1946, before Alger Hiss had officially joined the Endowment as its next president, the board met to elect three new members. Before any names were presented for discussion, Butler declared that Carnegie had stated on several occasions that the directors of the three divisions should always serve as Endowment trustees, and he therefore moved that Malcolm Davis, his successor at the Division of Intercourse and Education, be chosen. Others objected that they already had a slate of thirteen highly qualified men, but Butler persisted: "My point is, Mr. Carnegie's instructions were so definite that I think it is my duty and the duty of the Trustees to carry them out and the Directors have always been Trustees." The argument was made that Davis was as yet simply an acting director, awaiting the arrival of the new president to confirm the appointment, but Butler brushed this aside. The new president couldn't possibly know how the Endowment had operated in the past: "He could only tell of the future, and I think we should obey Mr. Carnegie's instructions.

That is my point. I have always done so, and it has been done in the other Trusts, with the greatest care." Faced with Butler's tenacity, the board voted to defer the election until the next regularly scheduled meeting in May. The motion carried, with Butler voicing the only "nay." "Mr. Carnegie is traduced," he declared.

The winter of 1946–47 was grim for Butler, for reasons other than the obtuseness of the Endowment's trustees. In early January, Kate underwent cancer surgery. Complications and recovery required eight weeks in the hospital, followed by sustained bed rest at home. Kate's slow convalescence meant that Butler's social life, so much a vital part of his existence, had come to an end, only deepening the isolation that his blindness and deafness had imposed on him. Life with Kate alone was never much fun, and now Butler had to accommodate himself to the reality that there would no longer be other people around to listen to him. Kate's frailty, he complained to his son-in-law, Neville Lawrence, meant that "we cannot have guests either in New York or at Southampton during the summer months. This is an odd change but one necessitated by the facts."

The illnesses of the old, if not pleasant, are at least to be expected; the death of a child seems a violation of the natural rhythm, a calamity for which there can be no consolation. On February 14, 1947, Neville cabled Butler that Sarah had suffered a bad heart attack. Writing the next day, Neville assured him that they had excellent doctors who were doing everything possible to aid in her recovery. Butler was horrified and bewildered; his beloved daughter had left New York several weeks before in apparently good health. He wondered whether she had perhaps overtaxed herself during her visit, or whether she might have "felt a great shock when she returned to England because of conditions existing there as to heat, light and food supply." Butler's attempts to understand poignantly revealed the distress he was experiencing at the news. But there was no way to explain it and, unfortunately, nothing to be done. On February 21, Neville, "heart broken at having to write the letter," told Butler that Sarah died at 2:10 that morning. He tried to comfort him by insisting that her visit to New York had not been responsible: "It was all the outcome of her devoted work from 1939 onwards looking after and helping the wives of soldiers, the poor and the sick."

Butler's grief at Sarah's death was profound. Although separated by an ocean, the two had remained close, corresponding every week, and her loss simply reduced the master rhetorician to clichés of muteness. "I have no words to tell you what her passing means to me," he wrote to Neville three days later. "The whole episode is so tragic that I have no words with which to write about it. All I can do is to tell you that we think of nothing else and of you and Murray." Sensitive to Butler's pain, and confident of the pleasure he would take in his grandson, Neville said he hoped he could take young Murray over to visit with his grandfather as soon as possible. Neville and Kate had never gotten along (Neville, in fact, detested her), and the convoluted logic of Butler's response suggested the terror Kate could still inspire in her husband. He would love to see Murray, he replied to Neville, but not too soon. Kate was still weak, and as she would be unable to do with Murray all the things she would like to do, it was therefore best not to bring him at all. Honoring less Kate's physical health than her antipathy toward his family, Butler thus managed to avoid the pleasure that his grandson would surely have given him.

Three months later, on May 8, Butler attended what would be his last Endowment meeting. His capacities might have eroded, but not his combativeness, and he pushed hard for his two obsessions: making Malcolm Davis the permanent director of the Division of Intercourse and Education and getting the Carnegie Corporation to recognize its financial commitment to the Endowment. It was a sad way for the man who had spent thirty-five years at the Endowment, twenty as its president, to end his connection, and no one in the boardroom could have taken pleasure at what occurred. When Butler proposed that Davis be made permanent, he couldn't get anyone to second the motion—the first time such a thing had ever happened to him. And when he interrupted Alger Hiss's explanation of the Endowment's new policies and direction with his standard cry, "Mr. Carnegie's whole idea was that we had not only our own Endowment, but we were entitled to grants from the Carnegie Corporation. All you have to do is ask for a hundred thousand or more and you will get it," he heard in explicit terms that the two decades of haggling with the Corporation over funds had come to an end. Hiss said he was satisfied that the Endowment was not entitled to receive money from the Corporation for grants abroad or for general purposes. Henceforth, it would recognize its budgetary constraints by becoming more of an operating than a granting agency, focusing its efforts on supporting the United Nations and leaving the awarding of grants to better-funded agencies. A new era had begun, and as the Endowment started to distance itself from Butler's influence, his insistence that one of Carnegie's favorite remarks was "'Don't save; spend, and ask me for more'" would no longer be heard.

With Kate still recovering, the burdens of caring for Butler and his affairs during the summer of 1947 fell increasingly to his personal secretary, Roberta Parker. Spending the time in Southampton to be near the Butler summer cottage, she labored tirelessly over the endless details involved in getting him the secretarial, nursing, bookkeeping, and bill-paying help he needed. Since she managed this well, Butler was free to meddle in university affairs. He fussed, for example, over the proposed title for Professor Albert Jacobs, whom Fackenthal had chosen to help him in the administration. Butler objected strongly to Jacobs's being called "Assistant to the President," finding it insufficiently academic. Fackenthal pointed out that Butler had himself suggested such a title for Fackenthal in 1922, but Butler persisted: it was acceptable in business or industry, but not in a university. Butler relented only when other trustees and the Education Committee unanimously supported Fackenthal; shortly thereafter, Jacobs was named provost.

And then there were the petty narcissistic matters. Having arranged to have the Columbia University Press publish a pamphlet containing photostatic copies of three tributes he had recently received—from Elizabeth, New Jersey, where he was born; from Paterson, where he grew up; and from New York, where his career was based—he wanted to send copies to the trustees, to other officers of the university, and to libraries across the country. The estimated cost for mailing was $200, and in July he wrote Fackenthal that he would be pleased if the expense might be met out of moneys the acting president now controlled. "I suppose," he explained, lest the point be missed, "that the same funds exist that were at my disposal when in active service . . ." Fackenthal responded that he would be happy to take care of the bill.

The fall was taken up with the Butlers' preparations to vacate 60 Morningside for Mamie and Ike and to move to an apartment the trustees had purchased for them at 620 Park Avenue. To leave the house they had occupied for thirty-five years was difficult, made more difficult by the loss of power it signified. In November the Butlers held their usual fall reception for faculty and staff. Kate could not successfully disguise her feelings about giving up the home they had built, and she decided that the kindest thing she could do for the Eisenhowers was not to invite them: "I would not *dare* put him in with a crowd," she explained to Philip Hayden. Hayden's argument that failing to extend an invitation might be misconstrued finally convinced Kate, and the Eisenhowers were permitted to receive one. (They were unable—or chose not—to attend.) Writing to Neville about the reception's success, Butler confessed what the loss of 60 Morningside meant to him:

> I hope the General and Mrs. Eisenhower will make as good use of it as Mrs. Butler has done in the interests of the University and the social life of New York. We have had among our guests, three kings and when he was a cardinal, the present Pope, who is the only Pope ever to cross the Atlantic. We have also in our house book the names of about twenty-seven heads of governments and hundreds of the great names of our times. It has been a wonderful experience and will be remembered as long as life lasts.

It was not to last much longer. On Thanksgiving Day, while still at 60 Morningside, Butler was admitted to St. Luke's Hospital with a severe attack of "indigestion." Confined to the hospital for tests and observation, he developed bronchial pneumonia a week later. Although doctors remained optimistic about his chances for recovery, his condition suddenly worsened on Saturday, when he fell into a coma and was placed in an oxygen tent. With Kate and his two physicians present, he died early Sunday morning, December 7, 1947. For a man who was fascinated by numerical coincidences, he would have been pleased to know that December 7 was a resonant Columbia date on which to die: On that day in 1891, Morningside Heights was chosen as Columbia's future site, and in 1895 the cornerstone of Low Library was laid.

The New York Times managed to run a front-page obituary in the late editions of the paper on the day of his death, and a second front-page article on December 8, the day before the funeral. Butler had left instructions that he did not want his body to lie in state; it was taken after his death to his home until it was moved to Columbia's St. Paul's Chapel for the service. According to the police, seven thousand people came to the campus to pay their final tribute, a thousand of whom jammed into the seven-hundred-seat chapel and another thousand into the rotunda of Low Library, where a public-address system broadcast the proceedings; the rest lingered respectfully to witness the casket being borne from the chapel to Low Library and down the steps across South Court to the waiting hearse. General Eisenhower, who had first said he would not be able to come, thought better of it and was present, along with Governor Dewey, Bernard Baruch, Alger Hiss, and assorted other dignitaries. Condolences were received from statesmen, educators, politicians, and religious leaders throughout the world, as well as from Presidents Hoover and Truman. After the service, Butler was buried in the family plot in Paterson's Cedar Lawn Cemetery, near his mother and father. Out of a substantial estate, he left $100,000 to his grandson. There was no evidence to suggest that his death precipitated any change in the configuration of the Holy Trinity.

Kate survived him by five months. A second major operation in February 1948 could not arrest the spread of her cancer, and she died on May 5. She wanted to live longer. Bequeathing $2,000 each to her two physicians, she promised them double if she should "survive the date of this will by five years or more." As the will was drawn in February of 1948, they failed to collect their bonuses.

The Disappearance

✤

Fame, the ancients assure us, is fleeting—a morally salubrious notion that is patently false, as any acquaintance with human consciousness or human history demonstrates. But if one wanted to defend the proposition, the case of Nicholas Murray Butler would offer compelling evidence. The formidable "Dr. Butler" of the first half of the twentieth century, the man described by *The New York Times* at his death as "one of the best known Americans of his generation the world over," earned instant oblivion in the second half. How was it that the person who had achieved greatness, according to his friend Charles Hilles, because he embodied the aspirations of his times, should be so quickly forgotten?

There are a number of ways to account for his disappearance. In part, the times and values he had come to represent no longer appeared relevant in post–World War II America. The perfect expression of an era when, according to E. Digby Baltzell, "Anglo-Saxon Protestants and gentlemen-businessmen ruled the nation and the world," Butler endured to find himself a splendid anachronism. The trope for human excellence that he located in the figure of the "educated gentleman," his antidote to the dishonesty, incompetence, and vulgarity he saw encroaching everywhere, had lost its resonance in an age that had ceased to revere gentlemen or cultured WASPs. Butler's cohort of best men, those sophisticated, articulate, influential friends whose company he enjoyed at Morningside Drive—the country's aristocrats, whom Butler felt Democracy had to produce if it was to survive—had failed to set things straight, and their time had passed. Butler helped to guarantee his own obsolescence by steadfastly supplying to a world in flux an immutable set of moral and political nostrums regarding the dependable rationality of public opinion, the need for statesmen to keep their word, the importance of international courts and arbitration to mediate international disputes.

George Kennan's pejorative assessment of America's foreign policy during the first half of the twentieth century as being dominated by a "legalistic-moralistic approach to international problems" neatly defined the limitations in Butler's understanding of foreign relations. Butler never questioned his presumptions that nations should be as subject to moral law as individuals were, and that they should willingly submit to juridical processes to maintain world harmony. Admirable as these ideas might be, they failed to address the realities of power, the pressures of national self-interest, the pathologies of political leaders. Butler's model of international cooperation, based as it was on the complicated trade-offs and compromises that permitted thirteen American Colonies to form a federal government, was inadequate for the international complexities of the twentieth century. He could not get beyond the notion, as he announced in a 1943 radio broadcast, that the "social, economic and political principles such as underlie the federal government of the United States must be repeated and reconstituted on a world wide scale . . . if we are to teach the world the lesson which the American people and the American government have to teach. That is their function."

As a political pundit, then, he ended up preaching a stale message to a world that didn't listen to him. People, it turned out, were not always wiser than their governments, and public opinion not the moderating moral force Butler believed in. To the degree that the Carnegie Endowment helped project Butler's views across the globe, it too rendered itself essentially inconsequential. International Relations Clubs in schools and International Mind Alcoves in libraries didn't make the world a more comprehensible or more accessible place, any more than the confidential reports filed by Butler's foreign correspondents during the 1920s and '30s enhanced America's understanding of the realities of European politics and how to deal with them. Alger Hiss's impatient dismemberment of Butler's programs suggested his own frustration with Butler's ideas. Besides the specific rebuilding projects (Rheims, Louvain, the commune of Fargniers) after World War I, it was not obvious what Butler could point to as significant accomplishments during his three decades at the Endowment.

Nor, despite his impressive credentials as an educator, would one want to characterize him as any sort of significant educational theorist. He left behind no body of innovative thought for the academic profession to which his name might properly be attached. He was responsible, as we have seen, for important educational and administrative achievements, as founder and first president of Columbia's Teachers College, as the organizing presence behind the formation of the College Entrance Examination Board, as the force pushing for reform of New York City's public school system, but none of these seem to have helped him to be remembered. Indeed, when Butler was enjoying his 1940 numerical calculation that put him in the company of four of the twentieth century's most powerful political leaders, it is difficult to imagine that even he had in mind his early successes as a committed educator. In any case, the world has certainly forgotten them.

His one conspicuous and lasting monument, of course, is Columbia. Whatever his failings, and whatever the contributions of others, Columbia was Butler's university, its stature a result of Butler's ability to goad, inspire, and sell it. Had Butler retired as Columbia's president in 1926, when he announced that he had finally reached his goal of having men in "America, Europe, Asia and Africa" testify that Morningside Heights contained "the greatest body of scholars, men of science, teachers, trained investigators, personalities and public servants within the confines of the civilized world," or, Nobel Prize in hand, in 1932, when the university honored his seventieth birthday with its worldwide Butler Day festivities, his deserved reputation as a dynamic university builder would be intact. But he stayed—well past the time he should have gone, in the process jeopardizing the institution he had worked to make distinguished and tarnishing his image as its indomitable advocate and guiding spirit. As the legal scholar Walter Gellhorn put it, he gave up his status as an elder statesman, "instead . . . just becoming an elder." "He is losing his gifts," Butler's bibliographer (and director of the Columbiana archives), M. Halsey Thomas, entered in his diary in 1937:

> He should have resigned as president some time ago, but he can't realize his usefulness is over, that he really does not know what is going on around the university, and that he is doing harm to the place as long as he stays on. Columbia is marking time and going downhill at present, and will continue to do so as long as we are deprived of a new and young and able president.

The cultural significance Butler forged for himself during his career depended as much on his capacity to keep himself before the public as on the nature of his individual achievements. As long as the dedicated Butler press agency was pumping out endless copy and distributing it across the globe, he retained his visibility. Once it stopped functioning and the newspapers were not saturated with his daily pronouncements, there seemed nothing solid to fall back on. Neither exclusively one thing or another—as the *Times* obituary noted, he was simultaneously an "educator, politician, world statesman and publicist"—he made it easy for licensed historians of different subspecialties to overlook him as belonging to someone else's turf. With his own passing and the passing of the generation that supported his rise to power, "Dr. Butler," like Alice's Cheshire cat, has faded into nothingness, leaving behind not a smile—the last thing he would ever leave behind—but a glowing résumé, recording the bare facts of one of the remarkable lives of the twentieth century.

Notes

❧

Butler's Columbia University papers are located in two places: the Rare Book and Manuscript Library (RBML) in Butler Library, and the Central Archives (CA) in the Columbiana Room in Low Library. Unless otherwise indicated, all references to Butler's papers are to those in the RBML, cataloged under correspondent or subject. Material in unprocessed files is cited by the box number in which it appears. Transcripts from the Columbia Oral History Project (COHP) are available in the Oral History Office, Butler Library. Carnegie Corporation and Carnegie Endowment for International Peace papers are also located in the RBML.

Introduction: The Sage

4 "three most": Frankel, 10.
6 Double Crostic quotation of March 23, 1940: "No man in my time has been so happy and on the whole so successful in public life as Theodore Roosevelt. He took his official tasks very seriously, but he always took them and made certain that they did not take him."
6 "for the reason": *Philadelphia Record*, January 29, 1928.
7 "the greatest savant": Howard Osterhout to NMB, January 26, 1920, Butler papers.
7 "no man in": H. S. Pritchett to George French, April 30, 1929, Butler papers, Pritchett file.
7 "of all the": Elihu Root, speech at American Society of International Law, April 30, 1921, Butler papers.
7 "nothing of human": editorial, *New York Times*, October 8, 1931.
7 "one of the": Cass Gilbert, on NMB being named president of the American Academy of Arts and Letters in 1928, Butler papers, Box 4.
7 "one of the great": Welles Bosworth to NMB, February 17, 1937, Butler papers.
7 "the one outstanding": Andrew West to NMB, July 30, 1942, Butler papers.
7 "the master interpreter": Owen Young, Lotos Club File, December 3, 1930, Butler papers.

7 "the nation's greatest": Louis Wiley to NMB, November 22, 1929, Butler papers.

7 "the incarnate combination": J. B. Scott to NMB, December 21, 1932, Butler papers.

7 "the most brilliant": James R. Sheffield to NMB, May 10, 1936, Butler papers.

8 "The effulgence of": Cromwell to NMB, April 2, 1942, Butler papers.

8 "one of the": Pound to NMB, July 27, 1934, Butler papers.

8 "the representative": Sinclair, 29–30.

9 "instinctive greed": Sinclair, 33.

9 "Of Dr. Nicholas": *Daily Worker*, September 7, 1937.

9 "the five thousand": *The New Republic*, September 4, 1915, IV, 121–23.

9 "but to gasp": Lippmann, *A Preface to Politics*, 72.

9 "When the history": Mencken, *Prejudices*, Third Series, 1922, 213–14.

10 "by sheer force": comments made at Waldorf dinner of 1932 celebrating Butler's 30-50-70th anniversaries, Butler Day dinner file, CA.

11 "We have, as": cited in Carson W. Ryan, 3.

11 "perhaps the": Shils, 171.

11 "the beginning of": Butler, "DC Gilman, Builder of Universities," *Review of Reviews* (November 1908), 552.

12 "To be concerned": D. C. Gilman, "University Problems in the United States," 45.

12 "The foundation of": David Starr Jordan, *Care and Culture of Men*, 75.

13 "Such language": Flexner, *Universities, American, English, German*, 212.

14 "The greatest power": Mark Levine, "Ivy Envy," *New York Times Magazine*, June 8, 2003, 76.

14 "What was in": NMB to trustees, April 5, 1937, Butler papers, GB 1–376.

14 "that a man": Wall, 349–50.

14 "the originator of": *College Humor*, June 30, 1932.

15 "who can merely": *Elkand* (Indiana) *Truth*, August 1, 1936.

15 "radiant beings": *The New Yorker*, November 21, 1935, 12.

16 "truly Butleriolic": *American Educational Review*, January 1924.

18 "Public Sage": *Muscatine Journal*, April 7, 1937.

18 "productive narcissists": Michael Maccoby, "Narcissistic Leaders: The Inevitable Pros, the Inevitable Cons," *The Harvard Business Review*, October 15, 2000, 68–79.

19 " 'Talking with Dr.': Edward Smith to Butler, January 29, 1919, quoting comment made by Fred Carpenter, Butler papers.

19 "magic of": Pupin to A.V.W. Jackson, March 26, 1933, Butler papers.

19 "For him words": Roger Howson, Miner papers, RBML.

20 "There was": interview with James Russell, COHP.

20 "it was possible": cited in Amory, 39.

20 "interminable miasmas of": *The American Mercury*, 1935, 298.

20 "wherever windbags": *The American Review*, November 1934–March 1935, 240.

20 "in phrases that": *Modern Quarterly: A Journal of Radical Opinion*, May 1933, 209.

20 "even the semi-colons": Mitchell, 26.

20 "indigestion, alcoholism": Mitchell, 28–29.

20 "must perforce": *The New Republic*, September 29, 1917, 251.

21 "I did not": Hall to NMB, Butler papers, September 24, 1923.

21 "like a dome": *Champion* magazine, October 1916.

21 "burly of figure": *Glasgow Bulletin*, June 5, 1923.

21 "energy exudes": *London Times*, June 10, 1923.

22 "looks too much": Auchincloss, 5.

22 "a high priest": *Spokane Spokesman Review*, March 25, 1916.

22 "a human power": *Seattle Post-Intelligencer*, March 19, 1916.

23 "the three greatest": *New York Journal*, October 8, 1929. Rating by Ernest Dimmet, author of *The Art of Thinking*.

23 "among the five": *Macon* (Georgia) *Telegraph*, February 10, 1932.

23 "the best thinkers": *Times News* (Iowa), August 23, 1932.

23 "five greatest contemporaries": *Minnesota Tribune*, June 4, 1933. Poll taken of graduating seniors from University of Minnesota.

23 "four good after-dinner": *Brooklyn Eagle*, February 5, 1928.

23 "the two greatest": *Southern Literary Messenger*, September 1939.

23 "whom all high": *Hearst* (California) *News*, October 13, 1933.

23 "greatest living American": *The Piedmont* (South Carolina), March 14, 1935. Poll of University of South Carolina professors.

23 "You and Edison": Edward Marshall to NMB, Butler papers, May 25, 1928.

23 "He is unique": *Brooklyn Eagle*, April 4, 1937.

24 "speaks with": *Manchester* (England) *Evening Chronicle*, August 13, 1934.

25 "untrammeled, unspoiled": Wills, 311.

25 The chart is located in Butler papers, Box 7.

26 "the foremost American": *New York Times*, January 4, 1932. Remarks by Bainbridge Colby at Lotos Club dinner in honor of NMB. Lotos Club file, Butler papers.

1. Flying the Union Jack

27 "Speaking some years": Butler, *Across the Busy Years*, I, 20.

27 "I was the": Butler papers, Box 7.

29 "It is not": Butler, *Across the Busy Years*, I, 35.

30 "greatest and most": *The Carpet and Upholstery Trade Review*, June 1, 1931.

31 "You seem to": Chalmers to NMB, November 22, 1873, Butler papers, Box 2.

31 "I was sorry": ibid., November 22, 1874.

31 "It is not": Butler, *Across the Busy Years*, I, 35.

31 "my mother's memory": ibid., 40.

31 "This much can": ibid.

32 "to live in New York City": Meldrum to Mrs. Leslie Meldrum, January 5, 1863, Butler papers, Box 15.

32 "to have them": ibid., December 16, 1873.

32 "Henry's boys are": ibid., May 24, 1866.

32 "I am always": Meldrum to Mrs. William Lindsay Boase, November 5, 1873, Butler papers, Box 15.

32 "Her boys are": ibid., December 16, 1873.

33 "that you are": Mary Butler to NMB, June 16, 1869, Butler papers, Box 15.

33 "I am sorry": ibid., July 26, 1871.

33 Butler's high school entrance examination is in Butler papers, Box 6.

33 "too amusing to": "On Getting a Good Old-fashioned Education," *CU Quarterly*, June 1936, 74.

34 "instruction for the": Butler, *Across the Busy Years*, I, 50.

36 "a never-ending": ibid., 54.

36 "I hope you": Chalmers to NMB, November 22, 1873, Butler papers, Box 2.

37 "four books of": Butler, *Across the Busy Years*, I, 58.

37 "to name, beginning": "On Getting a Good Old-fashioned Education," 77.

40 "Boeotian fogyism": Strong diary, January 17, 1854. This quotation, and the three that follow, are all taken from a typed manuscript, in the Columbiana collection, of material about Columbia that the editors omitted from the published diary.

40 "I have come": ibid., October 1, 1855.

40 "It is the": ibid., March 3, 1856.

41 "Imbecility, stagnation": ibid., April 8, 1856.

41 "one day the": Barnard, 1866 presidential report.

41 "Dr. Agnew in": Potter to Fish, July 19, 1874, Fish papers, RBML.

42 "from the level": Barnard to Agnew, October 26, 1879, Barnard papers, RBML.

42 "a school for": Barnard to Agnew, May 17, 1880, ibid.

42 "You can't imagine": *Columbia Alumni News*, XV, no. 31 (May 23, 1924), 451.

42 "a very simple": Butler, *Across the Busy Years*, I, 75.

43 "I was very": Nicholas Murray to NMB, March 20, 1879, Butler papers, Box 15.

43 "Murray we see": Meldrum to Mrs. William Lindsay Boase, March 11, 1881, Butler papers, Box 15.

43 "was full of": H. T. Peck, "The President in College," *Columbia Spectator*, April 19, 1902, 4.

43 "brazen, mannish": *Acta Columbiana*, November 7, 1879, CA.

44 "'runs the racket'": NMB to Mary Butler, November 2, 1879, Butler papers, Box 6.

44 "The sophomores must": *Acta Columbiana*, April 9, 1880, CA.

45 "A few men": ibid., June 1, 1880.

45 "the battle of": Wall, 126.

46 "occasionally summoned me": Butler, *Across the Busy Years*, I, 72.

46 "This happened some": ibid., 72–73.

47 "became an enthusiastic": ibid., 74–75.

47 "Murray now 20": Meldrum to Mrs. William Lindsay Boase, March 28, 1882, Butler papers, Box 15.

48 "he is the": ibid., October 19, 1882.

2. *"An Indubitable Genius"*

50 "the requirements for": Butler, *Across the Busy Years*, I, 93.

50 "lacked form": ibid., 69.

51 "The study of logic": Barnard, 1884 presidential report.

51 "At certain intervals": ibid.

51 "I enclose you": NMB to Harris, December 27, 1882, Butler papers.

52 "a bare outline": *New York School Journal*, December 15, 1884, 577.

52 "I assume that": Butler, *Across the Busy Years*, I, 94.

53 "We discussed and": ibid., 100.

53 "the whole theory": ibid.

53 "every hour of": ibid., 128.

53 "without a critical": ibid., 127.

54 "sister-in-law": Mary Butler to NMB, August 18, 1884, Butler papers, Box 2.

54 "for your wedding": ibid., April 7, 1885.

54 "It is twelve": NMB to Alice Haven, October 21, 1885, Butler papers. Cataloged correspondence, Box I.

55 "If you and": ibid., December 5, 1884.

55 "I am constrained": ibid., March 6, 1885.

55 "But you may": ibid., January 10, 1885.

58 "divination is": ibid., August 7, 1885.

60 "My special reason": Alexander to Dix, June 23, 1885, correspondence re. Philosophy Department, 1885–90, Butler papers, Box 7.

61 "we have . . . just": Barnard to Dix, July 11, 1885, Butler papers, Box 8.

61 "Nicholas Murray Butler": Satterlee to Dix, July 18, 1885, Miner papers, RBML.

61 "I have urged": Barnard to NMB, July 16, 1885, Butler papers, Box 8.

62 "But work, work": NMB to Haven, November 21, 1885.

62 "to ask for": Alexander to NMB, December 20, 1885, Butler papers, Box 7.

63 "I feel quite": NMB to Haven, January 26, 1886, Butler papers. Cataloged correspondence, Box I.

64 "to shoulder his": Barnard to NMB, September 10, 1886, Butler papers, Box 7.

65 "'How am I": Terhune, 62–63.

67 "bright courageous young": Huntington, Introduction.

68 "to have the": Dodge, 7.

68 First Annual Report of the IEA in Teachers College Library.

69 "which is neither": Second Annual IEA Report, ibid.

69 "a trained and": Third Annual IEA Report, ibid.

70 "the work of": Butler, *Across the Busy Years*, I, 181.

71 "The recognition of": ibid.

72 "nobody knew who": "The Origins of Teachers College and the Horace Mann School," address at the fortieth anniversary luncheon of the Horace Mann School, January 22, 1927, Butler speeches, Box 3, Folder 15, CA.

72 "The whole history": ibid.

3. A University Is Born

76 "If you wish": C. B. Hulbert, *The Distinctive Idea in Education*, cited in Veysey, 24.
76 "The prominence given": Porter, 73.
76 "A well-stored": Barnard, 1880 presidential report.
78 "recognition of the": Gilman, *The Launching of a University and Other Papers*, 105.
79 "in which provision": Barnard, 1866 presidential report.
80 "how to live": Burgess, *Reminiscences of An American Scholar*, 29.
81 "a new faculty": Burgess, ibid., 87.
81 "the superior class": Barnard, 1888 presidential report.
82 "but by a": report of the faculty of the School of Arts, miscellaneous documents, vol. I, CA.
83 "We consider that": reply of minority, ibid.
84 "were, with a": Butler, *Across the Busy Years*, I, 143.
84 "You will be": NMB to Harris, April 15, 1890, Butler papers.
85 "one of my": Burgess, *Reminiscences of An American Scholar*, 216.
86 "the splendid university": *Harper's Weekly*, May 16, 1896, XL, 485–86.
86 University of Columbia: Columbia librarian Melvil Dewey shared Eliot's distaste for Butler's suggested name. Writing to Seth Low, he expressed his hope that "you will not depart from what I infer is your own preference . . . and let Butler's heresy of the University of Columbia college get any foothold . . . A man like Butler can figure out a theory, but you can not send sandwich men up and down the street to explain to the public, and the name is incomparably inferior to the straight "Columbia University." Dewey to Low, January 20, 1896, Low papers, CA.
87 "No one who": Burgess, "Reminiscences of Columbia University in the Last Quarter of the Century," *Columbia University Quarterly*, XV (September 1913), 329.

4. Educator

90 "the most important": Charles W. Eliot, *American Education Since the Civil War*, Rice Institute pamphlet, Vol. 9, no. 1 (1922), 13.
91 "the first such": Sizer, 146.
91 "great army of": quoted in Kliebard, 12.
91 "It must stand": "The Reform of Secondary Education," *The Century Magazine*, XLVII, no. 2 (June 1894), 314.
93 "The President of": Butler, *Across the Busy Years*, I, 199.
93 "This might never": ibid., 200.
94 "To him is": Fuess, 77.
95 "Field Marshal": Ravitch, *The Great School Wars*, 144.
96 "to keep fire": NMB to parents, February 29, 1893, Butler papers, Box 2.
97 "tall, slender and": Scott to NMB, August 31, 1933, Butler papers.
98 "catarrh was at": NMB to parents, May 7, 1893, Butler papers, Box 2.
98 "to remove the": ibid., July 18, 1893.

98 "A meeting of": quoted in Sol Cohen, 27.

101 "only the Bull": *Educational Review*, 10 (June 1895), 102.

101 "was a virtuoso": Hammack, *Power and Society*, 285.

101 "the reformers were": NMB to Low, February 7, 1896, Butler papers, CA.

102 "Mr. Pulitzer has": Van Rensselaer to NMB, December 4, 1895, Butler papers.

103 "local home government": *School*, March 14, 1895.

106 "Gradually, to my": Gilman papers, May 18, 1896, Milton S. Eisenhower Library, Special Collections, Johns Hopkins University.

106 "New York has": NMB to Gilman, May 20, 1896, ibid.

106 "What I want": Low to Gilman, May 21, 1896, ibid.

106 "at one blow": Harris to Gilman, May 25, 1896, ibid.

106 "To lose you": NMB to Gilman, May 23, 1896, ibid.

107 "The members of": NMB to Gilman, May 29, 1896, ibid.

107 "to redeem the": Whittemore, *Nicholas Murray Butler and Public Education*, 68.

108 "I do not propose": *New York Tribune*, April 1, 1899.

108 "the absurd and monstrous": *New York Times*, March 30, 1899.

108 "one of those": *St. Paul* (Minnesota) *Pioneer Press*, April 4, 1899.

109 "It is becoming": *Milwaukee Sentinel*, February 10, 1899.

109 "President Little has": *New York Post*, April 6, 1899.

114 "I have read": NMB to Shepard, October 14, 1910, Butler papers.

114 "Personally I cannot": NMB to Brown, November 5, 1910, Butler papers.

114 "has not been": *Chicago Tribune*, November 23, 1910.

115 "I cannot understand": Young to Brown, January 21, 1911, Butler papers.

115 "I came on": *Chicago Tribune*, January 24, 1911.

115 "I am too": *Chicago Record Herald*, January 24, 1911.

116 "I am sorry": NMB to Shepard, July 1, 1911, Butler papers.

5. The Twelfth President

118 "The supposition that": *Educational Review*, XVI (November 1898), 406–7.

119 "I think that": questions put to him by Roger Howson, April 3, 1940, Miner papers, RBML.

119 "He would make": NMB to TR, February 23, 1900, presidential correspondence volumes, RBML.

119 "While Mr. Low": NMB to Holls, August, 15, 1901, Butler papers.

120 "in view of": Pine to NMB, April 6, 1917, Pine papers, CA.

120 "surprised and not": NMB to Low, May 2, 1893, Butler papers, CA.

120 "Alma Mater is": Low to NMB, May 22, 1893, ibid.

121 "apparently a haphazard": NMB to Low, October 18, 1894, ibid.

121 "so that you": Low to NMB, November 2, 1894, ibid.

122 "simply absurd": NMB to Low, July 3, 1897, ibid.

122 "would hurt": NMB to Low, July 5, 1897, ibid.

122 "only consolation is": NMB to Low, July 5, 1897, ibid.

122 "It is a": NMB to Low, July 21, 1897, ibid.

122 "Your own letter": Low to NMB, July 15, 1897, ibid.

123 "I am not": NMB to Low, July 21, 1897, ibid.

123 "accede to your": West to NMB, July 15, 1897, ibid.

123 "Had the situation": NMB to West, July 20, 1897, ibid.

125 "you believe it": NMB to Low, July 31, 1897, ibid.

125 "Seth Low . . . hated": George McAneny, COHP.

126 "Now the leaders": *Philadelphia Press*, September 26, 1897.

126 "Columbia University cannot": *New York Times*, November 8, 1901.

126 "Professor Butler is": William Schermerhorn to Pine, September 26, 1901, Rives papers, CA.

127 "If I am correct": Pine to Low, November 23, 1901, Butler papers, CA.

127 "the advocate of": Low to Pine, November 2, 1901, Low papers, CA.

128 The others endorsed: all these letters in Pine papers, CA.

129 "I have never": Low to Dix, December 26, 1901, Butler papers, CA.

129 "mature deliberation and": Columbia College papers, December 30, 1901, RBML.

129 "Your letter to": Pine to Low, January 3, 1902, Pine papers, CA.

130 "make my excuses": Low to Pine, January 4, 1902, Columbia College papers, RBML.

130 "The morning after": George McAneny, COHP.

130 "was influenced somewhat": Columbia College papers, February 3, 1902, RBML.

132 editorial writers tended: the following quotations come from the 1902 volume of NMB's clippings in RBML.

132 "When Mr. Butler": *Paterson News*, November 11, 1901.

132 "Nicholas Murray Butler": ibid., October 9, 1901.

133 "perambulating sycophant and": Mencken, *Prejudices*, first series, 1919, 82.

133 "an itinerant dispensary": Veblen, 285.

134 "the fanciest ear-benders": Mitchell, 8–9.

134 "if the Higher": *School*, February 21, 1895.

135 "The surest pledge": Theodore T. Munger, "A Significant Biography," *Atlantic Monthly*, 96 (October 1905), 561.

6. *"Great Personalities Make Great Universities"*

137 "What we do": NMB's concluding address at Columbia's 175th anniversary convocation, October 1, 1929, Butler papers, Box 210.

138 "seeking a multi-voiced": Bender, 279.

138 "the Governors of": Pine, 12.

138 "in all respects": ibid., 46.

139 "There is now": miscellaneous documents, 1891–1905, vol. 2, CA. Columbian University began as Columbian College in 1821, graduating its first class in 1824. In 1873 Congress rechartered it as Columbian University. It became George Washington University in 1904.

139 "possible complications growing": ibid.

139 "authoritative, expert": Bender, 284.

139–40 "Every city": Butler, *Scholarship and Service*, 14.

140 "would add to": NMB to Rives, June 23, 1911, Rives papers, CA.

140 "does not appeal": Rives to NMB, July 9, 1911, ibid.

140 "In plainest language": 1902 presidential report.

142 "You are in": NMB to August Belmont, December 1, 1902, Butler papers, CA.

143 "Few things are": Roosevelt to NMB, January 12, 1903, presidential correspondence volumes, RBML.

143 "great cities of": NMB to Rockefeller, February 5, 1903, Butler papers, CA.

144 "intention and purpose": NMB to Morgan, February 8, 1906, Butler papers, CA.

144 "under no actual": Morgan to NMB, February 15, 1906, Butler papers, CA.

145 "that any other": Low memorandum, "In Relation to the Hospital Land Directly to the South of the University," Low papers, CA.

146 "I find myself": Butler, 1902 presidential report.

147 "It would tend": Hobart College file, CA.

148 "in increasingly close": Butler, 1902 presidential report.

150 "It is not": *Columbia Spectator*, April 29, 1902.

151 "First, there must": transcript of Butler interview with Sutton, Woodberry papers, RBML.

153 "that I think": Woodberry to Spingarn, January 14, 1904, Woodberry papers, RBML.

154 "somewhat the nature": *New York Tribune*, February 9, 1904.

154 "I was wasting": ibid., February 3, 1904.

154 "as I was": *Evening Post*, February 10, 1904.

155 "as an offense": trustees to MacDowell, March 7, 1904, MacDowell papers, CA.

155 "a man's": MacDowell to trustees, March 11, 1904. Copy in Pine papers, CA.

7. An Old Shoe

156 "simple and direct": Fabian, 11.

157 "We might as": Carnegie, *Gospel of Wealth*, 19.

157 "I cannot understand": Carnegie to NMB, April 26, 1902, Butler papers.

157 "It rather pleases": NMB to Carnegie, April 28, 1902, ibid.

159 "to take under": NMB to Carnegie, April 4, 1908, ibid.

160 "strength and prowess": Eliot to Lucian Ward, December 16, 1902, Eliot papers, Harvard University.

160 "makes athletics impossible": NMB to Albert Shaw, October 28, 1909, Butler papers.

160 "moral and educational": *Review of Reviews*, vol. 33 (1906), 71–72.

160 "Columbia has gained": ibid.

161 "sheer hypocrisy": NMB to Carnegie, January 30, 1908, Carnegie papers, Library of Congress.

163 one historian: Patterson, 130.

164 "a magnificent appeal": Butler, *Across the Busy Years*, II, 87.

164 "had persuaded": ibid., 90.

165 "By persistent public": cited in Fabian, 31.

165 "I feel that": Carnegie to NMB, January 11, 1908, Carnegie papers, Library of Congress.

166 The new document: "Proposed Plan for the Establishment of a Carnegie International Institute," submitted by NMB with covering note, April 6, 1909, Carnegie papers, Library of Congress.

167 "But I do": see Fabian, 12.

167 "No words from": Fabian, ibid.

168 "believe that the": Butler, *The International Mind*, 73.

169 "the fundamental laws": Butler, *Why Should We Change Our Form of Government?*, 29.

169 "Who is it": ibid., 16.

170 "to regulate or": Butler, *The American as He Is*, 37.

170 "fixed and permanent": ibid., 38.

170 "The American cares": ibid., 39–40.

170 "hold fast with": ibid., 50.

171 "I would try": "Higher Preparedness," November 27, 1915, reprinted in Butler, *A World in Ferment*, 108–9.

171 "is nothing else": reprinted in Butler, *The International Mind*, 102.

8. Teddy Roosevelt and a Horse Called Nicoletta

172 "I suppose the": TR to NMB, October 12, 1901, Butler's presidential correspondence volumes, RBML.

172 "for I am": NMB to TR, October 14, 1901, ibid.

174 "Some one said": Sullivan, *Our Times*, volume I, *The Turn of the Century*, 88.

175 "To put you": NMB to TR, May 1, 1900, ibid.

176 "If you will": Butler, *Across the Busy Years*, I, 230.

176 "every friend of": ibid.

176 "The best we": quoted in Morris, 767.

177 "Words cannot express": NMB to TR, September 14, 1901, presidential correspondence volumes, RBML.

177 "I wish to": TR to NMB, September 14, 1901, ibid.

177 "Our intimacy was": Butler, *Across the Busy Years*, I, 312.

178 "He was not": *Review of Reviews*, October 1901, 435.

178 "against the urgent": ibid., 438.

178 "This strong, honest," ibid.

179 "I liked your": TR to NMB, October 1, 1901, presidential correspondence volumes, RBML.

180 "I simply report": NMB to TR, June 27, 1903, ibid.

180 "I hope to": TR to NMB, May 1, 1902, ibid.

180 "I most earnestly": TR to NMB, December 5, 1902, ibid.

180 "I should be": NMB to TR, March 26, 1903, ibid.

180 "In view of": NMB to William Loeb, March 23, 1903, ibid.

181 "provided appearances": NMB to TR, June 1, 1903, ibid.

181 "to create a": NMB to TR, June 3, 1903, ibid.

181 "some typical Jewish": TR to NMB, June 3, 1903, ibid.

181 "The dog has": TR to NMB, November 4, 1903, ibid.

181 "The danger": NMB to TR, November 4, 1903, ibid.

181–82 "Wall Street": NMB to TR, December 11, 1903, ibid.

182 "the diabolical skill": NMB to TR, January 2, 1904, ibid.

182 "Your relation to": NMB to TR, February 24, 1904, ibid.

183 "I am so": TR to NMB, May 27, 1904, ibid.

183 "absolutely the best": *Review of Reviews*, May 1904, 37.

183 "intuitive insight into": ibid., 39.

183 "emphasize its attractiveness": ibid., 42.

184 "'Standard Oil' tag": NMB to TR, August 4, 1904, presidential correspondence volumes, RBML.

184 "get the Standard": TR to NMB, August 6, 1904, ibid.

185 "No one in": *Philadelphia Press*, August 26, 1904.

186 Had he wanted the money: NMB to TR, August 28, 1904, presidential correspondence volumes, RBML.

186 "one of the": NMB to TR, November 19, 1904, ibid.

187 "wreck the whole": *Chicago Globe*, October 22, 1907.

189 "fond enough of": NMB to TR, February 4, 1907, presidential correspondence volumes, RBML.

189 "steadily growing": TR to NMB, February 6, 1907, ibid.

192 "I weigh my": "Politics and Business," reprinted in Butler, *Why Should We Change Our Form of Government?*, 82.

192 "change our representative": ibid., 4.

193 "The movement to": ibid., 14.

193 "much more than": ibid., 40.

193 "leads, in my": ibid., 47–48.

194 "refined and developed": *New York American*, April 10, 1912.

194 "the most astounding": *Boston Globe*, April 10, 1912.

195 "Roosevelt is no": *New York Press*, June 16, 1912.

196 "the greatest crisis": *New York Times*, June 25, 1912.

196–97 "not only as": *New York Times*, January 5, 1913.

9. *"Dear Tessie"*

199 "was morally certain": NMB to Rives, August 14, 1910, Butler papers, CA.

200 "He moved slowly": NMB to Rives, ibid.

201 The papers delighted: The following quotations all come from clippings in the Peck file, RBML.

201 "The newspaper men": NMB to Pine, July 4, 1910, Butler papers, CA.

201 "Knowledge of this": ibid.

202 "Peck's utter degeneracy": Pine to Rives, July 1, 1910, Pine papers, CA.

202 "disturbed by the": Matthews to NMB, July 4, 1910, Peck file, CA.

202 "You are cutting": NMB to Pine, July 4, 1910, Butler papers, CA.

202 "I have in": NMB to Pine, July 13, 1910, ibid.

202 "Of course, he": NMB to Pine, July 19, 1910, ibid.

203 "They revealed to": NMB to Arrowsmith, October 6, 1910, Butler papers.

203 "completely misled": Pine to NMB, July 11, 1910, Butler papers, CA.

203 "honor of the": NMB to Rives, September 22, 1910, ibid.

204 "Rives writes me": NMB to Pine, September 22, 1910, ibid.

204 "He is human": Arrowsmith to NMB, September 21, 1910, Peck file, CA.

204 "precisely the same": Peck to Arrowsmith, September 23, 1910, ibid.

204 "'Blackmail, backed up": Peck to trustees, September 21, 1910, Peck file, RBML.

205 "that the disagreeable": NMB to Pine, October 4, 1910, Butler papers, CA.

205 "best thing for": NMB to Pine, October 12, 1910, ibid.

205 "From my personal": NMB to Egbert, July 14, 1911, ibid.

206 "Harry is a": C. E. Bennett to Arrowsmith, April 19, 1913, Peck file, CA.

206 "a probably beginning": Caples to William Maxwell, July 29, 1913, ibid.

208 "I shall touch": Peck to NMB, October 31, 1913, ibid.

208 "it would be": NMB to Peck, December 15, 1913, Butler papers, CA.

209 "be surprised to": NMB to Pine, July 13, 1910, ibid.

209 Mrs. Peck 1: *New York American*, March 24, 1914.

210 "a natural anarchist": quoted in Van Deusen, 49.

211 "It appears that": memorandum of conversation with President Butler on reorganization of Comparative Literature Department, February 29, 1904, Butler papers, Box 8.

211 "While I dare": NMB to Spingarn, October 1, 1908, Butler papers.

212 "If the Trustees": Spingarn to NMB, February 3, 1910, Butler papers.

214 "I observe": NMB to Spingarn, February 3, 1911, in Spingarn.

214 "differences were amicably": ibid., Introduction.

214 "A threat that": Spingarn to NMB, February 8, 1911, ibid.

215 "He has stifled": *New York American*, April 10, 1911.

215 "A resolution introduced": NMB to Arrowsmith, April 1, 1911, Spingarn file, CA.

215 "sycophancy is a": Spingarn, 5.

216 "the word or": ibid., 8.

10. Mr. Butler's Asylum

218 "confidently predict international": *New York World*, January 24, 1912.

218 "the most far-sighted": *Providence* (Rhode Island) *Bulletin*, November 13, 1907.

222 "What the world": Butler, *The Basis of a Durable Peace*, 66.

223 "areas of jurisdiction": ibid., 95.

223 "As a matter": ibid., 102–03.

223 "domestic policies of": ibid., 122.

224 "Perhaps it would": CEIP Conferences, January 17, 1917, Box 138.

224 "I think it": ibid., February 17, 1917.

225 "What had been": *Columbia Alumni News*, VIII (July 1917), 883.

227 "a better president": Cattell to Gilman, June 2, 1884, Gilman papers, Johns Hopkins University.

227 "the twenty leading": Thorndike to NMB, May 12, 1913, Cattell file, CA.

227 "democracy of scholars": Cattell, *University Control*, 61.

227 "I once incited": ibid., 31.

228 "So long as": Pine to NMB, March 20, 1911, Butler papers.

228 "He is at": ibid.

229 "the expression of": Cattell to Rives, May 13, 1913, Cattell file, CA.

229 "there could be": ibid.

229 "are not free": Low to Rives, May 19, 1913, Cattell file, CA.

231 "If our many-talented": confidential memo, ibid.

232 "I had a": NMB to Pine, September 19, 1917, Samson file, CA.

233 "as much beyond": Cattell, *Memories of My Last Days*, 14.

234 "the impossibility of": Seligman papers, RBML.

234 "It is impossible": Seligman, memo to trustee subcommittee, June 18, 1917, Seligman papers, RBML.

235 "I do not": Kahn to NMB, August 27, 1917, Butler papers.

235 "lessened the power": COI to NMB, September 19, 1917, Butler papers.

235 "Words without deeds": NMB to Bangs, September 19, 1917, Bangs papers, CA.

235 "We have got": Pine to NMB, September 21, 1917, Pine papers, CA.

235 After twenty-six: Cattell later brought suit against Columbia seeking his pension benefits. Columbia settled before going to trial.

236 "the University is": Columbia *Alumni News*, IX (October 12, 1917), 59.

236 "As every man": *New York Times*, October 10, 1917.

237 "If Columbia University": NMB to Lawrence, October 23, 1917, Cattell file, CA.

238 "It is certainly": cited in Gruber, "Academic Freedom at Columbia University, 1917–1918: The Case of James McKeen Cattell," reprinted from the September 1972 *AAUP Bulletin*, 303.

238 "The source of": Woodbridge to NMB, November 22, 1917, Cattell file, CA.

238 "the conscious commission": NMB to Williams, March 5, 1917, Ryskin file, CA.

241 "'a Tammany politician'": cited in Bonner, xv.

241 "the vainest human": ibid., 230.

241 "We deem all": cited in Lamb, 130.

242 "this most notable": ibid., 262.

243 "war against war": *Columbia Spectator*, July 13, 1917.

243 "prepare to arm": *San Francisco Examiner*, August 9, 1917.

243 "What are they": *New York Times*, September 28, 1917.

245 "It is a": CEIP conference, October 25, 1918, Box 138.

245 "Get all the": ibid., November 14, 1918.

245 "These interesting and": Butler, *Across the Busy Years*, II, 122.

11. At Home—and Away

247 "a formal reception": Roger Howson, "Personal and Disjointed View on President Butler and his Presidency," Miner papers, RBML.

247 "exactly such a": NMB to Pine, March 7, 1911, president's house file, CA.

248 "who finds it difficult": Pine to NMB, September 30, 1911, ibid.

248 "clearing house": *The New Yorker*, November 15, 1930, 233.

248 "New York City's": *New York Journal American*, April 10, 1942.

249 "just about as": interview with George Ford, COHP.

249 "plates were changed": interview with Alan Nevins, COHP.

250 "champagne salesman": Mary Brown, conversation with author, March 16, 1994.

250 "utterly undetectable": Jacques Barzun to author, October 14, 1996.

250 "from the word": Mary Brown to author, March 16, 1994.

251 "'Before I can": Gildersleeve, 400.

251 "Sarah, you shouldn't": Lindsay Rogers, COHP.

253 "going up to": Associated Press interview with NMB, 1943.

255 Requests for information from Mudge and Winchell in Butler papers, Boxes 20 and 21.

257 "strongholds of our": Baltzell, 369.

258 "not a game": *New York Sun*, November 20, 1913.

258 "Golf has changed": "A Golfing Intellectual," *The American Golfer*, January 1945, 22.

258 In 1998: *New York Times* Business Section, May 31, 1998.

259 "of exceptional importance": Butler, *Across the Busy Years*, II, 423.

259 "both went": Chronicle of the Gin Mill Club, Butler papers.

260 "If you have": Annin to NMB, December 1, 1925, Butler papers.

261 "It seems to": NMB to Annin, December 4, 1926, ibid.

261 "what had": NMB to Annin, August 1, 1929, ibid.

261 "More of it": Annin to NMB, August 14, 1929, ibid.

261 "Think what": NMB to West, August 19, 1929, ibid.

261 "The contributions": West to NMB, September 2, 1929, ibid.

262 "an amorphous entity": roster of the Round Table Dining Club by Brander Matthews,
ibid.

263 "Perhaps the nearest": *Scribner's Magazine* XCVII, no. 2 (August 1935), 97.

263 "The Round Table," February 3, 1933, Butler papers.

264 "was to induce": Butler, *Across the Busy Years*, II, 425–26.

264 "replied that he": Ryder, 207.

265 "the best": Butler, *Across the Busy Years*, II, 424.

266 "to set standards": NMB speech of November 13, 1930, American Academy archives.

266 "Stuffed imbecile": quoted in Updike (ed.), 97.

266 "[Carl] Sandburg, a wretched": ibid.

269 "We are grown": announcement quoted in Sides, 41.

269 "Tacked to": Sides, 58.

270 "It disturbs me": NMB to Redding, June 13, 1898, Butler papers.

271 "one of the": Butler, *Across the Busy Years*, II, 422.

271 "to say that": ibid., 421.

271　"Bohemia means": NMB to Landfield, August 11, 1941, Butler papers.

271　"renowned and world": telegram from Crocker to NMB, informing him of election, October 16, 1918, Butler papers.

12. "Pick Nick for a Picnic in November"

274　"a wooden man": NMB to Lord Bryce, November 16, 1920, Butler papers.

275　when Mills began: Mills's remarks in 1920 Proceedings of Republican National Convention, 156–60.

277　"Accept my thanks": NMB to Marshall, February 25, 1915, Butler papers.

277　"it is on": Alexander to NMB, May 25, 1915, ibid.

277　"has been retailing": NMB to Alexander, June 14, 1915, ibid.

277　"You have made": Pritchett to NMB, September 4, 1918, ibid.

278　"clear vision": Smith to NMB, December 19, 1918, ibid.

278　"by the suggestions": NMB to Smith, December 23, 1918, ibid.

278　"under the handicap": Murphy to NMB, December 21, 1918, ibid.

279　"Quite apart from": NMB to Murphy, December 23, 1918, ibid.

279　"If there is": Marshall draft letter to C. H. Clark of Hartford Courant, July 13, 1919, ibid.

280　"Laugh and the": Marshall to NMB, February 11, 1919, ibid.

280　"some tenement section": Marshall to NMB, December 31, 1919, ibid.

281　"select as delegates": NMB to Smith, January 24, 1919, ibid.

282　"the holy effort": Marshall to NMB, October 29, 1919, ibid.

282　"you are the": Osterhout to NMB, February 25, 1919, ibid.

282　"is principally journalistic": draft of Marshall letter sent to Charles Scott, June 2, 1919, ibid.

283　"the common man": Attorney General Langer to Marshall, July 5, 1919, ibid.

283　"You will be": NMB to Osterhout, July 7, 1919, ibid.

284　"the one fact": Butler, Is America Worth Saving?, 9.

284　"the wage earner": ibid., 14.

285　"Our task": from speech "The High Cost of Living," ibid., 109.

285　"Take away": from speech "The Republican Party—Its Present Duty and Opportunity," ibid., 249.

285　"Oh, my friends": ibid., 250.

286　"our candidate is": Davies to NMB, August 16, 1919, Butler papers.

286　"thoroughly representative": NMB to Stephen Olin, October 3, 1919, ibid.

286　Davies comments from New York Times, December 24, 1919.

287　"I really do": NMB to Osterhout, January 6, 1920, ibid.

288　"has practically disappeared": NMB to Suzzallo, February 9, 1920, ibid.

289　"the situation": NMB to Suzzallo, April 30, 1920, ibid.

289　"the dance ": NMB to Smith, May 3, 1920, ibid.

289　"an Eastern man": Syracuse Post Standard, May 13, 1920.

289　"If I were": NMB to Thomas Proctor, May 13, 1920, ibid.

290　"One strong man": New York Evening Post, June 5, 1920.

290 "This is no": *Chicago Tribune*, June 7, 1920.

291 "about eleven minutes": *New York Times*, February 21, 1920.

291 "constant assurances": *New York Times*, June 8, 1920.

293 "It was": quoted in Sullivan, *Our Times: The Twenties*, 61.

293 "There ain't": quoted in Russell, 383.

294 "We three were": Butler, *Across the Busy Years*, I, 279.

294 "The New York Times": NMB to Olin, June 17, 1920, Butler papers.

295 "The chief task": For all of Butler's comments, see *The New York Times* of June 15, 1920.

295 "The statement is": *New York Times*, June 16, 1920.

296 "Answering your telegram": *New York Times*, June 23, 1920.

296 "Against my better judgment": NMB to Crocker, June 21, 1920, Butler papers.

296 "skillful and untiring": NMB to Charles Hilles, June 14, 1920, Butler papers.

13. *"Kid" Butler, the Columbia Catamount, vs. "Wild Bill" Borah, the Boise Bearcat*

297 "my time and": NMB to Harding, June 15, 1920, Butler papers, presidential correspondence volumes.

297 "good-natured": Butler, *Across the Busy Years*, I, 410.

298 "he said that": *Erie* (Pennsylvania) *Dispatch Herald*, October 21, 1945.

298 "looking at him": The exchange between Harding and Butler is in Butler, *Across the Busy Years*, I, 397–98.

299 "out of the": NMB to Harding, June 8, 1921, Butler papers.

300 "Was Nicholas Murray": Butler, *Across the Busy Years*, II, 123.

300 "The enclosed is": The memo to Marshall is in Butler papers, Box 6.

302 "pipe dream": *Montreal Gazette*, January 25, 1947.

302 "There is not": *Montreal Star*, January 23, 1947.

303 "endeavor to show": statement originally appeared in *New York Tribune*, February 27, 1919. Later reprinted as "Aloofness Is Impossible" in Butler, *Is America Worth Saving?*

303 Butler responded: NMB's letter to Hale of May 19, 1919, Butler papers.

304 "Do not forget": NMB to Kellogg, November 30, 1925, ibid.

305 "In their great": NMB to Coolidge, August 8, 1923, presidential correspondence volumes.

305 "The general feeling": NMB to Prince, February 5, 1926, ibid.

305 "During the past": NMB to Pritchett, September 4, 1928, ibid.

305 "The political situation": NMB to William Butler, May 23, 1932, ibid.

306 "The plain fact": NMB to Prince, May 15, 1924, ibid.

306 "One of the": *New York Telegram*, June 6, 1930.

307 "At the risk": Kirby to NMB, October 4, 1932, Butler papers.

307 "I have been": NMB to Kirby, October 4, 1932, ibid.

308 "the most intelligent": *New York Times*, May 20, 1932.

310 "It seemed almost": quoted in Behr, 238.

310 "I regard": NMB to Edwin Mead, March 7, 1927, Butler papers.

310 "So wet": *Waltham* (Massachusetts) *Tribune*, February 9, 1927.

310 "wetter than the": *St. Paul* (Minnesota) *Pioneer Press*, February 20, 1927.

310 "most responsible": *New York Times*, December 7, 1933.

311 "to take": Butler, *Faith of a Liberal*, 125.

311 In a passionate: speech reprinted in Butler, *Faith of a Liberal*, 271–82, from which the following quotations are taken.

311 "I should be": NMB to Pierre du Pont, January 7, 1930, Butler papers.

314 "more than half": *Pittsburgh Gazette Times*, June 1, 1925.

314 "with the boot-leggers": *New York Times*, February 13, 1927.

314 "should be tried": *Birmingham* (Alabama) *News*, March 12, 1927.

315 "In 1928 no": *New York Times*, February 8, 1927.

320 "It is primarily": The full texts of the Butler and Borah speeches are in Butler's papers on Prohibition in RBML, Box 209.

321 "of two of": *Watertown Times*, April 9, 1928.

321 "I suppose": *Syracuse Journal*, April 9, 1928.

322 "Resolved, all": *Binghampton Press*, January 25, 1928.

322 "of all those": *New York Times*, January 13, 1936.

322 "then it is": *Dayton News*, January 15, 1936.

322 "for reasons entirely": *New York Herald-Tribune*, June 5, 1936.

323 "The consideration of": *New York Times*, June 15, 1928.

324 "the clown show": *The Nation*, July 27, 1928.

325 "Dr. Butler's": *New York Times*, August 20, 1928.

325 "The New York": *New York Herald-Tribune*, August 21, 1928.

325 "the most extraordinary": *New York Telegram*, August 21, 1928.

326 "acquire a great": NMB to Pierre du Pont, November 12, 1928, Butler papers.

326 "to live in": *Boston American*, August 24, 1929.

327 "the only bootleggers": Kobler, 324.

327 "We haven't": Kobler, 327.

328 "Wet leaders": *New York Times*, June 6, 1932.

329 "There is something": ibid.

329 "It is a": ibid., June 13, 1932.

329 "worst plan": ibid, June 15, 1932.

330 "political blunder of": *New York Herald-Tribune*, June 19, 1932.

330 "all the saloon": *Detroit Times*, October 30, 1932.

330 "an infectious": *New York Herald-Tribune*, June 21, 1932.

330 "as sane and": *Fort Wayne Journal Gazette*, November 20, 1932.

14. "Jastrow Is, I'm Sorry to Say, a Hebrew"

332 "a most terrible": Horowitz, 231.

333 "is, I'm sorry": NMB to Low, August 26, 1897, Butler papers, CA.

333 "Do you not": NMB to Pine, December 14, 1909, Pine papers, CA.

333 "if he had": NMB to Pine, December 16, 1913, Butler papers, CA.

333 "leaders for anarchistic": NMB to Rives, November 13, 1913, Rives papers, CA.

333 "Personally, he is": NMB to McBain, February 14, 1934, Butler papers.

333 "could discover nothing": McBain to NMB, February 14, 1934, Butler papers.

333 "in regard to": Pine to NMB, November 8, 1902, Pine Papers, CA.

335 "escape . . . from": NMB to Jones, April 3, 1909, Jones papers, CA.

335 "I told him": Keppel to NMB, September 15, 1910, Keppel papers, CA.

336 "makes no discrimination": Low to trustee Education Committee, January 31, 1911, Low papers, CA.

337 "and it might": Keppel to NMB, January 27, 1912, Keppel papers, CA. Butler's 1912 presidential report, declaring Columbia's need "for more men, not fewer, who pursue a college course with no vocational aim in view, but who wish to furnish the mind for enjoyment, for happiness and for worth in later years," was another way of addressing the problem. Those wishing to go to college to become "liberally educated gentlemen" were not likely to be professionally ambitious Jews.

337 "To put it": Keppel to NMB, May 13, 1913, Keppel papers, CA.

337 "particularly desirable": NMB to Jones, November 19, 1913, Jones papers, CA.

338 "One of the": Keppel, 180.

338 "desirable students": ibid., 180.

339 "rapidly increasing in": Butler made no effort to conceal his enthusiasm for the former. Addressing the freshman class in the fall of 1916, he emphasized that "among all the purposes for which the College exists, and among all the things that it has done for nearly a hundred and sixty-five years, there is no purpose more dominant and controlling and no accomplishment more marked than that of making American gentlemen." *Columbia Spectator*, October 14, 1916.

340 "You are on": NMB to Jones, February 27, 1918, Jones papers, CA.

340 "depressing in the": NMB to Barclay Parsons, October 2, 1917, Butler papers, CA.

342 "actually and entirely": Wilson to Hawkes, June 9, 1922, Miner papers, RBML.

343 "to eliminate the": Hawkes to Wilson, June 16, 1922, Hawkes papers, CA.

348 "independent of": 1936–37 Seth Low *Bulletin of Information*, CA.

348 massive dropout rate: According to Blossom Caron's study, about 50 percent of Seth Low students left school when they became aware of what they were attending.

348 "As far as": Katz letter of December 12, 1932, in Seth Low folder, RBML.

349 "the most prestigious": Asimov, *In Memory Yet Green*, 139.

349 "was that the": ibid., 141.

350 "Very high Thorndike": report dated May 4, 1938, in Seth Low folder, RBML.

350 "the best type": Chappell to Harvey, March 2, 1934, in Seth Low folder, ibid.

15. *The Path to Peace*

355 "Don't save; spend": Carnegie Corp. minutes, May 28, 1947, Box 23, RBML.

355 "In order that": ibid.

356 "Butler looked him": Robert Lester, COHP.

356 "his great surprise": ibid.

357 "glorified office boy": ibid.

357 "as if he": John Russell, COHP.

357 "Butler just changes": Robert Lester, COHP.

357 "If anybody": Charles Dollard, COHP.

358 "Of all the": NMB to Pritchett, April 3, 1933, Butler papers.

358 "Everything they proposed": NMB to Pritchett, May 22, 1933, ibid.

359 "he ran it": Harvey Bundy, COHP.

359 "His method was": E. Berthol Sayre, COHP.

359 "He was *absolutely*": ibid.

359 "We have mattered": CEIP minutes, 1929, Box 21, 36–39.

359 "He didn't do": Alger Hiss, conversation with the author, August 19, 1995.

360 "I have been": Ramsay MacDonald, May 20, 1925, British Public Records Office, MacDonald papers, PRO30/69/1170/1.

361 "In the whole": MacDonald to MacAlister, November 6, 1925, British Public Records Office, PRO30/69/1435.

362 "it staggers me": NMB to Delano, November 7, 1929, CEIP, Box 26.

362 "From the purely": Davies to NMB, December 10, 1938, Butler papers.

363 "a policy, statement": CEIP minutes, May 4, 1933, Box 22.

364 "France would be": *New York Times*, April 6, 1927.

365 "to set down": Butler, *Across the Busy Years*, II, 202.

365 "Has not the": ibid., 203.

366 "On April 20": Ochs papers, Columbia University File, *New York Times* archives. See also Shotwell's comment in his oral history transcript that "when I came back from Paris I found that Butler had not noticed it and I wrote Butler's letter to the *Times*." Shotwell, COHP.

368 "I mentioned Butler": Stoner, 233.

368 "twenty-two states": NMB to John Finley, January 8, 1930, Butler papers, Box 7.

368 "first step in": ibid.

368 "huge bombs dropped": Butler, *The Path to Peace*, 80.

369 "We might as": comment made at American Club in Paris, *New York Herald-Tribune*, June 17, 1927.

369 "had been born": cited in Ferrell, 105.

370 "We have Monsieur": cited in Ferrell, 264.

370 "I do not": *New York Times*, August 30, 1928.

371 "in the moralistic": James Shotwell, COHP.

372 "the most stupendous": Butler address at Teachers College, "Education and World Citizenship," covered in *Columbia Spectator*, February 13, 1929.

372 "All this the": *International Conciliation*, no. 243 (October 28, 1929), 9.

372 "is of so": *New York Times*, February 26, 1930.

373 "no war ever": *New York Telegram*, November 29, 1930.

373 "at least half": Butler, *Across the Busy Years*, II, 211.

374 "quite unprecedented": ibid., 150.

374 "with any of": Montague to NMB, January 10, 1930, Butler papers.

374 "As you well": NMB to Montague, January 13, 1930, ibid.

375 "splendidly phrased and": NMB to Scott, January 20, 1930, ibid.

375 "Without intending to": Scott to Nobel Committee, January 17, 1930, ibid.

376 "To such an extent": Scott to Nobel Committee, January 27, 1931, ibid.

377 "Let me be": Dana letter of December 11, 1931, and NMB response of December 14 both in Nobel Peace Prize file of Butler's papers.

16. Perils of Bolshevism, Promises of Fascism

378 "a new political": Butler, A World in Ferment, 208.

378 "speeding toward the": ibid., 218.

379 "Public order": Butler, Is America Worth Saving?, 34.

380 "the greatest lesson": Chicago News, February 14, 1923.

380 "we have seen": New York Times, January 21, 1925.

380 "thought worthy of": NMB to Ochs, April 1, 1927, Butler papers.

381 "a full and accurate": Ochs to NMB, April 4, 1927, ibid.

381 "the amazing movement": "New Critics of Democracy" in Butler, Looking Forward, 190.

381 "in the service": ibid., 191.

381 "there is no": ibid., 190.

383 "I must say": Butler, Across the Busy Years, II, 155–56.

383 "there could scarcely": Spender to NMB, June 2, 1930, Butler papers.

384 "a distinguished man": NMB to Spender, June 13, 1930, ibid.

385 "Mussolini has endowed": New York Times, May 28, 1927.

385 "He thanks you": Sarfatti to NMB, November 29, 1933, ibid.

386 "Should I": NMB to Bigongiari, February 20, 1934, ibid.

386 "understands perfectly that": New York Sun, March 28, 1934.

386 "a curious hodge-podge": The Nation, vol. 139, no. 3619 (November 14, 1934), 550.

387 "whose high spiritual": NMB to Mussolini, January 26, 1926, Casa Italiana file, CA.

388 "has one of": NMB to Mrs. F. S. Bangs, February 4, 1925, ibid.

388 "As I have": Casa Italiana flyer, Casa Italiana file, CA.

388 "the study and teaching": NMB's Nation letter of November 14, 1934, p. 550.

388 "We are a": NMB to Luigi Criscuolo, February 11, 1928, Casa Italiana file, CA.

389 "What the Consul": Frank Fackenthal to NMB, March 24, 1928, Butler papers, CA.

389 "We run the": Fackenthal to NMB, March 29, 1932, Butler papers, CA.

390 "quite as warmly": NMB to Sforza, September 12, 1935, CEIP papers, Box 81.

390 "The Italian Soul": Sforza to NMB, February 23, 1935, Butler papers.

390 "I took no": NMB to Sarfatti, January 9, 1937, ibid.

390 "a peaceful way": New York Times, July 15, 1935.

390 "its own sacred": Misciatelli to NMB, August 16, 1935, CEIP papers, Box 81.

391 A month before the: NMB to Misciatelli, September 2, 1935, ibid.

391 "a victory for": Misciatelli to NMB, June 19, 1936, ibid.

394 "May that which": New York Times, May 17, 1937.

394 "no matter how": New York Herald-Tribune, September 23, 1937.

17. The Fund-raiser

395 "the intellectual center": statement to trustees at last meeting as president, January 10, 1945, Butler papers, Box 8.

396 "He did it for": Carlton Hayes, COHP.

396 "had this marvelous": Frederic Coudert, COHP.

396 "Mr. Harkness said": Columbia *Alumni News*, XXXVII (May 1946), 11.

398 "for the maintenance": First Annual Alumni Fund report, CA.

399 "for the increase": trustee minutes, May 1926, CA.

400 "cut out of": Williams to NMB, April 28, 1927, JPJ file, CA.

401 "preferable to continue": NMB to Jones, May 3, 1927, ibid.

401 "in the light of": Jones to NMB, May 17, 1927, ibid. I have been unable to locate a copy of the proposal.

402 "We should be": NMB to Bangs, February 10, 1908, Bangs papers, CA.

402 "a constant source": ibid.

403 "a literally stupendous": NMB to Goetze, May 5, 1926, Goetze papers, CA.

403 "which I submitted": Goetze to NMB, May 14, 1926, ibid.

403 On January 22: In the following discussion of Rockefeller Center, I am indebted to Dan Okrent's fine book, *Great Fortune*.

404 "It was missing": Okrent, 29.

405 "[The] damage being done": NMB to Goetze, Goetze papers, CA.

406 "And there in": *The New Yorker*, February 24, 1934, 47.

406 "Our needs multiply": *New York Times*, January 23, 1929.

408 "will at once": Butler, 1930 presidential report.

408 "The fortunes that": Butler, ibid.

409 "depend for its": *New York Times*, May 17, 1933.

410 "We had a": Frank Fackenthal, COHP.

410 "He didn't really": Fackenthal, ibid.

411 "If the amount": NMB to trustees, August 24, 1942, Box 8.

411 Columbia was the: see Geiger, 270.

412 "This is my": Fackenthal, COHP.

18. "Morningside's Miracle"

414 "The collapse at": NMB to Pritchett, February 20, 1930, Butler papers.

416 "délices of sole": It has been pointed out to me that chickens are not fed milk, but this is the way the dish is described in the dinner program.

417 "an exceptionally representative": *New York Times*, January 6, 1933.

417 "is in no": NMB to William Butler, October 13, 1933.

418 "genius for democratic": NMB quoted in *New York World-Telegram*, October 18, 1933.

418 "'It has got": *Chicago Tribune*, June 15, 1933.

419 "become so accustomed": *New York Herald-Tribune*, June 7, 1933.

419 "a magnificent and": *New York World-Telegram*, August 9, 1933.

419 "who carp at": *New York Times*, October 4, 1933.

420 "Nothing in the": *New York World-Telegram*, December 31, 1932.

421 "Nicholas, King of": Twelfth Night files, Century Association.

421 "Let care": ibid.

421 "The spirit of": Elihu Root, internal statement, Century Association.

422 "nothing more than": *The Woman Republican*, XI, no. 5 (January 28, 1933), 3.

422 "Columbia University has": NMB to Clark, written on January 11, 1933, and cited in the *Commercial Financial Chronicle* of January 21.

423 *New York Sun* parody of January 20, 1933.

423 "To use technical": *London Daily Herald*, January 26, 1933.

424 "It goes without": NMB to Landfield, November 19, 1931, Butler papers.

425 "One of the": United States District Court transcript, March 29, 1934, E.6968, 201.

426 "the Federal police": NMB letter to *New York Times*, December 28, 1933.

427 "the keystone of": quoted in Sheldon Stern, "The Evolution of a Reactionary, Louis Coolidge, 1900–1925," *Mid-America*, vol. 57, no. 2 (April 1975), 97.

427 "a more far-reaching": "The New American Revolution," *American Bar Association Journal*, X (December 1924), 849.

428 "into a mouthpiece": *Toledo Times*, January 3, 1934.

428 "Dr. Butler's letter": *Columbia Spectator*, January 4, 1934.

428 "attacking popular causes": *New Outlook*, March 1934.

428 "sincere, honest": *Hartford Courant*, April 24, 1934.

429 "There is no": James Wechsler, *Revolt on the Campus*, 419.

429 "I really think": NMB to Sherman, March 23, 1937, Butler papers.

430 "the home, the": form letters to governors, January 18, 1937, child labor file, RBML.

430 "The doctors and": NMB to E. D. Perry, February 18, 1935, Butler papers. The destruction of Butler's correspondence with Sarah has deprived us of an invaluable source of information about his emotional life.

431 "to see whether": *Daily News Chronicle* (London), March 1, 1935.

431 "the most important": *Chicago Tribune*, March 9, 1935.

432 "the applause which": CEIP minutes, December 11, 1939, Box 15.

433 "Is Dr. Butler": *Columbia Spectator*, April 3, 1935.

19. *Resignation, Retirements, and Death*

435 "typical contest between": *New York Times*, June 3, 1937.

435 "the abandonment of": *New York Herald Tribune*, November 5, 1938.

436 "that I do": *Congressional Record*, October 4, 1938, 13198.

437 "Before and above": "The True Function of a University in This World Crisis," delivered at General Assembly of the University Faculties, October 3, 1940. The full text was printed in the *New York Times* of October 4.

438 "That will make": *New York Journal-American*, October 6, 1940.

438 "by delivering his": *Chicago Tribune*, October 8, 1940.

438 "the right of": *Boston Globe*, October 5, 1940.

439 "I cannot understand": *Boston Herald*, October 5, 1940.

439 "I do not know": *New York Times*, October 5, 1940.

439 "a complete denial": *Boston Globe*, October 5, 1940.

439 "I hold that": NMB to Coe, November 5, 1910, CA.

440 "discretion, moderation, good": Butler 1915 presidential report.

441 The comments from the three deans all appear in the *New York Herald-Tribune* of October 4, 1940.

442 "a bit hasty": *New York Times*, November 8, 1940.

443 "President Nicholas Murray Butler": *New York Times*, November 12, 1940.

444 "are quite below": NMB to Johnson, April 4, 1934, Butler papers, American Academy.

445 "Whereas Nicholas Murray": Pound letter of April 7, 1940, in Pound file at American Academy.

446 "I have no": NMB to Canby, February 14, 1940, American Academy.

446 "was a clear": Grant to Walter Damrosch, April 26, 1940, American Academy.

446 "practically a majority": Charles Warren to Academy board, May 3, 1940, American Academy.

447 "Cross and Huntington": Damrosch to Gibson, December 21, 1940, American Academy.

448 "They'll have to": *New York Times*, April 2, 1941.

448 "Not until I": ibid., March 27, 1942.

448 "What's the use": ibid., April 2, 1943.

449 "completely abandoned": incident cited in Jacobs, 13.

450 "non-debating Board": Frederic Coudert, COHP.

450 enlisted the help: McGill, letter to the author, January 22, 1997.

451 "the most famous": *Life* magazine, November 12, 1945.

451 "He had come": *Paterson News*, May 2, 1945.

451 "At last they": *Quincy* (Massachusetts) *Patriot Ledger*, May 15, 1945.

452 "as the intellectual": NMB to the trustees, October 1, 1945, CA.

452 list of eight: The Columbia faculty on the list were historian Jacques Barzun; dean of the Business School Robert Calkins; professor of international law Philip C. Jessup; and John A. Krout, chairman of the History Department. The non-Columbians were Vannevar Bush, president of the Carnegie Institution; Lee Alvin DuBridge, president of the California Institute of Technology; William Pearson Tolley, chancellor of Syracuse University; and Senator J. William Fulbright, former president of the University of Arkansas. Travis Jacobs has the best discussion of the search process.

453 "the only one": see Jacobs, 24.

454 "Wild Bill Donovan": Robert Lester, COHP.

455 "with extreme delicacy": James Shotwell, COHP.

455 "My point is": CEIP minutes, Box 23, RBML.

456 "we cannot have": NMB to Neville Lawrence, October 13, 1947, Butler papers, Box 8.

456 "felt a great": NMB to Neville Lawrence, February 18, 1947, ibid.

458 "I suppose": NMB to Fackenthal, July 19, 1947, CA.

459 "I would not": Kate Butler to Philip Hayden, October 17, 1947, Kate Butler papers, CA.

459 "I hope the": NMB to Neville Lawrence, November 5, 1947, Box 8.

Epilogue: The Disappearance

461 "one of the": *New York Times*, December 7, 1947.

461 "Anglo-Saxon Protestants": Baltzell, 228.

462 "legalistic-moralistic": Kennan, 95.

462 "social, economic and political": taped radio broadcast, April 2, 1943.

463 "America, Europe, Asia": remarks at Columbia Alumni Luncheon, June 2, 1926, reported in *New York Evening Post*.

463 "instead . . . just becoming": Walter Gellhorn, COHP.

463 "He should have": M. Halsey Thomas, diary, February 2, 1937, New-York Historical Society.

Bibliography

Aaron, Daniel. *Men of Good Hope*. New York: Oxford University Press, 1951.

Adler, Cyrus. *Jacob Schiff: His Life and Letters*. New York: Doubleday, Doran, 1928.

Alogdelis, Joanne. "A Critical Evaluation of Selected Educational Speeches of Nicholas Murray Butler." (Ph.D. dissertation, University of Iowa, 1949).

Altschuler, Glenn S. *Andrew D. White: Educator, Historian, Diplomat*. Ithaca: Cornell University Press, 1979.

Ambrosius, Lloyd E. *Wilsonianism: Woodrow Wilson and His Legacy in American Foreign Relations*. New York: Palgrave Macmillan, 2002.

Amory, Cleveland. *The Last Resort*. New York: Harper & Bros., 1948.

Angell, James B. *Reminiscences*. New York: Longmans, Green, 1912.

Angoff, Charles. *H. L. Mencken: A Portrait from Memory*. New York: A. S. Barnes, 1956.

Asimov, Isaac. *A Memoir*. New York: Doubleday, 1994.

——. *In Memory Yet Green: The Autobiography of Isaac Asimov, 1920–1954*. New York: Doubleday, 1979.

Auchincloss, Louis. *The Rector of Justin*. Boston: Houghton Mifflin, 1964.

Auerbach, Jerold S. *Unequal Justice: Lawyers and Social Change in America*. New York: Oxford University Press, 1976.

Bagby, Wesley M. *The Road to Normalcy: The Presidential Campaign and the Election of 1920*. Baltimore: The Johns Hopkins University Press, 1962.

Bagg, Lyman H. *Four Years at Yale University*. New Haven: Charles C. Chatfield, 1871.

Baltzell, E. Digby. *The Protestant Establishment: Aristocracy and Caste in America*. New York: Random House, 1964.

Bardeen, C. W. "The New President of Columbia." Syracuse: *School Bulletin*, February 1902.

Barzun, Jacques, ed. *A History of the Faculty of Philosophy*. New York: Columbia University Press, 1957.

Beale, Howard K. *Theodore Roosevelt and the Rise of America to World Power*. Baltimore: The Johns Hopkins University Press, 1984.

Beard, Mary Ritter. *The Making of Charles A. Beard.* New York: Exposition Press, 1955.

Beck, Hubert. *Men Who Control Our Universities.* New York: King's Crown Press, 1947.

Beer, Thomas. *The Mauve Decade: American Life at the End of the Nineteenth Century.* New York: Alfred A. Knopf, 1926.

Behr, Edward. *Prohibition: Thirteen Years That Changed America.* New York: Arcade Publishing, 1996.

Bell, Daniel. *The Reforming of General Education.* New York: Columbia University Press, 1966.

Bender, Thomas. *New York Intellect: A History of Intellectual Life in New York City, from 1750 to the Beginnings of Our Own Time.* Baltimore: The Johns Hopkins University Press, 1987.

Bergdoll, Barry. *Mastering McKim's Plan.* New York: Columbia University Press, 1997.

Bernays, Edward L., ed. *The Engineering of Consent.* Norman: University of Oklahoma Press, 1968.

————. *Propaganda.* New York: Horace Liveright, 1928.

Bledstein, Burton J. *The Culture of Professionalism: The Middle Class and the Development of Higher Education in the United States.* New York: W. W. Norton, 1976.

Bonner, Thomas. *Iconoclast: Abraham Flexner and a Life in Learning.* Baltimore: The Johns Hopkins University Press, 2002.

Bosqui, Edward. *Memoirs of Edward Bosqui.* Oakland: Holmes, 1952.

Bourne, Randolph. *The History of a Literary Radical and Other Papers.* New York: S. A. Russell, 1956.

————. *The Radical Will: Selected Writings, 1911–1918,* ed. Olaf Hansen. New York: Urizen Books, 1977.

————. *War and the Intellectuals. Essays by Randolph S. Bourne, 1915–1919,* ed. Carl Resek. New York: Harper Torchbooks, 1964.

Boylan, James. *Pulitzer's School: Columbia University's School of Journalism, 1903–2003.* New York: Columbia University Press, 2003.

Breisner, Robert L. *Twelve Against Empire: The Anti-Imperialists, 1898–1900.* New York: McGraw-Hill, 1968.

Britton, Nan. *The President's Daughter.* New York: Elizabeth Ann Guild, 1927.

Bromley, Dorothy Dunbar. "Nicholas Murray Butler: Portrait of a Reactionary." *The American Mercury* (March 1935), 286–98.

Brooks, John Graham. *An American Citizen: The Life of William Henry Baldwin, Jr.* Boston: Houghton Mifflin, 1910.

Broun, Haywood Hale, and George Britt. *Christians Only: A Study in Prejudice.* New York: The Vanguard Press, 1931.

Brubacher, John S., and Willis Rudy. *Higher Education in Transition: A History of American Colleges and Universities, 1636–1976.* New York: Harper & Row, 1976.

Bryce, James. *The American Commonwealth.* London: Macmillan, 1888.

Burgess, J. W. *The American University: When Shall It Be? Where Shall It Be? What Shall It Be?* Boston: Ginn, Heath, 1884.

————. *Reminiscences of an American Scholar.* New York: Columbia University Press, 1934.

———. "Reminiscences of Columbia University in the Last Quarter of the Last Century." *Columbia University Quarterly* XV (1913), 321–335.

Burns, James MacGregor. *Leadership*. New York: Harper & Row, 1978.

Butler, Nicholas Murray. *Across the Busy Years*, vol. I. New York: Charles Scribner's Sons, 1939.

———. *Across the Busy Years*, vol. II. New York: Charles Scribner's Sons, 1940.

———. *The American as He Is*. New York: Macmillan, 1908.

———. *The Basis of a Durable Peace, Written at the Invitation of the* New York Times. New York: Charles Scribner's Sons, 1917.

———. *Between Two Worlds: Interpretations of the Age in Which We Live*. New York: Charles Scribner's Sons, 1934.

———. *Building the American Nation: An Essay of Interpretation*. New York: Charles Scribner's Sons, 1923.

———. *The Effect of the War of 1812 upon the Consolidation of the Union*. Baltimore: Johns Hopkins University Studies in Historical and Political Science, 1887.

———. *The Faith of a Liberal. Essays and Addresses on Political Principles and Public Policies*. New York: Charles Scribner's Sons, 1924.

———. *The International Mind: An Argument for the Judicial Settlement of International Disputes*. New York: Charles Scribner's Sons, 1913.

———. *Is America Worth Saving? Addresses on National Problems and Party Politics*. New York: Charles Scribner's Sons, 1920.

———. *Liberty-Equality-Fraternity: Essays and Addresses on the Problems of Today and Tomorrow*. New York: Charles Scribner's Sons, 1942.

———. *Looking Forward: What Will the American People Do About It? Essays and Addresses on Matters National and International*. New York: Charles Scribner's Sons, 1932.

———. *The Meaning of Education: Contributions to a Philosophy of Education*. New York: Charles Scribner's Sons, 1915.

———. *The Path to Peace: Essays and Addresses on Peace and Its Making*. New York: Charles Scribner's Sons, 1930.

———. *Philosophy*. New York: Columbia University Press, 1908.

———. *Scholarship and Service: The Policies and Ideals of a National University in a Modern Democracy*. New York: Charles Scribner's Sons, 1921.

———. *True and False Democracy*. New York: Macmillan, 1907.

———. *A World in Ferment: Interpretations of the War for a New World*. New York: Charles Scribner's Sons, 1917.

———. *Why Should We Change Our Form of Government?* New York: Charles Scribner's Sons, 1912.

Butts, R. Freeman. *The College Charts Its Course*. New York: McGraw-Hill, 1939.

Cady, Edwin H. *The Gentleman in America*. Syracuse: Syracuse University Press, 1949.

Cahan, Abraham. *The Rise of David Levinsky*. New York: Harper & Row, 1960.

Callahan, Raymond E. *Education and the Cult of Efficiency*. Chicago: University of Chicago Press, 1962.

Canby, Henry Seidel. *Alma Mater: The Gothic Age of the American College*. New York: Farrar & Rinehart, 1936.

Cannistraro, Philip V., and Brian R. Sullivan. *Il Duce's Other Woman*. New York: William Morrow, 1993.

Carnegie, Andrew. *The Empire of Business*. New York: Doubleday, Page, 1902.

——. *The Gospel of Wealth and Other Timely Essays*. New York: Century, 1900.

——. *Triumphant Democracy*. New York: Charles Scribner's Sons, 1886.

Caro, Robert. *The Power Broker: Robert Moses and the Fall of New York*. New York: Alfred A. Knopf, 1974.

Carron, Blossom R. "Seth Low Junior College of Columbia University." (Ed.D. dissertation, Teachers College, Columbia University, 1979).

Cattell, James McKeen. *University Control*. New York: Science Press, 1913.

Chace, James. *1912: Wilson, Roosevelt, Taft and Debs—The Election That Changed the Country*. New York: Simon & Schuster, 2004.

Chamberlain, W. H. *Confessions of an Individualist*. New York: Macmillan, 1940.

Chandler, Alfred D., Jr. *Strategy and Structure*. Cambridge: MIT Press, 1962.

——. *The Visible Hand: The Managerial Revolution in American Business*. Cambridge: Harvard University Press, 1977.

Clapp, Margaret, ed. *The Modern University*. Ithaca: Cornell University Press, 1950.

Cochran, Thomas C. *Railroad Leaders, 1845–1900: The Business Mind in Action*. New York: Russell and Russell, 1965.

—— and William Miller. *The Age of Enterprise: A Social History of Industrial America*. New York: Harper Torchbooks, 1961.

Cohen, Sol. *Progressives and Urban School Reform*. New York: Teachers College Press, 1964.

Coleman, McAlister. "Nicholas Murray Butler, the Open Mind of Morningside." *Modern Monthly* (May 1933), 200–209.

Collins, Randall. *The Credential Society*. New York: Academic Press, 1979.

Cooke, Morris. L. *Academic and Industrial Efficiency. Carnegie Foundation for the Advancement of Teaching, Report # 5*. Boston: Merrymount Press, 1910.

Coon, Horace. *Columbia, Colossus on the Hudson*. New York: E. P. Dutton, 1947.

——. *Money to Burn*. New York: Longmans, Green, 1938.

Cooper, John Milton, Jr. *Breaking the Heart of the World: Woodrow Wilson and the Fight for the League of Nations*. Cambridge: Cambridge University Press, 2001.

Corson, Louis D. "University Problems as Described in the Personal Correspondence among D. C. Gilman, A. D. White, and C. W. Eliot." (Ph.D. dissertation, Stanford University, 1951).

Counts, George S. *The Social Composition of Boards of Education*. Chicago: University of Chicago Press, 1927.

Cremin, Lawrence A. *American Education: The Metropolitan Experience, 1876–1980*. New York: Harper & Row, 1988.

——. *Transformation of the School*. New York: Random House, 1961.

——, David A. Shannon, and Mary Evelyn Townsend. *A History of Teachers College*. New York: Columbia University Press, 1954.

Croly, Herbert. *The Promise of American Life*. New York: Macmillan, 1909.

Cubberley, Ellwood. *Changing Conceptions of Education*. Boston: Houghton Mifflin, 1909.

Curti, Merle. *The Social Ideas of American Educators*. New York: Charles Scribner's Sons, 1935.

Davis, Hayne, ed. *Among the World's Peace Makers*. London: Garland, 1972.

Dewey, John. *Democracy and Education*. New York: Macmillan, 1916.

Diamond, Sigmund. *The Reputation of the American Businessman*. Cambridge: Harvard University Press, 1955.

Diggins, John P. *Mussolini and Fascism: The View from America*. Princeton: Princeton University Press, 1972.

Dodd, William E., Jr., and Martha Dodd, eds. *Ambassador Dodd's Diary, 1933–1938*. New York: Harcourt Brace, 1941.

Dodge, Grace H. *A Brief Sketch of the Early History of Teachers College*. New York: Maynard, Merrill, 1899.

Dolkart, Andrew S. *Morningside Heights: A History of Its Architecture and Development*. New York: Columbia University Press, 1998.

Domhoff, William G. *The Bohemian Grove and Other Retreats: A Study in Ruling-Class Cohesiveness*. New York: Harper & Row, 1974.

Dos Passos, John R. *The Anglo-Saxon Century*. New York: G. P. Putnam's Sons, 1903.

Douglas, William O. *Go East Young Man: The Early Years*. New York: Random House, 1974.

Drucker, Peter F. *Adventures of a Bystander*. New York: Harper & Row, 1978.

Duffus, R. L. *The Innocents at Cedro*. New York: Macmillan, 1944.

Duggan, Steven P. *A Professor at Large*. New York: Macmillan, 1943.

Dunkel, Harold B. *Herbart and Herbartianism: An Educational Ghost Story*. Chicago: University of Chicago Press, 1970.

Dykhuizen, George. *The Life and Mind of John Dewey*. Carbondale: Southern Illinois University Press, 1974.

Earnest, Ernest. *Academic Procession: An Informal History of the American College, 1636–1953*. Indianapolis: Bobbs-Merrill, 1953.

Eels, Walter C. *The Junior College*. Boston: Houghton-Mifflin, 1931.

Eliot, Charles W. *American Education Since the Civil War*. Houston: Rice Institute Pamphlet, 1922.

——. *Educational Reform: Essays and Addresses*. New York: Century, 1898.

——. "The Length of the College Course." *Education Review* (September 1903), 120–26.

——. "The New Education: Its Organization." *Atlantic Monthly* (February 1869), 203–20.

——. *A Turning Point in Higher Education: The Inaugural Address of Charles William Eliot as President of Harvard College, October 19, 1869*. Cambridge: Harvard University Press, 1969.

——. *University Administration*. Boston: Houghton Mifflin, 1908.

Eliott, Osborn. *Men at the Top*. New York: Harper, 1959.

Ely, Richard. *Ground Under Our Feet*. New York: Arno Press, 1977.

Erskine, John. *My Life as a Teacher*. Philadelphia: J. B. Lippincott, 1948.

Fabian, Larry L. *Andrew Carnegie's Peace Endowment: The Tycoon, the President, and Their Bargain of 1910*. Washington: Carnegie Endowment for International Peace, 1985.

Fass, Paula. *The Damned and the Beautiful: American Youth in the 1920s*. New York: Oxford University Press, 1977.

Ferrell, Robert H. *Peace in Their Time: The Origins of the Kellogg-Brand Pact*. New Haven: Yale University Press, 1952.

First, Wesley. *University on the Heights*. New York: Doubleday, 1969.

Fletcher, Robert H. *The Annals of the Bohemian Club*. San Francisco: Hicks-Judd, 1898.

Flexner, Abraham: *I Remember: The Autobiography of Abraham Flexner*. New York: Simon & Schuster: 1940.

———. *Medical Education in the United States and Canada*. New York: Carnegie Endowment for the Advancement of Teaching, Bulletin No. 4, 1910.

———. *Universities: American, English, German*. New York: Oxford University Press, 1930.

Foraker, Joseph. *Notes of a Busy Life*. Cincinnati: Stewart & Kidd, 1917.

Forbes, B. C. *Men Who Are Making America*. New York: B. C. Forbes, 1917.

Fox, Dixon Ryan. *The Decline of Aristocracy in the Politics of New York*. New York: Harper Torchbook, 1965.

Frankel, Max. *The Times of My Life and My Life with the Times*. New York: Random House, 1999.

Friess, Horace. *Felix Adler and Ethical Culture*. New York: Columbia University Press, 1981.

Fuess, Claude F. *The College Board: Its First Fifty Years*. New York: Columbia University Press, 1950.

Fulton, John, ed. *Memoirs of F.A.P. Barnard*. New York: Macmillan, 1896.

Gabler, Neal. *Winchell: Gossip, Power and the Culture of Celebrity*. New York: Alfred A. Knopf, 1994.

Geiger, Roger L. *To Advance Knowledge: The Growth of American Research Universities, 1900–1940*. New York: Oxford University Press, 1986.

Gelernter, David. *1939: The Lost World of the Fair*. New York: The Free Press, 1995.

Gettleman, Marvin E. *An Elusive Presence: The Discovery of John H. Finley and His America*. Chicago: Nelson-Hall, 1979.

Gildersleeve, Virginia C. *Many a Good Crusade*. New York: Macmillan, 1954.

Gilman, Daniel C. *The Launching of a University and Other Papers: A Sheaf of Remembrances*. New York: Dodd, Mead, 1906.

———. *A Plea for the Training of the Hand*, ed. N. M. Butler. New York: Industrial Education Association, 1888.

———. *University Problems in the United States*. New York: Arno Press (reprint), 1969.

Godkin, E. L. "Columbia College and the Public." *The Nation* (March 15, 1883), 226–27.

———. *Reflections and Comments, 1865–1895*. New York: Charles Scribner's Sons, 1895.

Gompers, Samuel. *Seventy Years of Life and Labor: An Autobiography*. New York: E. P. Dutton, 1925.

Goodspeed, Thomas Wakefield. *William Rainey Harper*. Chicago: University of Chicago Press, 1928.

Gorelick, Sherry. *City College and the Jewish Poor*. New Brunswick: Rutgers University Press, 1981.

Graham, Abbie. *Grace R. Dodge: Merchant of Dreams*. New York: The Women's Press, 1926.

Graybar, Lloyd J. *Albert Shaw of the* Review of Reviews: *An Intellectual Biography*. Lexington: University Press of Kentucky, 1974.

Grubar, Carol S. "Academic Freedom at Columbia University, 1917–1918: The Case of James McKeen Cattell." New York: *Bulletin of the American Association of University Professors*, No. 5, Autumn 1972.

Gutman, Herbert G. *Work, Culture and Society in Industrializing America*. New York: Alfred A. Knopf, 1976.

Hagedorn, Herman. *Leonard Wood*. New York: Harper & Bros., 1931.

Hall, Peter Dobkin. *The Organization of American Culture*. New York: New York University Press, 1982.

Hammack, David. "Elite Perceptions of Power in the Cities of the United States, 1880–1900." *Journal of Urban History*, 4 (1978), 363–96.

——. *Power and Society: Greater New York at the Turn of the Century*. New York: Columbia University Press, 1987.

Handlin, Oscar. *John Dewey's Challenge to Education*. New York: Harper & Bros., 1959.

Harper, William Rainey. *The Trend in Higher Education*. Chicago: University of Chicago Press, 1905.

Harris, Neil. *Humbug: The Art of P. T. Barnum*. Chicago: University of Chicago Press, 1973.

Harris, William T. "Nicholas Murray Butler." *The School Journal* (December 15, 1894), 577.

Haskell, Thomas, ed. *The Authority of Experts*. Bloomington: Indiana University Press, 1984.

Hawkins, Hugh D. *Between Harvard and America: The Educational Leadership of Charles W. Eliot*. New York: Oxford University Press, 1972.

——. "Three University Presidents." *American Quarterly*, XI (1959), 99–119.

Hays, Samuel L. *The Response to Industrialism*. Chicago: University of Chicago Press, 1957.

Healey, Mary Angelina. "The Educational Philosophy of Nicholas Murray Butler and Its Relevance for Contemporary Problems in Education." (Ph.D. dissertation, Catholic University of America, 1967).

Hendricks, Luther Virgil. *James Harvey Robinson, Teacher of History*. New York: King's Crown Press, 1946.

Herbst, Jurgen. "American Higher Education in the Age of the College." *History of Universities*, 7 (1988), 37–59.

Herman, Sondra. *Eleven Against War: Studies in American Internationalist Thought, 1898–1921*. Stanford: Hoover Institution Press, 1969.

Herring, Hubert. *And So to War*. New Haven: Yale University Press, 1938.

Higham, John. *Strangers in the Land*. New Brunswick: Rutgers University Press, 1955.

Hofstadter, Richard. *Academic Freedom in the Age of the College*. New York: Columbia University Press, 1961.

——, and Wilson Smith. *American Higher Education: A Documentary History*. Chicago: University of Chicago Press, 1961.

——, and C. DeWitt Hardy. *The Development and Scope of Higher Education in the United States*. New York: Columbia University Press, 1952.

Hollinger, David. *Morris R. Cohen and the Scientific Ideal*. Cambridge: MIT Press, 1985.

———. *Science, Jews and Secular Culture: Studies in Mid-Twentieth-Century American Intellectual History*. Princeton: Princeton University Press, 1996.

Holls, Frederick W. *The Peace Conference at The Hague*. New York: Macmillan, 1900.

Hook, Sidney. *Out of Step: An Unquiet Life in the 20th Century*. New York: Harper & Row, 1987.

Horner, Harlan. *The Life and Work of Andrew Sloan Draper*. Urbana: University of Illinois Press, 1934.

Horowitz, Helen Lefkowitz. *The Power and Passion of M. Carey Thomas*. New York: Alfred A. Knopf, 1994.

Hotchkiss, Willard E. *Higher Education and Business Standards*. Boston: Houghton Mifflin, 1918.

Howe, Mark DeWolfe, ed. *The Correspondence of Mr. Justice Holmes and Harold J. Laski, 1916–1935*. Cambridge: Harvard University Press, 1953.

Howson, Roger. *His Excellency, a Trustee*. New York: Columbia University Press, 1945.

Hoxie, R. Gordon. *History of the Faculty of Political Science*. New York: Columbia University Press, 1955.

Humphrey, David C. *From King's College to Columbia, 1746–1800*. New York: Columbia University Press, 1976.

Huntington, Emily. *The Kitchen Garden or Object Lessons in Household Work*. New York: Trow, 1878.

Hutchins, Robert M. *The Higher Learning in America*. New Haven: Yale University Press, 1936.

Iannaccone, Laurence. *Politics in Education*. New York: The Center for Applied Research in Education, 1967.

Israel, Jerry, ed. *Building the Organizational Society*. New York: The Free Press, 1972.

Jacobs, Travis Beal. *Eisenhower at Columbia*. New Brunswick: Transaction Publishers, 2001.

Jaher, Frederic C., ed. *The Rich, the Well-Born and the Powerful: Elites and Upper Classes in History*. Urbana: University of Illinois Press, 1973.

Jarausch, Konrad, ed. *The Transformation of Higher Learning, 1860–1930*. Chicago: University of Chicago Press, 1983.

Jencks, Christopher, and David Riesman. *The Academic Revolution*. New York: Doubleday, 1968.

Jensen, Gordon Maurice. "The National Civic Federation: American Business in an Age of Social Change and Social Reform, 1900–1910." (Ph.D. dissertation, Princeton University, 1956).

Jessup, Philip. *Elihu Root*. New York: Dodd, Mead, 1938.

Johnson, Alvin. *Pioneer's Progress*. New York: Viking, 1952.

Johnson, Henry. *The Other Side of Main Street*. New York: Columbia University Press, 1943.

Johnson, Robert U. *Remembered Yesterdays*. Boston: Little, Brown, 1923.

Johnston, Alva. "Fifteen Biggest Men in America." *The New Yorker* (January 25, 1930), 17–19.

Jordan, David Starr. *The Care and Culture of Men*. San Francisco: Whitaker & Roy, 1896.

———. *The Days of a Man*. New York: World Book Company, 1922.

Josephson, Matthew. *Robber Barons. The Great American Capitalists, 1861–1901*. New York: Harcourt, Brace & World, 1962.

――. *The Politicos*. New York: Harcourt, Brace & World, 1963.

Kadushin, Charles. *The American Intellectual Elite*. Boston: Little, Brown, 1974.

Kanigel, Robert. *The One Best Way: Frederick Winslow Taylor and the Enigma of Efficiency*. New York: Viking, 1997.

Keating, James M. "Seth Low and the Development of Columbia University, 1889–1901." (Ed.D. dissertation, Teachers College, 1973).

Kennan, George. *American Diplomacy, 1900–1950*. Chicago: University of Chicago Press, 1951.

Keppel, Frederick P. *Columbia*. New York: Columbia University Press, 1914.

Kerr, Clark. *The Uses of the University*. Cambridge: Harvard University Press, 1995.

Kessner, Thomas. *Fiorello La Guardia*. New York: Penguin, 1989.

Kliebard, Herbert M. *The Struggle for the American Curriculum, 1893–1958*. 2nd ed. New York: Routledge, 1995.

Knight, Edgar W. *Fifty Years of American Education*. New York: The Ronald Press, 1952.

Kobler, John. *Ardent Spirits: The Rise and Fall of Prohibition*. New York: G. P. Putnam's Sons, 1973.

Kohlsaat, Herman H. *From McKinley to Harding*. New York: Charles Scribner's Sons, 1923.

Konrad, George, and Ivan Szeleny. *The Intellectuals on the Way to Class Power*. New York: Harcourt Brace Jovanovich, 1979.

Kouwenhoven, John A. *The Columbia Historical Portrait of New York*. New York: Harper & Row, 1972.

Krutch, Joseph W. *More Lives Than One*. New York: William Sloan Associates, 1962.

Kuehl, Warren F. *Hamilton Holt: Journalist, Internationalist, Educator*. Gainesville: University of Florida Press, 1960.

――. *Seeking World Order: The United States and International Organization to 1920*. Nashville: Vanderbilt University Press, 1969.

Kuklick, Bruce. *The Rise of American Philosophy*. New Haven: Yale University Press, 1977.

Kurland, Gerald. *Seth Low: The Reformer in an Urban and Industrial Age*. New York: Twayne, 1971.

Lagemann, Ellen Condliffe. *A Generation of Women: Educators in the Lives of Progressive Reformers*. Cambridge: Harvard University Press, 1979.

――. *Private Power for the Public Good: A History of the Carnegie Foundation for the Advancement of Teaching*. Middletown: Wesleyan University Press, 1983.

Lamb, Albert R. *The Presbyterian Hospital and the Columbia-Presbyterian Medical Center, 1868–1943*. New York: Columbia University Press, 1955.

Landfield, Jerome. *The Story of the Land of Happiness*. Bohemian Grove, 1948.

Larson, Magali Sarfatti. *The Rise of Professionalism*. Berkeley: University of California Press, 1977.

Lasch, Christopher. *The Culture of Narcissism: American Life in an Age of Diminishing Expectations*. New York: W. W. Norton, 1978.

――. *New Radicalism in America, 1889–1963*. New York: Vintage Books, 1965.

Le Comte, Edward. *In and Out of the University and Adversity*. Lincoln (Nebraska): Writers Club Press, 2001.

Lemann, Nicholas. *The Big Test: The Secret History of the American Meritocracy*. New York: Farrar, Straus and Giroux, 1999.

Leopold, Richard W. *Elihu Root and the Conservative Tradition*. Boston: Little, Brown, 1954.

Levine, David O. *The American College and the Culture of Aspiration, 1915–1940*. Ithaca: Cornell University Press, 1986.

Link, Arthur S. *Wilson: The Road to the White House*. Princeton: Princeton University Press, 1947.

———. *Woodrow Wilson and the Progressive Era*. New York: Harper & Bros., 1947.

Lippmann, Walter. *Men of Destiny*. Seattle: University of Washington Press, 1969.

———. *A Preface to Politics*. New York: Mitchell Kennerley, 1913.

Low, Benjamin R. C. *Seth Low*. New York: G. P. Putnam's Sons, 1925.

Lowell, A. Lawrence. *At War with Academic Traditions in America*. Cambridge: Harvard University Press, 1934.

Lundberg, Ferdinand. *America's 60 Families*. New York: The Citadel Press, 1946.

Lutzker, Michael Arnold. "The 'Practical' Peace Advocates: An Interpretation of the American Peace Movement, 1898–1917." (Ph.D. dissertation, Rutgers University, 1969).

Lynch, Frederick. *The One Great Society*. New York: Fleming H. Revell Company, 1918.

Macmillan, Margaret. *Paris 1919: Six Months That Changed the World*. New York: Random House, 2001.

Mandelbaum, Michael. *The Ideas That Conquered the World*. New York: Public Affairs, 2002.

Marchand, C. Roland. *The American Peace Movement and Social Reform, 1898–1918*. Princeton: Princeton University Press, 1972.

Margulies, Herbert F. *The Mild Reservationists and the League of Nations Controversy in the Senate*. Columbia: University of Missouri Press, 1989.

Marrin, Albert. *Nicholas Murray Butler*. Boston: Twayne, 1976.

Masden, David. *The National University: Enduring Dream of the USA*. Detroit: Wayne State University Press, 1960.

Mason, A. T. *Harlan Fiske Stone*. New York: Viking, 1956.

Matthews, Brander, ed. *A History of Columbia University, 1754–1904*. New York: Columbia University Press, 1904.

———. *These Many Years: Recollections of a New Yorker*. New York: Charles Scribner's Sons, 1917.

May, Henry. *The End of American Innocence*. Chicago: Quadrangle Books, 1964.

McAllister, Ward. *Society as I Have Found It*. New York: Cassell, 1890.

McCaughey, Robert A. *Stand Columbia*. New York: Columbia University Press, 2003.

McClosskey, Robert Green. *American Conservatism in the Age of Enterprise, 1865–1910*. Cambridge: Harvard University Press, 1951.

McLachlan, James. "The American College in the Nineteenth Century: Toward a Reappraisal." *Teachers College Record* (December 1978), 287–306.

Mee, Charles. *The Ohio Gang*. New York: M. Evans, 1981.

Mencken, H. L. *Prejudices*. 6 series. New York: Alfred A. Knopf, 1919, 1920, 1922, 1924, 1926, 1927.

Merton, Thomas. *The Seven Storey Mountain*. New York: Harcourt Brace, 1948.

Metzger, Walter. *Academic Freedom in the Age of the University*. New York: Columbia University Press, 1951.

Meyer, Annie Nathan. *It's Been Fun*. New York: Henry Schuman, 1951.

Millhauser, Steven. *Martin Dressler: The Tale of an American Dreamer*. New York: Crown, 1996.

Mills, C. Wright. *The Power Elite*. New York: Oxford University Press, 1956.

Mitchell, Joseph. *My Ears Are Bent*. New York: Pantheon Books, 2001.

Morris, Edmund. *Theodore Rex*. New York: Random House, 2001.

Morrison, Charles C. *The Outlawry of War*. Chicago: Willett, Clark and Colby, 1927.

Morrison, Samuel Eliot, ed. *The Development of Harvard University Since the Inauguration of President Eliot, 1869–1929*. Cambridge: Harvard University Press, 1930.

Mowry, George E. *Theodore Roosevelt and the Progressive Movement*. Madison: University of Wisconsin Press, 1947.

Mumford, Lewis. *The Culture of Cities*. New York: Harcourt Brace, 1938.

Nasaw, David. *The Chief: The Life of William Randolph Hearst*. New York: Houghton Mifflin, 2000.

Nevins, Allan, and Milton Halsey Thomas, eds. *The Diary of George Templeton Strong*. New York: Macmillan, 1952.

———. *The State Universities and Democracy*. Urbana: University of Illinois Press, 1962.

Noble, David W. *The Paradox of Progressive Thought*. Minneapolis: University of Minnesota Press, 1958.

Nore, Ellen A. *Charles A. Beard: An Intellectual Biography*. Carbondale: Southern Illinois University Press, 1983.

Okrent, Daniel. *Great Fortune: The Epic of Rockefeller Center*. New York: Viking, 2003.

Oren, Dan A. *A History of the Jews at Yale*. New Haven: Yale University Press, 1985.

Parry, Albert. *Garrets and Pretenders: A History of Bohemianism in America*. New York: Covici Friede Publishers, 1933.

Patterson, David. *Toward a Warless World: The Travail of the American Peace Movement, 1887–1914*. Bloomington: Indiana University Press, 1976.

Paulson, Friedrich. *Autobiography*. New York: Columbia University Press, 1938.

Peck, Harry Thurston. "Twelve Years of the University." *Columbia University Quarterly* (December 1901), 12–17.

Perry, R. B. "Charles William Eliot." *The New England Quarterly* (January 1931), 5–29.

Pierson, George W. *Yale College: An Educational History, 1871–1921*. New Haven: Yale University Press, 1952.

Pine, John B., ed. *Charters, Acts of the Legislature, Official Documents and Records of Columbia University*. New York: Printed for the University, 1920.

Porter, Noah. *The American Colleges and the American Public*. New York: Arno Press (reprint), 1969.

Pringle, Henry F. *The Life and Times of William Howard Taft*. New York: Farrar & Rinehart, 1939.

———. *Theodore Roosevelt: A Biography*. New York: Harcourt Brace, 1931.

Pritchett, Henry S. "Shall the University Become a Business Corporation?" *Atlantic Monthly* (September 1905), 289–99.

Pupin, Michael. *From Immigrant to Inventor*. New York: Charles Scribner's Sons, 1929.

Ravitch, Diane. *The Great School Wars: New York City, 1805–1973*. New York: Basic Books, 1974.

———. *Left Back: A Century of Failed School Reforms*. New York: Simon & Schuster, 2000.

Reuben, Julie A. *The Making of the Modern University: Intellectual Transformation and the Marginalization of Morality*. Chicago: University of Chicago Press, 1996.

Rogers, Lindsay. "Reflections on Writing Biography of Public Men." *Political Science Quarterly* (December 1973), 725–33.

Rogers, Walter P. *Andrew D. White and the Modern University*. Ithaca: Cornell University Press, 1942.

Rosewater, Victor. *Backstage in 1912*. Philadelphia: Dorrance, 1932.

Ross, Edward A. *Seventy Years of It*. New York: D. Appleton-Century Company, 1936.

Rudolph, Frederick. *The American College and University: A History*. New York: Alfred A. Knopf, 1962.

Russell, Francis. *The Shadow of Blooming Grove: Warren G. Harding in His Times*. New York: McGraw-Hill, 1968.

Rutkoff, Peter, and William B. Scott. *New School: A History of the New School for Social Research*. New York: The Free Press, 1986.

Ryan, Alan. *John Dewey and the High Tide of American Liberalism*. New York: W. W. Norton, 1995.

Ryan, W. Carson. *Studies in Early Graduate Education*. New York: The Carnegie Foundation for the Advancement of Teaching, Bulletin No. 30, 1939.

Ryder, David Warren. *Great Citizen: A Biography of William H. Crocker*. San Francisco: Joseph H. Barry, 1962.

Sayre, Wallace, and Herbert K. Kaufman. *Governing New York City: Politics in the Metropolis*. New York: The Russell Sage Foundation, 1960.

Schaub, Edward, ed. *William Torry Harris, 1835–1935*. Chicago: Open Court, 1936.

Schiesel, Martin. *The Politics of Efficiency: Municipal Administration and Reform in America, 1880–1920*. Berkeley: University of California Press, 1977.

Schlesinger, Arthur M., Jr. *The Crisis of the Old Order, 1919–1933*. Boston: Houghton Mifflin, 1957.

Seitz, Don C. *Joseph Pulitzer: His Life and Letters*. New York: Simon & Schuster, 1924.

Selle, Erwin. *The Organization and Activities of the National Education Association*. New York: Teachers College, 1932.

Sexson, John A., and John W. Harbeson. *The New American College*. New York: Harper & Bros., 1946.

Shils, Edward. "The Order of Learning in the United States from 1865–1920: The Ascendency of the Universities." *Minerva* (Summer 1978), 159–95.

Shotwell, James T. *War as an Instrument of National Policy and Its Renunciation in the Pact of Paris*. New York: Harcourt Brace, 1929.

Sides, W. Hampton. *Stomping Grounds: A Pilgrim's Progress Through Eight American Subcultures*. William Morrow, 1992.

Sinclair, Upton. *The Goose Step: A Study of American Education*. Pasadena: Published by the author, 1922.

Sizer, Theodore. *Secondary Schools at the Turn of the Century*. New Haven: Yale University Press, 1964.

Slayton, Robert A. *Empire Statesman: The Rise and Redemption of Al Smith*. New York: The Free Press, 2001.

Sloan, Douglas. "Harmony, Chaos, and Consensus: The American College Curriculum." *Teachers College Record* (December 1971), 221–51.

Slosson, Edwin E. *Great American Universities*. New York: Macmillan, 1910.

Smith, Shirley W. *James Burrill Angell: An American Influence*. Ann Arbor: University of Michigan Press, 1955.

Snow, Louis F. *The College Curriculum in the United States*. New York: Teachers College, 1907.

Solomon, Barbara Miller. *Ancestors and Immigrants: A Changing New England*. Cambridge: Harvard University Press, 1957.

Spingarn, J. E. *A Question of Academic Freedom, Being the Official Correspondence Between Nicholas Murray Butler and J. E. Spingarn*. New York: Printed for Distribution Among the Alumni, 1911.

Spring, Joel H. *Education and the Rise of the Corporate State*. Boston: Beacon Press, 1972.

Sproat, John G. *"The Best Men": Liberal Reformers in the Gilded Age*. New York: Oxford University Press, 1968.

Stearns, Harold. *America and the Young Intellectuals*. New York: George H. Doran, 1921.

———, ed. *Civilization in the United States*. New York: Harcourt Brace, 1922.

Steffens, Lincoln. *The Autobiography of Lincoln Steffens*. New York: Harcourt Brace, 1931.

Stoner, John E. *S. O. Levinson and the Pact of Paris*. Chicago: University of Chicago Press, 1942.

Storr, Richard J. *The Beginnings of Graduate Education in America*. Chicago: University of Chicago Press, 1953.

Sullivan, Mark. *Our Times, 1900–1925*. 6 volumes. New York: Charles Scribner's Sons, 1926–35.

Summerscales, William. *Affirmation and Dissent: Columbia's Response to the Crisis of World War I*. New York: Teachers College Press, 1970.

Synnott, Marcia Graham. *The Half-Opened Door: Discrimination and Admissions at Harvard, Yale, and Princeton, 1900–1970*. Westport, Conn.: Greenwood Press, 1979.

Syrett, Harold C., ed. *The Gentleman and the Tiger: The Autobiography of George B. McClellan, Jr.* Philadelphia: J. B. Lippincott, 1956.

Tanenbaum, Samuel. *William Heard Kilpatrick, Trail Blazer in Education*. New York: Harper & Bros., 1951.

Tappan, Henry P. *University Education*. New York: G. P. Putnam, 1851.

Teachout, Terry. *The Skeptic: A Life of H. L. Mencken*. New York: HarperCollins, 2002.

Terhune, Albert Payson. *To the Best of My Memory*. New York: Harper & Bros., 1930.

Thompson, Daniel G. Brinton. *Ruggles of New York*. New York: Columbia University Press, 1946.

Thwing, Charles F. *The College President*. New York: Macmillan, 1926.

Trilling, Diana. *The Beginning of the Journey*. New York: Harcourt Brace, 1993.

Tugwell, Rexford. *To the Lesser Heights of Morningside: A Memoir*. Philadelphia: University of Pennsylvania Press, 1982.

Tyack, David. *The One Best System: A History of American Urban Education*. Cambridge: Harvard University Press, 1974.

——, and Elisabeth Hansot. *Managers of Virtue: Public School Leadership in America, 1820–1980*. New York: Basic Books, 1982.

Updike, John, ed. *A Century of Arts and Letters*. New York: Columbia University Press, 1998.

Vanderlip, Frank A. *Business and Education*. New York: Duffield, 1907.

Van der Zee, John. *Power at Ease: Inside the Greatest Men's Party on Earth*. New York: Harcourt Brace Jovanovich, 1974.

Van Deusen, Marshall. *J. E. Spingarn*. New York: Twayne, 1971.

Van Doren, Mark. *Autobiography*. New York: Harcourt Brace, 1939.

Veblen, Thorstein. *The Higher Learning in America*. Stanford: Academic Reprints, 1954.

Veysey, Laurence R. *The Emergence of the American University*. Chicago: University of Chicago Press, 1965.

Wall, Joseph. *Andrew Carnegie*. New York: Oxford University Press, 1970.

Wechsler, Harold. *The Qualified Student: A History of Selective Admissions in America*. New York: Wiley, 1977.

Wechsler, James. *Revolt on the Campus*. New York: Covici Friede Publishers, 1935.

Weinstein, James. *The Corporate Ideal in the Liberal State, 1900–1918*. Boston: Beacon Press, 1968.

Weld, William Ernest, and Kathryn W. H. Sewny. *Herbert E. Hawkes, Dean of Columbia College*. New York: Columbia University Press, 1958.

Wesley, Edgar B. *N.E.A.: The First Hundred Years, the Building of the Teaching Profession*. New York: Harper & Bros., 1957.

West, Andrew. *Present College Questions*. New York: Appleton, 1903

——. *Value of the Classics*. Princeton: Princeton University Press, 1917.

Wheatley, Steven C. *The Politics of Philanthropy: Abraham Flexner and Medical Education*. Wisconsin: University of Wisconsin Press, 1988.

Whittemore, Richard. *Nicholas Murray Butler and Public Education*. New York: Teachers College Press, 1970.

——. "Nicholas Murray Butler and the Teaching Profession." *History of Education Quarterly* (September 1961), 22–35.

Willis, Rudy S. "Eliot and Gilman: The History of an Academic Friendship." *Teachers College Record* (March 1953), 307–18.

Wills, Garry. *John Wayne's America: The Politics of Celebrity*. New York: Simon & Schuster, 1997.

Wyllie, Irvin. *The Self-made Man in America*. New Brunswick: Rutgers University Press, 1954.

Yardley, Jonathan, ed. *H. L. Mencken: My Life as Author and Editor*. New York: Alfred A. Knopf, 1993.

Zinsser, Hans. *As I Remember Him*. Boston: Little, Brown, 1940.

Acknowledgments

Some books have multiple and mysterious origins. *Nicholas Miraculous* had a single, explicit one: a phone call from a Columbia friend, Mary Dearborn, telling me that the Butler papers were open and that I was the person to write his biography. I am grateful for her suggestion, even if it occupied far more years of my life than I had imagined. At the outset of the project, the generous support of the Guggenheim and Spencer Foundations let me take time off from my teaching and devote myself entirely to the book. I could never have completed it without their help. I am especially indebted to the Spencer Foundation for permitting me to use my research money well beyond the date I had originally projected I would need it.

With the exception of those letters and documents that Butler chose to destroy at the end of his life, he was an inveterate saver of all scraps of paper, trivial or otherwise, relating to him and his activities, and together with his enormous correspondence, they constitute the bulk of the immense Butler collection—over 600 boxes of material, along with 144 volumes of clippings—housed in Columbia's Rare Book and Manuscript Library. No one has officially confirmed this, but I am confident that with the exception of the library staff, I have spent more time in the RBML than anyone else in its history. Although it would be foolish to suggest that long hours of research, day after day, are always exhilarating, they were helped to be pleasant and productive by the competence and friendliness of the librarians, who always saw that I had the materials I needed.

My gratitude to Bernie, Rudolph, Jane, Jenny, Kevin, Patrick, and the others who were with this enterprise from its start. I regret that Henry Rowland, who brought to my attention Butler's letters to Alice Haven, died before the book was finished. Ron Grele, the former director of Columbia's remarkable Oral History Collection, made its resources easily accessible to me.

Columbia's historical documents, trustee minutes and correspondence, and most of Butler's administrative papers are located in the Columbiana collection in Low Library, and here Jocelyn Baines was an invaluable ally in tracking things down. The professionalism of Columbia's librarians was matched (though, fortunately, no one was required to match their good-natured patience) by the archivists and librarians in other collections where I conducted research: Yale, Harvard, Princeton, Stanford, Berkeley, Johns Hopkins, the Library of Congress, the Bohemian Club, the Century Association, the American Academy of Arts and Letters, the Rockefeller Family Archive, the New York Historical Society, and the New York Public Library. My thanks to them all.

Gathering, photocopying, and organizing a vast amount of material over the ten years of active research for this book are not activities one can easily accomplish alone, and I was lucky to have a talented, conscientious series of Columbia undergraduates whom I was able to recruit every year to assist me. My gratitude to John Bennett, Mark Kuzmack, Wendy Lee, Kyu Li Oh, Rammy Park, Avani Patel, James Pulizzi, Joel Rubin, and Josh Shanker, for their efforts both large and small. My one graduate assistant, Tom Hill, performed a critical service by collecting all the references to Butler in Columbia's Oral History Project in Butler Library.

My enduring pursuit of Butler was immeasurably enhanced by friends and colleagues who, in addition to their enthusiasm, provided material support in the form of reading drafts of chapters, supplying me with bibliographic leads and gobbets of Butleriana, agreeing to be interviewed about Butler and Butler's Columbia, and sharing with me their rich knowledge of American culture. For these and other efforts on my behalf I am indebted to Jerold Auerbach, Ric Burns, Roger Blumberg. W. T. de Bary, Jacques Barzun, Paul Carter, Andrew Delbanco, Lucille Gudis, Jamie Katz, Herbert Leibowitz, James Pacey, Nick Platt, Carol Slade, Brian Sullivan, Frank Sypher, and Tom Vinciguerra. Special thanks to Dan Okrent for showing me his research notes on Rockefeller Center and Columbia, and for allowing me to read in draft several chapters of his *Great Fortune*. I am unhappy that a number of those who contributed to the book did not live to see it completed: Mary Mahoney Brown, Eli Ginzberg, Alger Hiss, Grayson Kirk, Ellen McGrath, Robert Merton, James Pacey, Pamela Richards, Edward Said, Jim Shenton, David Truman, and Warren Zimmerman.

One of the joys of teaching at "the house that Butler built" is the extraordinary people who are attracted to work there. The important help I received from five of these Columbians deserves particular mention. From the time he first learned that I was writing the biography, William J. McGill, president of the university from 1970 to 1980, eagerly followed its progress. His lengthy, wonderfully detailed e-mail correspondence about Columbia's fiscal difficulties, the trustees, and Rockefeller Center provided a unique source of information for me. He was fascinated by Butler, and I am deeply sorry that I was unable to finish the book while he was alive. Peter R. Pouncey has been an indomitable supporter of both project and author from the earliest days of gestation to completion. My only regret in completing the manuscript is that our weekly lunches will no longer begin with Peter's formulaic query, "And how is our good Dr. Butler today?" J. W. Smit read large portions of several early drafts and helped me to understand how historians looked at some of the issues I was examining. With characteristic generosity of spirit, Robert Ferguson took time out from his own research and writing to comment extensively on a number of draft chapters, in the process improving them all. E. W. Tayler knows as well as I do that there is no adequate way to thank him for what he has done for the book. He read every word—and then some—of an early draft, covering pages with comments that on occasion exceeded in length what I had written. His rigorous insistence on clarity never wavered—nor did his belief in what I was doing. I was blessed by both.

Rumors of the editorial talents of Elisabeth Sifton had reached me long before I had begun the book, but as a skeptical sort I resolved not to pay them any heed until I could judge for myself. I am now ready to testify: one could not possibly hope for a better editor. Her sublime judgment about matters both of style and substance was remarkable, and her therapeutic presence can be felt on every page. Any problems with the book that remain are exclusively my responsibility, not hers.

My wife, Judith, refers to the ménage a trois in which we have lived during the many years of research and writing of *Nicholas Miraculous*. She is right, and no one could have been more welcoming to the intruder than she. We greeted him together, shared the burdens of trying to understand him together, and finally sent him off to his rest together. In every aspect of this affair she was entirely enabling. For this, as for so many other gifts from her, I am the first to recognize my undeserved good fortune.

Index